# Handbook of Urban Inequalities

The Oxford India Handbooks are an important initiative in academic publishing. Each volume offers a comprehensive survey of research in a critical subject area and provides facts, figures, and analyses for a well-grounded perspective. The series provides scholars, students, and policy planners with a balanced understanding of a wide range of issues in the social sciences.

# Other Titles in the Series

HANDBOOK OF GENDER
Raka Ray (Editor)

HANDBOOK OF CLIMATE CHANGE AND INDIA
*Development, Politics, and Governance*
Navroz K. Dubash (Editor)

HANDBOOK OF MODERNITY IN SOUTH ASIA
*Modern Makeovers*
Saurabh Dube (Editor)

HANDBOOK OF PSYCHOLOGY IN INDIA
Girishwar Misra (Editor)

THE RIGHT TO INFORMATION ACT 2005
*A Handbook*
Sudhir Naib

HANDBOOK OF POPULATION AND
DEVELOPMENT IN INDIA (OIP)
A.K. Shiva Kumar, Pradeep Panda, and
Rajani R. Ved (Editors)

GLOBALIZATION AND DEVELOPMENT
*A Handbook of New Perspectives* (OIP)
Ashwini Deshpande (Editor)

HANDBOOK OF MUSLIMS IN INDIA
*Empirical and Policy Perspectives*
Rakesh Basant and Abusaleh Shariff (Editors)

HANDBOOK OF ENVIRONMENTAL
ECONOMICS IN INDIA
Kanchan Chopra and Vikram Dayal (Editors)

HANDBOOK OF AGRICULTURE IN INDIA (OIP)
Shovan Ray (Editor)

HANDBOOK OF ENVIRONMENTAL LAW
P.B. Sahasranaman

HANDBOOK OF LAW, WOMEN, AND
EMPLOYMENT
*Policies, Issues, Legislation, and Case Law*
Surinder Mediratta

HANDBOOK OF HUMAN DEVELOPMENT
*Concepts, Measures, and Policies*
Sakiko Fukuda-Parr and A.K. Shiva
Kumar (Editors)

HANDBOOK OF ENVIRONMENTAL
DECISION MAKING IN INDIA
*An EIA Model*
O.V. Nandimath

HANDBOOK OF URBANIZATION IN INDIA
(SECOND EDITION) (OIP)
K.C. Shivaramakrishnan, Amitabh
Kundu, and B.N. Singh

MAKING NEWS
*Handbook of the Media in Contemporary
India* (OIP)
Uday Sahay (Editor)

HANDBOOK OF INDIAN SOCIOLOGY (OIP)
Veena Das (Editor)

MANAGING BUSINESS IN THE
21ST CENTURY
*A Handbook* (OIP)
Anindya Sen and P.K. Sett (Editors)

# Handbook of Urban Inequalities

Darshini Mahadevia
Sandip Sarkar

OXFORD
UNIVERSITY PRESS

Oxford University Press is a department of the University of Oxford.
It furthers the University's objective of excellence in research, scholarship,
and education by publishing worldwide. Oxford is a registered trademark of
Oxford University Press in the UK and in certain other countries

Published in India by
Oxford University Press
YMCA Library Building, 1 Jai Singh Road, New Delhi 110001, India

ISBN-13: 978-0-19-808171-5
ISBN-10: 0-19-808171-5

Typeset in 11/13 Arno Pro
by Excellent Laser Typesetters, Pitampura, Delhi 110 034
Printed in India at Rakmo Press, New Delhi 110 020

# Contents

# Tables and Figures

## TABLES

## FIGURES

# Foreword

In contemporary times, more than half the world is living in urban areas. However, in India, only 32 per cent of the population, including those in the new towns that have emerged during the last decade, live in urban areas. At the same time, urban India's total population of 377.1 million is the largest in the world after China. In fact, urban India's population has surpassed the total population of USA.

Urban areas are considered important, as they tend to generate economic growth. In fact, a 2010 report by McKinsey Global Institute, *India's Urban Awakening: Building Inclusive Cities, Sustaining Economic Growth*, predicts that by 2030, cities could generate more than 70 per cent of India's net new employment and produce 70 per cent of its gross domestic product (GDP), while housing 40 per cent of its population. Currently, about 60 per cent of the country's GDP is generated from urban areas that house 32 per cent of the population. While these figures highlight the importance of urban areas, they also point to an unequal settlement pattern wherein cities produce a large proportion of the national income and wealth but do not contain the population in the same proportion. This can hardly be conducive to the concept of 'inclusive growth', which is the vision of the Twelfth Five Year Plan of India.

The idea of inclusive cities has to be located within the issue of equality in the patterns of urbanization and growth. This handbook by Darshini Mahadevia and Sandip Sarkar is important precisely because it focuses on the increasing rural–urban and intra-urban inequalities. For the first time, we have a book which presents a disaggregated picture of urban India, wherein the metro cities have been compared and contrasted with the non-metro cities both at the national and state levels. The data is drawn through reprocessing of the unit-level data of the National Sample Survey (NSS). While the earlier surveys facilitated a further disaggregate analysis of the non-metro segment of the urban population, since 2004–5, the sample of the non-metro segments has been reduced on account of an increasing emphasis on the metros and in order to better capture the trends and patterns in the metros. This has thus made it infeasible to acquire a disaggregated view of the non-metro sample. At the outset, the authors have pointed out that there has been an increase in inequality between the metros and the non-metros as well as across the percentile classes in all urban metros and non-metros. They contend that the beneficiaries of the economic reforms comprise the top 20 per cent and top 5 per cent of the population in the metros and non-metros, respectively, while the bottom 40 per cent of the population in both has seen a reducing rate of improvement in consumption. The suggestion made by both the McKinsey Global Institute report and that of India's High Powered Expert Committee (*Report on Indian Urban Infrastructure and Services*) to promote urbanization through metropolitanization and global linkages of large cities, which are the 'engines of growth', would only further exacerbate the inequalities in the urban system. This handbook also exposes the pro-metro bias in investments in urban infrastructure taken up through the first and the largest urban programme—the Jawaharlal Nehru National Urban Renewal Mission (JNNURM).

Exploring the areas of urban poverty, employment, and education to analyse inter-state and intra-state urban inequalities and the changes that have taken place therein over time, the authors argue that it is neither appropriate nor practical to have a uniform policy paradigm for the entire urban sector. As such, there is need for a much more disaggregated process of urban policymaking than has been hitherto pursued. The second important policy issue pertains to the need to recognize the immense diversity of non-metros, which range from populations of 5,000 to 1,000,000. It is thus imperative for policymaking to reflect the differences in the economies and infrastructure requirements of small towns as opposed to mid-sized towns and non-metro cities. The authors also discuss some of the policy imperatives emerging from the data analysis and suggest the way forward.

This book is a substantial revision of the study titled 'Poverty, Levels of Living and Employment Structure in the Small and Medium Size Towns', undertaken earlier at the Institute for Human Development (IHD), which was supported by the Central Statistical Organisation (CSO), Government of India. The authors have spent considerable time in further updating as well as analysing the enormous unit-level data available in the Employment–Unemployment and Consumption Expenditure surveys up to 2009–10, and the data on Housing and Basic Amenities Rounds up to 2008–9. The authors have kept the discussions on analysis emerging from the data to a minimum. This has been done with the belief that both academics and policymakers would use the data for conducting the much-needed in-depth research and analysis of various issues concerning the urban economy, poverty, infrastructure, and educational achievements.

I trust that with its rich data on various aspects of urbanization and urban development, discussions on challenges and strategies concerning inclusive urban development, and, above all, its extensive database, the book would be of immense value to the community of researchers, policymakers, and development practitioners, who are engaged with urban development issues in India. I congratulate the authors for bringing out this book at an opportune time, when India is poised for rapid urbanization while carrying forward its vision of inclusive growth.

August 2012

ALAKH N. SHARMA
Director
Institute for Human Development
New Delhi

# Preface

India is expected to experience an increase in the rate and level of urbanization, although the past three decades have indicated that economic growth is not necessarily translating into a higher rate of urbanization. In spite of this, there are many challenges in terms of employment and poverty, and levels of urban services. The inadequacies of this process are witnessed across all the urban centres—from metropolitan cities that are the focus of most policy and research, to small towns that often fall outside the radar of research and policymaking. The characteristics and dynamics of changes in the small and medium towns remain under-researched, and studies on these tend to be more micro-based (with a focus on individual towns) than holistic. In the last decade, there have been many changes experienced by the urban economy on account of increased manufacturing and tertiary sector investments. At the same time, the Jawaharlal Nehru National Urban Renewal Mission (JNNURM) has also brought significant investments in the infrastructure and housing sectors. It is not known in which all sectors changes have been experienced as a consequence. A disaggregated analysis of available data of the urban system, we hope, will help in sharper discussions on urban policies than what is possible today.

The idea about undertaking this research emanated from the necessity of creating a database for informed policymaking in urban areas. We were aware of the potential of re-processing the National Sample Survey (NSS) household-level data, which it had made available for use by the researchers. The Institute for Human Development (IHD) applied and obtained a research grant for this work from the Central Statistical Organisation (CSO). The study was largely limited to processing the unit-level data of household schedules of the NSS. This study was completed in early 2003 and the report submitted to the CSO carried data up to the 55th Round (1999–2000) of the NSS. Subsequently, when we decided to publish the work, we reprocessed the quinquennial NSS household schedule data of the 61st (2004–5) and the 66th Rounds (2009–10). Further, to capture the aspects of access to basic services, we used urban facility data of the 58th (2002) and

65th Rounds (2008–9). Hence, this book is now a revised and updated version of our earlier study supported by CSO. The urban facility data is from the housing survey rounds.

We are grateful to CSO for providing the initial funding for the research work. Subsequently, we are grateful to IHD for its support towards this endeavour. We are extremely grateful to Professor Alakh N. Sharma for his unending encouragement and support to us in all ways. His enthusiasm has rubbed on us and made us unflinchingly persevere in producing this book. The comments of two anonymous referees on the manuscript commissioned by the Oxford University Press (OUP) helped enormously in reorienting and substantiating the content of the book. We would like to place on record our gratitude to the OUP team for their continuous support through the various stages of production in giving the book its final shape. It goes without saying that any lacunae in the book are ours. We could be blamed for missing out on many other possible analyses of the available household schedule data. But, this is a call we took. We hope that the data presented in this book would be of use to the increasing body of urban researchers working in India.

DARSHINI MAHADEVIA
SANDIP SARKAR

# Abbreviations

| | |
|---|---|
| A/P | Administrative/Professional |
| ACA | Additional Central Assistance |
| APCE | Average Per Capita Consumption Expenditure |
| BIMARU | Bihar, Madhya Pradesh, Rajasthan, and Uttar Pradesh |
| BPL | Below Poverty Line |
| BSUP | Basic Services for the Urban Poor |
| C | Clerical |
| CA | Constitutional Amendment |
| CAA | Constitutional Amendment Act |
| CAGR | Compound Annual Growth Rate |
| CDP | Comprehensive Development Plan |
| CDS | Current Daily Status |
| CL | Casual Labour |
| CSMC | Central Sanctioning and Monitoring Committee |
| CSO | Central Statistical Organisation |
| CV | Coefficient of Variation |
| DPC | District Plannning Committee |
| DPR | Detailed Project Report |
| FSU | First Stage Unit |
| GDP | Gross Domestic Product |
| GSDP | Gross State Domestic Product |
| GoI | Government of India |
| HCR | Head Count Ratio |
| HPEC | High Powered Expert Committee |
| IDSMT | Integrated Development of Small and Medium Towns |

| IHD | Institute for Human Development |
| IT | Information Technology |
| ITES | IT Enabled Services |
| JNNURM | Jawaharlal Nehru National Urban Renewal Mission |
| KDF | Kernel Density Function |
| MGI | McKinsey Global Institute |
| ML | Manual Labour |
| MoA | Memorandum of Agreement |
| MoUD | Ministry of Urban Development |
| MPC | Metropolitan Planning Committee |
| MRP | Mixed Reference Period |
| NCO | National Classification of Occupations |
| NCU | National Commission on Urbanization |
| NE | North-East |
| NIC | National Industrial Classification |
| NSS | National Sample Survey |
| NSSO | National Sample Survey Organisation |
| PPP | Public Private Partnership |
| PURA | Providing Urban Facilities to Rural Areas |
| RE | Regularly Employed |
| SC | Scheduled Caste |
| SE | Self-employed |
| SFC | State Finance Commission |
| SIUC | Small and Intermediate Urban Centre |
| SLNA | State Level Nodal Agency |
| SMTs | Small and Medium Towns |
| ST | Scheduled Tribe |
| SWM | Solid Waste Management |
| TCPO | Town and Country Planning Organisation |
| TVEs | Town and Village Enterprises |
| UIDSSMT | Urban Infrastructure Development Scheme for Small and Medium Towns |
| UIG | Urban Infrastructure and Governance |
| ULB | Urban Local Body |
| ULCRA | Urban Land Ceiling and Regulation Act |
| UN | United Nations |
| UNCRD | United Nation Centre for Regional Development |
| UNFPA | United Nations Population Fund |
| UPSS | Usual Primary and Secondary Status |
| URIF | Urban Reform Incentive Fund |
| URP | Uniform Recall Period |
| WPR | Work Participation Rate |

# 1

## Urbanization, Urban Poverty, and Small and Medium Towns

### An Introduction

### INTRODUCTION

There is an increase in interest in the challenges of urbanization in India. This interest has increased on account of the announcement of the first and also a flagship programme of the national government, the Jawaharlal Nehru National Urban Renewal Mission (JNNURM). JNNURM's brochure[1] states that 'cities and towns have a vital role in India's socio-economic transformation and change', indicating that urbanization has many positive outcomes for the national development process. At the same time, urban areas also contribute significantly to the national domestic product, which is estimated at 50–5 per cent as per the JNNURM brochure. Consequently, there has been a spurt in reports on challenges of India's urbanization process. The most recent one is by the High Powered Expert Committee (HPEC) on status and investment requirements of urban infrastructure services. The McKinsey

Global Institute's (MGI) report on 'building inclusive cities' also focuses on infrastructure and housing markets (MGI 2010) and investments required therein. But these reflect on the aggregate picture of urbanization and development in cities and put forward future visions for them. At best, these reports put forward aggregate status of cities and at worst are documents to solicit private sector investments in cities. They do not give the actual database situation of urban development in India. They also do not reflect on the heterogeneity of urbanization and urban settlement systems. This handbook fills this gap in urban knowledge.

The urban system is heterogeneous all over the world and so also in India. It includes settlements with population sizes ranging from 5,000 to 20 million, logically mandating differential policy approaches to different size classes of urban centres. This is now being realized as evident from some recent researches

(Kundu and Sarangi 2005) and discussions. Importance of small and medium towns for urban policy has been identified by the United Nations Population Fund (UNFPA) in its *State of the World's Population* report (2007: 3):

Contrary to general belief, the bulk of urban population growth is likely to be in smaller cities and towns, whose capabilities for planning and implementation can be exceedingly weak. Yet the worldwide process of decentralizing governmental powers is heaping greater responsibility on them. As the population of smaller cities increases, their thin managerial and planning capacities come under mounting stress. New ways will have to be found to equip them to plan ahead for expansion, to use their resources sustainably and to deliver essential services. There are thus, multiple challenges facing the small and medium towns in the coming years; lack of economic base and employment opportunities for the population, lack of financial and managerial capacities, high incidence of poverty and low level of services.

The different capabilities of different sizes of urban centres are because of their different economic bases and dynamics. Smaller urban centres are influenced by the dynamics of agriculture development whereas metropolitan cities in the globalizing economic system are influenced by global economic dynamics. Long back, Minocha and Yadav (1989) had shown that Madhya Pradesh's agricultural development gave rise to the emergence of small towns whereas industrialization tended to strengthen agglomeration tendencies and greater concentration of population in a few cities. Increasing land prices in metropolitan cities, as has been the case in recent years, can push some of the economic activities to non-metropolitan cities. Deceleration or decline of the agriculture sector can adversely affect the economy and population growth of small urban centres even if the overall economy is doing well. If the global economy is robust, metropolitan cities can thrive even if the national or state economies are not doing well.[2]

The second issue is the large gap between small and medium towns (henceforth we call them non-metros) and metropolitan cities in terms of different indicators of development, namely, incidence of poverty, nature, type and quality of employment, wage rates, levels of services, and populations' capabilities such as literacy rate and education. There are large gaps between metros and non-metros in their financial bases and capabilities to deliver services to populations, the most basic function of any Urban Local Body (ULB). Thus, non-metros today are not in a position to even bridge their financial and administrative inadequacies, while the metros are struggling to do so. For example, JNNURM induced reforms and projects have been inadequately and unevenly implemented across states (Mahadevia 2010a). Thus, in spite of JNNURM, the image of any Indian city, whether a metro or a non-metro is Dickensian:

With its ubiquitous slums and squatter settlements; regular inundation in parts during monsoons; open sewerage and storm water drains, sometimes with water supply pipelines running through them; pot-holed roads and chaotic traffic; haphazard building construction in apparent violation of all planning norms and legislation; waste-pickers, children, and animals foraging amidst mounds of garbage; and the like. (Ibid.: 226)

Even at low level of urbanization there is chaos and high inter and intra urban inequalities on account of lack of service delivery, financial capability, and institutional inadequacy.

This brings us to the third issue of urban governance. Urban governments are weak institutionally as they do not have powers to legislate, as these are still held by state governments. The implementation of the 74th Constitutional Amendment (CA) of decentralized and participatory urban governance is still tardy, in spite of this being a mandatory reform under JNNURM. Two other governance reforms of the framing of the Community Participation

Law and the Public Disclosure Law are also tardy. Many states have weak State Finance Commissions (SFCs), which were expected to work on a formula of financial sustainability of cities and hence cities continue to depend upon state governments for funding, which has resulted in a situation of lack of any leader in any of the cities. Further, governance is hinged on successful partnerships between the three triads of state, market, and civil society, which do not seem to be building up yet. A part of the reason is lack of inclusion of urban poor and marginal sections in the system of urban governance. The governance approach continues to be that of fire-fighting rather than planning and anticipating bottlenecks well in advance. A lot has to be done on the urban governance side if poverty alleviation and development have to occur in urban areas.

The last issue connected with urban development is lack of integration of economic aspects such as employment issues with infrastructure issues such as housing and basic services; infrastructure with social development such as shelter security, basic services, and locational issues with access to and impact on health and education; and so on. There is lack of policy synergy in the urban sector, wherein urban development has only meant provision of housing and infrastructure and none of the other aspects of urban development. Therefore, this handbook is a first attempt to bring these various facets of urban areas together by reprocessing available datasets in the Indian system.

## EVIDENCE OF URBAN INEQUALITIES

The National Sample Survey Organisation's (NSSO's) consumption expenditure data gives us evidence of existing inequalities between rural and urban areas and within the urban sector, which have increased over time. These are broadly divided into two parts—pre-reforms, up to 1993–4 and reforms after 1993–4 to

2004–5.[3] Figure 1.1 shows that the Compound Annual Growth Rate (CAGR) of Average Per Capita Consumption Expenditure (APCE) was lower in the pre-reforms period as compared to the reforms period. But, what is interesting to note in this figure is that CAGR of APCE declined with an increase in APCE percentile in the 1983–94 period. This means that households at lower APCE percentiles experienced higher CAGR of APCE, that is, higher consumption expenditure growth than those at the higher percentile. In other words, economic growth in the pre-reforms period was distributed leading to larger increases in consumption expenditure at the bottom of the urban population as compared to the higher ends of the urban population. This situation changed after reforms. CAGR increased with an increase in the APCE percentile. In other words, economic growth in the reforms period benefitted higher percentiles of the urban population. Further, the population in the bottom 20 percentiles registered lower CAGR in the reforms period than in the pre-reforms period. In other words, the bottom 20 per cent of the urban population definitely experienced some regression in consumption expenditure.

The reforms period also shows a sudden jump in the growth in consumption expenditure among the top 20 per cent of the urban population and that the gap between the top and bottom 20 percentiles widened in the reforms period. The middle section also benefitted on account of reforms but its gains were lower than that of the top 20 per cent. Economic growth in the reforms period, therefore, was for the top 20 per cent of the urban population giving credence to the theory of elite benefit of reforms and elite capture of urban benefits.

CAGRs of APCE disaggregated by metros and non-metros (Figures 1.2 and 1.3) make the overall urban pattern clearer. In the pre-reforms period, the top 20 percentile's decline in APCE

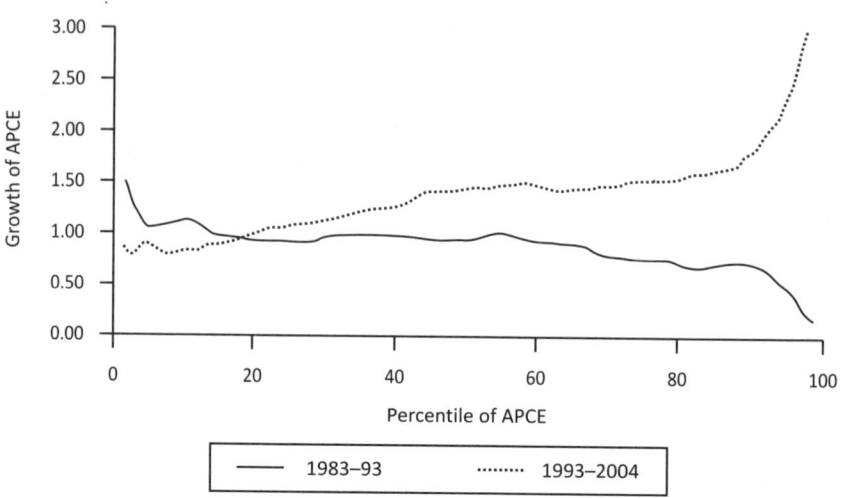

**Figure 1.1**  Compound Annual Growth Rate of APCE, All Urban

*Source*: Calculated from unit level data of consumption expenditure schedule of 38th (1983), 50th (1993–4), and 61st (2004–5) Rounds of NSSO and state specific official poverty line for the years 1983, 1993–4, and 2004–5.

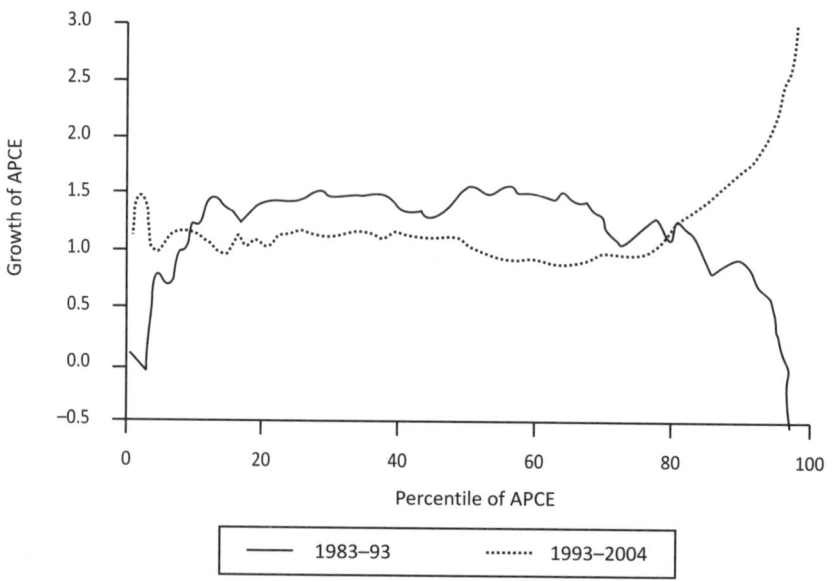

**Figure 1.2**  Compound Annual Growth Rate of APCE, Metros

*Source*: Calculated from unit level data of consumption expenditure schedule of 38th (1983), 50th (1993–4), and 61st (2004–5) Rounds of NSSO and state specific official poverty line for the years 1983, 1993–4, and 2004–5.

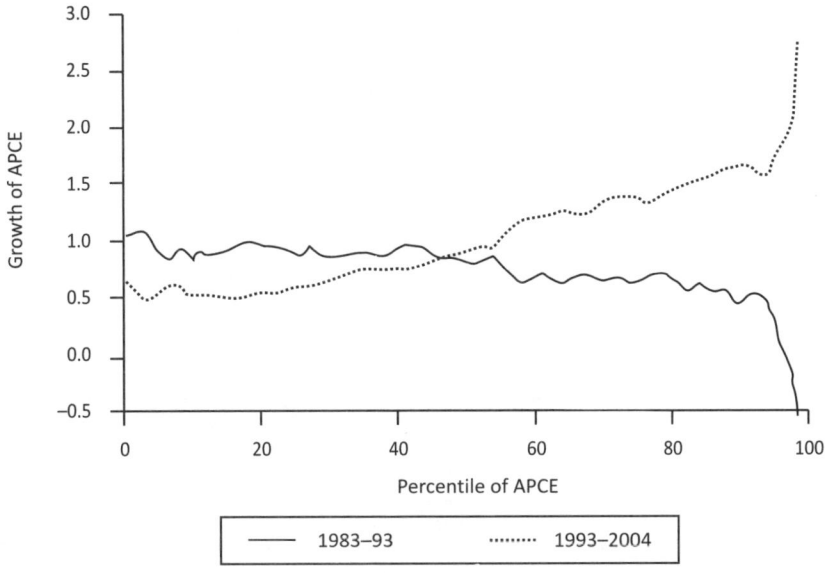

**Figure 1.3** CAGR of Average Per Capita Consumption Expenditure, Non-metros

*Source*: Calculated from unit level data of consumption expenditure schedule of 38th (1983), 50th (1993–4), and 61st (2004–5) Rounds of NSSO and state specific official poverty line for the years 1983, 1993–4, and 2004–5.

CAGR was on account of a very sharp decline in consumption in the same group in the metros. In the reforms period, the top 20 per cent's APCE CAGR shot up rapidly in the metros. CAGR of the middle consumption groups, 20 percentile to 80 percentile in the metros, went below their respective CAGRs in the pre-reforms period. Benefits accruing to the middle consumption classes after reforms were in non-metros, wherein from 40 percentile onwards the APCE CAGR graph rose rapidly. The top 5 per cent in non-metros also benefitted as much as the top 20 per cent in the metros after reforms. In the metros, the bottom 80 per cent registered a decline in APCE CAGR after the reforms whereas in non-metros it was the bottom 50 per cent that registered this decline. This means that consumption inequalities in the metros rose sharply and caused an increase in overall urban inequalities. At the same time, the bottom 50 per cent of the non-metro population

registered lower APCE CAGR as compared to the bottom 50 per cent of the metro population, suggesting that the bottom half of non-metros did not gain from the reforms process. In other words, only the top 20 per cent of the metro and the top 5 per cent of the non-metro population gained in the reforms process whereas others lost out.

The low APCE CAGR of the bottom 50 per cent of the population in non-metros explains the narrowing of rural–urban differential in the bottom 20 per cent of the respective population. Figure 1.4 shows the rural–urban differential in APCE for four consumption expenditure rounds. This figure shows that the rural–urban differential in APCE in the bottom 40 percentile groups reduced over time, and the difference was the lowest in 2004–5, indicating that the bottom 40 percentile in urban areas were as disadvantaged as those in rural areas in this year. In 2009–10, once again, the rural–urban

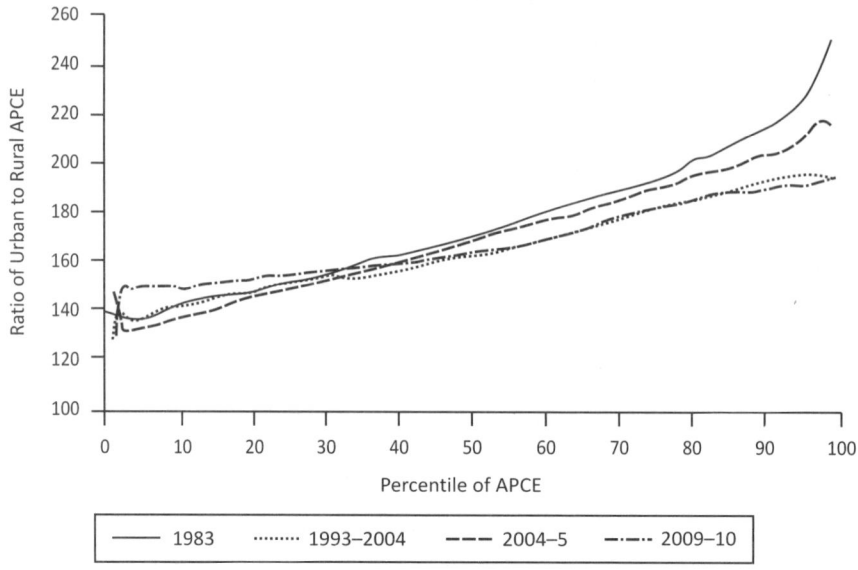

**Figure 1.4**    Ratio of Urban to Rural Average Per Capita Consumption Expenditure Over Time

*Source*: Calculated from unit level data of consumption expenditure schedule of 38th (1983), 50th (1993–4), 61st (2004–5), and 66th (2009–10) Rounds of NSSO.

difference in consumption expenditure by percentiles rose. This was because APCE of the bottom 40 per cent in the non-metros did not increase and that of the metros went down.

The gap between rural and urban APCE in the top 40 percentile increased continuously over the reforms period, with the curve registering an increasing slope from the 60th percentile onwards (Figure 1.4). This means that the top 40 percentile of the urban population was racing ahead of the top 40 percentile of the rural population. This was mainly on account of the top 20 percentile in urban areas which registered very high increase in average consumption in the last five years. Since consumerism increased all over, in rural as well as urban areas, the impact was mainly in the urban areas in the top 40 percentiles.

Lastly, there was also an increase in metro versus non-metro inequalities over time. On an average, the graph of ratio of metro to non-metro APCE by percentile moved up from 1987–8 onwards (Figure 1.5). In other words, the metro versus non-metro inequality in consumption expenditure increased continuously after reforms. In 1987–8 and 1993–4, the ratio, that is, the inequality between metro and non-metro consumption expenditure increased with an increase in the consumption percentile. Figure 1.5 shows an increasing slope in 1987–8 and 1993–4 across all the percentiles, indicating that the populations in the bottom percentiles were more equal across the two size classes than the populations in the top percentiles. In 2004–5, the graph went down from the 50th percentile to the 90th percentile but then increased sharply again. The same trend can be seen in 2009–10, except that the graph line is below that of 2004–5, indicating a slight decline in the metro versus non-metro inequality in consumption in the year. Probably on account of recession, consumption expenditures of all

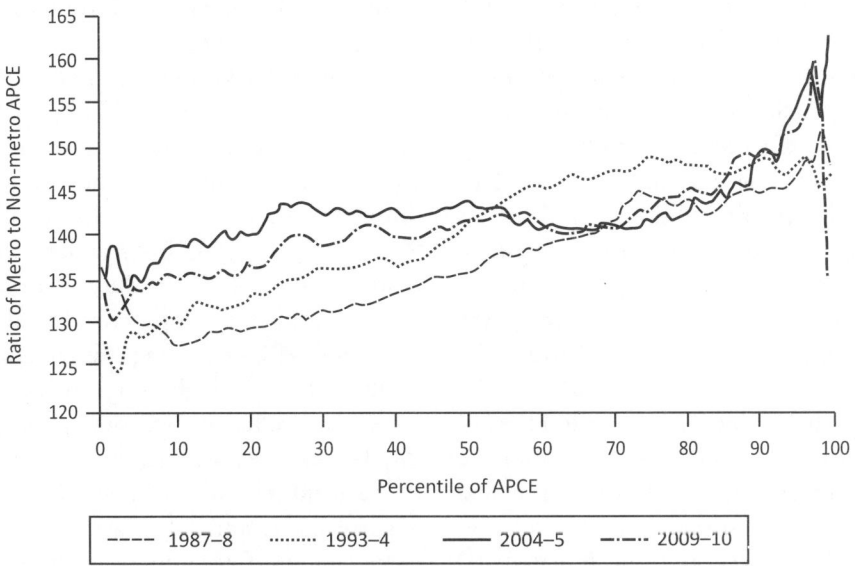

**Figure 1.5** Ratio of Metro to Non-metro Average Per Capita Consumption Expenditure Ratio Over Time

*Source*: Calculated from unit level data of consumption expenditure schedule of 38th (1983), 50th (1993–4), 61st (2004–5), and 66th (2009–10) Rounds of NSSO.

population percentiles declined and the de-cline was higher in metros than in non-metros. Recession depressed consumption in the met-ros more than in the non-metros. In the first decade of reforms, inequality between metros and non-metros rose, but the inequality increase was very high for the top 10 percentile followed by the middle 20 to 40 percentiles. However, in spite of these fluctuations, a consistent trend was that of increasing metro versus non-metro inequalities, with metros experiencing higher increase in consumption than non-metros in the wake of the reforms. The economic recession of 2008–9 somewhat depressed metro consump-tion leading to a slight decline in metro versus non-metro inequalities.

**THE POLICY CONTEXT**

The study of the urban system at a disaggre-gated level is important on account of urban reforms promoting decentralization wherein

ULBs have been mandated to take the full re-sponsibility of development projects at the city level, including finding resources for infrastruc-ture improvement and development; the onus of raising finances for infrastructure develop-ment has also been left to the ULBs. The 74th CA in a way supports this idea of decentraliza-tion of the responsibility of urban infrastruc-ture development to the ULBs. The Rakesh Mohan Committee Report (Expert Group on the Commercialization of Infrastructure 1996) had strongly recommended commercializa-tion and privatization of urban infrastructure. The HPEC (2011: xxv–xxvi) did not directly state commercialization but said: 'Improved tax revenues combined with rational user charges will enable cities to leverage their own resources to incur debt and also access new forms of financing through public private partnership (PPP)'. But, it did not negate the need for public finance, in particular national government funds for the same: 'The Committee believes that in view of the importance of urban infrastructure for economic growth and inclusion, the Government of India and state governments will have to step in, both by providing substantial funds and by facilitating the use of additional mechanisms for funding, which will require the strengthening of own finances of ULBs' (p. xxvi). In this context, would the Small and Medium Towns (SMTs) be able to stand up on their own, is the real question.

Since the beginning of economic reforms, several attempts have been made to improve municipal governance and finance. The first was the 74th Constitutional Amendment Act (CAA) introduced in 1994. It stated: (i) stability of ULBs through recognizing them as the third tier of the government and holding mandatory elections at the ULB level, (ii) one-third reservations for women in the elected wings of ULBs along with reservations for Scheduled Castes (SCs) and Scheduled Tribes (STs), (iii) formation of Metropolitan Planning Committees (MPCs) for all urban agglomerations over 1 million population and District Planning Committees (DPCs) for each administrative district, (iv) two-third of MPC members and four-fifth of DPC members to be made up of elected officials to give these committees political decision-making powers, (v) converging 18 major functions listed in the 12th Schedule of the legislation at the ULB level—functions include that of planning, service delivery, and poverty alleviation, (vi) formation of a ward or wards committees, with each committee for a population up to 300,000 for participation, (vi) mandatory constitution of SFCs to ensure adequate local government finance so that the functional devolution can match financial capabilities, and (vii) eventually all local policy decisions to be taken by elected councils of ULBs.

In 2002–3, the central government set up the Urban Reform Incentive Fund (URIF), with allocation of Rs 5,000 million (Rs 500 crore), to provide reform-linked central assistance to states. These reforms were market-linked: (i) enabling of housing and land markets through repeal of the Urban Land Ceiling and Regulation Act (ULCRA) at the state level, rationalization of stamp duty, reforming rent control laws, and computerized land registration; and (ii) increasing the financial base of the ULBs through property tax reforms, increasing collection efficiency of property tax, levying user charges on certain services to reach full recovery of operation and maintenance costs, and introduction of a double entry system of accounting in the ULBs. The funds were so small that URIF did not interest the states.

To make urban reforms successful, JNNURM was introduced as a major urban initiative of the central government in December 2005 to improve the infrastructure situation in 65 select cities, which included all metropolitan cities, state capitals, and some heritage cities. It was for the first time that the central government took on an important financial responsibility for urban development. JNNURM's overwhelming focus is on metropolitan and large cities. Rs 50,000 crore was promised by the central government as Additional Central Assistance (ACA) for mission cities over a period of time. The mission has two components: (i) Urban Infrastructure and Governance (UIG) for projects related to water supply and sanitation, sewerage, solid waste management, road network, urban transport, and redevelopment of old city areas, and (ii) Basic Services for the Urban Poor (BSUP) for integrated development of slums through projects for providing shelter, basic services, and other related civic amenities to urban poor. The former component is expected to get 60 per cent and the latter 40 per cent of the total ACA to be released.

Interestingly, the financing pattern took cognizance of the weak financial base of SMTs. Cities with populations more than 4 million would get only 35 per cent of the project funds as ACA; cities with populations between 1 to 4 million would get 50 per cent of the project funds as ACA; cities and towns in the north-east and Jammu and Kashmir would get 90 per cent of the project funds as ACA, and all others would get 80 per cent.[4]

A parallel programme of Urban Infrastructure Development Scheme for Small and Medium Towns (UIDSSMT) was also started to bridge the gap between metro and large cities and SMTs.[5] The objectives of the scheme are to: (i) improve infrastructural facilities and help create durable public assets and quality oriented services in cities and towns, (ii) enhance PPP in infrastructural development, and (iii) promote planned integrated development of towns and cities. ACA under this programme is 80 per cent of the project funds, another 10 per cent is to be state government funds, and only 10 per cent of the funds have to come from ULBs. Prior to UIDSSMT, a centrally sponsored scheme named Integrated Development of Small and Medium Towns (IDSMT) was meant for SMTs.

## Expenditures in UIG and UIDSSMT

The policy context presented here clearly indicates a bias in favour of metropolitan and large cities in terms of policies, understanding of urban development issues, and financing. Since national level compiled municipal finance data were not available, we used funding for two national programmes, UIG and UIDSSMT, for infrastructure development in metro and large cities and SMTs, respectively, as a representative of financial allocation to different size classes of urban centres. We used ACA approved and ACA released to the states for the UIG and UIDSSMT components at two time points for this purpose (Table 1.1).

To understand the data in Table 1.1 it is necessary to state the mechanisms of applications for the UIG and UIDSSMT projects. Both have similar mechanisms. After the preparation of a Comprehensive Development Plan (CDP) for a city, the city or the State Level Nodal Agency (SLNA) prepares a Detailed Project Report (DPR), which is then submitted to a Central Sanctioning and Monitoring Committee (CSMC). While the CDP and DPR are prepared and approved, states and cities/parastatals enter into a Memorandum of Agreement (MoA) with the Government of India (GoI) indicating their commitment to implementing identified reforms by spelling out specific milestones. The

**Table 1.1**  UIG and UIDSSMT ACA Approved and Released Over Time

|  | UIG | | UIDSSMT | | Ratio of UIG to UIDSSMT | |
|---|---|---|---|---|---|---|
|  | ACA approved | ACA released | ACA approved | ACA released | ACA approved | ACA released |
| Up to March 2009 (Rs crore)* | 23,411.09 | 7,428.40 | 10,311.76 | 5,820.71 | 3.2 | 1.8 |
| Up to August 10** (in crore) | 59,918.29 | 11,859.63 | 12,598.90 | 6,835.64 | 5.1 | 1.8 |
| GR from 2009 March to August 2010 (%) | 155.94 | 59.65 | 22.18 | 17.44 |  |  |

*Source:* * *Economic Survey 2008–9*, http://indiabudget.nic.in/es2008-09/chap2009/chap913.pdf (accessed on 12 May 2012).

** For UIG: http://jnnurm.nic.in/nurmudweb/Project/state.pdf (accessed on 15 February 2011) and for UIDSSMT: http://www.urbanindia.nic.in/programme/ud/uidssmtbody.htm#uidssmt (accessed on 15 February 2011).

central government gives the funds as ACA, as already mentioned, and a MoA is necessary to access ACA. Essentially, the project proposals and hence identification of the projects is done either by SLNA of the state or the concerned ULB (in states where the ULBs are powerful). The project proposals articulate the priority of the state and/or ULBs with regard to urban development. While the cities and towns prepare the project proposals, the state government sends them to the central government for funding. If a state gives priority to SMTs then a large number of applications will go for UIDSSMT funds and if a state gives priority to metros and large cities then the applications will go for UIG.

Table 1.1 gives the total ACA approved and released for two programmes at two time points. Up to August 2010, 640 towns and cities had been covered under UIDSSMT from 632 up to March 2009. This means that not many additional towns and cities were covered under UIDSSMT in this year. UIG was for 65 cities. ACA approved for UIDSSMT increased by 22.18 per cent from March 2010 to August 2010 (Table 1.1). But the increase in ACA released for UIDSSMT was only 17.44 per cent. In comparison, ACA approved and ACA released increased by 155.94 and 59.65 per cent, respectively, in the same period for UIG. Clearly, a larger proportion of central funds for urban development were going to UIG than to UIDSSMT projects, or to metros and large cities than to SMTs. This can also be seen from the figures of ACA approved and ACA released. The ratio of UIG to UIDSSMT ACA approved up to March 2009 was 3.2, which went up to 5.1 in the period up to August 2010. The ratio of UIG to UIDSSMT ACA released remained at 1.8 in the two periods mentioned. This means that the states had an overwhelming interest in projects in metros and large cities as compared to SMTs, but because of the funding pattern

biased in favour of SMTs, the gap narrowed down between UIG and UIDSSMT in the ACA released.

Kundu and Samanta (2011: 62–3) show that:

Only 58% of the urban population has been covered under JNNURM, the coverage being high in the developed states and metropolitan cities. Of the 5,161 towns/cities, 4,207 are yet to be covered under the programme. An analysis of the JNNURM funding pattern, which is inbuilt in the component-wise indicative allocation, clearly brings out the big-city bias. In fact, the developed states have had a larger share of the pie because of their ability to introduce the reforms as per their committed timeline. Moreover, a closer examination of the CDPs and DPRs, along with the mandatory reforms makes it obvious that the mission has a clear-cut mandate of producing 'global cities', disciplining them enough to adhere to the rigours of the credit rating agencies, which is a precondition to access capital market and other innovative sources of funding.

After the strong criticism of the mission on account of exclusions created through urban development processes (Mahadevia 2006a: 63), JNNURM included some pro-poor elements. But Kundu and Samanta (2011: 63) find that there was 'greater bias on improving the efficiency in the functioning of the overall city economy and meeting the infrastructural deficiencies at the macro-level rather than addressing the issues of distributional inadequacy and improving the access of the poor to these'.

In all, proposals had been sent for 640 towns under UIDSSMT by August end 2010 (Table 1.2) for 763 projects.[6] This means that of the approximate 5,000 towns and cities in India, only a few have sent funding applications (or DPRs) and average project proposals sent per SMT were 1.2. This was unlike the proposals sent under UIG for mission cities where there were many proposals per city sent for funding to the Ministry of Urban Development (MoUD).

**Table 1.2**    UIDSSMT versus UIG by States

| States | UIDSSMT to UIG (%age) (Total approved) | UIDSSMT to UIG (%age) (Total ACA released) |
|---|---|---|
| Andhra Pradesh | 54.1 | 174.6 |
| Assam | 65.8 | 70.0 |
| Bihar | 36.7 | 108.3 |
| Chhattisgarh | 82.8 | 37.0 |
| Gujarat | 8.2 | 21.9 |
| Haryana | 23.3 | 57.0 |
| Himachal | 13.2 | 37.2 |
| Jammu and Kashmir | 75.0 | 155.8 |
| Jharkhand | 12.7 | 33.2 |
| Karnataka | 20.8 | 63.7 |
| Kerala | 42.9 | 105.0 |
| Madhya Pradesh | 33.6 | 73.8 |
| Maharashtra | 23.9 | 51.9 |
| Orissa | 27.4 | 57.0 |
| Punjab | 54.6 | 122.2 |
| Rajasthan | 49.6 | 75.0 |
| Tamil Nadu | 14.9 | 59.0 |
| Uttarakhand | 15.4 | 19.4 |
| Uttar Pradesh | 21.7 | 51.4 |
| West Bengal | 8.0 | 33.6 |
| All-India | 21.0 | 57.6 |

*Source*: Mahadevia (2011: 58).

*Note*: 1. No parking projects sent for approval under UIDSSMT.

    2. Situation as on 31 August 2010.

But not all states had this dismal interest in UIDSSMT. Andhra Pradesh, Assam, Chhattisgarh, Jammu and Kashmir, Punjab, and Rajasthan, sent in UIDSSMT proposals equalling about 50 per cent and more of UIG funding requests (Tables 1.2 and 1.3). In fact, an old study on municipal finances found that per capita grants were the highest to small towns of population size up to 50,000 in Andhra Pradesh (if the municipal corporations were excluded). Punjab also had lower inequality among different size classes of towns in terms of per capita income and expenditure in this study (Mahadevia and Mukherjee 2003). Gujarat was the most unequal in terms of per capita income, per capita expenditure, per capita grant, and per capita debt, with SMTs at a great disadvantage as compared to metros (Mahadevia and Mukherjee 2003; Mahadevia 2006b). This is further supported by UIDSSMT proposals sent from Gujarat. The total funds applied for under UIDSSMT from Gujarat were just 8.2 per cent of the funds applied for under UIG! The other state which had such a poor interest in UIDSSMT was West Bengal, with UIDSSMT to UIG proportion in the project funds approved 8.0 per cent. In Gujarat and West Bengal, there was exclusive focus on metropolitan cities for infrastructure development.

**Table 1.3**    UIDSSMT as a Proportion of UIG, States

| Ratio | < 25% | 25–50% | 50–75% | 75–100% | >100% |
|---|---|---|---|---|---|
| UIDSSMT to UIG (%age) (Total approved) | Gujarat, Haryana Himachal, Jharkhand Karnataka, Maharashtra Tamil Nadu, Uttarakhand Uttar Pradesh, West Bengal | Bihar, Kerala Madhya Pradesh Orissa Rajasthan | Andhra Pradesh Assam Punjab | Chhattisgarh Jammu and Kashmir | |
| UIDSSMT to UIG (%age) (Total ACA released) | Gujarat Uttarakhand | Chhattisgarh Himachal Jharkhand West Bengal | Haryana, Karnataka Madhya Pradesh Maharashtra Orissa, Rajasthan Tamil Nadu Uttar Pradesh | Assam | Andhra Pradesh Bihar, Jammu and Kashmir Kerala, Punjab |

*Source*: Calculated by the authors from Mahadevia (2011).

When we look at ACA approved figures, the states which had a dismal record in terms of treating their SMTs were Gujarat, Haryana, Himachal Pradesh, Jharkhand, Karnataka, Maharashtra, Tamil Nadu, Uttarakhand, Uttar Pradesh, and West Bengal. These were states which either had one or more metropolitan cities and hence the state's attention was towards metro cities (Gujarat, Maharashtra, Karnataka, Tamil Nadu, Uttar Pradesh, and West Bengal). The other four states fall in this category because of their own reasons, which are not discussed here. Less developed states had a lower bias against SMTs and states such as Andhra Pradesh and Punjab were less unequal as shown

by Mahadevia and Mukherjee (2003) in the municipal finance analysis. Kerala's urbanization pattern was one continuum and there was very little difference in living standards in metros and non-metros.

With regard to ACA released, Gujarat and Uttarakhand remain laggards when the UIDSSMT to UIG proportion is viewed (Figure 1.6). Other laggards with respect to funds applied for but which did not improve in terms of ACA received were Haryana, Karnataka, Maharashtra, Tamil Nadu, and Uttar Pradesh. In terms of ACA released, the success in UIDSSMT was higher as compared to UIG because under the former the central

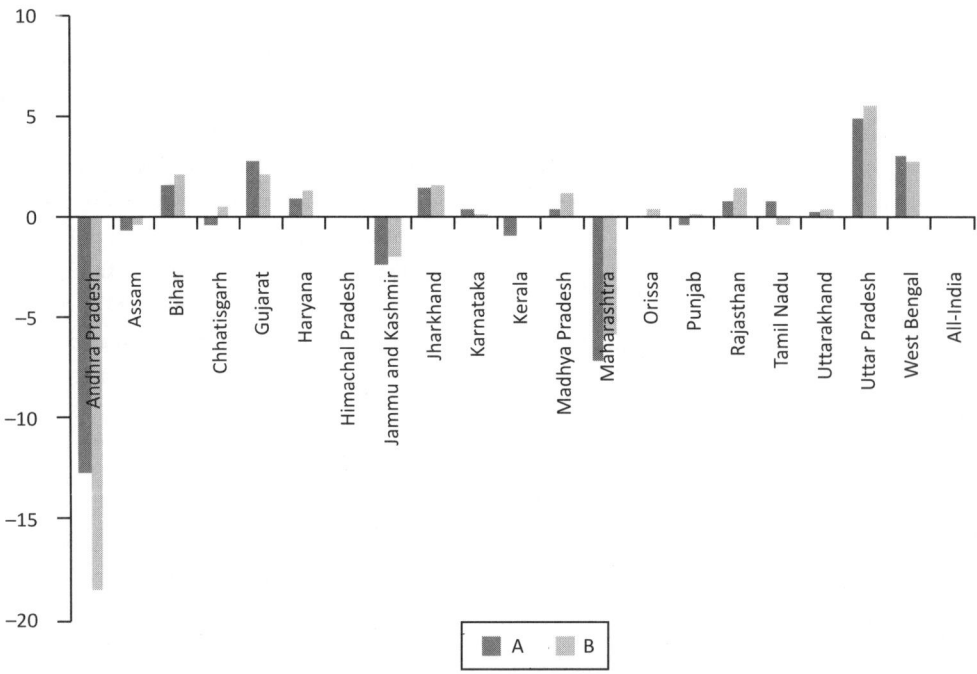

**Figure 1.6**   Difference between State's Share in Total Urban Population and State's Share in Total UIDSSMT ACA, Approved and Released

*Source*: Calculated by the authors from Mahadevia (2011).
*Note*: 1. A = ACA approved; B = ACA released. 2. If the sign is negative then the state has got higher approval or received ACA released to the total at the national level than its share in the total urban population, indicating that the state has given priority to SMTs. 3. Situation as on August 2010.

government contributes 80 per cent of the project costs and also releases ACA in two instalments, whereas in UIG the central share is only 35 per cent of the project cost and it releases ACA in four instalments. Hence, at the onset there was some equalization process instituted at the central government level to assist SMTs even if the states were not too keen to submit proposals. Thus, the proportion of ACA released for UIDSSMT to the proportion of ACA released for UIG projects was 58 per cent at the all-India level for the major states listed in Table 1.2 and for Andhra Pradesh, Bihar, Jammu and Kashmir, Kerala, and Punjab this proportion was more than 100 per cent. This means that

more funds to these states were released under UIDSSMT than under UIG. Thus, contrary to what has been argued by Kundu and Samantha (2011), in these states one observed lower bias against SMTs than in favour of metropolitan or main cities.

Figure 1.6 gives the difference between a state's share in the total urban population and its share in total UIDSSMT ACA, approved and released. Figure 1.6 shows that Andhra Pradesh, Jammu and Kashmir, and Maharashtra were the only three states where the sign was negative, indicating that the states had got more approval or received ACA released to the total at the national level than their share in the total

**Table 1.4**  Sectoral Share under UIDSSMT

| States | Water Supply | Sewerage | Storm Water | Water Body Management | Solid Waste Management | Heritage | Road | Total Approved | No. of Towns |
|---|---|---|---|---|---|---|---|---|---|
| Andhra Pradesh | 73.0 | 14.2 | 7.7 | 0.0 | 0.1 | 0.0 | 4.9 | 100.0 | 69 |
| Assam | 9.0 | 0.0 | 91.0 | 0.0 | 0.0 | 0.0 | 0.0 | 100.0 | 28 |
| Bihar | 37.8 | 0.0 | 0.0 | 0.0 | 3.8 | 0.0 | 58.4 | 100.0 | 11 |
| Chhattisgarh | 24.3 | 75.7 | 0.0 | 0.0 | 0.0 | 0.0 | 0.0 | 100.0 | 3 |
| Gujarat | 100.0 | 0.0 | 0.0 | 0.0 | 0.0 | 0.0 | 0.0 | 100.0 | 52 |
| Haryana | 0.0 | 66.4 | 0.0 | 0.0 | 33.6 | 0.0 | 0.0 | 100.0 | 7 |
| Himachal Pradesh | 0.0 | 0.0 | 26.0 | 1.3 | 0.0 | 0.0 | 63.4 | 100.0 | 3 |
| Jammu and Kashmir | 46.9 | 0.0 | 23.6 | 0.1 | 6.4 | 4.2 | 18.8 | 100.0 | 13 |
| Jharkhand | 83.6 | 0.0 | 0.0 | 0.0 | 16.4 | 0.0 | 0.0 | 100.0 | 4 |
| Karnataka | 61.3 | 11.4 | 10.7 | 0.0 | 0.0 | 0.0 | 16.6 | 100.0 | 30 |
| Kerala | 79.8 | 11.6 | 0.0 | 0.0 | 8.5 | 0.0 | 0.0 | 100.0 | 22 |
| Madhya Pradesh | 77.1 | 20.8 | 0.0 | 0.1 | 0.0 | 0.1 | 1.9 | 100.0 | 33 |
| Maharashtra | 76.8 | 18.0 | 3.2 | 0.0 | 0.0 | 0.1 | 1.9 | 100.0 | 86 |
| Orissa | 56.9 | 2.7 | 0.0 | 9.9 | 0.0 | 7.7 | 22.8 | 100.0 | 12 |
| Punjab | 15.0 | 85.0 | 0.0 | 0.0 | 0.0 | 0.0 | 0.0 | 100.0 | 14 |
| Rajasthan | 25.0 | 65.2 | 3.3 | 1.1 | 0.0 | 1.0 | 4.4 | 100.0 | 35 |
| Tamil Nadu | 53.6 | 34.5 | 0.4 | 0.0 | 0.4 | 0.0 | 11.1 | 100.0 | 115 |
| Uttarakhand | 0.0 | 100.0 | 0.0 | 0.0 | 0.0 | 0.0 | 0.0 | 100.0 | 1 |
| Uttar Pradesh | 41.6 | 24.7 | 1.9 | 0.0 | 14.5 | 0.0 | 17.5 | 100.0 | 46 |
| West Bengal | 82.1 | 3.2 | 12.8 | 0.0 | 0.0 | 0.0 | 1.9 | 100.0 | 25 |
| All-India | 61.2 | 22.5 | 5.8 | 0.2 | 2.5 | 0.3 | 7.4 | 100.0 | 640 |

*Source*: Mahadevia (2011: 58).

*Note*: 1. No parking projects sent for approval under UIDSSMT. 2. Situation as on 31 August 2010.

urban population. These states, therefore, gave priority to SMTs.

Interestingly and rightly so, about 84 per cent of the project funds applied for in UIDSSMT were for water supply and sewerage, the former having a share of 61 per cent and the latter 23 per cent (Table 1.4). Lack of city level infrastructure networks for water supply and sanitation are bottlenecks in improving basic services at the household level. It is too early to assess the impact of the 2008–9 NSS data on either JNNURM or UIDSSMT, but we expect that these investments will show results in the 2011 census[7] and certainly in the next NSS housing survey. There are a few states that deviate from this general behaviour—in Assam 91 per cent of the UIDSSMT approved project funds were for storm water drainage, in Haryana 34 per cent were for Solid Waste Management (SWM), in Himachal Pradesh 63 per cent were for roads, and in Orissa also 23 per cent were for roads. In Uttar Pradesh, water supply, sewerage, SWM, and roads were all important sectors, but water supply constituted only 42 per cent of the project funds approved, which was much lower than this sector's share at the national level. In other words, UIDSSMT projects will improve water and sewerage networks in SMTs.

## IMPORTANCE OF SMALL AND MEDIUM TOWNS

Interest in research in Small and Intermediate Urban Centres (SIUCs) or what we in India call SMTs, has been to seek alternatives to the processes of concentration of production, high-income jobs, and economic and social development in a few urban centres—large or metropolitan cities—in a country. In the developing countries, which have a colonial legacy, the metropolitan or large cities acted as primate cities organizing economies of imperial powers in colonized countries. Focussing

on the development of SMTs was meant to serve two purposes—directing growth away from centres of imperial power and at the same time achieving balanced regional economic and social development. Thus, national and international policies on SIUCs/SMTs carried both economic and social objectives (Hardoy and Satterthwaite 1986). But in practice not much has been achieved.

The UN's Conference on Human Settlements (Habitat Conference) in Vancouver in May-June 1976 made specific recommendations with regard to SIUCs/SMTs. The recommendations that were unanimously approved by the 132 governments, pointed to the urgent need for every government to establish a national policy on human settlements embodying the distribution of population and related economic and social activities over the national territory (Recommendation A.1) as an integral part of any national economic and social development policy (A.2) with the aim of improving the conditions of human settlements particularly promoting a more equitable distribution of benefits of development among regions and by making such benefits and public services equally accessible to all groups (A.4) (Ibid.).

In a seminar on Urban Development Strategies held by the UN Centre for Regional Development (UNCRD), Nagoya, Japan in 1974, development of SIUCs was emphasized because of the understanding that these towns: (i) have maximum employment multipliers, and (ii) provide possibility of amenity-based strategies of decentralizing social services in rural areas (Minocha and Yadav 1989: 11). Besides, SMTs could play the role of countering primacy, facilitating multiple growth via decentralization, offering rural areas accessibility to higher urban services, providing linkages to rural and urban areas, and promoting spatial integration via more dispersed populations (Minocha and

Yadav 1989). In India, in recognition of the latter, a new scheme 'Providing Urban Facilities to Rural Areas' (PURA) was announced in early 2004. Lastly, SMTs could act as food grain procurement centres for food security of the entire nation.

Hardoy and Satterthwaite (1986) give five reasons why developing country[8] governments would (should) consider the current and potential role of these centres in their national social and economic development plans: (i) SIUCs are places where rural people and rural enterprises interact and hence these centres can play a very important role in the development of rural areas by providing social and economic facilities, (ii) these settlements have local political importance, where the sub-national and sub-regional levels of government are located. It is through these centres that the needs and priorities of the sub-national and sub-regional populations get represented at the national levels. National governments have not been able to stimulate urban development away from large cities because of a poor understanding of local circumstances, local needs, and local possibilities in these urban centres that are meant to serve as growth centres, (iii) in developing countries, some of these centres can play an important role in many national priorities. For example, if a country has a national goal of increasing agricultural productivity or reducing food imports, some such centres can be provided with infrastructure to do so. In the current context in India where droughts and the spectre of hunger loom over a number of states and repeated disasters occur, these centres can be of importance in food distribution and disaster management away from state headquarters, (iv) long-term policies for the development of SIUCs can lessen the tendency towards undesirable concentration of industries, services, and government officials, and (v) in some countries nearby small and intermediate urban

settlements can be supported to support economic and social development in large cities or metropolitan centres. Hansen (1982) believes that urbanization from below will organically link the poor population with the development process.

In the context of China, researchers have argued that small towns have: (i) been beneficial to rational distribution of productive forces and control of size of large cities, (ii) led to favourable accumulation of large incidence of labour surplus through transfer of the population from agricultural to non-agricultural activities, (iii) been conducive to economic cooperation between the town and country-side as well as between workers and peasants, and (iv) led to a progressive rise in the level of health, education, and culture in rural areas (Deyin and Zongfen 1982).

SIUCs can play and will play different roles. Some will function as administrative headquarters, some will become industrial and commercial centres, some will be of tourist interest, and others may be market towns that can support agriculture. Some can help in the economic development of a region by locating industries. Some can be satellite towns for large cities, either in the immediate periphery or close by for guided urban/metropolitan development. They can be rural–urban interface settlements. They can promote local enterprises and local products and help in local wealth accumulation and therefore economic growth. They can absorb rural populations. They can spread social development and awareness, knowledge and information. They can decongest metros. They can absorb first generation migrants from rural areas and by that promote the process of urbanization.

Hardoy and Satterthwaite (1986: 5) believe that developing countries have not been successful in their attempts to divert urban growth and development to 'growth poles', 'growth centres', 'growth axes', and 'new towns'. In India too, the fate of SMTs has been similar.

## CLASSIFICATION OF URBAN CENTRES IN INDIA

The census of India classifies urban centres in six categories: (i) Class I, population 100,000 and above; (ii) Class II, population 50,000 to 99,999, (iii) Class III, population 20,000 to 49,999, (iv) Class IV, population 10,000 to 19,999, (v) Class V, population 5,000 to 9,999, and (vi) Class VI, population below 5,000.

The National Commission on Urbanization (NCU) proposed a different classification. It classified cities into six classes and towns into two. The classification of cities is: (i) C1, population 1 lakh to 5 lakh, (ii) C2, population 5 to 10 lakh, (iii) C3, population 10 to 20 lakh, (iv) C4, population 20 to 50 lakh, (v) C5, population 50 to 100 lakh, and (vi) C6, population 100 lakh and above. The classification of towns is: (i) T1, population 20,000 to 50,000, and (ii) T2, population 50,000 to 100,000.

As per the 74th CAA, urban centres are classified into four classes, M, A, B, and C for the purpose of urban governance and financial allocations. Class M cities are municipal corporations (population 3 lakh and above), class A are cities with municipalities (population 1 to 3 lakh), class B are towns with Nagar Panchayats (population 50,000 to 1 lakh), and class C are towns with populations less than 50,000.

The following classification of urban centres is available for the 1987–8 (43rd) and 1993–4 (50th) NSS Rounds.

i.    Small towns—Size class 4 (C4), up to population 50,000
ii.   Medium towns—Size class 3 (C3), population 50,000 to 200,000
iii.  Large cities—Size class 1 (C2), population 200,000 to 1 million

iv.   Metropolitan cities—Size class 1 (CM), population > 1 million

In the 1999–2000 (55th) Round, categories (ii) and (iii) mentioned above were merged together and the data for three stratums, of towns up to 50,000 population, towns between 50,000 and 1 million population, and cities with populations more than 1 million were available. In the 2004–5 and 2009–10 NSS Rounds, only two categories of disaggregation is possible, non-metro (all urban centres with population less than 1 million) and metro (urban centres with population more than 1 million). The categories were simplified because of the desire to increase the sample of individual metropolitan cities that would allow a city-wise analysis. Thus, although the study started with the purpose of comparing the different sizes of SMTs and metropolitan cities to observe their economic bases, employment situations, education levels, and levels of basic facilities, we were able to do this only till 1993–4, after which the study remains as a comparison between metros and non-metros with regard to these parameters.

Since the 61st Round, each district is treated as a separate strata and if there are one or more urban areas in a district with a population of 10 lakh or more as per the population census 2001, each of these forms a separate basic stratum and the remaining urban areas of the district are considered as another basic stratum (NSSO 2007: 5). Thus, in the NSS 61st and 66th Round surveys, estimates of each of the metros were directly available from the particular stratum estimate, whereas estimates for towns with populations between 50,000 and 1 million and less than 50,000 were not directly available as was possible in the previous Rounds. However, the NSSO did derive estimates of the last two categories from the First Stage Units (FSUs) and published them with a caveat that 'it is likely that the variability of the estimates for class 2 and class 3 towns in the 61st round may be on the higher side compared to those of 50th and 55th rounds' (NSSO 2007: 5). Class 2 and class 3 mentioned earlier refer to towns with populations between 50,000 and 1 million and less than 50,000, respectively. Similar possibility is there for the 66th Round data as well but NSSO has not yet processed these data.

The 65th Round, undertaken during July 2008 to June 2009 and which covered housing conditions and urban slums, had a different classification of urban strata: (i) < 50,000 population, (ii) 50,000 to 99,999 population, (iii) 100,000 to 499,000 population, (iv) 500,000 to 999,999 population, and (v) million and million plus cities. For this Round also, we restricted our processing to the metro and non-metro stratification and give additional data for small towns (population < 50,000).

Population distribution across the four urban size classes mentioned earlier was calculated for the 2001 census (Table 1.5). This data shows that among the 15 large states, Maharashtra had 51.30 per cent urban population living in metropolises (class CM), whereas just 14.70 per cent of the urban population lived in C4 (< 50,000 population) towns. The other state that had a very high proportion of the population living in metropolises was Gujarat (42.31 per cent). In contrast, Tamil Nadu, the state that had the highest urbanization level in 2001, had just 15.48 per cent of its urban population living in metropolises and as high as 42.95 per cent of its urban population living in C4 towns. Same was the case with Kerala, where 41.61 per cent of the urban population lived in C4 towns. These two states therefore had very broad-based urbanization whereas Maharashtra

**Table 1.5**　Population Distribution by City Size and States, 2001

| S. No. | Major States | C4 | C3 | C2 | CM | Total |
|--------|-------------|----|----|----|----|-------|
| | | Population < 50,000 | Population 50,000 to 200,000 | Population 200,000 to 1 million | Population 1 million | |
| 1 | Andhra Pradesh | 13.47 | 36.33 | 32.81 | 17.40 | 100.00 |
| 2 | Assam | 47.23 | 28.10 | 24.67 | – | 100.00 |
| 3 | Bihar | 29.18 | 34.53 | 20.21 | 16.08 | 100.00 |
| 4 | Gujarat | 19.59 | 26.87 | 11.23 | 42.31 | 100.00 |
| 5 | Haryana | 24.09 | 37.98 | 20.43 | 17.49 | 100.00 |
| 6 | Karnataka | 25.31 | 22.52 | 27.74 | 24.43 | 100.00 |
| 7 | Kerala | 41.61 | 25.31 | 33.08 | – | 100.00 |
| 8 | Madhya Pradesh | 36.01 | 25.16 | 19.69 | 19.14 | 100.00 |
| 9 | Maharashtra | 14.70 | 11.27 | 22.73 | 51.30 | 100.00 |
| 10 | Orissa | 37.76 | 26.92 | 35.32 | – | 100.00 |
| 11 | Punjab | 25.37 | 30.30 | 27.11 | 17.21 | 100.00 |
| 12 | Rajasthan | 29.58 | 23.09 | 29.66 | 17.67 | 100.00 |
| 13 | Tamil Nadu | 42.95 | 21.65 | 19.93 | 15.48 | 100.00 |
| 14 | Uttar Pradesh | 29.74 | 22.23 | 24.15 | 23.89 | 100.00 |
| 15 | West Bengal | 17.05 | 30.62 | 27.33 | 25.00 | 100.00 |
| 16 | India | 26.22 | 23.65 | 24.04 | 26.09 | 100.00 |

*Source*: Calculated by the authors using 2001 population census data procured from the census office.

and Gujarat had narrow-base urbanization. On the whole, about 26 per cent of the urban population lived in metropolises and the same percentage of the urban population lived in C4 towns. But otherwise there was high diversity in urban settlement patterns across states.

Figure 1.7 graphically presents the data of Table 1.5 for some of the states. Population distribution across the four size classes was relatively more balanced in India as a whole, and in Karnataka. Andhra Pradesh and Haryana had population concentration in the middle two

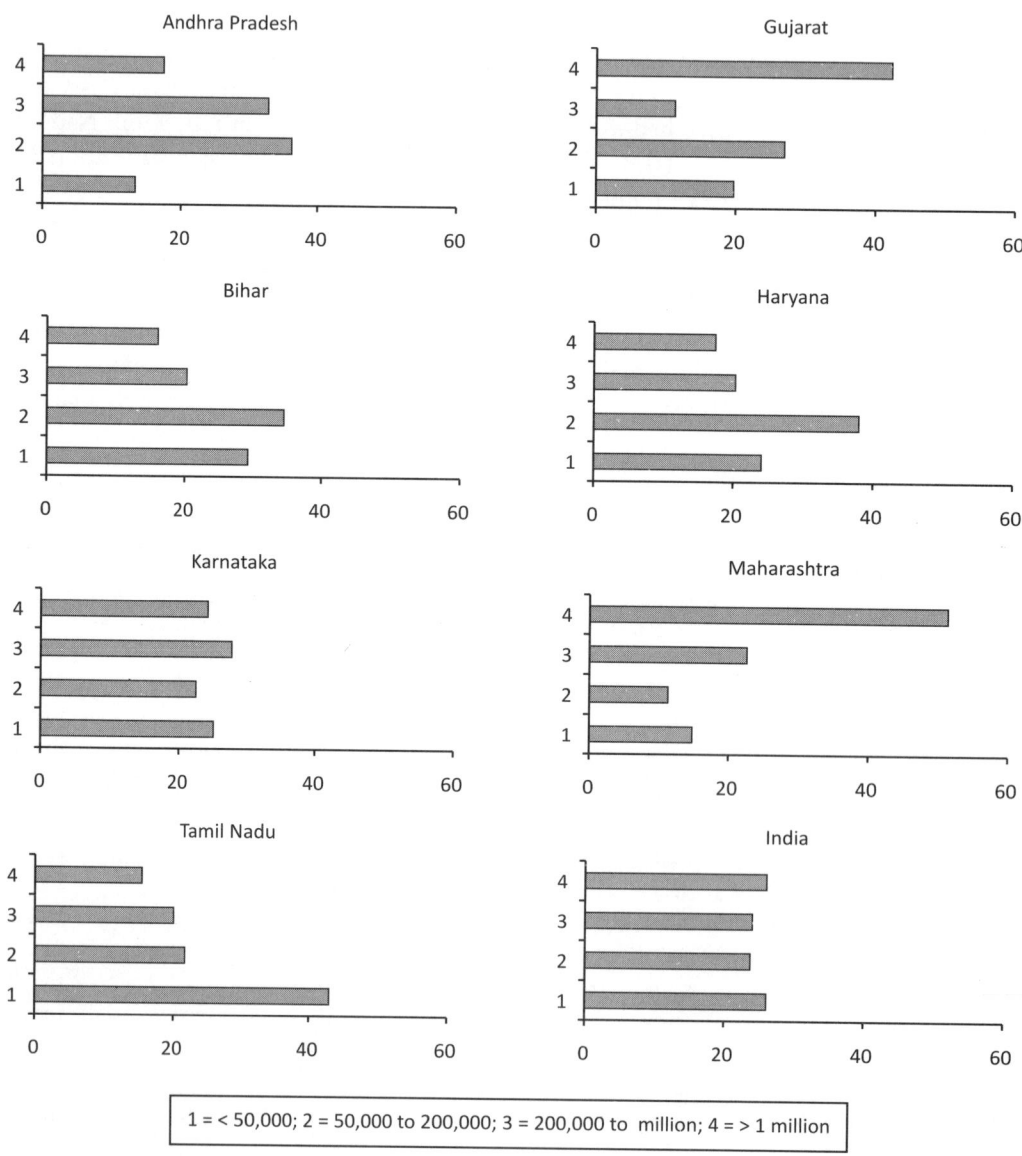

1 = < 50,000; 2 = 50,000 to 200,000; 3 = 200,000 to million; 4 = > 1 million

**Figure 1.7**    Population Distribution by Size Class of Urban Centres, 2001

*Source*: Data taken from Table 1.5.

categories, that is, in towns with population from 50,000 to 1 million. Top heavy states, that is, states with a concentration of population in metros were Gujarat and Maharashtra. A bottom heavy state was Tamil Nadu, with population concentration in small towns with population up to 50,000.

Table 1.6 shows that Gujarat's population was concentrated in metros. Hence it sent more funding proposals for metros. Conversely, Andhra Pradesh, Bihar, Haryana, Madhya Pradesh, Punjab, and Rajasthan had concentration of their populations in non-metros and hence these states had a higher proportion of UIDSSMT to UIG funds approved. Karnataka, Tamil Nadu, and West Bengal are interesting as they had a concentration of the population in non-metros but did not take much interest in sending proposals under UIDSSMT. There was a bias in these states against SMTs as far as new development investments were concerned. Lastly, although Maharashtra had a very high proportion of its population living in

metros, it continued to ask for central funds for SMTs. Thus, on the whole there was inequality between metros and non-metros which was increasing; states behaved entirely differently in terms of priorities in investments.

**URBAN POVERTY**

On the whole, while the proportion of the urban population below the poverty line declined from 49.01 per cent in 1973–4 to 25.70 per cent in 2004–5, the absolute number of urban poor increased from 600.46 lakh to 807.96 lakh (Table 1.7), an increase of 34.6 per cent over a 30-year period or an increase of 1 per cent per annum over the period. The absolute number of urban poor increased with an increase in urbanization levels. In contrast, in rural areas there was a consistent decline in the absolute number of poor except for an increase in 1993–4.

Though there was consistent decline in the incidence of urban poverty in India, represented by Head Count Ratios (HCRs) and in nearly all

**Table 1.6**   Matrix of % Population in Non-metros and % of UIDSSMT to UIG

| % Pop in Non-metros | UIDSSMT to UIG (%) in Approved ACA | |
|---|---|---|
| | Above India's average | Below India's average |
| Above India's Average | Andhra Pradesh, Bihar, Haryana, Madhya Pradesh, Punjab, Rajasthan | Karnataka, Tamil Nadu, West Bengal |
| Below India's Average | Maharashtra | Gujarat |

*Source*: Data taken from Tables 1.2 and 1.5.

**Table 1.7**   Trends in Poverty in India, Different Estimates

| Year | Number and Percentage of Poor | | | | | |
|---|---|---|---|---|---|---|
| | Rural | | Urban | | Combined | |
| | No. (lakh) | % | No. (lakh) | % | No. (lakh) | % |
| 1973–4 | 2612.9 | 56.4 | 600.5 | 49.0 | 3213.4 | 54.9 |
| 1977–8 | 2642.5 | 53.1 | 646.5 | 45.2 | 3289.0 | 51.3 |
| 1983 | 2519.6 | 45.7 | 709.4 | 40.8 | 3229.0 | 44.5 |
| 1987–8 | 2318.8 | 39.1 | 751.7 | 38.2 | 3070.5 | 38.9 |
| 1993–4 | 2440.3 | 37.3 | 763.4 | 32.4 | 3203.7 | 36.0 |
| 2004–5 | 2209.2 | 28.3 | 808.0 | 25.7 | 3017.2 | 27.5 |

*Source*: Press Information Bureau (1997, 2007).

**Table 1.8**   State-wise Urban Poverty Estimates

| S. No. | State | 1973–4* | 1977–8* | 1983* | 1987–8* | 1993–4* | 2004–5** |
|--------|-------|---------|---------|-------|---------|---------|----------|
| 1 | Andhra Pradesh | 50.6 | 43.6 | 36.3 | 40.1 | 38.3 | 28.0 |
| 2 | Assam | 36.9 | 32.7 | 21.7 | 9.9 | 7.7 | 3.3 |
| 3 | Bihar | 53.0 | 48.8 | 47.3 | 48.7 | 34.5 | 34.6 |
| 4 | Gujarat | 52.6 | 40.0 | 39.1 | 37.3 | 27.9 | 13.0 |
| 5 | Haryana | 40.2 | 36.6 | 24.2 | 18.0 | 16.4 | 15.1 |
| 6 | Himachal Pradesh | 13.2 | 19.4 | 9.4 | 6.3 | 9.2 | 3.4 |
| 7 | Karnataka | 52.5 | 50.4 | 42.8 | 48.4 | 40.1 | 32.6 |
| 8 | Kerala | 62.7 | 55.6 | 45.7 | 40.3 | 24.6 | 20.2 |
| 9 | Madhya Pradesh | 57.7 | 58.7 | 53.1 | 47.1 | 48.4 | 42.1 |
| 10 | Maharashtra | 43.9 | 40.1 | 40.3 | 39.8 | 35.2 | 32.2 |
| 11 | Orissa | 55.6 | 50.9 | 49.2 | 41.6 | 41.6 | 44.3 |
| 12 | Punjab | 28.0 | 27.3 | 23.8 | 14.7 | 11.4 | 7.1 |
| 13 | Rajasthan | 52.1 | 43.5 | 37.9 | 41.9 | 30.5 | 32.9 |
| 14 | Tamil Nadu | 49.4 | 48.7 | 47.0 | 38.6 | 39.8 | 22.2 |
| 15 | Uttar Pradesh | 60.1 | 56.2 | 49.8 | 43.0 | 35.4 | 30.6 |
| 16 | West Bengal | 34.7 | 38.2 | 32.3 | 35.1 | 22.4 | 14.8 |
| 17 | All-India | 49.0 | 45.2 | 40.8 | 38.2 | 32.4 | 25.7 |
|  | Coefficient of Variation | 28.1 | 25.0 | 32.7 | 40.5 | 43.3 | 55.6 |

*Source*: * Press Information Bureau (1997); ** Press Information Bureau (2007).

the states, the decline was not consistent (Table 1.8). In some states, urban poverty increased in some intervening years. For example, this happened in Andhra Pradesh, Rajasthan, and West Bengal from 1983 to 1987–8, and in Himachal Pradesh, Madhya Pradesh, and Tamil Nadu from 1987–8 to 1993–4. In Orissa, till 1987–8, there was a consistent decline, after which the incidence of urban poverty remained steady at about 40 per cent and increased to 44 per cent in 2004–5. In Maharashtra, there was near stagnation in urban poverty reduction between 1977–8 and 1987–8. In 1993–4, a significant decline occurred and thereafter the HCR decline continued. In 2004–5, among the 16 large states given in Table 1.8, Maharashtra was at the 6th position with a HCR of 32.20 per cent. States that had higher urban poverty incidence than Maharashtra in 2004–5 were Orissa (44.30 per cent), Madhya Pradesh

(42.10 per cent), Bihar (34.60 per cent), Rajasthan (32.90 per cent), and Karnataka (32.60 per cent) (Table 1.8 and Figure 1.6).

States that consistently registered lower incidence of urban poverty than the national level were Gujarat, Haryana, Himachal Pradesh, Assam, Punjab, and West Bengal, not particularly depicting any pattern in the matter. Kerala entered this list from 1993–4 onwards and Tamil Nadu in 2004–5. Occasionally, some other states entered and then left this list. Further, Tamil Nadu, Gujarat, and Andhra Pradesh registered the highest decline in urban poverty from 1993–4 to 2004–5 (Table 1.9). Among these, Gujarat had lower incidence of urban poverty compared to the other two and Andhra Pradesh and Tamil Nadu had nearly 40 per cent of population below poverty line in 1993–4 (Table 1.8). Incidence of urban poverty increased in Orissa and Rajasthan from 1993–4 to 2004–5 (Figure 1.8 and Table 1.9). These were the only two states where the incidence of urban poverty increased in this decade.

The Coefficient of Variation (CV) of HCRs across the states increased from 28.14 in 1973–4 to 55.63 in 2004–5. From 1977–8, there was consistent increase in inequality across the states with regard to incidence of urban poverty. This means that some states registered a faster reduction in urban poverty whereas other states registered lower reduction in urban poverty. Not only was urbanization uneven across states in India but urban poverty reduction was also uneven across the states. The unevenness in urban poverty reduction increased from the early 1990s, a period that coincided with economic reforms in India. Unevenness in urbanization also increased in the period of economic reforms, as seen before.

This book, however, only focuses on the inequalities between metros and non-metros with regard to poverty, employment, education levels, and services. Wherever needed, we discuss variations across the states. As Table 1.8 shows inequality across states with regard to the incidence of urban poverty and its reduction over time. We also expect that inequalities within a metro city also increased, which is evident from Figures 1.2 and 1.5. But, a scrutiny of other trends in the urban arena when urbanization and urban development processes are progressing on a highly unequal economic and social base and the inequality enhancing policy regime of the reforms period is kept for a future date and other studies. This book focuses only on inequalities between metros and non-metros over time, from 1987–8 to 2009–10.

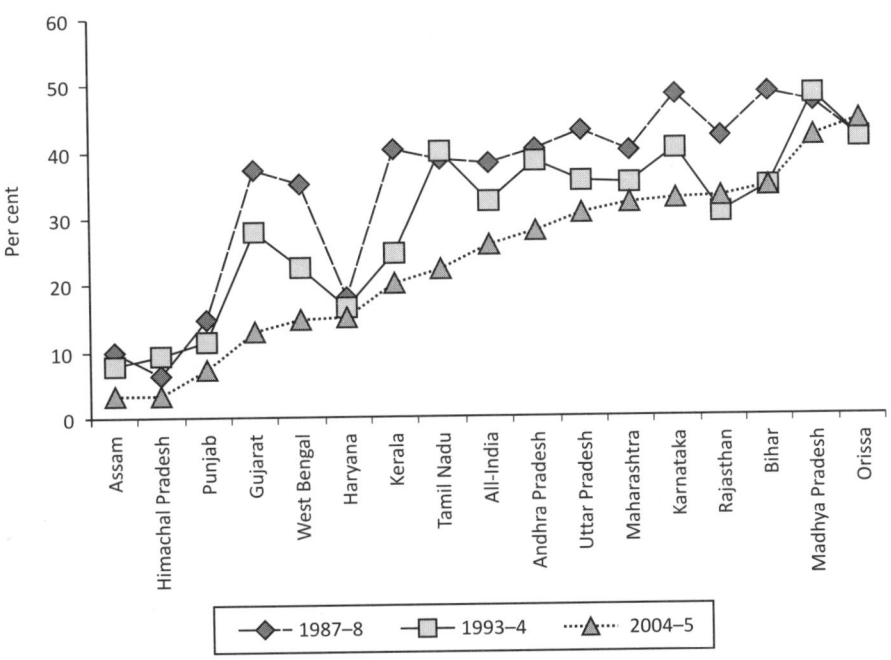

**Figure 1.8** Urban Poverty by States Over Time

*Source*: Data taken from Table 1.8.

**Table 1.9**   State-wise Decline in Urban Poverty (Percentage Points)

| S. No. | State | 1977–8* | 1983* | 1987–8* | 1993–4* | 1993–4—2004–5 |
|---|---|---|---|---|---|---|
| 1 | Andhra Pradesh | 7.06 | 7.25 | −3.81 | 1.78 | 10.33 |
| 2 | Assam | 4.21 | 10.98 | 11.79 | 2.21 | 4.43 |
| 3 | Bihar | 4.22 | 1.43 | −1.40 | 14.23 | −0.10 |
| 4 | Gujarat | 12.55 | 0.88 | 1.88 | 9.37 | 14.89 |
| 5 | Haryana | 3.61 | 12.42 | 6.16 | 1.61 | 1.28 |
| 6 | Himachal Pradesh | −6.27 | 10.01 | 3.14 | −2.89 | 5.78 |
| 7 | Karnataka | 2.17 | 7.54 | −5.60 | 8.28 | 7.54 |
| 8 | Kerala | 7.12 | 9.94 | 5.35 | 15.78 | 4.35 |
| 9 | Madhya Pradesh | −1.01 | 5.60 | 5.97 | −1.29 | 6.28 |
| 10 | Maharashtra | 3.78 | −0.17 | 0.48 | 4.63 | 2.95 |
| 11 | Orissa | 4.70 | 1.77 | 7.52 | −0.01 | −2.66 |
| 12 | Punjab | 0.64 | 3.53 | 9.12 | 3.32 | 4.25 |
| 13 | Rajasthan | 8.60 | 5.59 | −3.98 | 11.43 | −2.41 |
| 14 | Tamil Nadu | 0.71 | 1.73 | 8.32 | −1.13 | 17.57 |
| 15 | Uttar Pradesh | 3.86 | 6.41 | 6.86 | 7.57 | 4.79 |
| 16 | West Bengal | −3.53 | 5.88 | −2.76 | 12.67 | 7.61 |
| 17 | All-India | 3.77 | 4.45 | 2.59 | 5.84 | 6.66 |

*Source*: Calculated by the authors from data in Table 1.8.
*Note*: * Over previous round.

## DATA ISSUES

There are some shortcomings in NSS classifications. The 43rd Round (1987–8) town classification is based on the 1981 census while the 50th Round (1993–4) town classification is largely based on the 1991 census to the extent available in different states. The 55th Round (1999–2000) town classification is based on the 1991 census. All these have led to substantial underestimation of population of metropolitan cities in states where the 50th Round town classification was based on the 1981 census. As a consequence, the share of metro population in urban areas shows hardly any increase between the 43rd and 50th Rounds whereas in between the 50th and 55th Rounds the share shows substantial increase. Further, the population obtained from the NSS Rounds is generally lower than the interpolated census population and the gap between them is increasing over time.

NSS household schedule data was used for the entire analysis. Poverty incidence estimates and employment and education data were calculated for four NSS Rounds, starting from 1987–8 to 2009–10, covering almost two-and-a-half decades. However, a detailed analysis of the 2009–10 data is not presented but the data is given in annexures. The data from the 2009–10 Round is presented in Chapter 6 as we thought that a basic analysis of these data would give readers a broad idea of the trends observed in the last decade. The level of facilities status was calculated for four time points, 1993, 1998, 2002, and 2008 using NSS data.

Poverty estimates for small and medium towns were arrived at using the NSS consumption expenditure data of four quinquennial Rounds, the 43rd Round (1987–8), the 50th Round (1993–4), and the 61st Round (2004–5). Poverty estimates for each size class in the different rounds were arrived at using state level poverty lines of the Planning Commission. We could not estimate poverty incidence for 2009–10 because the official poverty line had not been released when this book went to press.

Historically, rural–urban price differential as incorporated in official poverty lines at the all-India level has been around the 15 per cent level. But the 1993 Expert Group Report recommended separate rates for each state (based on studies of inter-state price differentials) and did not explicitly consider urban to rural differentials. As a result, in 1999–2000, the urban to rural differential implicit in the official lines was around 39 per cent which was astonishingly large for some states (Deaton 2003). The effect of the adoption of the Expert Group's lines was to raise measured poverty in urban relative to rural areas. Further, within urban areas, the prices are not similar for different size classes of towns. In fact, there is substantial difference in prices in small towns and metropolitan cities for several goods and services. In all likelihood, the poverty line in metropolitan cities will be higher than that in small towns. The Tendulkar Committee revised rural poverty lines in 2009, which raised HCRs across all the states for rural areas (Planning Commission 2009). But, differential poverty lines across size classes of towns have not yet been calculated in India.

Of the various measures of poverty, only HCR has been used to estimate urban poverty. HCR gives the total population below the poverty line. Average per capita expenditure of the whole population in each of the town sizes in each of the states has also been calculated at current as well as constant (1993–4) prices.

Expenditures of all consumer items of 1987–8 and 1993–4 are based on a 30-day recall period, known as the Uniform Recall Period (URP). For 1999–2000 and 2004–5, all but five items were based on the 30-day recall period.

Expenditures on the five remaining items are based on the 365-day recall period. These items are clothing, footwear, education, institutional medical expenses, and consumer durables. So for 1999–2000 and 2004–5, the reference period is known as the Mixed Reference Period (MRP). The shift from URP to MRP increased APCE as can be observed from the higher value of APCE calculated on the basis of MRP compared to that of URP calculated for 1993–4 (Sundaram and Tendulkar 2003; Mazumdar and Sarkar 2004). In consequence, poverty figures in 1999–2000 based on MRP are over-estimated compared to 1987–8 and 1993–4 figures based on URP. Therefore, in our analysis we have not used APCE and poverty figures for 1999–2000. Sen and Himanshu (2004) found all-India HCR for all areas to be 35.9 per cent using URP and 30.6 per cent using MRP for 1993–4. For 2004–5, the Planning Commission has given two HCR estimates, those based on URP and those based on MRP. We have used HCR using URP for 2004–5 to make poverty estimates comparable to previous years.

Again for the 55th Round, the 7-day and 30-day period questions were canvassed side by side for food, *paan*, tobacco, and intoxicants. Sen and Himanshu (2004) raised the issue of possible contamination of 30-day data with 7-day data. They corrected the 55th Round (1999–2000) estimates for food and intoxicants for possible 'contamination' from a 7-day questionnaire. They used information from earlier NSS Rounds to arrive at some estimates. At the lower bound, they found the extent of such contamination to be small but even then it implied that the poverty incidence at all-India level using MRP for the 55th Round to be 27.8 per cent as against 26.1 per cent officially.

In 1993–4, there were 33 states and union territories. Their number increased to 35 in 1999–2000. The number remained the same in 2004–5. Of these, 17 were major states and the rest were smaller states and union territories. This analysis has been carried out for only 16 major states which have substantial urban populations and will therefore also have statistically significant sample sizes in different size classes of towns. All the north-eastern states except Assam were clubbed together and the group is called North-East (NE) states. All the other states were clubbed together as the 'rest of the states' category. Delhi and Goa, which were union territories earlier, are now states but are placed in the rest of the states category. Bihar, Uttar Pradesh, and Madhya Pradesh are represented here in their undivided forms, as the states of Jharkhand, Uttaranchal, and Chhattisgarh, respectively, were carved out from these in 2000 and therefore do not pose a problem of comparability of data.

## OUTLINE OF THE BOOK

This book focuses largely on bringing out disparities in urban systems between metros and non-metros. Hence, an overwhelming emphasis of the analysis across all the chapters is to bring out these disparities with regard to incidence of poverty, employment, education levels, and basic services. Therefore, we do not present many other possible analyses from the data presented in each chapter. By maintaining this focus, we have also tried to avoid the chapters becoming unwieldy. We, however, present the processed NSS data for use by other researchers as annexures.

The current chapter deals with the rationale for undertaking this study, the importance of SMTs in national urban systems, urban poverty trends across major states in India (over time), and data issues to generate the required data for a disaggregated analysis of the urban system in India. It also discusses current urban policies, with emphasis on SMTs in India. This chapter provides the background for the concluding chapter that discusses the policy implications of this study.

Then the disaggregated analysis of the urban sector begins. Poverty level, as expressed by HCR and per capita monthly consumption expenditures are calculated for each of the two size classes and are presented in Chapter 2. State level poverty lines of the Planning Commission are used for calculating HCRs. It is common knowledge that the cost of living in metropolitan cities is higher than in small towns mainly because of higher housing and transportation costs in the former; these are understated in consumption expenditure surveys. Thus, HCRs for metropolitan cities derived by using the state level urban poverty line will be lower than what they should be and in small towns HCRs would be higher than what they should be. Nothing much can be done about this and hence, the HCRs presented in Chapter 2 for different size classes of urban centres in 16 major states in India should be viewed with this limitation.

Employment patterns and unemployment levels across different size classes disaggregated by sex are taken up in Chapter 3. This chapter has data and analysis on firstly Work Participation Rates (WPRs), the nature of employment (self-employment, regular employment, and casual labour), sectors of employment namely primary, secondary, and tertiary (NIC [national industrial classification]), and the national occupation classification (NOC) of workers. A very high difference in quality of employment across different size classes is expected, with small towns being dependent on the primary sector and hence having a high proportion of the workers in the primary sector as against metropolitan cities which are expected to have a higher proportion of workers in the tertiary sector and that too in well paid tertiary employment. Lastly, unemployment rates for males and females are calculated separately in Chapter 3. Chronic unemployment is captured by the usual status employment rate (calculated for principal and subsidiary workers together) (called UPSS), and underemployment of casual workers is captured by the Current Daily Status (CDS).

Chapter 4 gives and analyses data on education levels across different size classes and by sex. From this data, the proportion of illiterates in the total population and the proportion of literates achieving different education levels are calculated. Education levels indicate the capability of residents to function in the employment market. The higher the capability, the higher the labour productivity, the higher the consumption levels, and the higher the ability to remain out of poverty.

Chapter 5 analyses the level of basic facilities in different size classes of urban centres. The data pertain to water supply, its quantity and quality, sanitation, its availability and crowding, and garbage collection. Access to these three facilities depends on two aspects—household incomes and ability of ULBs to provide these services. A ULB's ability to provide these services depends upon its financial status and the powers given to it to raise revenue income. In many states, in place of ULBs, state level parastatal agencies that are directly funded by state governments provide these basic services, especially water supply and sanitation, which are highly capital-intensive. The availability of such basic services in different size classes of urban centres is a reflection on state government finances. The level of basic facilities indirectly affects poverty levels. Basic facilities affect health and through that the capability of individuals to remain above (or below) the poverty line.

Chapter 6 is about trends in the last two and a half decades and their implications on policy. It presents the situation of consumption, employment, unemployment, and education by metro and non-metro disaggregation, using the 66th Round of NSS data. We do not attempt to estimate poverty using this round of data as the Planning Commission had not yet set the poverty lines for 2009–10 till this. This chapter does not undertake any extensive analysis of the 66th Round but has a discussion on the important findings from this Round. The chapter ends with a discussion on some important policy implications emerging from this handbook.

This handbook is, therefore, an attempt to present facts about urban centres in India, disaggregated by the two categories, metros; and non-metros. However, this database is not complete. There has to be a city-based data system as well, such as ward level data in metropolitan and large cities on all these aspects besides another one on incomes/expenditures, housing conditions, tax collections, birth rates and death rates, and many indicators of status of health and education. This handbook is a beginning in creating urban databases in India.

**NOTES**

1. Source: http://jnnurm.nic.in/wp-content/uploads/2010/12/broucher.pdf, accessed on 9 March 2012.

2. In case of some urban centres, extremely local factors will also play a significant role in their development dynamics, which in one city study are extremely important. At the same time, there are certain size-class commonalities that cannot be escaped.

3. Although, the 2009–10 NSS data on consumption expenditure is now available, we have not used them here as we would like to observe the decadal growth rates as we have done in Figure 1.1 and the price deflators were not available for the 2009–10 data at the time of finalizing this manuscript.

4. Source: http://jnnurm.nic.in/nurmudweb/toolkit/modified_guidelines.pdf, accessed on 26 March 2011.

5. For UIDSSMT details see: http://urbanindia.nic.in/programme/ud/uidssmt_guidelines.htm, accessed on 26 March 2011.

6. Source: http://www.urbanindia.nic.in/programme/ud/uidssmtbody.htm#uidssmt, accessed on 15 February 2011.

7. When this manuscript was completed, the housing data for 2011 were not available.

8. The term he uses is Third World.

# 2

# Consumption Patterns and Poverty

Consumption expenditure has been a long preferred measure of the household living standard. However, its accurate measurement through household expenditure surveys has always been a challenging exercise. Nonetheless, in India, detailed consumption expenditure surveys have been carried out quinquennially, which are also called thick rounds, undertaken roughly at five to six years' interval by the National Sample Survey Organisation (NSSO). Unit level data of several consumption expenditure rounds have been used for this chapter.

We took certain methodological decisions for the analysis presented in this chapter. The unit data is of the household level and each household is of a different size making household consumption data non-comparable. The household level data was normalized to Average Per Capita Consumption Expenditure (APCE) to do away with the impact of household size. The APCE figures in the chapter refer to monthly expenditures. Lastly, historically the NSSO consumption expenditure rounds collected data for a 30-day reference period. Since in the NSS Rounds APCE has been historically

based on a 30-day reference period, APCE is measured in monthly terms. In all discussions in this chapter on APCE, the figures are based for a month.

APCE gives normalized household consumption expenditure in a certain geographical region or in a certain segment of the population. It does not capture the variability of per capita consumption expenditure across households within the defined space. In this chapter we do not address the issue of inequality of consumption expenditure across households and only estimate the magnitude of households who are unable to meet the minimum consumption standard prescribed by a cut-off line which is known as the poverty line. The number of persons below the poverty line (certain per capita expenditure level) is considered to be poor and the share of these poor persons in the total population in the specified space is called poverty ratio or Head Count Ratio (HCR). Further, we have restricted our analysis to using the official poverty lines for 1987–8 and 1993–4; we have used the poverty line estimated by modified expert group commissioned by the Planning

Commission and the Planning Commission's official poverty line for 2004–5. For converting APCE at constant prices, the implicit price deflator derived from the state specific official poverty lines has been used.

For comparability purposes, APCE and HCR have been calculated for only two size classes for urban centres—metropolis (1 million or more population) and non-metropolis (cities and towns with less than a million population) for three quinquennial Rounds—43rd (1987–8), 50th (1993–4), and 61st (2004–5) NSSO Rounds. For the 43rd and 50th Rounds, further disaggregation of the urban sample by size class was available and hence APCE and HCR figures were calculated for C1 (<50,000), C2 (50,000 to 200,000), and C3 (200,000 to 1 million) classes separately as well. These estimates are presented in Tables A2.2 and A2.3, respectively. The discussion in the chapter is restricted to pointing out metro versus non-metro inequalities over time. Temporally, two time periods are used for analysis, pre-reforms (1987–8 to 1993–4) and the reforms period (1993–4 to 2004–5). This temporal division is maintained in all the subsequent chapters.

Unlike in Chapters 3 and 4, we could not include the 55th Round (1999–2000) data in our analysis. In all the quinquennial Rounds, except for the 55th Round, the reference period in the household questionnaire was 30-day for all items consumed. It is called the Uniform Reference Period (URP). But in the 55th Round different recall periods were used; 365-day recall period for expenditure on clothing, footwear, education, medical (institutional), and consumer durables and at most the 30-day reference period for other items of consumption. This is termed as the Mixed Reference Period (MRP). It led to substantial debate about comparability of consumption expenditure of this particular round of information with other

rounds. The conclusion of this debate is that estimation based on MRP led to an upward bias in the estimation of consumption expenditure for 1999–2000 and consequently it overestimated the decline in poverty in this year as compared to the prior round of 1993–4. This anomaly forced us to drop this year from our analysis.

It is, however, possible to calculate APCE on the basis of MRP for 1993–4 and 2004–5. The 2004–5 unit level data also gives APCE estimated using the MRP data and hence, it is also possible to get an estimate of APCE using MRP for this year. In 1993–4, for those five consumer items, expenditure data were collected for both 30-day and 365-day reference periods. Hence, the 1993–4 data can be made comparable with the 1999–2000 data by replacing 30-day expenditures of those five items with 365-day expenditure and get MRP estimates for 1993–4. A comparison of APCE on these five items by the 30-day and the 365-day reference periods for 1993–4 shows that in urban areas the change of the reference period from 30-day to 365-day made a substantial difference largely in clothing (Mazumdar and Sarkar 2008).

### AVERAGE PER CAPITA EXPENDITURES

Before undertaking an analysis of the poverty ratio it will be worthwhile to get a picture of the monthly APCE and the changes therein over time. APCE used here is at constant 1993–4 prices. It is derived by deflating average APCE obtained from unit level data of several NSSO quinquennial Rounds by the implicit price deflator.

At the all-India level, expectedly in all the years, APCEs in metros were higher than in non-metros. It can be seen from Figure 2.1 that the absolute difference of APCEs in metros and non-metros increased in the reforms period (1993–4 to 2004–5). Since the reforms period covers 11 years compared to six years of the

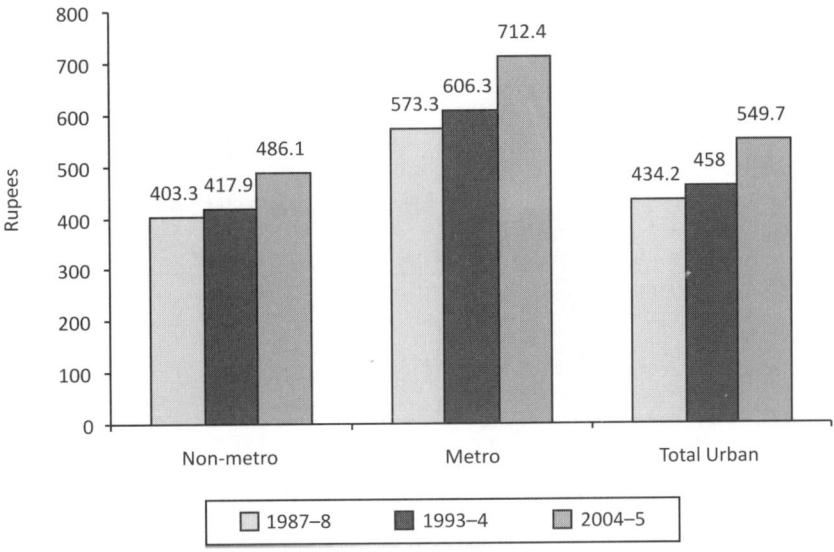

**Figure 2.1** APCE (at Constant 1993–4 Prices) Over Time by Size Class, All-India (in Rs)

*Source*: Unit level data of consumption expenditure schedule of 43rd (1987–8), 50th (1993–4), and 61st (2004–5) Rounds of NSSO and state specific official poverty line for the years 1987–8, 1993–4, and 2004–5.

pre-reforms period it will be useful to examine the APCE rate of growth.

Figure 2.2 and Table 2.1 show substantial rise in APCE growth in the reforms period compared to the pre-reforms period in non-metros, metros, and all areas. In the reforms period, APCE growth in urban areas was more than both non-metro and metro areas, as a few non-metro towns with low APCE levels were classified into metro areas in the reforms period, which pulled down the APCE growth rate in metro areas.

Figures 2.3 and 2.4 are scatter diagrams of the APCE level in the initial year of the period and the all-urban growth in APCE in the period. Thus, Figure 2.3 has the APCE levels in 1987–8 on the x-axis and per annum growth during 1987–8 to 1993–4 on the y-axis. Similarly, Figure 2.4 is constructed for the reforms period. In the pre-reforms period the scatter diagram between the initial level of APCE for

different states and subsequent growth does not show any relationship in the sense that these are neither convergent nor divergent. The correlation is insignificant with a value of –0.09. The low APCE level Bihar showed respectable growth in APCE and so also the high APCE states of Jammu and Kashmir and Maharashtra. However, in the reforms period, states with low level of APCE in 1993–4, that is, Bihar, Andhra Pradesh, Uttar Pradesh, Karnataka, and Rajasthan experienced higher rate of APCE growth as compared to states with a higher level of APCE such as Maharashtra and Jammu and Kashmir. Consequently, APCE of urban areas converged and the value of correlation was significant (r = –.54).

A similar analysis was carried out for metros (since non-metros is not given) separately to examine whether the convergence was stronger or weaker in the reforms period in metro or non-metro areas. Figures 2.5 and 2.6 are scatter

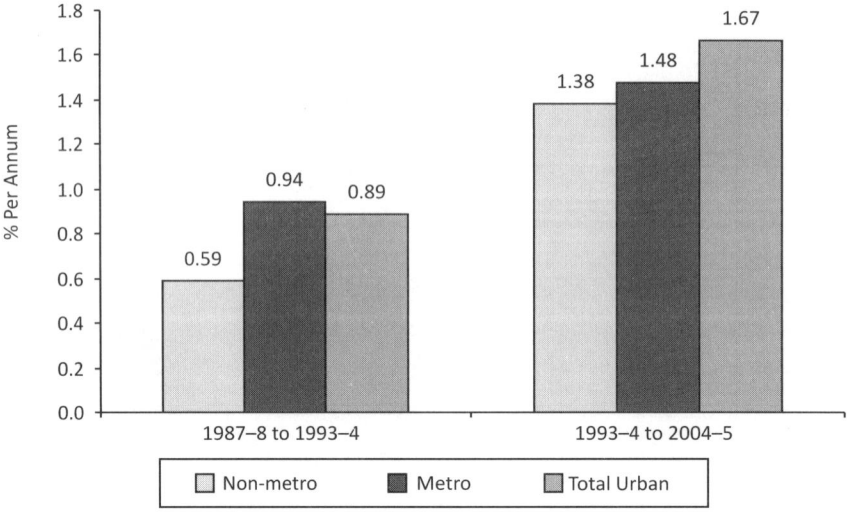

**Figure 2.2**    CAGR of APCE (Constant Prices) in Pre-reforms and Reforms Period by Size Class

*Source*: Data taken from Table 2.1.

**Table 2.1**    Compound Annual Growth Rate of Monthly APCE (Constant Prices), by States

| State | 1987–8 to 1993–4 | | | 1993–4 to 2004–5 | | |
|---|---|---|---|---|---|---|
| | Non-metro | Metro | Total Urban | Non-metro | Metro | Total Urban |
| Andhra Pradesh | −0.22 | −0.73 | −0.36 | 1.98 | 2.32 | 2.25 |
| Assam | 1.09 | | 1.09 | 2.37 | | 2.37 |
| Bihar | 2.91 | | 2.91 | 1.50 | | 2.01 |
| Gujarat | 1.47 | 2.74 | 2.05 | 2.58 | 2.49 | 2.76 |
| Haryana | 0.61 | | 0.61 | 2.08 | | 1.93 |
| Jammu and Kashmir | 3.32 | | 3.32 | −1.09 | | −1.09 |
| Karnataka | 1.07 | 1.53 | 1.13 | 1.18 | 2.69 | 1.92 |
| Kerala | 1.58 | | 1.58 | 2.49 | | 2.49 |
| Madhya Pradesh | −0.88 | | −0.25 | 1.54 | 4.03 | 2.08 |
| Maharashtra | 1.29 | 1.88 | 1.86 | 0.10 | 0.54 | 0.61 |
| Orissa | 0.09 | | 0.09 | 0.54 | | 0.54 |
| Punjab | 0.56 | | 0.96 | 2.34 | 5.72 | 3.19 |
| Rajasthan | −0.28 | | 0.34 | 0.97 | 1.21 | 1.19 |
| Tamil Nadu | −0.26 | 0.74 | −0.01 | 2.10 | 4.69 | 2.66 |
| Uttar Pradesh | 1.38 | 0.63 | 1.34 | 0.41 | 4.80 | 1.58 |
| West Bengal | 2.87 | 2.68 | 2.48 | 2.02 | 3.00 | 2.45 |
| Other NE States | −0.35 | | −0.35 | 2.37 | | 2.37 |
| Rest ST & UT | 3.92 | 0.91 | 1.49 | 0.84 | −1.17 | −0.78 |
| All-India | 0.59 | 0.94 | 0.89 | 1.38 | 1.48 | 1.67 |

*Source*: Unit level data of consumption expenditure schedule of 43rd (1987–8), 50th (1993–4), and 61st (2004–5) Rounds of NSSO and state specific official poverty line for the years 1987–8, 1993–4, and 2004–5.

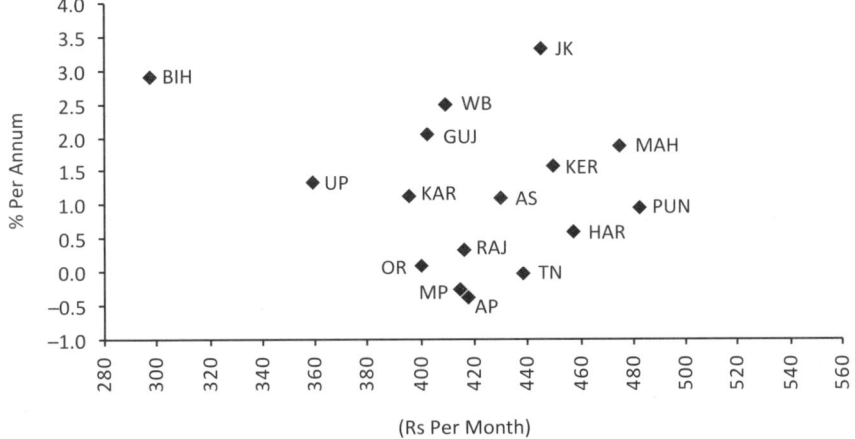

**Figure 2.3**   Scatter Diagram of Level of APCE in 1987–8 and Growth in APCE in the
Pre-reforms Period (1987–8 to 1993–4), All Urban

*Source*: Unit level data of consumption expenditure schedule of 43rd (1987–8) and 50th (1993–4) Rounds
of NSSO and state specific official poverty line for the years 1987–8 and 1993–4.

*Notes*: BIH: Bihar; JK: Jammu and Kashmir; WB: West Bengal; GUJ: Gujarat; UP: Uttar Pradesh;
KAR: Karnataka; MAH: Maharashtra; KER: Kerala; AS: Assam; RAJ: Rajasthan; OR: Orissa;
PUN: Punjab; AP: Andhra Pradesh; TN: Tamil Nadu; HAR: Haryana; and MP: Madhya Pradesh.

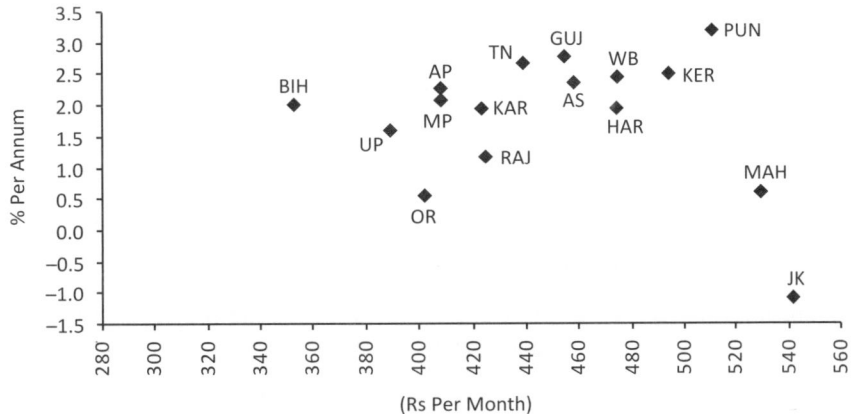

**Figure 2.4**   Scatter Diagram of Level of APCE in 1993–4 and Growth in APCE in the
Reforms Period (1993–4 to 2004–5), All Urban

*Source*: Unit level data of consumption expenditure schedule of 50th (1993–4) and 61st (2004–5) Rounds
of NSSO and state specific official poverty line for the years 1993–4 and 2004–5.

*Notes*: BIH: Bihar; JK: Jammu and Kashmir; WB: West Bengal; GUJ: Gujarat; UP: Uttar Pradesh;
KAR: Karnataka; MAH: Maharashtra; KER: Kerala; AS: Assam; RAJ: Rajasthan; OR: Orissa;
PUN: Punjab; AP: Andhra Pradesh; TN: Tamil Nadu; HAR: Haryana; and MP: Madhya Pradesh.

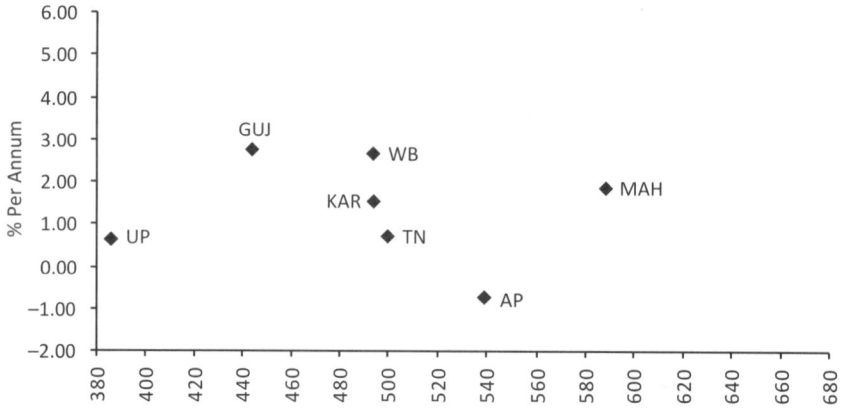

**Figure 2.5**    Scatter Diagram of Level of APCE in 1987–8 and Growth in APCE in the
Pre-reforms Period (1987–8 to 1993–4), Metros

*Source*: Unit level data of consumption expenditure schedule of 43rd (1987–8) and 50th (1993–4) Rounds
of NSSO and state specific official poverty line for the years 1987–8 and 1993–4.
*Notes*: UP: Uttar Pradesh; GUJ: Gujarat; WB: West Bengal; MAH: Maharashtra; KAR: Karnataka;
TN: Tamil Nadu; and AP: Andhra Pradesh;

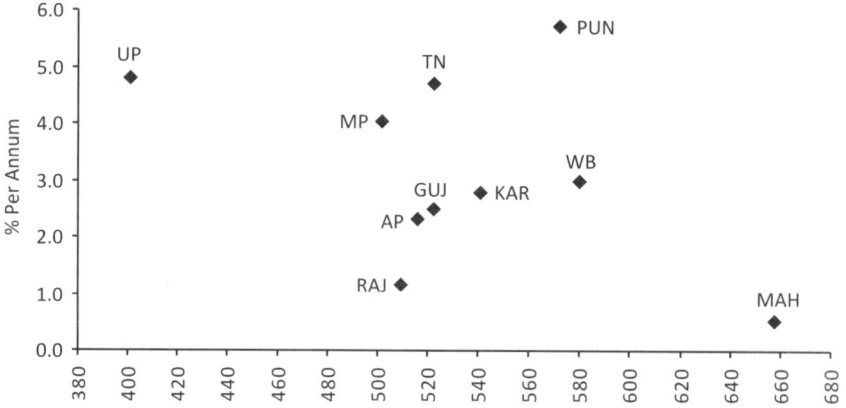

**Figure 2.6**    Scatter Diagram of Level of APCE in 1993–4 and Growth in APCE in the
Reforms Period (1993–4 to 2004–5), Metros

*Source*: Unit level data of consumption expenditure schedule of 50th (1993–4) and 61st (2004–5) Rounds
of NSSO and state specific official poverty line for the years 1993–4 and 2004–5.
*Notes*: UP: Uttar Pradesh; PUN: Punjab; TN: Tamil Nadu; MP: Madhya Pradesh; AP: Andhra Pradesh;
GUJ: Gujarat; KAR: Karnataka; WB: West Bengal; RAJ: Rajasthan; and MAH: Maharashtra.

diagrams for metro areas in the two periods. Similar to all urban areas in the pre-reforms period, no pattern can be seen and consequently the relationship between the level of APCE and growth in APCE in the metros is weak which is reflected in the low correlation value of –0.16. In the reforms period, the convergence pattern is sharper than even that of all urban areas in the metros, with the correlation coefficient value at a much higher level of –0.73. The convergence pattern is much stronger in metro areas than in all urban, indicating that the convergence is much stronger in metros than in non-metros.

This analysis shows that metro cities that were at a low level of APCE were able to grow at a faster rate to catch up with cities with a higher level of APCE thus leading to the convergence process. Stronger evidence of convergence in metro areas as compared to all urban areas also indicates that in states with a lower level of APCE in metro areas in 1993–4, the APCE gap between metro and non-metro cities increased in 2004–5. In contrast, states that had metro areas with a higher APCE level at the beginning of pre-reforms period, had an APCE gain which was more widely distributed between metro and non-metro cities.

The size distribution of towns beyond metros and non-metros is available only for two reform years of 1987–8 and 1993–4, which will at the least give an idea about the patterns of growth in this period. At the all-India level, in both years monthly APCE increased with the increase in size class of the urban centre. Hence, the monthly APCE was the least in small towns (C1 class) and the highest in metropolitan cities (CM class) (Figure 2.7). The gap between the two consecutive size classes increased with the increase in size class in 1981–8. To give an example, the ratio of APCE in C2 to APCE in C1 was 1.06 in 1987–8. In the same year, the ratio of APCE in C3 to APCE in C2 was 1.19, and the ratio of APCE in CM to APCE in C3 was 1.23. In 1993–4, the ratio of APCE in C2 to APCE in C1 and ratio of APCE in C3 to C2 were similar but the APCE of CM to APCE C3 was much higher at 1.29. Thus, nor did living standards improve with the increase in size class, but their improvement rate was also faster in higher size class of urban centres as compared to lower size

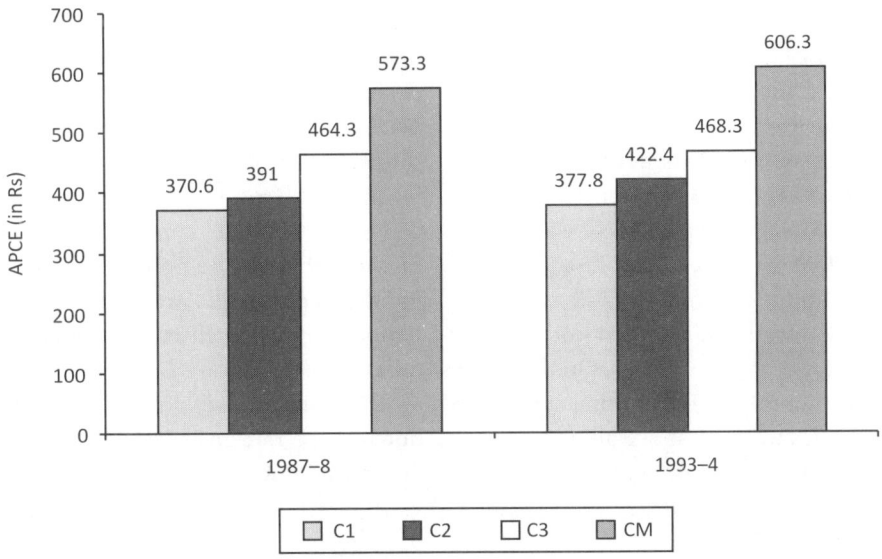

**Figure 2.7**   APCE by Size Class Over Time (Constant 1993–4 Prices)

*Source*: Unit level data of consumption expenditure schedule of 43rd (1987–8) and 50th (1993–4) Rounds of NSSO and state specific official poverty line for the years 1987–8 and 1993–4.

class. These ratios also indicate that APCE in metropolitan cities increased at a much faster rate than APCE in the small towns in the pre-reforms period indicating an increasing bias of the urban system toward metropolitan cities during this period. In 2004–5 we only had the metro and non-metro division. The ratio of metro to non-metro APCE in 2004–5 was 1.47 as compared to 1.45 in 1993–4. In the reforms period, the bias towards metros and large cities seems to have continued.

In most states, with the increase in size class, the monthly APCE increased. But there were also some exceptions. The states with exceptions in 1987–8 were: Assam, Gujarat, Haryana, Karnataka, and Punjab, all of which except Assam, are developed states. In 1993–4, the exception states were Gujarat, Haryana, Punjab, Orissa, and Uttar Pradesh, once again, the first three are developed states and the last two the less developed states.

Bihar lies at the bottom for all three years in non-metro size classes in APCE. Patna, the capital of Bihar was not classified as a metropolitan city in 1987–8 and 1993–4. Thus, Uttar Pradesh was at the bottom in these two years whereas Bihar was at the bottom in 2004–5 in the metro class. On the whole for all the urban areas, Bihar was at the bottom for two years— 1987–8 and 1993–4—and Orissa was at the bottom in 2004–5. Even in the disaggregated data for the non-metros, in 1987–8 as well as 1993–4, Bihar was the undisputed leader at the bottom in C1, C2, and C3 classes. On the other extreme, the monthly APCE of other states and union territories was way above all other states in all size classes of urban centres and in all urban areas in all the three years largely because of the presence of Delhi city.

The disparity of monthly APCE across state categories measured by the Coefficient of Variation (CV) shows that in each year under study the disparity was higher in metropolitan

size classes compared to non-metro size classes (for data see Tables A2.4 and A2.5). However, in metro areas the disparity declined from 21 to 18 in the pre-reforms period but marginally increased in the reforms period. In non-metro areas the disparity increased from 13 to 17 from 1987–8 to 1993–4 and further to 18 in 2004–5.

### LEVEL OF POVERTY (HCR)

As expected, the proportion of poor was much smaller in metro areas as compared to non-metros in all the years (Figure 2.8). At the same time, HCR declined at a faster rate in the metros as compared to non-metros in the pre-reforms period, the former registering a 7 percentage point decline whereas the latter had a 6 percentage point decline (Figure 2.8). However, in the reforms period, both the metros and non-metros experienced a similar rate of HCR decline—5 percentage points. What is clear, therefore, is that poverty as represented by HCRs declined in both the pre-reforms and reforms periods in non-metros, metros, and all urban areas at the all-India level; however, this decline was at a faster rate in the pre-reforms period than in the reforms period. Further, in the pre-reforms period, there was greater bias in favour of metros, which registered a faster rate of HCR decline as compared to non-metros. Figure 2.9 gives the annual rate of decline of HCR and clearly illustrates that in the reforms period overall as well as by class size, decline in urban HCR has slowed down.

The annual rate of decline of poverty slowed down in the reforms period in all urban, metro as well as non-metro. The rate of decline in HCR was 3.04 per cent per annum (p.a.) in the pre-reforms period which came down to 2.04 per cent per annum in the reforms period in all urban areas (Figure 2.9). In the case of metros, the rate of decline in the reforms period almost halved from that in the pre-reforms period, the

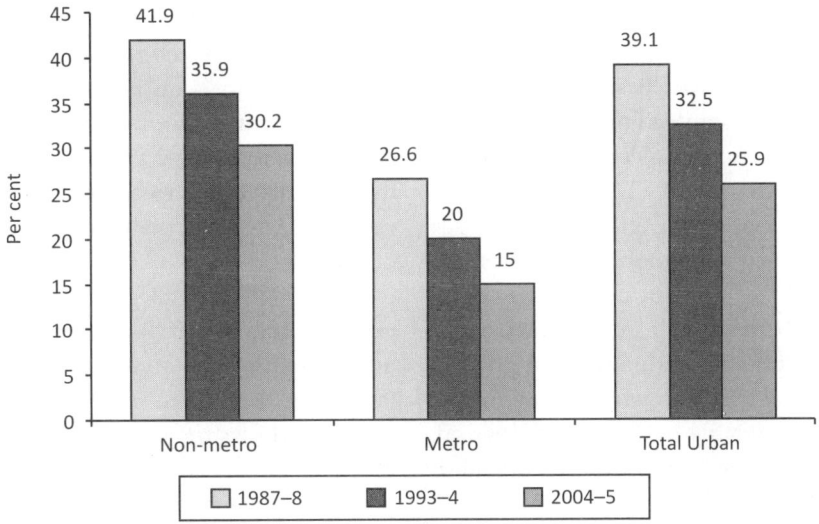

**Figure 2.8**   HCRs for Metro, Non-metro, and All Urban Over Time, All-India

*Source*: Data taken from Table 2.2.

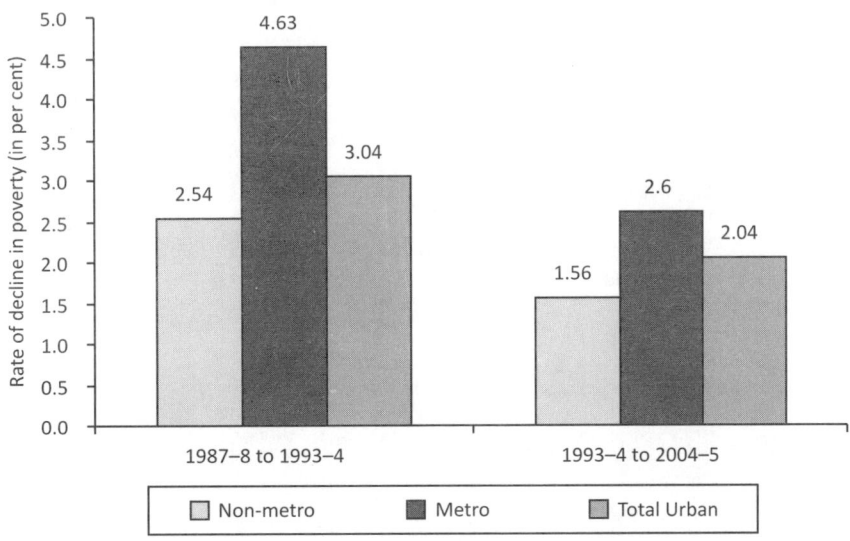

**Figure 2.9**   Rate of Decline in Poverty Over Time in Non-metro, Metro, and Urban areas

*Source*: Data taken from Table 2.3.

rate of decline in HCR being 4.63 per cent and 2.60 per cent per annum, respectively. The rate of decline in non-metros was the slowest among the three but it too slowed down in the reforms period to 1.56 per cent per annum from 2.54 per cent per annum in the pre-reforms period. The smaller rise in the rate of APCE growth in metro areas as compared to non-metro areas in the reforms period as observed earlier partially explains this. But in both metro and non-metro areas the growth in APCE was faster in the reforms period as compared to the pre-reforms period. This paradox, of slower decline in HCR but faster growth in APCE in the reforms period, shows that APCE growth took place in the higher consumption percentiles (as seen in Chapter 1) and not in the lower ones, indicating that the growth in both metro and non-metro areas in this period was anti-poor. In other words, the trickle-down effect of growth weakened considerably in the reforms period. We will analyse this issue in greater detail in next section.

The disparity across states with respect to metro and the non-metro areas for these three years shows an interesting picture. The disparity went up continuously over the years in non-metro, metro, and all-urban areas. But the disparity in metro areas across states went up much faster over the years from a lower level in 1987–8.

Tables 2.2 and 2.3 give the HCR and annual decline in HCR respectively for total urban, metro, and non-metro areas by states in India over three quinquennial Rounds. Table 2.4 shows the position of different states in achievements in terms of persons moving above the poverty line in metro and non-metro

**Table 2.2**  Head Count Ratios, Metro, Non-metro, and Total Urban, 1987–8, 1993–4, and 2004–5

| State | 1987–8 | | | 1993–4 | | | 2004–5 | | |
|---|---|---|---|---|---|---|---|---|---|
| | Non-metro | Metro | Total Urban | Non-metro | Metro | Total Urban | Non-metro | Metro | Total Urban |
| Andhra Pradesh | 42.4 | 31.3 | 41.1 | 40.7 | 19.6 | 38.5 | 28.4 | 22.7 | 27.4 |
| Assam | 11.3 | | 11.3 | 7.9 | | 7.9 | 3.6 | | 3.6 |
| Bihar | 51.9 | | 51.9 | 34.5 | | 34.5 | 32.9 | 12.9 | 30.3 |
| Gujarat | 40.6 | 32.4 | 38.5 | 29.5 | 25.4 | 28.2 | 16.7 | 8.6 | 13.3 |
| Haryana | 18.4 | | 18.4 | 16.5 | | 16.5 | 16.3 | 6.1 | 14.5 |
| Jammu and Kashmir | 14.9 | | 14.9 | 5.1 | | 5.1 | 7.4 | | 7.4 |
| Karnataka | 53.1 | 34.0 | 49.1 | 45.1 | 17.2 | 39.6 | 41.7 | 7.9 | 32.6 |
| Kerala | 38.5 | | 38.5 | 24.2 | | 24.2 | 20.0 | | 20.0 |
| Madhya Pradesh | 47.4 | | 47.4 | 49.5 | 38.2 | 47.9 | 45.9 | 24.2 | 42.6 |
| Maharashtra | 52.4 | 24.0 | 40.5 | 49.5 | 17.0 | 34.7 | 48.5 | 16.5 | 32.1 |
| Orissa | 42.6 | | 42.6 | 40.6 | | 40.6 | 44.7 | | 44.7 |
| Punjab | 13.7 | | 13.7 | 12.4 | 3.1 | 10.9 | 7.0 | 3.4 | 6.3 |
| Rajasthan | 37.9 | | 37.9 | 33.1 | 17.7 | 31.0 | 29.8 | 42.3 | 32.3 |
| Tamil Nadu | 42.1 | 32.7 | 40.2 | 41.2 | 32.0 | 39.2 | 25.5 | 8.7 | 22.5 |
| Uttar Pradesh | 45.6 | 38.2 | 45.0 | 35.8 | 25.3 | 34.6 | 34.0 | 17.7 | 30.5 |
| West Bengal | 36.2 | 27.0 | 33.7 | 25.7 | 10.4 | 22.6 | 16.9 | 3.2 | 13.5 |
| Other NE States | 5.7 | | 5.7 | 4.2 | | 4.2 | 1.7 | | 1.7 |
| Rest ST & UT | 26.6 | 16.7 | 18.9 | 17.7 | 15.9 | 16.3 | 9.7 | 16.3 | 15.8 |
| All-India | 41.9 | 26.6 | 39.1 | 35.9 | 20.0 | 32.5 | 30.2 | 15.0 | 25.9 |
| Coefficient of Variation | 44.5 | 22.8 | 44.7 | 52.7 | 48.3 | 51.2 | 63.4 | 73.4 | 60.0 |

*Source*: Unit level data of consumption expenditure schedule of 43rd (1987–8), 50th (1993–4), and 61st (2004–5) Rounds of NSSO and state specific official poverty line for the years 1987–8, 1993–4, and 2004–5.

**Table 2.3** Annual Decline in HCR, Metro, Non-metro, Total Urban

| State | 1987–8 to 1993–4 | | | 1993–4 to 2004–5 | | |
|---|---|---|---|---|---|---|
| | Non-metro | Metro | Total Urban | Non-metro | Metro | Total Urban |
| Andhra Pradesh | 0.68 | 7.49 | 1.10 | 3.23 | −1.34 | 3.05 |
| Assam | 5.88 | | 5.88 | 6.76 | | 6.76 |
| Bihar | 6.57 | | 6.57 | 0.43 | | 1.16 |
| Gujarat | 5.19 | 4.02 | 5.07 | 5.03 | 9.38 | 6.59 |
| Haryana | 1.86 | | 1.86 | 0.09 | | 1.16 |
| Jammu and Kashmir | 16.35 | | 16.35 | −3.41 | | −3.41 |
| Karnataka | 2.68 | 10.71 | 3.55 | 0.72 | 6.88 | 1.74 |
| Kerala | 7.47 | | 7.48 | 1.71 | | 1.70 |
| Madhya Pradesh | −0.72 | | −0.18 | 0.68 | 4.06 | 1.06 |
| Maharashtra | 0.94 | 5.56 | 2.53 | 0.18 | 0.28 | 0.71 |
| Orissa | 0.81 | | 0.81 | −0.89 | | −0.89 |
| Punjab | 1.60 | | 3.74 | 5.12 | −0.76 | 4.88 |
| Rajasthan | 2.21 | | 3.28 | 0.97 | −8.24 | −0.37 |
| Tamil Nadu | 0.38 | 0.37 | 0.41 | 4.26 | 11.12 | 4.94 |
| Uttar Pradesh | 3.95 | 6.64 | 4.28 | 0.46 | 3.21 | 1.15 |
| West Bengal | 5.54 | 14.76 | 6.43 | 3.72 | 10.07 | 4.59 |
| Other NE States | 4.94 | | 4.94 | 7.93 | | 7.93 |
| Rest ST and UT | 6.52 | 0.82 | 2.44 | 5.34 | −0.23 | 0.30 |
| All-India | 2.54 | 4.63 | 3.04 | 1.56 | 2.60 | 2.04 |

*Source*: Calculated by authors using data from Table 2.2.

cities. Table 2.4 depicts the proportion of the population above the poverty line. High and low mean the category of states that performed better and worse than the all-India level respectively for different years. States in bold reflect those states that improved their position with respect to the all-India average in the consecutive survey year. This means that in these states the proportion of population above the poverty line moved from high (more) to low (less) as compared to that of India and of states underlined are the ones where proportion of population above the poverty line has moved from low to high. The states that are in italics are those whose urbanization levels were higher than that at the all-India level in census 2001.

In 1987–8 in metro areas, only Maharashtra performed better than the all-India HCR level. In this year the rest of the seven states that reported metro cities performed worse than the all-India level. The more urbanized states of Gujarat, Karnataka, and Tamil Nadu reported proportionately more poor than the all-India level in this year; 1993–4 reported improvement in this regard and the more urbanized state of Karnataka along with Andhra Pradesh and West Bengal reported a less proportion of poor in metro areas than the all-India level. In this year two more states of Punjab and Rajasthan reported metro cities for the first time and both of them performed better than the all-India level. In 2004–5, the situation changed substantially. All six high urbanized states reported lower poverty rates than the all-India level. This shows that in the reforms period even the poor population in the metros of more urbanized states benefitted relatively

**Table 2.4**    Percentage of Persons above the Poverty Line

| | | Year | | |
|---|---|---|---|---|
| | | 1987–8 | 1993–4 | 2004–5 |
| Metro | High | *Maharashtra* | **Andhra Pradesh**, **Karnataka**, *Maharashtra*, *Punjab*, Rajasthan, **West Bengal** | Bihar, ***Gujarat***, *Haryana*, *Karnataka*, *Maharashtra*, *Punjab*, <u>*Tamil Nadu*</u> |
| | Low | Andhra Pradesh, *Gujarat*, *Karnataka*, *Tamil Nadu*, Uttar Pradesh, West Bengal | *Gujarat*, Madhya Pradesh, *Tamil Nadu*, Uttar Pradesh | <u>Andhra Pradesh</u>, Madhya Pradesh, <u>Rajasthan</u>, Uttar Pradesh |
| Non-metro | High | Assam, *Gujarat*, *Haryana*, Jammu and Kashmir, Kerala, *Punjab*, Rajasthan, West Bengal | Assam, **Bihar**, *Gujarat*, *Haryana*, Jammu and Kashmir, Kerala, *Punjab*, Rajasthan, **Uttar Pradesh**, West Bengal | **Andhra Pradesh**, Assam, *Gujarat*, *Haryana*, Jammu and Kashmir, Kerala, *Punjab*, Rajasthan, ***Tamil Nadu***, West Bengal |
| | Low | Andhra Pradesh, Bihar, *Karnataka*, Madhya Pradesh, *Maharashtra*, Orissa, *Tamil Nadu*, Uttar Pradesh | Andhra Pradesh, *Karnataka*, Madhya Pradesh, *Maharashtra*, Orissa, *Tamil Nadu* | <u>Bihar</u>, *Karnataka*, Madhya Pradesh, *Maharashtra*, Orissa, <u>Uttar Pradesh</u> |

*Source*: Data taken from Table 2.2.

*Notes*: 1. States marked in bold signify movement from low to high in the consecutive year and states that are underlined signify movement from high to low. The low is < all-India level and high is > all-India level.
2. States that are italicized were high on the level of urbanization in 2001 (> all-India level ).

more than the poor population in the metros of less urbanized states.

One notable exception was Bihar whose capital city Patna became a metro city for the first time in 2004–5 and it performed better than the all-India level in this regard. At the APCE level, Bihar and Haryana were far lower than the all-India APCE level but the proportion of poor in metro cities was far less in 2004–5. This reflects a more equitable distribution of APCE across different sections of the population in metro areas in these two states. In contrast, Rajasthan with a similar APCE level reported HCR of 42 per cent as against the all-India average of 15 per cent in the metro city category in 2004–5.

In the non-metro category, the less urbanized states of Assam, Jammu and Kashmir, and Kerala reported far lower HCR than the all-India average in all the three years by virtue of

their higher APCE level. In contrast, the more urbanized states of Karnataka and Maharashtra, where APCEs of non-metros were far less than their metro counterparts in all the three years, consequently had a high non-metro HCR, hovering within the range of 40–50 per cent along with the less urbanized states of Madhya Pradesh and Orissa.

This disparity in poverty levels becomes clearer when one examines the ratio of HCR of non-metro towns and metro cities across states (see Table 2.5). The HCR ratio of non-metros to HCR of metro areas worsened over the years. At the all-India level in the pre-reforms era it worsened from 1.57 in 1987–8 to 1.79 in 1993–4 but in the reforms period it worsened substantially to 2.02 in 2004–5. This is the pattern we see for individual states as well except for Andhra Pradesh, Punjab, and

Rajasthan. Clearly, the metro versus non-metro disparity worsened in the reforms period as far as HCR is concerned.

In 1987–8, the ratio of non-metro HCR to metro HCR was highest (worst) in Maharashtra but in 1993–4 Punjab (with 4.00) and Karnataka (2.62) overshadowed it. In 2004–5, the worst performing state was Karnataka whose ratio of non-metro HCR to metro HCR went up to 5.30 reflecting that the benefit of globalization through development of software services was concentrated in the capital city of Bangalore alone and did not trickle down to other cities and towns in the state. This was a consequence of the dualistic nature of tertiary sector led development (Mazumdar and Sarkar 2009). The same was the case with regard to West Bengal, where Kolkata city attracted software services. This state had low urbanization but high non-metro versus metro disparity in HCR. It is not a coincidence that except for Gujarat which achieved higher growth in the reforms period through widespread industrialization, all the other five more urbanized states reported higher disparity of HCR between non-metro

and metro areas compared to the all-India level in 2004–5. The less urbanized state of Bihar reported high disparity in 2004–5 as well.

The size distribution of towns beyond metros and non-metros is available for only two years—1987–8 and 1993–4. Nonetheless, it gives an idea about the patterns of change in HCR at least in the pre-reforms era. At the all-India level, in all the years HCR decreased with an increase in the size class of an urban centre. Hence, HCR was the highest in small towns (C1 class) and the lowest in metropolitan cities (CM class) (Figure 2.10). In 1987–8, the gap between the two consecutive size classes was the highest (with a value of 1.32) between C2 and C3 size classes of towns and in 1993–4 it was the highest (with a value of 1.40) between C3 and CM size class of towns (Table 2.6). These ratios also indicate that in pre-reforms period, APCE in metropolitan cities increased at a much faster rate than APCE in the small towns indicating an increasing bias of the urban system towards metropolitan cities during this period. In 2004–5 we had only metro and non-metro divisions. The ratio of

**Table 2.5**  Ratio of HCR of Non-metro to HCR of Metro

| State | 1987–8 | 1993–4 | 2004–5 |
|---|---|---|---|
| Andhra Pradesh | 1.36 | 2.08 | 1.25 |
| Bihar | – | – | 2.55 |
| Gujarat | 1.25 | 1.16 | 1.95 |
| Haryana | – | – | 2.66 |
| Karnataka | 1.56 | 2.62 | 5.30 |
| Madhya Pradesh | – | 1.30 | 1.90 |
| Maharashtra | 2.19 | 2.91 | 2.94 |
| Punjab | – | 4.00 | 2.07 |
| Rajasthan | – | 1.87 | 0.70 |
| Tamil Nadu | 1.29 | 1.29 | 2.92 |
| Uttar Pradesh | 1.19 | 1.41 | 1.92 |
| West Bengal | 1.34 | 2.48 | 5.26 |
| All-India | 1.57 | 1.79 | 2.02 |

*Source*: Calculated by authors using the data from Table 2.2.

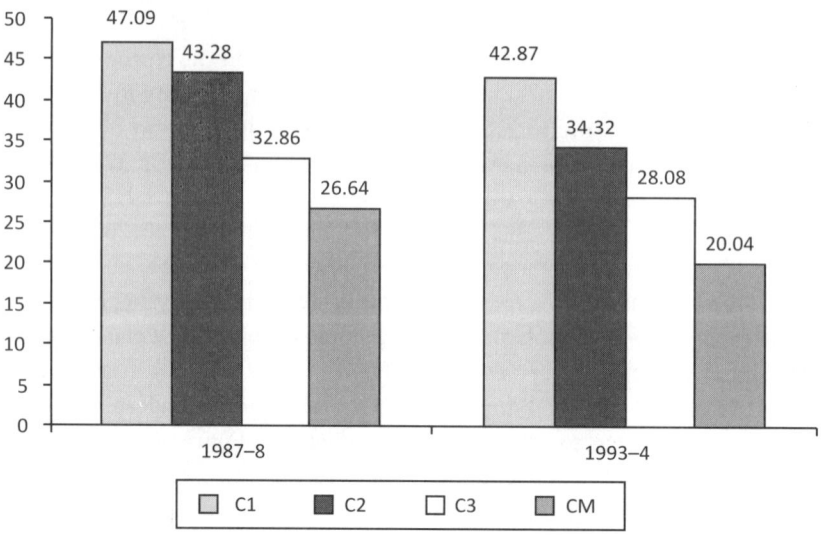

**Figure 2.10**   HCR by Size Class Over Time

*Source*: Calculated from Table A2.6.

**Table 2.6**   Gap between Two Consecutive Class Sizes

|        | Ratio of HCR of C1 to HCR of C2 | Ratio of HCR C2 to HCR C3 | Ratio of HCR C3 to HCR CM |
| ------ | ------------------------------- | ------------------------- | ------------------------- |
| 1987–8 | 1.09                            | 1.32                      | 1.23                      |
| 1993–4 | 1.25                            | 1.22                      | 1.40                      |

*Source*: Unit level data of consumption expenditure schedule of 43rd (1987–8), 50th (1993–4), and 61st (2004–5) Rounds of NSSO and state specific official poverty line for the years 1987–8, 1993–4, and 2004–5.

non-metro to metro HCR in 2004–5 was 2.02 as compared to 1.79 in 1993–4.

In most states, with the increase in size class, HCR decreased. There were few exceptions. In 1987–8, only for Punjab and the rest of the states and union territories HCR was higher in higher size class towns, and C2 was more than that of smaller size class of towns, C1. In 1993–4, similar patterns were observed in case of Gujarat and Haryana when one moved from C2 to C3 size class of towns. In 1987–8 states with highest HCR in C1, C2, C3, and CM size class of towns were Maharashtra, Karnataka, Bihar, and Karnataka respectively. In 1993–4, a similar position was occupied by Maharashtra

in all size classes except for Madhya Pradesh in the metropolitan size class. On the other extreme, HCR of other north-eastern states was way below all other states in C1 and C2 size classes of urban centres and in all urban areas in all the three years.

## RESPONSIVENESS OF DECLINE IN POVERTY TO RISE IN APCE

As seen earlier, a higher rise in APCE does not guarantee faster decline in HCR (poverty). This depends on how an increase in consumption expenditure (proxy for rise in income) percolates down to persons below the poverty line. If most of the increase in APCE is captured by persons above the poverty line it will have a comparatively lower impact on decline in poverty. To capture this aspect, we present elasticity of HCR with respect to APCE in Table 2.7. It estimates how much one percentage point increase in APCE impacts decline in poverty (HCR). It is measured as a ratio of rate of change of HCR to rate of change of APCE.

An increase in APCE normally leads to decline in HCR (poverty level) so the sign of elasticity would be negative. However, in cases where they move in the same direction, the sign of elasticity would be positive. All positive elasticity in the period 1987–8 to 1993–4 is consequences of negative growth of APCE (Table 2.1) accompanied by decline in HCR. In the next period (1993–4 to 2004–5)

all positive elasticities show increase in APCE accompanied by increase in HCR (Table 2.3).

In the pre-reforms period, HCR's elasticity with respect to APCE was much higher in both metro areas as well as non-metro areas with values over 4. It declined substantially to less than 2 in the reforms period in the both size classes. However, in non-metro towns the decline in elasticity was sharper and it was little over unity in the reforms period. This means that in non-metros, increase in APCE had a low impact on HCR. We saw earlier that APCE's growth in non-metros increased in the reforms period, but it did not translate into a reduction in HCR. The same was true in the metros as well. But the possibility of conversion of an increase in APCE into a reduction in HCR was higher in metros than in non-metros.

**Table 2.7**  Elasticity of HCR with respect to APCE

| State | 1987–8 to 1993–4 | | | 1993–4 to 2004–5 | | |
|---|---|---|---|---|---|---|
| | Non-metro | Metro | Total Urban | Non-metro | Metro | Total Urban |
| Andhra Pradesh | 3.12 | 10.27 | 3.01 | −1.63 | 0.58 | −1.35 |
| Assam | −5.42 | | −5.42 | −2.85 | | −2.85 |
| Bihar | −2.25 | | −2.26 | −0.29 | | −0.58 |
| Gujarat | −3.52 | −1.47 | −2.48 | −1.95 | −3.76 | −2.39 |
| Haryana | −3.05 | | −3.05 | −0.05 | | −0.60 |
| Jammu and Kashmir | −4.92 | | −4.92 | −3.13 | | −3.13 |
| Karnataka | −2.50 | −6.98 | −3.13 | −0.61 | −2.56 | −0.90 |
| Kerala | −4.74 | | −4.75 | −0.69 | | −0.68 |
| Madhya Pradesh | −0.82 | | −0.69 | −0.44 | −1.01 | −0.51 |
| Maharashtra | −0.73 | −2.96 | −1.37 | −1.84 | −0.51 | −1.16 |
| Orissa | −8.67 | | −8.63 | 1.64 | | 1.64 |
| Punjab | −2.83 | | −3.89 | −2.19 | 0.13 | −1.53 |
| Rajasthan | 8.00 | | −9.76 | −1.00 | 6.82 | 0.31 |
| Tamil Nadu | 1.46 | −0.50 | 34.09 | −2.03 | −2.37 | −1.86 |
| Uttar Pradesh | −2.86 | −10.55 | −3.19 | −1.13 | −0.67 | −0.72 |
| West Bengal | −1.93 | −5.51 | −2.59 | −1.85 | −3.36 | −1.87 |
| Other NE States | 14.05 | | 14.05 | −3.35 | | −3.35 |
| Rest ST & UT | −1.67 | −0.90 | −1.64 | −6.40 | −0.20 | 0.39 |
| All–India | −4.27 | −4.94 | −3.41 | −1.13 | −1.76 | −1.22 |

*Source*: Calculated by authors using the data from Tables 2.1 and 2.3.

*Note*: Elasticity measured here is the ratio of growth of HCR to the growth of corresponding APCE.

**Table 2.8** Classification of States by Elasticity of HCR

| | | Elasticity of HCR w.r.t. APCE | |
|---|---|---|---|
| | | 1987–8 to 1993–4 | 1993–4 to 2004–5 |
| Metro | High | Andhra Pradesh, *Karnataka*, Uttar Pradesh, West Bengal | *Gujarat*, *Karnataka*, <u>*Tamil Nadu*</u>, West Bengal |
| | Low | *Gujarat, Maharashtra, Tamil Nadu* | **Andhra Pradesh**, Madhya Pradesh, *Maharashtra*, **Punjab**, Rajasthan, **Uttar Pradesh** |
| Non-metro | High | Andhra Pradesh, Assam, Jammu and Kashmir, Kerala, Orissa, Rajasthan, *Tamil Nadu* | Andhra Pradesh, Assam, <u>*Gujarat*</u>, Jammu and Kashmir, *Maharashtra*, <u>*Punjab*</u>, <u>*Tamil Nadu*</u>, <u>Uttar Pradesh</u>, <u>West Bengal</u> |
| | Low | Bihar, *Gujarat*, *Haryana*, *Karnataka*, Madhya Pradesh, *Maharashtra*, Punjab, Uttar Pradesh, West Bengal | Bihar, *Haryana*, *Karnataka*, **Kerala**, Madhya Pradesh, **Orissa**, Rajasthan |

*Source*: Calculated from Table 2.6.

*Note*: 1. States marked in bold signify movement from high (> all-India level) to low (< all-India level) and the ones that are underlined indicate movement from low to high in consecutive years.

2. States that are italicized are high on level of urbanization in 2001 (> all-India level).

Table 2.8 shows the position of different states in terms of this measure of elasticity in metro and non-metro cities. In the metro city category, in the pre-reforms period only the more urbanized state of Karnataka had higher HCR elasticity. In the reforms period two more urbanized states of Gujarat and Tamil Nadu joined Karnataka in showing better responsiveness to a decline in poverty as compared to the all-India average. In the metro category, only West Bengal reported higher elasticity than the all-India level consistently in both the pre-reforms and reforms periods. Maharashtra, including its capital Mumbai fared badly in both periods showing far lower elasticity than the all-India level.

In the non-metro category as well a similar picture can be discerned. In the pre-reforms period only the more urbanized state of Tamil Nadu performed better than the all-India level. The rest of the six states were all less urbanized. But in the reforms period, Tamil Nadu got the company of the more urbanized states of Gujarat, Punjab, and Maharashtra. Among the less urbanized states, Andhra Pradesh, Assam, and Jammu and Kashmir consistently had much higher HCR elasticity as compared to the all-India level reflecting a much larger impact on decline in poverty with a similar rise in APCE growth.

From Table 2.7 it can be seen that all positive elasticity in the pre-reforms period reflects a scenario of negative APCE growth associated with a decline in poverty reflecting a high elasticity scenario or more equitable growth situation. This was the case in Andhra Pradesh, Rajasthan, Tamil Nadu, and other north-eastern states. In contrast, all cases of positive elasticity in the reforms period reflect a scenario of positive APCE growth (Table 2.1) associated with increase in poverty (Table 2.2) showing a very low elasticity scenario or an inequitable growth situation. Such cases were confined only to metro areas of Andhra Pradesh, Punjab, and Rajasthan. The overall finding of inequitable growth in the reforms period and equitable growth in the pre-reforms period corroborates our analysis in Chapter 1 (Figure 1.2), where we found that APCE growth was very high in the upper quintiles in the reforms period, in contrast to high APCE growth in the lower quintiles in the pre-reforms period.

## CONCLUSION

The analysis presented in this chapter indicates that in the reforms period there was a considerable increase in convergence across the more and less developed states with respect to APCE in the case of metros. In other words, metro cities became more alike in terms of average living standards irrespective of the level of development of the state they were in. At the same time, non-metros in the less developed states registered a lower APCE growth rate than the more developed states and thus in the less developed states the gap between metros and non-metros in terms of level of APCE has increased. The higher APCE growth in the reforms period in the less developed states had largely been captured by the population residing in metro areas. In more developed states the growth effect seems to have percolated down to non-metro areas in a better fashion.

But the disparity in the level of poverty (measured by HCR) across states in metro areas in the reforms period did not show any corresponding decline or convergence. There seems to be a considerable difference in various metro areas in response to change in HCR with respect to change in APCE.

Sarkar and Mehta (2010) plotted APCE of urban areas in Kernel Density Function (KDF) graphs for 1983, 1993–4, and 2004–5 at the all-India level. The kernel density plot showed concentration of urban persons at different APCE levels. Two interesting pictures were noted by them. First, the left side of the KDF graph showed a higher shift in the pre-reforms period (1983 to 1993–4) as compared to the reforms period (1993–4 to 2004–5). This indicated that in the former period households below the poverty line experienced relatively higher growth in APCE compared to households above the poverty line. We have already noted this as a slowing down of the trickle-down effect of growth in the reforms period.

The other interesting point in Sarkar and Mehta's (2010) study was that the poverty line was on the right side of the peak (highest concentration) of urban APCE and closer to it in both 1983 and 1993–4, but it shifted to the left side of the peak of the APCE graph in 2004–5 with a much smaller modal value. It showed that the advantage of having a high concentration of the urban population just below the poverty line which could go over the poverty line with a small increase in APCE in the pre-reforms period was no longer available in the reforms period. The implication of this is that the same growth in APCE in the reforms period would lead to lower decline of HCR by virtue of this factor only. The large decline in HCR's elasticity with respect to APCE that we observed in this chapter from the pre-reforms to the reforms period to a certain extent was also influenced by not having a large concentration of the urban population just below the poverty line.

Lastly, non-metro urban areas registered higher HCR and lower APCE in all the three quinquennial Rounds. A partial explanation can be found in accepting a uniform state level poverty line. The state level poverty line is estimated based on the average cost of living index in the state. However, in urban areas the cost of living is far higher in metropolitan cities than in small towns and hence a uniform poverty line tends to overestimate the incidence of poverty in small towns and underestimate it in metropolitan cities. The urban poverty line should also reflect the cost of accessing education and health facilities, which are not free and are to a great extent provided by the private sector. The same is the case with regard to housing and transport. These costs are far higher in metro cities than in non-metros. There is, therefore, a case for relooking at accepting a uniform state level urban poverty line.

# 3

# Employment and Unemployment Patterns

## INTRODUCTION

Participation in the labour market through employment is the single most important determinant of the level of living of a vast section of the population. Employment growth in urban areas is considerably higher than it is in rural areas in India because of growing and diversified work opportunities available in the former. However, in recent decades a new trend can be discerned within the urban system—of redistribution of population to smaller cities and towns as against a predominant concentration of urban population in metropolitan cities. There is growing concern that metropolitan cities are resisting in-migration of unskilled and low educated male workers due to changes in the requirements of the urban labour market reflected in the deceleration in the rate of population growth in these cities (Kundu and Mohanan 2009).

In the regional context, considerable variations exist among states in labour market outcomes. Some states have been able to provide significantly more employment opportunities and thus show higher employment and participation rates as compared to others. Ahmed and Pages (2008) found a significant relationship between Gross State Domestic Product (GSDP) growth and male employment growth in urban areas across the states. They did not find any pattern across states with regard to female employment, which is more influenced by cultural factors rather than by economic factors alone.

In this chapter we analyse whether changes in the employment structure differ substantially between non-metros and metros in terms of the nature and sector of employment and the relationship of the same with the level of urbanization. In examining regional differences in employment patterns, we categorize states into low and high level of urbanization, given that the higher level of urbanization is clearly associated with higher growth in GSDP over a longer period of time.

In this chapter we present the employment and unemployment situation from the National Sample Survey (NSS) 43rd (1987–8) Round to the 61st (2004–5) Round, disaggregated by available size classes. The analysis pertains to

Work Participation Rates (WPRs), nature of employment, industrial classification of workers, occupational classification of workers, and unemployment rates by usual status and current daily status of the population disaggregated by gender for major states in India. The data is for Usual Status (Principal + Subsidiary) (UPSS) workers. The industrial classification used is the National Industrial Classification (NIC), 1987 for the 43rd and 50th Rounds and revised NIC in 1998. Occupational classification used is the National Classification of Occupations (NCO) 1968 and both are restricted to just one-digit classification. For the purpose of analysis, one-digit categories are regrouped to get three basic categories in both the classifications. In the former the categories are: (i) primary (consisting of sections 0 and 1 of NIC 1987), (ii) secondary (sections 2, and 3, 4, and 5 of NIC 1987), and (iii) tertiary (sections 6, 7, 8, and 9 of NIC 1987).

In the latter, the reclassified categories are: (i) Administrative/Professional (A/P) (consisting of divisions 0, 1, and 2 of NCO), (ii) Clerical (consisting of divisions 3, 4, and 5), and (iii) Manual Labour (ML) (consisting of divisions 6, 7, 8, and 9 of NCO). The administrative/professional classification consists of all highly skilled professions and jobs, clerical of all semi-skilled activities, where education is required but not any specialized one and manual labour consists of all activities that involve physical labour. Some of the activities under ML, in fact, are skilled tasks such as carpentry, weaving, and tailoring which could have been classified as skilled manual labour activities. The clerical category consists of jobs that are more desk jobs. It is likely that those engaged in some skilled manual labour jobs would have higher wages than those employed in clerical type of jobs. As this is the first such analysis of its kind, the analytical categories have been kept simple.

The processed data is given in the Tables A3.1 to A3.39.

## OVERALL URBAN EMPLOYMENT

### Work Participation Rates

Urban areas are distinguished from rural areas on account of relatively very low female WPR as compared to males, a phenomenon observed on the whole as well in metros and non-metros. On the whole, 54.9 per cent of the urban males and 16.6 per cent of urban females were employed in 2004–5. This was an improvement in the WPR of 52.1 per cent for males and 15.5 per cent for females in 1993–4 (Figure 3.1). Thus, over the 11 years of the reforms period, male WPR improved by 2.8 percentage points and female WPR by just 1.1 percentage points. At the same time, there was a consistent increase in male and female WPRs (by 4.2 percentage points and 1.4 percentage points respectively) from 1987–8 onwards, albeit gradually among the latter. Thus, the gap between male and female WPR increased from 35.5 percentage points in 1987–8 to 38.3 percentage points in 2004–5. WPRs slightly dipped in 1999–2000. If this year is set aside from the analysis then we observe consistent increase in urban WPR over this period. In fact, throughout this chapter we have not included this year in the discussion.

If we divide the entire period of our analysis into two: (i) pre-reforms (1987–8 to 1993–4), and (ii) reforms (1993–4 to 2004–5), a different picture emerges. For whole urban, the employment growth was faster in the reforms period than in the pre-reforms period in terms of percentage points. Male WPR increased by 1.4 percentage point in the pre-reforms period and by 2.8 percentage points in the reforms period (Figure 3.1). Female WPR increased by 0.3 percentage points and 1.1 percentage points in the two periods, respectively.

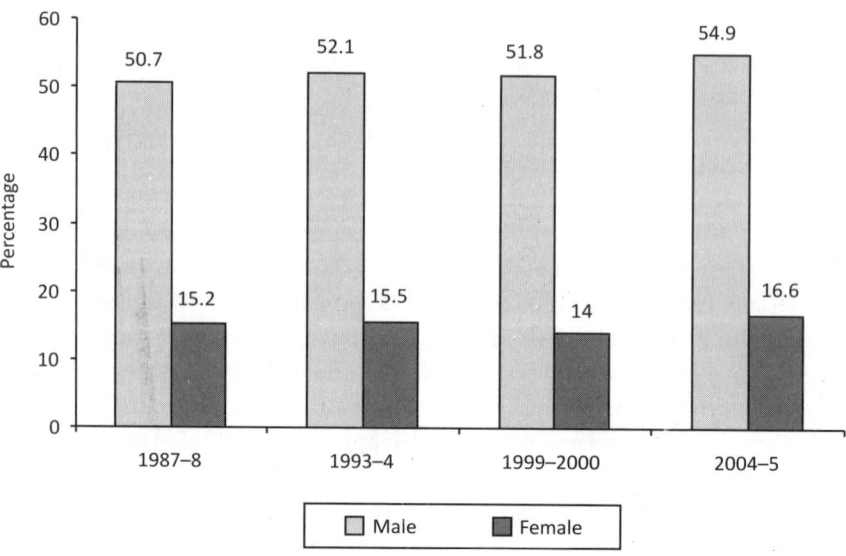

**Figure 3.1**    Male and Female WPRs Over Time, Urban India

*Source*: Data taken from Tables A3.1 to A3.3.

But, more important is to observe the Compound Annual Growth Rate (CAGR) of employment over the whole period (1987–8 to 2004–5). On the whole, CAGR of employment of females was higher (3.89 per cent) as compared to that of males (3.73 per cent) (Table 3.1). But disaggregated by time period, male and female employment growth slowed down to 3.15 per cent and 3.35 per cent,[1] respectively in the reforms period from 3.53 per cent and 3.57 per cent, respectively, in the pre-reforms period. It is interesting to note that CAGRs of female employment were higher than that of male employment in all sub-periods since 1987–8, primarily on account of a low base (see Table 3.1). However, it is also true and what is observed later in this chapter, that more work suitable for women was available in the labour market and improvement in female education facilitated this process. Besides, casualization of male employment also forced women to come out in the labour force. The plausibility of the last argument can be observed from a decline

in consumption expenditure growth rate in real terms in the bottom percentiles as shown in Chapter 1.

Most states presented in Figure 3.2 registered an increase in male WPR from 1993–4 except Haryana. In states such as Uttar Pradesh, Madhya Pradesh, and Bihar, male WPRs declined in the pre-reforms period and subsequently increased in the reforms period. Bihar had the lowest and extremely low male WPR followed by Madhya Pradesh and Uttar Pradesh. West Bengal followed by Tamil Nadu were at the top two spots in male WPR in 2004–5. What should also be noted is very rapid increase in male WPR in the reforms period in West Bengal and Gujarat, taking both the states to first and third positions in male WPRs among the major states in India. Male WPRs are influenced by level of economic development and level of urbanization.

Female WPRs were lower than male WPRs in all the states without any exception. But female WPRs registered a decline in only two

**Table 3.1**  Compound Annual Growth Rate of Employment (%)

| Period | Urban | | Non-metro | | Metro | |
|---|---|---|---|---|---|---|
| | Male | Female | Male | Female | Male | Female |
| 1987–8 to 1993–4 | 3.53 | 3.57 | 2.70 | 2.87 | 6.95 | 7.10 |
| 1993–4 to 1999–2000 | 2.45 | 0.85 | 1.49 | −0.53 | 5.24 | 6.15 |
| 1999–2000 to 2004–5 | 3.99 | 6.43 | 3.35 | 6.35 | 5.60 | 7.09 |
| 1993–4 to 2004–5 | 3.15 | 3.35 | 2.33 | 2.54 | 5.41 | 6.57 |
| 1987–8 to 2004–5 | 3.73 | 3.89 | 2.79 | 3.01 | 6.77 | 7.70 |

*Source*: Calculated from data of Tables A3.1 to A3.3 and census adjusted population of 1987–8, 1993–4, 1999–2000, and 2004–5.

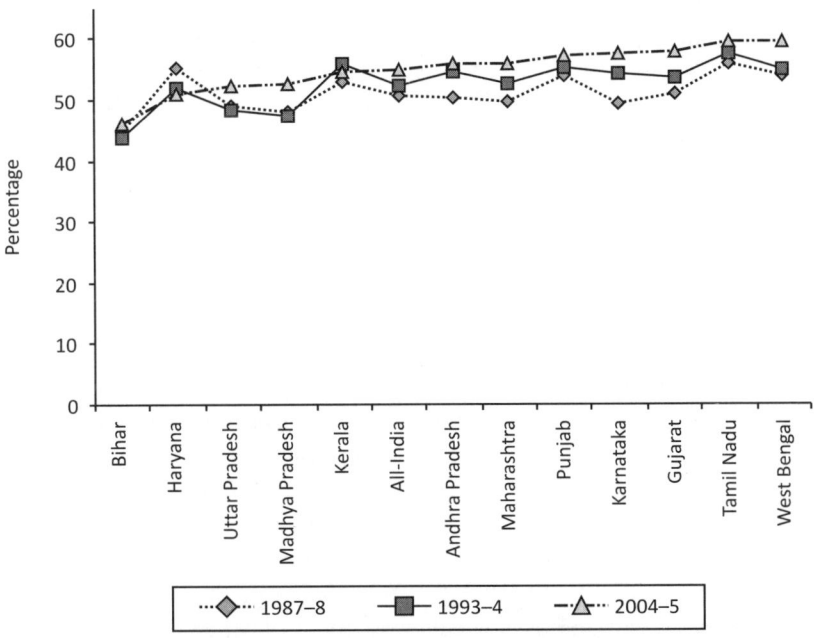

**Figure 3.2**  Male WPR Over Time, Select States

*Source*: Data taken from Tables A3.1 to A3.3.

states, Haryana and Karnataka (Figure 3.3). In a large number of states, namely Andhra Pradesh, Rajasthan, Madhya Pradesh, Punjab, and Bihar, female WPRs declined in the pre-reforms period and then increased in the reforms period. The three southern states of Tamil Nadu, followed by Andhra Pradesh and Kerala lead in female WPRs and Bihar, Uttar Pradesh, and Haryana in this order were the bottom three states in female WPRs. Thus, cultural and social factors along with economic factors influence female WPRs. Female WPR was relatively high in Maharashtra, which is the second most urbanized and third richest state in India while

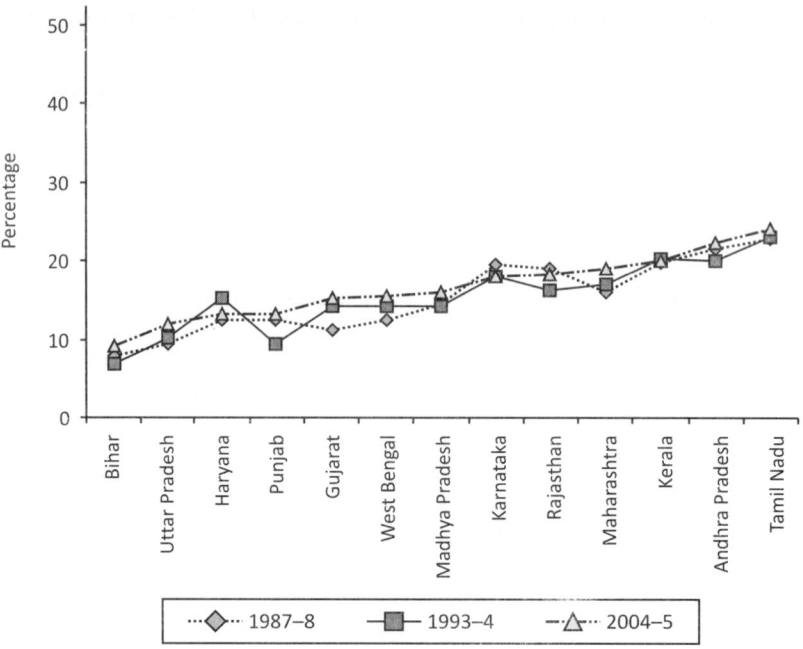

**Figure 3.3**   Female WPR Over Time, Select States

*Source*: Data taken from Tables A3.1 to A3.3.

WPR was relatively low in Gujarat which is the fourth richest and third most urbanized state in India.

### Nature of Work

There is an interesting change in the nature of work among males in urban India. In 1987–8, 43.7 per cent males were working as Regular Employed (RE) and 41.6 per cent as Self-Employed (SE) (Figure 3.4). In 2004–5, a larger proportion (44.8 per cent) were SE as compared to 1987–8 while RE declined to 40.6 per cent among males. Also, in the pre-reforms period, Casual Labour (CL) increased, SE remained constant, and RE decreased among males in all urban areas. But in the reforms period there was a significant increase in SE and decline in RE and CL among males. Thus, males shifted to the SE category post reforms, probably on the lower end shifting from CL and

on the higher end shifting from RE. It needs to be kept in mind that the SE category has a wide range of activities, with males having high earnings to low earnings. Further, in the first few years of reforms because of the economic crises, some males shifted to CL jobs from RE jobs. Subsequently, CL among males declined, reaching 14.6 per cent in 2004–5 and males shifted to SE. There was also a natural progression in the type of work; a new migrant to the city takes up whatever work is available, which is generally CL, and then shifts to permanent employment. Given that RE work has diminished males take to whatever is possible in the SE category. Hence, for the migrant population there is a natural progression in the nature of work from CL to SE.

A very different picture is seen among females. There was a consistent increase in RE among them—from 27.5 per cent in 1987–8

(Figure 3.4), to 29.2 per cent in 1993–4 and then to 35.6 per cent in 2004–5 (Figure 3.4). From where did this shift take place? Entirely from the CL type of work that declined from 25.4 per cent in 1987–8 to 16.7 per cent in 2004–5. In the pre-reforms period, like in case of male workers, CL employment increased marginally, SE declined significantly, and RE increased, the last category contributing to an increase in WPR. The same trend continued in the reforms period, with much larger increase in RE, sharper decline in CL, and noticeable increase in SE.

### Employment Sector

Among urban female workers, a large proportion of female workers, 18.3 per cent or two in every 11 workers were employed in the primary (P) sector in 2004–5 (Figure 3.5). However, this was a decline from 30.3 per cent in 1987–8 (Figure 3.5). Secondly, we also see concomitant

increase in female employment in the tertiary (T) sector, from 38.6 per cent in 1987–8 to 46.0 per cent in 1993–4, and to 49.5 per cent in 2004–5. There was also a slight increase in secondary (S) sector employment among females from 31.0 per cent in 1987–8 to 32.2 per cent in 2004–5. The proportion of secondary employment among females was only slightly less than the proportion among males. Looking at this more closely by two different periods, a decline in secondary and an increase in tertiary sector employment can be seen in the pre-reforms period and vice versa in the reforms period. It seems that the secondary sector has revived in urban India. Our understanding is that this is because of increase in employment in the construction sector.

Contrary to expectations and the general belief in a decline in secondary sector employment in urban India, the proportion of male workers employed in this sector remained

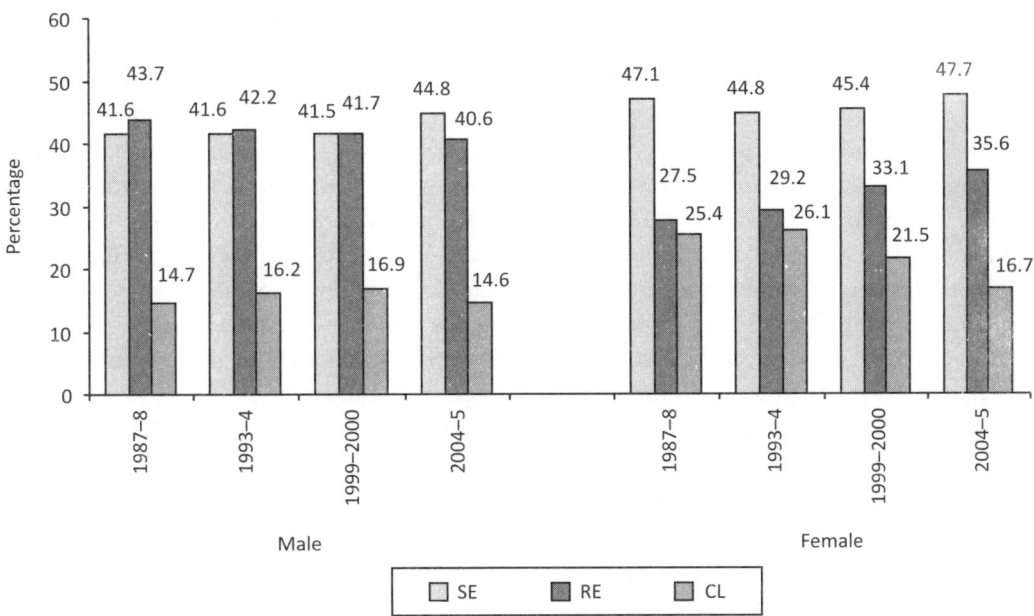

**Figure 3.4** Nature of Male and Female Employment Over Time, Urban India

*Source*: Data taken from Tables A3.4–A3.8, A3.10, A3.11, and A3.15.

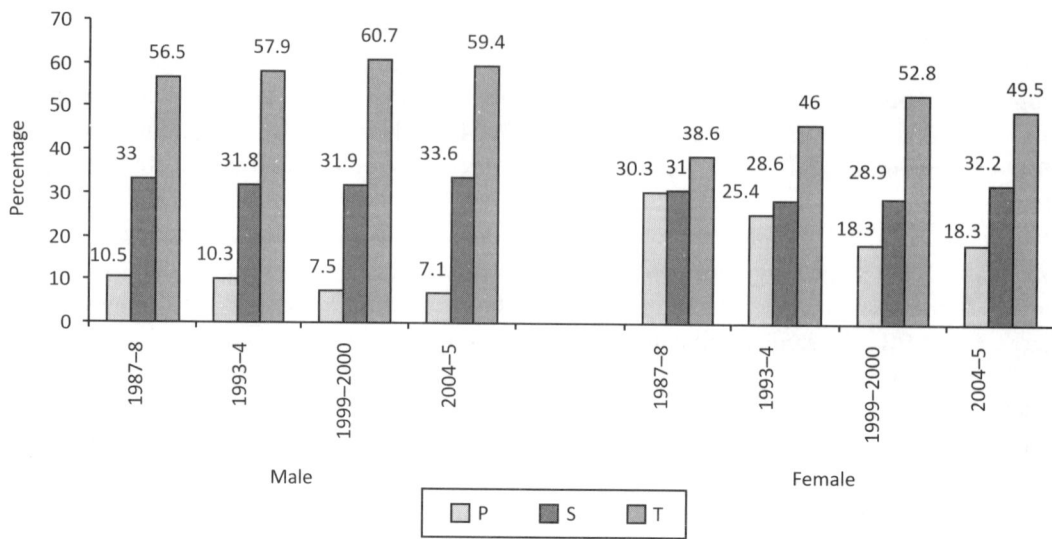

**Figure 3.5**   Industrial Classification of Male and Female Workers Over Time, Urban India

*Source*: Data taken from Tables A3.14, A3.15, A3.17, A3.18, A3.20, A3.21, and A3.23.

nearly the same in the entire study period (1987–8 to 2004–5). In 1987–8, 33.0 per cent males were employed in the secondary sector (Figure 3.5), which went up marginally to 33.6 per cent in 2004–5. In the intermediate year of 1993–4, secondary sector employment went down slightly among them to 31.8 per cent. There was a gradual increase in tertiary sector employment among urban males, from 56.5 per cent in 1987–8, to 57.9 per cent in 1993–4 to 59.4 per cent in 2004–5 (Figure 3.5). Thus, by mid-2000, three in every five employed urban males was working in the tertiary sector. The shift to tertiary sector employment was on account of a decline in primary sector employment and not due to a decline in secondary sector employment. Tertiary sector employment among males has become SE type and the CL, which could be in the secondary sector, has declined.

RE type of work increased for females in the tertiary sector as is evident from the cross tables of nature of work with sector of work (Table 3.2). More than half the females employed in

this sector were in RE jobs which increased to 60 per cent. Further, there was an increase in SE in the secondary sector, indicating that women were taking up sub-contracted work and were probably working from home on a piece rate basis. For example, Mahadevia and Shah (2010) find some textile industry work such as cutting threads for machine embroidered textiles, sub-contracted to women living in the slums in Surat. Similar sub-contracting occurred in the leather goods industry in Kanpur. It is possible that the option of taking up sub-contracted work and working from home brought some new women in the labour force, increasing their WPRs.

If we dissect male workers' sectoral distribution by two periods, we find that secondary sector employment declined in the pre-reforms period but increased in the reforms period reaching nearly 1987–8 level. When secondary sector employment declined in the pre-reforms period, tertiary sector employment increased. The opposite was true in the reforms period. In other words, a section of employment in

**Table 3.2**    Sectors of Work and Nature of Work, All Urban

| 1993–4 | Nature of Work | | | | | |
| | Male | | | Female | | |
| Sector | SE | RE | CL | SE | RE | CL |
| Primary | 53.5 | 13.7 | 32.7 | 56.5 | 1.9 | 41.6 |
| Secondary | 29.2 | 45.6 | 25.2 | 48.7 | 15.7 | 35.6 |
| Tertiary | 46.3 | 45.4 | 8.3 | 35.8 | 52.4 | 11.7 |
| 2004–5 | | | | | | |
| Primary | 62.0 | 14.5 | 23.5 | 62.2 | 2.4 | 35.4 |
| Secondary | 31.2 | 40.4 | 28.5 | 61.1 | 17.8 | 21.1 |
| Tertiary | 50.4 | 43.9 | 5.7 | 33.6 | 59.4 | 7.0 |

*Source*: Unit level data of employment–unemployment schedule of 50th (1993–4) and 61st (2004–5) Rounds of NSSO.

*Note*: The columns total 100 per cent.

the tertiary sector for males was residual employment, which was CL type in the pre-reforms period. A common trend across both the periods was a decline in primary sector employment, which is to be expected.

For males, a significant proportion (31 per cent) of secondary sector work was SE type in 2004–5, which was a slight increase from 1993–4. At the same time, there was an increase in CL type of work in this sector for males from 25.2 per cent in 1993–4 to 28.5 per cent in 2004–5. It is most probable that CL jobs in the secondary sector were in construction, which increased in the last decade-and-a-half on account of infrastructure development in urban areas. RE in the secondary sector decreased. In contrast to females, RE in the tertiary sector reduced and SE increased among males. It seems that males were replaced by females in certain regular work in the tertiary sector such as in clerical positions and as shop assistants.

**Quality of Employment**

There was improvement in the quality of urban employment in this entire period. Among males, those employed in A/P positions went up from 13.2 per cent in 1987–8 to 16.6 per cent in 1993–4 and to 18.0 per cent in 2004–5

(Figure 3.6). This category also includes other professional and technical persons. A part of the increase in SE in the tertiary sector among males in urban areas was with the emergence of professional and technical jobs. These are high salary jobs and this is one of the driver sectors of national income growth rates. This high paying urban sector emerged after 1993–4.

Manual Labour (ML) jobs declined somewhat among urban males, from 49.0 per cent in 1987–8 to 46.0 per cent in 2004–5, at a marginally faster rate in the reforms period than in the pre-reforms period. This explains the decline in CL jobs as well as primary sector jobs among males. At the same time, there was a slight shift from clerical (C) type of jobs to higher order, that is, A/P type of jobs among them—the percentage decline was from 37.8 per cent in 1987–8 to 36.6 per cent in 1993–4 to 36.0 per cent in 2004–5. Interestingly, females stepped into clerical type of jobs in place of males who moved up to A/P jobs. In spite of improvement in male employment, an overwhelming proportion of them (46 per cent) still continued in ML type of work which is low paying. This indicates that urban inequality in male employment increased.

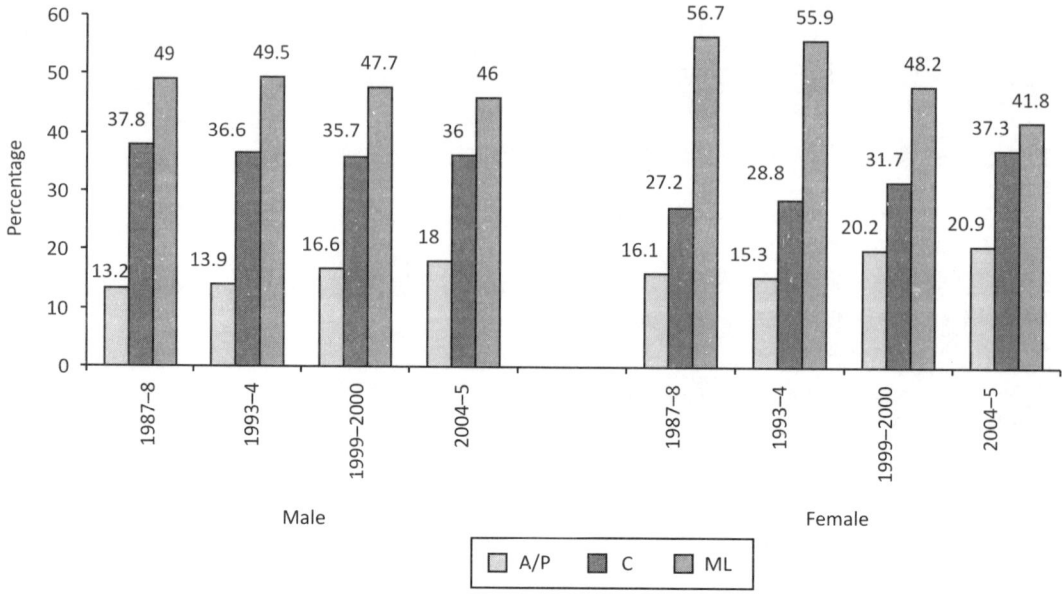

**Figure 3.6**   Occupational Classification of Male and Female Workers Over Time, Urban India

*Source*: Data taken from Tables A3.24, A3.25, A3.27, A3.28, A3.30, A3.31, and A3.33.

There was a much sharper decline in ML type of jobs among employed urban females—from 56.7 per cent in 1987–8 to 55.9 per cent in 1993–4 and then down to 41.8 per cent in 2004–5 (Figure 3.6), with a very sharp decline in the reforms period. Sectoral shift in jobs happened in favour of clerical type of jobs; their proportion in these jobs increased from 27.2 per cent in 1987–8 to just 28.8 per cent in 1993–4, but there was a significant increase in the reforms period to 37.3 per cent in 2004–5. Another significant sectoral shift in jobs occurred in favour of A/P type of jobs; their proportion increased from 16.1 per cent in 1987–8 to 20.9 per cent in 2004–5 with again a larger increase in the reforms period. In other words, in the reforms period, even the quality of female employment improved, with a shift from ML to clerical and clerical to A/P jobs. Interestingly, in 2004–5, the proportion of females employed in ML jobs was lower than

the proportion of males in such jobs. Female WPRs improved in the reforms period on account of availability of clerical jobs on the one hand and availability of home-based work on the other. Clerical jobs going to women could be because of low wage regular work in the tertiary sector.

**WORK PARTICIPATION RATES—METRO/ NON-METRO DIFFERENCES**

Male WPRs in metros were consistently higher than in non-metros and in all urban areas in all the years (Figure 3.7). This reached 56.6 per cent in 2004–5 from 52.5 per cent in 1987–8 or an increase of 4.1 percentage points, the same increase as observed for all urban areas. But the large WPR increase occurred in the pre-reforms period and not in the reforms period in the metros. Male employment CAGR in the pre-reforms period was 6.95 per cent and in the reforms period it was 5.41 per cent (Table 3.1).

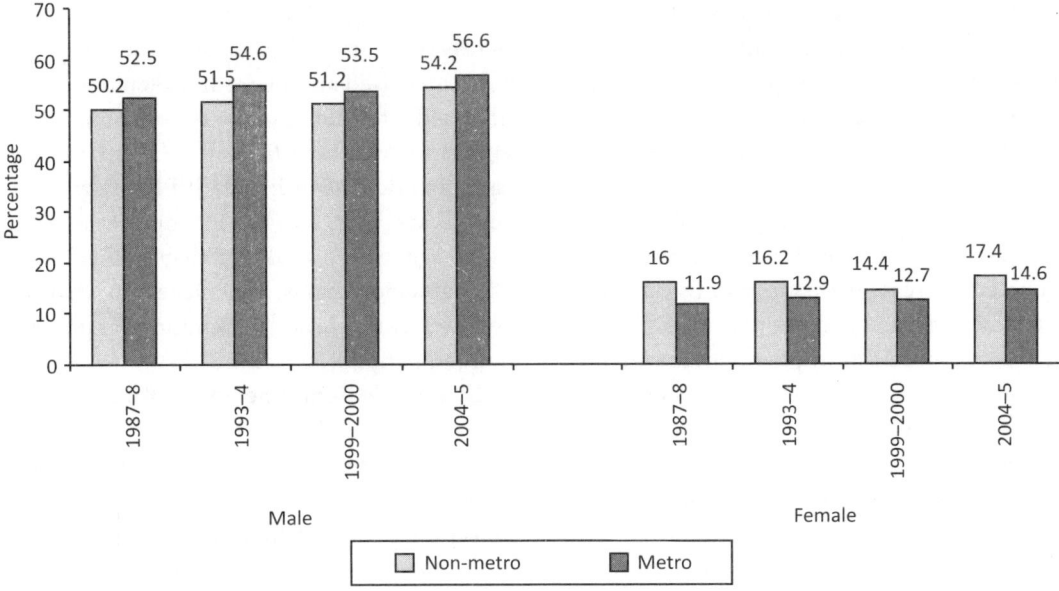

**Figure 3.7**  Work Participation Rates, Metros versus Non-metros

*Source*: Table A3.3.

Male WPR in non-metros has always been lower than the all-urban average and certainly lower than that in the metros as mentioned earlier. In 2004–5, male WPR in non-metros was 54.2 per cent, whereas in metros it was 56.6 per cent. Non-metro WPRs were closer to the average urban WPRs primarily because of its large share in total urban population (see Chapter 1). Over time, male WPRs in non-metros also improved from 50.2 per cent in 1987–8 to 51.5 per cent in 1993–4 and to 54.2 per cent in 2004–5, that is, an increase of 4.0 percentage points (nearly the same as the increase in WPRs in the metros and all urban areas) over the entire period.

In contrast, female WPR in the metros has been consistently lower than the female WPR in all urban and non-metros in all the years. In 2004–5, female WPR in non-metros was 17.4 per cent, that in metros was 14.6 per cent, and that in all urban areas was 16.6 per cent. With

higher household incomes, females tend to drop out of the labour market, a phenomenon we observe in urban India. Nonetheless, female WPRs in metros increased during this period, going up from 11.9 per cent in 1987–8 to 12.9 per cent in 1993–4 and to 14.6 per cent in 2004–5. Unlike males, female WPRs in the metros registered a comparatively larger increase in the 1993–4 to 2004–5 period as compared to the 1987–8 to 1993–4 period in percentage terms. But still female WPRs in metros were very low.

CAGRs of female workers were higher than that of male workers in all the periods in the metros. This was because of a low base of female workers. But CAGRs were higher in the pre-reforms period (7.10 per cent) than in the reforms period (6.57 per cent) in the metros. In the case of non-metros, female WPRs increased over the entire period, albeit much slowly registering an increase of only 1.4 percentage points. The change in female WPRs in non-metros was therefore the same as in all urban, suggesting a higher increase in employment in metros as compared to non-metros.

CAGRs of male and female employment in metros for each period were far higher than CAGRs of male and female employment in non-metros. Metros had a higher rate of employment increase than non-metros even in the pre-reforms period and this period had a higher increase in the rate of employment than it did in the reforms period. To sum up, in the reforms period there was higher employment growth for female workers than for male workers, but for both sexes, the pre-reforms period registered higher growth rate of employment. Besides employment growth slowing down, bias against non-metros continued in the reforms period.

The gap between male and female WPRs in non-metros also increased in percentage terms, from 34.2 in 1987–8 to 36.8 in 2004–5 (Figure 3.7). But this gap was lower than in the metros, where the gap increased from 40.6 percentage points in 1987–8 to 42.0 percentage points in 2004–5. Lastly, as in the case of males, females in non-metros registered faster increase in WPR in percentage terms after 1993–4 than in the 1987–8 to 1993–4 period.

A break-up of size classes is possible for first two NSS Rounds, for 1987–8 and 1993–4. Data shows that with an increase in the size of an urban centre, WPRs increased among males and declined among females at the aggregate level. As a result, with an increase in the size class of town, the gap between male and female WPRs increased, the gap becoming highest in metropolitan cities and lowest in the smallest size class of urban centres. This means that more work was available for females in smaller towns than in metropolitan cities and more work was available for males in metropolitan cities than in the smaller towns. Or females in smaller towns needed to work

to support family incomes whereas females in metros did not need to do so. When wages of males increased and hence household incomes increased, female members of households tended to withdraw from the labour market, leading to decline in female WPRs. Further, as we will see later, females in non-metros were also in agriculture work and they worked in the residual sector, that is, they picked up whatever work was available and agriculture was possible in urban peripheries in the SMTs.

There could be another reason for low female WPRs in metros. Is it that the types of jobs created in the metropolitan cities are not suitable for women? Women, who tend to have lower education levels than men and hence lower skill levels to negotiate the market economy, cannot access metropolitan labour markets that require higher order skills and levels of education. Hence, it is likely that women were unable to access the metropolitan labour market because employment was available in non-primary sectors and without skill training they were unable to access this market. Lastly, metropolitan cities also require that women travel longer distances to their work place as compared to small cities and towns. This means incurring time and financial costs. For many women this may not be easy, given their sole responsibility of household chores. Thus, many reasons explain why female WPRs tend to decline when the city size increases and why male WPRs tend to increase when the city size increases and each city would have a combination of these factors. More field research is required to find answers to this vexing situation in metropolitan cities.

### DIFFERENCES BY STATES

There are significant variations across states with regard to metro and non-metro differences. States with higher male WPRs in metros than in non-metros in 2004–5 were Gujarat, Karnataka, Maharashtra, West Bengal, Punjab,

Madhya Pradesh, Rajasthan, and Uttar Pradesh; these include both developed and less developed states (Table A3.3). The first four states have three of the seven largest metropolitan cities and Gujarat and Maharashtra also have high levels of urbanization. The state with the highest urbanization level in 2001, Tamil Nadu, however had nearly the same WPR for males in metros and non-metros. This was also true for Andhra Pradesh, which had a low level of urbanization. The states where non-metros had higher WPRs among males than in metros in 2004–5 were Bihar and Haryana, the former a part of the BIMARU states having one-third the per capita income of the latter. No clear pattern emerges here.

In 1993–4 there was a slight difference. The states where male WPRs in the metros were higher than in the non-metros were just Gujarat, Maharashtra, Punjab, West Bengal, and Madhya Pradesh. The states where the situation

was reverse were Andhra Pradesh, Karnataka, Rajasthan, and Uttar Pradesh. Tamil Nadu was the only large state which had the distinction of having no disparity in male WPRs in metros and non-metros. Certainly the richer states had a higher disparity in the urban system than the less developed states (Table A3.3).

Male WPRs in metros were high in states with high urbanization levels; and vice versa was also true in 2004–5 (Table 3.3). The terms high and low are in reference to the all-India average. Among females in metros, such a clear picture does not exist. Tamil Nadu, Haryana, and Punjab, the three developed states registered low female WPRs in their metros. Is this cultural or some other explanation needs to be sought? Like in the metros, even in non-metros male WPRs were closely related to the urbanization levels to a great extent, but with the exception of Andhra Pradesh, Kerala, and Assam, where in spite of low urbanization

**Table 3.3**   Distribution of States by WPR and Urbanization Levels, 2004–5

| | | Urbanization Level (2001) Metros | | Urbanization Level (2001) Non-metros | |
|---|---|---|---|---|---|
| | | High | Low | High | Low |
| Male WPRs | High | Gujarat, Karnataka, Maharashtra, Punjab, Tamil Nadu, West Bengal, | | Gujarat, Karnataka, Maharashtra, Punjab, Tamil Nadu, West Bengal | Andhra Pradesh, Assam, Kerala |
| | Low | Haryana | Andhra Pradesh, Bihar, Madhya Pradesh, Rajasthan, Uttar Pradesh | Haryana | Bihar, Jammu and Kashmir, Madhya Pradesh, Orissa Rajasthan, Uttar Pradesh |
| Female WPRs | High | Gujarat, Karnataka, Maharashtra, West Bengal | Madhya Pradesh, Rajasthan | Karnataka, Maharashtra, Tamil Nadu | Andhra Pradesh |
| | Low | Haryana, Punjab, Tamil Nadu | Andhra Pradesh, Bihar, Uttar Pradesh | Gujarat, Haryana, Punjab, West Bengal | Assam, Bihar, Jammu and Kashmir, Madhya Pradesh, Kerala, Orissa, Rajasthan, Uttar Pradesh |

*Source*: Table A3.3.
*Note*: High and low pertain to above and below the all-India average.

levels, male WPRs were high. Among females in non-metros, there was a slightly clearer picture than in the metros; WPRs among them were lower in the low urbanized states. This means that in the low urbanized states work was not available for females in non-metros. In the high urbanized states of Gujarat, Haryana, Punjab, and West Bengal, women chose to remain out of the labour force in the non-metros.

Metro-male WPRs increased in all the states in 2004–5 as compared to 1993–4. That was the case with regard to non-metro male WPRs as well with the exception of Kerala and Orissa, where there was only a marginal decline. In the case of metro-females, WPRs increased in all the states in 2004–5 as compared to 1993–4. In the case of non-metros, this was not the case in Haryana, Jammu and Kashmir, Karnataka, Kerala, Orissa, and Rajasthan. Lastly, at a further disaggregated level of size classes, the pattern of male WPR increasing with an increase in the size class of town was true for states that did not have metropolitan cities. In states that had metropolises, there was a mixed picture.

## NATURE OF EMPLOYMENT—METRO/ NON-METRO DIFFERENCES

At all urban level, up to 2000 the largest proportion of employed males was in the RE category, followed by the SE category (Tables A3.4, A3.7, and A3.10). In 2004–5, the SE category became the largest employer of working males (Table A3.12). In metros, the quality of employment was better than in all urban areas, indicating that in non-metros the quality of employment for males was relatively poor. In all the NSS Rounds, more than half the employed males in the metros were engaged in RE jobs. This indicates that RE had the largest share in metros (Figure 3.8). In the second position in terms of proportionate share in metros was SE among males. Further, in all the NSS Rounds,

the proportion of males employed as RE in metros was higher than the proportion of males employed as RE in all urban. The opposite was the case with regard to the proportion of males employed in SE and CL types of jobs. This means that metros had higher regular employment availability for males than all urban and lower need for males to work as self-employed or casual labour than all urban. Like for all urban, in the metros also RE and the CL among males went down over this period whereas SE went up.

In non-metros, the highest proportion of male workers was employed as SE (Figure 3.9), reaching 47.2 per cent in 2004–5 and its share significantly increased in the reforms period. RE was in the second position, which reduced in the pre-reforms period and then increased in the reforms period reaching 36.1 per cent in 2004–5. But this proportion was still less than 42.8 per cent in 1987–8. Interestingly, CL among males increased in the pre-reforms period, which came down in the reforms period. This means that the economic crises at the time of the economic reforms in 1991 was much severe in non-metros as compared to metros and that males in non-metros were forced to seek CL type of work. However, since 1993–4 the proportion of RE among males in non-metros has improved on the whole. Lastly, as compared to all urban, SE and CL employment among males was higher and RE lower in non-metros in all the years. This means that in contrast to metros, non-metros did not have opportunities for regular work and hence males were forced to work as SE and CL on the one hand and also have low WPRs than metros on the other.

Among females, the nature of employment in metros was quite different than that in non-metros. In the latter, the largest proportion of female workers was in SE category whereas in metros they were in RE, just as in the case of the male workers in metros. More than half the

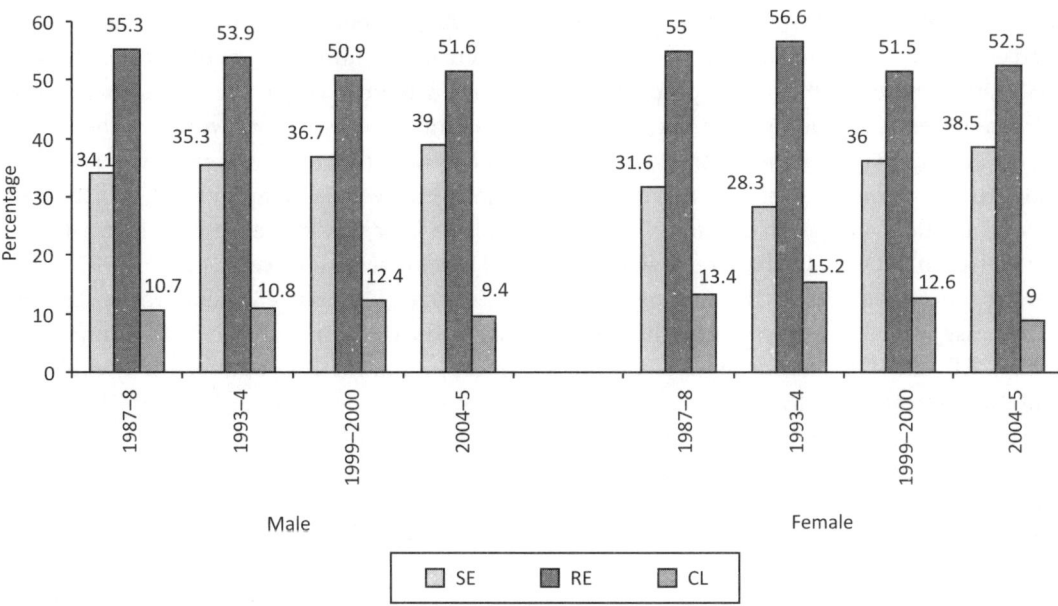

**Figure 3.8**  Nature of Employment in Metropolitan Cities

*Source*: Data taken from Tables A3.6, A3.9, and A3.13.

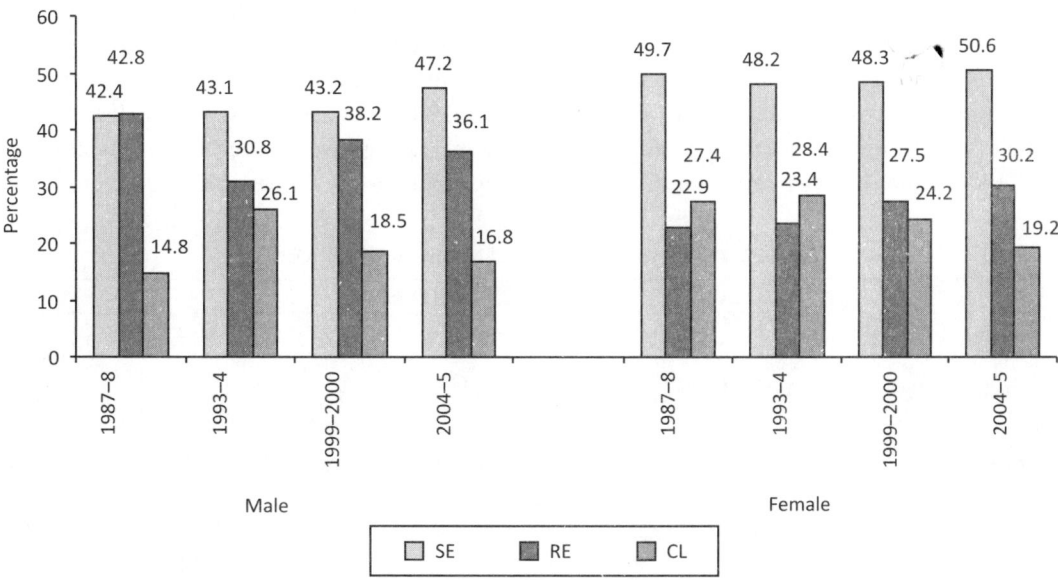

**Figure 3.9**  Nature of Employment in Non-metros

*Source*: Data taken from Tables A3.6, A3.9, and A3.12.

females in metros were employed as regular workers in all the rounds. In fact, in all the NSS rounds except 1987–8, the proportion of RE among females was higher than the what it was among males in the metros. Also, the proportion of SE among females in the metros was nearly the same as that among males in the metros in 2004–5. CL had the lowest share among female workers in the metros, just as in the case of males. Lastly, like in the case of males, RE and CL among females declined and SE increased in the metros. The only difference was that SE increased significantly among females in the metros after 1993–4 whereas among the males this increased after 1999–2000. Obviously, the difference between non-metros and metros in the case of females was because of non-metros, where one would find very high SE and relatively high CL and very low RE, as we will see later.

SE and CL employment was higher and RE lower in non-metros in all the years except 2004–5. But we cannot observe fluctuations in the RE category among females in non-metros as we saw for males. RE employment gradually increased among females in non-metros. But there was also a slight increase in SE among females in non-metros, reaching 50.6 per cent in 2004–5 from 49.7 per cent in 1987–8. The

SE category employed the largest proportion of females in non-metros contrary to the situation in metros where the largest proportion was employed as regular workers. The lack of availability of work in non-metros pushed the females to seek self-employment, which as we will see later was in the primary sector (Table 3.4). In the second place was CL in 1987–8 and 1993–4, which has been taken over by RE since then. Thus, the increase in WPRs among females in non-metros could be partly explained by an increase in the availability of RE in these urban centres. Regular work, as we will see later, is in the tertiary sector. This seems to be a positive trend. However, a very wide gap between metros and non-metros in terms of the nature of work for females continues to remain.

Evidently, more regular employment was available to males in large and metropolitan cities than in small and medium towns. Because of regular employment, income levels were higher in larger cities as compared to smaller towns. This explains why the incidence of poverty is higher in smaller towns as compared to larger cities.

Note that RE declined and CL increased from 1987–8 to 2004–5 among males, indicating increasing casualization of male workers in this period in the whole urban sector. However,

**Table 3.4**   Sectors of Work and Nature of Work, Metros

| 1993–4 | Nature of Work | | | | | |
|---|---|---|---|---|---|---|
|  | Male | | | Female | | |
| Sector | SE | RE | CL | SE | RE | CL |
| Primary | 55.6 | 25.9 | 18.5 | 71.9 | 0.0 | 28.0 |
| Secondary | 24.0 | 57.8 | 18.2 | 27.7 | 37.7 | 34.6 |
| Tertiary | 41.5 | 52.5 | 6.0 | 25.9 | 66.0 | 8.1 |
| 2004–5 |  |  |  |  |  |  |
| Primary | 71.8 | 23.0 | 5.2 | 78.4 | 0.8 | 20.8 |
| Secondary | 26.4 | 54.0 | 19.6 | 55.8 | 27.6 | 16.6 |
| Tertiary | 45.9 | 50.7 | 3.4 | 26.8 | 68.7 | 4.5 |

*Source*: Unit level data of employment–unemployment schedule of 50th (1993–4) and 61st (2004–5) Rounds of NSSO.

it seems that in the decade of 2000s some activities in the SE category also generated high paying employment among both males and females in all the urban areas.

Among females, a different pattern as compared to that among males was observed. In small towns (< 50,000 population), there was a stable proportion of RE from 1987–8 to 1993–4 and an increase in the proportion of CL labour in the same period. In metropolitan cities, there was an increase in RE and CL in the same period. Further, while the proportion employed as RE was the same among males and females in metropolitan cities, in small towns there was hardly any RE available for females. In small towns, therefore, more than half the females were engaged in SE type of activities and a large proportion was expected to be in the primary sector. The proportion of males engaged as RE was not as less as the proportion of females engaged as RE in small towns.

Summing up, one can say that the nature of employment among males and females in the metros was nearly the same although female WPRs were far lower than male WPRs. Also, there was higher RE and lower SE and CL employment among males in metros as compared to non-metros. The same was the case with regard to female employment. But in all urban SE dominated whereas in metros RE dominated for females in all the years. Lastly, among males in all urban RE dominated till 1993–4, but since then SE has dominated whereas in metros RE always dominated. RE however has declined and has been replaced by SE in metros among males as well as females.

### Differences by States

Across different states, the nature of employment varied greatly. But certain trends were clearly discernible. In metros in individual states, like at the all-India level, the largest proportion of working males were RE followed by

SE. There were no exceptions in 1987–8 and 1993–4. But in Uttar Pradesh the proportion of male workers employed as RE (48.4 per cent) was very close to the proportion of male workers working as SE (45.5 per cent). There was much larger SE among male workers in the less developed states than in the urbanized and developed states (Table 3.6) in metros. The exceptions appeared from 1993–4 onwards.

When data on the level of urbanization and percentage workers employed as RE are put together (Table 3.5), it is very clear that among males there was a close fit between the level of urbanization and the proportion employed as RE; in states where urbanization levels were high, employment as RE was also high. Among females in metros, this close fit disappeared and in the four urbanized states of Gujarat, Haryana, Punjab, and West Bengal, women exited out as RE. This could possibly be on account of high family incomes as well as cultural factors. In the less urbanized states of Andhra Pradesh and Bihar, women in RE was high. Thus, women seeking and getting regular work in the economy not only depends on the availability of work but also on the cultural disposition of households.

In non-metros, among the males the proportion of workers employed as RE was high in urbanized states and vice versa in the less urbanized states with the exception of Andhra Pradesh, Assam, and Madhya Pradesh where urbanization was low but male workers as RE was high. Among females, there was once again a mixed trend, the urbanization levels did not influence whether they came out to work regularly.

In all states except Gujarat and Tamil Nadu, regular employment among males in the metros decreased over time, similar to the trend at the all-India level (Figure 3.10). Except Uttar Pradesh and West Bengal, in all the other states, RE increased among females in metros over the whole period (Figure 3.11). In non-metros,

**Table 3.5**    Distribution of States by Proportion Employed as RE and
Urbanization Levels, 2004–5

| | | Urbanization Level (2001) Metros | | Urbanization Level (2001) Non-metros | |
| --- | --- | --- | --- | --- | --- |
| | | High | Low | High | Low |
| Males Employed as RE | High | Gujarat, Haryana, Maharashtra, Punjab, Tamil Nadu | | Gujarat, Haryana, Karnataka, Maharashtra, Punjab, Tamil Nadu | Andhra Pradesh, Assam, Madhya Pradesh |
| | Low | Karnataka, West Bengal | Andhra Pradesh, Bihar, Madhya Pradesh, Rajasthan, Uttar Pradesh | West Bengal | Bihar, Jammu and Kashmir, Kerala, Orissa, Rajasthan, Uttar Pradesh |
| Females Employed as RE | High | Karnataka, Tamil Nadu, Maharashtra | Andhra Pradesh, Bihar | Haryana, Punjab, Tamil Nadu, West Bengal | Assam, Kerala, Madhya Pradesh, Orissa |
| | Low | Gujarat, Haryana, Punjab, West Bengal | Madhya Pradesh, Rajasthan, Uttar Pradesh | Gujarat, Karnataka, Maharashtra | Andhra Pradesh, Bihar, Jammu and Kashmir, Rajasthan, Uttar Pradesh |

*Source*: Table A3.13.

*Note*: High and low pertain to above and below the all-India average.

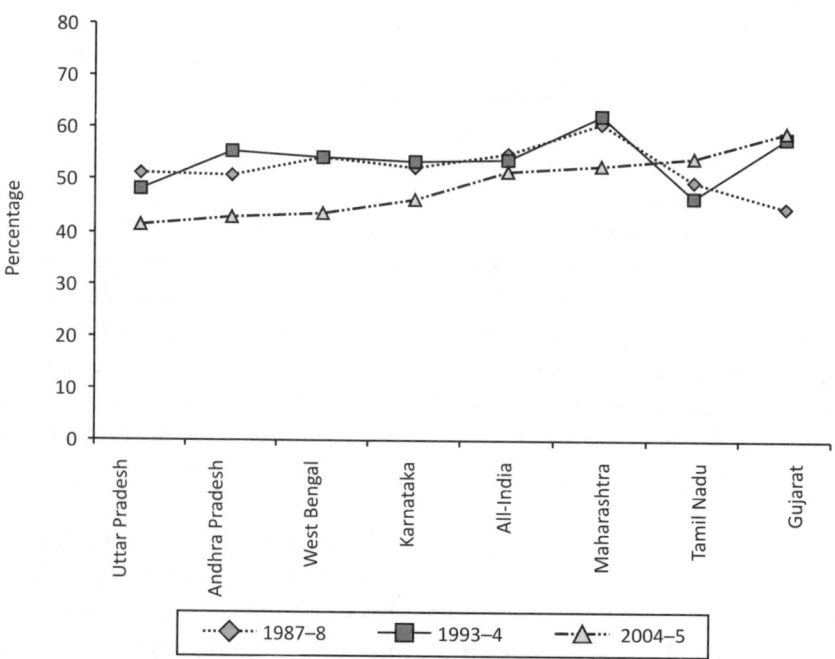

**Figure 3.10**    Percentage Males in Metros in RE, States

*Source*: Data taken from Tables A3.6, A3.9, and A3.13.

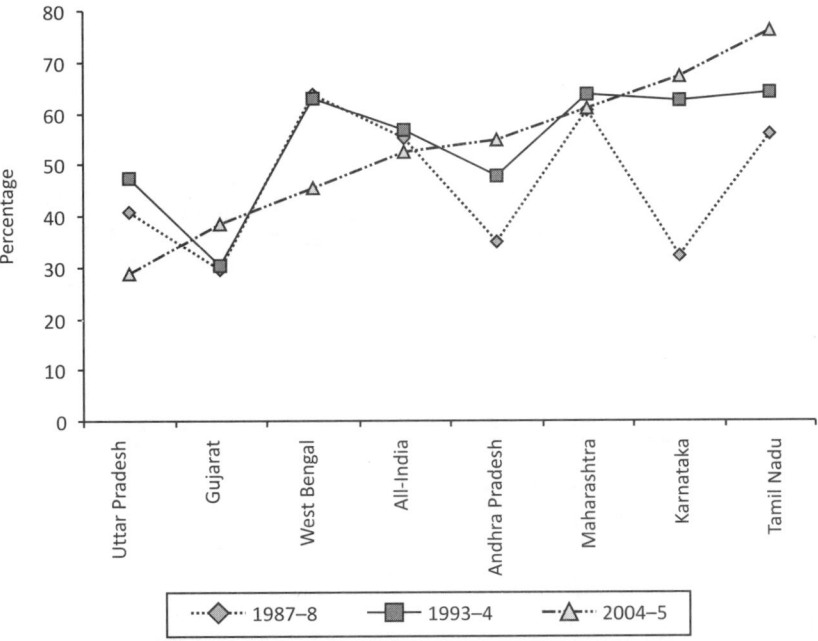

**Figure 3.11**    Percentage Females in Metros in RE, States

*Source*: Data taken from Tables A3.6, A3.9, and A3.13.

with the exception of Jammu and Kashmir and Kerala, RE declined in the pre-reforms period and then increased in the reforms period among males (Figure 3.12). Except Gujarat, Haryana, and West Bengal, RE increased over the whole period among females in non-metros (Figure 3.13).

Further, in metro cities in less developed states, there was high SE among males, indicating distress in the employment sector. This is supported by the fact that in all the four states where SE was higher than RE among males in metros in 2004–5, male WPRs were lower than the all-India metro WPRs. These states require immediate improvement in work availability in metro cities. It also indicates that migration to metro cities in these states was because of rural distress resulting in an increase in the population of these cities but not a concomitant increase in work availability.

Lastly, in some states a large proportion of male workers were engaged as CL in 2004–5 (Table A3.13). These are West Bengal (19.3 per cent), Karnataka (18.7 per cent), and Andhra Pradesh (12.7 per cent). RE among male workers in these three states was 43.8 per cent, 46.2 per cent, and 42.7 per cent, which was lower than the all-India metro average. These three states are known for information technology (IT) and IT enabled services (ITES) industries. Is it that the new economy creates higher inequalities and creates large CL type of jobs? This may be the case in Karnataka and West Bengal since WPRs in both these states were higher than the all-India metro average in 2004–5. Our experience tells us that CL employment would be in the construction sector, as the coming of IT and ITES industries in any city leads to the construction of IT enclaves that require new buildings.

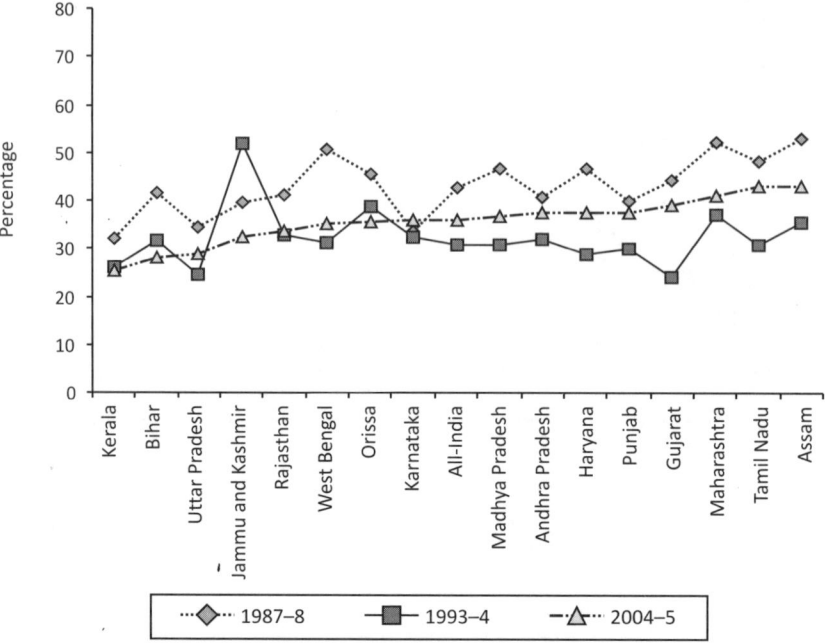

**Figure 3.12**    Percentage Males in Non-metros in RE, States

*Source*: Data taken from Tables A3.6, A3.9, and A3.12.

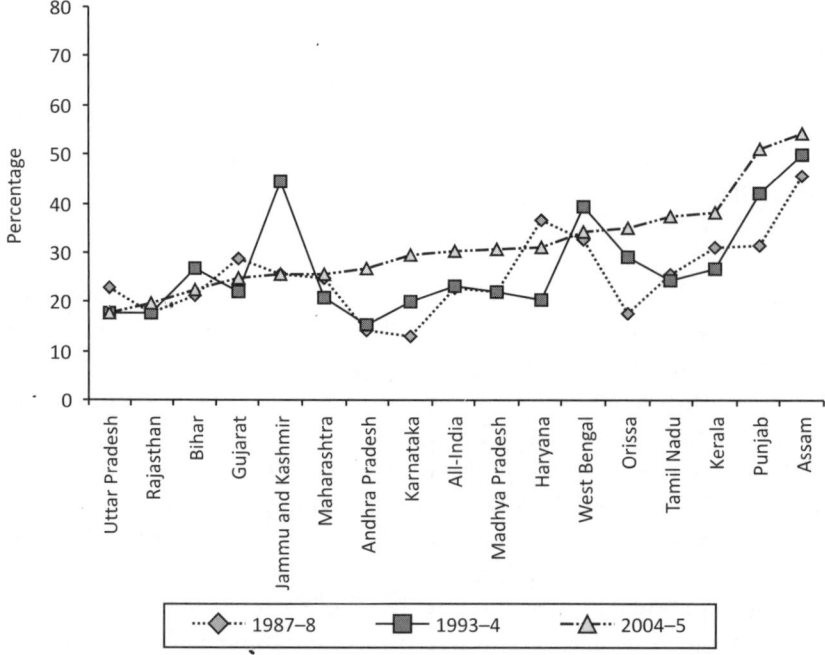

**Figure 3.13**    Percentage Females in Non-metros in RE, States

*Source*: Data taken from Tables A3.6, A3.9, and A3.12.

Among non-metros, the pattern of the highest share of SE followed by RE among males was not observed in Andhra Pradesh, Assam, Gujarat, Haryana, Madhya Pradesh, Maharashtra, Orissa, Tamil Nadu, and West Bengal in 1987–8 (Table A3.6); Jammu and Kashmir in 1993–4 (Table A3.9); and Maharashtra and Tamil Nadu in 2004–5 (Table A3.12). It seems that in Maharashtra and Tamil Nadu, RE employment was available to males even in non-metros. If we look at WPRs for the respective years, we can say that if WPRs were high in non-metros then RE was also high. Thus, the nature of employment among males was dependent on the availability of the work, whether in metros or in non-metros.

Increase in SE among males over time in metro cities can be seen in most of the states except in Andhra Pradesh, Tamil Nadu, Gujarat, and West Bengal between 1987–8 and 1993–4, and in Karnataka, Maharashtra, and Punjab between 1993–4 and 1999–2000. From 1993–4 to 2004–5, this was the case in all the states except Uttar Pradesh. Among female workers, the pattern of increase in SE in metros was the case in all the states with many more exceptions than in the case of males. The exceptions were: Andhra Pradesh, Karnataka, Maharashtra, Tamil Nadu, and West Bengal between 1987–8 and 1993–4; Karnataka, Punjab, and Rajasthan between 1993–4 and 1999–2000; and Gujarat, Karnataka, and Punjab between 1993–4 and 2004–5.

## INDUSTRIAL CLASSIFICATION—METRO/NON-METRO DIFFERENCES

The analysis in this section is limited to three broad industrial sectors—primary, secondary, and tertiary. Given that about 60 per cent of the male workers in urban India are employed in the tertiary sector, it is not surprising to find that in all the NSS Rounds more than 60 per cent of the male workers in metropolitan cities were employed in this sector (Figure 3.14). Also, there was a slight increase in the proportion of tertiary sector employment among male workers from 1987–8 to 2004–5 from 60.4 per cent to 61.0 per cent; however not from 1993–4 to 2004–5 (the economic reforms period), when there was marginal decline in the percentage from 61.5 to 61.0. Interestingly, in 2004–5, there was an increase in secondary sector employment in metros for males, an increase from 36.9 per cent in 1993–4 to 37.3 per cent in 2004–5. These changes were marginal and the trend of tertiarization of the metropolitan economy, which started in the 1980s, continued in the reforms period as well. However, the marginal increase in secondary sector employment in metros can be explained by the increase in work availability in the construction sector, which Mahadevia (2008) had shown for individual metros. The Jawaharlal Nehru National Urban Renewal Mission (JNNURM) and its investments concentrated in the metros might push this trend further.

Increase in secondary sector employment led to a decrease in tertiary sector employment in reform period. It seems that males from low wage informal employment may have shifted to the construction sector. It could be a positive trend as construction offers relatively better incomes (even for unskilled jobs) than all types of petty informal sector activities on which males would fall back on in times of no or loss of employment. This is what we saw in some cities which witnessed formal sector job loss because of restructuring of dominant economic units such as composite textile mills in Ahmedabad and Mumbai (see Mahadevia 2001, 2002 for Ahmedabad and Mahadevia 2008 for eight major metros). Increase in tertiary sector employment explains the increase in SE among males and employment in the construction sector seems to be of a regular kind in metros. Many metros such as Bangalore, Hyderabad,

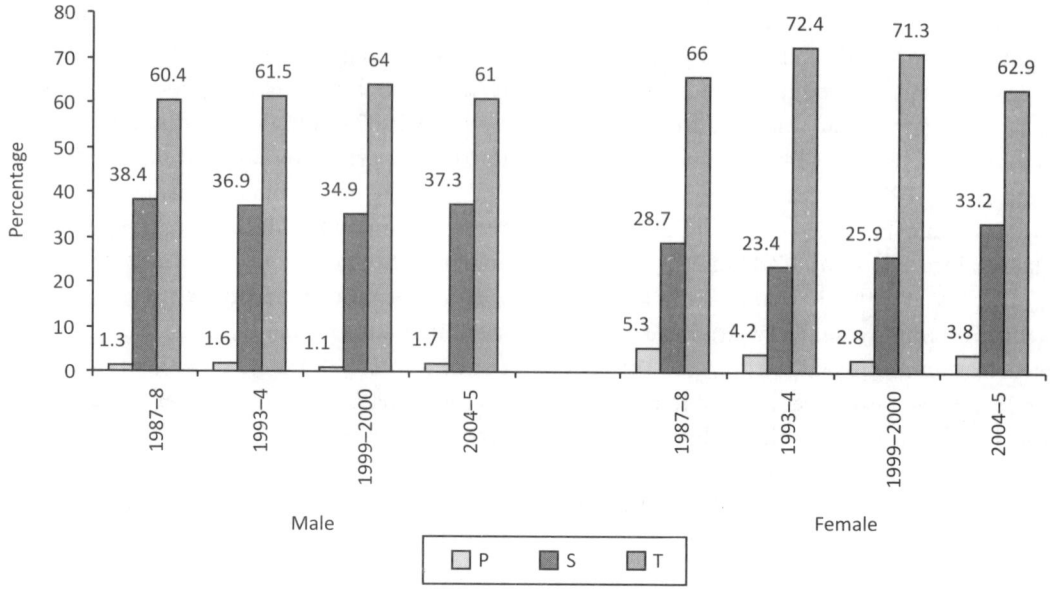

**Figure 3.14** Industrial Classification of Workers in Metropolitan Cities

*Source*: Data taken from Tables A3.16, A3.19, A3.20, A3.21, and A3.23.

Chennai, and Pune have seen increase in jobs in IT and ITES, which fall in the tertiary sector. However, there seems to be no discernible impact on the nature of employment as RE, as discussed in the previous section, has declined. One can therefore conclude that the loss of employment on account of the manufacturing sector decline, observed in all the metros, has not been filled up by the jobs in IT and ITES. As a result, males, particularly at the bottom end seem to have drifted to SE type tertiary sector work.

There was small primary sector employment among males in the metros, the figures remaining between 1 to 2 per cent over the entire period from 1987–8, but in urban India 7.1 per cent males were still employed in the primary sector. Clearly, this is the first distinguishing feature of employment in the metros as compared to overall urban India and non-metro urban areas. In all the years, secondary and tertiary sector employment among

males was higher in metros as compared to all urban.

In spite of a decline in the manufacturing sector employment in the metros, it is also important to see that still slightly more than one-third of the male workers were in the secondary sector. Further, Mahadevia (2008) has shown a significant proportion of male workers employed in the manufacturing sector in individual metro cities, indicating that even manufacturing activities are present in the metropolitan economy in India. Hence metropolitan cities in India cannot be called post-industrial cities.

Females in metropolitan cities were predominantly employed in the tertiary sector, as was the case in the entire urban economy—62.9 per cent females were employed in this sector in 2004–5, a decline from 66.0 per cent in 1987–8 and a significant decline from 72.4 per cent in 1993–4. During 1993–4 and 2004–5 there was a simultaneous increase in secondary sector employment among females in metros by

10 percentage points from 23.4 per cent to 33.2 per cent. Thus, an increase in female employment in the metros in the reforms period was on account of an increase in their employment in the secondary sector. However, Table 3.4 shows that secondary sector employment among females in the metros was in SE work, indicating that a part of the manufacturing work moved to homes through the process of sub-contracting and women were getting into such sub-contracting work carried out largely on a piece rate basis. This explains why there was an increase in female employment in the secondary sector in the metros. Table 3.4 also shows that RE of females in metros was in the tertiary sector, which was probably insecure work at low wages. Still about 4 per cent of the females in the metros were working in the primary sector. Thus, concerns with regard to female employment in metro cities are: continuing low WPRs, increased home-based sub-contracting work in the secondary sector and a significant

presence of low wage regular employment in the tertiary sector. Also, there was an increase in female workers in the metropolises and one can safely say that the work increase occurred because of increase in insecure employment in the secondary and tertiary sectors. This calls for social security for working women in metros.

Even in non-metros, there was an increase in secondary sector employment and a decline in tertiary sector employment among males in 2004–5 as compared to 1993–4 (Figure 3.15). There was also a simultaneous decline in primary sector employment among males. As seen earlier, WPRs among males also increased in 2004–5 as compared to 1993–4—an increase of 1.9 percentage points, which is a higher increase as compared to metros. Thus, it appears that some secondary sector establishments, and most likely among them manufacturing enterprises, shifted out of metros to non-metros and hence there was an increase in secondary sector employment among males in non-metros.

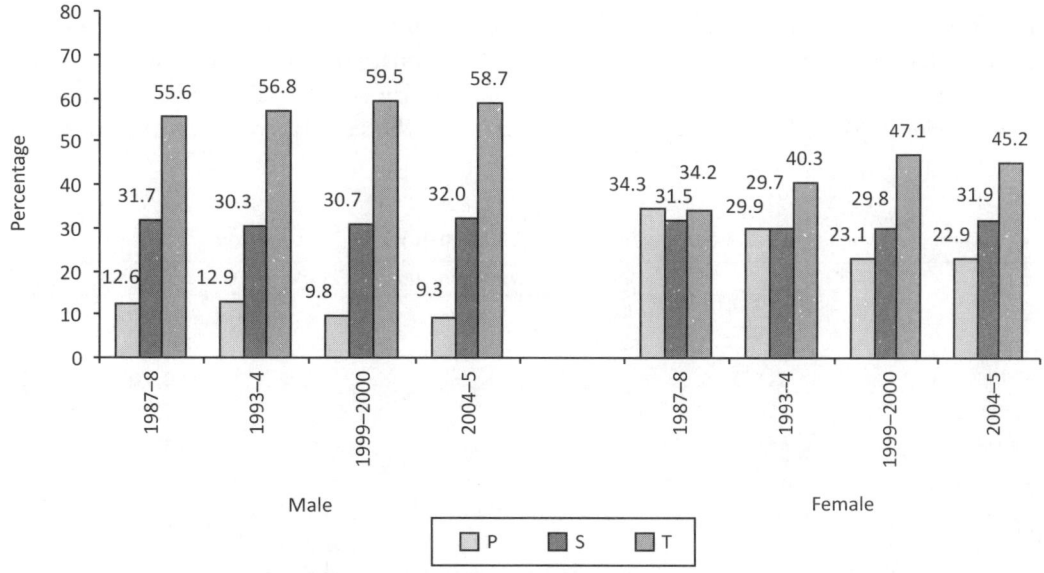

**Figure 3.15** Industrial Classification of Workers in Non-metros

*Source*: Data taken from Tables A3.16, A3.19, and A3.22.

However, secondary sector work was equally divided into SE, RE, and CL jobs. This was not true for females, whose employment in the secondary sector increased by 2.2 percentage points from 29.7 per cent in 1993–4 to 31.9 per cent in 2004–5, but once again in the SE category (Table 3.6), indicating that it moved to households through the sub-contracting route. Thus, the reforms process seems to have brought industrialization in non-metros, but more of the unorganized type, which requires a social security system in place.

Over the entire period, from 1987–8, there was an increase in tertiary sector employment among males from 55.6 per cent to 58.7 per cent in non-metros. That was also true for the economic reforms period, when in 1993–4 the proportion of males in the tertiary sector was 56.8 per cent, which increased to 58.7 per cent in 2004–5. In short, as compared to the pre-reforms period, tertiary sector employment among males increased faster in the reforms period. This employment was of SE as well as RE type. Secondary sector employment declined in the pre-reforms period and picked up during the reforms period for males in non-metros. Both these sectors in the post-reforms period expanded and hence there was a resultant decline in primary sector employment among males.

Tertiary sector employment in non-metros among females was lower than tertiary sector employment among them for all urban areas, and certainly for metros. This was because even such employment was not available to females in non-metros, who therefore continued to work in the primary sector; 22.9 per cent of them were thus employed in 2004–5, a decline from 29.9 per cent in 1993–4, and 34.3 per cent in 1987–8. The shifts in employment from primary to secondary and tertiary sectors for females in non-metros can be observed and there was a higher shift to the tertiary than to the secondary sector among them. In both, secondary and tertiary sectors, females shifted to RE as well as SE work categories and there was a decline in CL jobs. Also, their WPRs increased because of getting new RE type of jobs in the tertiary sector.

We now discuss some trends observed at a further disaggregated level of size classes. On the whole, at the all-India level, there was a decline in the percentage of workers employed in the primary sector and increase in secondary and tertiary sector male workers with an increase in the size class of towns. Among female

**Table 3.6**  Sectors of Work and Nature of Work, Non-metros

| 1993–4 | Nature of Work | | | | | |
|---|---|---|---|---|---|---|
| | Male | | | Female | | |
| Sector | SE | RE | CL | SE | RE | CL |
| Primary | 53.5 | 13.3 | 33.3 | 56.1 | 1.9 | 42.0 |
| Secondary | 31.1 | 41.1 | 27.8 | 52.3 | 12.0 | 35.8 |
| Tertiary | 47.9 | 43.1 | 9.0 | 39.6 | 47.3 | 13.1 |
| 2004–5 | | | | | | |
| Primary | 61.2 | 13.8 | 25.0 | 61.2 | 2.5 | 36.2 |
| Secondary | 33.5 | 33.7 | 32.8 | 62.9 | 14.5 | 22.6 |
| Tertiary | 52.4 | 40.9 | 6.7 | 36.6 | 55.3 | 8.1 |

*Source*: Unit level data of employment–unemployment schedule of 50th (1993–4) and 61st (2004–5) Rounds of NSSO.

workers, the pattern of employment was different. In small (< 50,000 population) towns, as mentioned earlier, a much higher proportion of females were employed in the primary sector as compared to male workers. These figures were higher than the figures for males in this sector in all the respective years. Recall that the female workers in this size class of urban centres were primarily engaged as self-employed workers. This was because they had been employed in primary sector activities. This shows that when settlements upgrade to urban status, the males are the first to make a transition to non-primary employment while females continue to work in the primary sector, in agriculture as well as livestock activities. Small town economies are transition economies. With an increase in size class of urban centres, female employment in secondary activities increases, but not when urban centres become metropolises. Then female workers tend to get overwhelmingly concentrated in the tertiary sector. Lastly, it is more probable for female workers to find employment in the secondary sector in medium sized towns and large cities than in metropolitan cities and small towns.

### Differences by States

States where employment of male workers in the secondary sector was high (higher than the all-India average for the size class) in metros in 2004–5 were Gujarat, Haryana, Punjab, and Rajasthan (Table A3.23). Metro cities in Gujarat, in particular Surat and Vadodara, continued to have a strong manufacturing base. In Punjab, Ludhiana was the sole metropolis and this is a manufacturing city. Haryana got secondary sector activities, both manufacturing and construction, because of Delhi, where manufacturing has not been allowed for many years and also spread of infrastructure development around it giving impetus to construction activities in the surrounding region including

in Haryana. Maharashtra was not there in this list, where 62.7 per cent males were employed in the tertiary sector in this year. Higher than the national average of all-urban male employment in the tertiary sector in metros can be seen in the less developed states of Bihar, Madhya Pradesh, Uttar Pradesh, and even in states with IT and ITES, namely Andhra Pradesh, Karnataka, Maharashtra, Tamil Nadu, and West Bengal in 2004–5. Maharashtra and Tamil Nadu were the two most urbanized states which also had one each mega city, namely Mumbai and Chennai. Is it that the high level of tertiary sector employment in metros in these two states was because of Mumbai and Chennai that might have a higher level of tertiary activities?

In 2004–5, the states with higher than national average of female workers in secondary sector in metros were Gujarat, Haryana, Madhya Pradesh, Punjab, Rajasthan, and Uttar Pradesh (Table A3.23). In Tamil Nadu just 12.8 per cent of the females were in the secondary sector in metros, whereas an overwhelming 87.2 per cent were in tertiary sector. The other states with a high proportion of females in the tertiary sector in the metros were Andhra Pradesh, Bihar, Karnataka, Maharashtra, and West Bengal.

Only in the three states, Gujarat, Uttar Pradesh, and West Bengal was there an increase in secondary sector employment among males in the metros in the reforms period (Figure 3.16). In all the states except Andhra Pradesh, the share of secondary sector employment among males in metros reduced in the pre-reforms period. In almost all the states, except Andhra Pradesh, the proportion of females employed in the secondary sector in the metros increased in the reforms period (Figure 3.17). Thus, at the national level among the metros we observe an increase in female employment in the secondary sector in the metros.

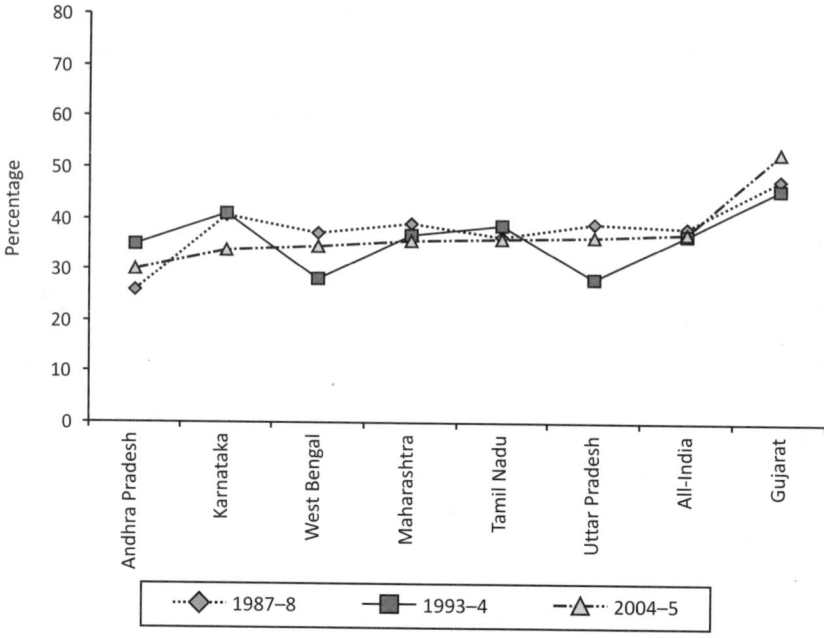

**Figure 3.16**    Percentage Male Workers in Secondary Sector Over Time, Metros
*Source*: Data taken from Tables A3.16, A3.19, A3.20, A3.21, and A3.23.

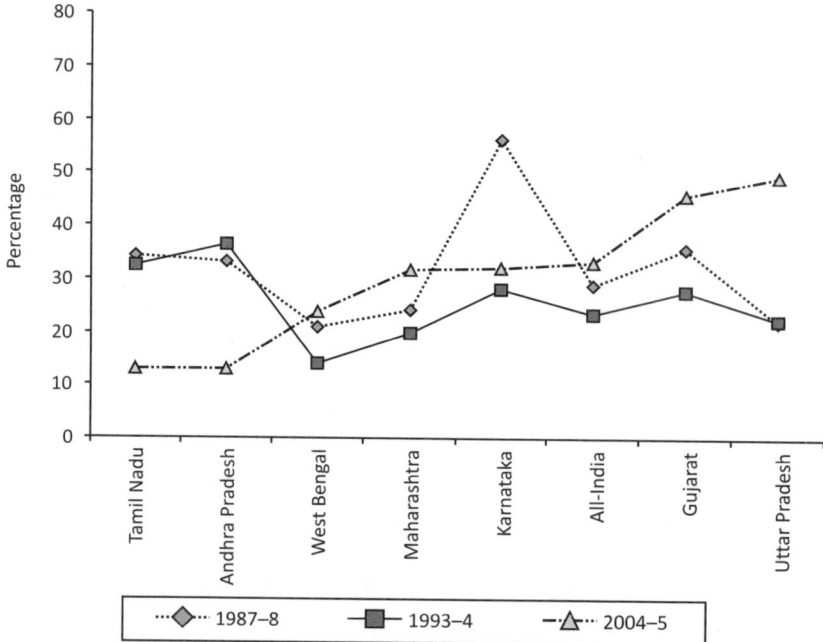

**Figure 3.17**    Percentage Female Workers in Secondary Sector Over Time, Metros
*Source*: Data taken from Tables A3.16, A3.19, A3.20, A3.21, and A3.23.

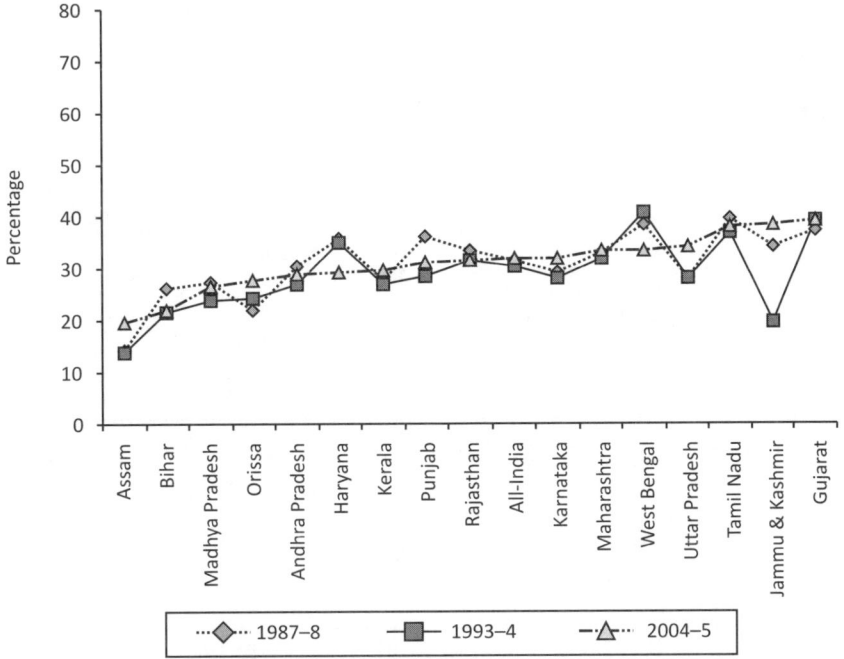

**Figure 3.18** Percentage Male Workers in Secondary Sector Over Time, Non-metros

*Source*: Data taken from Tables A3.16, A3.19, and A3.22.

States where secondary employment among males increased in non-metros in the reforms period as compared to the pre-reforms period were Assam, Jammu and Kashmir, Gujarat, Maharashtra, Karnataka, and Kerala (Figure 3.18). There is no common thread among these states. At the same time, there were very high fluctuations across the states in the proportion of males employed in the secondary sector in non-metros. Among females in non-metros also there were very high fluctuations in their proportion in secondary sector employment over time (Figure 3.19). In half the states, employment in the secondary sector dipped to a very low level in 1993–4 and then picked up by 2004–5 and in the other half; employment in the secondary sector increased in 1993–4 and then went down again in 2004–5.

We decided to look into the factors that might influence employment in the secondary sector. Is it high level of urbanization? Or conversely, does employment in the secondary sector lead to urbanization? We find that (Table 3.7 ), in metropolitan cities, urbanization levels do not explain male and female employment in the secondary sector; there are three states, Gujarat, Haryana, and Punjab, where both urbanization levels and secondary sector employment among males and females was high. Karnataka, Maharashtra, Tamil Nadu, and West Bengal had high urbanization but low secondary sector employment among males as well as females. This could probably be on account of high employment in the tertiary sector in the metros in these states. In non-metros, urbanization levels to a great extent explained the high employment in the secondary sector. This was truer for males than for females. But certainly higher employment among males in the secondary sector in non-metros probably

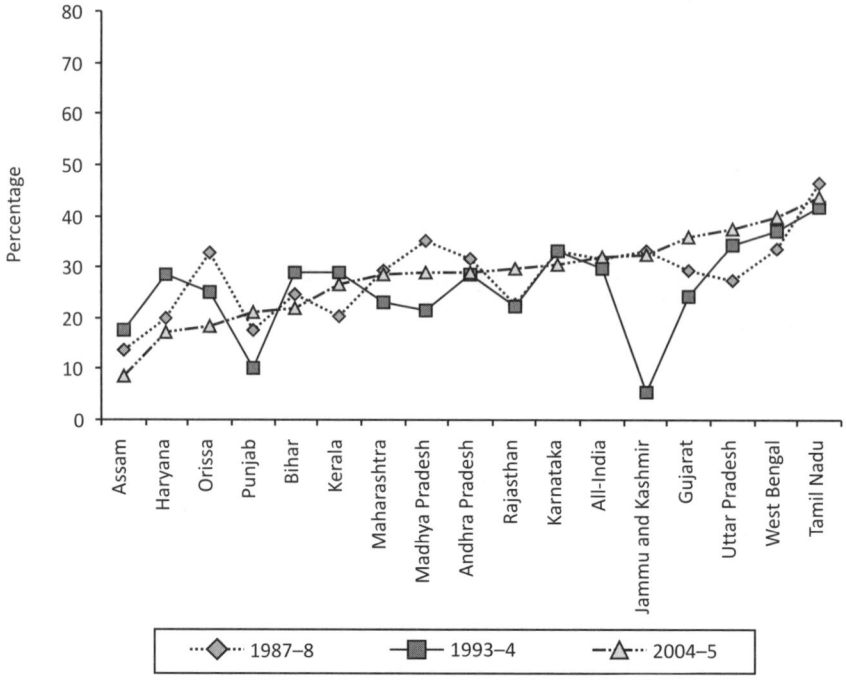

**Figure 3.19**     Percentage Female Workers in Secondary Sector Over Time, Non-metros

*Source*: Data taken from Tables A3.16, A3.19, and A3.22.

caused higher levels of urbanization in the states of Gujarat, Karnataka, Maharashtra, Tamil Nadu, and West Bengal. Conversely, if secondary sector employment is not available in non-metros then the urbanization levels in the states would be low.

Table 3.7 also gives us four categories of states: (i) Urbanization is high and the proportion of males and females employed in the secondary sector in metros is high, indicating that urbanization is driven by metro cities and through secondary sector employment in them. These states are Gujarat, Haryana and Punjab, the states in the top four in per capita income; (ii) Urbanization is high but secondary sector employment is low, indicating that urbanization is driven by the tertiary sector and these states are the IT states of Karnataka, Tamil Nadu, Maharashtra, and West Bengal,

which earlier had an extensive manufacturing base but then slipped behind. Manufacturing was displaced out of the Mumbai agglomeration area and replaced by the tertiary sector. Pune, the second largest metro in the state has a strong IT and ITES economy. Hence, metro-Maharashtra now has a high proportion of male as well as female workers in the tertiary sector. In a sense, metro-Maharashtra transited to the post-industrial economy. But non-metro Maharashtra still continues to be an industrial economy; (iii) Urbanization is low but secondary sector employment is high, which is in Rajasthan; and (iv) Urbanization and secondary sector employment are both low indicating that these are less developed states.

In highly urbanized states, except Haryana and Punjab, where secondary sector employment is high, non-metros are lagging behind.

**Table 3.7** Distribution of States by Proportion Employed in Secondary Sector and Urbanization Levels, 2004–5

| | | Urbanization Level (2001) Metros | | Urbanization Level (2001) Non-metros | |
| --- | --- | --- | --- | --- | --- |
| | | High | Low | High | Low |
| Males Employed in Secondary Sector | High | Gujarat, Haryana, Punjab | Rajasthan | Gujarat, Karnataka, Maharashtra Tamil Nadu, West Bengal | Jammu and Kashmir, Uttar Pradesh |
| | Low | Karnataka, Maharashtra, Tamil Nadu, West Bengal | Andhra Pradesh, Bihar, Madhya Pradesh, Uttar Pradesh | Haryana, Punjab | Andhra Pradesh, Assam, Bihar, Kerala, Madhya Pradesh, Orissa, Rajasthan |
| Females Employed in Secondary Sector | High | Gujarat, Haryana Punjab, | Madhya Pradesh, Rajasthan, Uttar Pradesh | Gujarat, Tamil Nadu, West Bengal | Jammu and Kashmir, Uttar Pradesh |
| | Low | Karnataka, Maharashtra, Tamil Nadu, West Bengal | Andhra Pradesh, Bihar | Haryana, Karnataka, Maharashtra, Punjab | Andhra Pradesh, Assam, Bihar, Kerala, Madhya Pradesh, Orissa, Rajasthan |

*Source*: Data taken from Tables A3.22 and A3.23.

*Note*: High and low pertain to above and below the all-India average.

Gujarat, another state where the urbanization level is high, the non-metros also have high secondary sector employment. The IT and ITES economy is largely in the metros in the states of Karnataka and Tamil Nadu and the non-metros are still based on secondary sector economy. There is a perfect fit between the level of urbanization and secondary sector employment in non-metros indicating that if the secondary sector is introduced in the non-metros, the chances of a state transiting to a higher level of urbanization are high.

What is the relationship between secondary sector employment and WPRs? No relationship exists in metropolitan cities. There are states such as Gujarat and Punjab where the higher secondary sector employment has caused higher male WPRs in metros (Table 3.8). In Karnataka, Maharashtra, Tamil Nadu, and West Bengal, male WPRs are high not on account of secondary sector employment but on account of tertiary sector employment. Same is nearly

true for female workers, with the exception of Rajasthan and Punjab; the former has high female WPRs and the latter low female WPRs, but both of them have a high proportion of women in the secondary sector. In non-metros we find no pattern in the relationship between secondary sector employment and WPRs. This was expected as probably it was tertiary sector employment that was linked to WPRs—the higher the tertiary sector employment, the higher is female WPR or vice versa given work is available only in the tertiary sector.

Tertiary sector employment among males in ·metros declined in the reforms period except in Karnataka and Tamil Nadu (Figure 3.20). This could probably be on account of an increase in IT and ITES services in these two states in the reforms period. Even Andhra Pradesh is expected to be an IT and ITES destination, but it has not seen an increase in tertiary employment among males in metros. Lastly, Maharashtra too saw an increase in tertiary sector employment

**Table 3.8**    Distribution of States by Proportion Employed in Secondary Sector and WPRs, 2004–5

| | | Metros Male WPR | | Non-metros Male WPR | |
|---|---|---|---|---|---|
| | | High | Low | High | Low |
| Males Employed in Secondary Sector | High | Gujarat, Punjab | Haryana, Rajasthan | Gujarat, Maharashtra, Tamil Nadu, West Bengal, Karnataka | Jammu and Kashmir, Uttar Pradesh |
| | Low | Karnataka, Maharashtra, Tamil Nadu, West Bengal | Andhra Pradesh, Bihar, Madhya Pradesh, Uttar Pradesh | Andhra Pradesh, Assam, Kerala, Punjab | Bihar, Haryana, Madhya Pradesh, Orissa, Rajasthan |
| | | Female WPR | | Female WPR | |
| Females Employed in Secondary Sector | High | Gujarat, Madhya Pradesh, Rajasthan | Haryana, Punjab, Uttar Pradesh | Tamil Nadu | Uttar Pradesh, West Bengal, Gujarat, Jammu and Kashmir |
| | Low | Karnataka, Maharashtra, West Bengal | Andhra Pradesh, Bihar, Tamil Nadu | Andhra Pradesh, Karnataka, Maharashtra | Assam, Bihar, Haryana, Kerala, Madhya Pradesh, Orissa, Punjab, Rajasthan |

*Source*: Data taken from Tables A3.3. A3.22, and A3.23.

*Note*: High and low pertain to above and below the all-India average.

among males in the reforms period and this could be on account of an increase in financial and real estate employment in Mumbai and IT and ITES employment in Pune. Karnataka, Tamil Nadu, and Andhra Pradesh, the three IT states, registered an increase in female employment in the tertiary sector in the metros (Figure 3.21). It is likely that they were employed in ITES firms. In non-metros, there was no particular pattern observed in male as well as female employment in the tertiary sector (Figure 3.22 and 3.23).

Table 3.9 is the converse of Table 3.7. States which had a higher level of secondary sector employment did not have a higher level of tertiary sector employment and hence the states switched the rectangles. In Karnataka, Maharashtra, and West Bengal, which had a high proportion of male and female workers in the tertiary sector in the metros also had high male and female WPRs, indicating that the tertiary sector in the metros in these states had

low-wage work and that the tertiarization was on account of lack of availability of secondary sector work. All the three states also had a high proportion of workers in IT and ITES as well as financial services in the metros and also a very high proportion of very low wage workers, indicating high inequality in the metro economies in these states.

## OCCUPATIONAL CLASSIFICATION—METRO/ NON-METRO DIFFERENCES

The proportion of male workers in A/P jobs in metros was larger than the same in all urban in all the National Sample Survey (NSS) Rounds and the proportion of male workers in ML type of jobs was consistently lower than non-metros and all urban (Tables A3.26 to A3.30 and A3.33). The same was true for clerical (C) type of jobs. In 2004–5, 21.7 male workers in metros, that is, one in every five male workers in metros was employed in such high paying jobs, when this figure for non-metros and

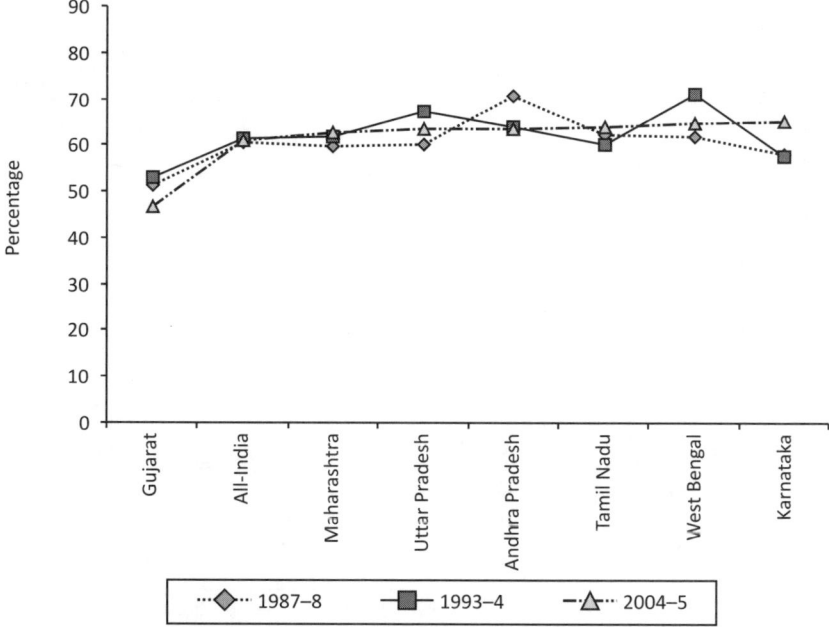

**Figure 3.20**    Percentage Male Workers in Tertiary Sector Over Time, Metros

*Source*: Data taken from Tables A3.16, A3.19, A3.20, A3.21, and A3.23.

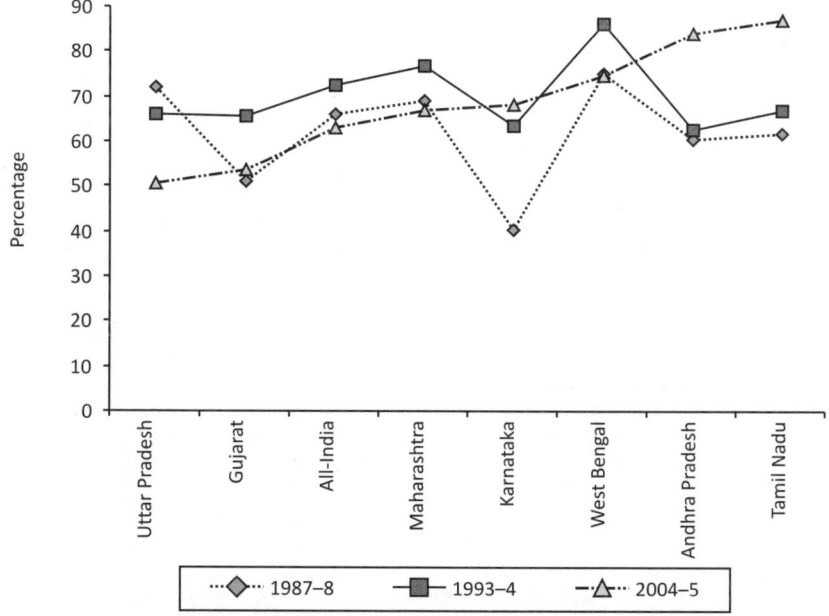

**Figure 3.21**    Percentage Female Workers in Tertiary Sector Over Time, Metros

*Source*: Data taken from Tables A3.16, A3.19, A3.20, A3.21, and A3.23.

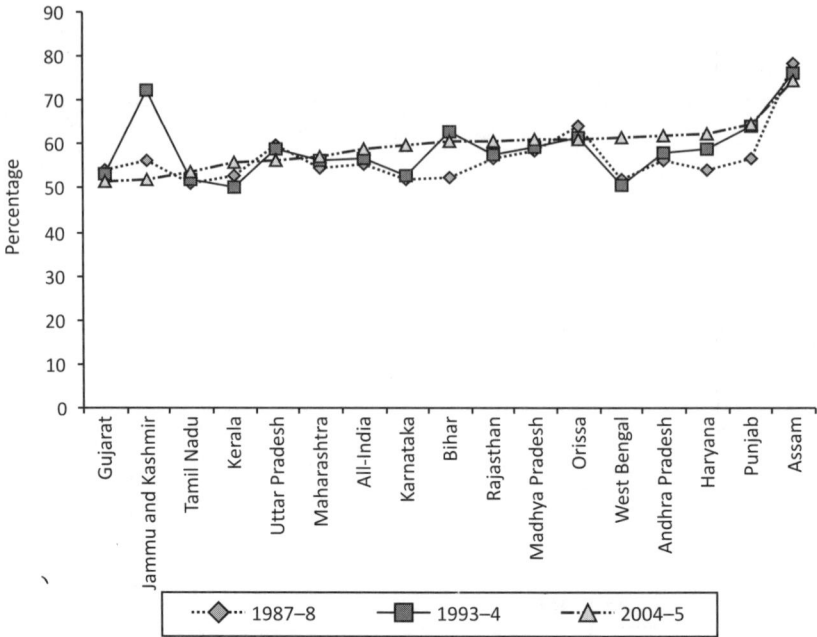

**Figure 3.22**　Percentage Male Workers in Tertiary Sector Over Time, Non-metros
*Source*: Data taken from Tables A3.16, A3.19, and A3.22.

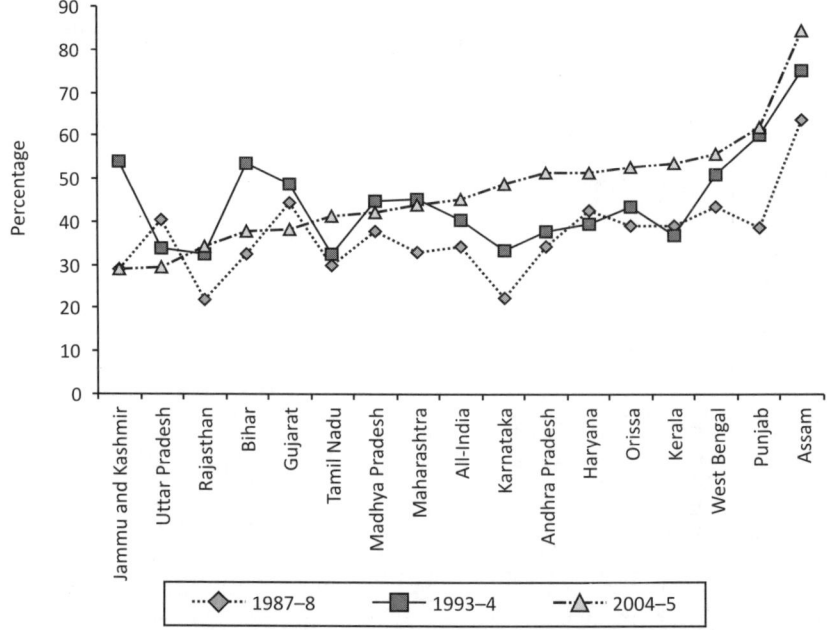

**Figure 3.23**　Percentage Female Workers in Tertiary Sector Over Time, Non-metros
*Source*: Data taken from Tables A3.16, A3.19, and A3.22.

**Table 3.9**   Distribution of States by Proportion Employed in Tertiary Sector and
Urbanization Levels, 2004–5

| | | Urbanization Level (2001) Metros | | Urbanization Level (2001) Non-metros | |
|---|---|---|---|---|---|
| | | High | Low | High | Low |
| Males Employed in Tertiary Sector | High | Karnataka, Maharashtra, Tamil Nadu, West Bengal | Andhra Pradesh, Bihar, Madhya Pradesh, Uttar Pradesh | Haryana, Karnataka, Punjab, West Bengal | Andhra Pradesh, Assam, Bihar, Madhya Pradesh, Orissa, Rajasthan |
| | Low | Gujarat, Haryana, Punjab | Rajasthan | Gujarat, Maharashtra, Tamil Nadu | Jammu and Kashmir, Kerala, Uttar Pradesh |
| Females Employed in Tertiary Sector | High | Karnataka, Maharashtra, West Bengal | Andhra Pradesh, Bihar | Haryana, Karnataka, Punjab, West Bengal | Andhra Pradesh, Assam, Kerala, Orissa |
| | Low | Gujarat, Haryana Punjab, Tamil Nadu | Madhya Pradesh Rajasthan, Uttar Pradesh | Gujarat, Maharashtra, Tamil Nadu | Bihar, Jammu and Kashmir, Madhya Pradesh, Rajasthan, Uttar Pradesh |

*Source*: Data taken from Tables A3.22 and A3.23.
*Note*: High and low pertain to above and below the all-India average.

all urban were only 16.4 and 18.0 per cent, respectively (Figures 3.6 and 3.25). In all urban, the proportion of males employed in ML jobs was 46.0 per cent and in clerical jobs it was 36.0 per cent in 2004–5. In metros, these figures were 40.6 and 37.6 per cent, respectively. Very clearly, the quality of employment available to males in the metros was far better and high paying as compared to all urban, and even more so when compared to non-metros.

The proportion of male worker in A/P jobs in the metros consistently increased over the period 1987–8 to 2004–5 (Figure 3.24) but much more after 1993–4. However, a very large proportion, two in every five, continued to be employed in ML type of jobs in 2004–5 in metros. And there was not much of a decline in the proportion of male workers in these type of jobs over the period; the figure was 41.9 per cent in 1987–8, 42.1 per cent in 1993–4 (the proportion went up at the time of the economic crisis), which then gradually came down to 40.6 per cent in 2004–5. Increase in A/P type of jobs among males was on account of a decrease in

clerical type of jobs among them. We will see later that clerical type of jobs were taken up by females in metros. Increase in A/P jobs that were high paying and not much decline in ML jobs indicate an increase in wage inequality in metropolitan cities. Further, as seen earlier, increase in secondary sector jobs in metropolitan cities, which was a welcome situation, was also in ML type of jobs, most likely as argued earlier, in the construction sector. There was a schism in the metropolitan labour market as far as males were concerned.

Nearly half the females in the metros were employed in clerical type of jobs in 2004–5, an increase from 47.7 per cent in 1993–4. Also, the proportion of females employed in clerical jobs in metros was higher than all urban and also higher than the proportion of males employed in clerical jobs in metros. These were white collar, low-paying, low-skill type of jobs in the positions of say sales girls, and so on or as self-employed in providing various types of semi-skilled services or engaging in some small businesses and so on.

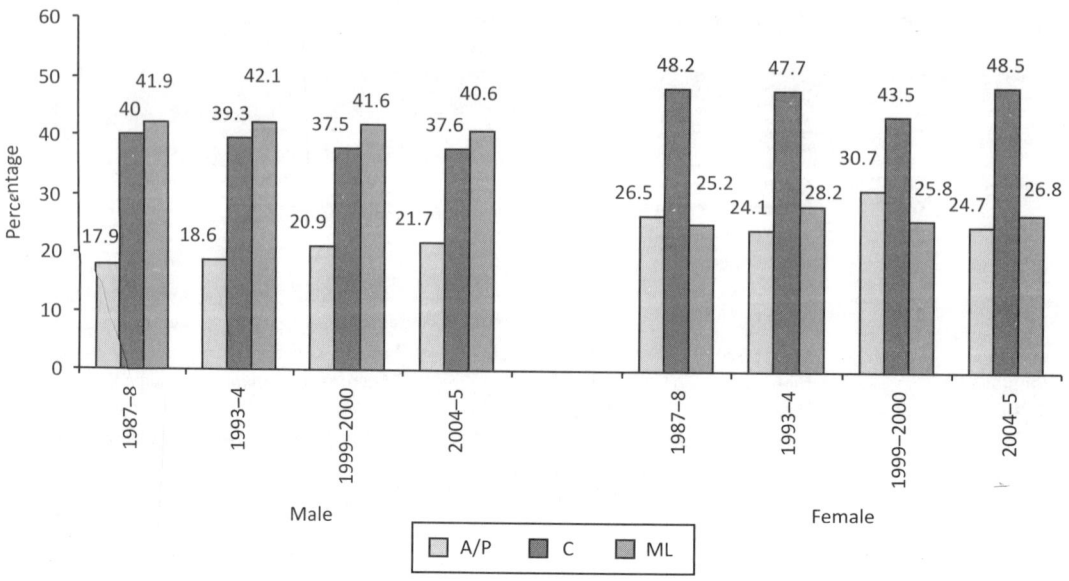

**Figure 3.24**  Occupational Classification of Workers in Metropolitan Cities

*Source*: Data taken from Tables A3.26, A3.29, and A3.33.

There was a very strange phenomenon of a decline in the proportion of females employed in A/P type of jobs in metros, from 26.5 per cent in 1987–8, to 24.1 per cent in 1993–4, which maintained the same level in 2004–5 (24.7 per cent)—a proportion even lower than that in 1987–8. But as compared to all urban, in all the years the proportion of females in A/P type of jobs in metros was higher. The possible explanation for this is that highly educated women, who could have been employed in A/P type of jobs were dropping out of the labour force on account of either high incomes of their spouses or lack of availability of suitable work or even both. In the wake of economic reforms high-end jobs became very competitive and also required long hours of work which were rewarded by very high salaries. In families, if a male member works long hours, the female member has to forgo a high stress job as she needs to take care of the family and cannot commute long distances to work, which is the

case in metros. Such women would prefer to work as SE from their homes.

Another noticeable trend in the quality of female employment in metros was the far lower proportion of females working in ML type of jobs as compared to all urban. In all urban, in 2004–5 this figure was 41.8 per cent whereas in metros it was 26.8 per cent. Further, there was not much of a change in the proportion of males and females depending on ML type of jobs over the reforms period. This had to do with both availability of jobs and the type of jobs created in metros and also education and skills of labour in metropolitan cities. We think that there has been the creation of jobs in the construction sector in a big way in metros since 2000 and that is reflected in the un-changing proportion of labour, male and female, employed in ML type of jobs. High CAGRs in female workers in metros is probably on account of an increase in the availability of regular clerical work.

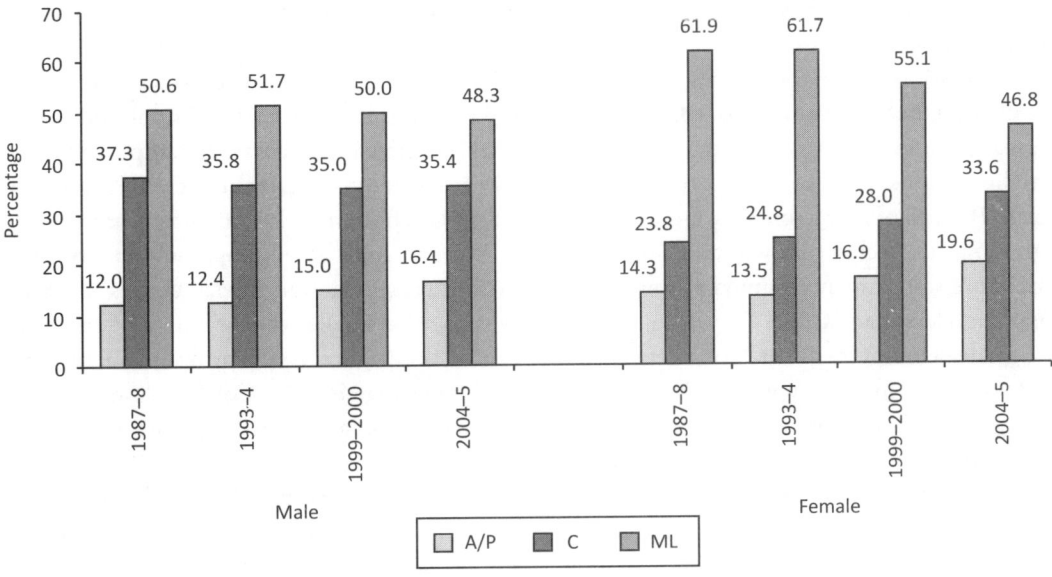

**Figure 3.25**   Occupational Classification of Workers in Non-metros

*Source*: Data taken from Tables A3.26, A3.29, and A3.32.

In non-metros, slightly more than half of the male workers were employed as ML till 1993–4, after which the proportion declined slightly to 48.3 per cent in 2004–5, which is higher than the proportion of males thus employed at the all urban level and far higher than the proportion of males thus employed in metros. Clearly, the quality of employment available in non-metros was poor and hence the increase in male WPRs in non-metros was accompanied by an increase in tertiary sector employment and a large proportion of males still remaining in ML jobs. But there was a small positive change as the share of male workers employed in A/P type of jobs increased to 16.4 per cent in 2004–5 from 12.4 per cent in 1993–4. There was the emergence of some tertiary sector high paying employment in the self-employment category. Also, as compared to all urban, non-metros had a lower proportion of employment in A/P and clerical type of jobs among males. A/P type of jobs in non-metros increased for males after 1993–4

when ML type jobs declined. Contrast this with an increase in A/P type of jobs and no change in ML type of jobs in metros. New opportunities in high paying A/P employment were also created to which a section from those who were regularly employed shifted in non-metros.

The gap between metros and non-metros in terms of male employment remained but narrowed down slightly. For example, in percentage terms, this gap was 5.9 in 1987–8, which came down to 5.3 per cent in 2004–5 with regard to A/P type of jobs. Also, the difference in employment in ML type of jobs came down from 9.6 percentage points in 1993–4 (their proportion being higher in non-metros than in metros) to 7.7 percentage points in 2004–5. Thus, better employment shifted to non-metros to some extent and improvement in the quality of employment in the metros was not as much. Anecdotal evidence suggests that extremely high land prices in the top eight metros led to non-viability of some of the new economy activities, which then have moved to smaller metros and non-metros. If we could divide non-metros into three size classes of towns— less than 50,000 population, 50,000 to 5 lakhs population, and more than 5 lakhs to less than 1 million population, we could possibly show that A/P types of employment were generated in the largest size class of towns and shift out of agriculture were largely confined to towns with population less than 50,000.

Female employment in non-metros was predominantly in ML type of jobs, just like among males, but surprisingly a lower propor- tion of females were in such jobs (46.8 per cent) as compared to males (48.3 per cent). In the second position in non-metros were clerical type of jobs—33.6 per cent in 2004–5, or a sig- nificant increase from 24.8 per cent in 1993–4. Interestingly, one in every five females in non- metros were employed in A/P type of jobs, the proportion being just slightly less than the all- India average for females in 2004–5. Also, this increase in the proportion of females employed in A/P type of jobs in non-metros occurred in the reforms period.

Compared to the metros, employment in ML type of jobs was higher and in clerical and A/P type of jobs it was lower among females in non-metros. On the whole, the proportion of ML jobs declined by 15 percentage points in the reforms period and that in the A/P and clerical jobs this proportion increased during the same period among females. This change set in after 1993–4. There has been a significant improvement in female employment in non- metros since the economic reforms. And this improvement was much more than in the met- ros. Thus, the gap between the proportion of females employed in A/P jobs in metros and the same in non-metros was 10.6 percent- age points in 1993–4, that came down to 5.1 percentage points in 2004–5. Also, the gap between the proportion of females employed

in ML jobs in non-metros and metros came down from 33.5 percentage points in 1993–4 to 20.0 percentage points in 2004–5. However, on the whole in both metros and non-metros, the quality of female employment improved since 1993–4 accompanied by high CAGR of female workers in both metros and non-metros.

We can look at employment quality by a further disaggregation of size classes of urban centres. The smaller the size class of an urban centre the higher is the proportion of male workers engaged as ML. Conversely, the smaller the size class of an urban centre the lower is the proportion of workers engaged in A/P services. Thus, with an increase in the size class of towns, more skilled and mental labour oriented jobs are available and in small towns more physi- cal labour oriented jobs are available to males. Improvement in the quality of employment among female workers with an increase in the size class of urban centres is also quite marked.

There was also an overwhelming concentra- tion of females in clerical jobs in metropolitan cities, which was not the case with smaller two size classes of urban centres where a very low proportion of females were in clerical type jobs. One can safely say that in small towns, there was an overwhelming concentration of females in manual jobs, mainly primary sector activi- ties, whereas in metropolitan cities, they were overwhelmingly concentrated in clerical jobs, which would be in the tertiary sector.

### Differences by States

Tamil Nadu (33.1 per cent), Andhra Pradesh (24.1 per cent), and West Bengal (22.1 per cent) were the states where the proportion of males employed in A/P type of employment was higher than the proportion of the same at the all-India level in metropolitan cities in 2004–5 (Figure 3.26). This means that the metros in these states, namely, Chennai, Hyderabad, and Kolkata offered better type of jobs to male workers than the other metros in India (Figure 3.26). Also note that metros in Gujarat had only 18 per cent males employed in the A/P employment category and about half the males employed in ML jobs in 2004–5. Also note that in metros in Maharashtra, the clerical category of employment (41.4 per cent) dominated followed by ML jobs (37.4 per cent) among males in 2004–5 (Table A3.33). Haryana, that benefitted because of its proximity to Delhi, had 72.9 per cent males employed as ML. Faridabad is the only metro city in Haryana, which is located next to Delhi and is an industrial town, which explains such a high proportion of ML. Gurgaon, which has attracted IT and ITES services is a non-metro and hence in the category of non-metros, Haryana had 16.3 per cent males employed in the A/P category of jobs when this figure for all-India in non-metros

was 16.4 per cent. This means that better quality jobs in Haryana were going to non-metros as compared to metros because of the former's geographical location. Other states where ML type of employment dominated among males in the metros were Rajasthan (58.9 per cent) and Punjab (57.0 per cent) in 2004–5. Metros in the BIMARU states of Bihar, Madhya Pradesh, and Uttar Pradesh had the highest proportion of male workers engaged in the clerical category of jobs. This means that the metros in these states, besides those in Gujarat and Maharashtra, remained laggards in attracting better paying employment in 2004–5. The contrast is noticeable, as Gujarat and Maharashtra are the two most industrialized states of India and are in the top four in per capita income as well as in urbanization, whereas Bihar, Madhya Pradesh, and Uttar Pradesh are the bottom most states

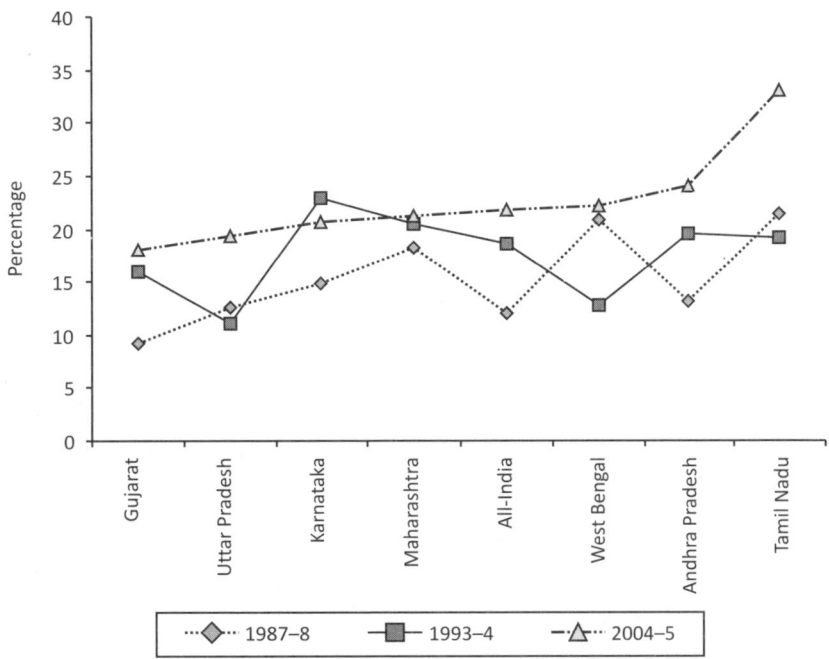

**Figure 3.26**   Percentage Male Workers in Administrative and Professional Services
Over Time, Metros

*Source*: Data taken from Tables A3.26, A3.29, and A3.33.

with regard to all indicators of development. There is a contrast between Maharashtra and Gujarat. In the former, clerical jobs dominated in metro cities whereas in the latter, ML jobs dominated. Besides, these were in the secondary sector. In other words, secondary sector jobs in metro-Gujarat were low skilled.

Among females in 2004–5, the states where A/P category of employment was high in the metros were Bihar, West Bengal, Tamil Nadu, Madhya Pradesh, Andhra Pradesh, and Uttar Pradesh. Rajasthan, Punjab, Uttar Pradesh, Madhya Pradesh, Haryana, Karnataka and Gujarat were the states where the proportion of females in ML was high in metros. We see no pattern either in terms of category of states or in terms of quality of employment among females, except that in Madhya Pradesh and

Uttar Pradesh there was very high disparity in the quality of employment of females in metro cities. We do not see such disparity among males in the metros in these two states.

Among non-metros, in Punjab, Haryana, and Assam females were employed in the A/P category of employment; their proportion was far higher in this category as compared to the all-India level in 2004–5 (Figure 3.28). This means that non-metros in these states had been able to provide better paying employment to females. In contrast, Bihar, Jammu and Kashmir, Madhya Pradesh, Maharashtra, Rajasthan, Tamil Nadu, and Uttar Pradesh provided largely ML type of jobs to females in non-metros in 2004–5 (Table A3.32). Among females, although the ML type of employment dominated at the all-India level in non-metros, Assam, Haryana, and

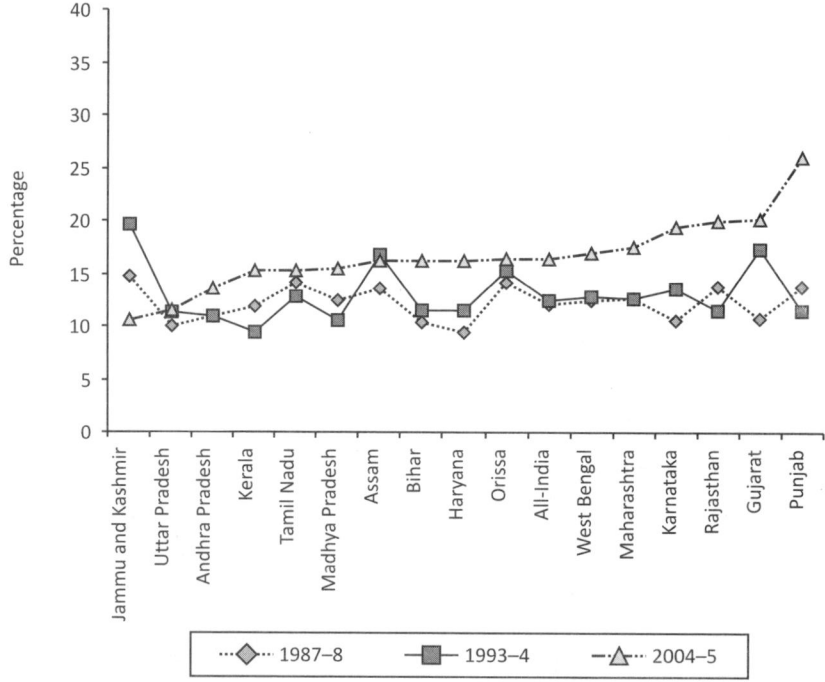

**Figure 3.27**   Percentage Male Workers in Administrative and Professional Services, Over Time, Non-metros

*Source*: Data taken from Tables A3.26, A3.29, and A3.32.

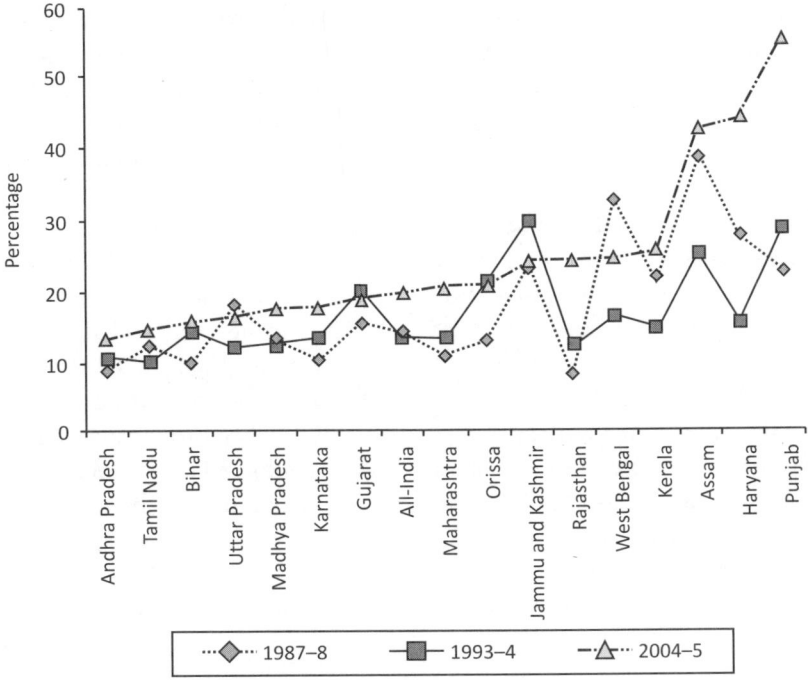

**Figure 3.28** Percentage Female Workers in Administrative and Professional Services, Over Time, Non-metros

*Source*: Data taken from Tables A3.26, A3.29, and A3.32.

Punjab had a very large proportion employed in A/P jobs in 2004–5. The other states where female employment share in A/P was higher than the all-India average in non-metros were Jammu and Kashmir, Kerala, Madhya Pradesh, Orissa, Rajasthan, and West Bengal.

In the case of male workers in metros, in all the states employment in A/P services increased in 2004–5 as compared to 1987–8 (Figure 3.26). But during the reforms period, 1993–4 to 2004–5 only Karnataka and Madhya Pradesh saw a decline in the same, indicating a decline in the quality of employment available to males in the metros in these two states. In Maharashtra and Gujarat, the improvement in the same slowed down in the reforms period and in Tamil Nadu, Uttar Pradesh, and Punjab, there was acceleration in the improvement

in the same in the reforms period. In the case of females in metro cities, employment in A/P services improved in only Uttar Pradesh, Andhra Pradesh, West Bengal, and Tamil Nadu in 2004–5 as compared to 1987–8. In all the states except Karnataka, Andhra Pradesh, and Uttar Pradesh, the decline was observed in the pre-reforms period.

A/P services among males in non-metros increased from 1987–8 to 2004–5 in all the states except Jammu and Kashmir (Figure 3.27). While the picture was mixed in the pre-reforms period, in the reforms period all the states registered an increase in high quality employment among males except Jammu and Kashmir and Assam in non-metros. Probably these states with high levels of political insecurity and ongoing insurgency may not have led to new economic activities penetrating down to smaller urban centres. Among female workers in non-metros in all the states except Uttar Pradesh and West Bengal high-end employment increased in 2004–5 as compared to 1987–8, but in most of them the improvement occurred in the reforms period.

The states with high level of urbanization but high employment in the ML category in metros were Gujarat, Haryana, Punjab, and West Bengal (Table 3.11). In the first three states, ML jobs were in the secondary sector whereas in West Bengal they were in the tertiary sector. A/P services were low, which means that in Bangalore, in spite of the IT and ITES boom, a large number of jobs were in the unskilled tertiary sector. Urban Maharashtra had tertiary sector clerical type of jobs available. Metro-

Tamil Nadu had tertiary sector jobs but in A/P services. In the metros in less developed states of Madhya Pradesh, and Uttar Pradesh, male presence in ML jobs was not so high but female presence in these types of jobs was high.

In non-metros, states with a higher level of urbanization, namely Gujarat, Karnataka, Maharashtra, Punjab, and West Bengal, a higher proportion of males were employed in the A/P services and they were probably employed in the tertiary sector (Table 3.10). Among females as well, in Haryana, Maharashtra, Punjab, and West Bengal a higher proportion was employed in high-end jobs and most probably in the tertiary sector. Conversely, all the states with low levels of urbanization except Orissa and Rajasthan in case of males and Orissa, Rajasthan, Assam, and Kerala in the case of females had high

**Table 3.10**   Distribution of States by Proportion Employed in Administrative and Professional Services and Urbanization Levels, 2004–5

| | | Urbanization Level (2001) Metros | | Urbanization Level (2001) Non-metros | |
|---|---|---|---|---|---|
| | | High | Low | High | Low |
| Males Employed in Administrative and Professional Services | High | Tamil Nadu, West Bengal | | Gujarat, Karnataka, Maharashtra, Punjab, West Bengal | Orissa, Rajasthan |
| | Low | Gujarat, Haryana, Karnataka, Maharashtra, Punjab | Andhra Pradesh, Bihar, Madhya Pradesh, Rajasthan, Uttar Pradesh | Haryana, Tamil Nadu | Andhra Pradesh, Assam, Bihar, Jammu and Kashmir, Kerala, Madhya Pradesh, Uttar Pradesh |
| Females Employed in Administrative and Professional Services | High | Maharashtra, Tamil Nadu, West Bengal | Andhra Pradesh, Bihar, Madhya Pradesh, Uttar Pradesh | Haryana, Maharashtra, Punjab, West Bengal | Assam, Kerala, Orissa, Rajasthan |
| | Low | Gujarat, Haryana, Karnataka, Punjab | Rajasthan | Gujarat, Karnataka, Tamil Nadu | Andhra Pradesh, Bihar, Jammu and Kashmir, Madhya Pradesh, Uttar Pradesh |

*Source*: Data taken from Tables A3.32 and A3.33.

*Note*: High and low pertain to above and below the all-India average.

**Table 3.11** Distribution of States by Proportion Employed in Manual Labour Jobs and Urbanization Levels, 2004–5

| | | Urbanization Level (2001) Metros | | Urbanization Level (2001) Non-metros | |
| --- | --- | --- | --- | --- | --- |
| | | High | Low | High | Low |
| Males Employed in Manual Labour Jobs | High | Gujarat, Haryana, Punjab, West Bengal | Andhra Pradesh, Rajasthan | Maharashtra, Tamil Nadu | Andhra Pradesh, Jammu and Kashmir, Kerala, Madhya Pradesh, Uttar Pradesh |
| | Low | Karnataka, Maharashtra, Tamil Nadu | Bihar, Madhya Pradesh, Uttar Pradesh | Gujarat, Haryana, Karnataka, Punjab, West Bengal | Assam, Bihar, Orissa, Rajasthan |
| Females Employed in Manual Labour Jobs | High | Gujarat, Haryana, Karnataka, Punjab | Madhya Pradesh, Rajasthan, Uttar Pradesh | Gujarat, Maharashtra, Tamil Nadu, | Bihar, Jammu and Kashmir, Madhya Pradesh, Rajasthan, Uttar Pradesh |
| | Low | Maharashtra, Tamil Nadu, West Bengal | Andhra Pradesh, Bihar | Haryana, Karnataka, Punjab, West Bengal | Andhra Pradesh, Assam, Kerala, Orissa |

*Source*: Data taken from Tables A3.32 and A3.33.

*Note*: High and low pertain to above and below the all-India average.

proportion of females in A/P services. These higher end jobs for females in non-metros were in both secondary and tertiary sectors. Further, the ML category of work in the high urbanized states was high in Tamil Nadu and Maharashtra in case of males and in addition Gujarat in case of females (Table 3.11).

## Unemployment Rates

In this section we consider two types of unemployment rates—the first one known as UPSS, which is usual status unemployment rate capturing the chronic unemployment throughout the year and Current Daily Status (CDS)[2] unemployment rate, which gives an idea about the extent of underemployment in the economy.[3] In general, CDS unemployment rates would be higher than UPSS unemployment rates.

Chronic unemployment in India has traditionally been very low. In the absence of universal social security measures, particularly unemployment allowance, most male workers are forced to do whatever work they might get in order to survive. The UPSS unemployment rate in urban areas for males was below 5 per cent in 1993–4 and went down to 3.8 per cent in 2004–5 (Figure 3.29). Only in 1987–8 was it a little over 5 per cent. The long-term female unemployment rate in urban areas has always been higher than that for males; it hovered around 5–6 per cent up to 2004–5 and in this year it increased to 6.9 per cent when it declined for males (Figure 3.30). We have already observed earlier in this chapter that WPR of females is much lower than that of males in urban areas. High unemployment rate and low WPR among females are interlinked. High unemployment rate among females reflects less opportunity to get jobs and it discouraged new entrants in the labour market.

Among males, there is very low difference between metro and non-metro UPSS unemployment rates. However, in the reforms period there was a higher reduction in this unemployment rate in metros than in non-metros. In

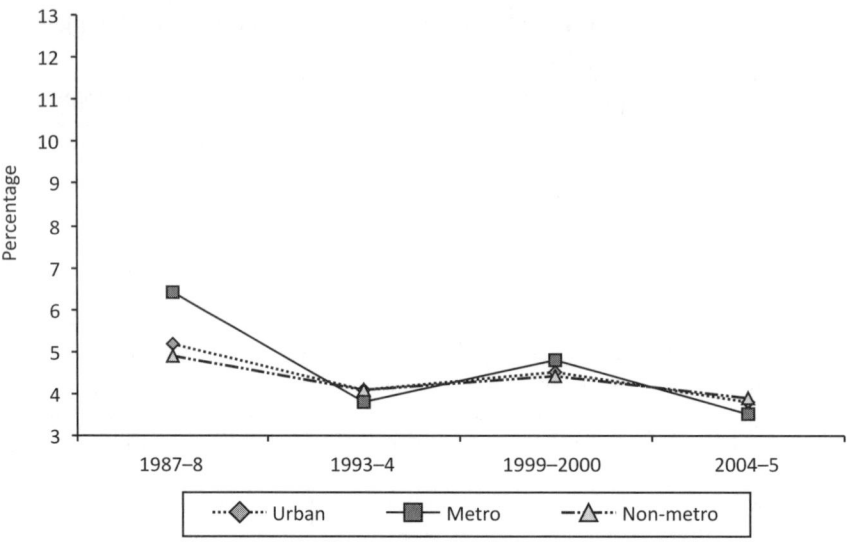

**Figure 3.29**    Usual Status Unemployment, Males

*Source*: Data taken from Tables A3.34 and A3.36.

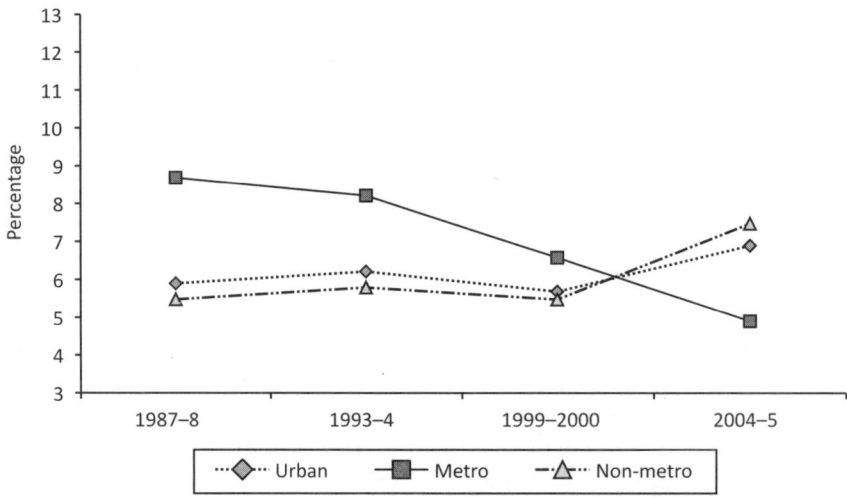

**Figure 3.30**    Usual Status Unemployment, Females

*Source*: Data taken from Tables A3.35 and A3.36.

case of female UPSS unemployment rates, there was a very wide gap between metros and non-metros; in the pre-reforms period, there was a very large gap between these two size classes of urban centres, with the metros displaying a much higher UPSS unemployment rate than non-metros. Post reforms, there was a very sharp decline in female UPSS unemployment in the metros but a sharp increase in the same in non-metros. This trend was observed in most of the states except Andhra Pradesh, Rajasthan, and Uttar Pradesh.

UPSS unemployment across town size classification is available for all years except for 2004–5. The town size class-wise data reveals that for both males and females long term unemployment increased with an increase in the size class of urban centres from 1987–8 to 1999–2000. The UPSS unemployment rate for males in 1987–8 across small towns, medium and large cities, and metropolises was 4.4, 5.2, and 6.4 per cent, respectively. The corresponding figures in 1999–2000 were 4.1, 4.6, and 4.8, respectively reflecting a decline in chronic unemployment among males in each size class of towns in the 12-year period. This led to a decline in total urban male unemployment rates from 5.2 to 4.5 per cent. In the case of females, a similar trend of rise in unemployment rate with an increase in the size of urban settlements could be observed with one important difference—the unemployment rate in large and metropolitan cities was considerably higher than that in small and medium towns.

In general, chronic unemployment in urban areas also had clear regional dimensions.

The whole eastern India (Assam, Bihar, Orissa, West Bengal, and other north-eastern states) and Kerala showed a much higher level of chronic unemployment. In these states female chronic unemployment rates were also much above male chronic unemployment rates and in several cases female unemployment was observed to be well above the 2-digit level in several years. In contrast, in Uttar Pradesh some of the size classes in all the three Rounds up to 1999–2000 had low male and female UPSS unemployment rates.

CDS unemployment rates were higher largely due to the absence of regular employment for many workers on account of increasing levels of casualization. At the all-India level, in all survey years CDS unemployment rates for male and females fluctuated between 6–8 and 10–12 per cent, respectively. Since 1993–4, CDS unemployment has been higher in non-metros as compared to metro areas and the gap widened in 2004–5 (Figures 3.31 and 3.32).

Like the chronic unemployment scenario there was a regional dimension to CDS

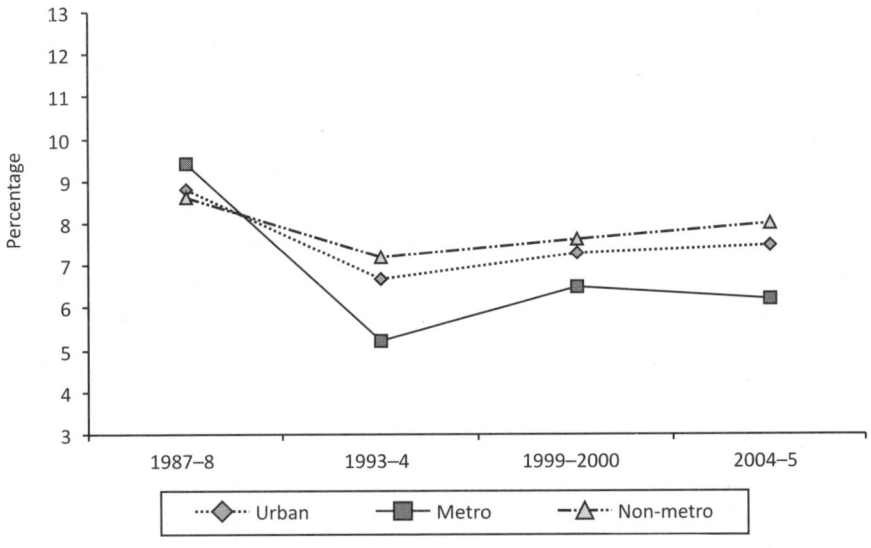

**Figure 3.31** CDS Unemployment, Males

*Source*: Data taken from Tables A3.37 and A3.39.

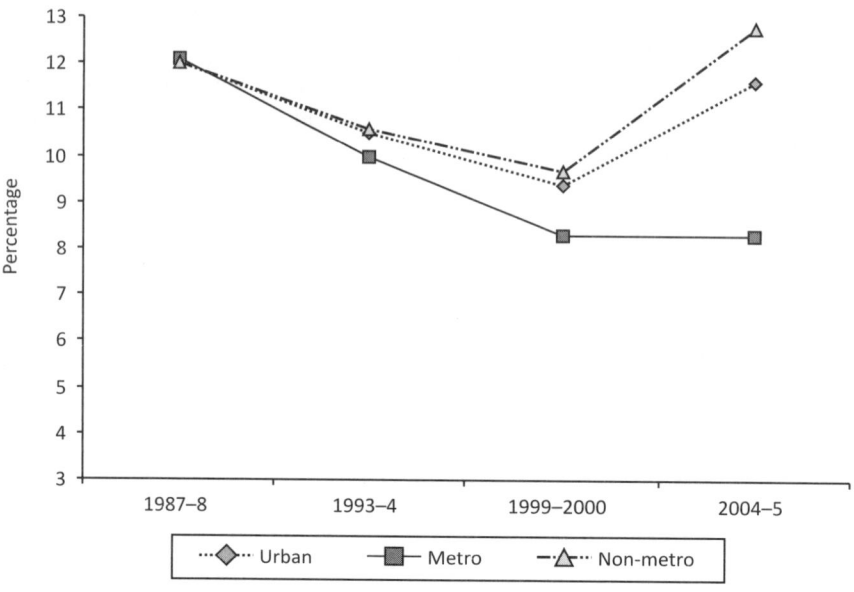

**Figure 3.32**    CDS Unemployment, Females

*Source*: Data taken from Tables A3.38 and A3.39.

unemployment as well. In the case of males, double digit high CDS unemployment was confined to the two states, Kerala and West Bengal. In the case of females, in addition to these two states a high CDS unemployment rate was also found in Assam in all the years. In contrast, similar to the scenario in chronic unemployment, Uttar Pradesh recorded much lower CDS unemployment in all the years for both males and females.

**CONCLUSIONS**

This analysis shows that there was a gradual increase in WPRs in urban India over the entire study period. But employment increase in CAGRs was higher in the pre-reforms period than in the reforms period on account of a low base in the pre-reforms period. Even in percentage points, the growth rate was higher in the pre-reforms period than in the reforms period. Compared to males, female workers' CAGR was high once again on account of a low base to

start with. Compared to non-metros, CAGRs of workers in metros was higher for all the periods, indicating that more work was generated and available in metros than in non-metros, and thus, the employment situation was better and it improved much more in the metros than in the non-metros over time. The period of economic reforms also shows that this trend continued and the metros benefitted more than the non-metros. Also, females in metros benefitted on account of reforms. This is reflected in unemployment rates; the post reforms unemployment rates came down sharply in metros than in non-metros for males and females. In fact, in the UPSS as well as CDS unemployment rates among females went down in metros and went up in non-metros in the reforms period.

We will see later in this book (in the education chapter), that education levels improved in non-metros but better quality jobs were not available there. This means that the educated youth in non-metros were not taking up employment on account of suitable jobs not being available.

The nature of work changed in the reforms period. Males shifted to SE, females shifted to RE, and this shift was from CL. RE was high in metros as compared to non-metros. RE dominated male employment in metros and SE dominated male employment in non-metros. RE among males in non-metros was in the secondary as well as tertiary sectors. RE among females in non-metros was in the tertiary sector. In metros also, RE was equally high in the secondary and tertiary sectors for males. RE for females in the tertiary sector increased in the reforms period. Lastly, SE increased among females in the secondary sector indicating that part of the manufacturing was getting sub-contracted to females and this entire work was likely to be home-based and piece rate in nature. Thus, there was an increase in casualization of work in the reforms period and the additional females coming into the labour force was entirely unprotected labour. The protected secondary sector also shifted to unprotected work. This happened in both metros and non-metros. There is a dire need to increase social security coverage of urban workers.

Lastly, we do not find much decline in ML employment in the metros and those workers remained as high as before even though better quality employment (A/P type) increased in these cities in the wake of economic reforms. Some of the IT and ITES economy states also continued to have a very large proportion of manual labour in their metros, which was most likely to be construction labour. Many large metro cities experienced high construction activities such as construction of spaces and parks for IT and ITES, and malls and high-end residential complexes. JNNURM also resulted in increased construction activities in metros. But nonetheless, manual labour employment dominated the non-metro economy and it is partly due to large female manual labour employment in agriculture. There is an urgent need to intervene in the non-metro economy to improve work opportunities and quality of work available in them. As we will see in Chapter 4 on education, there is qualified labour available in these cities and towns to support new economic activities.

## NOTES

1. Population data have been adjusted for NSS years. The 1993–4 urban sample was drawn based on the 1981 population census data. This means that in the metro sample, there was under-representation of cities and in the non-metro sample there were some metro cities also.

2. The daily status concept incorporates changes in the activity status of persons by taking into account half-day data during the seven days of the reference week. In situations where large scale seasonal unemployment exists, the CDS measure gives a better picture of the unemployment situation than one relating to unemployed persons.

3. CDS unemployment fully captures underemployment among casual workers. Regular workers, by definition, are fully employed. CDS unemployment only partially captures underemployment among self-employed. In urban areas, part-time self-employed workers get captured by it. But, say a self-employed real estate agent might spend the whole day in the shop but might get customers for only a few hours of the day but the real estate agent will report working for a full day. However, casual workers are hired for half/full day depending on the work requirement and normally they are not allowed to stay idle for long hours.

# 4

# Educational Opportunities and Economic Well-being

In economic literature, from Adam Smith onwards, there have been discussions on the relationship between education and economic growth. T.A. Schultz was perhaps the first economist who presented a theory in the early 1960s in which education was presented not merely as a consumption activity but also as an investment in forming human capital, which along with physical capital contributes to economic growth. Education is considered a tool of empowerment and building of human capabilities. Education, particularly elementary education, is therefore viewed as an important input in the development of a society. In summary, education is important in five distinct ways (Drèze and Sen 1995):

1. *Intrinsic importance*—being educated is an achievement in itself and an opportunity to being educated is important for a person's effective freedom.
2. *Instrumental personal role*—education can help a person do many things (other than being educated) that are also valuable. For example, education can lead to economic opportunities and income can lead to increase in other choices in life.
3. *Instrumental social role*—education can lead to awareness about social needs and participation in a collective decision-making process.
4. *Instrumental process role*—process of schooling, which can have other benefits. For example, schooling can bring children in contact with others, which can broaden their horizons. Exposure to other cultures and ways of living can do away with social maladies such as untouchability, caste and culture biases, communal divide, and so on.
5. *Empowerment and distributive role*—education can lead to disadvantaged groups getting enabled to resist oppression, organize themselves politically, and get a fairer deal. The redistributive effects can be important not only between social groups and households, but also within a family, especially with respect to gender inequalities.

In the urban context as well, education is important in these five distinct ways. But the difference with rural areas is that urban settlements open up diversified work opportunities, access to which is linked to the level of education of a worker. In other words, in the context of the labour market, education plays an instrumental role. Also in the urban context, the differential impact of the level of education on workforce participation and earnings becomes more marked as compared to rural areas. In the latter, improvement in the level of education leads to out-migration to urban areas on account of lack of diversified employment opportunities. Similarly, the differences in labour market outcomes between small and large settlements with similar levels of education also get magnified on account of lack of opportunities in the former. In this chapter we make an effort to relate educational attainment with workforce participation and nature of employment across gender and by types of urban settlements.

As in the chapter on employment, this chapter also uses the National Sample Survey (NSS) data from four Rounds and analyses the literacy levels and levels of education disaggregated by gender at the national level and by states for total urban, metro, and non-metro areas up to 2004–5. The household schedule data is taken from the NSS's employment-unemployment rounds and reprocessed as in Chapter 3. The entire data generated is given in Tables A4.1 to A4.15.

**Literacy/Illiteracy Rates**

On the whole illiteracy rates decline with an increase in the size class of an urban centre (Figure 4.1). Or literacy rates increase with an increase in the size of an urban centre. Figure 4.1 shows such a clear pattern emerging when non-metro and metro literacy rates for all the four NSS Rounds are compared among males. The data for females is given in Figure 4.2, which also shows that literacy rates increase

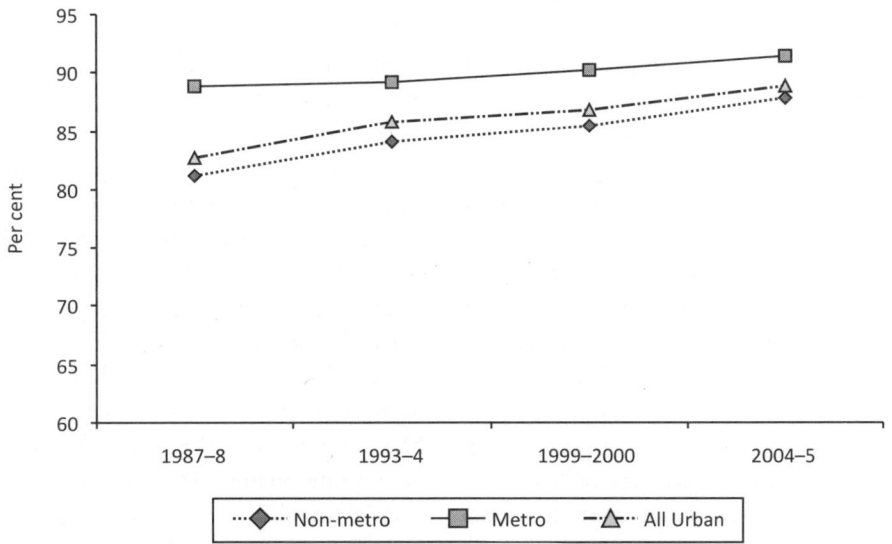

**Figure 4.1**    Literacy Rates (of 7 +) by Size Class, Males, All-India

*Source*: Data taken from Tables A4.3, A4.4, A4.7, A4.8, A4.13, A4.14, and A4.15.

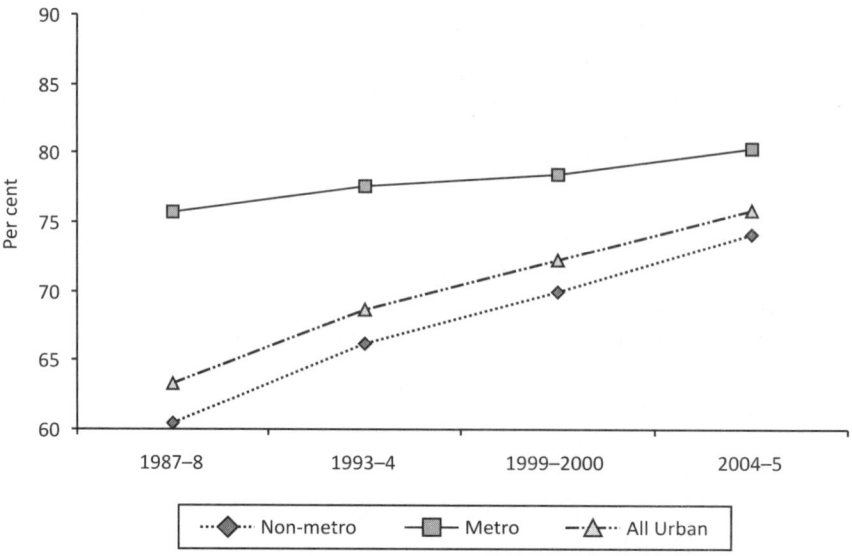

**Figure 4.2**    Literacy Rates (of 7 +) by Size Class, Females, All-India

*Source*: Data taken from Tables A4.3, A4.4, A4.7, A4.8, A4.13, A4.14, and A4.15.

with an increase in the size class of an urban centre. Literacy rates in non-metros for males were 81.2, 84.1, and 87.8 per cent, respectively for 1987–8, 1993–4, and 2004–5 respectively. These figures in metros for males were 88.9, 89.2, and 91.4 per cent respectively. It is encouraging to observe that the gap between non-metros and metros reduced with time. Nonetheless, it is also disheartening to observe that males in metros have not yet reached full literacy.

Female literacy rates were far lower than male literacy rates in both non-metros and metros for all the four NSS Rounds. Female literacy rates in non-metros were 60.5, 66.2, and 74.1 per cent in 1987–8, 1993–4, and 2004–5, respectively. Figures 4.1 and 4.2 for metros were 75.7, 77.6, and 80.4 per cent, respectively.

About 20 per cent females in metros and 26 per cent females in non-metros were still illiterate. The metro non-metro gap reduced considerably in the case of male literacy. But with regard to female literacy, although the

metro to non-metro gap reduced, it still remained large. Improvements in male literacy were spread evenly across the pre-reforms and reforms periods in both metros and non-metros. But improvements in female literacy in non-metros were faster in the pre-reforms period than in the reforms period.

The gap in literacy rates between metros and non-metros narrowed over time. This can be seen when we look at the ratio of metro literacy rates to non-metro literacy rates; these were 1.09, 1.06, and 1.04 for the three NSS Rounds in 1987–8, 1993–4, and 2004–5 for males and 1.25, 1.17, and 1.09 for the same years for females. Thus, there was higher inequality in metro/non-metro literacy rates among females than among males. We can say the same when literacy rates in metros are compared with those in small towns.

Even in the years when further disaggregation of non-metro data is possible, it can be observed that male and female literacy rates improved with the size class of towns and in each size class these improved over time. However, a gender gap in literacy rates was higher in the smaller size class of towns than in the larger size class of towns.

Two important observations can be made from this data. First, that the gap between metros and non-metros with regard to literacy rates was higher for females than for males. The metro to non-metro inequity index was 1.04 for males and 1.09 for females in 2004–5 (Table 4.1). At the same time, there was a sharper decline in this inequity among females than among males over time, as the male ratio improved from 1.09 to 1.04 whereas the female ratio improved from 1.25 to 1.09.

The other observation is that the gender gap was higher in the case of non-metros than in case of metros. The gender inequity ratio, which is the ratio of the male and female literacy rates, came down in metros as well as in non-metros from 1.17 in 1987–8 to 1.14 in 2004–5 in the metros and from 1.34 in 1987–8 to 1.18 in 2004–5 in non-metros. The decline in gender inequality was higher in non-metros over time. Nonetheless, non-metros continued to discriminate against women much more than the metros in their access to education. This also means that women had better chances of improving in their education levels in metros than in non-metros.

This pattern of improving literacy rates over the NSS Rounds for males as well as for females, higher literacy rates (male and female) in metro cities as compared to non-metro cities,

improvement in literacy rates with increase in the urban settlement size, higher gender disparity in literacy rates in smaller towns than in metro cities, and higher improvement in female literacy rates in metro cities than in smaller towns can be seen for individual states as well.

There were, however, a few exceptions to this trend. In the metro category, there were four exceptions wherein Andhra Pradesh, West Bengal, Punjab, and Rajasthan male and female literacy rates declined in 2004–5 as compared to 1993–4 (Tables A4.7, A4.8, A4.13, and A4.14 and Figures 4.3 and 4.4). It needs to be stated here that there was no metros in Punjab and Rajasthan in 1987–8. There is no explanation for decline in literacy rates in metropolitan cities in Andhra Pradesh and West Bengal during 1993–4 and 2004–5. Also, Rajasthan and Punjab had only one metropolitan city, Jaipur and Ludhiana, respectively, and there is no reason for decline in literacy rates in these two cities as well in the 1993–4 and 2004–5 period.

Because the non-metros started from a low literacy base, particularly with regard to female literacy, the improvement in literacy rates were quite steep over this entire period of 1987–8 to 2004–5. In the case of males, the states that registered a steep improvement in literacy rates were Gujarat, Karnataka, Bihar, Jammu and Kashmir, and Uttar Pradesh (Figure 4.5). In the case of females, improvements in literacy rates in this period were steep in almost all the states except Kerala, which already had high literacy rates in 1987–8. Among females, the

**Table 4.1**    Metro to Non-metro and Gender Inequity Ratios Over Time

|  | Metro to Non-metro Inequity | | Gender Inequity | |
|  | Male | Female | Non-metro | Metro |
|---|---|---|---|---|
| 1987–8 | 1.09 | 1.25 | 1.34 | 1.17 |
| 1993–4 | 1.06 | 1.17 | 1.27 | 1.15 |
| 2004–5 | 1.04 | 1.09 | 1.18 | 1.14 |

*Source*: Data taken from Tables A4.3, A4.4, A4.7, A4.8, A4.13, and A4.14.

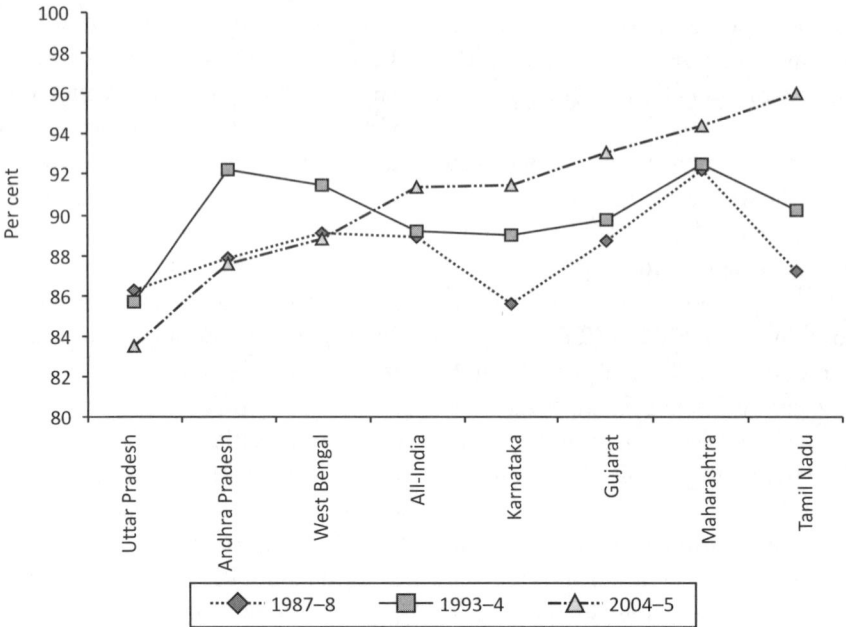

**Figure 4.3**    Male Literacy Rates by States, Metros, Over Time

*Source*: Data taken from Tables A4.3, A4.7, and A4.13.

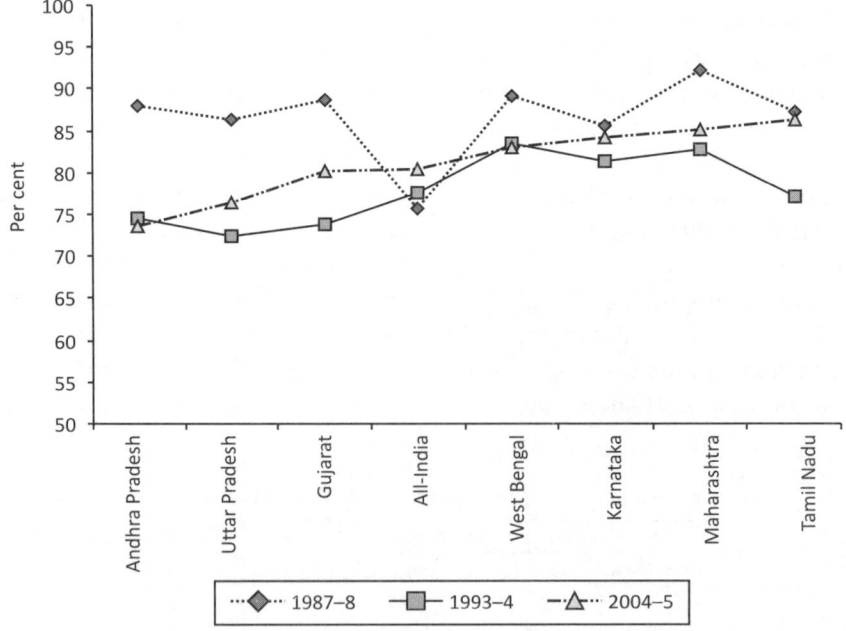

**Figure 4.4**    Female Literacy Rates, Metros, Over Time

*Source*: Data taken from Tables A4.4, A4.8, and A4.14.

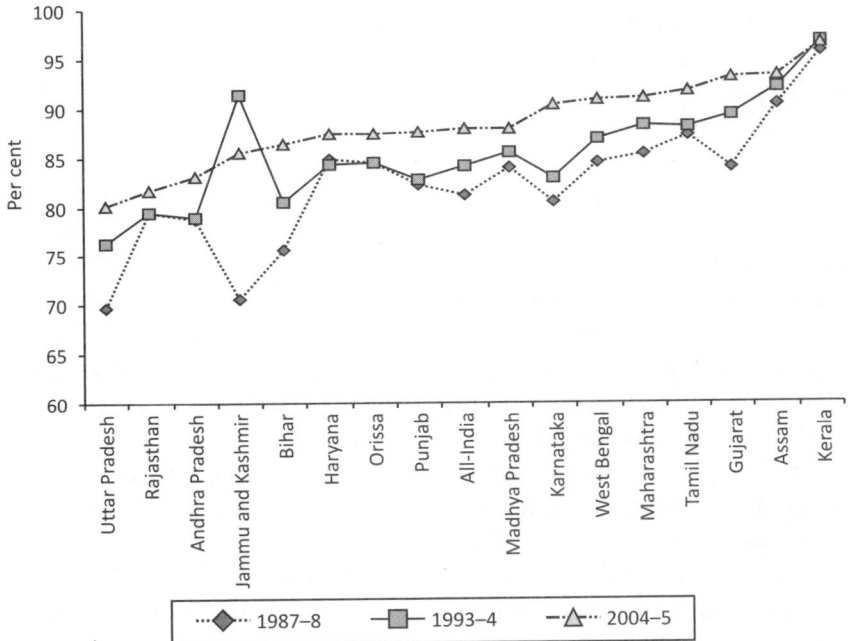

**Figure 4.5**   Male Literacy Rates, Non-metros, Over Time

*Source*: Data taken from Tables A4.3, A4.7, and A4.13.

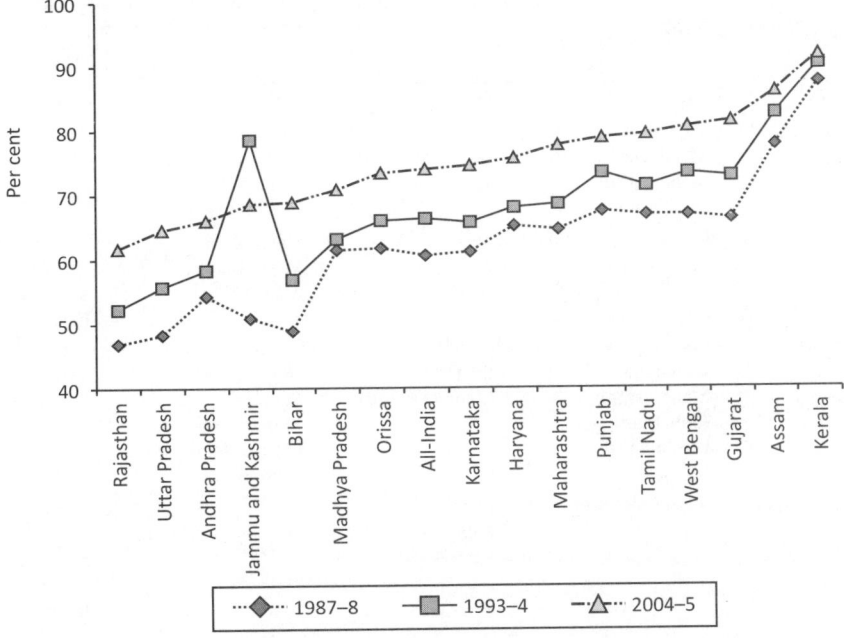

**Figure 4.6**   Female Literacy Rates, Non-metros, Over Time

*Source*: Data taken from Tables A4.4, A4.8, and A4.14.

states which observed steep improvements over time were Rajasthan, Uttar Pradesh, Bihar, Gujarat, West Bengal, and Jammu and Kashmir (Figure 4.6). In all the states, improvements in literacy rates were faster in the reforms period as compared to the pre-reforms period except Assam and Jammu and Kashmir.

There is higher disparity across states with respect to literacy rates in the non-metros than in metros. The Coefficient of Variation (CV) for male literacy across the states was 8.07, 6.38, and 5.04, respectively, for 1987–8, 1993–4, and 2004–5 in case of non-metros and 2.47, 2.36, and 4.84 in case of metros. This means that the metros tended to be similar in providing educational opportunities than non-metros. Also, there was very high variation in availability of educational facilities across the states in non-metros. Even if a state had low literacy rates, the metros would be well ahead of non-metros.

This means that the states where literacy rates were low also had higher intra-state inequality across different size classes of urban centres with regard to literacy. The states where the ratio of metro literacy to non-metro literacy (in the case of males) was high were Bihar in 2004–5, and Rajasthan, Andhra Pradesh, and Uttar Pradesh in previous years. The last important point is that there was an increase in disparity across the states in case of metro male literacy rates whereas there was a decrease in disparity across the states in the case of non-metro male literacy rates.

CV for female literacy across the states were 17.46, 14.84, and 10.79, respectively, for 1987–8, 1993–4, and 2004–5 in the case of non-metros and 4.44, 7.05, and 12.11 in the case of metros. In the case of females also, metros were more egalitarian than non-metros. But there was much higher disparity with

**Table 4.2** Distribution of States by Literacy Rates and Urbanization Levels, 2004–5

| | | Urbanization Level (2001) Metros | | Urbanization Level (2001) Non-metros | |
|---|---|---|---|---|---|
| | | High | Low | High | Low |
| Male Literacy Rate | High | Gujarat, Haryana, Karnataka, Maharashtra, Tamil Nadu | Bihar, Madhya Pradesh | Gujarat, Karnataka, Maharashtra, Tamil Nadu, West Bengal | Assam, Kerala, Madhya Pradesh |
| | Low | Punjab, West Bengal | Andhra Pradesh, Rajasthan, Uttar Pradesh | Haryana, Punjab | Andhra Pradesh, Bihar, Jammu and Kashmir, Orissa, Rajasthan, Uttar Pradesh |
| Female Literacy Rate | High | Karnataka, Maharashtra, Tamil Nadu, West Bengal | Bihar, Madhya Pradesh | Gujarat, Haryana, Karnataka, Maharashtra, Punjab, Tamil Nadu, West Bengal | Assam, Kerala |
| | Low | Gujarat, Haryana, Punjab | Andhra Pradesh, Rajasthan, Uttar Pradesh | | Andhra Pradesh, Bihar, Jammu and Kashmir, Madhya Pradesh, Orissa, Rajasthan, Uttar Pradesh |

*Source*: Data taken from Tables A4.13 and A4.14.

*Note*: High and low pertain to above and below the all-India average.

regard to female literacy rates across the states in both metros as well as non-metros. Like in case of males, there was an increase in disparity in metro female literacy over time, particularly in the reforms period and a decline in disparity in non-metro female literacy rates in the pre-reforms period. Lastly, achievements of states with regard to female literacy rates were quite varied and there was also very high intra-state disparity. There may be many other factors that influenced achievements with regard to female literacy rates such as government policies, culture, and economic development. Of these, government policies seem to be playing a very important role, as we can see substantial improvement in female literacy rates in metros and non-metros in Madhya Pradesh in the last decade.

Observing the relationship of literacy levels with urbanization levels (Table 4.2) we find that it was weak in the case of metros where states with high as well as low levels of urbanization had both high and low literacy rates. In the case of non-metros, we see some relationship emerging in the case of females, where states with a high level of urbanization had high female literacy rates in non-metros. Once again, it stands proved that literacy rates are a largely a function of state policy and not just market dynamics.

We also attempted to observe the relationship between literacy levels and work participation rates (WPRs) and we find a strong relationship only in the case of males in non-metros (Table 4.3), with states having higher literacy rates also having higher WPRs. This analysis, however, does not explore the cause and impact of this relationship. In the case of females in non-metros, there were many states which were exceptions to this fact because in some of the developed states such as Gujarat, Haryana, and Punjab female literacy rates in

**Table 4.3**  Distribution of States by Literacy Rates and WPRs, 2004–5

| | | Metros Male WPR (2004–5) | | Non-metros Male WPR (2004–5) | |
|---|---|---|---|---|---|
| | | High | Low | High | Low |
| Male Literacy Rate | High | Gujarat, Karnataka, Maharashtra, Tamil Nadu | Bihar, Haryana, Madhya Pradesh | Assam, Gujarat, Karnataka, Kerala, Maharashtra, Tamil Nadu, West Bengal | Madhya Pradesh |
| | Low | Punjab, West Bengal | Andhra Pradesh, Rajasthan, Uttar Pradesh | Andhra Pradesh, Punjab | Bihar, Haryana, Jammu and Kashmir, Orissa, Rajasthan, Uttar Pradesh |
| | | Female WPR (2004–5) | | Female WPR (2004–5) | |
| Female Literacy Rate | High | Karnataka, Madhya Pradesh, Maharashtra, West Bengal | Bihar, Tamil Nadu | Karnataka, Maharashtra, Tamil Nadu | Assam, Gujarat, Haryana, Kerala, Punjab, West Bengal |
| | Low | Gujarat, Rajasthan | Andhra Pradesh, Haryana, Punjab, Uttar Pradesh | Andhra Pradesh | Bihar, Jammu and Kashmir, Madhya Pradesh, Orissa, Rajasthan, Uttar Pradesh |

*Source*: Data taken from Tables A3.3, A4.13, and A4.14.

*Note*: High and low pertain to above and below the all-India average.

non-metros were higher but the women did not go out in the labour force to earn for their families. In metros we did not find any relationship.

## PRIMARY EDUCATION

Though the NSS data give four different levels of education, up to primary, from primary up to middle, from middle up to higher secondary, and from higher secondary to graduate and above in discussions, the two extreme levels of education—up to primary and graduate and above—have been covered. The two cases provide an interesting contrast with regard to the education situation.

The literate population whose education level was up to primary and below primary level was the highest in the smallest size class of urban centres (Figure 4.7). With the increase in size class of an urban centre, the per cent literate population educated with such low levels of education declined. This means that education levels of the literate increased with an increase

in the size class of urban centres. Metropolitan cities had the lowest proportion of the literate population that remained up to just the primary or below level. This group also contained those who had earned literacy through adult literacy classes, such as total literacy campaigns. In 2004–5, for example, 37 per cent of the males in non-metros and 30 per cent males in metro cities had such low levels of education among those who were literate. Among females, these figures were 43 and 34 per cent, respectively (Figure 4.8). Obviously, the proportion which had low levels of education among females was higher than that among males in all size classes and over time.

There was a decline in the proportion of literate who had studied up to the primary and below levels over time. This was true with regard to males as well as females and in case of metros as well as non-metros. Further, decline in this proportion among females was larger in metros than in non-metros and as a result

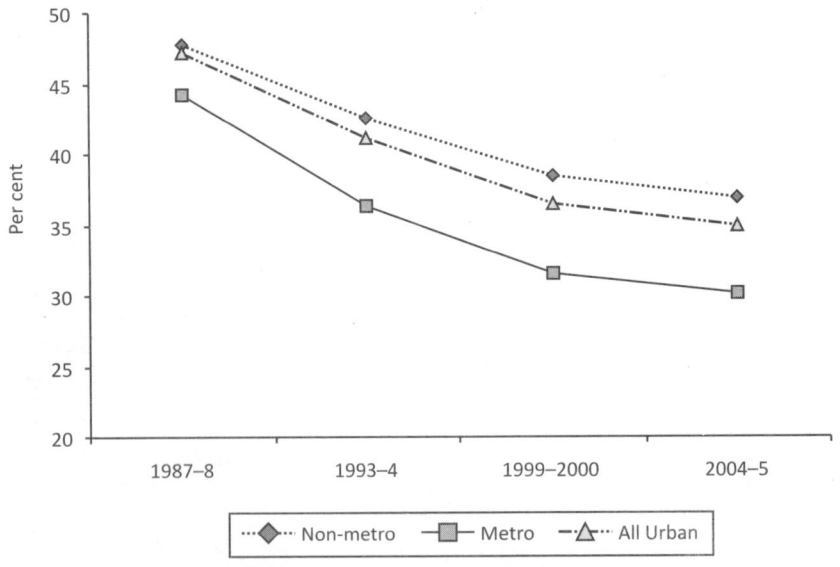

**Figure 4.7**  Percentage Male Literates Educated up to Primary, Over Time

*Source*: Calculated by authors taking data from Tables A4.3, A4.4, A4.7, A4.8, A4.13, A4.14, and A4.15.

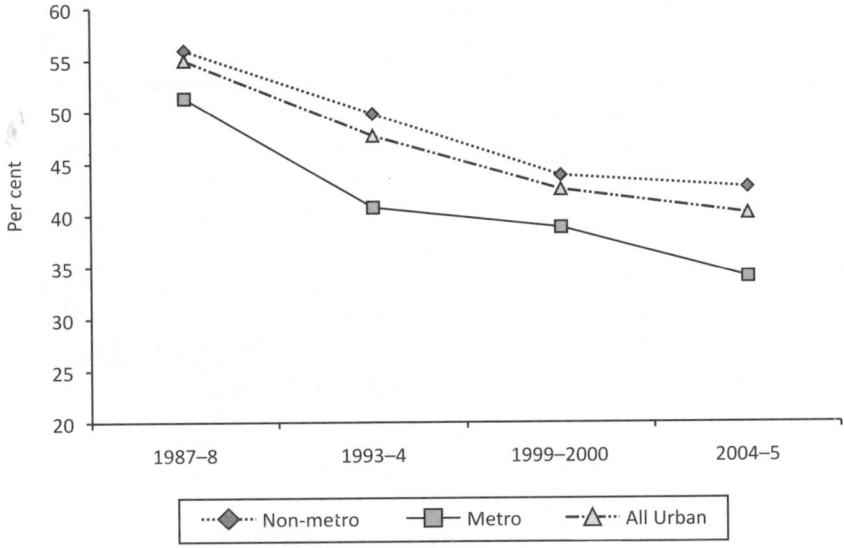

**Figure 4.8**   Percentage Female Literates Educated up to Primary, Over Time

*Source*: Calculated by authors taking data from Tables A4.3, A4.4, A4.7, A4.8, A4.13, A4.14, and A4.15.

the gap between metros and non-metros with regard to per cent literate with education up to the primary and below levels increased in the case of females. To a lesser extent, this was true also for males. The ratios of the proportion of literate with education below primary levels in non-metros to the same in metros were 1.08, 1.17, and 1.23 in 1987–8, 1993–4, and 2004–5, respectively, in the case of males and 1.09, 1.22, and 1.26, respectively, for the same years in case of females (Table 4.4). Thus, while literacy rates improved and the gap between metros and non-metros reduced over time, the educational attainment among literates in non-metros remained poor and the gap between metros and non-metros increased over time in the case of both males as well as females. In other words, there was a higher probability of children getting out of the education system after completing primary school in non-metros than in metros because of lack of educational facilities in non-metros beyond primary schools. This could also be attributed to the lack of household demand

for beyond primary education among a set of households in non-metros on account of either lack of ability to incur expenditure or lack of future employment prospects after attaining higher education. These are conjectures, which need to be researched in future.

A similar pattern of decline in the proportion of literates up to the primary level over time among males as well as females and in metros and non-metros can be observed across the states. It can also be observed that non-metros and females have a higher proportion of such low levels of education as compared to metros and males respectively. Over time, the non-metro to metro ratio in proportion of literates educated up to the primary level increased, which means that inequality also increased. In Gujarat, the ratio was less than 1 in 1987–8 and 1993–4, but became more than 1 in 2004–5 (Table 4.4). This means that in Gujarat, a higher proportion of the educated had such low levels of education in metros as compared to non-metros up to 1993–4, after which the

**Table 4.4**    Ratio of Non-metro to Metro of Percentage Educated up to Primary Level, by States

| State | Male | | | Female | | |
|---|---|---|---|---|---|---|
| | 1987–8 | 1993–4 | 2004–5 | 1987–8 | 1993–4 | 2004–5 |
| Andhra Pradesh | 1.10 | 1.12 | 1.23 | 1.09 | 1.32 | 1.64 |
| Gujarat | 0.84 | 0.91 | 1.12 | 0.89 | 0.91 | 1.40 |
| Karnataka | 1.20 | 1.33 | 1.40 | 1.22 | 1.34 | 1.32 |
| Maharashtra | 0.96 | 1.22 | 1.21 | 1.05 | 1.25 | 1.07 |
| Tamil Nadu | 1.32 | 1.35 | 1.68 | 1.18 | 1.28 | 1.36 |
| Uttar Pradesh | 1.07 | 1.13 | 1.26 | 0.94 | 1.21 | 1.31 |
| West Bengal | 1.16 | 1.19 | 1.16 | 1.19 | 1.07 | 1.41 |
| All-India | 1.08 | 1.17 | 1.23 | 1.09 | 1.22 | 1.26 |

*Source*: Data taken from Tables A4.3, A4.4, A4.7, A4.8, A4.13, and A4.14.

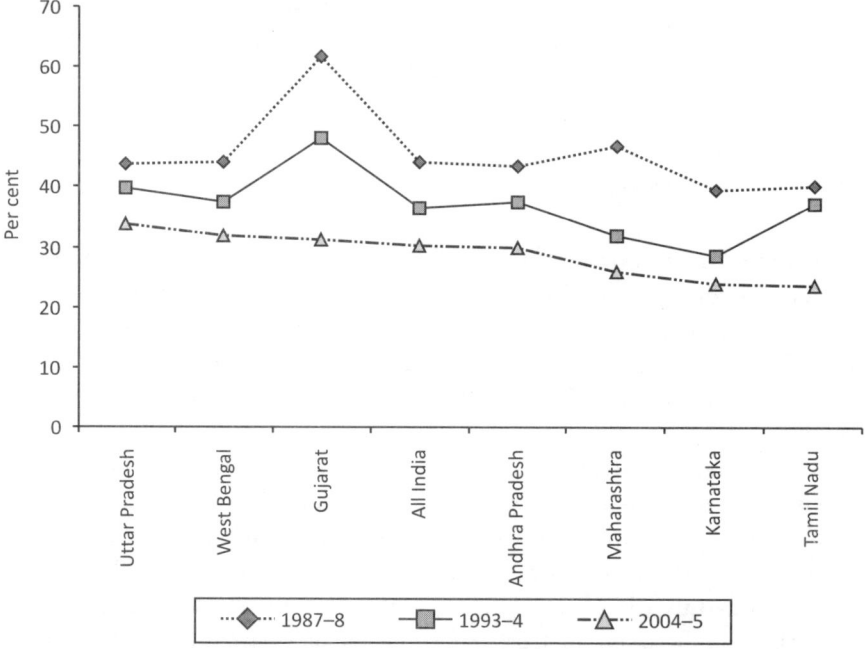

**Figure 4.9**    Percentage Male Literates in Metros Educated up to Primary, by States, Over Time

*Source*: Calculated by authors using data taken from Tables A4.3, A4.7, and A4.13.

metros reduced this proportion at a faster rate than non-metros.

In both males as well as females, there were high income as well as low income states at the top and the bottom with regard to the proportion of literates with low levels of education in metros (Figures 4.9 and 4.10). Gujarat was third from the bottom in the case of metro males and Maharashtra being the second from the bottom in the case of metro females. In the case of non-metro males, Orissa, Assam, and Kerala with low income levels were towards the top and in case of non-metro females, Kerala and Assam were towards the top. In the case of non-metros

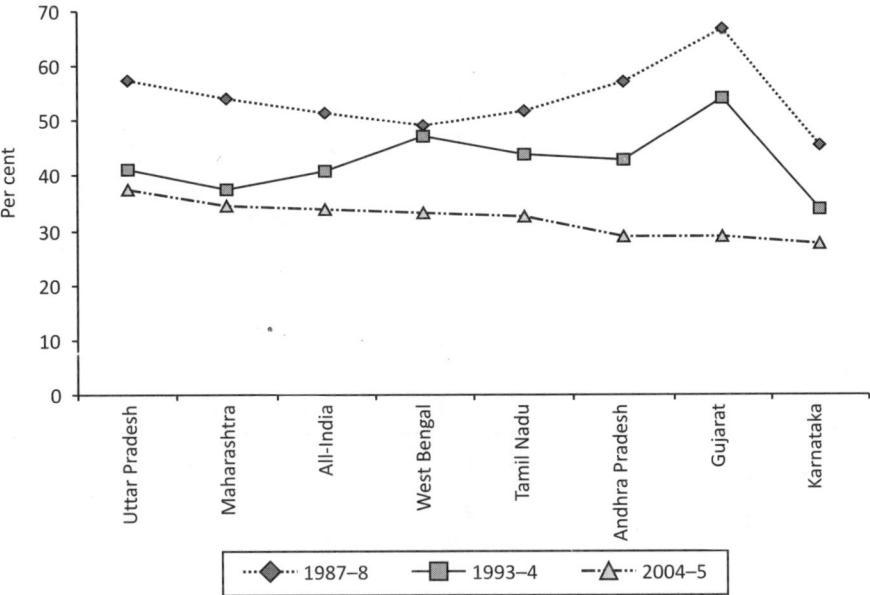

**Figure 4.10**    Percentage Female Literates in Metros Educated up to Primary, by States, Over Time
*Source*: Calculated by authors using data taken from Tables A4.4, A4.8, and A4.14.

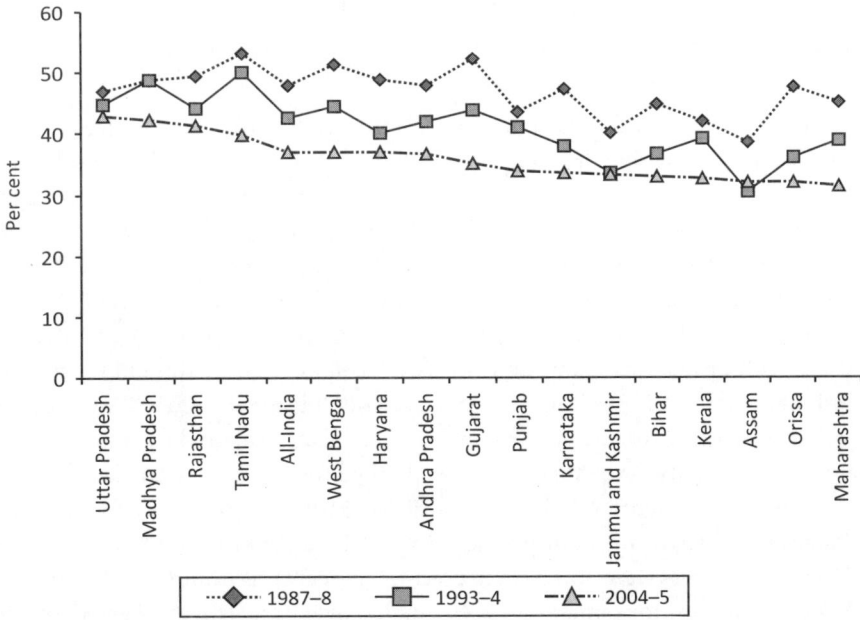

**Figure 4.11**    Percentage Male Literates in Non-metros Educated up to Primary, by States, Over Time
*Source*: Calculated by authors using data taken from Tables A4.3, A4.7, and A4.13.

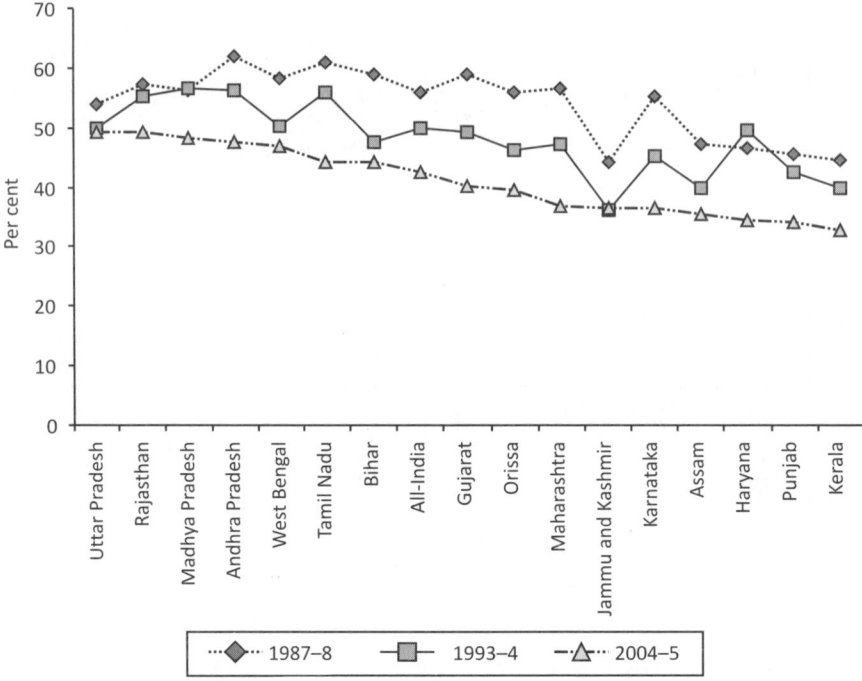

**Figure 4.12**    Percentage Female Literates in Non-metros Educated up to Primary,
by States, Over Time

*Source*: Calculated by authors using data taken from Tables A4.4, A4.8, and A4.14.

at the bottom were all less developed states in the case of males as well as females (Figures 4.11 and 4.12).

Such low levels of education fetches only unskilled, low wage jobs (Figures 4.13 and 4.14). An illiterate population would also get similar jobs. If the proportion of illiterate and the proportion of those with primary or below education are combined then 44.6 per cent males and 57.5 per cent females in non-metros in 2004–5 were at a capability level that would fetch them unskilled jobs (Figure 4.13). This is a very significant proportion. In metropolitan cities in 2004–5, these figures were 36.1 per cent for males and 46.9 per cent for females. These are also very high. One in every three males in metros and nearly half the males in non-metros and nearly three in every five females in non-

metros and nearly half the females in metros, did not qualify for any jobs other than unskilled ones. This was the situation in spite of the fact that since 2000, greater attention is being paid to the education sector in India.

There was significant decline in illiteracy rates across size classes of towns for males as well as females over time but a similar decline was not observed when illiterates and those with education up to the primary or below were clubbed together. For example, from 1987–8 to 2004–5, those with low or no literacy declined by 13.1 percentage points in non-metros and 14.3 percentage points in the metros among males over this 18-year period of 1987–8 to 2004–5. This is very slow progress. A very significant proportion of the male population in all size classes of urban centres, but more so

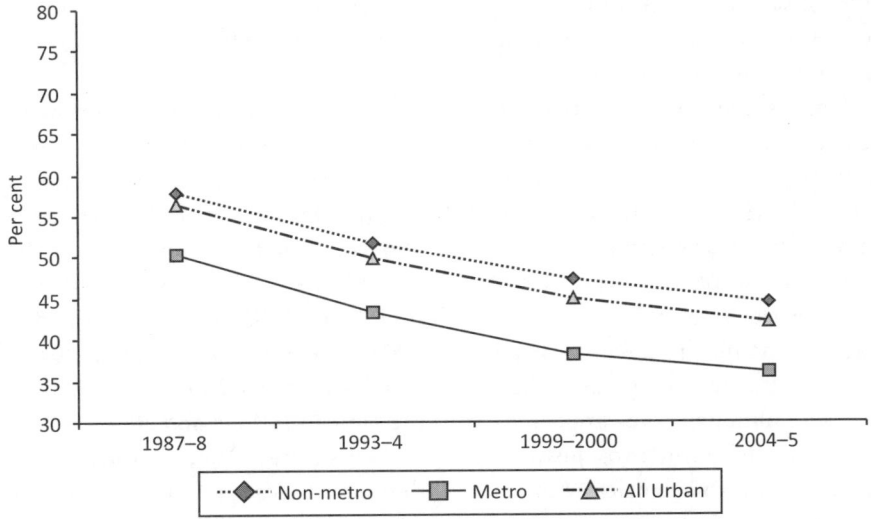

**Figure 4.13**   Percentage Males with No or Low Education Levels, Over Time

*Source*: Data taken from Tables A4.3, A4.4, A4.7, A4.8, A4.13, A4.14, and A4.15.

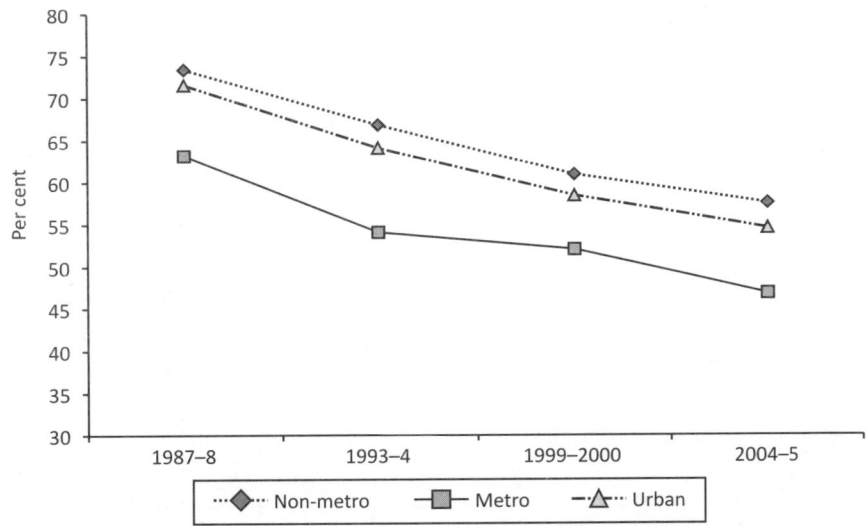

**Figure 4.14**   Percentage Females with No or Low Education Levels, Over Time

*Source*: Data taken from Tables A4.3, A4.4, A4.7, A4.8, A4.13, A4.14, and A4.15.

in non-metros, were not even completing the primary level of education or were still illiterate. Further, the reduction in proportion of males with no or low levels of education was slightly more in metros than in non-metros, even though non-metros started with much poorer levels of educational achievements and high levels of illiteracy. In other words, there was a widening of the gap between metros and non-metros with regard to the proportion of the population that was illiterate and with education only up to the primary level. The gap become wider in the case of females than in the case of males.

Among females, the situation was worse in terms of current status and improvement registered in literacy rates and level of education in urban India. In 1987–8, as high as 73.3 per cent of the females in non-metros, that is, three in every four, had no or low levels of education, which improved to only 57.5 per cent, by 15.8 percentage points in 2004–5. Even in the metros, the situation for females did not improve much, although the improvement was more than that in non-metros, just like for males. The proportion of females with no or low levels of education in metros came down from 63.2 per cent in 1987–8 to 46.9 per cent in 2004–5, a decline of just 16.3 percentage points. Progress towards the target of universalization of elementary education, that is,

education up to Class 8 is very slow even in metropolitan India; it is very slow for all and slower for females.

Gender gap increased in non-metros as well as metros with regard to the percentage of the population with no or low literacy rates. For example, the ratio of per cent females with no or low education to per cent males with no or low education was 1.27 in 1987–8, which increased to 1.29 in 1993–4, and remained at 1.29 in 2004–5 in non-metros. In metros, this ratio increased from 1.25 in 1987–8, and remained the same in 1993–4 and 2004–5 at 1.30.

Across the states, in the case of metros, there was a clear pattern; the worst performing states, which are, those with high illiteracy plus education only up to the primary level, were those with low income states (Figures 4.15 and 4.16). In non-metros, for the males as well as the females, the better performing states were of

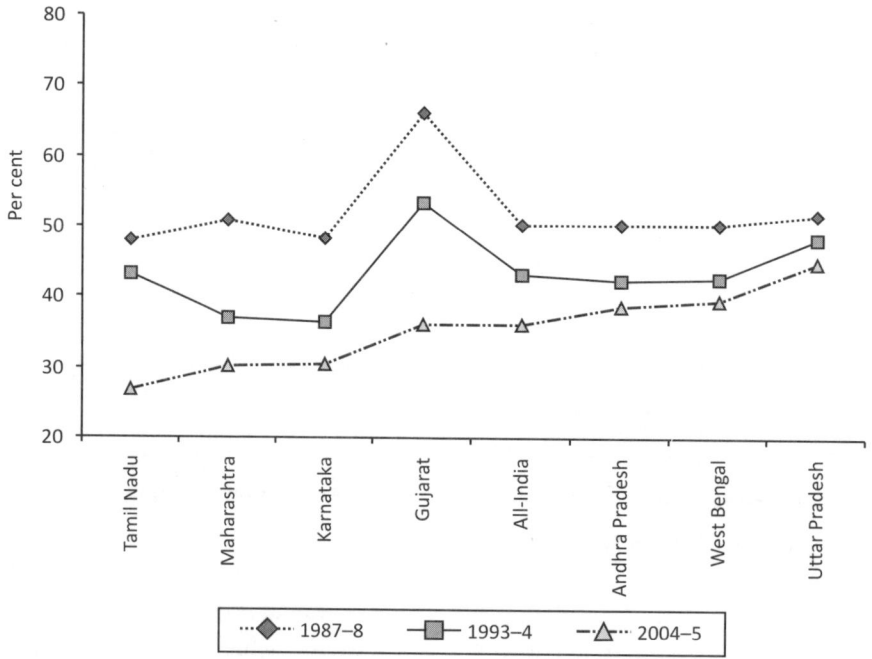

**Figure 4.15**   Percentage Males in Metros with No or Low Education Levels, by States, Over Time
*Source*: Data taken from Tables A4.3, A4.7, and A4.13.

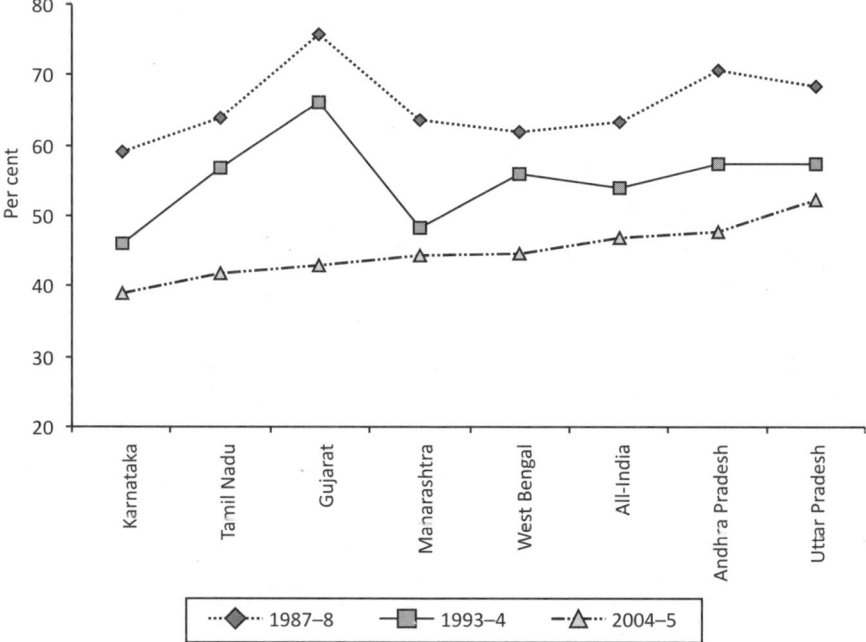

**Figure 4.16**  Percentage Females in Metros with No or Low Education Levels, by States, Over Time

*Source*: Data taken from Tables A4.4, A4.8, and A4.14.

two types; low income but with a long history of social sector intervention and high income (Figures 4.17 and 4.18). But among the worst performing states, in the case of males both low-income and high-income states were present whereas among females only low income states were present.

Low levels of education and low levels of regular employment and vice versa are what we would have expected. This means that if a state has a high proportion of those with no or low education, there would be low regular employment (these states are in bold letters in Table 4.5) and conversely if the state had low illiteracy and high education, the proportion of workers in regular employment will be high (these states are in italics in Table 4.5). However, we do not see such a clear pattern across the states in Table 4.5 except in the case of males and females in metros.

We also analysed the relationship between low levels of education and employment in ML jobs, as no or low level of education would fetch unskilled work (Table 4.6). There was a closer fit in this relationship than with regular employment. High manual labour correlating with a high proportion of the population with no or low education was expected and both developed and less developed states showed this relationship. The converse situation, where there was low manual labour and a low proportion of the population with no or low education, also existed in both developed as well as less developed states. These states are in italics in Table 4.6.

**HIGHER EDUCATION**

The proportion of the literate population educated up to the graduate level and above, that is, those who reached the tertiary level of

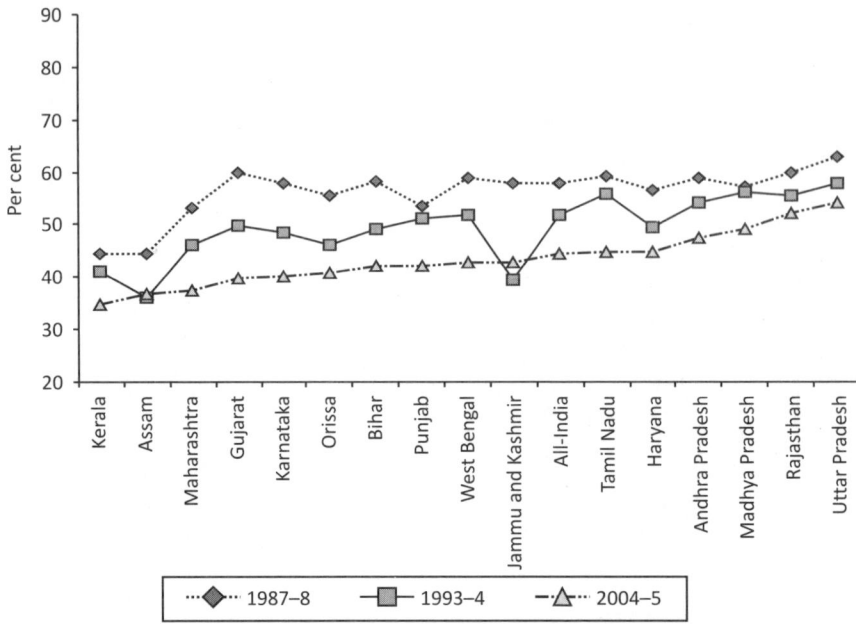

**Figure 4.17**    Percentage Males in Non-metros with No or Low Education Levels, by States, Over Time
*Source*: Data taken from Tables A4.3, A4.7, and A4.13.

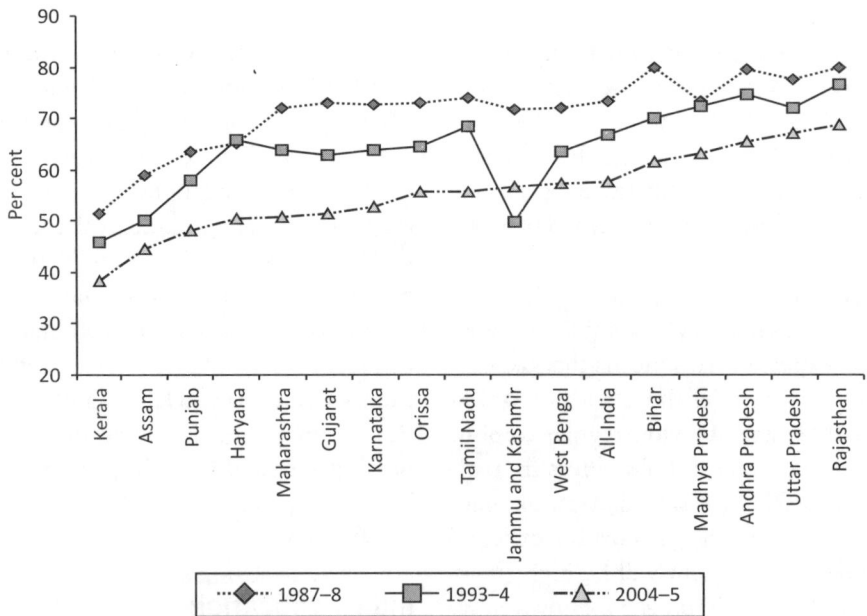

**Figure 4.18**    Percentage Females in Non-metros with No or Low Education Levels, by States, Over Time
*Source*: Data taken from Tables A4.4, A4.8, and A4.14.

**Table 4.5**    Distribution of States by No or Low Education Levels and Proportion of Regular Employed, 2004–5

| | | Metros<br>Male Regular Employed | | Non-metros<br>Male Regular Employed | |
| --- | --- | --- | --- | --- | --- |
| | | High | Low | High | Low |
| Males with No or Low Education | High | Haryana, Punjab | **Andhra Pradesh, Madhya Pradesh, Rajasthan, Uttar Pradesh, West Bengal** | Andhra Pradesh, Haryana, Madhya Pradesh, Tamil Nadu | **Rajasthan, Uttar Pradesh** |
| | Low | *Gujarat, Maharashtra, Tamil Nadu* | Bihar, Karnataka | *Assam, Gujarat, Karnataka, Maharashtra, Punjab* | Bihar, Jammu and Kashmir, Kerala, Orissa, West Bengal |
| | | Female Regular Employed | | Female Regular Employed | |
| Females with No or Low Education | High | Andhra Pradesh, Bihar | **Haryana, Punjab, Rajasthan, Uttar Pradesh** | Madhya Pradesh | **Andhra Pradesh, Bihar, Rajasthan, Uttar Pradesh** |
| | Low | *Karnataka, Maharashtra, Tamil Nadu* | Gujarat, Madhya Pradesh, West Bengal | *Assam, Haryana, Kerala, Orissa, Punjab, Tamil Nadu, West Bengal* | Gujarat, Jammu and Kashmir, Karnataka, Maharashtra |

*Source*: Data taken from Tables A3.12, A3.13, A4.13, and A4.14.
*Note*: High and low pertain to above and below the all-India average.

**Table 4.6**    Distribution of States by No or Low Education Level and Proportion Employed as Manual Labour, 2004–5

| | | Metros<br>Male Manual Labour | | Non-metros<br>Male Manual Labour | |
| --- | --- | --- | --- | --- | --- |
| | | High | Low | High | Low |
| Males with No or Low Education | High | **Andhra Pradesh, Haryana, Punjab, Rajasthan, West Bengal** | Madhya Pradesh, Uttar Pradesh | **Andhra Pradesh, Madhya Pradesh, Tamil Nadu, Uttar Pradesh** | Jammu and Kashmir, Kerala, Maharashtra |
| | Low | Gujarat | *Bihar, Karnataka, Maharashtra, Tamil Nadu* | Haryana, Rajasthan | *Assam, Bihar, Gujarat, Karnataka, Orissa, Punjab, West Bengal* |
| | | Female Manual Labour | | Female Manual Labour | |
| Females with No or Low Education | High | **Haryana, Punjab, Rajasthan, Uttar Pradesh** | Andhra Pradesh, Bihar | **Bihar, Madhya Pradesh, Rajasthan, Uttar Pradesh** | Andhra Pradesh |
| | Low | Gujarat, Karnataka, Madhya Pradesh | *Maharashtra, Tamil Nadu, West Bengal* | Gujarat, Jammu and Kashmir, Maharashtra, Tamil Nadu | *Assam, Haryana, Karnataka, Kerala, Orissa, Punjab, West Bengal* |

*Source*: Data taken from Tables A3.32, A3.33, A4.13, and A4.14.
*Note*: High and low pertain to above and below the all-India average.

education, increased with an increase in the size class of urban centres and was higher among males than among females in all the size classes of urban centres. The trend of an increasing proportion of tertiary level of education with time and a higher proportion of these people in larger cities than in smaller ones is clear in Figures 4.19 and 4.20. In this figure one can see that: (i) metro cities had a consistently higher proportion of those educated up to the tertiary level among the literates than non-metros in all the years, (ii) over time, this proportion increased in both metros and non-metros, (iii) over time this proportion increased for both males and females, (iv) in all the years, a higher proportion of literate males than literate females reached the tertiary level of education, and (v) the gap between metros and non-metros increased in the reforms period as compared to the pre-reforms period in the case of females and reduced in the case of males (Table 4.7). The proportion of literates

reaching tertiary level increased by 5.2 percentage points among males and by 6.8 percentage points among females in this entire period of 18 years. This is very slow progress in achieving the tertiary level of education among metro cities in India.

**Table 4.7**    Ratio of Metro to Non-metro in Percentage Literates Reaching Graduate Level

|        | 1987–8 | 1993–4 | 2004–5 |
|--------|--------|--------|--------|
| Male   | 1.45   | 1.46   | 1.41   |
| Female | 1.56   | 1.92   | 1.60   |

*Source*: Calculated by authors using data taken from Tables A4.3, A4.4, A4.7, A4.8, A4.13, and A4.14.

In non-metros, the proportion of literates reaching the tertiary level of education in 2004–5 was just 13.3 per cent among males and 10.5 per cent among females. This was an increase of 4.0 percentage points for males from 9.3 per cent in 1987–8 and 4.0 percentage points for females from 6.5 per cent in 1987–8.

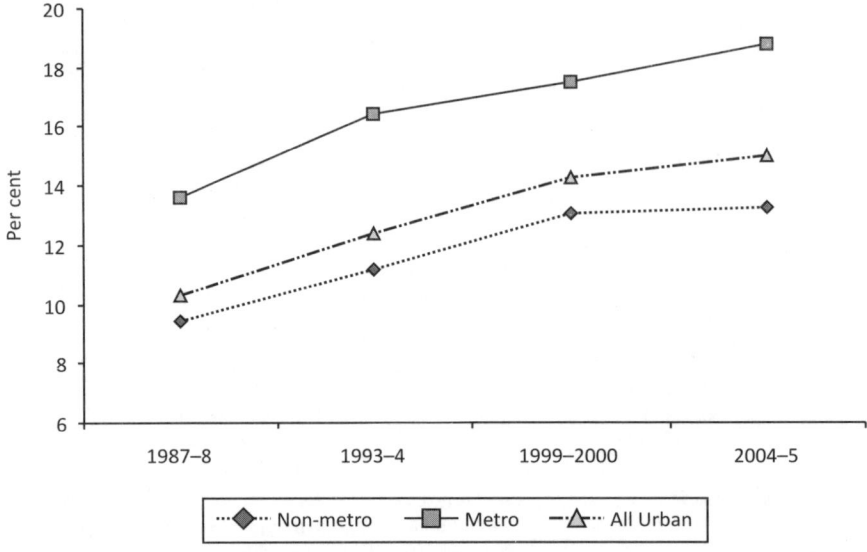

**Figure 4.19**    Percentage Male Literates Studied up to Graduate and Above Levels, Over Time

*Source*: Calculated by authors using data taken from Tables A4.3, A4.4, A4.7, A4.8, A4.13, A4.14, and A4.15.

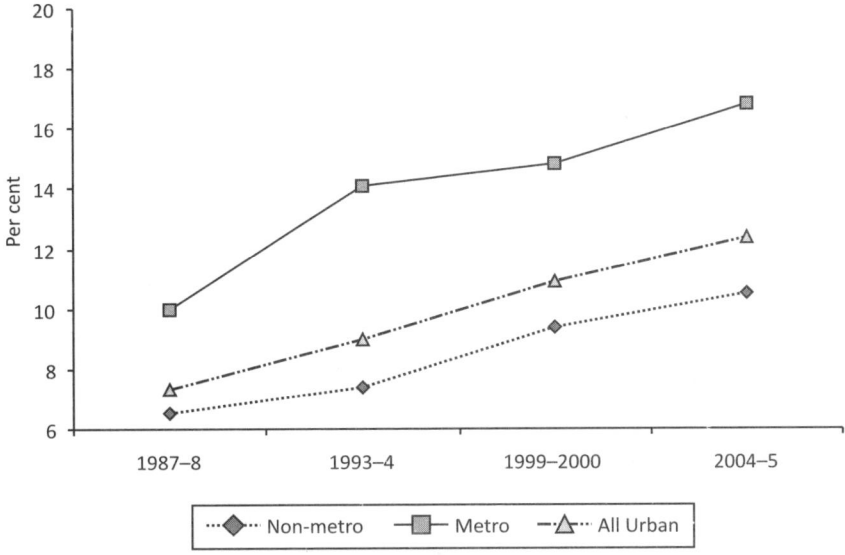

**Figure 4.20**   Percentage Female Literates Studied up to Graduate and Above Levels, Over Time

*Source*: Calculated by authors using data taken from Tables A4.3, A4.4, A4.7, A4.8, A4.13, A4.14, and A4.15.

This means that opportunities to reach and also demand tertiary level education were higher in metros than in non-metros and that these improved over time. As with other aspects of education, females in non-metros achieved the slowest progress in education attainments in the last 18 years in urban India.

It is interesting to note that the gender gap (proportion of literate males reaching the tertiary level of education divided by the proportion of literate females reaching the tertiary level of education) declined over time and it also declined with an increase in size classes of urban centres. For example, in non-metros in 1987–8 the gender gap was 1.45, which reduced to 1.27 in 2004–5 (Table 4.8). In metros in 1987–8, this ratio was 1.36, which reduced to 1.12 in 2004–5. There was therefore a significant narrowing of the gender gap with regard to higher education in metropolitan cities in 2004–5 as compared to non-metros. In the case of metros, the gender gap reduced

faster in the pre-reforms period whereas in the case of non-metros, it reduced faster in the reforms period.

**Table 4.8**   Gender Gap in Percentage Literates Reaching Graduate Level

|            | 1987–8 | 1993–4 | 2004–5 |
|------------|--------|--------|--------|
| Metro      | 1.36   | 1.15   | 1.12   |
| Non-metros | 1.45   | 1.51   | 1.27   |

*Source*: Data taken from Tables A4.3, A4.4, A4.7, A4.8, A4.13, and A4.14.

It is surprising to note that Gujarat, Maharashtra, and Karnataka, the three developed and high urbanized states were at the bottom with regard to literate males reaching the tertiary level of education in their metros (Figure 4.21). In contrast, the states of Tamil Nadu, Andhra Pradesh, and Uttar Pradesh performed better in this indicator of education (for males) in metros. In the case of females in metros, once again Gujarat and Maharashtra

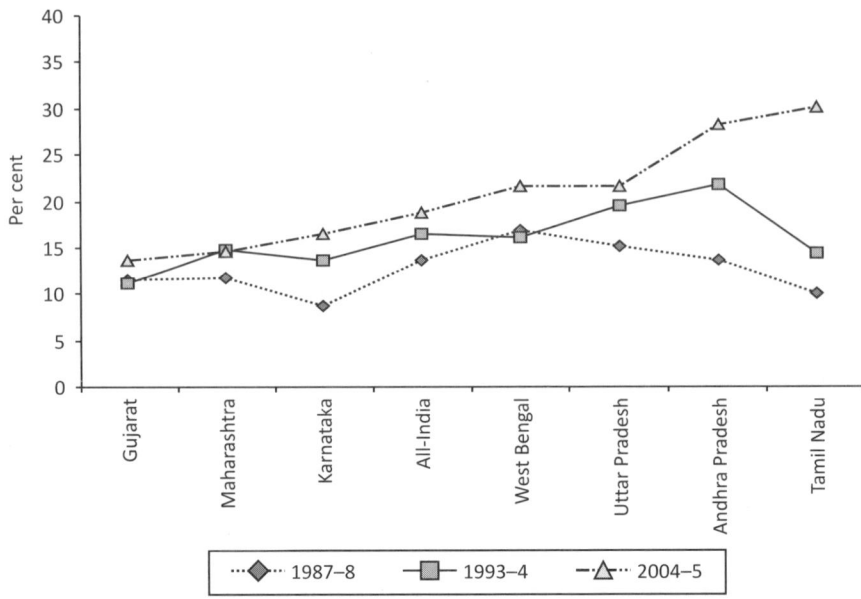

**Figure 4.21**    Percentage Male Literates Studied up to Graduate and Above Levels in Metros, by States, Over Time

*Source*: Calculated by authors using data taken from Tables A4.3, A4.7, and A4.13.

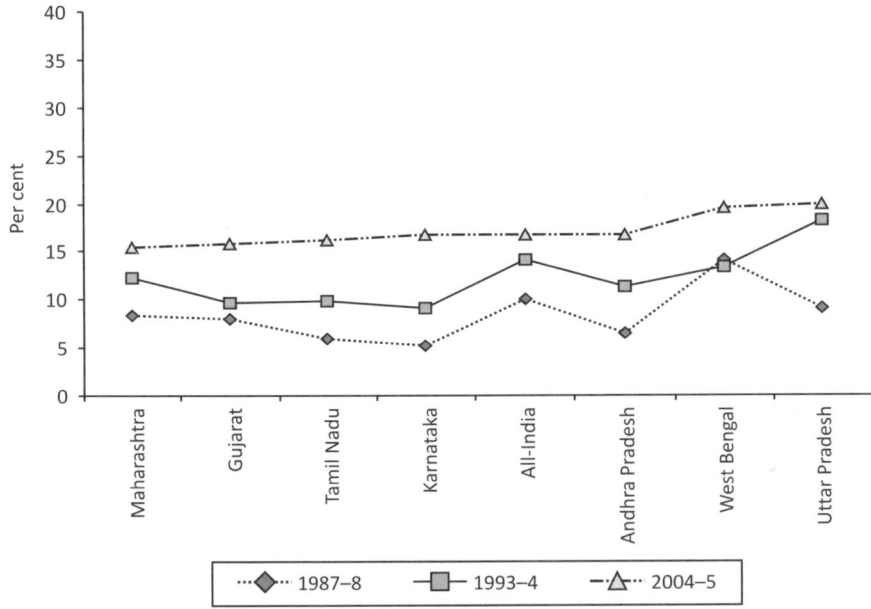

**Figure 4.22**    Percentage Female Literates Studied up to Graduate and Above Levels in Metros, by States, Over Time

*Source*: Calculated by authors using data taken from Tables A4.4, A4.8, and A4.14.

found themselves at the bottom along with Tamil Nadu, whereas Uttar Pradesh, West Bengal, and Andhra Pradesh were towards the top (Figure 4.22). However, if we observe the extent of improvement in this indicator of education then we see the fastest change in Andhra Pradesh, Tamil Nadu, and Karnataka for males as well as females. Probably, the coming of information technology (IT) and IT enabled services (ITES) in metro cities in these states was because of availability of a tertiary level educated population. In Gujarat and Maharashtra, the change was very little in case of males and among the lowest in the case of females in metros. This probably is one reason why new economy activities have not come to Gujarat.

The non-metro situation is very interesting. In the case of males, the less developed states such as Assam, Bihar, Madhya Pradesh, and Orissa were at the top with regard to literates reaching the tertiary level (Figure 4.23). It seems that the population in these states considers education as a way of getting access to better employment opportunities and through that of moving out of low-income conditions. Gujarat, Maharashtra, and Tamil Nadu were in the league of five worst performing states in this indicator in the case of males. In the case of females, the most urbanized and high-income states, namely, Gujarat, Maharashtra, Tamil Nadu, and Karnataka along with Andhra Pradesh were in the bottom five (Figure 4.24). At the top, there was no particular pattern. It is to be noted that industrial leaders in India—Gujarat and Maharashtra—were laggards in their urban population reaching the tertiary level of education in both metros as well as non-metros.

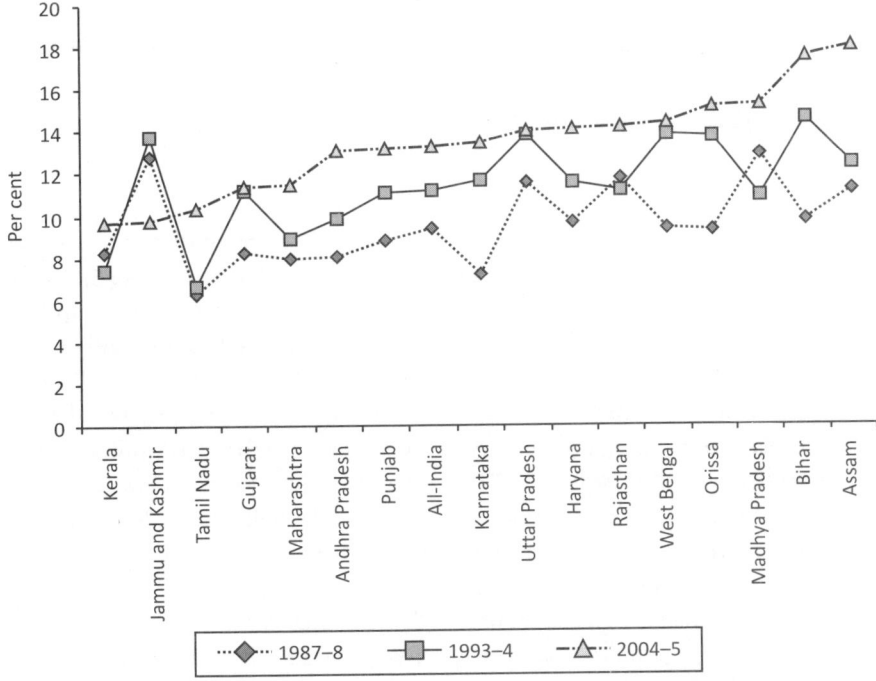

**Figure 4.23**  Percentage Male Literates Studied up to Graduate and Above Levels in Non-metros, by States, Over Time

*Source*: Calculated by authors using data taken from Tables A4.3, A4.7, and A4.13.

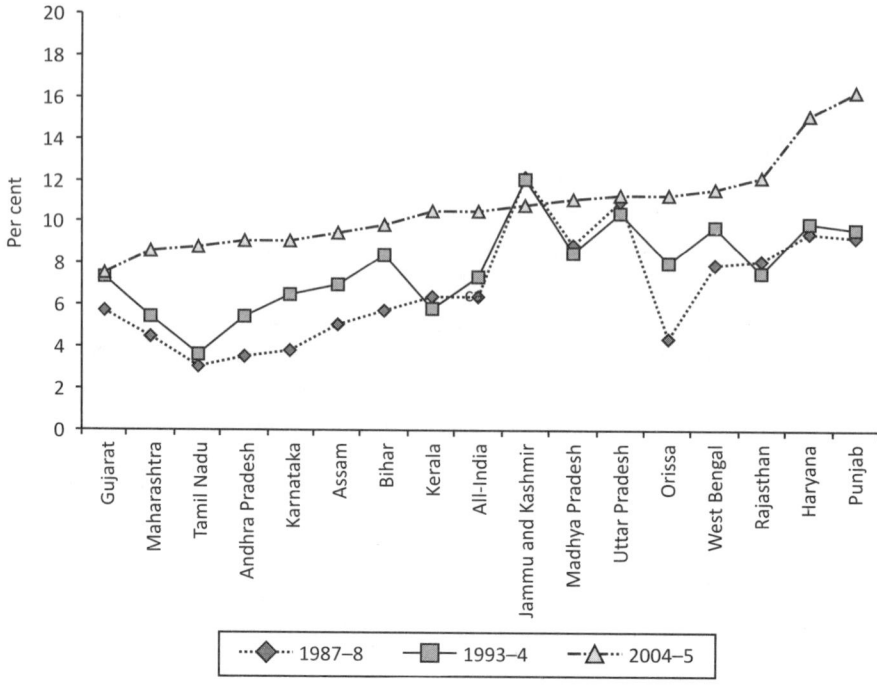

**Figure 4.24**    Percentage Female Literates Studied up to Graduate and Above Levels in Non-metros, by States, Over Time

*Source*: Calculated by authors using data taken from Tables A4.4, A4.8, and A4.14.

Lastly, in the case of all the states, improvements were observed in all the states except in Jammu and Kashmir in 2004–5 as compared to previous years.

In general, there was a positive relationship between the proportion of literates with graduate and above levels of education and employment in Administrative/Professional (A/P) jobs (Table 4.9). This linkage was stronger in metros than in non-metros. Also, it was stronger for males in metros than for females in metros. The less developed states had a high proportion of males and females with graduate and above levels of education in their non-metros. But they did not find employment in high skilled jobs because these are not located in these cities. Probably such levels of employment would

be located where infrastructure is available and not just an educated population. Conversely, there was a negative relationship between the tertiary level of education and employment in Manual Labour (ML) type of jobs. We have not shown this in a figure but the correlations presented in Table 4.10 indicate this. The correlation values in this table are not significant, but they do point towards the direction of the relationship.

**CONCLUSIONS**

This chapter shows that literacy rates as well as levels of education attained by the population living in non-metros, and in particular in Small and Medium Towns (SMTs) was lower than that in metros. This was primarily due to

**Table 4.9**    Distribution of States by Graduate and Above Education Levels and Proportion Employed in Administrative and Professional Services, 2004–5

| | | Metros Male Administrative and Professional Services | | Non-metros Male Administrative and Professional Services | |
|---|---|---|---|---|---|
| | | High | Low | High | Low |
| Males with Graduate and Above Education | High | Tamil Nadu, West Bengal | Andhra Pradesh, Bihar, Madhya Pradesh, Uttar Pradesh | Karnataka, Orissa, Rajasthan, West Bengal | Assam, Bihar, Haryana, Madhya Pradesh, Uttar Pradesh |
| | Low | | Gujarat, Haryana, Karnataka, Maharashtra, Punjab, Rajasthan | Gujarat, Maharashtra, Punjab | Andhra Pradesh, Jammu and Kashmir, Kerala, Tamil Nadu |
| | | Female Administrative and Professional Services | | Female Administrative and Professional Services | |
| Females with Graduate and Above Education | High | Andhra Pradesh, Madhya Pradesh, Uttar Pradesh, West Bengal | Punjab | Haryana, Kerala, Orissa, Punjab, Rajasthan, West Bengal | Jammu and Kashmir, Madhya Pradesh, Uttar Pradesh |
| | Low | Bihar, Maharashtra, Tamil Nadu | Gujarat, Haryana, Karnataka, Rajasthan | Assam, Maharashtra | Andhra Pradesh, Bihar, Gujarat, Karnataka, Tamil Nadu |

*Source*: Data taken from Tables A3.32, A3.33, A4.13, and A4.14.

*Note*: High and low pertain to above and below the all-India average.

two reasons: low demand for education, in particular for higher education, and low supply. Demand for education, in particular for higher education, could have been low because of the following reasons: (i) high poverty (an aspect we see in Chapter 2) and hence inability to sustain children in the educational system for long years as compared to metropolitan cities, (ii) lack of employment opportunities and hence families getting dissuaded to invest more years in education, and (iii) lack of employment opportunities requiring high levels of education and skills. For women, in addition to these reasons there may also be other social reasons: (i) families not wanting to invest in a girl's education as she may not be useful to the parental family after she gets married, and (ii) difficulty in finding a husband for a well educated girl in a situation where demand for education among young males is low.

The low supply of education infrastructure in SMTs as compared to metropolitan cities, and in particular of higher order education facilities is because of the following reasons: (i) economies of scale; as a higher order of settlements tends to attract a higher order of facilities as smaller settlements do not have the threshold population to sustain higher order facilities, (ii) low financial capabilities of SMTs to invest in social facilities due to their low economic base and particular inability to attract investments in higher order social facilities, and (iii) low attractiveness of the place for professionals to seek jobs and resultant shortage of skilled human resources to operate higher order social facilities. Through policy, some of the supply as

**Table 4.10**  Correlations of Different Indicators of Education with that of Employment

| | | | | Correlation Value with | | |
|---|---|---|---|---|---|---|
| | WPR | % Employed as Regular Workers | % Employed in Secondary Sector | % Employed in Tertiary Sector | % Employed Administrative in & Professional Services | % Employed as Manual Labour |
| **Non-metro males** | | | | | | |
| % literates reaching tertiary level of education | −0.47 | 0.05 | −0.81 | 0.78 | 0.13 | −0.52 |
| % literates with low levels of education | −0.29 | −0.14 | 0.16 | −0.10 | −0.23 | 0.28 |
| % literate | 0.53 | 0.25 | −0.02 | 0.01 | 0.22 | −0.20 |
| % with no or low levels of education | −0.29 | −0.14 | 0.16 | −0.10 | −0.23 | 0.28 |
| **Non-metro females** | | | | | | |
| % literates reaching tertiary level of education | −0.33 | 0.29 | −0.34 | 0.17 | 0.74 | −0.55 |
| % literates with low levels of education | −0.01 | −0.68 | 0.39 | −0.60 | −0.53 | 0.63 |
| % literate | 0.13 | 0.69 | −0.17 | 0.62 | 0.37 | −0.55 |
| % with no or low levels of education | −0.01 | −0.68 | 0.39 | −0.60 | −0.53 | 0.63 |
| **Metro males** | | | | | | |
| % literates reaching tertiary level of education | −0.06 | −0.64 | −0.69 | 0.72 | 0.70 | −0.73 |
| % literates with low levels of education | 0.13 | 0.10 | 0.39 | −0.45 | −0.51 | 0.57 |
| % literate | −0.28 | 0.11 | −0.18 | 0.21 | 0.18 | −0.31 |
| % with no or low levels of education | 0.13 | 0.10 | 0.39 | −0.45 | −0.51 | 0.57 |
| **Metro females** | | | | | | |
| % literates reaching tertiary level of education | 0.31 | −0.09 | 0.10 | 0.08 | −0.43 | 0.08 |
| % literates with low levels of education | 0.10 | 0.52 | −0.41 | 0.44 | 0.30 | −0.35 |
| % literate | −0.08 | −0.22 | −0.27 | −0.23 | −0.16 | −0.12 |
| % with no or low levels of education | −0.13 | −0.17 | −0.21 | 0.09 | 0.36 | −0.29 |

*Source*: Calculated by the authors using data from Tables A4.13, A4.14, A3.12, A3.13, A3.22, A3.23, A3.32, and A3.33.

well as demand side problems can be resolved but only if we look at the urban economy in a disaggregated manner.

Metropolitan India, which is to lead India's global economic integration, has still not achieved full literacy. About 8 per cent of the males and 20 per cent of the females are still illiterate. It might be argued that full literacy is not there because of new migrants. We might recall, and as Mahadevia (2008) has argued elsewhere, metropolitan cities in India have seen a deceleration in population growth. Thus, new migrants are not responsible for the metros not reaching a full literacy situation. The answer has to be sought in both demand for education from the low income urban population and also supply of primary education.

The less developed states, or those that are part of the BIMARU states (except Bihar), namely Uttar Pradesh and Rajasthan, have high illiteracy rates among males as well as females in metros cities. In Jaipur, 44 per cent females and 15 per cent males are illiterate. What is surprising is that metropolitan Punjab, namely Ludhiana, has very high illiteracy levels—15 per cent among males and 25 per cent among females. Is this a problem of a small sample in Ludhiana? May be not, because 13 per cent of the males and 22 per cent of the females in the whole of urban Punjab were illiterate in 2004–5. Punjab ranks number one in per capita gross domestic product (GDP) among the large Indian states. The second richest state in terms of per capita GDP is Haryana, where also female illiteracy rates were 27 per cent for the whole urban, 24 per cent in non-metros, and 37 per cent in metros. The metros in Haryana are Faridabad and Gurgaon, both close to Delhi, and even then they perform dismally on literacy rates for females. In the case of Haryana, high female illiteracy in urban areas could be because of cultural factors.

The metro non-metro gap in literacy rates still exists but it is heartening to know that it came down to 1.04 in 2004–5 from 1.09 in 1987–8 for males and from 1.25 to 1.09 for females in the same period. But females in non-metros are at the greatest disadvantage with regard to literacy and have witnessed the slowest improvement in literacy rates.

While literacy rates have improved in non-metros over time, this improvement has been more in the case of males than in the case of females. The other observation is that the gender gap is higher in the case of non-metros than in the case of metros.

It would be interesting to see how education indicators relate with those for employment. The correlations are given in Table 4.10. Employment in the secondary sector has a negative relationship with the tertiary level of education and the relationship is significant in case of non-metro males. In the case of metro as well as non-metro males, we observe a positive relationship between the tertiary level of education and employment in the tertiary sector. In the case of females, in metros as well as non-metros all the relationships are weak and hence whether females get literate or reach higher levels of education, whether they are in gainful employment or the type of employment women choose is influenced by factors not under study in this book.

Further, we also find in this chapter that while there has been a significant decline in illiteracy rates across size classes of towns for males as well as females over time a similar decline is not observed when illiterates and those with education up to the primary or below levels are clubbed together. This is more in the case of non-metros, particularly with regard to females—45 per cent of the males in non-metros and 36 per cent of them in metros are either not literate or had not even completed the primary level of education in 2004–5. The percentages for females were even higher— 58 per cent in non-metros and 47 per cent in metros.

The proportion of the literate population which reached the tertiary level of education is still very low in urban India. In 2004–5, 19 per cent males and 17 per cent females among the literate population in the metros had reached the tertiary level of education. This is quite low. Obviously and expectedly, in non-metros these figures were just 13 and 11 per cent for males and females respectively. Further, metro/non metro disparity with regard to reaching the tertiary level education reduced for males over time but increased for females. As with other aspects of education, females in non-metros achieved the slowest progress in education attainments in the last 18 years in urban India.

Although in Indian policy discussions it is widely accepted that growth of the manufacturing sector is essential for generating adequate employment this does not let India give up on the advantage she has in the tertiary sector and to maintain that advantage, urban India will need tertiary sector employment at the high end. However, a large part of the tertiary sector is a residual sector and employment is in low-paid services. And hence, to not just maintain this advantage but also make a transition to a developed economy, it is essential that not just literacy rates but educational attainments of the entire urban population, metro and non-metro, males and females, be improved to at least the elementary level.

This analysis shows that urban development is biased wherein education opportunities, that is, opportunities to improve human capabilities are found more in large cities and metropolises than in small towns. This implies that those in large cities have better and higher wage jobs than those in small towns. This means that those in large cities have higher capability and get better opportunities to come out of poverty than those in small towns. This situation of lop-sided development in the urban system is changing, but very slowly.

# 5

# Access to Water and Sanitation

Urban poverty is multi dimensional. Reduction in deprivation does not mean just employment at an income to ensure living above the poverty line but also acceptable living conditions—access to an adequate and clean water supply, availability of sanitation, accessibility to work and other basic needs—availability of primary healthcare and access to primary education. Urban areas also pose another problem, of vulnerabilities, on account of fluctuations in the labour market resulting in temporary loss of employment and lack of access to water and sanitation resulting in an increase in the health burden, resulting in the household slipping down into poverty, loss of shelter on account of slum demolitions and displacements, and urban violence. Lack of access to basic services is deprivation as well as a cause for increase in household vulnerability.

Safe water and sanitation are basic requirements for a dignified and healthy life for all, women and men, and are therefore entitlements that every Indian citizen should enjoy. In the Indian context, they are an extension of the fundamental right to life. These entitlements

contribute directly and indirectly to achieving the Millennium Development Goals (MDGs) by 2015 and also to the goals of the Eleventh Five Year Plan by 2012 based on an approach of 'inclusive growth'. Safe water and sanitation are extremely important in the urban context because of the high density of living.

Safe water and sanitation have very large positive externalities and by that they qualify to be public goods. Lack of safe water and sanitation cause outbreaks of epidemics and Indian cities are every year affected by these. The impact of epidemics on the poor is much larger than it is on non-poor for many reasons; firstly epidemics break out in areas where the poor live, their access to safe water and sanitation is far lower than non-poor, and since their nutritional status is poor they succumb more easily to epidemics than non-poor. Thus, lack of safe water and sanitation cause health disorders and keep mortality rates high in general and among the poor in particular.

Lack of storm water drains leads to water logging every monsoon and outbreak of vector diseases such as malaria, dengue, and leptospirosis that afflict the poor the most as they live in settlements that are in low-lying and unserviced areas.

Lack of solid waste management also leads to the outbreak of numerous diseases and causes clogging of drains that lead to water logging and subsequent problems. In all, safe water and sanitation for all urban residents is the key to improving the urban health situation, a path which all developed countries took before medicines were even invented to address the disease burden.

There is a very strong gender dimension to safe water and sanitation. Women bear the maximum brunt if these are not available. They are forced to spend time and energy collecting water for household use and by that are forced to give up on income-generating opportunities and leisure time. There are severe health consequences of such work on women. In the absence of sanitation they have to go out for defecation in the dark, increasing risks of sexual violence. They are unable to go out in the day time for defecation, which also has adverse health consequences. Higher morbidity rates within families because of lack of these services forces women to spend time on caring for the sick within the family and thereby increase their burden. This also leads to poor health status of women and lower incomes in their hands.

This chapter deals with the level of services across different size classes of urban centres. This analysis of access to various urban facilities in different size classes of towns across states in India is based on four Rounds of the NSS data; the 49th Round (January–June 1993), the 54th Round (January–June 1998), the 58th Round (July–December 2002), and the 65th Round (2008–9 surveys). The facilities covered are drinking water, bathrooms, drainage, toilets, and garbage collection. Data on garbage collection is not available in the 49th

Round. Under each of the facilities, firstly we compare and contrast two periods: (i) 49th to 54th Rounds, and (ii) 58th to 65th Rounds at the all-India level and by states. For facilities for which data is not available for all the four years we first present the status for the latest Round and then compare it with the earlier Round's status. The data are given in Tables A5.1 to A5.21.

The focus of all the four Rounds was not similar. The NSS 49th Round enquired about household conditions and migration, the NSS 54th Round centred on sanitation and hygiene and services, and the 58th and 65th Rounds concentrated on housing conditions. However, there are few common aspects on urban facilities covered by all these rounds which have been comparatively analysed in this chapter. It will be interesting to examine improvement/deterioration in urban facilities in different size classes of towns across different states.

There is another limitation of this exercise. Firstly, the NSS 49th Round is largely based on size classification of towns as in the 1981 population census and the NSS 54th and 58th Rounds are based on size classification of towns as in the 1991 census. The 65th Round is based on size classification of census 2001. Certain surveyed towns may fall in different size classes of towns in the earlier two Rounds of the survey. Thus, the universe in the 54th and 58th Rounds is not the same as in the 49th Round and that in the 65th Round is not the same as that in the 54th and 58th Rounds. Secondly, the overall sample size and sample distribution of households across different size classes of towns were different in different surveys making the results not strictly comparable. These methodological anomalies have to be kept in mind while analysing the data. Lastly, the analysis gives us a very broad picture of the metro versus non-metro situation given the anomalies in the data.

## DRINKING WATER FACILITIES

Urban households that had access to tap water stood at 70 per cent in 1993. Hardly any improvement in access to tap water was observed from 1993 to 1998. But in the present decade, in 2002 and 2008–9, some improvement in access to tap water at all-India level can be seen (Figure 5.1). In 2008–9, 23 per cent of the households did not have access to tap water at the all-India level. In 1998, no change from the 1993 situation can be observed because there was a decline in the proportion of metro households that had access to tap water. The main factor seems to be the reclassification of some of the larger sized towns to the metropolis category in the states of Bihar and Uttar Pradesh. However, substantial improvement in access to tap water was observed in these newly classified metropolises from 2002 to 2008–9, and metropolises in these states reached the level of access to tap water that existed in 1993. But improvements over the entire period were marginal, from 85.1 per cent to 85.8 per cent only. Thus, 14 per cent

of the households in the metros continued to remain without access to tap water.

The difference between metro and non-metro towns was substantial in 1993, which reduced substantially in 1998 but thereon maintained a trend of a declining gap. This was on account of improvements in this service in non-metros where non-availability of tap water for households reduced from 34 per cent to 26 per cent. Contrary to expectations, improvements in non-metros were higher than in metros with regard to access to tap water. But the improvements were much less than desired. In the metros, which are the JNNURM mission cities, we should have expected 100 per cent tap water coverage.

The lowest sized (C1) towns were most constrained in this regard as compared to larger sized towns. In the former, just 53 per cent of the households had access to tap water supply in 1993. This situation hardly changed in 1998 but substantial improvements were observed in 2008–9 when 69 per cent of the households

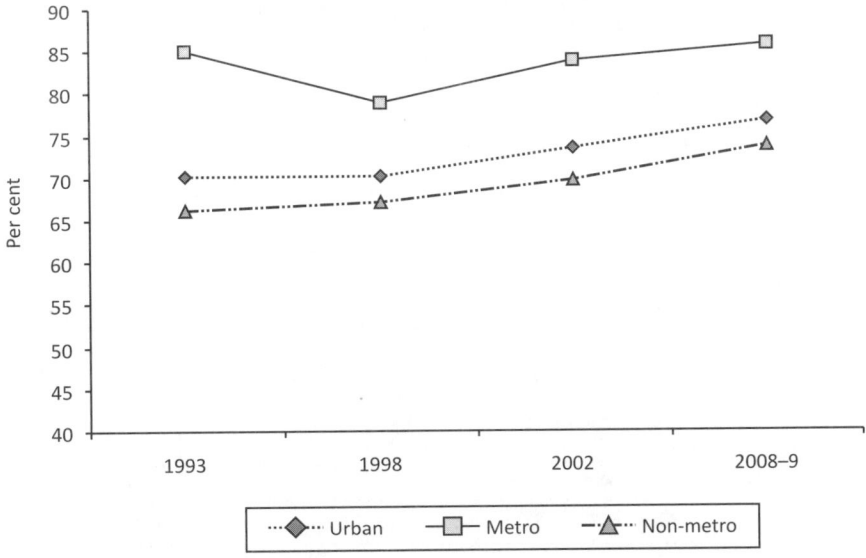

**Figure 5.1**   Access to Tap Water by Size Class, Over Time

*Source*: Data taken from Table A5.2.

residing in this size class of towns had access to tap water and the difference with larger-sized non-metro towns considerably reduced.

Karnataka leads in percentage households having access to tap water among the metros (Figure 5.2). Bangalore, the metro in the state reached nearly 100 per cent access to tap water in 2008–9. This was followed by Maharashtra where 97 per cent households in the metros had access to tap water. In all the states except West Bengal, Maharashtra, and Karnataka, there was worsening of the access to this service in 2008–9 as compared to either 2002 or any of the previous years of data (Figure 5.2). Metros in all the states registered extension of their boundaries and the peri-urban areas merged within the boundaries could be deficit in water supply infrastructure. This is one explanation. But Bangalore too registered expansion of her boundaries and even then, the metro reached

near 100 per cent access to tap water. The explanation therefore lies in lack of priority for water supply services in metropolitan cities, which probably deteriorated over time. It is also possible that water supply lines may have been laid out in a city but its slum settlements and low income groups may not have got connections in their houses. The NSSO's slum data shows that only 78 per cent of the slum households had access to tap water (NSSO 2010: 17), and slums are largely a metropolitan phenomenon. JNNURM funding does not seem to have improved access to tap water for a section of households in metro cities and these households are the ones living in the slums and on pavements. Slums have to be connected to the existing water supply network. If a slum is considered illegal then Urban Local Bodies (ULBs) often do not want to extend water supply to it. The Basic Services for the Urban Poor

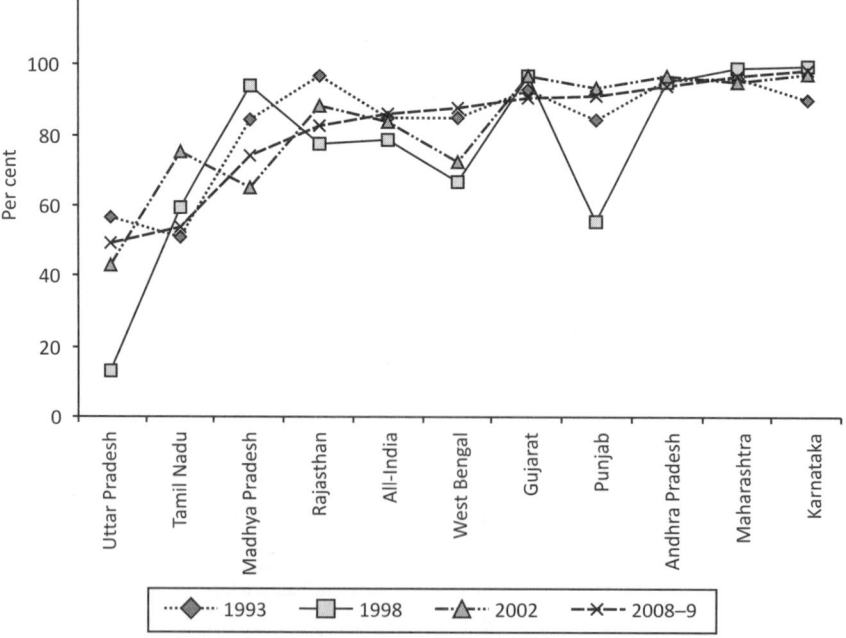

**Figure 5.2**    State-wise Access to Tap Water (% Households) in Metros, Over Time

*Source*: Data taken from Table A5.2.

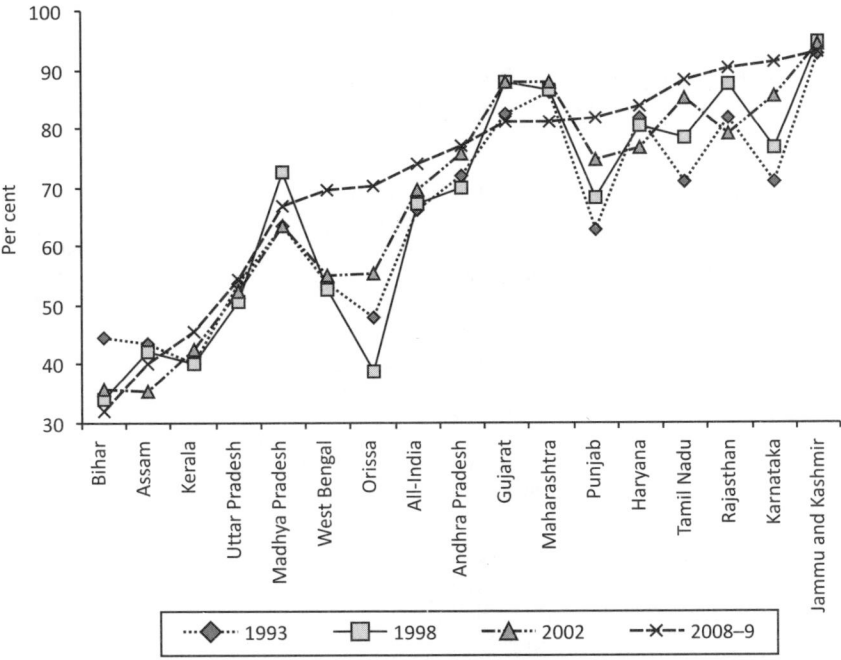

**Figure 5.3**　State-wise Access to Tap Water (% Households) Non-Metros, Over Time

*Source*: Data taken from Table A5.2.

(BSUP) programme under JNNURM is for this purpose but it has been utilized for constructing new houses rather than for extending basic services in existing slums. Mahadevia (2010b) has argued that connecting a slum settlement with water supply and sewerage lines gives a sense of *de facto* tenure security to the dwellers and that the ULBs do not intend to extend even this level of tenure security for fear that slum dwellers will permanently stake their claims on the city's land.

In non-metros, the worst performing states were Bihar, followed by Assam, Kerala, Uttar Pradesh, and Madhya Pradesh in an ascending order (Figure 5.3), and the best were Jammu and Kashmir, Karnataka, Rajasthan, Tamil Nadu, and Haryana in descending order. In Bihar, Assam, Gujarat, and Maharashtra the situation deteriorated in 2008–9 as compared to previous years. This also means that in all the states, although the gap between metros and non-metros declined somewhat, in the latter half of the decade of 2000, non-metros lost their capability to increase coverage of tap water to households. UIDSSMT also has not helped in improving the situation in non-metros, most likely because it has focussed on extending networks in cities and not connecting existing households to the network.

Table 5.1 shows the position of different the achievements of states in terms of households that had access to drinking water through taps in metro and non-metro cities. High and low means category of states that performed better and worse than the all-India level respectively. States in bold reflect those states that either improved/deteriorated their positions with respect to the all-India average in consecutive survey years. The italicized states are those where urbanization levels were higher than all-India

**Table 5.1**    Percentage of Households having Water Supply through Tap by States

|  |  | 1993 | 1998 | 2002 | 2008–9 |
|---|---|---|---|---|---|
| Metro | High | Andhra Pradesh, *Gujarat, Karnataka, Maharashtra,* Rajasthan | Andhra Pradesh, *Gujarat, Karnataka, Maharashtra,* **Madhya Pradesh** | Andhra Pradesh, *Gujarat, Karnataka, Maharashtra,* **Punjab, Rajasthan** | Andhra Pradesh, *Gujarat, Karnataka, Maharashtra, Punjab,* **West Bengal** |
|  | Low | Madhya Pradesh, *Punjab, Tamil Nadu,* Uttar Pradesh, West Bengal | Bihar, *Punjab,* **Rajasthan**, *Tamil Nadu,* Uttar Pradesh, West Bengal | Bihar, **Madhya Pradesh**, *Tamil Nadu,* Uttar Pradesh, West Bengal | Bihar, *Haryana,* Madhya Pradesh, **Rajasthan**, *Tamil Nadu,* Uttar Pradesh |
| Non-Metro | High | Andhra Pradesh, *Gujarat, Haryana,* Jammu and Kashmir, *Karnataka, Maharashtra,* Rajasthan, *Tamil Nadu* | Andhra Pradesh, *Gujarat, Haryana,* Jammu and Kashmir, *Karnataka, Maharashtra,* **Madhya Pradesh**, *Punjab*, Rajasthan, Tamil Nadu | Andhra Pradesh, *Gujarat, Haryana,* Jammu and Kashmir, *Karnataka, Maharashtra,* Punjab, Rajasthan, *Tamil Nadu* | Andhra Pradesh, *Gujarat, Haryana,* Jammu and Kashmir, *Karnataka, Maharashtra,* Punjab, Rajasthan, *Tamil Nadu* |
|  | Low | Assam, Bihar, Kerala, Madhya Pradesh, Orissa, *Punjab,* Uttar Pradesh, West Bengal | Assam, Bihar, Kerala, Orissa, Uttar Pradesh, West Bengal | Assam, Bihar, Kerala, **Madhya Pradesh**, Orissa, Uttar Pradesh, West Bengal | Assam, Bihar, Kerala, Madhya Pradesh, Orissa, Uttar Pradesh, West Bengal |

*Source*: Based on data from Table A5.2.

*Notes*: 1. States in bold signify movement from high (> all-India level) to low (< all-India level) or low to high in consecutive years.

2. Italicized states were high on the level of urbanization in 2001 (> all-India level).

(high) in census 2001. We have highlighted these states to check whether or not more urbanized states performed better than the less urbanized states in providing different types of urban facilities in general and here with regard to access to tap water for drinking purposes in particular.

In metro areas in 1990s the more urbanized states of Punjab and Tamil Nadu performed below the national average in providing tap water. In subsequent years only Punjab improved its position in metro areas. Among low urbanized states only Andhra Pradesh performed well throughout the period under study. The performance of less urbanized states of Madhya Pradesh and Rajasthan fluctuated in different years. Only in the last survey year of 2008–9,

did West Bengal shift to the category of better performing states.

In non-metro areas, the picture is clearer. Except for Punjab in 1993, in all the other years the more urbanized states performed better than the all-India average. Among the low urbanized states, Andhra Pradesh, Jammu and Kashmir, and Rajasthan performed better than the national average in all the years. The states which consistently performed badly on access to tap water were Assam, Bihar, Kerala, Orissa, Uttar Pradesh, West Bengal, and Madhya Pradesh in all years except one, in the case of non-metros.

At the all-India level a similar picture to that observed for access to tap water emerged with regard to the proportion of households having a drinking water source within the premises whether it was a tap, hand pump, or well in different years. At the all-India level, 66 per cent had a drinking water source within the premises in 1998. This percentage was the highest in metropolitan cities (76 per cent) and lowest in small (C1) towns (56 per cent). The corresponding figures for 2008–9 were 83.6 and 66 per cent, respectively (Figure 5.4 and Table A5.3). Unlike access to tap water, there was consistent improvement in availability of water within the premises in metros, non-metros, and all urban areas.

Unlike at the all-India level, the pattern of access to drinking water within the premises differed substantially across states (Figures 5.5 and 5.6). In Assam, Bihar, Kerala, Uttar Pradesh, and Punjab, a much larger proportion of the households reported access to drinking water supply within the premises than access to tap water. The reason lies in substantial reliance on other sources of drinking water within the premises—hand pumps and wells. In contrast, households in Andhra Pradesh, Karnataka, and Tamil Nadu reported far higher access to tap water than any other in-premises source. Further, households from small and medium towns in these states had much lower access to any source of drinking water within the premises than households in larger sized towns.

Having a drinking water source within the premises does not mean that households do not share the source of drinking water. At the all-India level in 2008–9, the proportion of households that had an exclusive source of drinking was much less—less than half of all the households and the difference in this regard across size classes of towns was much less (Table A5.5). In Andhra Pradesh and Tamil Nadu, where households relied largely on municipality taps as a source of drinking water, about three-fourth of all the households shared the source of drinking water in 2008–9. That is, just one-third of all the households had an

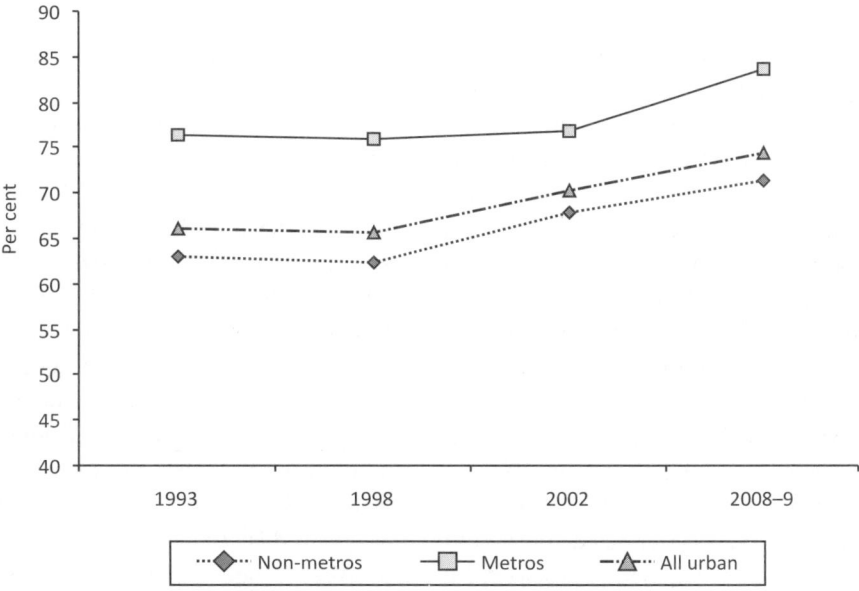

**Figure 5.4**    Access to Water within Premises, Over Time

*Source*: Data taken from Table A5.4.

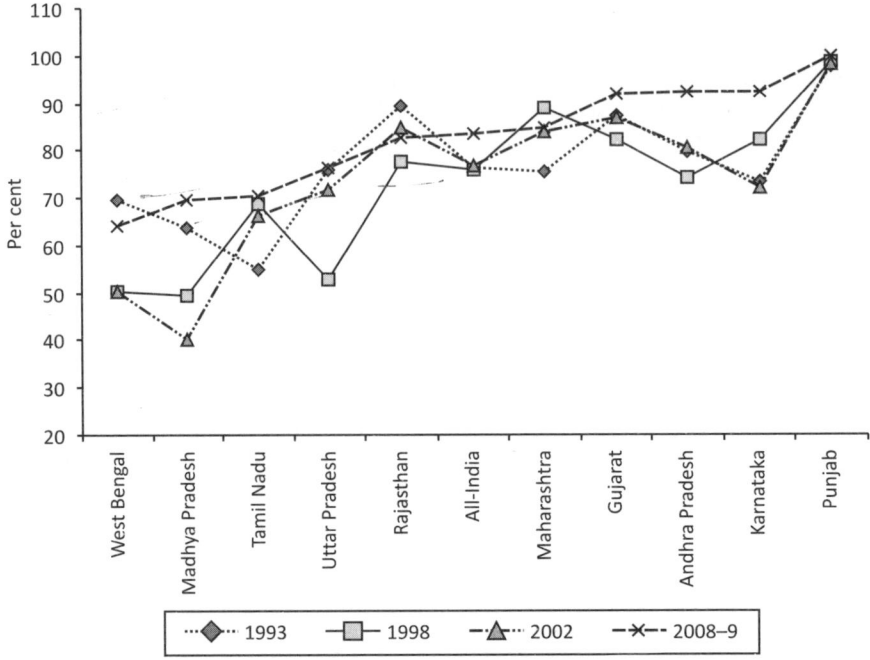

**Figure 5.5**    Access to Water within Premises in Metros by States, Over Time

*Source*: Data taken from Table A5.4.

individual source of drinking water. In states like Orissa and West Bengal, hardly one-fourth of all the households reported not sharing the source of drinking water. In Orissa and West Bengal, the phenomenon of multiple households staying in the same premises sharing a common source of drinking water seemed to be the most prevalent. In Assam, Kerala, and Uttar Pradesh where a much larger proportion of the households reported drinking water supply within the premises than access to tap water, more than half the households had individual access to drinking water in 2008–9. In these states the smaller size classes of towns performed better than larger sized towns and metros in this regard. Further, states where a higher proportion of households had access to taps for drinking water, a lesser proportion of the households in small and medium towns

compared to larger ones had an exclusive source of drinking water.

With regard to adequacy of drinking water available throughout the year, just one-tenth of all the households reported inadequacy in 2008–9 at the all-India level in case of all urban areas (Table A5.7). Among size classes of urban centres, at the all-India level as well as across the states there was no substantial difference in this regard, although after 2002 the difference between metros and non-metros widened somewhat (Figure 5.7). Even among the states variations with regard to adequacy at the all urban level as well as across the size classes was less in this year. However, Assam, Gujarat, and West Bengal reported very high level of drinking water adequacy. In contrast, at least one-fourth of all the households in Madhya Pradesh and other north-eastern (NE) states

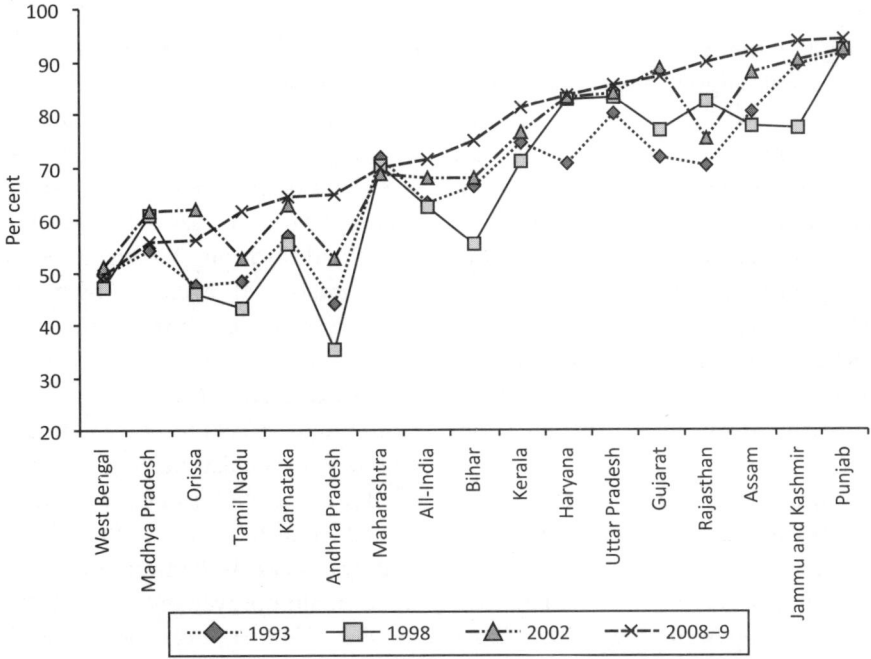

**Figure 5.6** Access to Water within Premises in Non-metros by States, Over Time

*Source*: Data taken from Table A5.2.

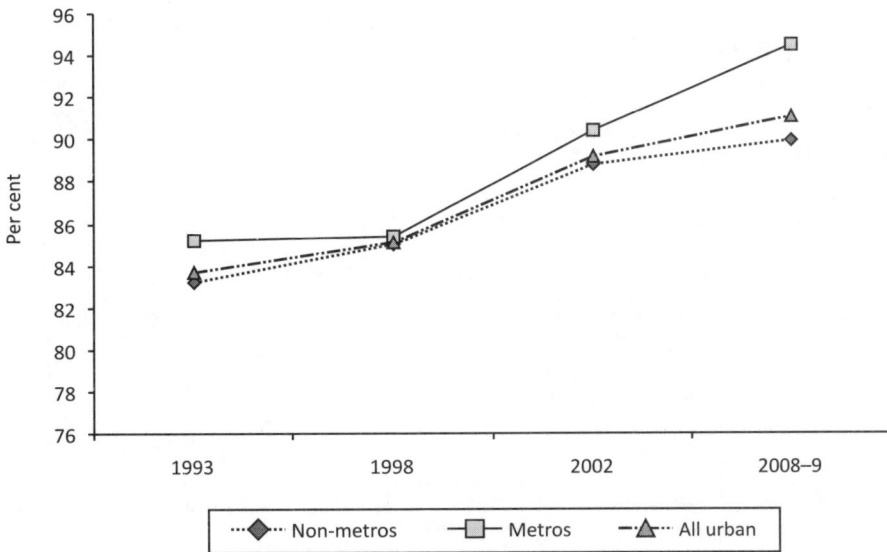

**Figure 5.7** Percentage Households Reporting Adequacy of Drinking Water, Over Time

*Source*: Data taken from Table A5.8.

reported inadequacy of drinking water availability throughout the year.

There was some improvement in adequacy of drinking water availability at the all-India level particularly in all size classes of towns from 1993 to 2008–9. At the state level, however, substantial improvements in drinking water supply were observed in metropolises in Tamil Nadu. In contrast, metropolises in Madhya Pradesh showed deterioration in this regard (Figure 5.8). Even with respect to non-metros, there was very little variation across states and over time in adequacy of drinking water (Figure 5.9).

To sum up, after examining different aspects of drinking water facilities namely access to tap water, availability of drinking water within the premises, sharing of drinking water source, and adequacy of drinking water, some

improvements were observed in urban areas in India in the 1990s. The overall improvement was faster in non-metros as compared to metros. But still significant inadequacies remain and improvement has been slow. Also, there was deterioration in drinking water facilities only in the metro areas of Madhya Pradesh and Uttar Pradesh during 2002 to 2008–9; this phenomenon is partly explained by the definitional issues of metros and non-metros.

**BATHROOM FACILITIES**

Households' access to bathroom facilities was quite low in the early 1990s—a little over half of all the households in urban areas had access to bathroom facilities. Unlike drinking water facilities, access to bathroom facilities showed substantial improvements from 1993 to 1998. At the all-India level, access to bathroom

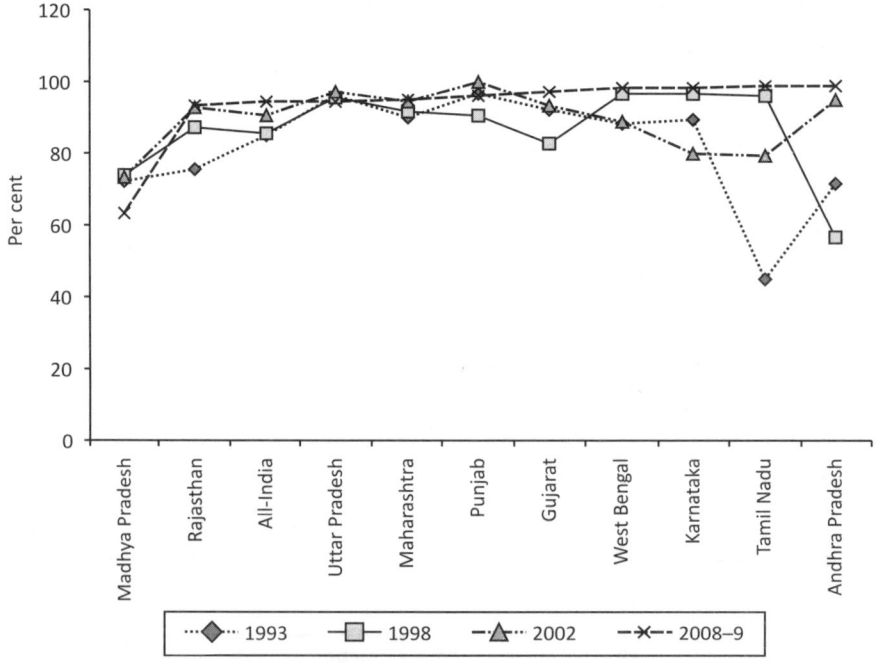

**Figure 5.8**   Percentage Households Stating Adequacy of Drinking Water in Metros by States, Over Time

*Source*: Data taken from Table A5.8.

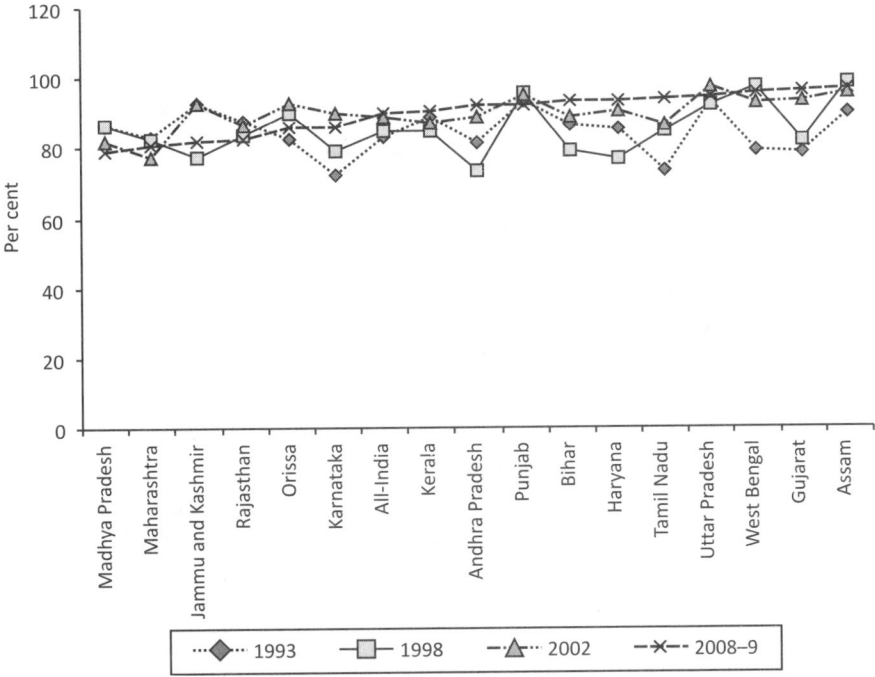

**Figure 5.9**    Percentage Households Stating Adequacy of Drinking Water in
Non-metros by States, Over Time

*Source*: Data taken from Table A5.8.

facilities improved from little more than half to two-third of all households in this period. This improvement was observed almost uniformly in all size classes of towns at the all-India level. Considerable improvement in this access took place also in this decade and in 2008–9 over three-fourth of all urban households had access to bathroom facilities. The substantial difference in access to bathroom facilities that existed between metro and non-metro cities in 1993 virtually disappeared in 2008–9 (Figure 5.10).

The lowest sized (C1) towns were most constrained in this regard as compared to larger sized towns. In the former, just 44 per cent of the households had access to bathroom facilities in 1993. This improved in a consistent manner to 56 per cent in 1998 and further to 71 per cent in 2008–9 (Table A5.9). However,

absolute difference with larger-sized non-metro towns (C3) did not considerably reduce as the latter size class of towns experienced the maximum improvement in access to bathroom facilities and households accessing bathroom facilities in this size classes of towns in 2008–9 was better than those in metro towns.

Access to bathroom facilities did not improve with an increase in the size class of towns across all the states (Tables A5.9 and A.5.10). This was probably because availability of bathroom facilities is a function of availability of space at the dwelling unit level and metropolises with much higher densities (or crowding) have smaller dwelling unit sizes, which do not make it possible for each household to have a separate bathroom facility. Further, in metros, in low income settlements, households tend to share a dwelling space and hence would

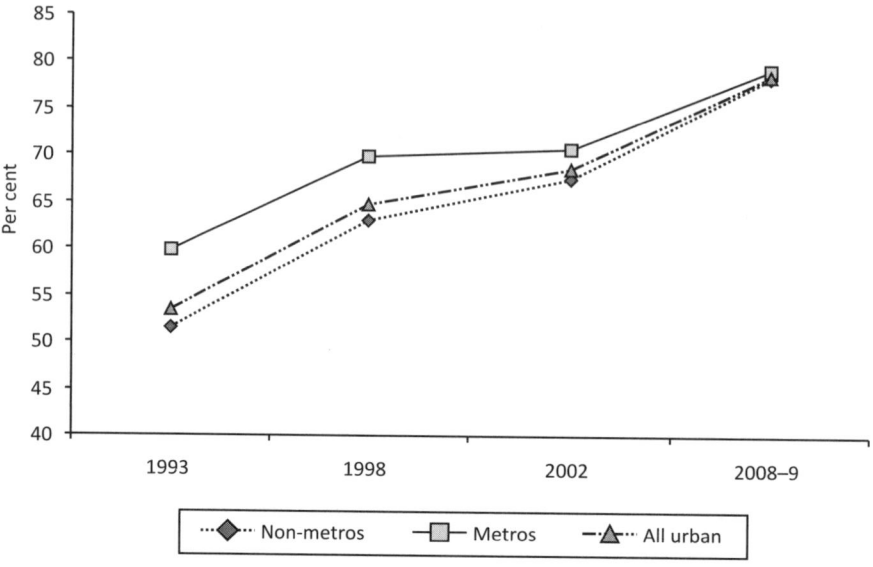

**Figure 5.10**    Percentage Households with Access to Bathroom Facilities, Over Time

*Source*: Data taken from Table A5.10.

share a facility. Low income settlements also have shared facilities such as common toilets and common bathrooms, say in the *chawls* of Mumbai. Thus, lack of availability of space for individual facilities, high densities, and sharing of housing, all contribute towards shared facilities in metro cities.

In all the years in metro as well as non-metro areas, one of the most urbanized states of Maharashtra performed well below the national average in providing bathroom facilities to households except for non-metro areas in 2008–9. The other states that performed badly in metros were Gujarat and West Bengal (Figure 5.11). In contrast, the low urbanized state of Andhra Pradesh performed well throughout the study period in its metros. In 2008–9, out of 12 states that had metro cities, only three were below the all-India average. The non-performance of these three states actually stands out in this year.

In the non-metro areas, the picture was mixed. Except for Maharashtra, in all the other

years the more urbanized states performed better than the all-India average (Table 5.2). But, the states at the top were not the most urbanized states of Gujarat and Tamil Nadu, which were in the middle (Figure 5.12). The less urbanized states of Assam, Jammu and Kashmir, and Kerala performed much better than the all-India average in all the years in the non-metro category. None of these three states had any metro cities. It can be seen that the number of states which performed below the national average in providing bathroom facilities has declined substantially in recent years (Table 5.2).

**DRAINAGE FACILITIES**

Unlike bathroom and toilet facilities where individual households can play an active role in providing these facilities, drainage facility needs to be provided by local governments. In 1993, one-fourth of all households in urban areas in India did not have drainage facilities (Figure 5.13). In 2008–9, this proportion declined to

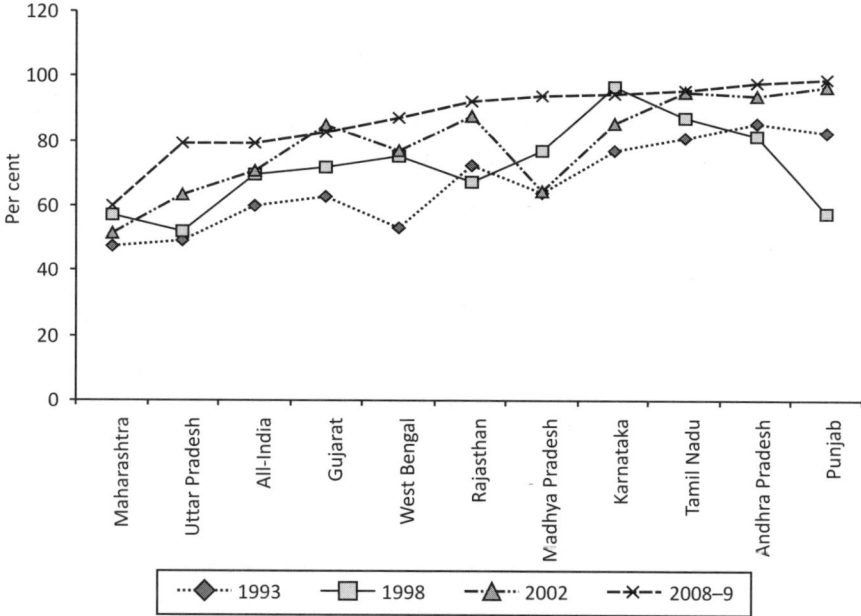

**Figure 5.11**    Percentage Households with Access to Bathrooms in Metros by States, Over Time

*Source*: Data taken from Table A5.10.

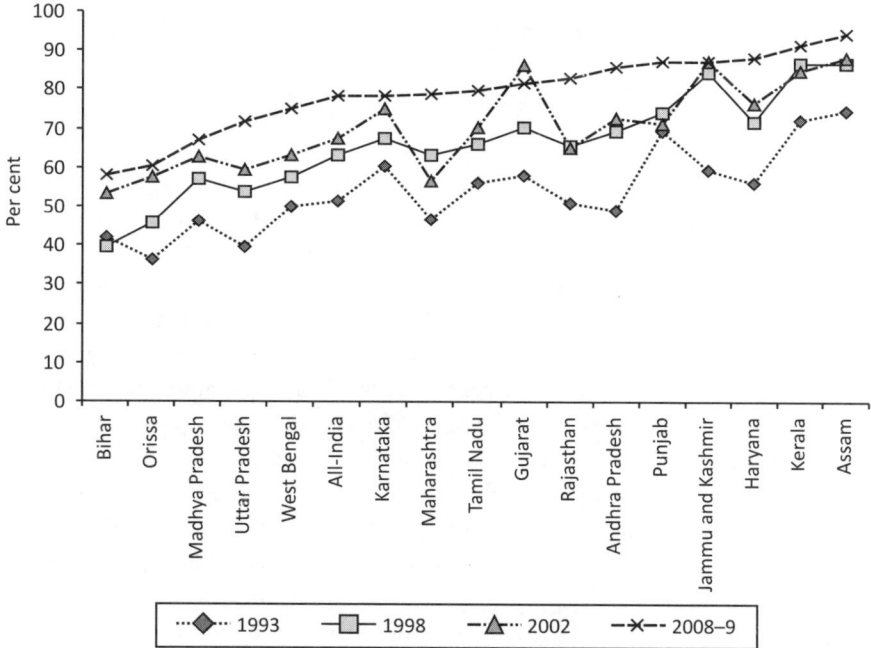

**Figure 5.12**    Percentage Households with Access to Bathrooms in Non-metros by States, Over Time

*Source*: Data taken from Table A5.10.

**Table 5.2**    Percentage Households Having Access to Bathroom Facilities by States

| | | 1993 | 1998 | 2002 | 2008–9 |
|---|---|---|---|---|---|
| Metro | High | Andhra Pradesh, *Gujarat, Karnataka,* Madhya Pradesh, *Punjab,* Rajasthan, *Tamil Nadu* | Andhra Pradesh, *Gujarat, Karnataka,* Madhya Pradesh, *Tamil Nadu,* **West Bengal** | Andhra Pradesh, *Gujarat, Haryana, Karnataka,* **Punjab,** **Rajasthan,** *Tamil Nadu,* West Bengal | Andhra Pradesh, *Gujarat, Haryana, Karnataka,* **Madhya Pradesh,** *Punjab,* Rajasthan, *Tamil Nadu,* West Bengal |
| | Low | *Maharashtra,* Uttar Pradesh, West Bengal | Bihar, *Maharashtra,* **Punjab, Rajasthan,** Uttar Pradesh | Bihar, **Madhya Pradesh,** *Maharashtra,* Uttar Pradesh | Bihar, *Maharashtra,* Uttar Pradesh |
| Non-Metro | High | Assam, *Gujarat, Haryana,* Jammu and Kashmir, *Karnataka,* Kerala, *Punjab, Tamil Nadu,* West Bengal | **Andhra Pradesh,** Assam, *Gujarat, Haryana,* Jammu and Kashmir, *Karnataka,* Kerala, Punjab, Rajasthan, *Tamil Nadu* | Andhra Pradesh, Assam, *Gujarat, Haryana,* Jammu and Kashmir, *Karnataka,* Kerala, Punjab, *Tamil Nadu* | Andhra Pradesh, Assam *Gujarat, Haryana,* Jammu and Kashmir, *Karnataka,* Kerala, **Maharashtra,** *Punjab,* **Rajasthan,** *Tamil Nadu* |
| | Low | Andhra Pradesh, Bihar, Madhya Pradesh, Orissa, *Maharashtra,* Rajasthan, Uttar Pradesh | Bihar, Madhya Pradesh, Orissa, *Maharashtra,* Uttar Pradesh, **West Bengal** | Bihar, Madhya Pradesh, Orissa, *Maharashtra,* West Bengal, Rajasthan, Uttar Pradesh | Bihar, Madhya Pradesh, Orissa, Uttar Pradesh, West Bengal |

*Source*: Based on data from Table A5.12.

*Notes*: 1. States in bold signify movement from high (> all-India level) to low (< all-India level) or low to high in consecutive years.

2. Italicized states were high on the level of urbanization in 2001 (> all-India level).

just 15 per cent, indicating that providing this facility to an increasing number of urban households was not as high a priority as it should have been even in the following 15 years. With regard to drainage facilities there were substantial improvements with an increase in size classes of towns; the smaller towns had poorer drainage facilities as compared to metropolis in all four years of our study (Table A5.11).

Small rural towns (C1) fared far worse than other higher size classes of towns. In 1993, 40 per cent of all households in the C1 size class of towns did not have any drainage facility whereas one-tenth of all households in metropolis lacked this facility. This could be because with an increase in the size class of towns, the capacity of ULBs to provide drainage facilities

increases, especially in states where ULBs are powerful. Even in states where state level agencies and not ULBs provide drainage facilities the per capita expenditure on drainage facilities in metropolises tended to be larger than that in small towns. In 2008–9 for which the most recent data is available, one-fourth of all households in small towns (C1) did not have drainage facilities. In the same year, in metropolis hardly 3 per cent of all households lacked this facility. Further, in the decade of 2000, there was faster improvement in drainage coverage in metros. Such faster improvement in drainage coverage in non-metros occurred in the decade of the 1990s (Table A5.12).

Substantial differences existed with regard to access to drainage facilities in 1998 across

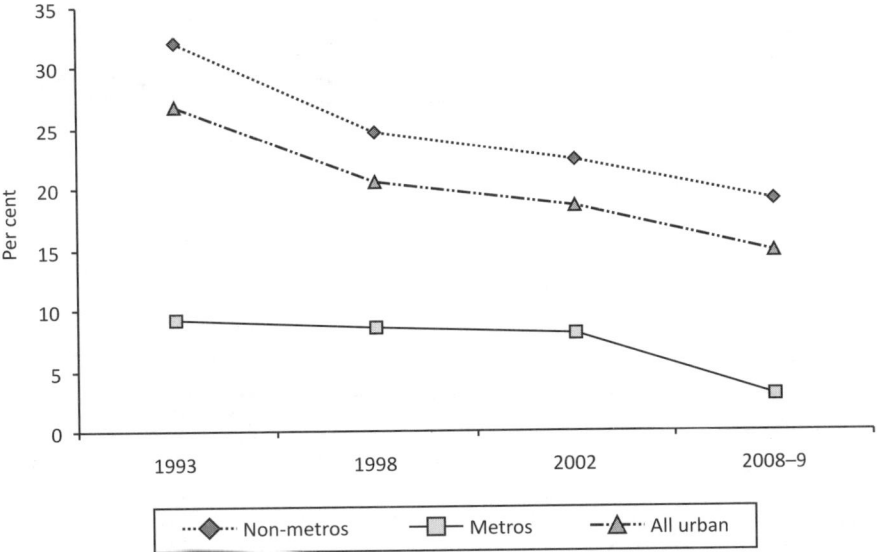

**Figure 5.13**  Percentage Households without Access to Drainage, Over Time

*Source*: Data taken from Table A5.12.

the states. In Jammu and Kashmir, Maharashtra, and Punjab more than 90 per cent of all the urban households had some kind of drainage facility. In contrast, in Assam, Bihar, Kerala, Orissa, and other NE states more than one-third of all urban households lacked any drainage facility. Surprisingly, half of the households in Kerala did not have any drainage facility. In 2008–9, four more states, Gujarat, Haryana, Rajasthan, and Uttar Pradesh joined the league of states where more than 90 per cent of all urban households had some kind of drainage facility. Surprisingly the two states of Kerala and Orissa did not have any improvement in providing this facility to a large proportion of the households in the whole decade (1998 to 2008–9).

In 1998, households residing in metropolises in Gujarat, Karnataka, Maharashtra, and Punjab had almost universal access to drainage facilities. By 2008–9 this facility had virtually spread to all metropolitan households (Figure 5.14). But substantial differences still existed in non-metropolitan towns across states in India in all the four years. The proportion of households which did not have any drainage facility declined at a lower rate; from one-third in 1993 to one-fifth in 2008–9 (Figure 5.15). Table 5.3, which only covers non-metros, shows that even in 2008–9, the most urbanized states of Maharashtra and Tamil Nadu still fared worse than the all-India average with regard to availability of drainage facilities in non-metros. In contrast, the low urbanized states of Jammu and Kashmir, Madhya Pradesh, Rajasthan, and Uttar Pradesh performed better than the national average in providing drainage facilities to a larger proportion of households. Andhra Pradesh presents an interesting case where in each subsequent year of the survey it either fared better or worse than the all-India average.

Access to *pucca* covered or underground drainage was largely limited to metropolises and to a certain extent to large cities in 1998 as well

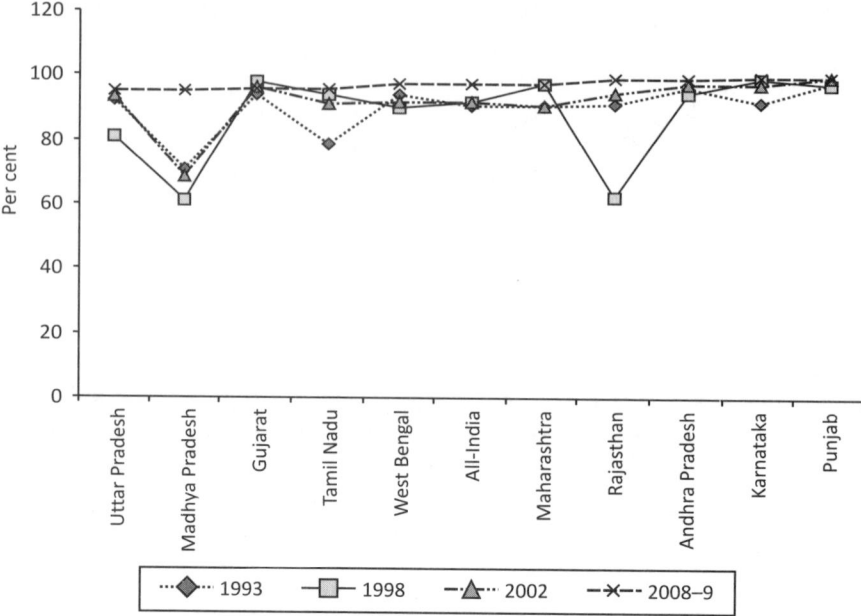

**Figure 5.14**    Percentage Households Not Having Access to Drainage in Metros by States, Over Time

*Source*: Data taken from Table A5.12.

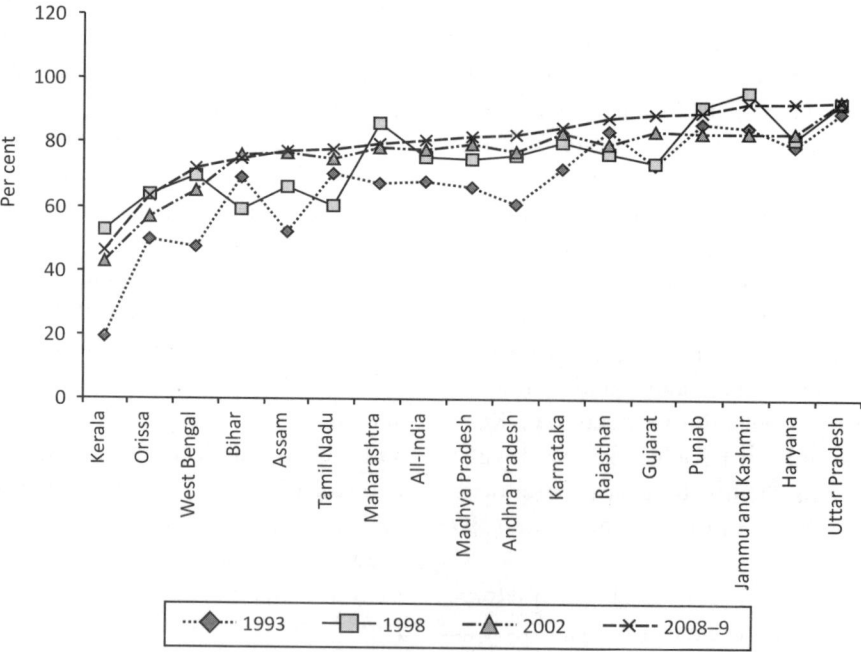

**Figure 5.15**    Percentage Households Having Access to Drainage in Non-metros by States, Over Time

*Source*: Data taken from Table A5.12.

**Table 5.3** Percentage of Households Having Drainage Facilities by States

|  |  | 1993 | 1998 | 2002 | 2008–9 |
|---|---|---|---|---|---|
| Non-Metro | High | Bihar, *Gujarat*, *Haryana*, Jammu and Kashmir, *Karnataka*, *Punjab*, Rajasthan, *Tamil Nadu*, Uttar Pradesh | **Andhra Pradesh**, *Gujarat*, *Haryana*, Jammu and Kashmir, *Karnataka*, ***Maharashtra***, *Punjab*, Rajasthan, Uttar Pradesh | *Gujarat*, *Haryana*, Jammu and Kashmir, *Karnataka*, **Madhya Pradesh**, *Maharashtra*, *Punjab*, Rajasthan, Uttar Pradesh | **Andhra Pradesh**, *Gujarat*, *Haryana*, Jammu and Kashmir, *Karnataka*, Madhya Pradesh, *Punjab*, Rajasthan, Uttar Pradesh |
|  | Low | Andhra Pradesh, Assam, Kerala, Madhya Pradesh, *Maharashtra*, Orissa, West Bengal | Assam, **Bihar**, Kerala, Madhya Pradesh, Orissa, ***Tamil Nadu***, West Bengal | **Andhra Pradesh**, Assam, Bihar, Kerala, Orissa, *Tamil Nadu*, West Bengal | Assam, Bihar, Kerala, ***Maharashtra***, Orissa, *Tamil Nadu*, West Bengal |

*Source*: Based on data from Table A5.12.

*Notes*: 1. States in bold signify movement from high (> all-India level) to low (< all-India level) or low to high in consecutive years.

2. Italicized states were high on the level of urbanization in 2001 (> all-India level).

as in 1993 (Table A5.13). At the all-India level, 31 per cent of all drainage facilities availed by households were *pucca* covered or underground in 1998. In this year, this percentage was as high as 60 per cent in the metropolises. There was substantial improvement in coverage in this regard from small towns to metropolises, once again for the same reason as discussed earlier of metropolises getting preferential treatment or having higher capacity for taking care of drainage facilities in both the years. Thus, the gap between metros and non-metros increased in the decade of 2000 (Figure 5.16). Barring Gujarat, in no other states did small towns have this facility to a considerable extent in both the years—in that state one-third of all drainage facilities for households were either *pucca* covered or underground in 1998. In 1993, the percentage figures for small and medium towns (C1 and C2) were much higher in this state. In urban Gujarat and Maharashtra, half of all drainage facilities accessed by households were *pucca* covered or underground in 1998. In all the other states a large disparity existed between metropolis and large cities in 1998 as well as in1993.

There were improvements in access to drainage facilities from 1993 to 1998. But most of this was of the type open *katcha/pucca* variety. This can be seen from the substantial increase in the share of *pucca* covered/underground drainage in all drainage facilities at the all-India level (Figure 5.16) in this period. The increase in the share of *pucca* covered/underground drainage was the most striking in small and medium sized categories of towns at the all-India level which experienced substantial rise in households' access to drainage facilities. It becomes clearer from the high inverse relationship between rise in access to drainage facilities with a fall in the share of *open katcha/pucca* drainage in states which experienced substantial expansion in households' access to drainage facilities in tiny and small towns.

Access to *pucca* covered or underground drainage showed substantial improvements in 2002 and further improvements in 2008. The coverage of this type of drainage in total drainage facilities went up to 51 and 59 per cent of all urban households in 2002 and 2008–9, respectively (Figure 5.16). At the all-India level, between

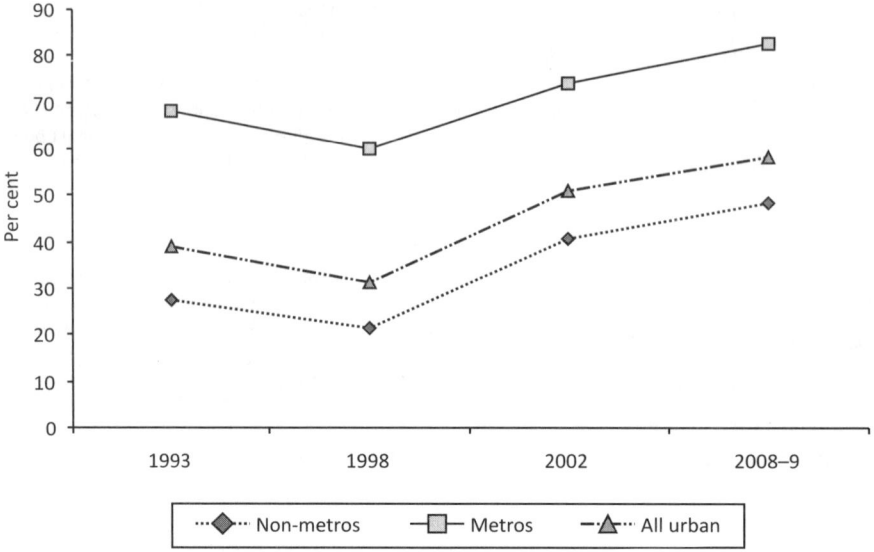

**Figure 5.16**　Percentage Households with Access to Covered Drains, Over Time

*Source*: Data taken from Table A5.14.

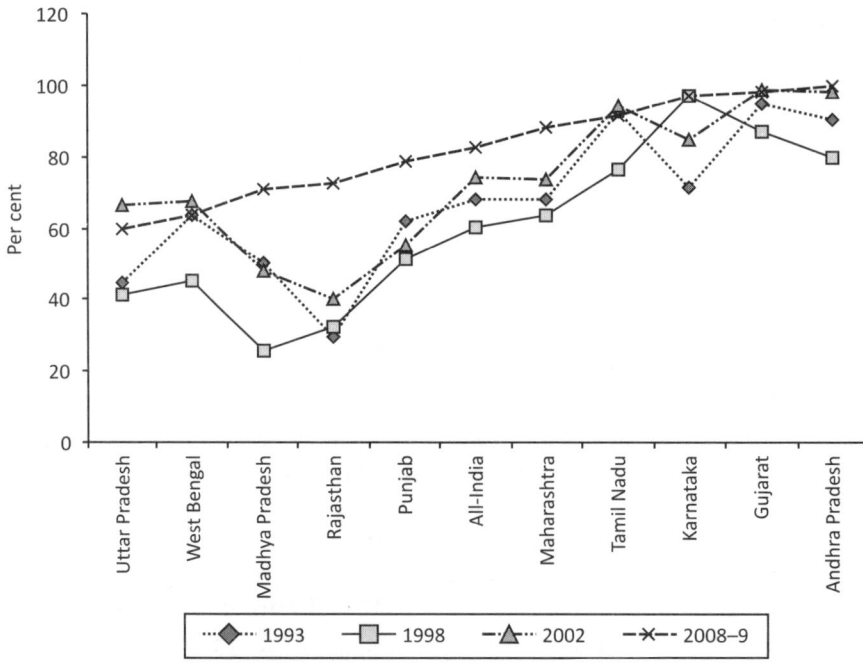

**Figure 5.17**　Percentage Households with Access to Covered Drains in Metros by States, Over Time

*Source*: Data taken from Table A5.14.

1998 and 2002 this improvement was propelled largely by increased coverage in metropolises and between 1998 and 2008–9 improvements were observed in all size classes of towns in the non-metro category. In small town size class (C1) the coverage more than doubled between 1998 and 2008–9 (Table A5.13). Kerala was an exceptional case where only half of all the urban households had drainage facilities but more than two-third of these households had access to pucca or underground drainage virtually in all size classes of towns (Figures 5.17 and 5.18).

## TOILET FACILITIES

At the all-India level in 1993, 30 per cent of all urban households did not have access to toilet facilities. Households' access to toilet facilities at the all-India level improved consistently and in 2008–9 only 11 per cent of all urban households did not have access to toilet facilities

(Figure 5.19). The difference between metropolises and non-metropolises was substantial in 1998 and this gap showed a significant decline over the 10 years. In 1998, in metropolises 13 per cent of the households did not have access to toilet facilities but by 2008–9 virtually all households in metropolitan areas had access to toilet facilities except for Bihar, Rajasthan, and Uttar Pradesh where one-sixteenth of the households still did not have access to this facility (Figure 5.20).

Across size classes of towns, access to toilet facilities showed substantial improvements from small towns to large cities. This phenomenon can be observed virtually in all the states over different years. Again, in small size class of towns (C1) considerable improvements in accessing toilet facilities can be observed from 1993 to 2008–9. Even in 2008–9, around one-fifth of the households in this size class of

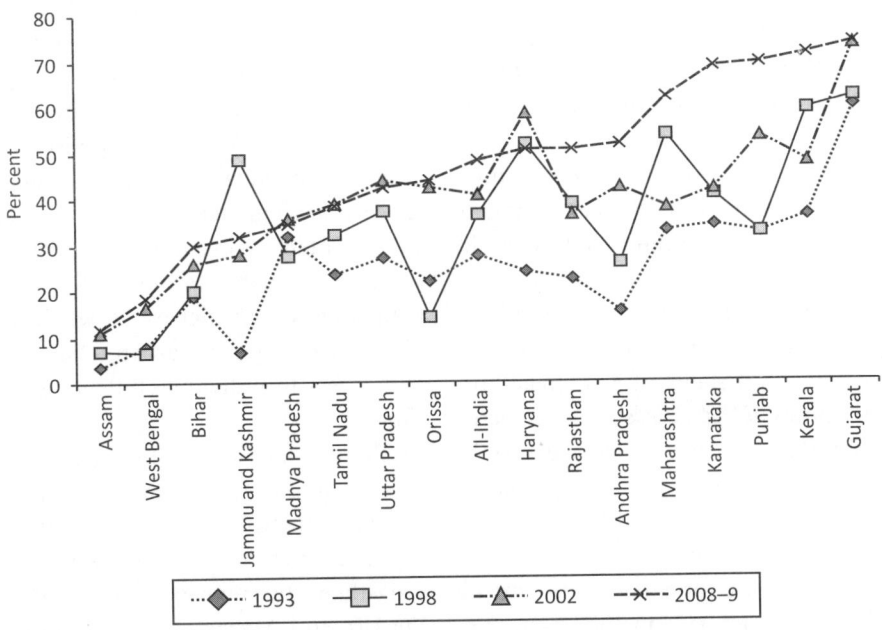

**Figure 5.18**   Percentage Households with Access to Covered Drains in Non-metros by States, Over Time

*Source*: Data taken from Table A5.14.

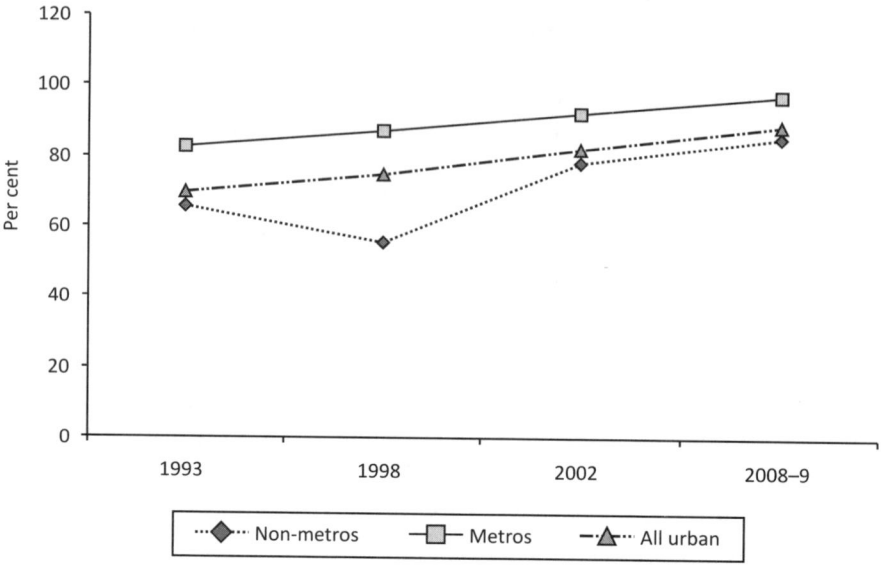

**Figure 5.19**  Percentage Households with Access to Toilets, Over Time

*Source*: Data taken from Table A5.16.

towns did not have access to toilet facilities. During 1993 to 2008–9 (Table A5.15), in the non-metropolitan category larger size towns experienced substantial improvements in this facility.

The states where non-metros also had a high proportion of households with access to toilets were Assam, Kerala, Punjab, and West Bengal in that order in 2008–9 (Figure 5.21). The worst performing states were Bihar, Madhya Pradesh, Orissa, and Tamil Nadu in that order. Thus in the highly urbanized states of Karnataka and Tamil Nadu households' access to toilet facilities was lower than the national average in 1993 as well as in 2008–9. Their relative performance remained poor regardless of their higher urbanization status. Even in the high urbanized state of Maharashtra, the performance in this regard was not all that satisfactory—in 2002 its performance was worse than the all-India average.

At the all-India level nearly two-third of the households that had toilet facilities had

exclusive access to it in 2008–9 (Figure 5.22). This access was higher at 68 per cent in non-metros as compared to metros (60 per cent). Individual access to toilets showed a decline from small towns to metropolises. As in the case of individual bathroom facilities, where sharing was higher in metros as compared to non-metros, even in the case of toilets, sharing was higher in metros (Figure 5.22) as compared to non-metros. However, in metros, non-metros, and all urban, sharing declined and access to individual toilets increased over time.

Sharing of toilet facilities by different households was the most common in Maharashtra and West Bengal and least common in Jammu and Kashmir, Madhya Pradesh, Orissa, and Rajasthan. In metropolises in West Bengal, Punjab, and Maharashtra less than one-third of all the households with toilet facilities had individual access to toilets (Figure 5.23). Metropolises in Karnataka (Bangalore),

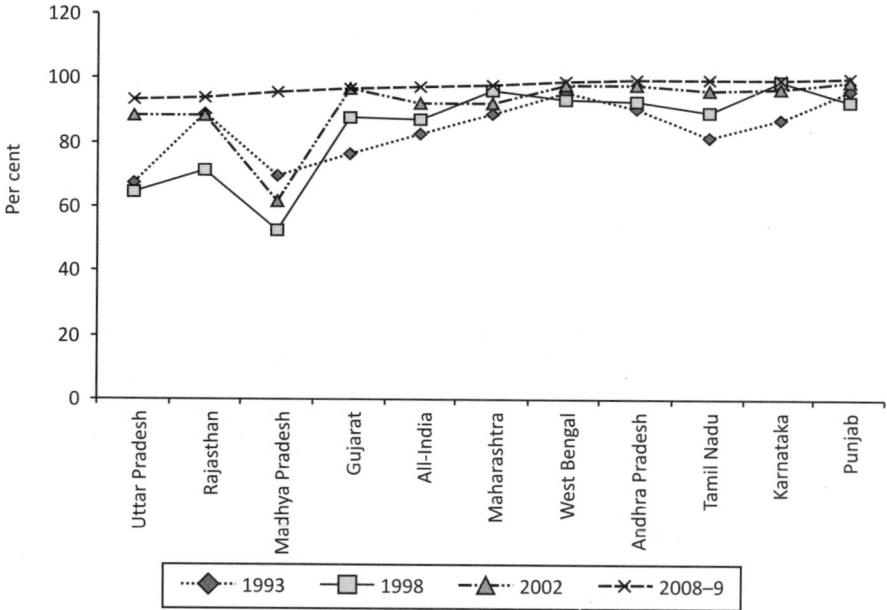

**Figure 5.20**    Percentage Households with Access to Toilets in Metros by States, Over Time

*Source*: Data taken from Table A5.16.

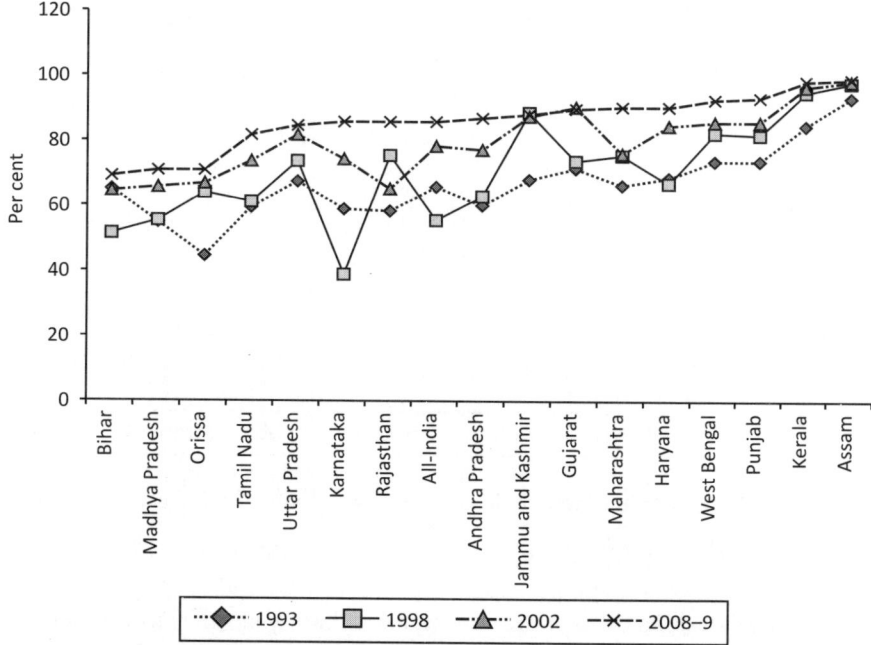

**Figure 5.21**    Percentage Households with Access to Toilets in Non-metros by States, Over Time

*Source*: Data taken from Table A5.16.

**Table 5.4**     Percentage Households Having Access to Toilet Facilities

|  |  | 1993 | 1998 | 2002 | 2008–9 |
|---|---|---|---|---|---|
| Non-metro | High | Andhra Pradesh, Assam, *Gujarat*, *Haryana*, Jammu and Kashmir, Kerala, *Maharashtra*, *Punjab*, Uttar Pradesh, West Bengal | Andhra Pradesh, Assam, *Gujarat*, *Haryana*, Jammu and Kashmir, Kerala, *Maharashtra*, **Orissa**, *Punjab*, **Rajasthan**, *Tamil Nadu*, Uttar Pradesh, West Bengal | Assam, *Gujarat*, *Haryana*, Jammu and Kashmir, Kerala, *Punjab*, Uttar Pradesh, West Bengal | **Andhra Pradesh**, Assam, *Gujarat*, *Haryana*, Jammu and Kashmir, Kerala, **Maharashtra**, *Punjab*, West Bengal |
| | Low | Bihar, *Karnataka*, Madhya Pradesh, Orissa, Rajasthan, *Tamil Nadu* | Bihar, *Karnataka*, Madhya Pradesh | **Andhra Pradesh**, Bihar, *Karnataka*, Madhya Pradesh, **Maharashtra**, **Orissa**, Rajasthan, *Tamil Nadu* | Bihar, *Karnataka*, Madhya Pradesh, Orissa, Rajasthan, *Tamil Nadu*, **Uttar Pradesh** |

*Source*: Based on data from Table A5.16.

*Notes*: 1. States in bold signify movement from high (> all-India level) to low (< all-India level) or low to high in consecutive years.

2. Italicized states were high on the level of urbanization in 2001 (> all-India level).

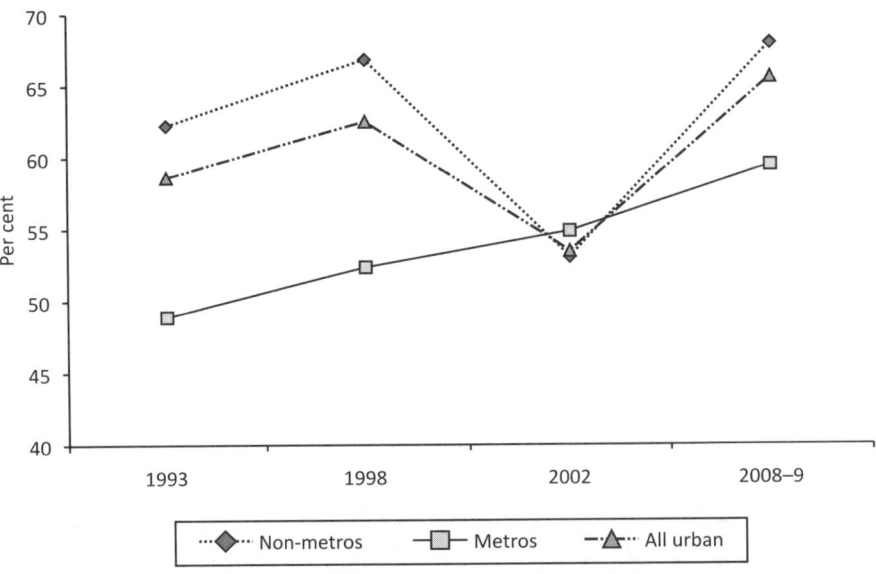

**Figure 5.22**     Percentage Households with Access to Individual Toilets, Over Time

*Source*: Data taken from Table A5.18.

Gujarat, and Uttar Pradesh had a high proportion of households with access to individual toilets. In the case of non-metros, Maharashtra, West Bengal, Tamil Nadu, Andhra Pradesh, and Bihar were the worst performing and Kerala, Jammu and Kashmir, Orissa, Assam, and Haryana were better performing (Figure 5.24). At the top as well as the bottom, there

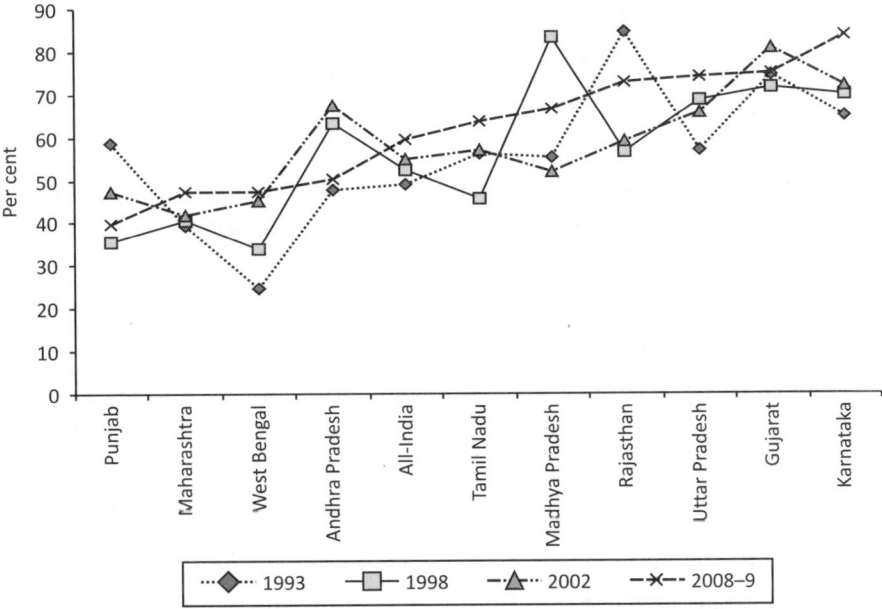

**Figure 5.23** Percentage Households with Access to Individual Toilets in Metros by States, Over Time

*Source*: Data taken from Table A5.18.

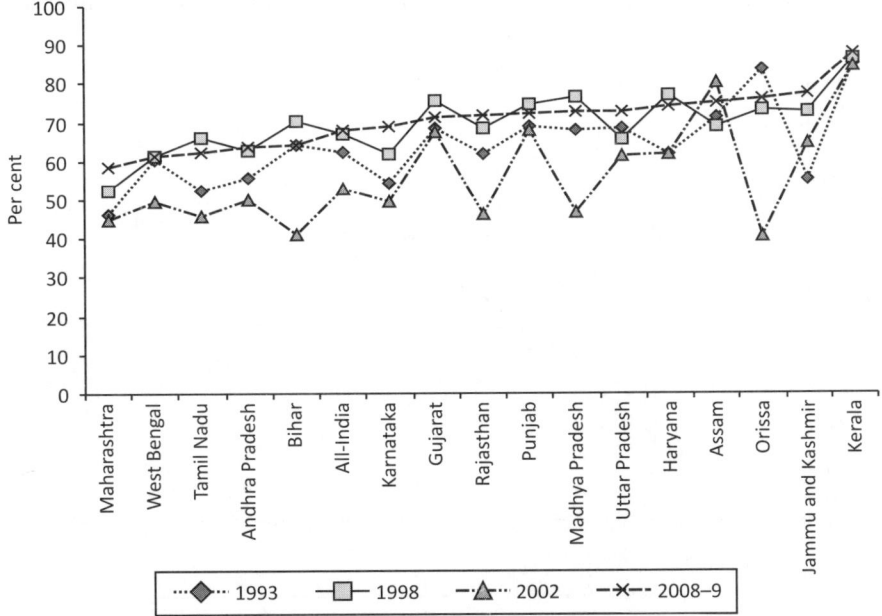

**Figure 5.24** Percentage Households with Access to Individual Toilets in Non-metros by States, Over Time

*Source*: Data taken from Table A5.18.

were urbanized and less urbanized states and high-income and low-income states.

The proportion of households that had individual access to toilet facilities showed marginal improvement in the 1990s (Figure 5.22). The improvements were almost uniformly spread out across different size classes of towns. This analysis shows that individual household's access to toilet facilities more or less moved at the same pace as the rise in proportion of households with access to toilet facilities. Surprisingly, individual access to toilet facilities experienced substantial deterioration in 2002 but improved in 2008–9 to reach a slightly higher level than what it was in 1998.

## GARBAGE COLLECTION SYSTEM

Garbage collection data is available only from 1998. In that year garbage collection by local authorities was undertaken at a small scale in urban India. Hardly, one-seventh of all households reported garbage being collected by

local authorities (Figure 5.25). ULBs were not performing this function in most states and in states where they were performing this function, it was not done satisfactorily.

Substantial improvements can be observed in 2002 when more than half of all the households in non-metro areas and nearly two-third of all the households in metro areas reported garbage collection by local authorities (Table A5.20). In this vast improved scenario the two most urbanized states of Maharashtra and Tamil Nadu stood out in the improved collection of garbage by local authorities in metro as well as non-metro areas. In 2008–9, garbage collection by local authorities showed further moderate improvements (Table A5.21). In addition to Maharashtra and Tamil Nadu another high urbanized state of Karnataka also showed vast improvements in this regard in 2008–9. In this year in metropolitan areas in these three states, garbage collection by local authorities almost became universal. In small

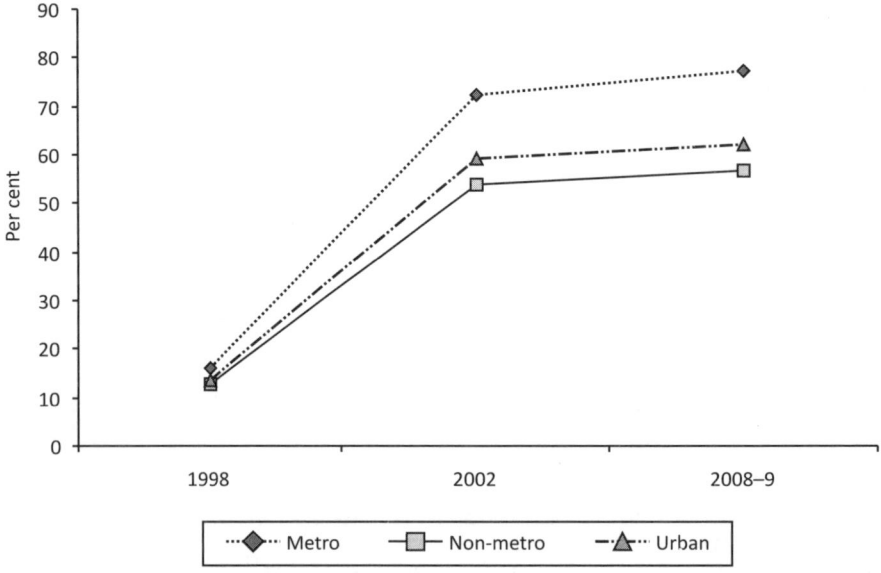

**Figure 5.25**　Percentage Households Reporting Garbage Collection by Local Authority, Over Time

*Source*: Data taken from Tables A5.20 and A5.21.

towns (C1) in 1998 hardly one-tenth of the households reported garbage collection by local authorities. In 2008–9, even in this size class nearly half of all the households reported garbage collection by local authorities. This improvement in metropolitan cities was on account of the Supreme Court Rule of 1999, Solid waste management Guidelines in Class-1 cities, and subsequently the Municipal Solid Waste (Management and Handling) Rules, 2000 under the Environment Protection Act.

## CONCLUSIONS

The size class disaggregated urban services data presented in this chapter indicate that metro cities have consistently better access to urban facilities as compared to non-metros with the overall urban somewhere in the middle but closer to non-metros than metros as the latter houses about two-third of the urban population. The exception is with regard to the quality of the service. For example, if a service such as bathrooms or toilets are available than there is higher incidence of sharing in metros than in non-metros, primarily on account of lack of availability of space for individual bathrooms and toilets in metropolitan cities. Further, in metros in low-income settlements, households tend to share a dwelling space and hence would share a facility. Low-income settlements also have shared facilities such as common toilets and common bathrooms, say in *chawls* in Mumbai. Thus, lack of availability of space for individual facilities, high densities, and sharing of housing, all contribute towards shared facilities in metro cities. With regard to individual services, metro and non-metro differences in access over time are very different.

With regard to access to tap water, the metros did not improve over time, from 1993 to 2008–9, whereas non-metros improved reducing the gap. Access to bathrooms improved at a faster rate in non-metros than in metros and in 2008–9 access became nearly the same. Improvement in access to drainage was marginally faster in non-metros than in metros but the gap between the two remained nearly as wide as it was in the early 1990s. Provision of covered drains improved faster in metros than in non-metros and the gap between the two which was beginning to narrow in the 1990s grew wider in the decade of 2000. Was this on account of JNNURM, whose Urban Infrastructure and Governance (UIG) component is only for metros and the large cities? Also, access to toilets became near universal in metros and the metro non-metro gap reduced over time.

Last, all the services in metros as well as in non-metros improved from either 1998 or 2002 onwards. This could be on account of an improved financial base in urban areas due to their sourcing funds from other than budgetary support, and since latter half of the decade of 2000 from the JNNURM. But metros improved faster with regard to certain services such as access to drainage and covered drainage, where local authorities or state level parastatal agencies need to invest through their respective budgetary resources. To some extent even access to tap water is contingent upon a local authority's initiative as tap water comes in if there is an extension of the city level water supply network, a responsibility of the local authority. But after that households have not been connected to the water network on account of multiple hurdles such as legality of housing settlements and the affordability of households. Metros and large cities were more successful than non-metros and among the latter the small towns, as the metros have higher capability than the latter in extending services. Similarly, garbage collection improved because of concerted efforts of local governments after the enforcement of a central legislation on

**Table 5.5**    Ranking of States in Access to Different Services, Metros

| State | % ACA/% Urban Pop.* | %age Households with Access to | | | |
|---|---|---|---|---|---|
| | | Tap water | Bathroom | Toilet | Drainage |
| Andhra Pradesh | 3 | 3 | 2 | 3 | 3 |
| Bihar | 12 | 8 | 11 | 10 | 10 |
| Gujarat | 1 | 5 | 9 | 7 | 8 |
| Haryana | 11 | 10 | 6 | 8 | 5 |
| Karnataka | 6 | 1 | 4 | 2 | 1 |
| Madhya Pradesh | 2 | 2 | 12 | 6 | 6 |
| Maharashtra | 8 | 9 | 5 | 9 | 11 |
| Punjab | 10 | 4 | 1 | 1 | 2 |
| Rajasthan | 9 | 7 | 7 | 11 | 4 |
| Tamil Nadu | 4 | 11 | 3 | 4 | 9 |
| Uttar Pradesh | 7 | 12 | 10 | 12 | 12 |
| West Bengal | 5 | 6 | 8 | 5 | 7 |

*Source*: Data taken from Tables A5.2, A5.10, A5.12, and A5.16, and Mahadevia (2011).
*Notes*: * Based on JNNURM data for the UIG component. This indicator is calculated using the following formula: %age share of state in the ACA released divided by the %age share of the state in total urban population of India. The data is from: http://www.urbanindia.nic.in/programme/ud/uidssmtbody.htm#uidssmt accessed on 15 February 2010) and its status up to 31 August 2010.

**Table 5.6**    Ranking of States in Access to Different Services, Non-metros

| State | % ACA/% Urban Pop.* | %age Households with Access to | | | |
|---|---|---|---|---|---|
| | | Tap water | Bathroom | Toilet | Drainage |
| Andhra Pradesh | 1 | 9 | 6 | 9 | 8 |
| Assam | 4 | 15 | 1 | 1 | 12 |
| Bihar | 16 | 16 | 16 | 16 | 13 |
| Gujarat | 12 | 8 | 8 | 7 | 5 |
| Haryana | 15 | 5 | 3 | 5 | 2 |
| Jammu and Kashmir | 2 | 1 | 4 | 8 | 3 |
| Karnataka | 7 | 2 | 11 | 10 | 7 |
| Kerala | 6 | 14 | 2 | 2 | 16 |
| Maharashtra | 3 | 12 | 14 | 15 | 9 |
| Madhya Pradesh | 9 | 7 | 10 | 6 | 10 |
| Orissa | 10 | 10 | 15 | 14 | 15 |
| Punjab | 8 | 6 | 5 | 3 | 4 |
| Rajasthan | 11 | 3 | 7 | 11 | 6 |
| Tamil Nadu | 5 | 4 | 9 | 13 | 11 |
| Uttar Pradesh | 13 | 13 | 13 | 12 | 1 |
| West Bengal | 14 | 11 | 12 | 4 | 14 |

*Source*: Data taken from Tables A5.2, A5.10, A5.12, and A5.16 and Mahadevia (2011).
*Note*: * Based on JNNURM data for the UIG component. This indicator is calculated using the following formula: %age share of state in the ACA released divided by the %age share of the state in total urban population of India. The data is from: http://www.urbanindia.nic.in/programme/ud/uidssmtbody.htm#uidssmt accessed on 15 February 2010) and its status up to 31 August 2010.

solid waste management on the one hand and improved awareness about the service from the beginning of the decade of 2000.

We do not find any pattern in the performance of states with regard to each of these services and we find both urbanized and less urbanized states at the top as well as the bottom with regard to availability of these services in metros and non-metros (Tables 5.5 and 5.6). Besides, each state had varying levels of performance in case of each of the services. Lastly, we do not find any direct connection of a state's performance with regard to a service and the state's ability to access JNNURM funds. We have assumed that a state's ability to access JNNURM funds is indicated by its ability to access Additional Central Assistance (ACA) and to make this data neutral for the size of the urban population we devised a ratio which is obtained by the percentage share of a state in the ACA released divided by the percentage share of the state in the total urban population of India. Thus, for each state further investigations into what causes an improvement in service levels in a particular city or size classes of cities need to be investigated separately.

# 6

# Emerging Patterns and Policy Implications

This chapter became a necessity to include the NSS's 66th Round data (2009–10) on Average Per Capita Consumption Expenditure (APCE), employment, and education. The analysis presented in the previous chapters is up to 2004–5, that is, till the 61st NSS Round using detailed unit-level data available from the 'thick' rounds up till then. By including an analysis of the 66th Round, we are now able to cover the trends in this decade, when the economic growth in India picked up to about 8 per cent per annum. While completing this manuscript, unit-level data of the 66th Round, for 2009–10 were released by the NSSO. We processed the unit-level data of the employment-unemployment survey and household consumption expenditure survey in the 66th Round to generate relevant tables. This chapter presents the latest data along with data from previous years to observe trends in consumption expenditure, employment and unemployment, and education over about a two-decade period. Like in the other chapters, state-wise detailed data is given in the Tables (A6.1 to A6.11). But, unlike the previous chapters,

we have not analysed state-wise trends in this chapter.

## EMPLOYMENT AND UNEMPLOYMENT

Compared to the previous rounds of the employment-unemployment survey, the latest survey stands out; the overall urban, metro, and non-metro WPRs of males and females came down in 2009–10 (66th Round) in contrast to an increasing trend in these WPRs observed since 1987–8 (Table 6.1). Male WPRs declined by 0.6 percentage points for all urban, 1.3 percentage points for metros, and 0.3 percentage points for non-metros. The decline in female WPRs was higher as compared to that of males—by 2.8 percentage points in all urban, 2.2 percentage points in metros, and 3.2 percentage points in non-metros. In other words, work availability for females declined and/or females withdrew from the labour force in the urban economy in the last five years. It also needs to be observed that this is a very large decline in WPRs as far as females are concerned and the decline was the largest in the non-metro sector of the urban economy. In contrast, a decline in male WPRs was higher in metros than in non-metros.

**Table 6.1**   Trends in WPR (in percentages)

|  | Non-metro | Metro | Urban |
|---|---|---|---|
| **Male** | | | |
| 1987–8 | 50.2 | 52.5 | 50.7 |
| 1993–4 | 51.5 | 54.6 | 52.1 |
| 2004–5 | 54.2 | 56.6 | 54.9 |
| 2009–10 | 53.9 | 55.3 | 54.3 |
| **Female** | | | |
| 1987–8 | 16.0 | 11.9 | 15.2 |
| 1993–4 | 16.2 | 12.9 | 15.5 |
| 2004–5 | 17.4 | 14.6 | 16.6 |
| 2009–10 | 14.2 | 12.4 | 13.8 |

*Source*: Data taken from Tables A3.3 and A6.1.

It must be kept in mind that 1987–8 was a drought year and all over India, in rural as well as urban areas, work availability declined. Subsequently, over the entire reforms period, there was an improvement in male as well as female WPRs, all the way up to the most recent Round. Evidently, this was an impact of the global recession and the drought year as well as probably the growth path selected by India which was not employment intensive. There was a larger impact on work availability for females in both non-metros and metros, with non-metros registering a higher percentage point decline than the metros. Among the males, the percentage decline was higher in the metros than in the non-metros. Some view this decline as a withdrawal from the workforce because of enrolment of the youth in education and by others because of a shift to unpaid self-employment or family employment which is not captured in the labour force statistics. What really happened may need to be viewed by analysing time use data which is now being collected by NSSO. We have not done so for want of time and the need to limit the scope of our analysis.

**Table 6.2**   Unemployment Rate (in percentages)

|  | Male | | Female | |
|---|---|---|---|---|
|  | Usual Status | CDS | Usual Status | CDS |
| **Non-Metro** | | | | |
| 1987–8 | 4.9 | 8.6 | 5.5 | 12.0 |
| 1993–4 | 4.1 | 7.2 | 5.8 | 10.6 |
| 2004–5 | 3.9 | 8.0 | 7.5 | 12.8 |
| 2009–10 | 2.6 | 5.4 | 5.7 | 9.5 |
| **Metro** | | | | |
| 1987–8 | 6.4 | 9.4 | 8.7 | 12.1 |
| 1993–4 | 3.8 | 5.2 | 8.2 | 10.0 |
| 2004–5 | 3.5 | 6.2 | 4.9 | 8.3 |
| 2009–10 | 3.4 | 4.6 | 5.7 | 7.8 |
| **All Urban** | | | | |
| 1987–8 | 5.2 | 8.8 | 5.9 | 12.0 |
| 1993–4 | 4.1 | 6.7 | 6.2 | 10.5 |
| 2004–5 | 3.8 | 7.5 | 6.9 | 11.6 |
| 2009–10 | 2.8 | 5.1 | 5.7 | 9.1 |

*Source*: Data taken from Tables A3.34, A 3.35, A3.36, and A6.8.

Unemployment rates too declined significantly for males as well as females in all urban, on account of a substantial decline in non-metro unemployment rates when the metros' usual status unemployment increased by 0.8 percentage points for females. The usual status unemployment rate in all urban declined by 1.0 percentage points in the case of males and by 1.2 percentage points in the case of females (Table 6.2). These figures for non-metros were 1.3 and 1.8 percentage points, respectively. This means that like WPRs unemployment rates too declined sharply for females in case of non-metro urban centres. But while in the metros WPRs for females declined by 2.2 percentage points, unemployment rate increased by 0.8 percentage points. This means that a decline in WPR in the metros led to an increase in usual status unemployment for females. In the non-metros, a large chunk of the females exited the labour force, indicating that they were not interested in employment, either on account of non-availability of work or because of an increase in incomes of households. Further analysis of the NSS data, by disaggregating by age-groups and wage rates will be required to understand this phenomenon in the non-metros.

Male unemployment rates by usual status declined at a higher rate in the non-metros than in the metros, by just 0.1 percentage points in case of the latter, but male WPRs declined at a faster rate in the metros than in the non-metros. In totality, the size of the labour force shrunk relatively more in non-metros in the case of males. It needs to be further investigated as to who withdrew from the labour market and why; did some males move to education, did some of them give up hopes of availability of employment and became non-workers, did some move into work categories with no payment and hence were not captured in the labour force survey or was it a combination of factors as mentioned earlier for females. In the metros, while WPRs declined, unemployment hardly increased, indicating that a smaller proportion (than in the non-metros) moved out of the labour force, and this could probably be explained by a shift to education in the young age groups. Current Daily Status (CDS) unemployment rates followed the same pattern as the usual status unemployment rates except that these declined for the metros as well as for the non-metros for males as well as females unlike the usual status where unemployment rates increased for females in the metros.

## NATURE OF EMPLOYMENT

On the whole, at the all urban level in the last five years, both Regular Employment (RE) as well as Casual Labour (CL) employment among males increased bringing down self-employment work among them. This showed a widening disparity among males in terms of work quality. For the first time since the reforms, RE among males showed some improvement,

which led to a decline in Self-Employment (SE) among them. At the same time even CL work availability increased and it seems that as a result a shift to CL occurred in the last five years.

**Table 6.3**    Nature of Employment (in percentages), All Urban

|  | SE | RE | CL |
|---|---|---|---|
| **Male** | | | |
| 1987–8 | 41.6 | 43.7 | 14.7 |
| 1993–4 | 41.6 | 42.2 | 16.2 |
| 2004–5 | 44.8 | 40.6 | 14.6 |
| 2009–10 | 41.1 | 41.9 | 17.0 |
| **Female** | | | |
| 1987–8 | 47.1 | 27.5 | 25.4 |
| 1993–4 | 44.8 | 29.2 | 26.1 |
| 2004–5 | 47.7 | 35.6 | 16.7 |
| 2009–10 | 41.1 | 39.3 | 19.6 |

*Source*: Data taken from Tables A3.4, A3.5, A3.7, A3.8, A3.13, A6.2, and A6.3.
*Note*: Rows add up to 100.

A somewhat different trend can be observed among females. In the last five years, like in case of males, the shares of RE and CL increased while that of SE declined. Over the last two decades, there was an increasing trend of RE among urban females while the shares of SE and CL fluctuated over time. In the years when SE declined, CL increased and vice versa. Up to 2004–5, an increase in the proportion of females engaged as RE went hand-in-hand with an increase in female WPRs. In 2009–10, while female WPRs substantially declined in all urban areas, RE continued to increase. We may therefore be inclined to conclude that a decline in WPRs was on account of loss of SE opportunities for urban women and hence some took up whatever casual work was available.

Metro and non-metro differences in the nature of work were substantial. Among males in non-metros, the trend was somewhat similar to what was observed for females at the all urban level—RE started increasing since 1993–4, however not reaching the 1987–8 level when 42.8 per cent males were engaged as RE (Figure 6.1). In fact, at the time of economic reforms and in a few years after that, non-metro males lost regular work and the proportion of males employed as RE reached only 30.8 per cent. Subsequently, WPRs also increased along with improvement in availability of RE up to 2009–10 when WPRs declined but the proportion of RE increased. With an increase in WPRs up to 2004–5, SE also increased among males in non-metros. As a result, in the reforms period, CL declined. In 2009–10, the proportion engaged as CL increased to 19.9 per cent while WPRs and SE declined. It seems that in the last five years, work availability for males declined in the SE category and those who would like to and can are taking up CL work. Otherwise, others just dropped out of the labour force. Data also shows that both RE and CL increased indicating an emerging schism in the quality of work available in non-metros. Because non-metros include a wide spectrum of urban settlements, there is a need to look at the situation in a more disaggregated manner as to in which size of urban settlements, RE is being generated.

In the metros, CL type of work for males always remained low at around 10 per cent (Figure 6.2). RE consistently declined whereas SE consistently increased up to 2004–5, after which the trend altered—RE marginally increased and SE marginally declined. The increase in SE up to 2004–5 among males in metros was along with an increase in WPRs. In fact, increase in SE work availability seems to have resulted in improvements in WPRs among metro males. In 2009–10, it seems that there was no substantial change in SE work availability to metro males and as a result WPRs declined. In other words, in the reforms period, SE opportunities for males in metros increased. Once again, SE work could be at high as well as low-income levels.

Among females, the trends are close to those among males in their respective classes

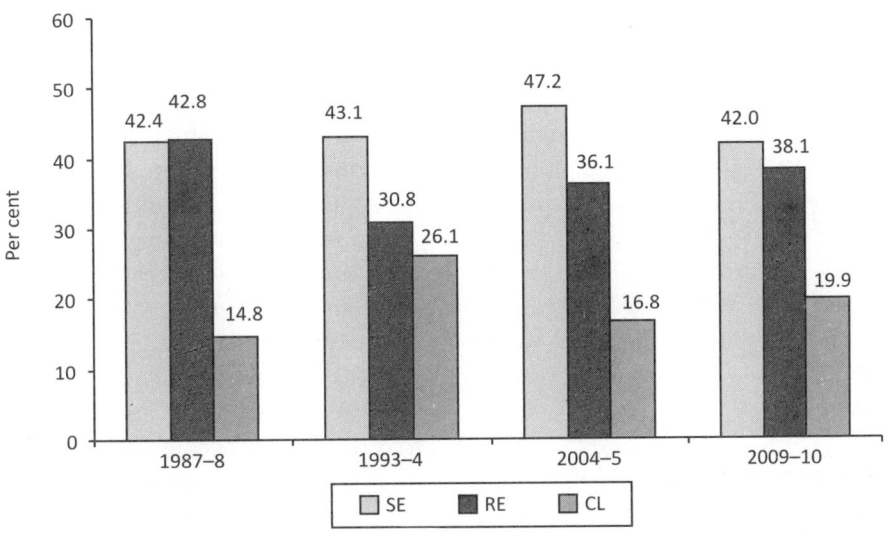

**Figure 6.1** Nature of Employment in Non-metros, Males

*Source*: Data taken from Tables A3.6, A3.9, A3.12, and A6.2.

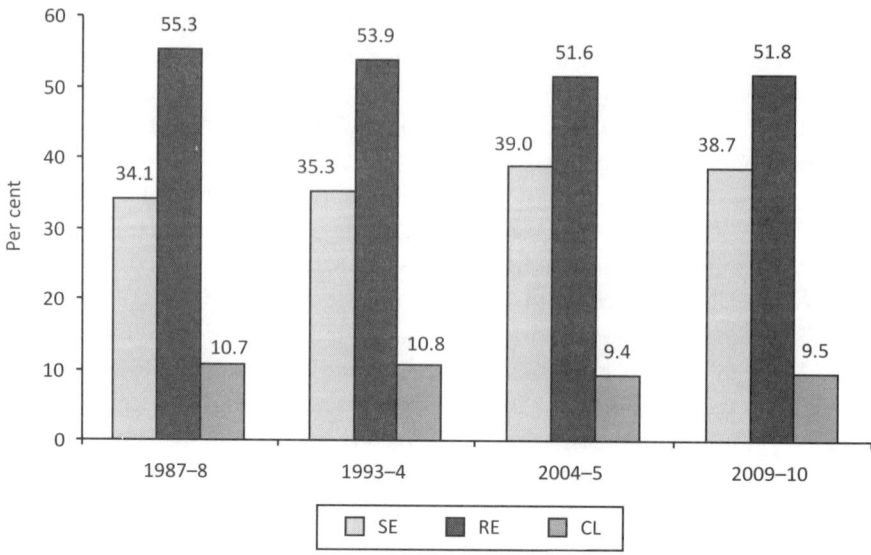

**Figure 6.2**    Nature of Employment in Metros, Males

*Source*: Data taken from Tables A3.6, A3.9, A3.13, and A6.2.

of urban centres. For example, in non-metros, females employed as CL substantially increased in 2009–10, in fact, it stood at as high as 22.8 per cent (Figure 6.3). SE reduced substantially from 50.6 per cent in 2004–5 to 43.3 per cent, and was probably the reason for a substantial decline in WPRs among females. RE continued to increase over time and also during the last five years. Like metro males, metro females were also not getting into CL. Their proportion in RE consistently increased and reached 57.2 per cent in 2009–10 (Figure 6.4). In fact, SE declined and RE increased among them in spite of a decline in WPRs. Again, availability of SE work is important for the urban workers in general but female workers in particular in metro economies.

## SECTORAL DISTRIBUTION OF THE WORKFORCE

At the all urban level, as expected employment in the primary sector for males as well as for females declined over the entire period, but the

decline was faster in the reforms period (Table 6.4). In the last five years, the same trend continued. Nonetheless, 14.2 per cent employed females in all urban were in the primary sector in 2009–10 (Table 6.4) on account of non-metros where 17.8 per cent of the females were still in this sector (Figure 6.7). As expected, the share of employment of the tertiary sector increased over time for males as well as for females. But in the 2004–5 to 2009–10 period the proportion of males in the tertiary sector remained unchanged whereas females experienced a 3.4 percentage points increase in tertiary employment in all urban. Note that males experienced a marginal decline in WPRs whereas females experienced a drastic decline in WPRs. Female WPRs in urban areas seem to have declined on account of a decline in the primary sector. Females released from agriculture probably shifted to the tertiary sector to the extent that they could get absorbed. Often in this process of transition when agriculture land was in disuse particularly in the drought year of

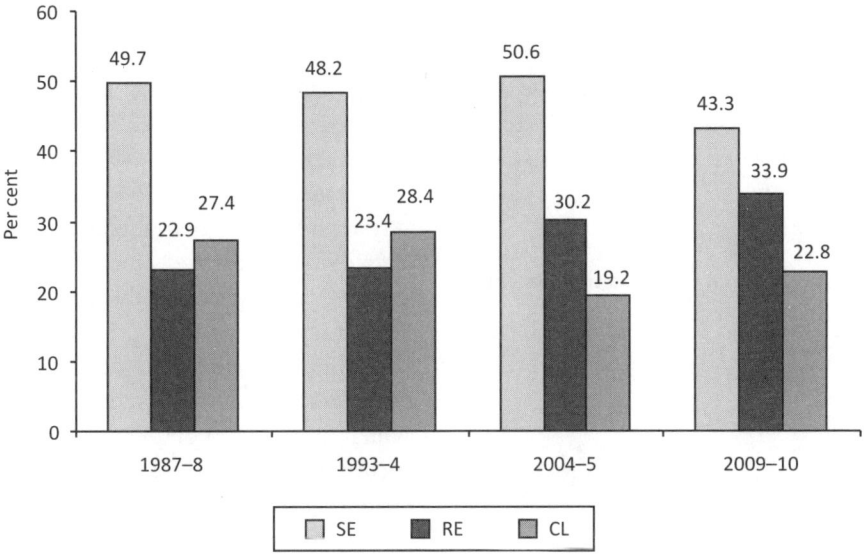

**Figure 6.3** Nature of Employment in Non-metros, Females

*Source*: Data taken from Tables A3.6, A3.9, A3.12, and A6.3.

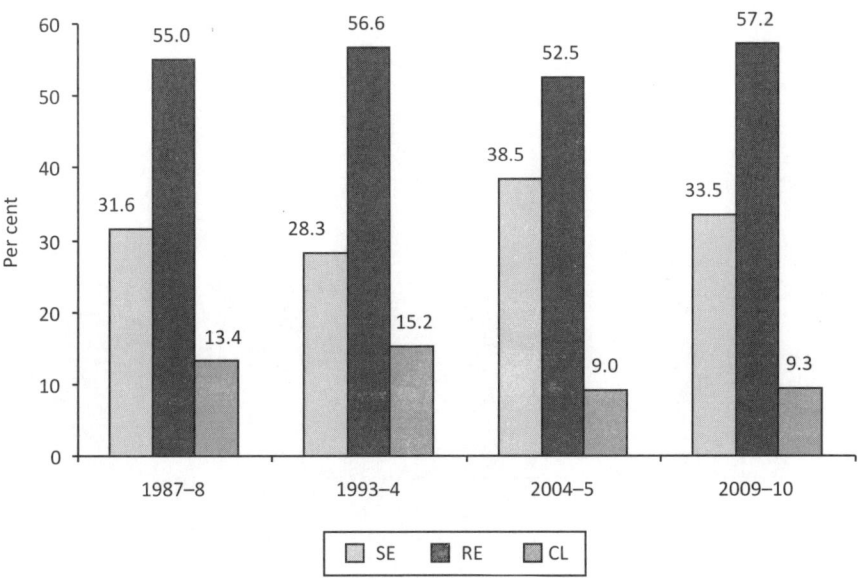

**Figure 6.4** Nature of Employment in Metros, Females

*Source*: Data taken from Tables A3.6, A3.9, A3.13, and A6.3.

2009–10, women lost their employment. At the same time, if the land was sold and the family earned a fortune then women dropped out of the labour force. Decline in primary sector employment for females resulted in a sharp decline in SE among them in 2009–10 as compared to 2004–5 (Table 6.3).

**Table 6.4** Sectoral Share of Employment (in percentages), All Urban

|  | P | S | T |
| --- | --- | --- | --- |
| **Male** | | | |
| 1987–8 | 10.5 | 33.0 | 56.5 |
| 1993–4 | 10.3 | 31.8 | 57.9 |
| 2004–5 | 7.1 | 33.6 | 59.4 |
| 2009–10 | 6.7 | 34.0 | 59.3 |
| **Female** | | | |
| 1987–8 | 30.3 | 31.0 | 38.6 |
| 1993–4 | 25.4 | 28.6 | 46.0 |
| 2004–5 | 18.3 | 32.2 | 49.5 |
| 2009–10 | 14.2 | 32.9 | 52.9 |

*Source*: Data taken from Tables A3.14, A3.15, A3.17, A3.18, A3.23, A6.4, and 6.5.
*Note*: Rows add up to 100.

For males as well as for females there was a marginal increase in the share of secondary sector employment. The increase in regular employment for females was in the tertiary sector. There was also casual labour increase for females and that too seems to be in the tertiary sector. Cross tabulation of sectors of employment with the nature of work would tell us the type of work available in the tertiary and secondary sectors.

Although male WPRs declined in the metros there was an increase in the share of RE, which was on account of an increase in tertiary sector work in 2009–10 (Figure 6.6). This was a trend in the previous years as well. The share of secondary sector employment among males consistently declined over time, with a marginal increase in 2004–5 and then a decline in 2009–10. Nonetheless, 34.4 per cent employed males in 2009–10 were in the secondary sector. Probably a large proportion of this would be in the construction sector, which has seen phenomenal increase on account of infrastructure projects

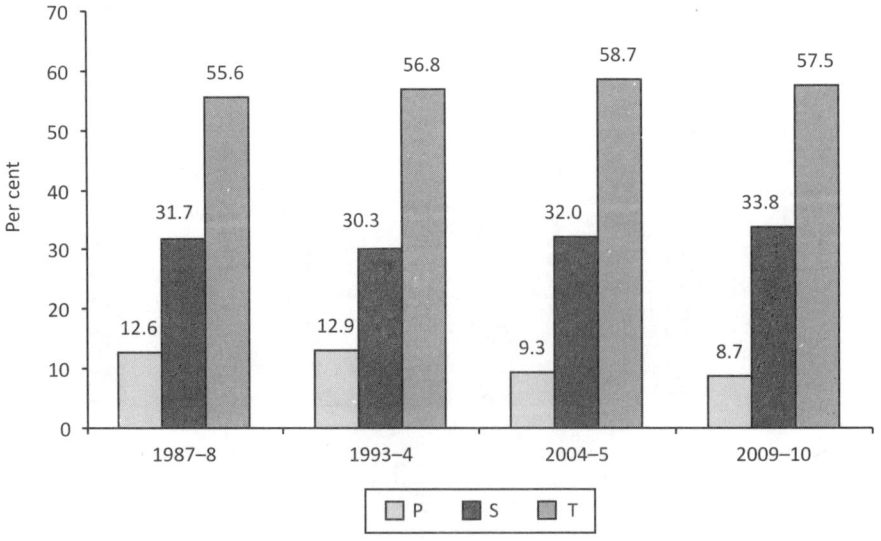

**Figure 6.5**　Sectoral Employment Share, Non-metros, Males

*Source*: Data taken from Tables A3.16, A3.19, A3.22, and A6.4.

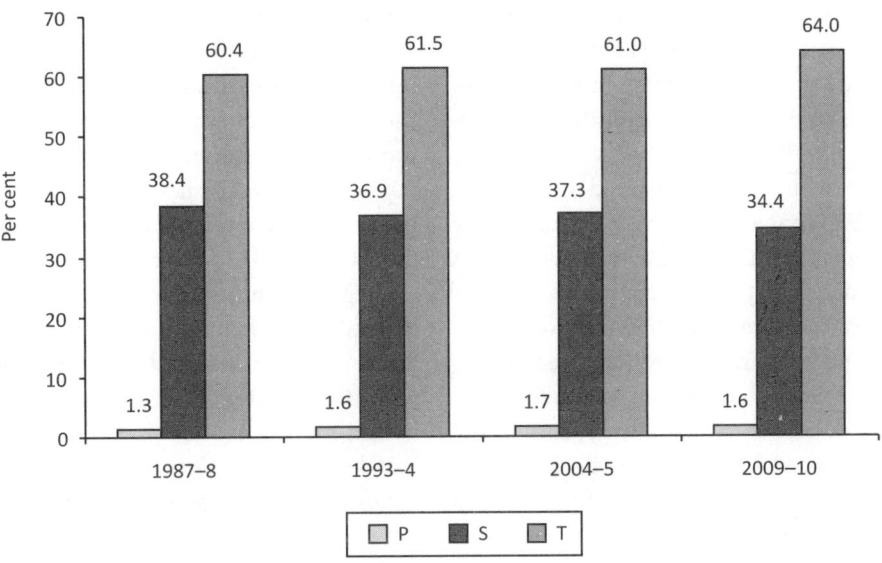

**Figure 6.6**    Sectoral Employment Share, Metros, Males

*Source*: Data taken from Tables A3.16, A3.19, A3.23, and A6.4.

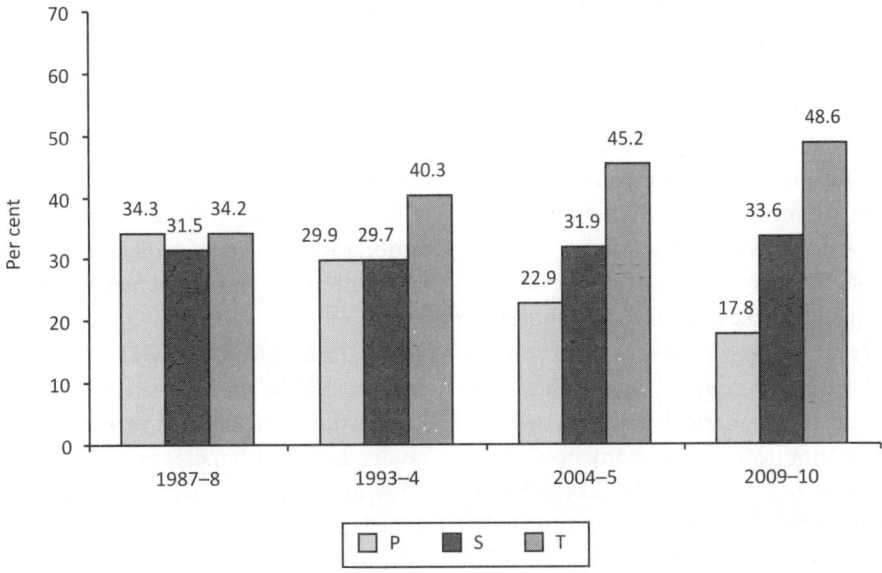

**Figure 6.7**    Sectoral Employment Share, Non-metros, Females

*Source*: Data taken from Tables A3.16, A3.19, A3.22, and A6.5.

in metro cities under the JNNURM. Among females in metros, as compared to 2004–5 there was a significant increase in the share of tertiary sector employment from 63 to 67 per cent and a simultaneous decline in the secondary sector, which had registered increase in 2004–5 (Figure 6.8). For females also, tertiary sector employment was of a regular type. In other words, metropolitan economies are transiting to tertiarization, with one-third of the workers remaining in the secondary sector.

Female WPRs declined in non-metros because of a decline in availability of work in the primary sector, which also led to a decline in SE. Nonetheless, about 18 per cent of the females worked in the primary sector in the non-metros (Figure 6.7). There was a consistent increase in the share of secondary sector employment among non-metro females, reaching 33.6 per cent in 2009–10, nearly the same proportion as that among males in non-metros (whose proportion in secondary sector was 33.8 per cent). Work in the secondary sector increased for non-metro males in 2009–10, which was of regular as well as casual labour type as both these types of work increased in 2009–10 as compared to 2004–5 for males.

In the non-metros, although employment in the primary sector reduced among females, those remaining in the sector showed a shift towards casual labour from 36.2 per cent (Table 3.6) in 2004–5 to 46 per cent in 2009–10 (Figure 6.6), at the cost of SE. It seems that in this class of towns, on account of industrialization, peripheral agricultural land was diverted to non-agricultural purposes and hence it was not possible for many households to remain in agriculture. It is also likely that agriculture households in the non-metros either sold or were waiting to sell their land leading to a decline in agriculture. Thus, SE among women in agriculture households declined. While the males transited out to the non-

primary sector (Figure 6.5), women continued in agriculture but as daily wage labour in the remaining farms, leading to an increase in CL in the primary sector. CL in the secondary sector too increased in non-metros in 2009–10 from 2004–5, when SE in this sector declined for males as well as females. Hence, even though industrialization occurred in non-metros (or a category of non-metros), the nature of work here was informal and of the daily wage type. These workers would have very poor social security. The extent of RE in the secondary sector in non-metros did not change much in the last half decade. In the tertiary sector for non-metro males regular employment increased from 40.9 per cent (Table 3.6) to 44 per cent (Table 6.5) and for non-metro females it increased from 55 per cent to 59 per cent. In other words, some dynamics of the metros penetrated down to some non-metros, while there was overall casualization of non-metro employment.

In the metros the nature of work in the secondary sector did not change much in the last five years both for males and females. It also did not change in the tertiary sector among males. The only change observed in this period was an increase in RE among females in the tertiary sector—an increase from 68.7 per cent in 2004–5 (Table 3.4) to 73 per cent in 2009–10 (Table 6.5). Increase in regular employment among females in metros (Figure 6.4) was on account of an increase in tertiary sector work.

**QUALITY OF EMPLOYMENT**

On the whole, in all urban areas in spite of casualization, ML type of work declined among males as well as females and high quality of employment in Administrative and Professional (A/P) services increased over the entire period of the study (Table 6.6). The exception is of females which registered a slight increase in ML employment in 2009–10 as compared to 2004–5. Interestingly, the 2004–5 to 2009–10

**Table 6.5**    Nature of Employment for Each Sector, 2009–10

|  | Non-Metros | | | | Metros | | | |
|---|---|---|---|---|---|---|---|---|
|  | SE | RE | CL | Total Workers | SE | RE | CL | Total Workers |
| **Male** | | | | | | | | |
| Primary | 57.1 | 11.5 | 31.4 | 100.0 | 73.9 | 18.2 | 8.0 | 100.0 |
| Secondary | 26.9 | 35.0 | 38.1 | 100.0 | 27.2 | 53.9 | 18.9 | 100.0 |
| Tertiary | 48.5 | 44.0 | 7.5 | 100.0 | 44.0 | 51.5 | 4.4 | 100.0 |
| **Female** | | | | | | | | |
| Primary | 51.7 | 2.4 | 45.9 | 100.0 | 72.8 | 9.4 | 17.8 | 100.0 |
| Secondary | 56.5 | 14.7 | 28.9 | 100.0 | 56.0 | 26.1 | 17.9 | 100.0 |
| Tertiary | 31.2 | 58.8 | 10.0 | 100.0 | 22.0 | 72.9 | 5.0 | 100.0 |

*Source*: Calculated by authors from the unit level data of Employment and Unemployment Schedule of 66th Round (2009–10) of NSSO.

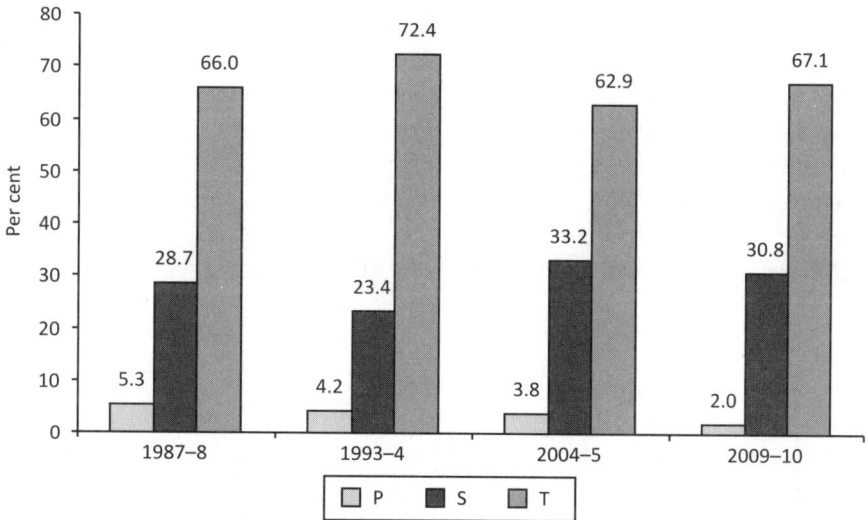

**Figure 6.8**    Sectoral Employment Share, Metros, Females
*Source*: Data taken from Tables A3.16, A3.19, A3.23, and A6.5.

period registered the largest percentage increase in A/P type of jobs; about 10 percentage point increase among males and 7 percentage point increase among females. The reduction in ML type of jobs was just 2.2 percentage points among males and an increase of 0.4 percentage points among females. This implies that employment in the middle category declined significantly. This shows continuation in the trend of increasing inequality in the quality of employment in the urban sector, with high increases in high quality-high income employment on the one hand and a continuing large proportion of workers remaining in unskilled jobs. These inequalities translated into consumption inequalities on the whole, but in particular among the top 20 percentiles in the urban sector, as observed in Chapter 1.

**Table 6.6**    Quality of Employment, All Urban

|  | A/P | C | ML |
|---|---|---|---|
| **Male** | | | |
| 1987–8 | 13.2 | 37.8 | 49.0 |
| 1993–4 | 13.9 | 36.6 | 49.5 |
| 2004–5 | 18.0 | 36.0 | 46.0 |
| 2009–10 | 28.3 | 28.0 | 43.8 |
| **Female** | | | |
| 1987–8 | 16.1 | 27.2 | 56.7 |
| 1993–4 | 15.3 | 28.8 | 55.9 |
| 2004–5 | 20.9 | 37.3 | 41.8 |
| 2009–10 | 27.9 | 29.9 | 42.2 |

*Source*: Data taken from Tables A3.24, A3.25, A3.27, A3.28, A3.33, A6.6, and A6.7.
*Note*: Rows add up to 100.

There was a vast difference between the quality of work in the metros and non-metros (Figures 6.9 to 6.12). Among males, there was about a 10 percentage point difference between metros and non-metros with regard to the proportion employed in A/P jobs, the former having a higher proportion than the latter in 2009–10. The distance between metros and non-metros increased in 2009–10 as compared to 2004–5, when the gap was just 5.3 percentage points. The point to note is that in 1993–4, the gap was about 6.2 percentage points, which declined in 2004–5, indicating that non-metros were moving closer to metros with regard to high quality employment. But, once again the gap increased. The same is true for females as well for the years 2009–10 and 2004–5. The gap between metros and non-metros widened to 10 percentage points in 2009–10 as compared to 5 percentage points in 2004–5. Females in metros did not register any change with regard to the proportion employed in A/P jobs from 1993–4 to 2004–5. Thus, in case of females too the gap declined in 2004–5 as compared to 1993–4 and then increased in 2009–10 as compared to the previous Round. One reason for this could be the sample itself, as explained in Chapter 1, where we state that metros and non-metros over the NSS years are not strictly comparable, as these are not the same cities in the different sample rounds.

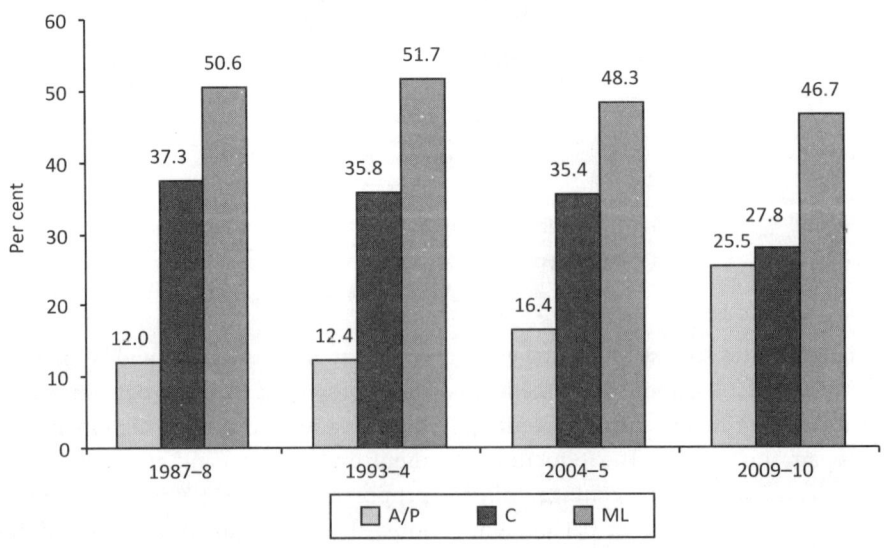

**Figure 6.9**    Employment Quality, Non-metros, Males

*Source*: Data taken from Tables A3.26, A3.29, A3.32, and A6.6.

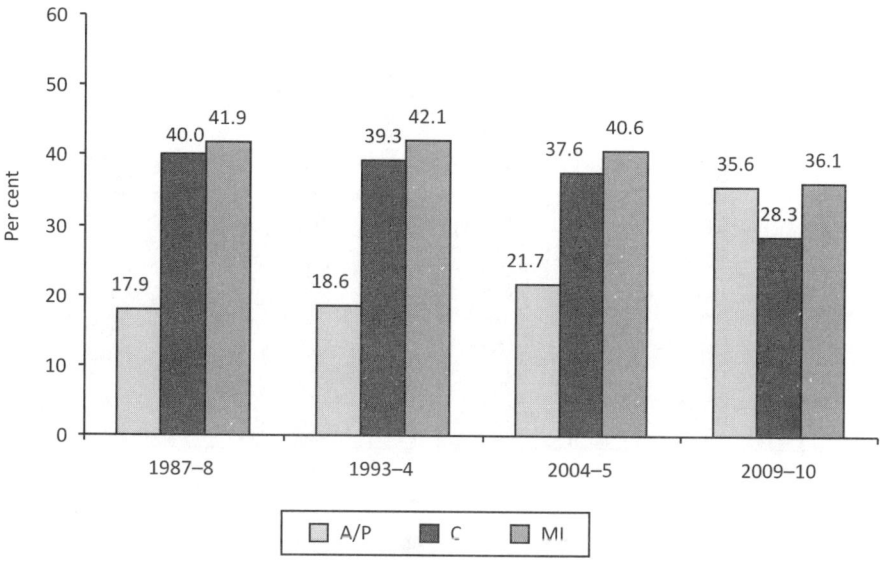

**Figure 6.10**  Employment Sectors, Metros, Males

*Source*: Data taken from Tables A3.26, A3.29, A3.33, and A6.6.

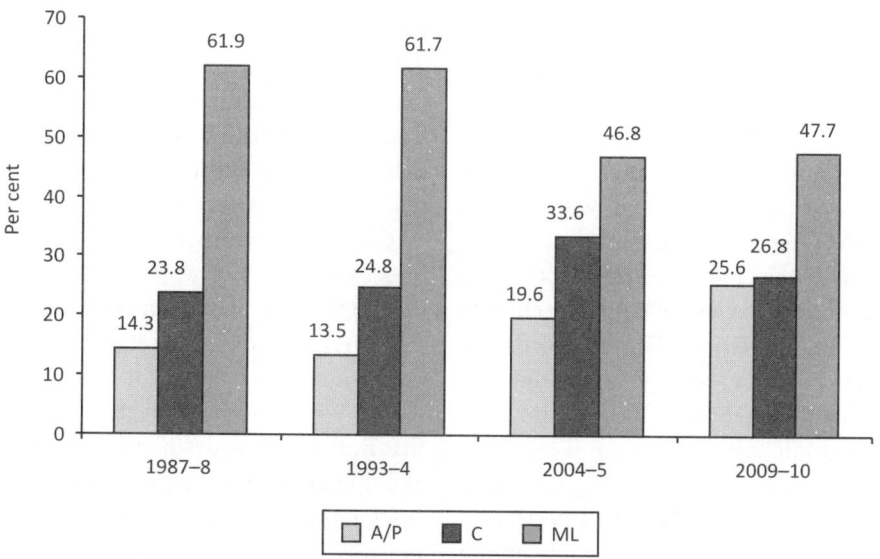

**Figure 6.11**  Employment Quality, Non-metros, Females

*Source*: Data taken from Tables A3.26, A3.29, A3.32, and A6.7.

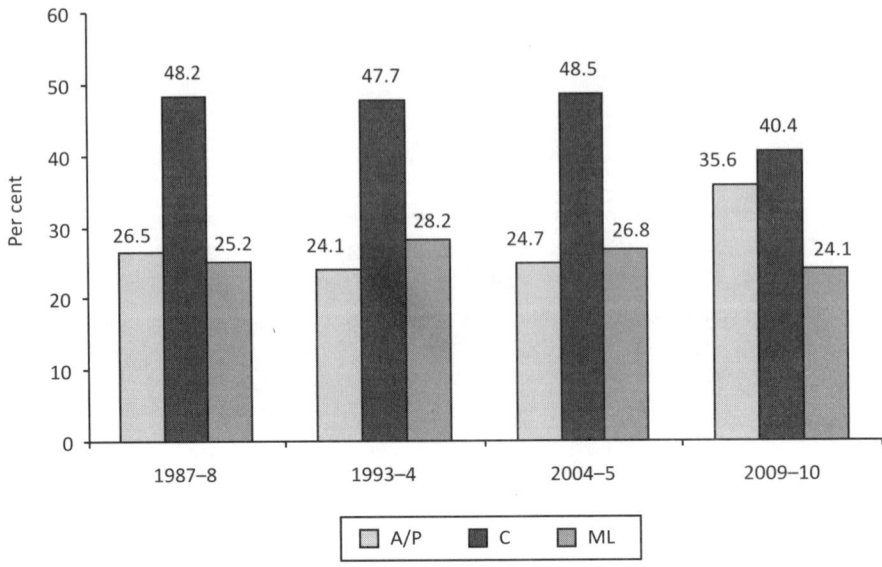

**Figure 6.12**   Employment Sectors, Metros, Females

*Source*: Data taken from Tables A3.26, A3.29, A3.33, and A6.7.

ML type of jobs continued to dominate the non-metro economy, wherein 46.7 per cent among males and 47.7 per cent among females were in such type of employment. In the metros, ML jobs dominated among males and clerical type of jobs dominated among females. As we have observed for all urban, A/P type of employment among females increased at the time when clerical jobs declined, with a small decline in ML type of jobs in the metros. Among males also, A/P jobs increased on account of a substantial decline in clerical employment and a smaller decline in ML jobs. In other words, the metropolitan economy became highly unequal in terms of employment over time, particularly in the last half a decade.

### LITERACY RATES AND EDUCATION LEVELS

It goes without saying that literacy rates among males as well as females improved over the NSS Rounds, reaching 93.6 per cent in the metros and 89.7 per cent in the non-metros among males and 84.8 per cent and 77.7 per cent, respectively among females in 2009–10 (Figures 6.13 and 6.14). Even in the metros, the males have not reached 100 per cent literacy, when the definition of literacy is very minimal—ability to read and write. Improvements in literacy rates have been very slow among females in the last half a decade, and they have not crossed the 90 per cent mark as yet.

Over time, non-metro to metro inequality in literacy rates as well as female to male inequality in the same has decreased (Table 6.7). In 1993–4, at the onset of reforms, non-metro to metro inequality ratios for males and females were 0.94 and 0.85, respectively, which means that non-metro males had reached 94 per cent and females had reached 85 per cent of the literacy rates of their counterparts in the metros. In 2009–10, the ratio improved to 0.96 and 0.92 for males and females, respectively. Similarly, we calculated female to male ratios of literacy, which too improved from 0.87 in

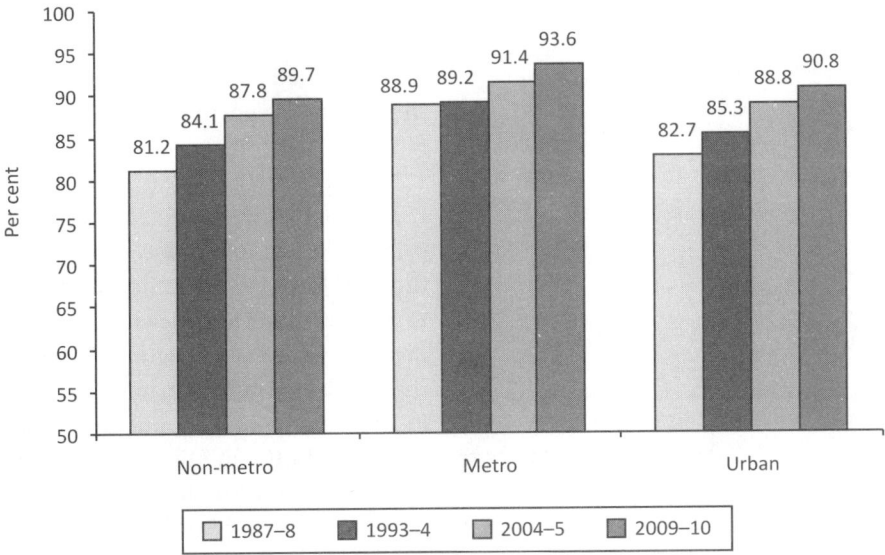

**Figure 6.13** Literacy Rates, Males

*Source*: Data taken from Tables A4.3, A4.7, A4.13, and A6.9.

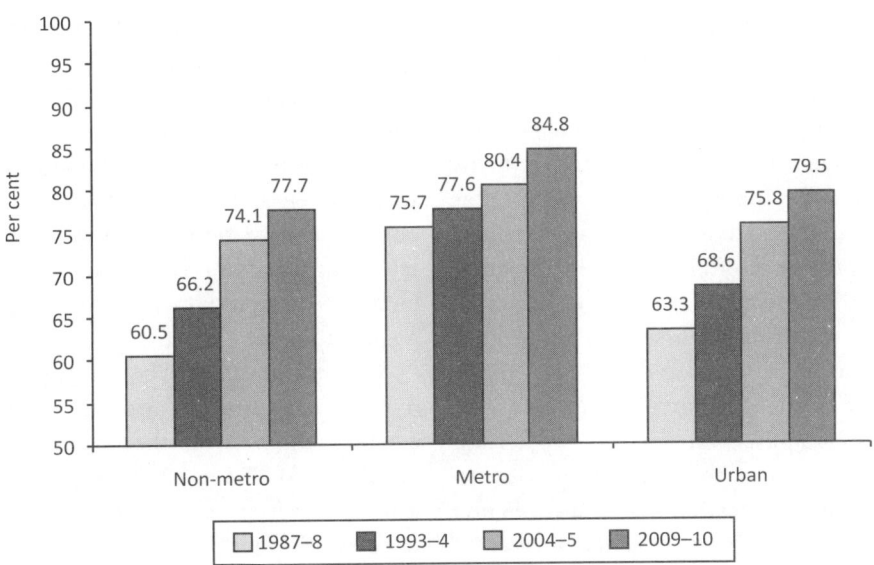

**Figure 6.14** Literacy Rates, Females

*Source*: Data taken from Tables A4.4, A4.8, A4.14, and A6.10.

**Table 6.7**    Equality Ratios in Literacy Rate

|         | Non-metro/Metro | Female/Male |
|---------|-----------------|-------------|
|         | Male            | Metro       |
| 1987–8  | 0.91            | 0.85        |
| 1993–4  | 0.94            | 0.87        |
| 2004–5  | 0.96            | 0.88        |
| 2009–10 | 0.96            | 0.91        |
|         | Female          | Non-metro   |
| 1987–8  | 0.80            | 0.75        |
| 1993–4  | 0.85            | 0.79        |
| 2004–5  | 0.92            | 0.84        |
| 2009–10 | 0.92            | 0.87        |

*Source*: Calculated by the authors taking data from Tables A4.3, A4.4, A4.7, A4.8, A4.13, A4.14, A6.9, and A6.10.

1993–4 to 0.91 in 2009–10 in the metros and from 0.79 to 0.87 in the same period in the non-metros. The gender gap was higher in non-metros and the class-gap was higher among females than among males. This means that there was higher gender inequality in literacy rates in non-metros and there was higher inequality between non-metros and metros among females. This was the case in all the NSS Rounds and it continued even till the end of the last decade.

Literacy rates have improved but a substantial proportion of the urban population remains nearly illiterate. Children who drop out after primary school tend to move close to illiterates. Their proportion continues to remain quite high, at 38.7 per cent in non-metros and 31.2 per cent in metros in the case of males (Figure 6.15) and as high as 50.6 and 39.3 per cent in the case of females (Figure 6.16) in 2009–10. There has certainly been a significant decline in the proportion of the population with no literacy or low education over time. While non-metro versus metro and female versus male inequality in literacy rates declined over time, these ratios worsened with regard to no or low literacy rates (Table 6.8). Non-metro to

metro inequality in no or low literacy was 1.20 in 1993–4, which increased to 1.24 in 2004–5, and remained at the same level in 2009–10 in the case of males. In the case of females these ratios for the three years were 1.23, 1.23, and 1.29. Thus, a large proportion of the population in non-metros was unable to move beyond the primary level of education, which suggests that the quality of labour in non-metros continues to be very poor. Gender inequality in this indicator of education increased in non-metros; the inequality ratio remained constant at 1.29 in 1993–4 and 2004–5, but increased to 1.31 in 2009–10. In the metros, between 2004–5 and 2009–10, the inequality ratio in this indicator came down from 1.30 to 1.26, which was a marginal increase from a ratio of 1.25 in 1993–4.

The number of those reaching higher education (university education) was still low at 18.0 per cent among males and 15.5 per cent among females in all the urban areas together (Figures 6.17 and 6.18). As in the previous Rounds, in 2009–10 as well, the proportion of literates reaching higher education levels was higher in the metros as compared to the non-metros; the figures being 22.3 and 21.5 per cent, respectively, for males and females in metros and 16.3 and 13.3 per cent, respectively, for non-metros. In non-metros, five in six literate males and seven in eight literate females still dropped out of the education system by the time their schooling was complete. For non-metros to get high quality employment therefore is going to be big problem.

The non-metro to metro gap marginally reduced over time in the case of males, the equality ratio between the two rising from 0.68 in 1993–4 to 0.73 in 2009–10 (Table 6.9). The gap nonetheless remains quite high. Among females, the ratio fluctuated over different rounds and between 2004–5 and 2009–10 the ratio marginally declined from 0.63 to 0.62. A more worrying figure is that the ratio was 0.65

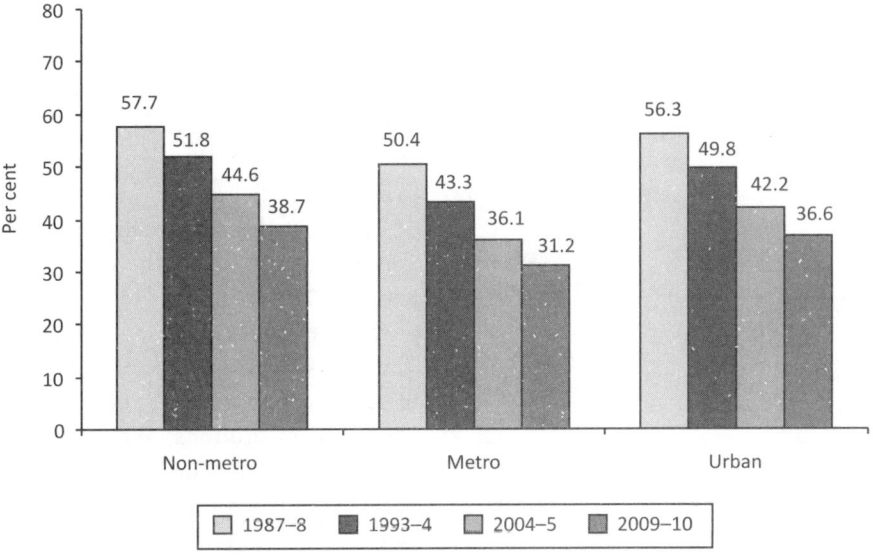

**Figure 6.15** No Literacy and Low Education, Males

*Source*: Data taken from Tables A4.3, A4.7, A4.13, and A6.9.

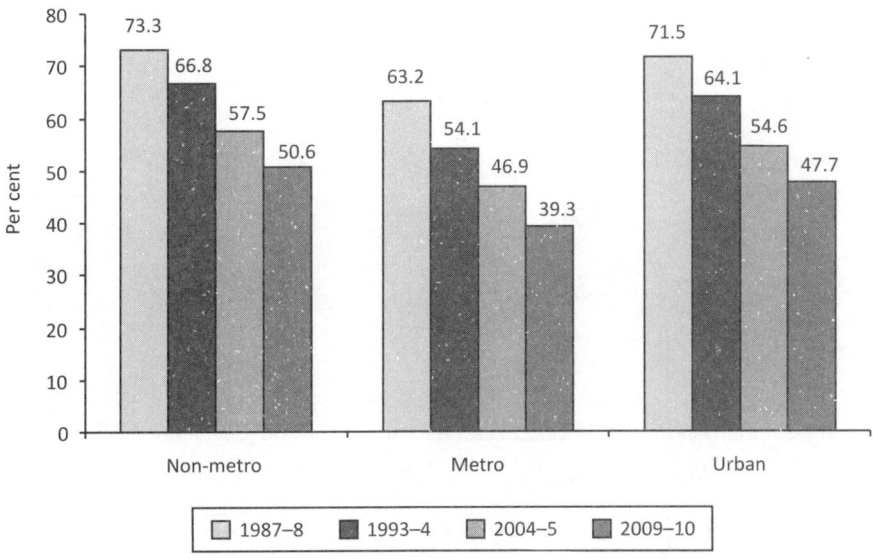

**Figure 6.16** No Literacy and Low Education, Females

*Source*: Data taken from Tables A4.4, A4.8, A4.14, and A6.10.

**Table 6.8**    Inequality Ratios in No or Low
Education Levels

|  | Non-Metro/Metro | Female/Male |
|---|---|---|
|  | Male | Metro |
| 1987–8 | 1.14 | 1.25 |
| 1993–4 | 1.20 | 1.25 |
| 2004–5 | 1.24 | 1.30 |
| 2009–10 | 1.24 | 1.26 |
|  | Female | Non-Metro |
| 1987–8 | 1.16 | 1.27 |
| 1993–4 | 1.23 | 1.29 |
| 2004–5 | 1.23 | 1.29 |
| 2009–10 | 1.29 | 1.31 |

*Source*: Calculated by the authors taking data from Tables A4.3, A4.4, A4.7, A4.8, A4.13, A4.14, A6.9, and A6.10.

in 1987–8, a Round before the reforms began. Therefore, in the reforms period while entry into higher education increased among the population in non-metros, the improvement was only among males and not among females. Was this because higher education facilities were not yet available in non-metros and hence the youth had to move to metros to access them? If so then there are more possibilities of young males moving to metros than young females moving to metros.

Those in higher quality employment in non-metros was nearly the same for males and females (25.5 per cent [Figure 6.9] and 25.6 per cent [Figure 6.11], respectively) in 2009–10. Thus, it was not on account of non-availability of such work that females did not enter higher education institutions. Therefore lack of easy access to higher education institutions was a probable reason for females dropping out of the system after school education was completed. Secondly, there certainly is a big gender dimension to such decisions by families; families even in urban areas do not expect female household members to make careers and would want them to be married off as soon as the match was fixed. There was also a fear that more educated

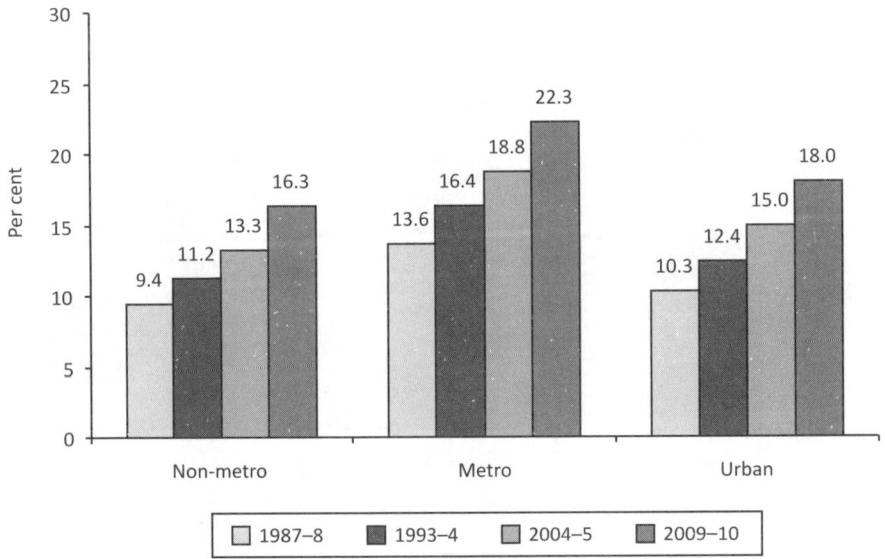

**Figure 6.17**    Proportion of Literates in Higher Education, Males

*Source*: Calculated by authors using data taken from Tables A4.3, A4.7, A4.13, and A6.9.

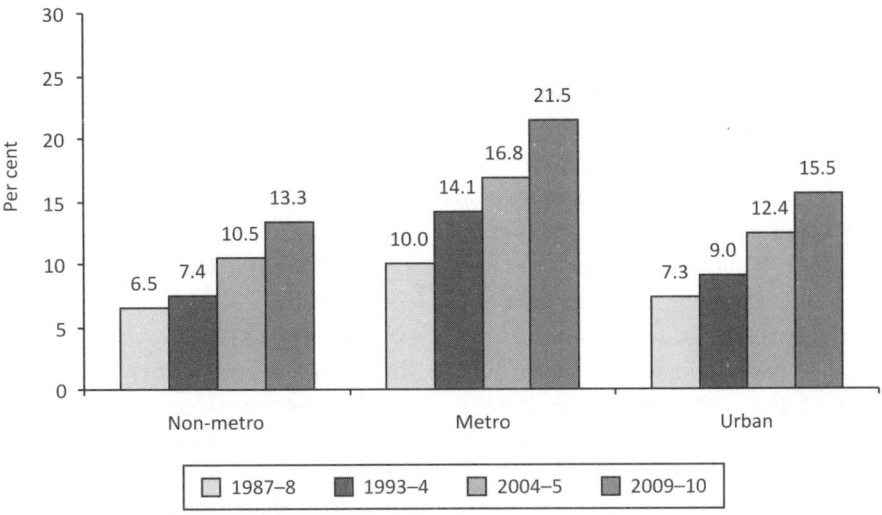

**Figure 6.18**   Proportion of Literates in Higher Education, Females

*Source*: Calculated by authors using data taken from Tables A4.4, A4.8, A4.14, and A6.10.

**Table 6.9**   Equality Ratios in Higher Education

|  | Non-metro/Metro | Female/Male |
|---|---|---|
|  | Male | Metro |
| 1987–8 | 0.69 | 0.74 |
| 1993–4 | 0.68 | 0.86 |
| 2004–5 | 0.71 | 0.89 |
| 2009–10 | 0.73 | 0.96 |
|  | Female | Non-metro |
| 1987–8 | 0.65 | 0.69 |
| 1993–4 | 0.52 | 0.66 |
| 2004–5 | 0.63 | 0.79 |
| 2009–10 | 0.62 | 0.82 |

*Source*: Calculated by the authors taking data from Tables A4.3, A4.4, A4.7, A4.8, A4.13, A4.14, A6.9, and A6.10.

females would not get suitable grooms. For various cultural and economic reasons, females in non-metros may have dropped out of the education system after completing schooling besides the possible reason of non-availability of higher education facilities in this size class of urban centres.

Gender equality in the proportion of literate reaching higher education increased over time. It needs to be mentioned that this ratio is only the proportion of females in higher education divided by the proportion of males in higher education and not the ratio of actual numbers. In the metros, the ratio increased to 0.96 and in the non-metros it reached 0.82 in 2009–10.

**AVERAGE CONSUMPTION EXPENDITURES**

By the time this handbook went to print, official poverty lines had not been declared by the Government of India (GoI). Hence, we refrained from estimating overall Head Count Ratios (HCRs) as well as the ones disaggregated by size classes of urban centres. Poverty lines are estimated applying price inflators on the previous NSS Round's state-wise poverty line. Since the poverty line and price deflators were not available, we were also not been able to calculate the Compound Annual Growth Rate (CAGR) of consumption expenditures. We only report the APCE by states (see Table

A6.11), a comparison of metro to non-metro APCE changes over time (Table 6.10), and Coefficient of Variation (CV) of APCE over the states (Table 6.10) also over time. The metro to non-metro ratio of APCE fluctuated, increasing in the first decade of the reforms and declining in the last half a decade. The ratio however increased from 1987–8, which is the only pre-reforms period data presented in this book.

Inequality across states, represented by the CV of APCE, increased over time in total urban, the values of CV increased from 17.6 in 1987–8 to 20.7 in 2009–10. There was a larger increase in the CV in non-metro sample, where the CV in 2009–10 was 25.6. This can be explained by non-metros of some states having high APCE. For example, in Haryana, Punjab, and the rest of the states and union territories, the ratio was less than 1, indicating that the per capita APCE in non-metros was higher than it was in the metros. On the other extreme were Rajasthan, Madhya Pradesh, West Bengal, and Karnataka where the ratio was high—2.18, 1.77, 1.64, and 1.63, respectively, when the average ratio was 1.44 (Table 6.10). In other words, metro cities across the states were similar than non-metros across the states. We observed this in earlier

chapters as well that the developed states and developed urban centres were more alike in nature whereas less developed states and less developed urban centres were more diverse in nature. 'Happy families are all alike; every unhappy family is unhappy in its own way', a famous quote from Leo Tolstoy's 'Anna Karenina', is quite relevant in this context.

## POLICY IMPLICATIONS

This handbook is written to point out that there are very large differences in metros and non-metros in an urban system. This is as true at the national level as it is at the state level in India. It is therefore inappropriate to have a uniform policy paradigm for the entire urban sector. Having established this need for more disaggregated urban policymaking than we see currently in India, the second important policy issue is recognizing that there is a great deal of diversity in the non-metros, they range from population of 5,000 (in case a census town has been declared an urban centre) to 1 million. In 2001 (since the 2011 census town data was not available), 26 per cent of the urban population was in small towns with populations less than 50,000. The same proportion of the population

**Table 6.10**    Monthly APCE (current prices), Metro, Non-metro, and Total Urban, 2009–10

|  | Non-Metro | Metro | Total Urban | Metro to Non-Metro Ratio |
|---|---|---|---|---|
| Average Consumption Expenditure (Current Prices in Rs) |  |  |  |  |
| 1987–8 | 228.21 | 324.39 | 245.71 | 1.42 |
| 1993–4 | 417.92 | 606.32 | 458.04 | 1.45 |
| 2004–5 | 930.54 | 1363.71 | 1052.35 | 1.47 |
| 2009–10 | 1603.51 | 2301.83 | 1785.81 | 1.44 |
| Coefficient of Variation |  |  |  |  |
| 1987–8 | 12.46 | 20.11 | 17.58 | – |
| 1993–4 | 17.26 | 18.02 | 19.51 | – |
| 2004–5 | 18.24 | 16.21 | 14.96 | – |
| 2009–10 | 25.59 | 20.99 | 20.67 | – |

*Source*: Data taken from Tables A2.4 and A6.11.

was in million plus or metro cities. In other words, little less than three-fourth of the urban population lived in urban centres with populations less than 1 million. There is therefore a need to have more nuanced policymaking even if one were to have separate policies for non-metros.

A disaggregated analysis and following from policymaking for non-metros has not remained a possibility since 1999–2000. After 1999–2000, in the name of getting correct estimates for each individual metro, all other urban centres which constitute large diversity in settlement sizes and about three-fourth of the urban population, has been put into a residual block termed as 'non-metro'. Hence we are unable to look closely at the specific problems of small towns, mid-sized towns and so on. And without any database, what is actually happening in these towns cannot be discerned, let alone be used for taking sound policy measures. In a sense, NSS's urban database has been made metro-centric in the reforms period, which was not the case earlier. The possibility of disaggregating non-metro size classes needs to be brought back in NSS's sampling frame.

The economic dynamics in the reforms period seem to have been metro-centric, indicated by increasing metro and non-metro inequalities with regard to consumption expenditure, reflected by increase in ratio of average metro consumption to average non-metro consumption and increasing curve of these ratios calculated for each percentile. This inequality increased because of non-metros in less developed states being left behind whereas metros in the less developed states benefitted from reforms. Also, poverty reduction was higher in the metros than in the non-metros.

There was also an increase in inequality of consumption in the metros in the reforms period, with top 20 percentile racing ahead in consumption while the bottom 40 percentile

experiencing lower or no real growth in consumption as compared to the pre-reforms decade. It is clear from consumption data that the top 20 percentile of the metros benefited the most because of the reforms. The inequality penetrated down to non-metros as well, wherein the top 20 percentile moved ahead. The top 20 percentile moved ahead in both the metros as well as non-metros because of higher quality employment generated in the service sector. While a section of the metro and non-metro population benefitted from the new high paying service sector employment, a significant proportion in both was in low quality employment. In non-metros nearly half the employed were in low quality employment and in the metros this proportion was one-third. The proportion in low quality employment did not decline much in non-metros and saw a small decline in the metros. Hence, intra-metro and intra-non-metro inequality increased in the reforms period. If that is the case, then those in poor quality employment need to be protected through social security measures. Currently, social security schemes are targeted towards only those who hold a Below Poverty Line (BPL) cards. Besides the massive problem of exclusion of the real poor, protection is required not only by those who are at or below the poverty line but also all those who are in poor quality employment.

In the reforms period, HCR elasticity with respect to APCE not just declined but was showing a positive sign, indicating that the increase in APCE resulted in an increase in HCR in some states. In other states where the sign was negative (with an increase in APCE HCR declined), the elasticity values declined in the reforms period as compared to the pre-reforms period, which shows that the increase in consumption is not automatically translating into poverty reduction. The non-metros experienced higher disconnect between consumption and poverty reduction. This could be because of a continuing high proportion of the population still having access to very poor quality employment in a condition of lack of social security and social protection measures. WPRs went down in 2009–10; this was more in the case of non-metros than metros, meaning that a section of those in the workforce moved out and those in the labour force moved to marginal economic activities and they were not captured in the data. There was an impact of the economic recession that started in 2008 also in 2009–10. Policy emphasis on poverty reduction should not be on increase in consumption levels alone for the average population but it should also be on consumption redistribution and social security and protection measures to see that in times of transition as well as recession, the population does not fall below the poverty level.

With regard to consumption there was higher inequality among states in case of non-metros as compared to metros and the agricultural states had higher per capita consumption in non-metros as compared to industrial states. An agriculture based economic development strategy would bring about reduction in poverty in non-metros at a faster rate than any other strategy. Variations across metros were less than those across non-metros, given that the metropolitan economy on the whole transited to the tertiary sector.

The decline in WPRs in non-metros, and among the females in particular in the last half a decade was as much an outcome of a decline of agriculture in some of the peripheral areas in non-metros as women pulling out of the labour force at the first instance of households gaining prosperity on account of land sales. Also, with urbanization expected in urban peripheries, agriculture ceased and households were in the process of selling land. As a result, self-employment significantly declined and women moved out of the labour force. Some among them who

were not in a position to sustain livelihoods moved into casual labour and some got into unpaid or low paid work often not captured in labour force surveys. In periods of transition in non-metros, there have to be employment support programmes. In times of non-availability of work, households shift to self-employment and policy should be concerned with supporting possibilities of self-employment. This means that credit must be available and there should be market support. There must also be retraining for self-employed service sector work. The best policy option however would be to support industrialization in non-metros through proactive state policies, which are based on an equitable land policy. Generation of secondary employment in non-metros will go a long way in reducing metro versus non-metro inequality.

This analysis also brought out that in non-metros secondary sector work shifted to casual labour. In 1993–4, 27.8 per cent males in the secondary sector were employed as casual labour. This proportion increased to 32.8 per cent in 2004–5 and to 38.1 per cent in 2009–10. This was all unprotected labour. Hence, even if industrialization has to be induced in non-metros, it must be ensured that regular work is available along with social security measures. Only then will wages improve and HCRs in non-metros decline. Even among females in non-metros, secondary sector work became increasingly CL type, the proportions increasing from 22.6 per cent in 2004–5 to 28.9 per cent in 2009–10. In the 1993–4 to 2004–5 period secondary sector work in non-metros for females saw an increase in SE, indicating that secondary work moved to home-based type of work, where the wages were paid on a piece rate basis. This was not a method of improving consumption and reducing poverty. Attention will have to paid to the quality of work in non-metros. There has also been an increase in regular work in the tertiary sector among females since 1993–4, and this could be seen as a positive trend. However, we suspect that this regular work is without any protection and might be in low salary jobs, which have gone to females replacing men in the labour market, for the reason that females can be paid lower wages than males.

In the metros there was high increase in administrative and profession type of jobs of the regular type, which led to a high increase in per capita consumption expenditures for the top 20 percentile of the population. Such a trend was observed also among females. Hence, total household consumption would have gone up. In the metropolitan economy, such high increase in income resulted in inflation caused by high demand. One of the areas where inflation hit hard was the urban land market, where prices skyrocketed (Mahadevia 2009). Basic housing became unaffordable for a large section of the population. Shelter security is fundamental to accessing other services in urban areas (Mahadevia 2010b). More than a third of the metropolitan workers are in manual labour jobs, which has not seen much decline in the decade of the 2000 and they were adversely hit on account of high inflation rates. They are also not in a position to access urban basic services. The implication of such a situation is that metropolitan cities have become classic dual economies and there is a schism between urban elites and urban poor. In metropolitan cities we also need to see urban poverty in its multidimensional form. Hence, it is recommended that a strong shelter programme, which is inclusive and is based on making land accessible to urban poor is designed and implemented to address the question of poverty.

Lastly, given increasing inequalities in the overall urban system between metros and non-metros, the national level urban development programme, JNNURM, should think of increasing funding to non-metros. Currently, the total funds approved for non-metros under Urban Infrastructure Development Scheme for Small and Medium Towns (UIDSSMT) are just 20 per cent of the funds approved for the Urban Infrastructure and Governance (UIG) component, which is for mission cities which are largely metros and main cities in the states. However, the funds disbursed to UIDSSMT towns are about 58 per cent of those disbursed to UIG cities. UIDSSMT cities form about 70 per cent of the urban population and such a skewed approach to urban development will enhance rather than reduce inequalities in the urban system.

# Annexures

**Table A2.1** State Specific Poverty Line for Urban Areas

| State | Poverty Line (in Rs) | | | Implicit Price Deflator at 1993–4 = 100 | | |
|---|---|---|---|---|---|---|
| | 1987–8 | 1993–4 | 2004–5 | 1987–8 | 1993–4 | 2004–5 |
| Andhra Pradesh | 151.88 | 278.14 | 542.89 | 54.61 | 100 | 195.19 |
| Assam | 126.60 | 212.42 | 378.84 | 59.60 | 100 | 178.34 |
| Bihar | 150.25 | 238.49 | 435.00 | 63.00 | 100 | 182.40 |
| Gujarat | 173.18 | 297.22 | 541.16 | 58.27 | 100 | 182.07 |
| Haryana | 143.22 | 258.23 | 504.49 | 55.46 | 100 | 195.36 |
| Jammu and Kashmir | 148.10 | 248.45 | 553.77 | 59.61 | 100 | 222.89 |
| Karnataka | 171.18 | 302.89 | 599.66 | 56.52 | 100 | 197.98 |
| Kerala | 163.29 | 280.54 | 559.39 | 58.21 | 100 | 199.40 |
| Madhya Pradesh | 178.35 | 317.16 | 570.15 | 56.23 | 100 | 179.77 |
| Maharashtra | 189.17 | 328.56 | 665.90 | 57.58 | 100 | 202.67 |
| Orissa | 165.40 | 298.22 | 528.49 | 55.46 | 100 | 177.21 |
| Punjab | 144.98 | 253.61 | 466.16 | 57.17 | 100 | 183.81 |
| Rajasthan | 165.38 | 280.85 | 559.63 | 58.89 | 100 | 199.26 |
| Tamil Nadu | 165.82 | 296.63 | 547.42 | 55.90 | 100 | 184.55 |
| Uttar Pradesh | 154.15 | 258.65 | 483.26 | 59.60 | 100 | 186.84 |
| West Bengal | 149.96 | 247.53 | 449.32 | 60.58 | 100 | 181.52 |
| Other NE States | 126.60 | 212.42 | 378.84 | 59.60 | 100 | 178.34 |
| Rest ST & UT | 164.30 | 288.44 | 544.59 | 56.96 | 100 | 188.81 |
| All-India | 159.20 | 281.35 | 538.60 | 56.58 | 100 | 191.43 |

*Source*: Press Information Bureau (1997, 2007).

**Table A2.2**    Monthly APCE across Different City Size, 1987–8

| State | Current Prices (Rs) | | | | Constant (1993–4) Prices | | | |
|---|---|---|---|---|---|---|---|---|
| | < 50,000 | 50,000 to 200,000 | 200,000 to 1 million | 50,000 to 1 million | < 50,000 | 50,000–200,000 | 200,000–1 million | 50,000 to 1 million |
| Andhra Pradesh | 201.68 | 211.53 | 252.96 | 230.23 | 369.35 | 387.34 | 463.21 | 421.62 |
| Assam | 225.63 | 313.81 | 291.15 | 302.93 | 378.59 | 526.53 | 488.50 | 508.28 |
| Bihar | 171.77 | 181.80 | 213.94 | 198.17 | 272.65 | 288.57 | 339.59 | 314.55 |
| Gujarat | 213.21 | 208.13 | 264.26 | 235.81 | 365.92 | 357.18 | 453.51 | 404.71 |
| Haryana | 259.79 | 253.55 | 241.64 | 250.24 | 468.42 | 457.18 | 435.70 | 451.20 |
| Jammu and Kashmir | 234.86 | | 283.79 | 283.79 | 394.00 | | 476.08 | 476.08 |
| Karnataka | 198.02 | 193.19 | 259.03 | 221.43 | 350.38 | 341.80 | 458.29 | 391.80 |
| Kerala | 232.92 | 285.67 | 296.56 | 293.02 | 400.17 | 490.75 | 509.46 | 503.43 |
| Madhya Pradesh | 206.49 | 211.89 | 277.45 | 249.96 | 367.20 | 376.82 | 493.42 | 444.51 |
| Maharashtra | 201.37 | 224.02 | 257.62 | 239.94 | 349.76 | 389.06 | 447.41 | 416.74 |
| Orissa | 194.00 | 246.05 | 252.26 | 249.03 | 349.79 | 443.66 | 454.85 | 449.00 |
| Punjab | 270.42 | 265.32 | 284.96 | 278.64 | 473.03 | 464.09 | 498.45 | 487.41 |
| Rajasthan | 215.31 | 266.16 | 274.76 | 271.95 | 365.64 | 451.96 | 466.56 | 461.82 |
| Tamil Nadu | 232.55 | 231.66 | 256.82 | 239.37 | 416.01 | 414.41 | 459.43 | 428.20 |
| Uttar Pradesh | 188.87 | 194.79 | 250.18 | 229.19 | 316.90 | 326.83 | 419.77 | 384.56 |
| West Bengal | 203.22 | 224.81 | 290.09 | 244.28 | 335.45 | 371.09 | 478.85 | 403.21 |
| Other NE States | 272.52 | 281.91 | 0.00 | 281.90 | 457.25 | 473.00 | | 473.00 |
| Rest ST and UT | 287.37 | 271.67 | 435.60 | 334.37 | 504.49 | 476.94 | 764.74 | 587.01 |
| All-India | 209.68 | 221.21 | 262.70 | 241.71 | 370.56 | 390.97 | 464.29 | 427.16 |
| Coefficient of Variation | 14.41 | 29.73 | 30.36 | 12.99 | 15.45 | 15.87 | 17.50 | 13.35 |

*Source:* Unit level data of consumption expenditure schedule of 43rd (1987–8) Round of NSSO and state specific official poverty line for the year 1987–8.

**Table A2.3**  Monthly APCE across Different City Size, 1993–4

| State | Current Prices (Rs) | | | | Constant (1993–4) Prices | | | |
|---|---|---|---|---|---|---|---|---|
| | < 50,000 | 50,000 to 200,000 | 200,000 to 1 million | 50,000 to 1 million | < 50,000 | 50,000–200,000 | 200,000–1 million | 50,000 to 1 million |
| Andhra Pradesh | 366.03 | 398.97 | 427.82 | 411.16 | 366.03 | 398.97 | 427.82 | 411.16 |
| Assam | 419.16 | 448.57 | 566.67 | 508.98 | 419.16 | 448.57 | 566.67 | 508.98 |
| Bihar | 283.99 | 346.38 | 403.66 | 383.89 | 283.99 | 346.38 | 403.66 | 383.89 |
| Gujarat | 396.88 | 460.61 | 379.28 | 443.23 | 396.88 | 460.61 | 379.28 | 443.23 |
| Haryana | 463.66 | 490.34 | 440.41 | 477.74 | 463.66 | 490.34 | 440.41 | 477.74 |
| Jammu and Kashmir | 455.42 | | 619.53 | 619.53 | 455.42 | | 619.53 | 619.53 |
| Karnataka | 372.24 | 373.71 | 455.07 | 413.54 | 372.24 | 373.71 | 455.07 | 413.54 |
| Kerala | 460.12 | 515.95 | 554.06 | 536.12 | 460.12 | 515.95 | 554.06 | 536.12 |
| Madhya Pradesh | 350.22 | 405.68 | 458.93 | 428.05 | 350.22 | 405.68 | 458.93 | 428.05 |
| Maharashtra | 375.18 | 423.90 | 468.69 | 453.38 | 375.18 | 423.90 | 468.69 | 453.38 |
| Orissa | 392.38 | 383.08 | 432.94 | 410.29 | 392.38 | 383.08 | 432.94 | 410.29 |
| Punjab | 467.38 | 518.75 | 502.26 | 510.43 | 467.38 | 518.75 | 502.26 | 510.43 |
| Rajasthan | 372.06 | 397.06 | 473.25 | 435.49 | 372.06 | 397.06 | 473.25 | 435.49 |
| Tamil Nadu | 379.65 | 408.18 | 487.21 | 441.04 | 379.65 | 408.18 | 487.21 | 441.04 |
| Uttar Pradesh | 343.95 | 370.55 | 460.21 | 421.37 | 343.95 | 370.55 | 460.21 | 421.37 |
| West Bengal | 400.23 | 449.60 | 497.97 | 468.28 | 400.23 | 449.60 | 497.97 | 468.28 |
| Other NE States | 419.72 | 504.85 | | 504.85 | 419.72 | 504.85 | | 504.85 |
| Rest ST and UT | 504.85 | 826.86 | 804.71 | 812.44 | 504.85 | 826.86 | 804.71 | 812.44 |
| All-India | 377.76 | 422.41 | 468.34 | 444.45 | 377.76 | 422.41 | 468.34 | 444.45 |
| Coefficient of Variation | 13.50 | 24.16 | 20.07 | 20.77 | 13.50 | 24.16 | 20.07 | 20.77 |

*Source:* Unit level data of consumption expenditure schedule of 50th (1993–4) Round of NSSO and state specific official poverty line for the year 1993–4.

**Table A2.4**  Monthly APCE (current prices), Metro, Non-metro, and Total Urban, 1987–8, 1993–4, and 2004-5

| State | 1987–8 | | | 1993–4 | | | 2004–5 | | |
|---|---|---|---|---|---|---|---|---|---|
| | Non-metro | Metro | Total Urban | Non-metro | Metro | Total Urban | Non-metro | Metro | Total Urban |
| Andhra Pradesh | 219.07 | 294.32 | 228.07 | 395.93 | 515.83 | 408.60 | 958.65 | 1296.33 | 1018.55 |
| Assam | 256.15 | | 256.15 | 458.57 | | 458.57 | 1057.98 | – | 1057.98 |
| Bihar | 187.21 | | 187.21 | 353.03 | | 353.03 | 758.86 | 1092.13 | 801.73 |
| Gujarat | 226.11 | 258.86 | 234.32 | 423.59 | 522.49 | 454.18 | 1020.81 | 1247.43 | 1115.20 |
| Haryana | 253.45 | | 253.46 | 473.92 | | 473.92 | 1161.76 | 1053.20 | 1142.35 |
| Jammu and Kashmir | 265.39 | | 265.39 | 541.58 | | 541.58 | 1070.12 | – | 1070.12 |
| Karnataka | 209.16 | 278 | 223.50 | 394.54 | 538.94 | 423.14 | 888.38 | 1428.71 | 1033.21 |
| Kerala | 261.71 | | 261.70 | 493.84 | | 493.83 | 1290.89 | – | 1290.89 |
| Madhya Pradesh | 232.97 | | 232.98 | 393.02 | 501.63 | 408.06 | 835.99 | 1392.89 | 920.04 |
| Maharashtra | 225.96 | 338.76 | 273.18 | 423.79 | 657.87 | 529.80 | 868.28 | 1414.27 | 1148.25 |
| Orissa | 222.01 | | 222.01 | 402.54 | | 402.54 | 757.31 | – | 757.31 |
| Punjab | 275.68 | | 275.67 | 498.74 | 571.64 | 510.73 | 1182.40 | 1936.49 | 1326.09 |
| Rajasthan | 245.12 | | 245.11 | 409.38 | 520.99 | 424.73 | 907.32 | 1184.83 | 964.02 |
| Tamil Nadu | 236.30 | 279.28 | 245.19 | 416.19 | 522.23 | 438.29 | 965.25 | 1596.00 | 1079.65 |
| Uttar Pradesh | 212.75 | 230.06 | 214.00 | 387.62 | 400.83 | 388.97 | 757.34 | 1254.90 | 863.91 |
| West Bengal | 229.02 | 299.46 | 247.98 | 448.02 | 579.35 | 474.19 | 1012.98 | 1455.37 | 1123.61 |
| Other NE States | 276.54 | | 276.54 | 454.29 | | 454.29 | 1048.13 | – | 1048.13 |
| Rest ST and UT | 313.82 | 428.86 | 403.36 | 693.73 | 794.95 | 773.67 | 1435.29 | 1319.31 | 1340.67 |
| All-India | 228.21 | 324.39 | 245.71 | 417.92 | 606.32 | 458.04 | 930.54 | 1363.71 | 1052.35 |
| Coefficient of Variation | 12.46 | 20.11 | 17.58 | 17.26 | 18.02 | 19.51 | 18.24 | 16.21 | 14.96 |

*Source*: Unit level data of consumption expenditure schedule of 43rd (1987–8), 50th (1993–4), and 61st (2004–5) Rounds of NSSO.

**Table A2.5**  Monthly APCE (constant prices), Metro, Non-metro, and Total Urban, 1987–8, 1993–4, and 2004–5

| State | 1987–8 | | | 1993–4 | | | 2004–5 | | |
|---|---|---|---|---|---|---|---|---|---|
| | Non-metro | Metro | Total Urban | Non-metro | Metro | Total Urban | Non-metro | Metro | Total Urban |
| Andhra Pradesh | 401.15 | 538.99 | 417.66 | 395.93 | 515.83 | 408.60 | 491.15 | 664.15 | 521.84 |
| Assam | 429.78 | | 429.79 | 458.57 | | 458.57 | 593.22 | | 593.22 |
| Bihar | 297.15 | | 297.15 | 353.03 | | 353.03 | 416.05 | 598.76 | 439.55 |
| Gujarat | 388.04 | 444.27 | 402.15 | 423.59 | 522.49 | 454.18 | 560.66 | 685.12 | 612.50 |
| Haryana | 457.00 | | 457.00 | 473.92 | | 473.92 | 594.66 | 539.10 | 584.73 |
| Jammu and Kashmir | 445.22 | | 445.22 | 541.58 | | 541.58 | 480.11 | | 480.11 |
| Karnataka | 370.06 | 491.89 | 395.46 | 394.54 | 538.94 | 423.14 | 448.72 | 721.65 | 521.88 |
| Kerala | 449.59 | | 449.61 | 493.84 | | 493.83 | 647.40 | | 647.40 |
| Madhya Pradesh | 414.32 | | 414.30 | 393.02 | 501.63 | 408.06 | 465.04 | 774.83 | 511.79 |
| Maharashtra | 392.43 | 588.37 | 474.47 | 423.79 | 657.87 | 529.80 | 428.42 | 697.81 | 566.56 |
| Orissa | 400.30 | | 400.29 | 402.54 | | 402.54 | 427.34 | | 427.34 |
| Punjab | 482.21 | | 482.22 | 498.74 | 571.64 | 510.73 | 643.27 | 1053.53 | 721.45 |
| Rajasthan | 416.24 | | 416.25 | 409.38 | 520.99 | 424.73 | 455.34 | 594.60 | 483.80 |
| Tamil Nadu | 422.72 | 499.6 | 438.61 | 416.19 | 522.23 | 438.29 | 523.04 | 864.82 | 585.03 |
| Uttar Pradesh | 356.96 | 386.02 | 359.08 | 387.62 | 400.83 | 388.97 | 405.34 | 671.64 | 462.38 |
| West Bengal | 378.05 | 494.3 | 409.32 | 448.02 | 579.35 | 474.19 | 558.05 | 801.76 | 619.00 |
| Other NE States | 464.00 | | 464.00 | 454.29 | | 454.29 | 587.70 | | 587.70 |
| Rest ST and UT | 550.96 | 752.9 | 708.13 | 693.73 | 794.95 | 773.67 | 760.19 | 698.77 | 710.08 |
| All-India | 403.33 | 573.29 | 434.24 | 417.92 | 606.32 | 458.04 | 486.09 | 712.37 | 549.72 |
| Coefficient of Variation | 13.21 | 20.97 | 18.45 | 17.26 | 18.02 | 19.51 | 18.55 | 18.48 | 15.30 |

*Source:* Unit level data of consumption expenditure schedule of 43rd (1987–8), 50th (1993–4), and 61st (2004–5) Rounds of NSSO and state specific official poverty line for the years 1987–8, 1993–4, and 2004–5.

**Table A2.6**  Head Count Ratios for Different Size Classes, 1987–8 and 1993–4

| State | Current Prices (Rs) | | | | Constant (1993–4) Prices | | | |
|---|---|---|---|---|---|---|---|---|
| | < 50,000 | 50,000 to 200,000 | 200,000 to 1 million | 50,000 to 1 million | < 50,000 | 50,000–200,000 | 200,000–1 million | 50,000 to 1 million |
| Andhra Pradesh | 45.45 | 45.88 | 33.88 | 40.46 | 44.41 | 41.06 | 35.76 | 38.81 |
| Assam | 13.23 | 12.59 | 3.80 | 8.38 | 8.90 | 6.59 | 6.48 | 6.53 |
| Bihar | 56.41 | 51.20 | 46.12 | 48.62 | 49.11 | 36.01 | 23.71 | 27.96 |
| Gujarat | 44.13 | 43.63 | 31.94 | 37.87 | 36.37 | 21.83 | 33.76 | 24.38 |
| Haryana | 19.34 | 18.41 | 16.84 | 17.97 | 12.59 | 13.51 | 30.95 | 17.91 |
| Jammu and Kashmir | 24.01 | | 9.47 | 9.47 | 9.14 | | 1.49 | 1.49 |
| Karnataka | 56.10 | 57.37 | 39.80 | 49.85 | 51.78 | 47.34 | 31.24 | 39.47 |
| Kerala | 42.63 | 35.74 | 33.15 | 33.99 | 28.47 | 23.20 | 14.79 | 18.75 |
| Madhya Pradesh | 55.06 | 52.04 | 35.58 | 42.49 | 57.41 | 45.03 | 40.16 | 42.98 |
| Maharashtra | 59.75 | 52.64 | 43.33 | 48.22 | 58.39 | 49.84 | 41.13 | 44.10 |
| Orissa | 51.37 | 34.03 | 34.17 | 34.09 | 44.71 | 38.72 | 36.29 | 37.39 |
| Punjab | 14.61 | 16.22 | 11.75 | 13.18 | 14.92 | 13.54 | 9.52 | 11.51 |
| Rajasthan | 43.66 | 37.74 | 30.27 | 32.69 | 38.09 | 34.28 | 25.13 | 29.66 |
| Tamil Nadu | 46.20 | 41.48 | 32.77 | 38.88 | 44.05 | 44.52 | 31.80 | 39.23 |
| Uttar Pradesh | 53.58 | 50.45 | 33.65 | 40.02 | 47.23 | 35.22 | 20.52 | 26.89 |
| West Bengal | 42.91 | 34.45 | 26.94 | 32.21 | 33.56 | 25.01 | 18.16 | 22.36 |
| Other NE States | 6.55 | 4.62 | 5.76 | 4.62 | 5.89 | 1.77 | | 1.77 |
| Rest ST and UT | 22.81 | 44.17 | 5.76 | 29.48 | 18.38 | 18.52 | 16.67 | 17.32 |
| All-India | 47.09 | 43.28 | 32.86 | 38.14 | 42.87 | 34.32 | 28.08 | 31.32 |
| Coefficient of Variation | 44.26 | 41.96 | 47.46 | 46.29 | 52.87 | 51.10 | 48.86 | 55.48 |

*Source*: Unit level data of consumption expenditure schedule of 43rd (1987–8) and 50th (1993–4) Rounds of NSSO.

**Table A3.1** Work Participation Rates by Usual (Principal + Subsidiary) Status, Male

| States | 1987–8 | | | | | 1993–4 | | | | | 1999–2000 | | |
|---|---|---|---|---|---|---|---|---|---|---|---|---|---|
| | C1 | C2 | C3 | C2+C3 | TU | C1 | C2 | C3 | C2+C3 | TU | C1 | C2+C3 | TU |
| Andhra Pradesh | 48.6 | 52.6 | 49.8 | 51.4 | 50.3 | 54.9 | 55.2 | 54.4 | 54.8 | 54.4 | 52.2 | 51.6 | 51.1 |
| Assam | 48.8 | 49.0 | 60.9 | 54.6 | 51.2 | 52.9 | 51.8 | 53.6 | 52.7 | 52.8 | 51.2 | 53.4 | 52.2 |
| Bihar | 46.0 | 43.2 | 44.7 | 44.0 | 44.8 | 47.6 | 44.8 | 41.0 | 42.3 | 43.9 | 47.1 | 41.3 | 43.2 |
| Gujarat | 50.8 | 49.6 | 55.1 | 52.3 | 51.0 | 54.7 | 50.4 | 53.3 | 51.0 | 53.5 | 52.8 | 53.4 | 53.6 |
| Haryana | 51.4 | 51.3 | 71.0 | 57.2 | 55.3 | 50.7 | 50.7 | 57.2 | 52.3 | 51.9 | 45.5 | 52.7 | 50.6 |
| Jammu and Kashmir | 53.5 | 0.0 | 52.9 | 52.9 | 53.1 | 46.4 | | 51.6 | 51.6 | 49.1 | 49.8 | 46.3 | 47.8 |
| Karnataka | 49.7 | 48.8 | 50.9 | 49.7 | 49.4 | 56.2 | 51.2 | 53.9 | 52.6 | 54.2 | 53.6 | 53.2 | 54.5 |
| Kerala | 53.4 | 54.0 | 51.8 | 52.5 | 53.0 | 54.5 | 53.8 | 61.3 | 57.7 | 55.9 | 55.2 | 56.7 | 55.9 |
| Madhya Pradesh | 48.6 | 46.7 | 48.3 | 47.6 | 48.0 | 48.6 | 44.3 | 47.5 | 45.6 | 47.2 | 49.2 | 48.1 | 48.8 |
| Maharashtra | 50.5 | 46.0 | 48.3 | 47.1 | 49.6 | 48.3 | 50.1 | 52.1 | 51.4 | 52.6 | 50.5 | 51.5 | 53.2 |
| Orissa | 48.2 | 49.8 | 50.7 | 50.3 | 49.3 | 51.1 | 52.2 | 49.9 | 50.9 | 51.0 | 47.9 | 47.1 | 47.5 |
| Punjab | 53.4 | 51.7 | 55.5 | 54.3 | 54.0 | 54.0 | 51.5 | 56.0 | 53.8 | 55.3 | 51.0 | 54.7 | 54.9 |
| Rajasthan | 45.8 | 47.9 | 48.6 | 48.4 | 47.1 | 49.7 | 50.1 | 47.5 | 48.8 | 49.0 | 47.0 | 48.9 | 48.6 |
| Tamil Nadu | 55.6 | 56.7 | 58.0 | 57.1 | 55.8 | 56.4 | 56.3 | 61.2 | 58.3 | 57.5 | 55.4 | 58.0 | 56.4 |
| Uttar Pradesh | 48.0 | 48.6 | 49.7 | 49.3 | 48.9 | 47.7 | 49.6 | 48.6 | 49.0 | 48.2 | 46.4 | 51.4 | 49.0 |
| West Bengal | 52.8 | 51.9 | 53.4 | 52.3 | 53.9 | 51.0 | 53.3 | 54.5 | 53.8 | 55.0 | 56.6 | 54.2 | 56.7 |
| Other NE States | 47.5 | 44.4 | 48.6 | 44.4 | 46.2 | 48.0 | 44.6 | 47.5 | 44.6 | 46.6 | 45.1 | 43.6 | 44.5 |
| Rest ST and UT | 47.8 | 49.0 | 49.3 | 49.2 | 53.1 | 51.0 | 51.8 | 59.2 | 56.6 | 53.9 | 52.0 | 52.4 | 52.8 |
| All-India | 49.9 | 49.9 | 51.0 | 50.4 | 50.7 | 51.4 | 51.2 | 51.8 | 51.4 | 52.1 | 50.5 | 51.6 | 51.8 |

*Source:* Unit level data of employment and unemployment schedule of 43rd (1987–8), 50th (1993–4), and 55th (1999–2000) Rounds of NSSO.

*Notes:* C1 = towns with population up to 50,000 (called small town);

C2 = towns with population of 50,000 to 2 lakhs (called medium towns);

C3 = cities with population of 2 lakhs to 10 lakhs (called large cities);

CM = cities with population > 10 lakhs (called metropolitan cities or metros);

TU = total urban.

**Table A3.2** Work Participation Rates by Usual (Principal + Subsidiary) Status, Female

| States | 1987-8 | | | | | 1993-4 | | | | | 1999-2000 | | |
|---|---|---|---|---|---|---|---|---|---|---|---|---|---|
| | C1 | C2 | C3 | C2+C3 | TU | C1 | C2 | C3 | C2+C3 | TU | C1 | C2+C3 | TU |
| Andhra Pradesh | 26.9 | 22.9 | 18.0 | 20.6 | 21.5 | 25.6 | 20.2 | 16.3 | 18.6 | 20.0 | 25.4 | 17.2 | 17.8 |
| Assam | 6.9 | 9.5 | 11.9 | 10.7 | 8.4 | 7.0 | 11.1 | 13.0 | 12.1 | 9.2 | 8.5 | 14.3 | 11.2 |
| Bihar | 10.2 | 5.2 | 7.3 | 6.3 | 7.9 | 7.2 | 6.5 | 5.9 | 6.8 | 6.9 | 7.1 | 8.2 | 7.5 |
| Gujarat | 13.7 | 9.6 | 10.8 | 10.2 | 11.2 | 19.6 | 10.6 | 13.3 | 11.2 | 14.2 | 15.0 | 12.4 | 13.6 |
| Haryana | 12.5 | 10.2 | 18.1 | 12.1 | 12.3 | 17.3 | 15.6 | 11.0 | 14.5 | 15.2 | 17.1 | 8.4 | 11.0 |
| Jammu and Kashmir | 17.9 | 0.0 | 12.5 | 12.5 | 14.5 | 15.5 | | 10.7 | 10.7 | 13.0 | 7.6 | 5.4 | 6.3 |
| Karnataka | 25.8 | 20.0 | 12.6 | 16.7 | 19.6 | 22.5 | 18.2 | 16.4 | 17.3 | 18.1 | 20.1 | 15.7 | 17.9 |
| Kerala | 20.7 | 20.7 | 18.0 | 18.8 | 19.8 | 22.2 | 21.3 | 15.1 | 18.0 | 20.3 | 22.2 | 18.4 | 20.5 |
| Madhya Pradesh | 17.0 | 12.0 | 13.3 | 12.8 | 14.4 | 18.6 | 10.0 | 12.1 | 10.9 | 14.2 | 15.8 | 11.5 | 13.5 |
| Maharashtra | 23.4 | 15.5 | 14.2 | 14.9 | 16.0 | 21.9 | 15.3 | 14.8 | 15.0 | 16.9 | 18.4 | 12.6 | 13.7 |
| Orissa | 14.7 | 11.2 | 9.5 | 10.4 | 12.5 | 20.8 | 10.6 | 10.9 | 10.8 | 15.1 | 18.5 | 11.7 | 14.7 |
| Punjab | 16.5 | 12.8 | 8.7 | 10.0 | 12.4 | 9.4 | 10.5 | 9.3 | 9.9 | 9.4 | 17.3 | 11.0 | 12.6 |
| Rajasthan | 24.9 | 16.4 | 12.5 | 13.8 | 19.1 | 19.6 | 17.1 | 14.2 | 15.7 | 16.3 | 16.5 | 13.6 | 13.9 |
| Tamil Nadu | 27.3 | 21.4 | 25.1 | 22.5 | 22.7 | 27.1 | 23.5 | 21.6 | 22.7 | 23.0 | 25.1 | 19.8 | 21.6 |
| Uttar Pradesh | 10.4 | 10.9 | 8.2 | 9.2 | 9.4 | 12.3 | 11.3 | 8.2 | 9.5 | 10.2 | 11.8 | 7.9 | 9.5 |
| West Bengal | 10.8 | 12.6 | 11.4 | 12.3 | 12.5 | 17.2 | 13.8 | 12.0 | 13.1 | 14.3 | 15.2 | 9.5 | 11.7 |
| Other NE States | 17.1 | 20.2 | | 20.2 | 18.5 | 18.1 | 17.3 | | 17.3 | 17.8 | 17.1 | 18.5 | 17.7 |
| Rest ST and UT | 15.6 | 16.4 | 19.9 | 17.7 | 10.7 | 18.7 | 21.1 | 16.0 | 17.7 | 11.5 | 12.8 | 10.5 | 11.2 |
| All-India | 18.7 | 15.1 | 12.8 | 14.0 | 15.2 | 19.2 | 15.2 | 13.0 | 14.2 | 15.5 | 17.1 | 12.7 | 14.0 |

*Source:* Unit level data of employment and unemployment schedule of 43rd (1987–8), 50th (1993–4) and 55th (1999–2000) Rounds of NSSO.

**Table A3.3**  Work Participation Rates by Usual (Principal + Subsidiary) Status, Metro and Non-metro

| States | Male | | | | | | | | | Female | | | | | | | | |
|---|---|---|---|---|---|---|---|---|---|---|---|---|---|---|---|---|---|---|
| | 1987-8 | | 1993-4 | | 1999-2000 | | 2004-5 | | | 1987-8 | | 1993-4 | | 1999-2000 | | 2004-5 | | |
| | NM | M | NM | M | NM | M | NM | M | TU | NM | M | NM | M | NM | M | NM | M | TU |
| Andhra Pradesh | 50.3 | 50.4 | 54.9 | 50.7 | 51.7 | 47.9 | 56.0 | 56.1 | 56.0 | 23.1 | 10.9 | 21.0 | 11.3 | 19.2 | 11.1 | 24.4 | 13.7 | 22.4 |
| Assam | 51.2 | | 52.8 | | 52.2 | – | 55.1 | | 55.1 | 8.4 | | 9.2 | | 11.2 | – | 10.9 | | 10.9 |
| Bihar | 44.8 | | 43.9 | | 43.5 | 41.7 | 47.2 | 37.5 | 45.9 | 7.9 | | 6.9 | | 7.8 | 6.2 | 10.2 | 1.2 | 9.2 |
| Gujarat | 51.7 | 49.0 | 52.6 | 55.3 | 53.1 | 54.4 | 56.5 | 59.5 | 57.8 | 11.7 | 9.6 | 14.7 | 12.9 | 13.5 | 13.8 | 15.1 | 15.1 | 15.1 |
| Haryana | 55.3 | | 51.9 | | 50.6 | – | 51.6 | 49.0 | 51.1 | 12.3 | | 15.2 | | 10.9 | – | 14.3 | 8.1 | 13.2 |
| Jammu and Kashmir | 53.1 | | 49.1 | | 47.8 | – | 52.6 | | 52.6 | 14.5 | | 13.0 | | 6.3 | – | 11.2 | | 11.2 |
| Karnataka | 49.7 | 48.5 | 54.2 | 53.9 | 53.4 | 58.1 | 55.2 | 64.5 | 57.6 | 21.5 | 12.3 | 19.7 | 11.3 | 17.7 | 18.3 | 19.1 | 15.1 | 18.1 |
| Kerala | 53.0 | | 55.9 | | 55.9 | – | 54.7 | | 54.7 | 19.8 | | 20.3 | | 20.5 | – | 20.0 | | 20.0 |
| Madhya Pradesh | 48.0 | | 47.0 | 48.2 | 48.7 | 50.0 | 51.9 | 55.9 | 52.6 | 14.4 | | 14.3 | 13.6 | 13.8 | 11.2 | 15.8 | 16.6 | 15.9 |
| Maharashtra | 48.3 | 51.3 | 50.3 | 55.4 | 51.2 | 55.3 | 55.1 | 56.8 | 56.0 | 18.0 | 12.9 | 17.6 | 15.9 | 14.4 | 13.0 | 18.6 | 19.4 | 19.0 |
| Orissa | 49.3 | | 51.0 | | 47.5 | – | 50.4 | | 50.4 | 12.5 | | 15.1 | | 14.7 | – | 14.8 | | 14.8 |
| Punjab | 54.0 | | 53.9 | 62.6 | 53.5 | 61.2 | 55.3 | 65.1 | 57.2 | 12.4 | | 9.8 | 7.1 | 13.0 | 9.6 | 14.3 | 9.2 | 13.3 |
| Rajasthan | 47.1 | | 49.2 | 47.9 | 48.1 | 52.2 | 50.2 | 52.7 | 50.8 | 19.1 | | 17.3 | 8.9 | 14.8 | 7.8 | 16.1 | 24.3 | 18.2 |
| Tamil Nadu | 56.4 | 53.6 | 57.6 | 57.1 | 56.9 | 54.9 | 59.2 | 59.9 | 59.3 | 24.7 | 15.2 | 24.6 | 16.7 | 22.2 | 19.9 | 26.7 | 12.7 | 24.1 |
| Uttar Pradesh | 48.8 | 50.2 | 48.5 | 46.4 | 49.2 | 48.4 | 51.8 | 54.1 | 52.3 | 9.7 | 6.2 | 10.7 | 6.7 | 9.6 | 9.1 | 12.4 | 9.7 | 11.8 |
| West Bengal | 52.5 | 57.8 | 53.0 | 62.9 | 54.9 | 62.2 | 58.6 | 62.0 | 59.5 | 11.7 | 14.6 | 14.3 | 14.3 | 11.1 | 13.4 | 15.5 | 15.5 | 15.5 |
| Other NE States | 46.2 | | 46.6 | | 44.5 | – | 47.2 | | 47.2 | 18.5 | | 17.8 | | 17.7 | – | 21.4 | | 21.4 |
| Rest ST and UT | 48.5 | 54.4 | 54.4 | 53.8 | 52.3 | 53.1 | 55.2 | 53.5 | 53.8 | 16.8 | 9.0 | 18.1 | 9.6 | 11.2 | 11.3 | 17.6 | 8.8 | 10.5 |
| All-India | 50.2 | 52.5 | 51.5 | 54.6 | 51.2 | 53.5 | 54.2 | 56.6 | 54.9 | 16.0 | 11.9 | 16.2 | 12.9 | 14.4 | 12.7 | 17.4 | 14.6 | 16.6 |

*Source:* Unit level data of employment and unemployment schedule of 43rd (1987–8), 50th (1993–4), 55th (1999–2000), and 61st (2004–5) Rounds of NSSO.

*Notes:*  NM = Non-metro and M = Metro.

**Table A3.4** Nature of Employment, Usual (Principal + Subsidiary) Status, Male, 1987–8

(in per cent)

| States | <50,000 | | | 50,000–200,000 | | | 200,000–1 million | | | 50,000–1 million | | | Total Urban | | |
|---|---|---|---|---|---|---|---|---|---|---|---|---|---|---|---|
| | SE | RE | CL | SE | RE | CL | SE | RE | CL | SE | RE | CL | SE | RE | CL |
| Andhra Pradesh | 44.1 | 33.1 | 22.8 | 34.7 | 45.4 | 20.0 | 34.7 | 45.4 | 20.0 | 39.4 | 39.1 | 21.6 | 40.6 | 38.5 | 20.9 |
| Assam | 46.0 | 45.1 | 8.9 | 26.3 | 63.3 | 10.4 | 26.3 | 63.3 | 10.4 | 34.7 | 55.0 | 10.3 | 41.1 | 49.3 | 9.5 |
| Bihar | 47.7 | 32.2 | 20.2 | 39.0 | 48.2 | 12.7 | 39.0 | 48.2 | 12.7 | 44.7 | 43.4 | 11.9 | 45.9 | 38.8 | 15.3 |
| Gujarat | 39.8 | 40.7 | 19.5 | 39.3 | 47.3 | 13.5 | 39.3 | 47.3 | 13.5 | 39.8 | 47.8 | 12.4 | 38.6 | 44.8 | 16.6 |
| Haryana | 61.2 | 31.3 | 7.5 | 23.2 | 53.3 | 23.5 | 23.2 | 53.3 | 23.5 | 45.5 | 40.4 | 14.2 | 50.2 | 37.7 | 12.2 |
| Jammu and Kashmir | 54.1 | 35.2 | 10.7 | 52.4 | 42.2 | 5.5 | 52.4 | 42.2 | 5.5 | 52.4 | 42.2 | 5.4 | 53.0 | 39.7 | 7.3 |
| Karnataka | 46.4 | 27.7 | 25.9 | 46.8 | 40.1 | 13.1 | 46.8 | 40.1 | 13.1 | 41.5 | 39.6 | 18.9 | 40.8 | 37.4 | 21.8 |
| Kerala | 44.9 | 28.6 | 26.5 | 35.0 | 36.1 | 28.8 | 35.0 | 36.1 | 28.8 | 36.8 | 36.7 | 26.4 | 41.0 | 32.5 | 26.5 |
| Madhya Pradesh | 46.5 | 38.6 | 14.8 | 38.9 | 51.8 | 9.3 | 38.9 | 51.8 | 9.3 | 40.2 | 49.1 | 10.7 | 42.6 | 45.0 | 12.3 |
| Maharashtra | 41.8 | 39.1 | 19.1 | 28.2 | 60.4 | 11.5 | 28.2 | 60.4 | 11.5 | 29.2 | 54.5 | 16.3 | 33.1 | 54.1 | 12.8 |
| Orissa | 45.4 | 38.3 | 16.3 | 36.9 | 52.2 | 10.9 | 36.9 | 52.2 | 10.9 | 41.0 | 49.2 | 9.9 | 43.1 | 44.0 | 12.9 |
| Punjab | 54.6 | 34.6 | 10.8 | 46.8 | 43.1 | 10.1 | 46.8 | 43.1 | 10.1 | 49.7 | 40.1 | 10.2 | 51.4 | 38.2 | 10.4 |
| Rajasthan | 53.0 | 30.4 | 16.6 | 39.1 | 50.1 | 10.8 | 39.1 | 50.1 | 10.8 | 43.6 | 45.0 | 11.4 | 48.0 | 38.2 | 13.8 |
| Tamil Nadu | 33.7 | 45.5 | 20.9 | 31.7 | 50.5 | 17.8 | 31.7 | 50.5 | 17.8 | 35.5 | 47.7 | 16.8 | 33.8 | 47.4 | 18.9 |
| Uttar Pradesh | 63.8 | 23.1 | 13.0 | 48.8 | 42.3 | 8.9 | 48.8 | 42.3 | 8.9 | 52.3 | 38.1 | 9.6 | 55.5 | 33.5 | 11.0 |
| West Bengal | 41.1 | 42.8 | 16.1 | 34.0 | 55.0 | 11.0 | 34.0 | 55.0 | 11.0 | 34.5 | 52.6 | 12.9 | 36.9 | 50.5 | 12.6 |
| Other NE States | 45.7 | 41.4 | 12.9 | | | | | | | 41.0 | 47.9 | 11.1 | 43.8 | 44.0 | 12.2 |
| Rest ST and UT | 36.6 | 47.7 | 15.7 | 21.6 | 77.3 | 1.1 | 21.6 | 77.3 | 1.1 | 24.6 | 54.8 | 20.6 | 36.6 | 56.8 | 6.6 |
| All-India | 47.0 | 35.0 | 18.0 | 39.1 | 48.3 | 12.6 | 39.1 | 48.3 | 12.6 | 40.9 | 45.1 | 14.0 | 41.6 | 43.7 | 14.7 |

*Source*: Unit level data of employment and unemployment schedule of 43rd (1987–8) Round of NSSO.

*Notes*: SE = Self-employed; RE = Regular Employed; and CL = Casual Labour.

**Table A3.5**  Nature of Employment, Usual (Principal + Subsidiary) Status, Female, 1987–8

(in per cent)

| States | <50,000 | | | 50,000–200,000 | | | 200,000–1 million | | | 50,000–1 million | | | Total Urban | | |
|---|---|---|---|---|---|---|---|---|---|---|---|---|---|---|---|
| | SE | RE | CL | SE | RE | CL | SE | RE | CL | SE | RE | CL | SE | RE | CL |
| Andhra Pradesh | 49.3 | 10.1 | 40.6 | 46.6 | 15.0 | 38.4 | 47.1 | 21.5 | 31.5 | 46.8 | 17.6 | 35.7 | 47.3 | 15.5 | 37.2 |
| Assam | 62.6 | 31.0 | 6.4 | 44.2 | 42.7 | 13.1 | 4.9 | 76.2 | 18.8 | 22.8 | 60.9 | 16.2 | 43.0 | 45.7 | 11.2 |
| Bihar | 46.3 | 17.0 | 36.7 | 46.5 | 17.3 | 36.3 | 43.5 | 32.2 | 24.2 | 44.7 | 26.2 | 29.1 | 45.5 | 21.3 | 33.2 |
| Gujarat | 38.7 | 23.9 | 37.4 | 41.4 | 25.2 | 33.4 | 43.5 | 41.5 | 15.0 | 42.5 | 33.6 | 23.9 | 40.1 | 28.9 | 31.1 |
| Haryana | 67.2 | 25.4 | 7.4 | 31.0 | 52.2 | 16.8 | 30.7 | 26.4 | 42.9 | 30.9 | 42.6 | 26.5 | 43.9 | 36.5 | 19.6 |
| Jammu and Kashmir | 82.4 | 14.3 | 3.3 | | | | 62.8 | 35.2 | 2.0 | 62.8 | 35.2 | 2.0 | 71.9 | 25.6 | 2.6 |
| Karnataka | 36.6 | 9.7 | 53.7 | 33.9 | 14.8 | 51.3 | 42.8 | 26.8 | 30.4 | 36.8 | 18.7 | 44.5 | 36.0 | 15.5 | 48.5 |
| Kerala | 56.6 | 22.1 | 21.4 | 54.2 | 26.6 | 19.3 | 40.4 | 50.5 | 9.1 | 45.3 | 42.0 | 12.7 | 51.5 | 31.1 | 17.4 |
| Madhya Pradesh | 59.8 | 11.7 | 28.6 | 51.1 | 23.5 | 25.4 | 48.3 | 35.2 | 16.5 | 49.4 | 30.6 | 20.0 | 54.2 | 21.9 | 23.9 |
| Maharashtra | 44.2 | 11.5 | 44.3 | 31.0 | 34.6 | 34.5 | 30.8 | 40.3 | 29.0 | 30.9 | 37.1 | 32.0 | 35.5 | 36.7 | 27.8 |
| Orissa | 57.7 | 13.8 | 28.5 | 50.4 | 25.1 | 24.5 | 25.3 | 19.4 | 55.3 | 39.7 | 22.7 | 37.6 | 50.1 | 17.6 | 32.4 |
| Punjab | 62.0 | 27.3 | 10.7 | 64.8 | 22.6 | 12.6 | 47.9 | 44.2 | 7.9 | 55.0 | 35.2 | 9.9 | 58.4 | 31.4 | 10.3 |
| Rajasthan | 80.2 | 6.7 | 13.1 | 64.3 | 25.6 | 10.1 | 44.3 | 42.4 | 13.3 | 52.2 | 35.8 | 12.0 | 69.7 | 17.7 | 12.7 |
| Tamil Nadu | 48.0 | 21.2 | 30.9 | 48.8 | 34.3 | 16.9 | 50.3 | 21.7 | 28.0 | 49.3 | 30.1 | 20.6 | 45.5 | 29.8 | 24.7 |
| Uttar Pradesh | 71.2 | 15.3 | 13.5 | 66.0 | 19.9 | 14.1 | 54.4 | 36.4 | 9.2 | 59.6 | 29.0 | 11.4 | 63.5 | 23.8 | 12.7 |
| West Bengal | 59.9 | 20.6 | 19.5 | 50.7 | 32.0 | 17.4 | 31.3 | 59.2 | 9.5 | 45.5 | 39.3 | 15.3 | 44.5 | 42.6 | 12.9 |
| Other NE States | 66.5 | 25.7 | 7.8 | 61.5 | 30.7 | 7.8 | | | | 61.5 | 30.7 | 7.8 | 64.0 | 28.2 | 7.8 |
| Rest ST and UT | 49.5 | 31.3 | 19.2 | 26.2 | 29.4 | 44.4 | 19.3 | 80.7 | | 23.5 | 49.9 | 26.6 | 31.6 | 58.3 | 10.1 |
| All-India | 53.7 | 15.3 | 31.0 | 47.2 | 26.5 | 26.4 | 44.1 | 35.3 | 20.6 | 45.8 | 30.5 | 23.8 | 47.1 | 27.5 | 25.4 |

*Source*: Unit level data of employment and unemployment schedule of 43rd (1987–8) Round of NSSO.

**Table A3.6**  Nature of Employment, Usual (Principal + Subsidiary) Status, Metro, and Non-metro, 1987–8

(in per cent)

| States | Male | | | | | | Female | | | | | |
|---|---|---|---|---|---|---|---|---|---|---|---|---|
| | Non-metro | | | Metro | | | Non-metro | | | Metro | | |
| | SE | RE | CL | SE | RE | CL | SE | RE | CL | SE | RE | CL |
| Andhra Pradesh | 38.3 | 40.7 | 21.1 | 36.4 | 51.1 | 12.5 | 47.9 | 14.2 | 37.9 | 38.1 | 34.8 | 27.1 |
| Assam | 37.5 | 52.9 | 9.5 | | | | 43.1 | 45.7 | 11.2 | | | |
| Bihar | 42.6 | 41.6 | 15.8 | | | | 45.6 | 21.2 | 33.2 | | | |
| Gujarat | 39.5 | 44.5 | 16.0 | 34.7 | 44.9 | 20.4 | 40.6 | 28.7 | 30.7 | 38.2 | 29.5 | 32.3 |
| Haryana | 34.5 | 46.7 | 18.7 | | | | 43.9 | 36.5 | 19.6 | | | |
| Jammu and Kashmir | 53.0 | 39.6 | 7.4 | | | | 71.9 | 25.5 | 2.6 | | | |
| Karnataka | 46.6 | 33.6 | 19.8 | 28.6 | 52.4 | 19.0 | 36.7 | 13.0 | 50.3 | 31.5 | 32.2 | 36.3 |
| Kerala | 40.2 | 32.2 | 27.6 | | | | 51.4 | 31.1 | 17.4 | | | |
| Madhya Pradesh | 41.9 | 46.7 | 11.4 | | | | 54.2 | 21.9 | 23.9 | | | |
| Maharashtra | 33.2 | 52.4 | 14.3 | 32.0 | 60.8 | 7.2 | 37.3 | 24.9 | 37.9 | 32.1 | 60.5 | 7.4 |
| Orissa | 40.9 | 45.6 | 13.5 | | | | 50.0 | 17.6 | 32.4 | | | |
| Punjab | 49.6 | 40.1 | 10.3 | | | | 58.3 | 31.4 | 10.3 | | | |
| Rajasthan | 45.5 | 41.0 | 13.5 | | | | 69.6 | 17.7 | 12.7 | | | |
| Tamil Nadu | 32.6 | 48.3 | 19.1 | 30.1 | 49.8 | 20.1 | 48.6 | 25.6 | 25.7 | 26.0 | 56.1 | 17.8 |
| Uttar Pradesh | 54.9 | 34.6 | 10.6 | 37.2 | 51.2 | 11.6 | 64.7 | 23.0 | 12.3 | 39.0 | 40.6 | 20.5 |
| West Bengal | 36.6 | 50.5 | 12.9 | 36.7 | 54.2 | 9.1 | 50.5 | 32.8 | 16.7 | 31.7 | 63.7 | 4.6 |
| Other NE States | 45.7 | 41.4 | 12.9 | | | | 64.0 | 28.2 | 7.8 | | | |
| Rest ST and UT | 28.1 | 64.5 | 7.4 | 38.3 | 58 | 3.6 | 33.9 | 42.5 | 23.6 | 30.4 | 66.7 | 2.9 |
| All-India | 42.4 | 42.8 | 14.8 | 34.1 | 55.3 | 10.7 | 49.7 | 22.9 | 27.4 | 31.6 | 55.0 | 13.4 |

*Source:* Unit level data of employment and unemployment schedule of 43rd (1987–8) Round of NSSO.

**Table A3.7** Nature of Employment, Usual (Principal + Subsidiary) Status, Male, 1993–4

(in per cent)

| States | <50,000 | | | 50,000–200,000 | | | 200,000–1 million | | | 50,000–1 million | | | Total Urban | | |
|---|---|---|---|---|---|---|---|---|---|---|---|---|---|---|---|
| | SE | RE | CL | SE | RE | CL | SE | RE | CL | SE | RE | CL | SE | RE | CL |
| Andhra Pradesh | 39.8 | 29.7 | 30.5 | 34.3 | 22.7 | 40.1 | 36.7 | 46.4 | 16.9 | 38.7 | 42.7 | 18.6 | 38.3 | 40.1 | 21.7 |
| Assam | 54.4 | 36.0 | 9.7 | 45.7 | 10.2 | 49.7 | 29.3 | 60.9 | 9.8 | 39.3 | 49.8 | 11.0 | 47.8 | 42.0 | 10.3 |
| Bihar | 51.2 | 27.2 | 21.7 | 38.2 | 11.1 | 54.9 | 42.1 | 47.4 | 10.5 | 46.7 | 41.0 | 12.3 | 48.2 | 36.5 | 15.4 |
| Gujarat | 39.2 | 36.5 | 24.4 | 48.3 | 11.3 | 41.4 | 42.8 | 25.6 | 31.6 | 41.7 | 40.0 | 18.3 | 37.3 | 44.9 | 17.8 |
| Haryana | 49.0 | 41.4 | 9.6 | 32.8 | 8.7 | 39.3 | 39.1 | 51.6 | 9.4 | 39.3 | 46.7 | 14.0 | 41.9 | 45.3 | 12.8 |
| Jammu and Kashmir | 44.9 | 51.9 | 3.2 | | | | 44.0 | 51.5 | 4.5 | 44.0 | 51.5 | 4.5 | 44.4 | 51.7 | 3.9 |
| Karnataka | 41.7 | 35.5 | 22.9 | 39.2 | 23.5 | 38.5 | 45.3 | 35.9 | 18.8 | 41.9 | 39.2 | 18.9 | 39.8 | 40.6 | 19.6 |
| Kerala | 38.3 | 24.5 | 37.2 | 38.0 | 21.4 | 38.5 | 35.0 | 33.2 | 31.8 | 36.6 | 29.5 | 33.9 | 37.5 | 26.8 | 35.7 |
| Madhya Pradesh | 48.6 | 32.6 | 18.8 | 45.3 | 12.7 | 36.2 | 33.1 | 48.6 | 18.3 | 34.9 | 48.6 | 16.5 | 40.5 | 42.1 | 17.4 |
| Maharashtra | 41.3 | 34.7 | 24.0 | 48.9 | 20.8 | 43.4 | 37.9 | 49.5 | 12.6 | 39.7 | 48.1 | 12.2 | 36.7 | 52.5 | 10.9 |
| Orissa | 36.3 | 42.7 | 21.0 | 46.2 | 8.9 | 40.1 | 35.5 | 56.0 | 8.5 | 37.5 | 52.3 | 10.2 | 37.0 | 48.1 | 14.9 |
| Punjab | 54.9 | 30.0 | 15.1 | 33.0 | 10.5 | 56.3 | 44.1 | 47.9 | 8.1 | 49.8 | 42.2 | 8.0 | 48.7 | 39.8 | 11.5 |
| Rajasthan | 56.2 | 33.5 | 10.3 | 34.2 | 12.7 | 46.6 | 41.1 | 50.1 | 8.8 | 43.9 | 44.6 | 11.5 | 47.1 | 43.0 | 9.9 |
| Tamil Nadu | 37.6 | 35.3 | 27.1 | 46.4 | 16.3 | 36.5 | 33.7 | 43.6 | 22.8 | 35.3 | 40.5 | 24.2 | 34.6 | 40.3 | 25.2 |
| Uttar Pradesh | 61.2 | 23.9 | 14.9 | 31.0 | 10.8 | 60.3 | 55.1 | 35.8 | 9.1 | 57.3 | 32.5 | 10.2 | 57.3 | 31.3 | 11.4 |
| West Bengal | 41.5 | 39.9 | 18.6 | 51.5 | 13.7 | 37.1 | 37.7 | 48.8 | 13.5 | 37.4 | 47.7 | 15.0 | 37.4 | 47.6 | 15.0 |
| Other NE States | 45.2 | 42.9 | 12.0 | 47.9 | 11.1 | 38.1 | | | | 38.1 | 56.0 | 5.9 | 42.5 | 47.9 | 9.6 |
| Rest ST and UT | 37.5 | 45.8 | 16.7 | 38.8 | 34.5 | 27.2 | 29.3 | 56.2 | 14.4 | 28.6 | 55.9 | 15.5 | 41.7 | 46.6 | 11.8 |
| All-India | 46.0 | 32.7 | 21.3 | 41.8 | 15.5 | 43.0 | 40.8 | 44.6 | 14.6 | 42.0 | 42.4 | 15.6 | 41.6 | 42.2 | 16.2 |

*Source*: Unit level data of employment and unemployment schedule of 50th (1993–4) Round of NSSO.

**Table A3.8**  Nature of Employment, Usual (Principal + Subsidiary) Status, Female, 1993–4

(in per cent)

| States | <50,000 | | | 50,000–200,000 | | | 200,000–1 million | | | 50,000–1 million | | | Total Urban | | |
|---|---|---|---|---|---|---|---|---|---|---|---|---|---|---|---|
| | SE | RE | CL | SE | RE | CL | SE | RE | CL | SE | RE | CL | SE | RE | CL |
| Andhra Pradesh | 40.0 | 8.7 | 51.2 | 53.4 | 20.6 | 26.0 | 52.7 | 19.7 | 27.6 | 53.2 | 20.2 | 26.6 | 46.2 | 17.4 | 36.5 |
| Assam | 42.3 | 43.3 | 14.4 | 19.5 | 44.2 | 36.3 | 16.7 | 63.5 | 19.8 | 17.9 | 55.0 | 27.1 | 28.2 | 50.1 | 21.7 |
| Bihar | 42.9 | 24.1 | 33.1 | 47.8 | 17.5 | 34.7 | 39.7 | 33.7 | 26.6 | 42.5 | 28.2 | 29.3 | 42.6 | 26.9 | 30.6 |
| Gujarat | 49.8 | 13.2 | 37.0 | 31.9 | 38.9 | 29.2 | 42.9 | 15.1 | 42.1 | 34.5 | 33.1 | 32.3 | 42.5 | 24.3 | 33.2 |
| Haryana | 76.0 | 13.8 | 10.3 | 47.4 | 23.7 | 28.9 | 57.6 | 22.6 | 19.8 | 49.3 | 23.5 | 27.2 | 57.4 | 20.6 | 22.1 |
| Jammu and Kashmir | 47.1 | 41.3 | 11.6 | | | | 49.4 | 48.8 | 1.8 | 49.4 | 48.8 | 1.8 | 48.1 | 44.5 | 7.4 |
| Karnataka | 49.7 | 14.4 | 35.9 | 47.1 | 23.7 | 29.2 | 46.5 | 29.9 | 23.6 | 46.8 | 26.5 | 26.6 | 46.0 | 25.4 | 28.7 |
| Kerala | 49.4 | 22.7 | 27.9 | 39.5 | 28.1 | 32.4 | 41.1 | 38.4 | 20.5 | 40.2 | 32.7 | 27.1 | 45.8 | 26.6 | 27.6 |
| Madhya Pradesh | 51.4 | 13.6 | 35.1 | 36.3 | 35.0 | 28.7 | 42.1 | 32.7 | 25.2 | 39.1 | 33.9 | 27.0 | 44.9 | 24.2 | 30.9 |
| Maharashtra | 40.9 | 10.5 | 48.6 | 53.3 | 20.7 | 26.0 | 39.0 | 35.6 | 25.4 | 44.0 | 30.4 | 25.6 | 36.5 | 38.9 | 24.6 |
| Orissa | 35.9 | 23.3 | 40.9 | 32.1 | 42.6 | 25.3 | 49.1 | 33.9 | 16.9 | 41.0 | 38.1 | 20.9 | 37.9 | 29.2 | 32.8 |
| Punjab | 66.1 | 26.1 | 7.8 | 44.2 | 47.0 | 8.7 | 41.9 | 48.8 | 9.3 | 43.2 | 47.8 | 9.0 | 49.8 | 41.4 | 8.9 |
| Rajasthan | 75.3 | 8.1 | 16.6 | 64.6 | 13.8 | 21.5 | 45.5 | 41.6 | 12.9 | 55.9 | 26.5 | 17.6 | 63.7 | 20.3 | 16.0 |
| Tamil Nadu | 44.1 | 20.0 | 36.0 | 43.7 | 24.9 | 31.5 | 45.6 | 33.2 | 21.1 | 44.4 | 28.2 | 27.4 | 39.6 | 30.2 | 30.2 |
| Uttar Pradesh | 71.2 | 11.0 | 17.9 | 66.9 | 18.1 | 14.9 | 62.8 | 29.4 | 7.8 | 65.0 | 23.5 | 11.5 | 65.8 | 19.9 | 14.3 |
| West Bengal | 46.0 | 22.4 | 31.6 | 32.5 | 51.8 | 15.7 | 37.1 | 42.7 | 20.2 | 34.1 | 48.7 | 17.2 | 36.4 | 43.8 | 19.8 |
| Other NE States | 67.0 | 24.2 | 8.9 | 51.2 | 45.0 | 3.9 | | | | 51.2 | 45.0 | 3.9 | 60.7 | 32.4 | 6.9 |
| Rest ST and UT | 50.2 | 31.6 | 18.2 | 24.1 | 49.5 | 26.4 | 33.9 | 51.0 | 15.1 | 29.9 | 50.4 | 19.7 | 29.4 | 52.2 | 18.3 |
| All-India | 50.4 | 15.5 | 34.0 | 46.8 | 28.1 | 25.2 | 45.7 | 33.3 | 21.1 | 46.3 | 30.3 | 23.4 | 44.8 | 29.2 | 26.1 |

*Source:* Unit level data of employment and unemployment schedule of 50th (1993–4) Round of NSSO.

**Table A3.9**  Nature of Employment, Usual (Principal + Subsidiary) Status, Metro and Non-metro, 1993–4

(in per cent)

| States | Male | | | | | | Female | | | | | |
|---|---|---|---|---|---|---|---|---|---|---|---|---|
| | Non-metro | | | Metro | | | Non-metro | | | Metro | | |
| | SE | RE | CL | SE | RE | CL | SE | RE | CL | SE | RE | CL |
| Andhra Pradesh | 37.2 | 32.1 | 30.7 | 31.4 | 55.4 | 13.2 | 47.7 | 15.5 | 36.8 | 21.4 | 47.8 | 30.8 |
| Assam | 46.4 | 35.6 | 18.0 | | | | 28.2 | 50.1 | 21.7 | | | |
| Bihar | 43.7 | 31.6 | 24.7 | | | | 42.6 | 26.8 | 30.6 | | | |
| Gujarat | 43.3 | 24.2 | 32.4 | 30.7 | 58.0 | 11.4 | 43.1 | 22.0 | 34.9 | 41.1 | 30.4 | 28.5 |
| Haryana | 42.8 | 29.1 | 28.1 | | | | 57.4 | 20.6 | 22.1 | | | |
| Jammu and Kashmir | 44.4 | 51.7 | 3.9 | | | | 48.1 | 44.6 | 7.3 | | | |
| Karnataka | 41.9 | 32.4 | 25.8 | 31.7 | 53.4 | 14.9 | 48.3 | 20.2 | 31.5 | 29.3 | 62.4 | 8.3 |
| Kerala | 37.6 | 26.2 | 36.2 | | | | 45.8 | 26.7 | 27.6 | | | |
| Madhya Pradesh | 44.9 | 30.7 | 24.4 | 35.6 | 48.5 | 15.9 | 46.2 | 22.2 | 31.7 | 36.3 | 37.7 | 26.1 |
| Maharashtra | 40.3 | 37.1 | 22.6 | 32.8 | 62.4 | 4.8 | 42.5 | 21.0 | 36.5 | 28.2 | 63.6 | 8.3 |
| Orissa | 39.0 | 39.0 | 22.0 | | | | 37.9 | 29.2 | 32.9 | | | |
| Punjab | 43.2 | 30.2 | 26.5 | 38.6 | 43.4 | 18.0 | 49.2 | 42.2 | 8.7 | 54.1 | 35.8 | 10.1 |
| Rajasthan | 46.2 | 32.7 | 21.1 | 36.0 | 60.9 | 3.1 | 65.0 | 17.9 | 17.1 | 46.8 | 53.3 | |
| Tamil Nadu | 39.7 | 31.0 | 29.3 | 28.7 | 46.7 | 24.6 | 44.3 | 24.3 | 31.4 | 12.6 | 64.2 | 23.1 |
| Uttar Pradesh | 51.0 | 24.4 | 24.6 | 45.5 | 48.4 | 6.1 | 67.9 | 17.7 | 14.5 | 40.1 | 47.5 | 12.5 |
| West Bengal | 44.2 | 31.1 | 24.7 | 33.8 | 54.3 | 12.0 | 38.3 | 39.3 | 22.3 | 28.3 | 62.9 | 8.9 |
| Other NE States | 46.7 | 31.0 | 22.3 | | | | 60.7 | 32.4 | 6.9 | | | |
| Rest ST and UT | 34.3 | 47.9 | 17.8 | 44.1 | 45.2 | 10.8 | 37.8 | 43.1 | 19.1 | 24.9 | 57.2 | 17.9 |
| All-India | 43.1 | 30.8 | 26.1 | 35.3 | 53.9 | 10.8 | 48.2 | 23.4 | 28.4 | 28.3 | 56.6 | 15.2 |

*Source:* Unit level data of employment and unemployment schedule of 50th (1993–4) Round of NSSO.

**Table A3.10**  Nature of Employment, Usual (Principal + Subsidiary) Status, Male, 1999–2000

(in per cent)

| States | < 50,000 | | | 50,000–1 million | | | > 1 million | | | Total Urban | | |
|---|---|---|---|---|---|---|---|---|---|---|---|---|
| | SE | RE | CL | SE | RE | CL | SE | RE | CL | SE | RE | CL |
| Andhra Pradesh | 40.9 | 31.8 | 27.3 | 35.2 | 43.5 | 21.4 | 32.2 | 49.0 | 18.9 | 35.8 | 42.0 | 22.2 |
| Assam | 55.7 | 32.8 | 11.5 | 39.1 | 50.2 | 10.7 | – | – | – | 48.3 | 40.5 | 11.2 |
| Bihar | 56.9 | 24.9 | 18.2 | 52.5 | 32.7 | 14.8 | 52.9 | 40.7 | 6.5 | 54.1 | 31.0 | 14.9 |
| Gujarat | 49.2 | 31.5 | 19.3 | 39.3 | 37.3 | 23.4 | 36.0 | 37.7 | 26.3 | 40.8 | 35.9 | 23.3 |
| Haryana | 52.5 | 27.1 | 20.4 | 40.1 | 50.6 | 9.4 | – | – | – | 43.3 | 44.4 | 12.3 |
| Jammu and Kashmir | 49.7 | 36.2 | 14.0 | 48.3 | 43.6 | 8.1 | – | – | – | 48.9 | 40.4 | 10.7 |
| Karnataka | 43.2 | 32.2 | 24.6 | 40.6 | 39.1 | 20.4 | 27.0 | 58.3 | 14.8 | 37.9 | 41.7 | 20.4 |
| Kerala | 39.6 | 23.0 | 37.4 | 35.2 | 33.6 | 31.2 | – | – | – | 37.4 | 28.0 | 34.6 |
| Madhya Pradesh | 47.0 | 32.6 | 20.4 | 44.8 | 40.1 | 15.0 | 40.0 | 43.3 | 16.8 | 45.3 | 36.9 | 17.8 |
| Maharashtra | 42.5 | 35.3 | 22.2 | 31.9 | 48.2 | 19.9 | 31.2 | 63.1 | 5.7 | 33.0 | 54.0 | 13.0 |
| Orissa | 45.1 | 36.6 | 18.3 | 39.1 | 42.7 | 18.2 | – | – | – | 41.9 | 39.9 | 18.3 |
| Punjab | 53.0 | 27.2 | 19.8 | 49.5 | 42.9 | 7.6 | 34.8 | 50.0 | 15.3 | 47.4 | 40.4 | 12.2 |
| Rajasthan | 53.4 | 33.7 | 12.9 | 43.0 | 40.8 | 16.2 | 38.6 | 55.6 | 5.8 | 46.1 | 40.4 | 13.6 |
| Tamil Nadu | 32.9 | 38.8 | 28.4 | 34.6 | 48.9 | 16.6 | 30.7 | 47.6 | 21.7 | 33.0 | 45.4 | 21.6 |
| Uttar Pradesh | 63.4 | 22.5 | 14.1 | 51.2 | 37.8 | 11.0 | 45.0 | 38.5 | 16.5 | 53.2 | 33.4 | 13.4 |
| West Bengal | 44.4 | 34.7 | 20.9 | 42.2 | 40.7 | 17.1 | 43.8 | 42.4 | 13.8 | 43.1 | 39.9 | 17.0 |
| Other NE States | 39.3 | 44.5 | 16.3 | 33.4 | 55.7 | 10.9 | – | – | – | 36.9 | 49.1 | 14.1 |
| Rest ST and UT | 34.1 | 51.3 | 14.7 | 31.2 | 55.0 | 13.9 | 43.8 | 53.6 | 2.6 | 39.7 | 53.7 | 6.6 |
| All-India | 47.4 | 31.5 | 21.1 | 40.6 | 42.5 | 16.9 | 36.7 | 50.9 | 12.4 | 41.5 | 41.7 | 16.9 |

*Source*: Unit level data of employment and unemployment schedule of 55th (1999–2000) Round of NSSO.

**Table A3.11**  Nature of Employment, Usual (Principal + Subsidiary) Status, Female, 1999–2000

(in per cent)

| States | < 50,000 | | | 50,000–1 million | | | > 1 million | | | Total Urban | | |
|---|---|---|---|---|---|---|---|---|---|---|---|---|
| | SE | RE | CL | SE | RE | CL | SE | RE | CL | SE | RE | CL |
| Andhra Pradesh | 43.2 | 26.1 | 30.8 | 38.8 | 28.0 | 33.2 | 31.6 | 38.1 | 30.3 | 39.3 | 28.5 | 32.2 |
| Assam | 38.5 | 52.5 | 9.1 | 16.2 | 57.6 | 26.2 | – | – | – | 25.2 | 55.5 | 19.3 |
| Bihar | 49.8 | 12.7 | 37.5 | 56.2 | 25.0 | 18.8 | 31.9 | 58.4 | 9.7 | 51.3 | 25.2 | 23.5 |
| Gujarat | 47.5 | 25.1 | 27.4 | 29.4 | 30.3 | 40.3 | 50.9 | 23.1 | 26.0 | 42.2 | 26.3 | 31.5 |
| Haryana | 48.9 | 22.1 | 29.0 | 53.0 | 35.1 | 11.9 | – | – | – | 51.1 | 29.0 | 19.9 |
| Jammu and Kashmir | 45.3 | 32.6 | 22.1 | 37.9 | 49.4 | 12.7 | – | – | – | 41.8 | 40.7 | 17.6 |
| Karnataka | 55.1 | 13.5 | 31.5 | 39.2 | 34.4 | 26.5 | 26.9 | 56.0 | 17.1 | 41.7 | 32.5 | 25.7 |
| Kerala | 55.2 | 25.4 | 19.5 | 45.9 | 40.8 | 13.3 | – | – | – | 51.5 | 31.6 | 17.0 |
| Madhya Pradesh | 51.1 | 10.8 | 38.1 | 53.2 | 19.0 | 27.8 | 38.5 | 42.0 | 19.5 | 50.4 | 17.1 | 32.5 |
| Maharashtra | 43.8 | 14.3 | 41.9 | 40.8 | 31.4 | 27.8 | 32.1 | 60.2 | 7.6 | 37.5 | 41.0 | 21.6 |
| Orissa | 40.5 | 19.6 | 39.9 | 51.5 | 22.3 | 26.2 | – | – | – | 45.3 | 20.8 | 33.9 |
| Punjab | 71.3 | 22.7 | 6.0 | 42.1 | 49.1 | 8.8 | 6.4 | 86.3 | 7.3 | 49.3 | 43.2 | 7.5 |
| Rajasthan | 69.1 | 13.0 | 17.9 | 66.4 | 22.9 | 10.8 | 36.7 | 54.7 | 8.7 | 65.5 | 20.7 | 13.8 |
| Tamil Nadu | 39.5 | 32.2 | 28.2 | 45.2 | 39.1 | 15.7 | 29.9 | 57.7 | 12.4 | 39.5 | 40.7 | 19.8 |
| Uttar Pradesh | 80.8 | 10.8 | 8.4 | 55.6 | 35.6 | 8.9 | 58.3 | 33.9 | 7.8 | 65.9 | 25.7 | 8.4 |
| West Bengal | 61.7 | 24.0 | 14.4 | 42.7 | 39.0 | 18.3 | 28.5 | 56.4 | 15.1 | 43.7 | 40.0 | 16.3 |
| Other NE States | 55.3 | 34.6 | 10.1 | 41.4 | 49.8 | 8.8 | – | – | – | 49.1 | 41.3 | 9.6 |
| Rest ST and UT | 49.2 | 36.1 | 14.8 | 31.0 | 56.6 | 12.4 | 36.0 | 60.1 | 3.9 | 36.4 | 56.2 | 7.4 |
| All-India | 52.7 | 20.8 | 26.6 | 44.5 | 33.3 | 22.2 | 36.0 | 51.5 | 12.6 | 45.4 | 33.1 | 21.5 |

*Source:* Unit level data of employment and unemployment schedule of 55th (1999–2000) Round of NSSO.

**Table A3.12**  Nature of Employment, Usual (Principal + Subsidiary) Status, Non-metros, 1999–2000 and 2004–5

(in per cent)

| States | Male | | | | | | Female | | | | | |
|---|---|---|---|---|---|---|---|---|---|---|---|---|
| | 1999–2000 | | | 2004–5 | | | 1999–2000 | | | 2004–5 | | |
| | SE | RE | CL | SE | RE | CL | SE | RE | CL | SE | RE | CL |
| Andhra Pradesh | 36.6 | 40.6 | 22.9 | 42.4 | 37.6 | 19.9 | 40.2 | 27.4 | 32.4 | 51.0 | 26.7 | 22.3 |
| Assam | 48.3 | 40.6 | 11.1 | 45.3 | 43.3 | 11.4 | 25.2 | 55.5 | 19.3 | 26.4 | 54.5 | 19.1 |
| Bihar | 54.3 | 29.5 | 16.2 | 55.0 | 28.0 | 17.0 | 54.0 | 20.7 | 25.3 | 48.1 | 22.6 | 29.3 |
| Gujarat | 43.5 | 34.8 | 21.6 | 46.7 | 39.4 | 13.9 | 37.7 | 27.9 | 34.4 | 47.1 | 24.8 | 28.2 |
| Haryana | 43.3 | 44.4 | 12.3 | 53.8 | 37.6 | 8.6 | 51.1 | 29.2 | 19.7 | 58.4 | 31.3 | 10.3 |
| Jammu and Kashmir | 48.9 | 40.4 | 10.7 | 56.1 | 32.5 | 11.4 | 41.7 | 40.7 | 17.6 | 71.5 | 25.5 | 3.0 |
| Karnataka | 41.8 | 35.9 | 22.3 | 44.3 | 36.1 | 19.6 | 47.5 | 23.4 | 29.1 | 48.8 | 29.4 | 21.8 |
| Kerala | 37.6 | 27.9 | 34.5 | 40.5 | 25.2 | 34.2 | 51.4 | 31.6 | 17.0 | 42.6 | 38.1 | 19.3 |
| Madhya Pradesh | 46.0 | 36.0 | 17.9 | 47.1 | 36.9 | 16.1 | 51.9 | 14.0 | 34.0 | 42.7 | 30.9 | 26.5 |
| Maharashtra | 34.9 | 44.5 | 20.6 | 39.5 | 41.2 | 19.2 | 42.0 | 24.7 | 33.3 | 42.1 | 25.8 | 32.1 |
| Orissa | 41.9 | 39.9 | 18.2 | 46.2 | 35.7 | 18.1 | 45.3 | 20.8 | 33.9 | 37.9 | 35.2 | 26.9 |
| Punjab | 50.6 | 38.0 | 11.4 | 52.7 | 37.6 | 9.6 | 54.6 | 37.8 | 7.6 | 44.6 | 51.4 | 4.0 |
| Rajasthan | 47.3 | 37.9 | 14.8 | 52.5 | 33.8 | 13.7 | 67.6 | 18.2 | 14.1 | 68.8 | 19.8 | 11.5 |
| Tamil Nadu | 33.8 | 44.6 | 21.6 | 38.7 | 43.1 | 18.2 | 42.3 | 35.6 | 22.1 | 46.6 | 37.5 | 15.9 |
| Uttar Pradesh | 56.2 | 31.6 | 12.3 | 59.0 | 28.9 | 12.1 | 68.9 | 22.5 | 8.6 | 73.0 | 17.6 | 9.5 |
| West Bengal | 42.8 | 39.0 | 18.2 | 47.4 | 35.1 | 17.5 | 50.0 | 33.2 | 16.8 | 53.1 | 34.1 | 12.8 |
| Other NE States | 36.9 | 49.1 | 14.1 | 48.3 | 42.8 | 8.9 | 49.1 | 41.4 | 9.5 | 52.5 | 42.3 | 5.2 |
| Rest ST and UT | 32.1 | 53.8 | 14.1 | 31.7 | 48.5 | 19.8 | 37.1 | 49.7 | 13.2 | 30.9 | 54.7 | 14.4 |
| All-India | 43.2 | 38.2 | 18.5 | 47.2 | 36.1 | 16.8 | 48.3 | 27.5 | 24.2 | 50.6 | 30.2 | 19.2 |

*Source:* Unit level data of employment and unemployment schedule of 55th (1999–2000) and 61st (2004–5) Rounds of NSSO.

**Table A3.13**   Nature of Employment, Usual (Principal + Subsidiary) Status, Metros and All Urban, 2004–5

(in per cent)

| States | Male | | | | | | Female | | | | | |
|---|---|---|---|---|---|---|---|---|---|---|---|---|
| | Metro | | | All Urban | | | Metro | | | All Urban | | |
| | SE | RE | CL | SE | RE | CL | SE | RE | CL | SE | RE | CL |
| Andhra Pradesh | 44.5 | 42.7 | 12.7 | 42.8 | 38.6 | 18.6 | 31.7 | 54.7 | 13.6 | 48.7 | 30.0 | 21.2 |
| Assam | | | | 45.3 | 43.3 | 11.4 | | | | 26.4 | 54.5 | 19.1 |
| Bihar | 50.8 | 40.2 | 9.0 | 54.5 | 29.3 | 16.2 | 26.4 | 73.6 | | 47.8 | 23.3 | 28.9 |
| Gujarat | 34.6 | 59.4 | 5.9 | 41.4 | 48.2 | 10.4 | 36.7 | 38.5 | 24.8 | 42.9 | 30.3 | 26.8 |
| Haryana | 23.1 | 74.3 | 2.6 | 47.8 | 44.7 | 7.5 | 61.5 | 37.6 | 0.8 | 58.7 | 32.0 | 9.2 |
| Jammu and Kashmir | | | | 56.1 | 32.5 | 11.4 | | | | 71.5 | 25.5 | 3.0 |
| Karnataka | 35.1 | 46.2 | 18.7 | 41.6 | 39.0 | 19.4 | 23.6 | 67.3 | 9.1 | 43.7 | 37.1 | 19.2 |
| Kerala | | | | 40.5 | 25.2 | 34.2 | | | | 42.6 | 38.1 | 19.3 |
| Madhya Pradesh | 52.3 | 39.8 | 7.8 | 48.0 | 37.4 | 14.7 | 50.2 | 42.5 | 7.4 | 44.0 | 32.9 | 23.1 |
| Maharashtra | 37.9 | 52.8 | 9.3 | 38.7 | 47.3 | 14.1 | 30.5 | 60.9 | 8.6 | 36.1 | 43.8 | 20.1 |
| Orissa | | | | 46.2 | 35.7 | 18.1 | | | | 37.9 | 35.2 | 26.9 |
| Punjab | 34.5 | 60.5 | 5.0 | 48.6 | 42.8 | 8.6 | 39.5 | 50.8 | 9.7 | 44.0 | 51.4 | 4.7 |
| Rajasthan | 43.2 | 48.8 | 8.0 | 50.3 | 37.4 | 12.3 | 80.4 | 16.4 | 3.3 | 72.7 | 18.6 | 8.7 |
| Tamil Nadu | 35.1 | 54.5 | 10.4 | 38.0 | 45.2 | 16.7 | 22.8 | 76.0 | 1.2 | 44.3 | 41.2 | 14.5 |
| Uttar Pradesh | 50.7 | 41.5 | 7.8 | 57.1 | 31.7 | 11.2 | 61.7 | 28.8 | 9.5 | 70.9 | 19.6 | 9.5 |
| West Bengal | 36.9 | 43.8 | 19.3 | 44.7 | 37.3 | 17.9 | 50.1 | 45.3 | 4.6 | 52.4 | 36.7 | 10.9 |
| Other NE States | | | | 48.3 | 42.8 | 8.9 | | | | 52.5 | 42.3 | 5.2 |
| Rest ST and UT | 35.5 | 59.6 | 4.8 | 34.8 | 57.5 | 7.7 | 19.1 | 75.4 | 5.5 | 23.0 | 68.6 | 8.4 |
| All-India | 39.0 | 51.6 | 9.4 | 44.8 | 40.6 | 14.6 | 38.5 | 52.5 | 9.0 | 47.7 | 35.6 | 16.7 |

*Source*: Unit level data of employment and unemployment schedule of 61st (2004–5) Round of NSSO.

**Table A3.14**  Distribution of Workers by Industrial Categories, Usual (Principal + Subsidiary) Status, Male, 1987–8

(in per cent)

| States | <50,000 | | | 50,000–200,000 | | | 200,000–1 million | | | 50,000–1 million | | | Total Urban | | |
|---|---|---|---|---|---|---|---|---|---|---|---|---|---|---|---|
| | P | S | T | P | S | T | P | S | T | P | S | T | P | S | T |
| Andhra Pradesh | 21.7 | 29.9 | 48.4 | 11.3 | 29.2 | 59.6 | 5.2 | 32.3 | 62.4 | 8.7 | 30.5 | 60.8 | 12.5 | 29.8 | 57.8 |
| Assam | 11.1 | 14.0 | 75.0 | 2.8 | 16.3 | 80.9 | 2.5 | 13.4 | 84.1 | 2.6 | 14.8 | 82.6 | 7.4 | 14.3 | 77.8 |
| Bihar | 32.2 | 18.8 | 49.0 | 20.6 | 19.8 | 59.6 | 7.7 | 41.8 | 50.5 | 14.0 | 31.1 | 54.9 | 21.5 | 26.0 | 52.4 |
| Gujarat | 14.4 | 34.1 | 51.5 | 5.9 | 30.8 | 63.3 | 3.3 | 47.3 | 49.3 | 4.6 | 39.5 | 55.9 | 6.9 | 39.7 | 53.3 |
| Haryana | 11.1 | 23.7 | 65.2 | 4.3 | 32.3 | 63.5 | 19.6 | 55.3 | 25.1 | 9.9 | 40.8 | 49.3 | 10.3 | 35.7 | 54.0 |
| Jammu and Kashmir | 19.3 | 27.5 | 53.2 | | | | 4.1 | 37.8 | 58.1 | 4.1 | 37.8 | 58.1 | 9.6 | 34.0 | 56.4 |
| Karnataka | 25.8 | 26.5 | 47.8 | 13.3 | 32.0 | 54.7 | 8.6 | 31.8 | 59.6 | 11.3 | 31.9 | 56.8 | 15.1 | 31.5 | 53.4 |
| Kerala | 24.4 | 33.3 | 42.3 | 10.7 | 22.0 | 67.3 | 16.3 | 21.4 | 62.3 | 14.5 | 21.6 | 63.9 | 19.7 | 27.7 | 52.6 |
| Madhya Pradesh | 26.9 | 20.5 | 52.7 | 8.6 | 21.9 | 69.5 | 3.9 | 38.7 | 57.4 | 5.8 | 31.7 | 62.4 | 14.0 | 27.3 | 58.5 |
| Maharashtra | 22.3 | 24.5 | 53.2 | 9.6 | 32.9 | 57.5 | 2.7 | 44.0 | 53.3 | 6.3 | 38.3 | 55.5 | 7.4 | 35.7 | 56.9 |
| Orissa | 23.7 | 22.2 | 54.1 | 8.4 | 17.2 | 74.4 | 1.0 | 27.1 | 71.9 | 4.8 | 22.1 | 73.1 | 13.7 | 22.2 | 64.1 |
| Punjab | 12.5 | 28.8 | 58.6 | 7.2 | 28.1 | 64.7 | 3.3 | 45.0 | 51.7 | 4.5 | 40.0 | 55.5 | 7.4 | 36.0 | 56.7 |
| Rajasthan | 18.0 | 31.9 | 50.1 | 4.8 | 28.2 | 66.9 | 2.9 | 37.4 | 59.7 | 3.5 | 34.5 | 62.0 | 10.2 | 33.3 | 56.5 |
| Tamil Nadu | 15.2 | 39.4 | 45.4 | 6.3 | 39.8 | 53.9 | 2.2 | 40.3 | 57.5 | 5.0 | 40.0 | 55.0 | 7.8 | 39.1 | 53.0 |
| Uttar Pradesh | 21.8 | 23.3 | 54.9 | 8.8 | 24.8 | 66.4 | 4.4 | 35.1 | 60.5 | 6.0 | 31.3 | 62.7 | 11.5 | 28.9 | 59.6 |
| West Bengal | 15.6 | 38.1 | 46.3 | 6.3 | 36.3 | 57.4 | 4.9 | 44.4 | 50.6 | 5.9 | 38.9 | 55.2 | 7.1 | 38.2 | 54.7 |
| Other NE States | 22.4 | 12.8 | 64.8 | 16.0 | 11.2 | 72.9 | 0.0 | | 72.9 | 16.0 | 11.2 | 72.9 | 19.7 | 12.0 | 67.3 |
| Rest ST and UT | 11.5 | 33.0 | 55.5 | 9.1 | 32.9 | 58.1 | 1.2 | 20.4 | 78.4 | 5.8 | 27.7 | 66.5 | 2.4 | 36.2 | 60.8 |
| All-India | 20.6 | 28.2 | 51.2 | 9.0 | 30.1 | 60.9 | 5.0 | 38.3 | 56.7 | 7.0 | 34.2 | 58.8 | 10.5 | 33.0 | 56.5 |

*Source:* Unit level data of employment and unemployment schedule of 43rd (1987–8) Round of NSSO.

*Notes:* P = Primary, S = Secondary, and T = Tertiary.

**Table A3.15**  Distribution of Workers by Industrial Categories, Usual (Principal + Subsidiary) Status, Female, 1987–8

(in per cent)

| States | <50,000 | | | 50,000–200,000 | | | 200,000–1 million | | | 50,000–1 million | | | Total Urban | | |
|---|---|---|---|---|---|---|---|---|---|---|---|---|---|---|---|
| | P | S | T | P | S | T | P | S | T | P | S | T | P | S | T |
| Andhra Pradesh | 44.2 | 29.4 | 26.4 | 31.2 | 31.5 | 37.3 | 18.4 | 35.9 | 45.7 | 26.1 | 33.2 | 40.7 | 32.5 | 31.6 | 35.9 |
| Assam | 31.2 | 24.4 | 44.5 | 24.8 | 6.0 | 69.2 | 4.9 | 0.0 | 95.1 | 14.0 | 2.7 | 83.3 | 22.2 | 13.3 | 62.2 |
| Bihar | 58.9 | 19.4 | 21.8 | 36.1 | 12.4 | 51.6 | 16.4 | 43.2 | 40.5 | 24.3 | 30.8 | 44.9 | 42.2 | 24.0 | 32.2 |
| Gujarat | 38.5 | 28.4 | 33.1 | 22.6 | 32.1 | 45.3 | 5.9 | 28.5 | 65.6 | 14.0 | 30.2 | 55.8 | 23.6 | 30.6 | 45.6 |
| Haryana | 63.8 | 8.7 | 27.5 | 15.1 | 20.4 | 64.5 | 37.1 | 35.6 | 27.3 | 23.0 | 25.8 | 51.2 | 38.0 | 20.3 | 41.7 |
| Jammu and Kashmir | 66.5 | 14.8 | 18.8 | | | | 13.2 | 48.9 | 37.9 | 13.2 | 48.9 | 37.9 | 37.8 | 33.0 | 29.2 |
| Karnataka | 53.6 | 28.5 | 17.9 | 36.8 | 39.9 | 23.3 | 12.8 | 44.1 | 43.1 | 29.0 | 41.3 | 29.8 | 39.3 | 36.1 | 24.6 |
| Kerala | 52.4 | 22.9 | 24.8 | 27.7 | 19.0 | 53.3 | 25.6 | 16.3 | 58.1 | 26.4 | 17.2 | 56.4 | 40.5 | 20.4 | 39.1 |
| Madhya Pradesh | 45.6 | 28.6 | 25.8 | 20.4 | 36.8 | 42.8 | 4.4 | 43.9 | 51.8 | 10.6 | 41.1 | 48.3 | 26.8 | 35.1 | 37.9 |
| Maharashtra | 60.0 | 17.3 | 22.7 | 27.1 | 32.5 | 40.5 | 6.1 | 49.7 | 44.2 | 17.6 | 40.3 | 42.2 | 27.6 | 27.5 | 44.8 |
| Orissa | 41.5 | 24.1 | 34.5 | 12.9 | 48.2 | 38.8 | 8.4 | 38.3 | 53.3 | 11.0 | 44.0 | 45.0 | 28.4 | 32.6 | 39.0 |
| Punjab | 52.9 | 13.8 | 33.3 | 50.6 | 14.8 | 34.6 | 24.2 | 26.1 | 49.7 | 35.3 | 21.3 | 43.4 | 43.7 | 17.6 | 38.6 |
| Rajasthan | 69.2 | 21.5 | 9.3 | 46.7 | 22.9 | 30.5 | 22.5 | 25.9 | 51.6 | 31.9 | 24.7 | 43.3 | 55.0 | 22.7 | 22.2 |
| Tamil Nadu | 33.1 | 43.1 | 23.8 | 15.4 | 51.0 | 33.6 | 12.3 | 48.2 | 39.5 | 14.4 | 50.0 | 35.6 | 21.0 | 44.9 | 34.2 |
| Uttar Pradesh | 43.6 | 23.5 | 32.9 | 39.4 | 27.3 | 33.3 | 10.0 | 32.4 | 57.6 | 23.2 | 30.1 | 46.7 | 31.0 | 26.9 | 42.2 |
| West Bengal | 30.3 | 33.1 | 36.6 | 19.1 | 36.7 | 44.2 | 18.3 | 25.6 | 56.2 | 18.9 | 33.3 | 47.9 | 17.5 | 28.7 | 53.8 |
| Other NE States | 44.6 | 7.7 | 47.6 | 45.5 | 5.4 | 49.1 | | | | 45.5 | 5.4 | 49.1 | 45.3 | 6.5 | 47.6 |
| Rest ST and UT | 42.8 | 13.5 | 43.7 | 31.6 | 15.3 | 53.1 | 0.0 | 18.4 | 81.6 | 19.0 | 16.5 | 64.5 | 11.4 | 18.9 | 69.3 |
| All-India | 47.9 | 27.3 | 24.8 | 27.1 | 34.5 | 38.4 | 13.5 | 37.0 | 49.5 | 21.0 | 35.6 | 43.4 | 30.3 | 31.0 | 38.6 |

*Source:* Unit level data of employment and unemployment schedule of 43rd (1987–8) Round of NSSO.

**Table A3.16** Distribution of Workers by Industrial Categories, Usual (Principal + Subsidiary) Status, Metro and Non-metro, 1987–8

(in per cent)

| States | Male | | | | | | Female | | | | | |
|---|---|---|---|---|---|---|---|---|---|---|---|---|
| | Non-metro | | | Metro | | | Non-metro | | | Metro | | |
| | P | S | T | P | S | T | P | S | T | P | S | T |
| Andhra Pradesh | 13.6 | 30.3 | 56.1 | 3.2 | 26.0 | 70.8 | 34.3 | 31.5 | 34.2 | 6.3 | 33.3 | 60.4 |
| Assam | 7.5 | 14.3 | 78.2 | | | | 22.7 | 13.7 | 63.5 | | | |
| Bihar | 21.5 | 26.1 | 52.5 | | | | 42.9 | 24.6 | 32.5 | | | |
| Gujarat | 8.7 | 37.2 | 54.1 | 1.1 | 47.8 | 51.2 | 26.3 | 29.3 | 44.4 | 13.5 | 35.7 | 50.9 |
| Haryana | 10.3 | 35.7 | 54.0 | | | | 37.7 | 19.8 | 42.4 | | | |
| Jammu and Kashmir | 9.6 | 34.1 | 56.3 | | | | 37.8 | 33.1 | 29.1 | | | |
| Karnataka | 18.8 | 29.1 | 52.1 | 1.2 | 40.6 | 58.2 | 44.5 | 33.2 | 22.3 | 3.5 | 56.1 | 40.4 |
| Kerala | 19.7 | 27.7 | 52.6 | | | | 40.5 | 20.3 | 39.2 | | | |
| Madhya Pradesh | 14.0 | 27.3 | 58.6 | | | | 26.7 | 35.3 | 37.9 | | | |
| Maharashtra | 12.2 | 33.2 | 54.6 | 1.4 | 39.0 | 59.6 | 37.9 | 29.3 | 32.8 | 6.7 | 24.2 | 69.1 |
| Orissa | 13.7 | 22.1 | 64.2 | | | | 28.5 | 32.6 | 38.9 | | | |
| Punjab | 7.3 | 36.0 | 56.7 | | | | 43.7 | 17.7 | 38.5 | | | |
| Rajasthan | 10.2 | 33.3 | 56.5 | | | | 55.2 | 22.7 | 22.1 | | | |
| Tamil Nadu | 9.4 | 39.7 | 50.9 | 1.4 | 36.5 | 62.1 | 23.8 | 46.6 | 29.7 | 3.7 | 34.4 | 61.9 |
| Uttar Pradesh | 12.4 | 28.1 | 59.5 | 0.6 | 39.1 | 60.2 | 32.2 | 27.2 | 40.6 | 5.9 | 22.1 | 72.0 |
| West Bengal | 9.5 | 38.6 | 52.0 | 1.1 | 37.2 | 61.7 | 22.9 | 33.5 | 43.6 | 4.0 | 20.9 | 75.1 |
| Other NE States | 19.9 | 12.2 | 68.0 | | | | 45.1 | 6.6 | 48.4 | | | |
| Rest ST and UT | 8.3 | 30.0 | 61.8 | 0.9 | 38.0 | 61.1 | 28.5 | 15.3 | 56.2 | 2.4 | 21.5 | 76.2 |
| All-India | 12.6 | 31.7 | 55.6 | 1.3 | 38.4 | 60.4 | 34.3 | 31.5 | 34.2 | 5.3 | 28.7 | 66.0 |

*Source:* Unit level data of employment and unemployment schedule of 43rd (1987–8) Round of NSSO.

**Table A3.17**   Distribution of Workers by Industrial Categories, Usual (Principal + Subsidiary) Status, Male, 1993–4

(in per cent)

| States | <50,000 | | | 50,000–200,000 | | | 200,000–1 million | | | 50,000–1 million | | | Total Urban | | |
|---|---|---|---|---|---|---|---|---|---|---|---|---|---|---|---|
| | P | S | T | P | S | T | P | S | T | P | S | T | P | S | T |
| Andhra Pradesh | 25.8 | 28.8 | 45.4 | 10.5 | 24.9 | 64.6 | 8.4 | 27.9 | 63.8 | 9.5 | 26.2 | 64.3 | 13.6 | 27.8 | 58.5 |
| Assam | 16.2 | 15.1 | 68.8 | 1.3 | 17.1 | 81.7 | 1.4 | 8.4 | 90.2 | 1.3 | 12.5 | 86.2 | 9.8 | 13.9 | 76.3 |
| Bihar | 26.0 | 20.0 | 54.0 | 10.3 | 19.6 | 70.1 | 10.3 | 24.2 | 65.5 | 10.3 | 22.6 | 67.1 | 15.5 | 21.7 | 62.8 |
| Gujarat | 13.2 | 39.6 | 47.2 | 3.1 | 37.2 | 59.7 | 2.5 | 45.9 | 51.6 | 3.0 | 39.2 | 57.8 | 5.5 | 41.6 | 53.0 |
| Haryana | 16.0 | 31.3 | 52.7 | 2.6 | 34.4 | 63.1 | 3.2 | 41.5 | 55.3 | 2.7 | 36.3 | 60.9 | 6.3 | 35.0 | 58.7 |
| Jammu and Kashmir | 11.0 | 17.8 | 71.2 | | | | 5.3 | 21.5 | 73.2 | 5.3 | 21.5 | 73.2 | 7.9 | 19.8 | 72.3 |
| Karnataka | 27.8 | 28.3 | 43.9 | 13.2 | 28.9 | 57.9 | 9.4 | 26.9 | 63.7 | 11.2 | 27.9 | 60.9 | 15.6 | 30.6 | 53.7 |
| Kerala | 24.9 | 29.4 | 45.7 | 25.9 | 25.7 | 48.3 | 16.1 | 22.8 | 61.1 | 20.5 | 24.1 | 55.4 | 22.9 | 27.0 | 50.1 |
| Madhya Pradesh | 29.4 | 18.3 | 52.3 | 7.9 | 25.0 | 67.1 | 4.1 | 33.1 | 62.8 | 6.3 | 28.4 | 65.3 | 15.4 | 24.0 | 60.6 |
| Maharashtra | 23.3 | 23.0 | 53.7 | 9.0 | 28.0 | 63.0 | 4.1 | 41.1 | 54.9 | 5.7 | 36.7 | 57.6 | 6.9 | 34.2 | 58.9 |
| Orissa | 29.3 | 23.5 | 47.2 | 4.5 | 22.5 | 73.0 | 1.7 | 27.1 | 71.2 | 2.9 | 25.1 | 72.0 | 14.3 | 24.4 | 61.3 |
| Punjab | 15.7 | 23.5 | 60.8 | 4.7 | 26.5 | 68.9 | 5.0 | 33.3 | 61.8 | 4.8 | 30.1 | 65.1 | 6.6 | 33.7 | 59.8 |
| Rajasthan | 18.3 | 28.8 | 52.9 | 8.8 | 36.6 | 54.6 | 2.7 | 30.0 | 67.3 | 5.7 | 33.4 | 60.9 | 9.5 | 31.6 | 58.9 |
| Tamil Nadu | 17.0 | 31.5 | 51.5 | 9.7 | 36.2 | 54.2 | 3.7 | 46.0 | 50.3 | 7.1 | 40.5 | 52.5 | 8.8 | 37.4 | 53.8 |
| Uttar Pradesh | 23.2 | 25.6 | 51.2 | 10.2 | 26.1 | 63.7 | 4.1 | 31.9 | 63.9 | 6.7 | 29.4 | 63.8 | 12.3 | 27.9 | 59.8 |
| West Bengal | 16.8 | 34.4 | 48.8 | 6.1 | 40.9 | 53.1 | 4.9 | 46.7 | 48.4 | 5.6 | 43.2 | 51.2 | 6.9 | 37.7 | 55.3 |
| Other NE States | 25.0 | 13.3 | 61.7 | 2.7 | 11.5 | 85.8 | 2.7 | 11.5 | 85.8 | 2.7 | 11.5 | 85.8 | 16.3 | 12.6 | 71.1 |
| Rest ST and UT | 13.7 | 26.3 | 60.0 | 8.2 | 25.5 | 66.2 | 2.9 | 35.1 | 62.0 | 4.6 | 32.0 | 63.4 | 2.6 | 36.6 | 60.8 |
| All-India | 22.2 | 27.0 | 50.8 | 8.5 | 30.3 | 61.2 | 5.5 | 34.5 | 60.1 | 7.0 | 32.3 | 60.7 | 10.3 | 31.8 | 57.9 |

*Source:* Unit level data of employment and unemployment schedule of 50th (1993–4) Round of NSSO.

**Table A3.18**  Distribution of Workers by Industrial Categories, Usual (Principal + Subsidiary) Status, Female, 1993–4

(in per cent)

| States | <50,000 | | | 50,000–200,000 | | | 200,000–1 million | | | 50,000–1 million | | | Total Urban | | |
|---|---|---|---|---|---|---|---|---|---|---|---|---|---|---|---|
| | P | S | T | P | S | T | P | S | T | P | S | T | P | S | T |
| Andhra Pradesh | 52.8 | 21.5 | 25.7 | 25.9 | 30.9 | 43.1 | 10.8 | 38.1 | 51.2 | 20.5 | 33.5 | 46.0 | 32.0 | 29.0 | 39.1 |
| Assam | 15.7 | 23.3 | 60.9 | 1.8 | 17.0 | 81.2 | | 11.0 | 89.1 | 0.7 | 13.4 | 85.9 | 7.2 | 17.7 | 75.1 |
| Bihar | 34.1 | 24.6 | 41.3 | 11.5 | 36.8 | 51.8 | 9.0 | 27.6 | 63.5 | 9.8 | 30.7 | 59.5 | 17.9 | 28.7 | 53.5 |
| Gujarat | 41.6 | 21.6 | 36.9 | 11.1 | 15.1 | 73.8 | 1.4 | 65.8 | 32.9 | 8.7 | 27.4 | 63.8 | 21.6 | 25.1 | 53.3 |
| Haryana | 53.9 | 10.4 | 35.7 | 21.1 | 40.9 | 38.0 | 27.7 | 17.4 | 55.0 | 22.3 | 36.4 | 41.2 | 31.9 | 28.6 | 39.6 |
| Jammu and Kashmir | 48.8 | 6.4 | 44.8 | | | | 30.0 | 4.4 | 65.5 | 30.0 | 4.4 | 65.5 | 40.7 | 5.5 | 53.8 |
| Karnataka | 44.1 | 29.9 | 26.1 | 24.7 | 41.4 | 33.9 | 18.7 | 31.7 | 49.5 | 21.8 | 37.2 | 40.9 | 30.5 | 32.6 | 36.9 |
| Kerala | 44.0 | 29.5 | 26.6 | 19.1 | 32.5 | 48.4 | 18.4 | 22.8 | 58.8 | 18.8 | 28.2 | 53.0 | 34.0 | 29.0 | 37.0 |
| Madhya Pradesh | 51.7 | 19.1 | 29.3 | 11.1 | 29.7 | 59.2 | 8.2 | 18.7 | 73.1 | 9.7 | 24.4 | 65.9 | 30.8 | 22.6 | 46.6 |
| Maharashtra | 50.2 | 14.1 | 35.7 | 28.5 | 23.4 | 48.1 | 7.9 | 35.4 | 56.8 | 15.1 | 31.2 | 53.7 | 19.8 | 21.8 | 58.4 |
| Orissa | 47.7 | 20.8 | 31.4 | 5.3 | 29.5 | 65.3 | 10.5 | 32.2 | 57.3 | 8.1 | 30.9 | 61.0 | 31.7 | 24.9 | 43.4 |
| Punjab | 54.8 | 8.8 | 36.3 | 26.8 | 5.6 | 67.7 | 14.6 | 15.9 | 69.5 | 21.1 | 10.4 | 68.5 | 27.7 | 12.1 | 60.2 |
| Rajasthan | 60.7 | 12.5 | 26.8 | 42.8 | 38.9 | 18.3 | 18.2 | 21.6 | 60.2 | 31.5 | 30.9 | 37.6 | 42.9 | 22.7 | 34.4 |
| Tamil Nadu | 34.6 | 37.9 | 27.5 | 25.0 | 44.0 | 31.1 | 7.3 | 47.3 | 45.4 | 18.1 | 45.2 | 36.7 | 22.0 | 40.5 | 37.5 |
| Uttar Pradesh | 45.2 | 29.9 | 24.8 | 27.7 | 43.8 | 28.5 | 11.8 | 32.0 | 56.2 | 20.2 | 38.1 | 41.7 | 30.4 | 33.4 | 36.2 |
| West Bengal | 22.4 | 46.9 | 30.7 | 7.9 | 34.1 | 58.0 | 3.5 | 26.1 | 70.5 | 6.4 | 31.3 | 62.3 | 9.9 | 32.5 | 57.6 |
| Other NE States | 36.5 | 17.6 | 45.9 | 4.5 | 20.6 | 75.0 | | | | 4.4 | 20.5 | 75.0 | 23.5 | 18.8 | 57.7 |
| Rest ST and UT | 42.2 | 16.9 | 40.9 | 24.8 | 6.4 | 68.9 | 3.6 | 15.3 | 81.0 | 12.3 | 11.7 | 76.1 | 10.1 | 15.4 | 74.5 |
| All-India | 44.5 | 25.7 | 29.8 | 22.0 | 33.9 | 44.1 | 10.5 | 32.6 | 57.0 | 17.0 | 33.3 | 49.7 | 25.4 | 28.6 | 46.0 |

*Source:* Unit level data of employment and unemployment schedule of 50th (1993–4) Round of NSSO.

**Table A3.19** Distribution of Workers by Industrial Categories, Usual (Principal + Subsidiary) Status, Metro and Non-metro, 1993–4

(in per cent)

| States | Male | | | | | | Female | | | | | |
|---|---|---|---|---|---|---|---|---|---|---|---|---|
| | Non-metro | | | Metro | | | Non-metro | | | Metro | | |
| | P | S | T | P | S | T | P | S | T | P | S | T |
| Andhra Pradesh | 15.0 | 27.0 | 57.9 | 1.1 | 34.8 | 64.1 | 33.8 | 28.5 | 37.6 | 1.0 | 36.3 | 62.7 |
| Assam | 9.7 | 14.0 | 76.3 | | | | 7.1 | 17.7 | 75.2 | | | |
| Bihar | 15.4 | 21.7 | 62.9 | | | | 17.9 | 28.7 | 53.5 | | | |
| Gujarat | 7.5 | 39.4 | 53.1 | 1.2 | 46.0 | 52.8 | 27.1 | 24.2 | 48.7 | 6.9 | 27.7 | 65.5 |
| Haryana | 6.3 | 35.0 | 58.7 | | | | 31.9 | 28.5 | 39.6 | | | |
| Jammu and Kashmir | 7.9 | 19.8 | 72.3 | | | | 40.7 | 5.5 | 53.8 | | | |
| Karnataka | 19.1 | 28.1 | 52.8 | 1.6 | 40.9 | 57.5 | 33.6 | 33.2 | 33.2 | 8.3 | 28.2 | 63.6 |
| Kerala | 22.9 | 27.0 | 50.1 | | | | 34.0 | 29.0 | 37.0 | | | |
| Madhya Pradesh | 17.2 | 23.7 | 59.2 | 4.7 | 26.1 | 69.3 | 33.9 | 21.3 | 44.7 | 10.8 | 31.1 | 58.1 |
| Maharashtra | 12.1 | 31.8 | 56.2 | 1.4 | 36.8 | 61.8 | 31.7 | 23.1 | 45.2 | 3.4 | 20.0 | 76.6 |
| Orissa | 14.3 | 24.4 | 61.3 | | | | 31.8 | 24.9 | 43.3 | | | |
| Punjab | 7.8 | 28.3 | 63.9 | 1.6 | 55.7 | 42.8 | 29.9 | 10.0 | 60.1 | 10.8 | 28.4 | 60.9 |
| Rajasthan | 11.0 | 31.5 | 57.5 | 0.7 | 32.6 | 66.7 | 45.2 | 22.3 | 32.5 | 15.5 | 26.8 | 57.7 |
| Tamil Nadu | 10.8 | 37.1 | 52.1 | 1.1 | 38.6 | 60.3 | 25.7 | 41.8 | 32.4 | 0.6 | 32.5 | 66.9 |
| Uttar Pradesh | 13.3 | 27.9 | 58.8 | 4.5 | 28.2 | 67.3 | 31.9 | 34.3 | 33.8 | 11.7 | 22.3 | 66.0 |
| West Bengal | 8.8 | 40.7 | 50.5 | 0.9 | 28.2 | 71.0 | 12.1 | 36.9 | 51.0 | 0.2 | 13.9 | 86.0 |
| Other NE States | 16.4 | 12.6 | 71.0 | | | | 23.8 | 18.8 | 57.4 | | | |
| Rest ST and UT | 8.0 | 29.9 | 62.1 | 1.3 | 38.3 | 60.4 | 23.9 | 13.7 | 62.5 | 2.6 | 16.3 | 81.1 |
| All-India | 12.9 | 30.3 | 56.8 | 1.6 | 36.9 | 61.5 | 29.9 | 29.7 | 40.3 | 4.2 | 23.4 | 72.4 |

*Source:* Unit level data of employment and unemployment schedule of 50th (1993–4) Round of NSSO.

**Table A3.20** Distribution of Workers by Industrial Categories, Usual (Principal + Subsidiary) Status, Male, 1999–2000

(in per cent)

| States | < 50,000 | | | 50,000–1 million | | | > 1 million | | | Total Urban | | |
|---|---|---|---|---|---|---|---|---|---|---|---|---|
| | P | S | T | P | S | T | P | S | T | P | S | T |
| Andhra Pradesh | 17.3 | 32.0 | 50.8 | 7.2 | 31.7 | 61.1 | 0.6 | 26.4 | 73.0 | 8.1 | 30.8 | 61.1 |
| Assam | 10.8 | 13.6 | 75.6 | 1.4 | 14.9 | 83.7 | – | – | – | 6.6 | 14.2 | 79.2 |
| Bihar | 20.6 | 18.8 | 60.6 | 11.4 | 23.5 | 65.1 | 3.0 | 41.7 | 55.3 | 13.6 | 24.2 | 62.2 |
| Gujarat | 22.0 | 21.9 | 56.0 | 3.9 | 35.5 | 60.6 | 1.2 | 45.9 | 52.9 | 7.9 | 35.5 | 56.6 |
| Haryana | 13.9 | 26.7 | 59.4 | 6.0 | 30.7 | 63.3 | – | – | – | 8.1 | 29.7 | 62.3 |
| Jammu and Kashmir | 20.8 | 21.4 | 57.8 | 5.2 | 22.4 | 72.4 | – | – | – | 12.1 | 22.0 | 66.0 |
| Karnataka | 15.5 | 27.4 | 57.2 | 7.2 | 33.9 | 59.0 | 1.3 | 42.7 | 56.0 | 8.5 | 33.9 | 57.6 |
| Kerala | 10.4 | 35.3 | 54.4 | 5.2 | 28.4 | 66.4 | – | – | – | 8.0 | 32.1 | 60.0 |
| Madhya Pradesh | 20.6 | 24.5 | 54.9 | 8.6 | 25.7 | 65.7 | 5.5 | 29.9 | 64.6 | 13.9 | 25.6 | 60.4 |
| Maharashtra | 16.0 | 21.4 | 62.7 | 3.1 | 40.3 | 56.6 | 1.2 | 34.7 | 64.2 | 3.9 | 34.8 | 61.3 |
| Orissa | 17.3 | 26.8 | 55.9 | 9.1 | 28.8 | 62.1 | – | – | – | 12.9 | 27.9 | 59.2 |
| Punjab | 16.2 | 25.2 | 58.6 | 4.4 | 28.4 | 67.3 | 0.1 | 54.8 | 45.1 | 6.5 | 32.9 | 60.6 |
| Rajasthan | 10.9 | 31.4 | 57.7 | 10.5 | 35.5 | 54.0 | 0.7 | 27.3 | 71.9 | 9.3 | 32.9 | 57.8 |
| Tamil Nadu | 12.1 | 34.9 | 53.0 | 6.8 | 37.3 | 55.9 | 1.1 | 34.9 | 64.0 | 7.0 | 35.9 | 57.1 |
| Uttar Pradesh | 15.3 | 28.5 | 56.2 | 6.3 | 33.3 | 60.5 | 1.1 | 33.0 | 65.9 | 7.6 | 31.8 | 60.7 |
| West Bengal | 11.9 | 34.9 | 53.2 | 3.0 | 34.4 | 62.6 | 0.4 | 32.0 | 67.7 | 4.1 | 33.8 | 62.1 |
| Other NE States | 19.9 | 11.9 | 68.2 | 4.2 | 14.4 | 81.4 | – | – | – | 13.4 | 12.9 | 73.6 |
| Rest ST and UT | 6.9 | 33.5 | 59.7 | 1.8 | 35.8 | 62.4 | 0.6 | 29.8 | 69.7 | 1.6 | 31.6 | 66.8 |
| All-India | 15.7 | 27.5 | 56.8 | 6.1 | 32.8 | 61.2 | 1.1 | 34.9 | 64.0 | 7.5 | 31.9 | 60.7 |

*Source:* Unit level data of employment and unemployment schedule of 55th (1999–2000) Round of NSSO.

**Table A3.21**  Distribution of Workers by Industrial Categories, Usual (Principal + Subsidiary) Status, Female, 1999–2000

(in per cent)

| States | <50,000 | | | 50,000–1 million | | | >1 million | | | Total Urban | | |
|---|---|---|---|---|---|---|---|---|---|---|---|---|
| | P | S | T | P | S | T | P | S | T | P | S | T |
| Andhra Pradesh | 26.6 | 39.5 | 34.0 | 15.4 | 31.6 | 53.0 | 0.5 | 26.9 | 72.6 | 17.0 | 33.4 | 49.6 |
| Assam | 10.8 | 14.6 | 74.6 | 3.4 | 1.3 | 95.3 | – | – | – | 6.4 | 6.7 | 86.9 |
| Bihar | 39.9 | 24.3 | 35.8 | 22.6 | 21.5 | 55.9 | 4.2 | 25.9 | 69.9 | 25.7 | 22.9 | 51.4 |
| Gujarat | 41.4 | 10.3 | 48.4 | 16.2 | 28.9 | 54.8 | 2.3 | 26.4 | 71.3 | 19.0 | 22.5 | 58.5 |
| Haryana | 51.2 | 7.7 | 41.1 | 20.7 | 14.5 | 64.8 | – | – | – | 34.9 | 11.3 | 53.8 |
| Jammu and Kashmir | 33.3 | 23.9 | 42.8 | 14.5 | 25.5 | 60.0 | – | – | – | 24.3 | 24.7 | 51.1 |
| Karnataka | 36.7 | 30.6 | 32.7 | 15.0 | 30.6 | 54.4 | 0.9 | 48.8 | 50.4 | 19.2 | 35.7 | 45.1 |
| Kerala | 18.0 | 35.6 | 46.4 | 11.6 | 20.2 | 68.2 | – | – | – | 15.4 | 29.4 | 55.2 |
| Madhya Pradesh | 40.3 | 29.2 | 30.6 | 22.3 | 29.5 | 48.2 | 8.4 | 34.2 | 57.4 | 30.4 | 29.9 | 39.7 |
| Maharashtra | 49.0 | 12.3 | 38.7 | 13.6 | 23.7 | 62.7 | 1.3 | 19.9 | 78.9 | 15.5 | 19.5 | 65.0 |
| Orissa | 22.5 | 37.2 | 40.3 | 19.8 | 41.0 | 39.3 | – | – | – | 21.3 | 38.9 | 39.9 |
| Punjab | 31.6 | 7.2 | 61.3 | 16.6 | 11.8 | 71.6 | – | 59.8 | 40.2 | 20.5 | 15.4 | 64.1 |
| Rajasthan | 50.4 | 26.0 | 23.6 | 32.4 | 36.0 | 31.7 | 23.4 | 9.8 | 66.8 | 39.7 | 29.8 | 30.5 |
| Tamil Nadu | 24.7 | 37.1 | 38.2 | 14.7 | 40.4 | 45.0 | 1.6 | 31.7 | 66.7 | 15.6 | 37.1 | 47.3 |
| Uttar Pradesh | 33.2 | 41.4 | 25.5 | 9.7 | 35.5 | 54.9 | 5.3 | 22.3 | 72.5 | 17.4 | 34.0 | 48.6 |
| West Bengal | 8.6 | 52.1 | 39.3 | 1.1 | 29.6 | 69.3 | – | 11.7 | 88.4 | 2.8 | 30.4 | 66.7 |
| Other NE States | 31.8 | 10.2 | 58.0 | 4.5 | 13.3 | 82.2 | – | – | – | 19.6 | 11.6 | 68.8 |
| Rest ST and UT | 27.2 | 17.4 | 55.4 | 2.5 | 26.2 | 71.2 | 7.0 | 23.3 | 69.7 | 8.5 | 23.3 | 68.3 |
| All-India | 32.4 | 30.2 | 37.4 | 14.9 | 29.5 | 55.6 | 2.8 | 25.9 | 71.3 | 18.3 | 28.9 | 52.8 |

*Source:* Unit level data of employment and unemployment schedule of 55th (1999–2000) Round of NSSO.

**Table A3.22** Distribution of Workers by Industrial Categories, Usual (Principal + Subsidiary) Status, Non-metros, 1999–2000 and 2004–5

| States | Male | | | | | | Female | | | | | |
|---|---|---|---|---|---|---|---|---|---|---|---|---|
| | 1999–2000 | | | 2004–5 | | | 1999–2000 | | | 2004–5 | | |
| | P | S | T | P | S | T | P | S | T | P | S | T |
| Andhra Pradesh | 9.7 | 31.8 | 58.5 | 9.3 | 29.0 | 61.7 | 19.1 | 34.2 | 46.7 | 19.8 | 29.0 | 51.2 |
| Assam | 6.6 | 14.2 | 79.2 | 5.9 | 19.7 | 74.4 | 6.4 | 6.7 | 86.9 | 7.3 | 8.6 | 84.1 |
| Bihar | 15.2 | 21.6 | 63.2 | 17.5 | 22.1 | 60.4 | 28.7 | 22.5 | 48.9 | 40.6 | 21.8 | 37.6 |
| Gujarat | 11.6 | 29.7 | 58.7 | 9.2 | 39.2 | 51.5 | 27.7 | 20.4 | 51.9 | 25.8 | 35.9 | 38.3 |
| Haryana | 8.1 | 29.7 | 62.3 | 8.6 | 29.2 | 62.1 | 34.6 | 11.4 | 54.0 | 31.6 | 17.0 | 51.4 |
| Jammu and Kashmir | 12.1 | 22.0 | 66.0 | 9.5 | 38.6 | 51.9 | 24.2 | 24.7 | 51.1 | 38.7 | 32.3 | 29.0 |
| Karnataka | 11.0 | 30.9 | 58.1 | 8.4 | 32.1 | 59.5 | 26.4 | 30.6 | 43.0 | 20.7 | 30.4 | 48.8 |
| Kerala | 8.0 | 32.1 | 59.9 | 14.7 | 29.5 | 55.8 | 15.4 | 29.4 | 55.1 | 19.8 | 26.5 | 53.7 |
| Madhya Pradesh | 15.1 | 25.0 | 59.8 | 12.7 | 26.5 | 60.8 | 33.2 | 29.3 | 37.5 | 29.0 | 28.9 | 42.1 |
| Maharashtra | 6.8 | 34.9 | 58.3 | 9.5 | 33.5 | 57.0 | 27.5 | 19.2 | 53.3 | 27.7 | 28.6 | 43.7 |
| Orissa | 12.9 | 27.9 | 59.2 | 11.2 | 27.6 | 61.2 | 21.3 | 38.8 | 39.8 | 28.9 | 18.3 | 52.8 |
| Punjab | 8.1 | 27.4 | 64.5 | 4.7 | 31.0 | 64.3 | 23.0 | 9.8 | 67.2 | 17.3 | 20.9 | 61.8 |
| Rajasthan | 10.7 | 33.8 | 55.5 | 7.6 | 31.7 | 60.7 | 40.9 | 31.3 | 27.9 | 36.2 | 29.7 | 34.1 |
| Tamil Nadu | 9.1 | 36.3 | 54.7 | 8.2 | 38.1 | 53.7 | 19.8 | 38.7 | 41.5 | 15.3 | 43.6 | 41.2 |
| Uttar Pradesh | 10.0 | 31.3 | 58.7 | 9.3 | 34.2 | 56.4 | 22.1 | 38.6 | 39.4 | 33.0 | 37.4 | 29.6 |
| West Bengal | 5.5 | 34.5 | 59.9 | 4.7 | 33.6 | 61.6 | 4.0 | 38.3 | 57.8 | 4.3 | 40.0 | 55.6 |
| Other NE States | 13.4 | 12.9 | 73.6 | 15.6 | 14.1 | 70.3 | 19.6 | 11.6 | 68.8 | 20.0 | 14.1 | 65.9 |
| Rest ST and UT | 3.4 | 35.1 | 61.5 | 4.6 | 33.6 | 61.8 | 10.8 | 23.3 | 65.9 | 11.8 | 20.6 | 67.6 |
| All-India | 9.8 | 30.7 | 59.5 | 9.3 | 32.0 | 58.7 | 23.1 | 29.8 | 47.1 | 22.9 | 31.9 | 45.2 |

*Source:* Unit level data of employment and unemployment schedule of 55th (1999–2000) and 61st (2004–5) Rounds of NSSO.

Table A3.23 Distribution of Workers by Industrial Categories, Usual (Principal + Subsidiary) Status, Metros and all Urban, 2004–5

(in per cent)

| States | Male | | | | | | Female | | | | | |
|---|---|---|---|---|---|---|---|---|---|---|---|---|
| | Metro | | | All Urban | | | Metro | | | All Urban | | |
| | P | S | T | P | S | T | P | S | T | P | S | T |
| Andhra Pradesh | 6.6 | 29.9 | 63.6 | 8.8 | 29.2 | 62.0 | 2.8 | 13.1 | 84.1 | 17.8 | 27.1 | 55.1 |
| Assam | | | | 5.9 | 19.7 | 74.4 | | | | 7.3 | 8.6 | 84.1 |
| Bihar | 7.6 | 19.0 | 73.4 | 16.4 | 21.8 | 61.8 | 0.0 | 19.6 | 80.4 | 40.0 | 21.8 | 38.2 |
| Gujarat | 0.5 | 52.8 | 46.7 | 5.4 | 45.2 | 49.4 | 0.8 | 45.8 | 53.4 | 15.7 | 39.9 | 44.4 |
| Haryana | 3.0 | 70.2 | 26.8 | 7.6 | 37.2 | 55.3 | 11.3 | 34.4 | 54.3 | 29.3 | 19.0 | 51.7 |
| Jammu and Kashmir | | | | 9.5 | 38.6 | 51.9 | | | | 38.7 | 32.3 | 29.0 |
| Karnataka | 1.1 | 33.8 | 65.1 | 6.2 | 32.6 | 61.1 | 0.1 | 32.0 | 68.0 | 16.5 | 30.7 | 52.7 |
| Kerala | | | | 14.7 | 29.5 | 55.8 | | | | 19.8 | 26.5 | 53.7 |
| Madhya Pradesh | 3.0 | 29.5 | 67.5 | 11.1 | 27.0 | 61.9 | 8.1 | 35.6 | 56.3 | 25.4 | 30.1 | 44.6 |
| Maharashtra | 1.7 | 35.7 | 62.7 | 5.4 | 34.6 | 59.9 | 1.6 | 31.7 | 66.7 | 14.3 | 30.2 | 55.5 |
| Orissa | | | | 11.2 | 27.6 | 61.2 | | | | 28.9 | 18.3 | 52.8 |
| Punjab | 1.7 | 55.9 | 42.4 | 4.0 | 36.6 | 59.3 | 1.1 | 54.4 | 44.5 | 15.2 | 25.1 | 59.6 |
| Rajasthan | 9.5 | 38.1 | 52.5 | 8.0 | 33.3 | 58.7 | 29.5 | 55.4 | 15.1 | 33.9 | 38.4 | 27.7 |
| Tamil Nadu | 0.3 | 35.9 | 63.8 | 6.7 | 37.7 | 55.6 | 0.0 | 12.8 | 87.2 | 13.8 | 40.6 | 45.6 |
| Uttar Pradesh | 0.4 | 36.3 | 63.4 | 7.3 | 34.7 | 58.0 | 0.0 | 49.3 | 50.7 | 26.9 | 39.6 | 33.5 |
| West Bengal | 0.9 | 34.5 | 64.7 | 3.7 | 33.8 | 62.4 | 1.8 | 23.7 | 74.5 | 3.8 | 36.3 | 59.9 |
| Other NE States | | | | 15.6 | 14.1 | 70.3 | | | | 20.0 | 14.1 | 65.9 |
| Rest ST and UT | 0.2 | 33.5 | 66.3 | 1.0 | 33.5 | 65.4 | 0.0 | 19.8 | 80.2 | 3.9 | 20.1 | 76.1 |
| All-India | 1.7 | 37.3 | 61.0 | 7.1 | 33.6 | 59.4 | 3.8 | 33.2 | 62.9 | 18.3 | 32.2 | 49.5 |

*Source:* Unit level data of employment and unemployment schedule of 61st (2004–5) Round of NSSO.

**Table A3.24** Distribution of Workers by Occupational Categories, Usual (Principal + Subsidiary) Status, Male, 1987–8

(in per cent)

| States | <50,000 | | | 50,000–200,000 | | | 200,000–1 million | | | 50,000–1 million | | | Total Urban | | |
|---|---|---|---|---|---|---|---|---|---|---|---|---|---|---|---|
| | A/P | C | ML | A/P | C | ML | A/P | C | ML | A/P | C | ML | A/P | C | ML |
| Andhra Pradesh | 8.5 | 33.4 | 57.7 | 11.7 | 38.6 | 49.8 | 13.8 | 36.3 | 50.0 | 11.7 | 37.9 | 50.4 | 11.3 | 37.4 | 51.2 |
| Assam | 13.3 | 47.9 | 38.8 | 14.2 | 57.8 | 28.1 | 13.6 | 53.5 | 32.9 | 10.9 | 56.9 | 32.1 | 13.6 | 51.2 | 35.3 |
| Bihar | 7.4 | 34.7 | 57.8 | 12.1 | 38.4 | 49.4 | 12.8 | 36.8 | 50.4 | 12.0 | 37.8 | 50.2 | 10.4 | 36.4 | 53.1 |
| Gujarat | 12.9 | 29.7 | 57.4 | 6.8 | 50.6 | 42.7 | 11.2 | 38.1 | 50.7 | 8.4 | 44.3 | 47.3 | 10.3 | 37.8 | 51.7 |
| Haryana | 10.0 | 44.4 | 45.6 | 11.7 | 43.9 | 44.4 | 4.6 | 25.7 | 69.7 | 7.9 | 37.7 | 54.3 | 9.3 | 39.3 | 51.3 |
| Jammu and Kashmir | 13.8 | 37.2 | 49.0 | | | | 15.4 | 40.7 | 43.8 | 15.1 | 40.8 | 44.0 | 14.8 | 39.5 | 45.7 |
| Karnataka | 11.0 | 33.0 | 55.8 | 11.9 | 40.3 | 47.8 | 7.9 | 42.9 | 49.1 | 8.2 | 42.3 | 49.4 | 11.5 | 37.9 | 50.5 |
| Kerala | 8.5 | 26.3 | 65.1 | 17.1 | 40.3 | 42.7 | 14.7 | 39.9 | 45.5 | 14.4 | 40.4 | 45.2 | 11.8 | 32.9 | 55.3 |
| Madhya Pradesh | 12.4 | 33.3 | 54.2 | 13.2 | 42.8 | 44.0 | 11.8 | 39.8 | 48.5 | 11.8 | 41.3 | 46.9 | 12.4 | 38.0 | 49.6 |
| Maharashtra | 9.6 | 36.5 | 54.0 | 14.2 | 34.5 | 51.2 | 14.5 | 36.0 | 49.5 | 13.9 | 35.4 | 50.8 | 15.1 | 36.9 | 48.0 |
| Orissa | 11.9 | 35.3 | 52.8 | 20.2 | 42.2 | 37.3 | 11.7 | 44.0 | 44.4 | 15.7 | 43.3 | 41.0 | 14.1 | 39.4 | 46.5 |
| Punjab | 13.1 | 40.1 | 46.8 | 15.3 | 43.4 | 41.2 | 13.7 | 37.4 | 48.8 | 13.0 | 39.8 | 47.2 | 13.8 | 39.5 | 46.6 |
| Rajasthan | 12.5 | 33.1 | 54.4 | 13.0 | 44.6 | 42.4 | 15.8 | 40.6 | 43.6 | 14.6 | 42.0 | 43.4 | 13.8 | 37.8 | 48.4 |
| Tamil Nadu | 13.9 | 30.9 | 54.9 | 15.1 | 35.9 | 49.0 | 12.9 | 40.8 | 46.2 | 14.1 | 37.6 | 48.2 | 15.7 | 35.2 | 49.1 |
| Uttar Pradesh | 7.9 | 37.6 | 54.2 | 10.1 | 42.3 | 47.6 | 12.2 | 40.2 | 47.5 | 10.8 | 41.3 | 47.9 | 10.2 | 39.4 | 50.2 |
| West Bengal | 11.0 | 32.1 | 56.9 | 12.8 | 36.1 | 51.1 | 14.0 | 39.8 | 46.1 | 11.6 | 38.0 | 50.5 | 14.8 | 37.7 | 47.4 |
| Other NE States | 16.1 | 40.8 | 41.6 | 27.0 | 41.3 | 30.6 | | | | 22.0 | 45.0 | 33.0 | 20.4 | 41.0 | 37.2 |
| Rest ST and UT | 15.5 | 34.2 | 50.2 | 17.4 | 33.6 | 49.0 | 22.8 | 51.4 | 25.8 | 19.1 | 41.3 | 39.6 | 19.7 | 40.3 | 39.8 |
| All-India | 10.8 | 34.3 | 54.7 | 13.0 | 39.7 | 47.3 | 12.8 | 39.1 | 48.1 | 12.1 | 39.7 | 48.2 | 13.2 | 37.8 | 49.0 |

*Source*: Unit level data of employment and unemployment schedule of 43rd (1987–8) Round of NSSO.

*Notes*: A/P = Administrative and Professional; C = Clerical; and ML = Manual Labour.

**Table A3.25** Distribution of Workers by Occupational Categories, Usual (Principal + Subsidiary) Status, Female, 1987–8

(in per cent)

| States | <50,000 | | | 50,000–200,000 | | | 200,000–1 million | | | 50,000–1 million | | | Total Urban | | |
|---|---|---|---|---|---|---|---|---|---|---|---|---|---|---|---|
| | A/P | C | ML | A/P | C | ML | A/P | C | ML | A/P | C | ML | A/P | C | ML |
| Andhra Pradesh | 5.7 | 23.6 | 70.7 | 10.1 | 28.4 | 61.5 | 12.6 | 34.1 | 53.3 | 10.0 | 31.0 | 58.9 | 9.1 | 29.0 | 62.0 |
| Assam | 40.3 | 21.8 | 35.6 | 42.2 | 37.7 | 20.1 | 31.7 | 50.8 | 17.6 | 29.6 | 49.7 | 20.7 | 38.4 | 33.1 | 27.3 |
| Bihar | 8.4 | 20.9 | 70.7 | 10.6 | 43.3 | 46.1 | 11.1 | 41.0 | 47.9 | 8.6 | 43.0 | 48.4 | 9.6 | 30.6 | 59.8 |
| Gujarat | 12.6 | 21.9 | 65.6 | 11.1 | 29.9 | 59.1 | 24.5 | 43.8 | 31.7 | 14.6 | 38.6 | 46.8 | 16.5 | 30.6 | 52.9 |
| Haryana | 34.6 | 8.9 | 56.5 | 30.1 | 32.8 | 37.1 | 12.6 | 14.7 | 72.7 | 22.8 | 25.1 | 52.1 | 27.6 | 19.9 | 52.5 |
| Jammu and Kashmir | 16.6 | 3.4 | 80.0 | | | | 29.5 | 11.2 | 59.4 | 28.9 | 11.6 | 59.6 | 23.5 | 7.6 | 68.9 |
| Karnataka | 7.2 | 13.3 | 79.5 | 16.5 | 15.3 | 68.2 | 12.0 | 34.1 | 54.0 | 8.2 | 23.1 | 68.6 | 10.1 | 20.0 | 70.0 |
| Kerala | 9.8 | 15.3 | 75.0 | 25.7 | 30.9 | 43.5 | 40.8 | 38.9 | 20.3 | 27.2 | 40.7 | 32.0 | 21.4 | 24.7 | 53.8 |
| Madhya Pradesh | 7.0 | 16.8 | 76.2 | 14.8 | 25.6 | 59.6 | 20.3 | 32.8 | 46.9 | 17.0 | 30.6 | 52.4 | 13.1 | 23.9 | 63.0 |
| Maharashtra | 8.4 | 15.5 | 76.1 | 11.8 | 30.0 | 57.9 | 14.3 | 32.9 | 52.2 | 11.2 | 32.1 | 56.7 | 16.5 | 32.7 | 50.6 |
| Orissa | 11.4 | 22.9 | 65.7 | 16.5 | 32.2 | 51.4 | 13.6 | 36.9 | 49.6 | 15.2 | 34.2 | 50.6 | 13.0 | 27.7 | 59.3 |
| Punjab | 19.5 | 17.4 | 63.0 | 19.2 | 16.0 | 64.8 | 30.4 | 25.6 | 44.1 | 24.6 | 21.8 | 53.6 | 22.7 | 19.6 | 57.7 |
| Rajasthan | 3.5 | 6.4 | 90.1 | 7.4 | 24.0 | 68.6 | 19.5 | 33.3 | 47.2 | 14.2 | 29.6 | 56.2 | 7.7 | 15.2 | 77.1 |
| Tamil Nadu | 10.9 | 17.8 | 71.3 | 14.7 | 23.6 | 61.8 | 10.3 | 35.3 | 54.5 | 12.3 | 28.0 | 59.8 | 13.9 | 25.7 | 60.4 |
| Uttar Pradesh | 11.0 | 23.1 | 65.9 | 16.7 | 20.8 | 62.6 | 28.7 | 28.8 | 42.5 | 22.0 | 25.5 | 52.4 | 17.6 | 26.0 | 56.5 |
| West Bengal | 32.3 | 30.8 | 36.9 | 33.5 | 30.9 | 35.7 | 30.8 | 39.9 | 28.8 | 21.3 | 37.8 | 40.9 | 32.9 | 39.1 | 28.0 |
| Other NE States | 36.8 | 29.4 | 33.7 | 35.5 | 33.2 | 30.5 | | | | 17.2 | 43.4 | 39.4 | 36.2 | 31.3 | 32.1 |
| Rest ST and UT | 16.2 | 28.5 | 55.1 | 20.6 | 33.4 | 46.0 | 39.7 | 44.0 | 16.3 | 28.2 | 37.6 | 34.1 | 31.5 | 40.4 | 27.6 |
| All-India | 10.5 | 17.8 | 71.6 | 16.6 | 26.3 | 57.0 | 19.9 | 33.6 | 46.4 | 15.3 | 30.6 | 54.1 | 16.1 | 27.2 | 56.7 |

*Source:* Unit level data of employment and unemployment schedule of 43rd (1987–8) Round of NSSO.

**Table A3.26** Distribution of Workers by Occupational Categories, Usual (Principal + Subsidiary) Status, Metro and Non-metro, 1987–8

(in per cent)

| States | Male | | | | | | Female | | | | | |
|---|---|---|---|---|---|---|---|---|---|---|---|---|
| | Non-metro | | | Metro | | | Non-metro | | | Metro | | |
| | A/P | C | ML | A/P | C | ML | A/P | C | ML | A/P | C | ML |
| Andhra Pradesh | 11.0 | 36.0 | 52.9 | 13.1 | 48.4 | 38.3 | 8.7 | 27.5 | 63.9 | 14.8 | 51.6 | 33.6 |
| Assam | 13.5 | 51.2 | 35.3 | | | | 38.9 | 33.5 | 27.6 | | | |
| Bihar | 10.4 | 36.4 | 53.2 | | | | 9.6 | 30.6 | 59.8 | | | |
| Gujarat | 10.7 | 37.9 | 51.3 | 9.2 | 37.5 | 52.8 | 15.3 | 29.4 | 55.3 | 21.1 | 34.8 | 44.0 |
| Haryana | 9.4 | 39.3 | 51.3 | | | | 27.6 | 20.0 | 52.5 | | | |
| Jammu and Kashmir | 14.8 | 39.5 | 45.7 | | | | 23.5 | 7.6 | 68.9 | | | |
| Karnataka | 10.6 | 37.1 | 52.3 | 14.8 | 41.1 | 44.0 | 10.1 | 16.3 | 73.6 | 9.8 | 45.4 | 44.9 |
| Kerala | 11.8 | 32.9 | 55.3 | | | | 21.5 | 24.7 | 53.8 | | | |
| Madhya Pradesh | 12.4 | 38.0 | 49.6 | | | | 13.0 | 23.9 | 63.1 | | | |
| Maharashtra | 12.6 | 35.7 | 51.7 | 18.2 | 38.4 | 43.4 | 10.8 | 23.8 | 65.4 | 28.2 | 51.0 | 20.8 |
| Orissa | 14.1 | 39.4 | 46.5 | | | | 13.0 | 27.7 | 59.3 | | | |
| Punjab | 13.8 | 39.5 | 46.7 | | | | 22.7 | 19.6 | 57.7 | | | |
| Rajasthan | 13.8 | 37.8 | 48.4 | | | | 7.7 | 15.1 | 77.1 | | | |
| Tamil Nadu | 14.2 | 34.7 | 51.1 | 21.4 | 37.2 | 41.4 | 12.1 | 22.6 | 65.3 | 25.1 | 45.4 | 29.6 |
| Uttar Pradesh | 10.0 | 39.7 | 50.3 | 12.5 | 37.3 | 50.3 | 17.9 | 24.3 | 57.8 | 11.7 | 59.4 | 28.9 |
| West Bengal | 12.4 | 35.4 | 52.3 | 20.9 | 43.7 | 35.2 | 32.6 | 32.5 | 34.9 | 33.6 | 53.3 | 13.1 |
| Other NE States | 20.7 | 41.6 | 37.8 | | | | 36.3 | 31.4 | 32.3 | | | |
| Rest ST and UT | 17.9 | 38.1 | 44.1 | 20.2 | 40.9 | 38.7 | 23.4 | 34.0 | 42.6 | 35.7 | 43.8 | 19.8 |
| All-India | 12.0 | 37.3 | 50.6 | 17.9 | 40.0 | 41.9 | 14.3 | 23.8 | 61.9 | 26.5 | 48.2 | 25.2 |

*Source:* Unit level data of employment and unemployment schedule of 43rd (1987–8) Round of NSSO.

**Table A3.27** Distribution of Workers by Occupational Categories, Usual (Principal + Subsidiary) Status, Male, 1993–4

(in per cent)

| States | < 50,000 | | | 50,000–200,000 | | | 200,000–1 million | | | 50,000–1 million | | | Total Urban | | |
|---|---|---|---|---|---|---|---|---|---|---|---|---|---|---|---|
| | A/P | C | ML | A/P | C | ML | A/P | C | ML | A/P | C | ML | A/P | C | ML |
| Andhra Pradesh | 9.0 | 25.4 | 65.6 | 13.0 | 37.2 | 49.9 | 10.2 | 38.8 | 51.1 | 11.9 | 37.8 | 50.3 | 11.7 | 34.4 | 53.9 |
| Assam | 17.3 | 53.9 | 28.8 | 14.6 | 56.7 | 28.8 | 17.1 | 48.2 | 34.8 | 15.9 | 52.2 | 31.9 | 16.7 | 53.2 | 30.1 |
| Bihar | 7.1 | 34.3 | 58.6 | 9.9 | 45.6 | 44.6 | 15.8 | 39.8 | 44.5 | 13.7 | 41.8 | 44.5 | 11.5 | 39.4 | 49.2 |
| Gujarat | 10.2 | 27.6 | 62.2 | 25.8 | 36.2 | 38.1 | 14.8 | 30.3 | 55.0 | 23.2 | 34.8 | 42.0 | 16.9 | 30.7 | 52.4 |
| Haryana | 8.0 | 34.1 | 58.0 | 14.0 | 37.7 | 48.2 | 10.1 | 41.1 | 48.8 | 12.9 | 38.7 | 48.4 | 11.6 | 37.4 | 51.0 |
| Jammu and Kashmir | 14.6 | 49.1 | 36.3 | | | | 23.7 | 45.6 | 30.7 | 23.7 | 45.6 | 30.7 | 19.6 | 47.2 | 33.2 |
| Karnataka | 14.3 | 30.1 | 55.7 | 9.2 | 39.6 | 51.2 | 16.7 | 36.3 | 47.0 | 13.0 | 37.9 | 49.1 | 15.5 | 34.5 | 50.0 |
| Kerala | 7.0 | 26.6 | 66.5 | 10.7 | 30.9 | 58.5 | 13.6 | 37.5 | 48.9 | 12.3 | 34.6 | 53.2 | 9.4 | 30.2 | 60.4 |
| Madhya Pradesh | 9.3 | 31.4 | 59.3 | 10.6 | 44.7 | 44.7 | 12.9 | 34.9 | 52.2 | 11.6 | 40.5 | 47.9 | 11.3 | 36.8 | 51.8 |
| Maharashtra | 11.0 | 31.7 | 57.3 | 12.8 | 38.2 | 49.0 | 14.0 | 36.4 | 49.7 | 13.6 | 37.0 | 49.4 | 16.4 | 37.6 | 45.9 |
| Orissa | 15.3 | 24.5 | 60.3 | 17.8 | 39.8 | 42.4 | 13.0 | 45.4 | 41.6 | 15.1 | 43.0 | 42.0 | 15.1 | 35.0 | 49.9 |
| Punjab | 12.6 | 37.3 | 50.2 | 11.9 | 49.2 | 38.9 | 10.4 | 40.0 | 49.6 | 11.1 | 44.3 | 44.6 | 11.2 | 41.4 | 47.4 |
| Rajasthan | 9.3 | 33.5 | 57.2 | 8.8 | 35.8 | 55.5 | 17.7 | 36.7 | 45.6 | 13.2 | 36.2 | 50.6 | 11.8 | 36.4 | 51.9 |
| Tamil Nadu | 11.9 | 33.9 | 54.2 | 14.9 | 32.7 | 52.4 | 11.9 | 32.2 | 55.9 | 13.6 | 32.5 | 54.0 | 14.3 | 33.4 | 52.3 |
| Uttar Pradesh | 9.4 | 34.8 | 55.8 | 12.3 | 41.8 | 45.8 | 13.2 | 42.3 | 44.5 | 12.8 | 42.1 | 45.1 | 11.4 | 39.8 | 48.8 |
| West Bengal | 13.0 | 30.7 | 56.3 | 11.3 | 35.7 | 53.0 | 14.8 | 36.6 | 48.6 | 12.7 | 36.1 | 51.2 | 12.8 | 38.6 | 48.6 |
| Other NE States | 13.4 | 35.5 | 51.0 | 21.3 | 53.2 | 25.5 | | | | 21.3 | 53.2 | 25.5 | 16.5 | 42.4 | 41.1 |
| Rest ST and UT | 13.8 | 39.5 | 46.7 | 14.4 | 40.5 | 45.2 | 19.7 | 40.5 | 39.7 | 18.0 | 40.5 | 41.5 | 21.9 | 38.0 | 40.1 |
| All-India | 10.7 | 31.9 | 57.4 | 13.4 | 38.7 | 47.9 | 13.7 | 38.0 | 48.3 | 13.6 | 38.4 | 48.1 | 13.9 | 36.6 | 49.5 |

*Source*: Unit level data of employment and unemployment schedule of 50th (1993–4) Round of NSSO.

**Table A3.28**  Distribution of Workers by Occupational Categories, Usual (Principal + Subsidiary) Status, Female, 1993–4

(in per cent)

| States | <50,000 | | | 50,000–200,000 | | | 200,000–1 million | | | 50,000–1 million | | | Total Urban | | |
|---|---|---|---|---|---|---|---|---|---|---|---|---|---|---|---|
| | A/P | C | ML | A/P | C | ML | A/P | C | ML | A/P | C | ML | A/P | C | ML |
| Andhra Pradesh | 6.9 | 18.3 | 74.8 | 14.7 | 29.9 | 55.4 | 10.8 | 38.4 | 50.8 | 13.4 | 33.0 | 53.6 | 11.3 | 27.4 | 61.3 |
| Assam | 27.1 | 38.9 | 34.0 | 27.2 | 42.9 | 29.9 | 21.1 | 63.2 | 15.7 | 23.7 | 54.3 | 22.0 | 25.1 | 47.8 | 27.1 |
| Bihar | 11.1 | 32.9 | 56.0 | 8.4 | 44.2 | 47.5 | 19.8 | 41.8 | 38.4 | 15.9 | 42.6 | 41.5 | 14.3 | 39.4 | 46.3 |
| Gujarat | 9.4 | 22.6 | 68.1 | 31.7 | 30.0 | 38.3 | 35.3 | 18.3 | 46.4 | 32.6 | 27.1 | 40.3 | 17.8 | 28.4 | 53.9 |
| Haryana | 7.3 | 16.8 | 75.9 | 16.7 | 12.5 | 70.9 | 27.7 | 20.1 | 52.2 | 18.8 | 13.9 | 67.3 | 15.3 | 14.8 | 69.9 |
| Jammu and Kashmir | 26.7 | 17.4 | 55.9 | | | | 33.9 | 27.7 | 38.4 | 33.9 | 27.7 | 38.4 | 29.8 | 21.9 | 48.3 |
| Karnataka | 10.8 | 18.5 | 70.7 | 8.9 | 22.4 | 68.6 | 23.9 | 28.4 | 47.8 | 15.8 | 25.1 | 59.2 | 13.8 | 25.0 | 61.2 |
| Kerala | 11.2 | 15.3 | 73.5 | 19.2 | 18.7 | 62.1 | 19.8 | 35.2 | 45.0 | 19.5 | 26.0 | 54.5 | 14.5 | 19.5 | 66.0 |
| Madhya Pradesh | 6.5 | 16.7 | 76.8 | 21.0 | 30.8 | 48.2 | 19.4 | 45.0 | 35.6 | 20.2 | 37.6 | 42.1 | 13.8 | 26.3 | 59.9 |
| Maharashtra | 11.7 | 18.6 | 69.7 | 13.0 | 34.1 | 53.0 | 15.1 | 36.7 | 48.2 | 14.4 | 35.8 | 49.8 | 18.6 | 38.5 | 42.9 |
| Orissa | 17.8 | 15.8 | 66.4 | 35.0 | 28.4 | 36.6 | 17.2 | 42.9 | 40.0 | 25.5 | 36.1 | 38.4 | 20.9 | 24.0 | 55.1 |
| Punjab | 21.4 | 13.4 | 65.2 | 31.1 | 30.6 | 38.3 | 31.1 | 38.8 | 30.1 | 31.1 | 34.5 | 34.4 | 27.1 | 29.1 | 43.8 |
| Rajasthan | 7.0 | 13.6 | 79.4 | 11.3 | 6.8 | 81.9 | 21.8 | 26.7 | 51.5 | 16.2 | 16.0 | 67.8 | 13.5 | 15.0 | 71.5 |
| Tamil Nadu | 10.0 | 19.2 | 70.8 | 7.8 | 24.1 | 68.2 | 12.7 | 31.9 | 55.5 | 9.7 | 27.2 | 63.1 | 11.1 | 27.2 | 61.8 |
| Uttar Pradesh | 7.6 | 12.3 | 80.0 | 9.3 | 17.9 | 72.8 | 22.9 | 30.0 | 47.1 | 15.8 | 23.7 | 60.5 | 13.7 | 19.7 | 66.6 |
| West Bengal | 12.5 | 18.6 | 68.9 | 15.0 | 42.6 | 42.4 | 25.6 | 48.0 | 26.4 | 18.7 | 44.5 | 36.8 | 17.9 | 39.6 | 42.5 |
| Other NE States | 16.7 | 26.8 | 56.5 | 18.8 | 55.2 | 25.9 | | | | 18.8 | 55.2 | 25.9 | 17.5 | 38.4 | 44.1 |
| Rest ST and UT | 16.3 | 22.5 | 61.2 | 10.5 | 54.0 | 35.6 | 25.4 | 47.6 | 27.0 | 19.3 | 50.2 | 30.5 | 27.6 | 45.9 | 26.5 |
| All-India | 10.0 | 18.0 | 72.0 | 14.6 | 27.2 | 58.2 | 19.0 | 35.6 | 45.4 | 16.5 | 30.9 | 52.6 | 15.3 | 28.8 | 55.9 |

*Source*: Unit level data of employment and unemployment schedule of 50th (1993–4) Round of NSSO.

**Table A3.29**  Distribution of Workers by Occupational Categories, Usual (Principal + Subsidiary) Status, Metro and Non-metro, 1993–4

| States | Male | | | | | | Female | | | | | |
| --- | --- | --- | --- | --- | --- | --- | --- | --- | --- | --- | --- | --- |
| | Non-metro | | | Metro | | | Non-metro | | | Metro | | |
| | A/P | C | ML | A/P | C | ML | A/P | C | ML | A/P | C | ML |
| Andhra Pradesh | 10.9 | 33.7 | 55.5 | 19.5 | 41.3 | 39.2 | 10.6 | 26.9 | 62.5 | 21.4 | 35.7 | 42.9 |
| Assam | 16.7 | 53.2 | 30.1 | | | | 25.2 | 47.8 | 27.0 | | | |
| Bihar | 11.5 | 39.4 | 49.1 | | | | 14.3 | 39.4 | 46.3 | | | |
| Gujarat | 17.4 | 31.6 | 51.0 | 15.9 | 28.8 | 55.4 | 19.6 | 24.6 | 55.8 | 12.8 | 38.5 | 48.7 |
| Haryana | 11.6 | 37.4 | 51.0 | | | | 15.3 | 14.8 | 69.9 | | | |
| Jammu and Kashmir | 19.6 | 47.2 | 33.2 | | | | 29.8 | 21.9 | 48.3 | | | |
| Karnataka | 13.6 | 34.2 | 52.2 | 23.0 | 35.9 | 41.1 | 13.2 | 21.7 | 65.2 | 18.3 | 49.1 | 32.6 |
| Kerala | 9.4 | 30.2 | 60.4 | | | | 14.5 | 19.6 | 66.0 | | | |
| Madhya Pradesh | 10.5 | 36.2 | 53.3 | 16.5 | 40.5 | 43.1 | 12.3 | 25.6 | 62.1 | 23.8 | 31.4 | 44.8 |
| Maharashtra | 12.7 | 35.1 | 52.3 | 20.5 | 40.4 | 39.1 | 13.1 | 27.6 | 59.3 | 26.1 | 53.5 | 20.4 |
| Orissa | 15.2 | 35.0 | 49.9 | | | | 21.0 | 23.9 | 55.1 | | | |
| Punjab | 11.5 | 42.4 | 46.1 | 10.1 | 37.2 | 52.7 | 28.6 | 28.9 | 42.5 | 15.6 | 30.5 | 53.9 |
| Rajasthan | 11.6 | 35.1 | 53.3 | 13.2 | 43.7 | 43.1 | 11.8 | 14.8 | 73.3 | 34.4 | 16.7 | 48.9 |
| Tamil Nadu | 12.9 | 33.0 | 54.0 | 19.1 | 34.9 | 46.0 | 9.9 | 23.4 | 66.7 | 18.0 | 48.8 | 33.3 |
| Uttar Pradesh | 11.4 | 39.2 | 49.4 | 11.0 | 44.5 | 44.5 | 12.0 | 18.4 | 69.7 | 34.5 | 35.8 | 29.7 |
| West Bengal | 12.8 | 34.5 | 52.7 | 12.7 | 51.8 | 35.5 | 16.4 | 35.2 | 48.4 | 24.4 | 60.2 | 15.4 |
| Other NE States | 16.5 | 42.4 | 41.2 | | | | 17.5 | 38.1 | 44.4 | | | |
| Rest ST and UT | 16.4 | 40.1 | 43.4 | 23.2 | 37.5 | 39.3 | 18.1 | 39.5 | 42.4 | 32.8 | 49.4 | 17.8 |
| All-India | 12.4 | 35.8 | 51.7 | 18.6 | 39.3 | 42.1 | 13.5 | 24.8 | 61.7 | 24.1 | 47.7 | 28.2 |

*Source:* Unit level data of employment and unemployment schedule of 50th (1993–4) Round of NSSO.

**Table A3.30**  Distribution of Workers by Occupational Categories, Usual (Principal + Subsidiary) Status, Male, 1999–2000

| States | < 50,000 | | | 50,000–1 million | | | Metro | | | Total Urban | | |
|---|---|---|---|---|---|---|---|---|---|---|---|---|
| | A/P | C | ML | A/P | C | ML | A/P | C | ML | A/P | C | ML |
| Andhra Pradesh | 13.4 | 29.5 | 57.1 | 16.8 | 35.8 | 47.4 | 20.5 | 40.0 | 39.5 | 16.7 | 35.2 | 48.0 |
| Assam | 18.8 | 50.4 | 30.9 | 19.6 | 51.9 | 28.5 | – | – | – | 19.2 | 51.1 | 29.8 |
| Bihar | 11.0 | 43.7 | 45.4 | 15.7 | 39.8 | 44.5 | 21.2 | 30.6 | 48.2 | 14.8 | 40.0 | 45.3 |
| Gujarat | 17.5 | 32.0 | 50.6 | 16.7 | 34.6 | 48.8 | 22.4 | 31.2 | 46.4 | 19.0 | 32.7 | 48.4 |
| Haryana | 9.4 | 34.3 | 56.3 | 12.8 | 33.3 | 54.0 | – | – | – | 11.9 | 33.5 | 54.6 |
| Jammu and Kashmir | 13.5 | 43.5 | 43.0 | 15.2 | 50.9 | 33.8 | – | – | – | 14.5 | 47.6 | 37.9 |
| Karnataka | 16.0 | 33.4 | 50.7 | 19.2 | 36.1 | 44.8 | 23.9 | 32.3 | 43.8 | 19.3 | 34.2 | 46.5 |
| Kerala | 9.3 | 24.4 | 66.3 | 15.7 | 33.3 | 51.1 | – | – | – | 12.3 | 28.5 | 59.3 |
| Madhya Pradesh | 12.0 | 32.8 | 55.2 | 12.5 | 39.9 | 47.7 | 13.4 | 31.0 | 55.7 | 12.4 | 35.4 | 52.3 |
| Maharashtra | 14.5 | 32.9 | 52.6 | 19.0 | 31.5 | 49.5 | 20.1 | 35.3 | 44.6 | 18.9 | 33.6 | 47.5 |
| Orissa | 10.6 | 40.5 | 48.9 | 16.0 | 32.7 | 51.3 | – | – | – | 13.5 | 36.4 | 50.2 |
| Punjab | 19.8 | 27.2 | 53.0 | 18.5 | 37.4 | 44.1 | 19.5 | 27.6 | 52.9 | 19.0 | 32.9 | 48.1 |
| Rajasthan | 13.6 | 33.6 | 52.8 | 15.9 | 30.3 | 53.8 | 28.7 | 44.3 | 27.0 | 16.9 | 33.4 | 49.6 |
| Tamil Nadu | 12.2 | 29.3 | 58.5 | 17.4 | 33.8 | 48.8 | 24.3 | 31.1 | 44.6 | 17.5 | 31.7 | 50.8 |
| Uttar Pradesh | 9.0 | 38.2 | 52.8 | 11.6 | 38.4 | 49.9 | 10.9 | 45.8 | 43.3 | 10.7 | 40.4 | 49.0 |
| West Bengal | 19.2 | 27.8 | 53.0 | 17.5 | 37.8 | 44.7 | 23.9 | 38.4 | 37.7 | 19.7 | 35.9 | 44.4 |
| Other NE States | 16.5 | 36.1 | 47.4 | 23.9 | 45.0 | 31.1 | – | – | – | 19.6 | 39.8 | 40.6 |
| Rest ST and UT | 20.0 | 32.9 | 47.0 | 13.6 | 37.0 | 49.4 | 28.3 | 46.5 | 25.2 | 23.8 | 42.7 | 33.5 |
| All-India | 13.2 | 33.6 | 53.2 | 16.1 | 35.9 | 48.0 | 20.9 | 37.5 | 41.6 | 16.6 | 35.7 | 47.7 |

*Source:* Unit level data of employment and unemployment schedule of 55th (1999–2000) Round of NSSO.

**Table A3.31**  Distribution of Workers by Occupational Categories, Usual (Principal + Subsidiary) Status, Female, 1999–2000

(in per cent)

| States | <50,000 | | | 50,000–1 million | | | Metro | | | Total Urban | | |
|---|---|---|---|---|---|---|---|---|---|---|---|---|
| | A/P | C | ML | A/P | C | ML | A/P | C | ML | A/P | C | ML |
| Andhra Pradesh | 13.1 | 25.4 | 61.5 | 14.4 | 36.3 | 49.3 | 24.8 | 45.1 | 30.2 | 15.2 | 34.1 | 50.7 |
| Assam | 40.4 | 23.9 | 35.7 | 26.9 | 53.8 | 19.2 | – | – | – | 32.3 | 41.8 | 25.8 |
| Bihar | 11.5 | 24.1 | 64.3 | 21.4 | 38.4 | 40.2 | 7.3 | 61.0 | 31.7 | 16.6 | 36.8 | 46.6 |
| Gujarat | 18.2 | 25.2 | 56.6 | 17.4 | 32.5 | 50.1 | 30.4 | 34.4 | 35.2 | 22.0 | 30.9 | 47.0 |
| Haryana | 19.7 | 15.6 | 64.7 | 26.6 | 27.0 | 46.4 | – | – | – | 23.4 | 21.6 | 55.0 |
| Jammu and Kashmir | 29.5 | 12.7 | 57.8 | 33.8 | 21.6 | 44.7 | – | – | – | 31.5 | 16.9 | 51.6 |
| Karnataka | 11.4 | 21.8 | 66.8 | 23.0 | 30.6 | 46.4 | 31.5 | 37.4 | 31.1 | 21.0 | 29.1 | 49.9 |
| Kerala | 13.5 | 18.8 | 67.8 | 21.1 | 39.0 | 40.0 | – | – | – | 16.5 | 26.9 | 56.6 |
| Madhya Pradesh | 8.9 | 13.2 | 77.9 | 12.9 | 32.1 | 55.1 | 24.3 | 32.5 | 43.2 | 12.0 | 21.9 | 66.1 |
| Maharashtra | 12.3 | 21.5 | 66.2 | 24.3 | 33.8 | 41.9 | 30.8 | 49.3 | 20.0 | 24.7 | 38.3 | 37.0 |
| Orissa | 11.5 | 33.7 | 54.8 | 12.7 | 34.5 | 52.8 | – | – | – | 12.1 | 34.1 | 53.9 |
| Punjab | 21.7 | 20.0 | 58.4 | 27.1 | 35.6 | 37.4 | 28.3 | 25.8 | 45.9 | 25.6 | 29.5 | 45.0 |
| Rajasthan | 11.4 | 8.6 | 80.0 | 17.2 | 17.0 | 65.8 | 38.8 | 25.8 | 35.4 | 16.1 | 13.9 | 70.0 |
| Tamil Nadu | 18.3 | 21.3 | 60.4 | 18.1 | 30.2 | 51.7 | 25.4 | 45.5 | 29.1 | 19.8 | 30.1 | 50.0 |
| Uttar Pradesh | 6.7 | 18.0 | 75.3 | 23.2 | 30.5 | 46.4 | 27.0 | 42.4 | 30.6 | 18.2 | 29.3 | 52.5 |
| West Bengal | 13.0 | 28.0 | 59.1 | 22.9 | 47.9 | 29.2 | 25.7 | 63.0 | 11.4 | 21.0 | 46.8 | 32.2 |
| Other NE States | 20.4 | 34.0 | 45.5 | 26.6 | 53.5 | 19.9 | – | – | – | 23.2 | 42.7 | 34.1 |
| Rest ST and UT | 22.2 | 32.8 | 45.0 | 24.6 | 49.7 | 25.8 | 52.3 | 30.8 | 17.0 | 41.5 | 35.8 | 22.7 |
| All-India | 13.6 | 20.9 | 65.5 | 19.8 | 34.2 | 46.0 | 30.7 | 43.5 | 25.8 | 20.2 | 31.7 | 48.2 |

*Source:* Unit level data of employment and unemployment schedule of 55th (1999–2000) Round of NSSO.

**Table A3.32**  Distribution of Workers by Occupational Categories, Usual (Principal + Subsidiary) Status, Non-metros, 1999–2000, and 2004–5

| State | Male | | | | | | Female | | | | | |
|---|---|---|---|---|---|---|---|---|---|---|---|---|
| | 1999–2000 | | | 2004–5 | | | 1999–2000 | | | 2004–5 | | |
| | A/P | C | ML | A/P | C | ML | A/P | C | ML | A/P | C | ML |
| Andhra Pradesh | 16.0 | 34.2 | 49.8 | 13.6 | 33.5 | 52.9 | 14.0 | 32.7 | 53.3 | 13.4 | 41.8 | 44.8 |
| Assam | 19.1 | 51.0 | 29.8 | 16.3 | 48.2 | 35.4 | 32.4 | 41.7 | 25.9 | 42.9 | 45.2 | 11.9 |
| Bihar | 13.8 | 41.4 | 44.9 | 16.3 | 36.3 | 47.4 | 17.9 | 33.4 | 48.6 | 15.6 | 29.9 | 54.6 |
| Gujarat | 17.0 | 33.5 | 49.5 | 20.1 | 33.8 | 46.1 | 17.8 | 29.2 | 53.1 | 18.8 | 26.2 | 55.1 |
| Haryana | 11.9 | 33.5 | 54.6 | 16.3 | 38.4 | 45.3 | 23.5 | 21.8 | 54.7 | 44.2 | 37.0 | 18.8 |
| Jammu and Kashmir | 14.5 | 47.7 | 37.9 | 10.5 | 38.1 | 51.4 | 31.6 | 17.0 | 51.4 | 24.0 | 18.5 | 57.5 |
| Karnataka | 17.7 | 34.8 | 47.5 | 19.5 | 35.6 | 44.9 | 16.9 | 26.0 | 57.1 | 17.9 | 40.6 | 41.6 |
| Kerala | 12.3 | 28.5 | 59.2 | 15.2 | 32.9 | 52.0 | 16.5 | 26.9 | 56.6 | 25.5 | 40.9 | 33.5 |
| Madhya Pradesh | 12.2 | 36.0 | 51.8 | 15.5 | 35.4 | 49.1 | 10.5 | 20.6 | 68.9 | 17.4 | 29.3 | 53.2 |
| Maharashtra | 17.7 | 31.9 | 50.4 | 17.5 | 32.5 | 49.9 | 19.6 | 29.0 | 51.4 | 20.6 | 27.4 | 52.0 |
| Orissa | 13.5 | 36.3 | 50.2 | 16.4 | 38.1 | 45.5 | 12.0 | 34.1 | 53.9 | 20.9 | 41.3 | 37.7 |
| Punjab | 18.9 | 34.2 | 46.9 | 26.1 | 36.7 | 37.2 | 24.8 | 28.9 | 46.4 | 55.6 | 31.9 | 12.5 |
| Rajasthan | 15.0 | 31.7 | 53.4 | 20.0 | 37.2 | 42.8 | 14.5 | 13.0 | 72.5 | 24.4 | 21.7 | 53.8 |
| Tamil Nadu | 15.2 | 31.9 | 52.9 | 15.3 | 34.7 | 50.1 | 18.2 | 25.7 | 56.1 | 14.4 | 32.0 | 53.6 |
| Uttar Pradesh | 10.5 | 38.3 | 51.1 | 11.6 | 35.0 | 53.4 | 14.5 | 23.9 | 61.6 | 16.0 | 23.1 | 60.9 |
| West Bengal | 18.0 | 35.0 | 47.0 | 17.0 | 37.0 | 46.0 | 19.1 | 40.2 | 40.7 | 24.7 | 41.7 | 33.6 |
| Other NE States | 19.5 | 39.8 | 40.7 | 19.6 | 41.1 | 39.3 | 23.2 | 42.7 | 34.1 | 25.8 | 46.1 | 28.1 |
| Rest ST and UT | 15.6 | 35.7 | 48.7 | 21.7 | 37.1 | 41.2 | 23.8 | 44.0 | 32.2 | 30.5 | 44.1 | 25.4 |
| All-India | 15.0 | 35.0 | 50.0 | 16.4 | 35.4 | 48.3 | 16.9 | 28.0 | 55.1 | 19.6 | 33.6 | 46.8 |

*Source:* Unit level data of employment and unemployment schedule of 55th (1999–2000) and 61st (2004–5) Rounds of NSSO.

**Table A3.33**  Distribution of Workers by Occupational Categories, Usual (Principal + Subsidiary) Status, Metros and All Urban, 2004–5

(in per cent)

| States | Male | | | | | | Female | | | | | |
|---|---|---|---|---|---|---|---|---|---|---|---|---|
| | Metro | | | All Urban | | | Metro | | | All Urban | | |
| | A/P | C | ML | A/P | C | ML | A/P | C | ML | A/P | C | ML |
| Andhra Pradesh | 24.1 | 35.1 | 40.8 | 15.5 | 33.8 | 50.7 | 25.8 | 49.8 | 24.4 | 15.0 | 42.8 | 42.3 |
| Assam | | | | 16.3 | 48.2 | 35.4 | | | | 42.9 | 45.2 | 11.9 |
| Bihar | 18.2 | 43.5 | 38.3 | 16.5 | 37.1 | 46.4 | 89.9 | 10.1 | 0.0 | 16.6 | 29.6 | 53.8 |
| Gujarat | 18.0 | 32.9 | 49.1 | 19.2 | 33.4 | 47.4 | 16.3 | 54.7 | 29.1 | 17.7 | 38.3 | 44.0 |
| Haryana | 7.1 | 20.0 | 72.9 | 14.5 | 34.8 | 50.8 | 9.7 | 53.4 | 36.9 | 38.4 | 39.8 | 21.8 |
| Jammu and Kashmir | | | | 10.5 | 38.1 | 51.4 | | | | 24.0 | 18.5 | 57.5 |
| Karnataka | 20.6 | 40.2 | 39.3 | 19.8 | 36.9 | 43.2 | 18.5 | 50.8 | 30.7 | 18.0 | 42.7 | 39.3 |
| Kerala | | | | 15.2 | 32.9 | 52.0 | | | | 25.5 | 40.9 | 33.5 |
| Madhya Pradesh | 15.7 | 45.8 | 38.5 | 15.5 | 37.2 | 47.3 | 26.5 | 34.9 | 38.6 | 19.1 | 30.4 | 50.5 |
| Maharashtra | 21.2 | 41.4 | 37.4 | 19.5 | 37.2 | 43.4 | 23.5 | 53.3 | 23.2 | 22.1 | 41.0 | 36.8 |
| Orissa | | | | 16.4 | 38.1 | 45.5 | | | | 20.9 | 41.3 | 37.7 |
| Punjab | 17.2 | 25.9 | 57.0 | 24.1 | 34.2 | 41.7 | 15.6 | 27.4 | 57.0 | 49.4 | 31.2 | 19.3 |
| Rajasthan | 16.6 | 24.5 | 58.9 | 19.2 | 34.1 | 46.7 | 8.0 | 13.7 | 78.4 | 20.2 | 19.7 | 60.1 |
| Tamil Nadu | 33.1 | 33.2 | 33.7 | 18.6 | 34.4 | 47.0 | 26.7 | 63.2 | 10.0 | 15.7 | 35.2 | 49.1 |
| Uttar Pradesh | 19.3 | 42.0 | 38.7 | 13.3 | 36.6 | 50.1 | 25.4 | 34.1 | 40.5 | 18.0 | 25.5 | 56.4 |
| West Bengal | 22.1 | 35.8 | 42.1 | 18.3 | 36.7 | 45.0 | 39.6 | 47.8 | 12.5 | 28.6 | 43.3 | 28.1 |
| Other NE States | | | | 19.6 | 41.1 | 39.3 | | | | 25.8 | 46.1 | 28.1 |
| Rest ST and UT | 27.3 | 38.0 | 34.7 | 26.3 | 37.8 | 35.9 | 38.5 | 49.9 | 11.6 | 35.9 | 48.0 | 16.1 |
| All-India | 21.7 | 37.6 | 40.6 | 18.0 | 36.0 | 46.0 | 24.7 | 48.5 | 26.8 | 20.9 | 37.3 | 41.8 |

*Source*: Unit level data of employment and unemployment schedule of 61st (2004–5) Round of NSSO.

**Table A3.34**  Unemployment Rates by States, Usual Status, Male

| States | 1987–8 | | | | | 1993–4 | | | | | 1999–2000 | | |
|---|---|---|---|---|---|---|---|---|---|---|---|---|---|
| | C1 | C2 | C3 | C2+C3 | TU | C1 | C2 | C3 | C2+C3 | TU | C1 | C2+C3 | TU |
| Andhra Pradesh | 4.6 | 4.5 | 6.1 | 5.2 | 4.9 | 2.6 | 2.6 | 3.9 | 3.1 | 2.9 | 3.8 | 3.4 | 4.0 |
| Assam | 6.0 | 3.1 | 2.6 | 2.8 | 4.7 | 5.7 | 3.8 | 6.6 | 5.2 | 5.5 | 8.9 | 6.2 | 7.7 |
| Bihar | 5.0 | 5.8 | 6.6 | 6.2 | 5.7 | 4.2 | 6.5 | 9.0 | 8.1 | 6.9 | 5.6 | 8.5 | 7.3 |
| Gujarat | 3.9 | 3.6 | 1.7 | 2.6 | 4.2 | 1.9 | 3.5 | 2.0 | 3.1 | 3.0 | 2.3 | 2.2 | 2.0 |
| Haryana | 4.8 | 4.8 | 0.6 | 3.3 | 3.7 | 3.5 | 1.9 | 2.7 | 2.1 | 2.5 | 4.2 | 2.2 | 2.7 |
| Jammu and Kashmir | 3.8 | | 4.3 | 4.3 | 4.2 | 8.5 | | 3.7 | 3.7 | 5.9 | 2.9 | 5.7 | 4.5 |
| Karnataka | 4.3 | 5.8 | 4.6 | 5.3 | 5.0 | 2.0 | 3.4 | 3.3 | 3.4 | 2.9 | 4.2 | 2.2 | 3.0 |
| Kerala | 9.8 | 11.1 | 10.3 | 10.5 | 10.1 | 6.7 | 8.6 | 5.0 | 6.6 | 6.7 | 6.0 | 5.0 | 5.6 |
| Madhya Pradesh | 2.3 | 4.8 | 4.7 | 4.8 | 3.8 | 3.5 | 7.2 | 7.0 | 7.1 | 5.3 | 3.9 | 3.9 | 4.1 |
| Maharashtra | 3.1 | 5.8 | 4.5 | 5.2 | 5.8 | 4.2 | 3.1 | 3.2 | 3.2 | 4.3 | 4.5 | 4.9 | 5.6 |
| Orissa | 5.9 | 5.3 | 6.9 | 6.1 | 6.0 | 7.8 | 5.6 | 5.9 | 5.8 | 6.7 | 7.3 | 6.8 | 7.1 |
| Punjab | 4.2 | 7.4 | 3.3 | 4.5 | 4.4 | 2.7 | 2.5 | 5.5 | 4.1 | 3.1 | 3.6 | 3.2 | 2.8 |
| Rajasthan | 3.7 | 3.5 | 4.8 | 4.4 | 4.1 | 1.6 | 0.9 | 3.6 | 2.2 | 1.7 | 2.3 | 2.6 | 2.6 |
| Tamil Nadu | 6.0 | 4.5 | 5.7 | 4.9 | 6.2 | 3.5 | 4.4 | 4.2 | 4.3 | 4.3 | 3.8 | 3.1 | 3.6 |
| Uttar Pradesh | 1.9 | 3.2 | 4.3 | 3.9 | 3.0 | 3.0 | 2.9 | 3.4 | 3.2 | 3.2 | 2.2 | 4.2 | 4.3 |
| West Bengal | 6.3 | 8.5 | 8.9 | 8.7 | 7.5 | 7.0 | 7.7 | 5.1 | 6.7 | 6.3 | 5.7 | 9.1 | 7.2 |
| Other NE States | 2.8 | 5.8 | | 5.8 | 4.0 | 2.2 | 6.5 | | 6.5 | 3.9 | 2.7 | 9.5 | 5.6 |
| Rest ST and UT | 5.3 | 8.4 | 8.6 | 8.5 | 4.6 | 6.1 | 3.9 | 4.2 | 4.1 | 1.7 | 3.3 | 8.6 | 4.0 |
| All-India | 4.4 | 5.4 | 5.1 | 5.2 | 5.2 | 3.7 | 4.3 | 4.5 | 4.4 | 4.1 | 4.1 | 4.6 | 4.5 |

*Source:* Unit level data of employment and unemployment schedule of 43rd (1987–8), 50th (1993–4), and 55th (1999–2000) Rounds of NSSO.

*Notes:*  C1 = towns with population upto 50,000 (called small town);

C2 = towns with population of 50,000 to 2 lakhs (called medium towns);

C3 = cities with population of 2 lakhs to 10 lakhs (called large cities);

CM = cities with population > 10 lakhs (called metropolitan cities or metros); and

TU = total urban.

**Table A3.35**  Unemployment Rates by States, Usual Status, Female

| States | 1987–8 | | | | | 1993–4 | | | | | 1999–2000 | | |
|---|---|---|---|---|---|---|---|---|---|---|---|---|---|
| | C1 | C2 | C3 | C2+C3 | TU | C1 | C2 | C3 | C2+C3 | TU | C1 | C2+C3 | TU |
| Andhra Pradesh | 2.5 | 2.1 | 11.1 | 5.9 | 4.5 | 1.5 | 3.9 | 7.6 | 5.2 | 3.5 | 2.6 | 3.5 | 3.7 |
| Assam | 19.8 | 11.5 | 19.0 | 15.7 | 17.8 | 25.5 | 16.0 | 31.9 | 25.7 | 25.6 | 30.8 | 8.2 | 18.9 |
| Bihar | 0.7 | 7.8 | 4.0 | 5.5 | 3.0 | 2.5 | 6.5 | 14.9 | 12.2 | 9.3 | 6.4 | 6.8 | 8.1 |
| Gujarat | 1.9 | 0.9 | 0.5 | 0.7 | 1.4 | 1.1 | 4.7 | | 3.6 | 4.4 | 1.0 | 3.1 | 2.0 |
| Haryana | 2.3 | 8.2 | 4.7 | 6.9 | 5.3 | 3.6 | 2.7 | 4.9 | 3.1 | 3.3 | 2.0 | 2.8 | 2.5 |
| Jammu and Kashmir | 5.4 | | 10.3 | 10.3 | 8.1 | 13.3 | | 3.0 | 3.0 | 9.1 | 4.3 | 13.2 | 8.8 |
| Karnataka | 1.7 | 5.3 | 4.7 | 5.1 | 3.2 | 3.0 | 7.8 | 3.7 | 6.0 | 5.6 | 4.0 | 2.2 | 4.4 |
| Kerala | 24.9 | 24.8 | 21.8 | 22.9 | 24.0 | 18.8 | 11.6 | 25.9 | 18.6 | 18.7 | 15.3 | 25.7 | 19.8 |
| Madhya Pradesh | 2.8 | 4.3 | 5.5 | 5.0 | 4.0 | 0.9 | 8.6 | 6.3 | 7.5 | 3.9 | 1.0 | 1.9 | 1.4 |
| Maharashtra | 1.2 | 1.0 | 3.1 | 1.9 | 4.2 | 0.7 | 7.0 | 2.4 | 4.1 | 4.7 | 3.4 | 3.3 | 6.6 |
| Orissa | 2.9 | 7.8 | 22.0 | 14.4 | 8.1 | 5.3 | 8.4 | 5.9 | 7.1 | 6.1 | 5.7 | 4.6 | 5.2 |
| Punjab | 4.9 | 9.6 | 7.8 | 8.6 | 6.8 | 5.7 | 4.1 | 7.0 | 5.5 | 5.3 | 0.9 | 3.1 | 2.1 |
| Rajasthan | 0.6 | 1.0 | 1.8 | 1.5 | 0.9 | 0.7 | 0.2 | 0.7 | 0.4 | 0.6 | 0.0 | 4.0 | 2.1 |
| Tamil Nadu | 3.9 | 6.4 | 10.1 | 7.7 | 6.5 | 6.9 | 3.1 | 8.0 | 5.1 | 6.8 | 3.8 | 6.0 | 5.1 |
| Uttar Pradesh | 1.7 | 0.3 | 2.2 | 1.4 | 1.6 | 1.2 | 1.2 | 0.8 | 1.0 | 1.1 | 0.8 | 6.2 | 3.2 |
| West Bengal | 13.5 | 14.2 | 18.6 | 15.4 | 13.9 | 7.2 | 18.2 | 16.2 | 17.5 | 14.2 | 4.8 | 13.2 | 9.5 |
| Other NE States | 3.4 | 8.2 | | 8.2 | 5.8 | 5.3 | 7.0 | | 7.0 | 6.0 | 4.7 | 8.1 | 6.2 |
| Rest ST and UT | 7.8 | 6.5 | 2.0 | 4.7 | 7.8 | 12.6 | 7.3 | 15.8 | 12.5 | 8.6 | 13.3 | 13.2 | 7.3 |
| All-India | 4.2 | 5.7 | 7.8 | 6.7 | 5.9 | 4.6 | 6.3 | 7.6 | 6.9 | 6.2 | 4.4 | 6.3 | 5.7 |

*Source:* Unit level data of employment and unemployment schedule of 43rd (1987–8), 50th (1993–4), and 55th (1999–2000) Rounds of NSSO.

**Table A3.36**  Unemployment Rates by States, Usual Status, by Sex, Metro and Non-metro

| States | Male | | | | | | | | | Female | | | | | | | | |
|---|---|---|---|---|---|---|---|---|---|---|---|---|---|---|---|---|---|---|
| | 1987-8 | | 1993-4 | | 1999-2000 | | 2004-5 | | | 1987-8 | | 1993-4 | | 1999-2000 | | 2004-5 | | |
| | NM | M | NM | M | NM | M | NM | M | TU | NM | M | NM | M | NM | M | NM | M | TU |
| Andhra Pradesh | 5.0 | 4.5 | 3.0 | 2.0 | 3.5 | 6.1 | 3.6 | 3.5 | 3.6 | 4.4 | 5.9 | 3.7 | 0.6 | 3.2 | 7.1 | 3.5 | 5.8 | 3.8 |
| Assam | 4.7 | | 5.5 | | 7.7 | – | 6.9 | | 6.9 | 17.8 | | 25.6 | | 18.9 | – | 9.1 | | 9.1 |
| Bihar | 5.7 | | 6.9 | | 7.3 | 7.4 | 6.5 | 11.3 | 7.0 | 3.0 | | 9.3 | | 6.6 | 17.7 | 2.8 | 20.4 | 3.1 |
| Gujarat | 3.1 | 7.3 | 2.6 | 3.8 | 2.2 | 1.7 | 2.3 | 2.2 | 2.3 | 1.3 | 1.6 | 2.2 | 9.7 | 2.2 | 1.7 | 2.3 | 3.7 | 2.9 |
| Haryana | 3.7 | | 2.5 | | 2.7 | – | 3.6 | 1.5 | 3.2 | 5.3 | | 3.3 | | 2.8 | – | 8.4 | | 7.5 |
| Jammu and Kashmir | 4.2 | | 5.9 | | 4.5 | – | 3.7 | | 3.7 | 8.1 | | 9.1 | | 8.9 | – | 10.9 | | 10.9 |
| Karnataka | 4.8 | 6.1 | 2.7 | 3.8 | 3.1 | 2.8 | 2.2 | 1.2 | 1.9 | 3.0 | 4.6 | 4.5 | 13.2 | 3.1 | 7.5 | 3.6 | 12.3 | 5.7 |
| Kerala | 10.1 | | 6.7 | | 5.6 | – | 6.2 | | 6.2 | 24.0 | | 18.7 | | 20.0 | – | 33.4 | | 33.4 |
| Madhya Pradesh | 3.8 | | 5.4 | 4.5 | 3.9 | 5.2 | 3.3 | 3.3 | 3.3 | 4.0 | | 3.8 | 5.1 | 1.4 | 1.9 | 2.1 | | 1.8 |
| Maharashtra | 4.4 | 7.4 | 3.5 | 5.1 | 4.8 | 6.3 | 3.3 | 3.7 | 3.5 | 1.6 | 9.2 | 2.5 | 7.5 | 3.3 | 10.1 | 3.2 | 5.0 | 4.1 |
| Orissa | 6.0 | | 6.7 | | 7.0 | – | 9.0 | | 9.0 | 8.1 | | 6.1 | | 5.3 | – | 26.6 | | 26.6 |
| Punjab | 4.4 | | 3.7 | 0.6 | 3.3 | 0.9 | 3.2 | 1.8 | 2.9 | 6.8 | | 5.5 | 3.4 | 2.2 | 1.7 | 15.8 | | 14.0 |
| Rajasthan | 4.1 | | 2.0 | 0.2 | 2.5 | 3.3 | 2.9 | 2.6 | 2.8 | 0.9 | | 0.6 | 0.6 | 2.2 | 1.5 | 3.8 | 1.1 | 2.9 |
| Tamil Nadu | 5.4 | 9.2 | 4.0 | 5.4 | 3.4 | 4.3 | 2.9 | 3.0 | 2.9 | 5.8 | 10.7 | 6.0 | 11.2 | 4.9 | 5.6 | 5.0 | 2.1 | 4.8 |
| Uttar Pradesh | 3.1 | 2.4 | 3.1 | 4.1 | 3.4 | 6.4 | 3.7 | 2.8 | 3.5 | 1.5 | 1.9 | 1.1 | 1.4 | 3.4 | 2.9 | 3.2 | 1.8 | 3.0 |
| West Bengal | 7.8 | 6.6 | 6.7 | 5.0 | 8.1 | 4.8 | 5.7 | 5.4 | 5.6 | 14.8 | 11.9 | 14.1 | 14.6 | 10.1 | 7.9 | 8.1 | 9.4 | 8.4 |
| Other NE States | 4.0 | | 3.9 | | 5.6 | – | 7.4 | | 7.4 | 5.8 | | 6.0 | | 6.2 | – | 16.3 | | 16.3 |
| Rest ST and UT | 7.1 | 4.0 | 4.8 | 0.9 | 6.9 | 2.4 | 3.8 | 4.6 | 4.4 | 6.0 | 8.8 | 12.5 | 6.2 | 13.3 | 3.3 | 12.5 | 6.4 | 8.5 |
| All-India | 4.9 | 6.4 | 4.1 | 3.8 | 4.4 | 4.8 | 3.9 | 3.5 | 3.8 | 5.5 | 8.7 | 5.8 | 8.2 | 5.5 | 6.5 | 7.5 | 4.9 | 6.9 |

*Source:* Unit level data of employment and unemployment schedule of 43rd (1987–8), 50th (1993–4), 55th (1999–2000), and 61st (2004–5) Rounds of NSSO.

*Notes:* NM = Non-metro and M = Metro.

**Table A3.37**  Unemployment Rates by States, Current Daily Status, Male

| States | 1987–8 | | | | | 1993–4 | | | | | 1999–2000 | | |
|---|---|---|---|---|---|---|---|---|---|---|---|---|---|
| | C1 | C2 | C3 | C2+C3 | TU | C1 | C2 | C3 | C2+C3 | TU | C1 | C2+C3 | TU |
| Andhra Pradesh | 11.5 | 9.4 | 10.3 | 9.8 | 10.0 | 9.0 | 6.9 | 8.2 | 7.5 | 7.5 | 8.6 | 6.8 | 7.2 |
| Assam | 7.1 | 4.9 | 3.2 | 4.0 | 5.8 | 6.8 | 4.7 | 7.2 | 6.0 | 6.5 | 12.7 | 6.3 | 9.9 |
| Bihar | 7.3 | 8.1 | 9.0 | 8.5 | 8.1 | 6.3 | 7.9 | 10.0 | 9.2 | 8.3 | 7.2 | 10.1 | 8.7 |
| Gujarat | 7.3 | 5.2 | 4.0 | 4.5 | 7.1 | 5.6 | 7.0 | 4.5 | 6.4 | 5.7 | 4.9 | 4.2 | 4.0 |
| Haryana | 8.6 | 6.2 | 5.5 | 6.0 | 6.8 | 9.5 | 6.1 | 3.6 | 5.4 | 6.5 | 8.1 | 3.2 | 4.5 |
| Jammu and Kashmir | 7.4 | | 5.4 | 5.4 | 6.1 | 9.8 | – | 4.9 | 4.9 | 7.1 | 4.9 | 6.8 | 6.0 |
| Karnataka | 10.4 | 9.1 | 7.6 | 8.4 | 9.5 | 4.9 | 6.9 | 5.6 | 6.2 | 5.6 | 7.0 | 4.5 | 5.3 |
| Kerala | 23.3 | 21.1 | 21.8 | 21.6 | 22.4 | 14.8 | 14.0 | 12.6 | 13.3 | 14.1 | 16.3 | 14.6 | 15.5 |
| Madhya Pradesh | 5.0 | 7.3 | 6.4 | 6.7 | 6.1 | 5.5 | 9.3 | 8.6 | 9.0 | 7.1 | 7.8 | 6.1 | 7.3 |
| Maharashtra | 6.9 | 8.5 | 7.7 | 8.1 | 8.6 | 7.6 | 5.0 | 5.1 | 5.1 | 6.0 | 8.6 | 6.8 | 7.7 |
| Orissa | 9.4 | 8.2 | 7.4 | 7.8 | 8.6 | 13.0 | 7.4 | 7.4 | 7.4 | 9.9 | 10.6 | 9.1 | 9.8 |
| Punjab | 7.5 | 10.8 | 4.6 | 6.5 | 6.9 | 3.6 | 4.1 | 5.6 | 4.9 | 3.9 | 6.8 | 5.4 | 4.8 |
| Rajasthan | 7.3 | 7.0 | 7.4 | 7.3 | 7.3 | 2.6 | 1.6 | 4.5 | 3.0 | 2.6 | 6.2 | 4.0 | 4.7 |
| Tamil Nadu | 12.7 | 10.6 | 9.9 | 10.3 | 12.4 | 8.0 | 8.7 | 8.5 | 8.6 | 8.7 | 10.9 | 7.6 | 9.0 |
| Uttar Pradesh | 4.7 | 5.5 | 5.7 | 5.6 | 5.2 | 5.2 | 4.4 | 4.5 | 4.5 | 4.8 | 4.9 | 6.5 | 6.3 |
| West Bengal | 11.4 | 12.9 | 12.3 | 12.7 | 11.7 | 10.8 | 12.7 | 8.0 | 10.8 | 10.2 | 8.1 | 12.1 | 10.1 |
| Other NE States | 3.4 | 6.8 | | 6.8 | 4.8 | 3.2 | 7.0 | – | 7.0 | 4.7 | 3.0 | 9.5 | 5.8 |
| Rest ST and UT | 9.6 | 14.2 | 11.2 | 12.9 | 5.9 | 8.0 | 7.2 | 9.9 | 9.0 | 3.0 | 6.8 | 11.2 | 5.5 |
| All-India | 9.0 | 9.0 | 7.8 | 8.4 | 8.8 | 7.2 | 7.4 | 6.9 | 7.1 | 6.7 | 8.1 | 7.3 | 7.3 |

*Source:* Unit level data of employment and unemployment schedule of 43rd (1987–8), 50th (1993–4), and 55th (1999–2000) Rounds of NSSO.

**Table A3.36** Unemployment Rates by States, Usual Status, by Sex, Metro and Non-metro

| States | Male | | | | | | | | | Female | | | | | | | | |
|---|---|---|---|---|---|---|---|---|---|---|---|---|---|---|---|---|---|---|
| | 1987-8 | | 1993-4 | | 1999-2000 | | 2004-5 | | | 1987-8 | | 1993-4 | | 1999-2000 | | 2004-5 | | |
| | NM | M | NM | M | NM | M | NM | M | TU | NM | M | NM | M | NM | M | NM | M | TU |
| Andhra Pradesh | 5.0 | 4.5 | 3.0 | 2.0 | 3.5 | 6.1 | 3.6 | 3.5 | 3.6 | 4.4 | 5.9 | 3.7 | 0.6 | 3.2 | 7.1 | 3.5 | 5.8 | 3.8 |
| Assam | 4.7 | | 5.5 | | 7.7 | – | 6.9 | | 6.9 | 17.8 | | 25.6 | | 18.9 | – | 9.1 | | 9.1 |
| Bihar | 5.7 | | 6.9 | | 7.3 | 7.4 | 6.5 | 11.3 | 7.0 | 3.0 | | 9.3 | | 6.6 | 17.7 | 2.8 | 20.4 | 3.1 |
| Gujarat | 3.1 | 7.3 | 2.6 | 3.8 | 2.2 | 1.7 | 2.3 | 2.2 | 2.3 | 1.3 | 1.6 | 2.2 | 9.7 | 2.2 | 1.7 | 2.3 | 3.7 | 2.9 |
| Haryana | 3.7 | | 2.5 | | 2.7 | – | 3.6 | 1.5 | 3.2 | 5.3 | | 3.3 | | 2.8 | – | 8.4 | | 7.5 |
| Jammu and Kashmir | 4.2 | | 5.9 | | 4.5 | – | 3.7 | | 3.7 | 8.1 | | 9.1 | | 8.9 | – | 10.9 | | 10.9 |
| Karnataka | 4.8 | 6.1 | 2.7 | 3.8 | 3.1 | 2.8 | 2.2 | 1.2 | 1.9 | 3.0 | 4.6 | 4.5 | 13.2 | 3.1 | 7.5 | 3.6 | 12.3 | 5.7 |
| Kerala | 10.1 | | 6.7 | | 5.6 | – | 6.2 | | 6.2 | 24.0 | | 18.7 | | 20.0 | – | 33.4 | | 33.4 |
| Madhya Pradesh | 3.8 | | 5.4 | 4.5 | 3.9 | 5.2 | 3.3 | 3.3 | 3.3 | 4.0 | | 3.8 | 5.1 | 1.4 | 1.9 | 2.1 | | 1.8 |
| Maharashtra | 4.4 | 7.4 | 3.5 | 5.1 | 4.8 | 6.3 | 3.3 | 3.7 | 3.5 | 1.6 | 9.2 | 2.5 | 7.5 | 3.3 | 10.1 | 3.2 | 5.0 | 4.1 |
| Orissa | 6.0 | | 6.7 | | 7.0 | – | 9.0 | | 9.0 | 8.1 | | 6.1 | | 5.3 | – | 26.6 | | 26.6 |
| Punjab | 4.4 | | 3.7 | 0.6 | 3.3 | 0.9 | 3.2 | 1.8 | 2.9 | 6.8 | | 5.5 | 3.4 | 2.2 | 1.7 | 15.8 | | 14.0 |
| Rajasthan | 4.1 | | 2.0 | 0.2 | 2.5 | 3.3 | 2.9 | 2.6 | 2.8 | 0.9 | | 0.6 | 0.6 | 2.2 | 1.5 | 3.8 | 1.1 | 2.9 |
| Tamil Nadu | 5.4 | 9.2 | 4.0 | 5.4 | 3.4 | 4.3 | 2.9 | 3.0 | 2.9 | 5.8 | 10.7 | 6.0 | 11.2 | 4.9 | 5.6 | 5.0 | 2.1 | 4.8 |
| Uttar Pradesh | 3.1 | 2.4 | 3.1 | 4.1 | 3.4 | 6.4 | 3.7 | 2.8 | 3.5 | 1.5 | 1.9 | 1.1 | 1.4 | 3.4 | 2.9 | 3.2 | 1.8 | 3.0 |
| West Bengal | 7.8 | 6.6 | 6.7 | 5.0 | 8.1 | 4.8 | 5.7 | 5.4 | 5.6 | 14.8 | 11.9 | 14.1 | 14.6 | 10.1 | 7.9 | 8.1 | 9.4 | 8.4 |
| Other NE States | 4.0 | | 3.9 | | 5.6 | – | 7.4 | | 7.4 | 5.8 | | 6.0 | | 6.2 | – | 16.3 | | 16.3 |
| Rest ST and UT | 7.1 | 4.0 | 4.8 | 0.9 | 6.9 | 2.4 | 3.8 | 4.6 | 4.4 | 6.0 | 8.8 | 12.5 | 6.2 | 13.3 | 3.3 | 12.5 | 6.4 | 8.5 |
| All-India | 4.9 | 6.4 | 4.1 | 3.8 | 4.4 | 4.8 | 3.9 | 3.5 | 3.8 | 5.5 | 8.7 | 5.8 | 8.2 | 5.5 | 6.5 | 7.5 | 4.9 | 6.9 |

*Source:* Unit level data of employment and unemployment schedule of 43rd (1987–8), 50th (1993–4), 55th (1999–2000), and 61st (2004–5) Rounds of NSSO.

*Notes:* NM = Non-metro and M = Metro.

**Table A3.37**  Unemployment Rates by States, Current Daily Status, Male

| States | 1987–8 | | | | | 1993–4 | | | | | 1999–2000 | | |
|---|---|---|---|---|---|---|---|---|---|---|---|---|---|
| | C1 | C2 | C3 | C2+C3 | TU | C1 | C2 | C3 | C2+C3 | TU | C1 | C2+C3 | TU |
| Andhra Pradesh | 11.5 | 9.4 | 10.3 | 9.8 | 10.0 | 9.0 | 6.9 | 8.2 | 7.5 | 7.5 | 8.6 | 6.8 | 7.2 |
| Assam | 7.1 | 4.9 | 3.2 | 4.0 | 5.8 | 6.8 | 4.7 | 7.2 | 6.0 | 6.5 | 12.7 | 6.3 | 9.9 |
| Bihar | 7.3 | 8.1 | 9.0 | 8.5 | 8.1 | 6.3 | 7.9 | 10.0 | 9.2 | 8.3 | 7.2 | 10.1 | 8.7 |
| Gujarat | 7.3 | 5.2 | 4.0 | 4.5 | 7.1 | 5.6 | 7.0 | 4.5 | 6.4 | 5.7 | 4.9 | 4.2 | 4.0 |
| Haryana | 8.6 | 6.2 | 5.5 | 6.0 | 6.8 | 9.5 | 6.1 | 3.6 | 5.4 | 6.5 | 8.1 | 3.2 | 4.5 |
| Jammu and Kashmir | 7.4 | | 5.4 | 5.4 | 6.1 | 9.8 | – | 4.9 | 4.9 | 7.1 | 4.9 | 6.8 | 6.0 |
| Karnataka | 10.4 | 9.1 | 7.6 | 8.4 | 9.5 | 4.9 | 6.9 | 5.6 | 6.2 | 5.6 | 7.0 | 4.5 | 5.3 |
| Kerala | 23.3 | 21.1 | 21.8 | 21.6 | 22.4 | 14.8 | 14.0 | 12.6 | 13.3 | 14.1 | 16.3 | 14.6 | 15.5 |
| Madhya Pradesh | 5.0 | 7.3 | 6.4 | 6.7 | 6.1 | 5.5 | 9.3 | 8.6 | 9.0 | 7.1 | 7.8 | 6.1 | 7.3 |
| Maharashtra | 6.9 | 8.5 | 7.7 | 8.1 | 8.6 | 7.6 | 5.0 | 5.1 | 5.1 | 6.0 | 8.6 | 6.8 | 7.7 |
| Orissa | 9.4 | 8.2 | 7.4 | 7.8 | 8.6 | 13.0 | 7.4 | 7.4 | 7.4 | 9.9 | 10.6 | 9.1 | 9.8 |
| Punjab | 7.5 | 10.8 | 4.6 | 6.5 | 6.9 | 3.6 | 4.1 | 5.6 | 4.9 | 3.9 | 6.8 | 5.4 | 4.8 |
| Rajasthan | 7.3 | 7.0 | 7.4 | 7.3 | 7.3 | 2.6 | 1.6 | 4.5 | 3.0 | 2.6 | 6.2 | 4.0 | 4.7 |
| Tamil Nadu | 12.7 | 10.6 | 9.9 | 10.3 | 12.4 | 8.0 | 8.7 | 8.5 | 8.6 | 8.7 | 10.9 | 7.6 | 9.0 |
| Uttar Pradesh | 4.7 | 5.5 | 5.7 | 5.6 | 5.2 | 5.2 | 4.4 | 4.5 | 4.5 | 4.8 | 4.9 | 6.5 | 6.3 |
| West Bengal | 11.4 | 12.9 | 12.3 | 12.7 | 11.7 | 10.8 | 12.7 | 8.0 | 10.8 | 10.2 | 8.1 | 12.1 | 10.1 |
| Other NE States | 3.4 | 6.8 | | 6.8 | 4.8 | 3.2 | 7.0 | – | 7.0 | 4.7 | 3.0 | 9.5 | 5.8 |
| Rest ST and UT | 9.6 | 14.2 | 11.2 | 12.9 | 5.9 | 8.0 | 7.2 | 9.9 | 9.0 | 3.0 | 6.8 | 11.2 | 5.5 |
| All-India | 9.0 | 9.0 | 7.8 | 8.4 | 8.8 | 7.2 | 7.4 | 6.9 | 7.1 | 6.7 | 8.1 | 7.3 | 7.3 |

*Source:* Unit level data of employment and unemployment schedule of 43rd (1987–8), 50th (1993–4), and 55th (1999–2000) Rounds of NSSO.

**Table A3.38**   Unemployment Rates by States, Current Daily Status, Female

| States | 1987-8 | | | | | 1993-4 | | | | | 1999-2000 | | |
|---|---|---|---|---|---|---|---|---|---|---|---|---|---|
| | C1 | C2 | C3 | C2+C3 | TU | C1 | C2 | C3 | C2+C3 | TU | C1 | C2+C3 | TU |
| Andhra Pradesh | 12.4 | 10.6 | 20.0 | 14.8 | 13.3 | 9.4 | 9.9 | 10.0 | 9.9 | 9.5 | 5.5 | 10.1 | 8.9 |
| Assam | 27.7 | 18.3 | 19.6 | 19.1 | 22.6 | 27.5 | 15.5 | 29.8 | 24.5 | 25.7 | 38.5 | 8.6 | 21.9 |
| Bihar | 3.0 | 15.9 | 7.5 | 10.7 | 7.0 | 3.2 | 10.4 | 19.0 | 16.3 | 12.3 | 11.5 | 10.2 | 13.5 |
| Gujarat | 7.9 | 6.0 | 3.9 | 4.9 | 5.8 | 7.5 | 7.4 | – | 6.0 | 7.8 | 5.0 | 8.1 | 5.4 |
| Haryana | 7.5 | 6.4 | 15.7 | 9.3 | 8.9 | 8.1 | 6.8 | 7.6 | 6.9 | 7.3 | 3.3 | 6.1 | 4.9 |
| Jammu and Kashmir | 16.6 | | 14.5 | 14.5 | 15.1 | 19.5 | – | 6.6 | 6.5 | 14.0 | 7.4 | 18.1 | 13.4 |
| Karnataka | 11.5 | 10.7 | 9.8 | 10.4 | 11.1 | 5.4 | 12.1 | 7.2 | 9.9 | 8.9 | 6.6 | 3.1 | 5.9 |
| Kerala | 46.9 | 36.7 | 30.0 | 32.6 | 40.0 | 28.8 | 19.3 | 33.6 | 26.3 | 27.8 | 24.1 | 33.0 | 28.2 |
| Madhya Pradesh | 7.3 | 7.8 | 8.5 | 8.2 | 7.9 | 2.9 | 10.9 | 7.0 | 8.9 | 5.9 | 7.6 | 3.7 | 5.7 |
| Maharashtra | 8.7 | 5.1 | 6.0 | 5.5 | 8.8 | 5.7 | 10.0 | 5.3 | 6.9 | 7.8 | 11.0 | 6.9 | 10.0 |
| Orissa | 7.7 | 16.7 | 30.6 | 22.8 | 14.7 | 7.1 | 13.9 | 9.9 | 11.8 | 9.3 | 8.5 | 7.7 | 8.2 |
| Punjab | 14.1 | 13.6 | 9.7 | 11.4 | 12.5 | 7.2 | 4.9 | 7.9 | 6.4 | 5.8 | 3.1 | 7.4 | 5.3 |
| Rajasthan | 4.6 | 2.1 | 4.2 | 3.5 | 4.1 | 1.9 | 0.3 | 2.2 | 1.2 | 1.5 | 1.1 | 5.3 | 3.5 |
| Tamil Nadu | 12.0 | 10.9 | 18.0 | 13.3 | 13.2 | 12.8 | 9.2 | 15.3 | 11.7 | 12.7 | 8.9 | 10.0 | 8.6 |
| Uttar Pradesh | 2.6 | 2.7 | 5.1 | 4.1 | 3.4 | 7.1 | 5.3 | 1.5 | 3.6 | 4.9 | 2.0 | 7.6 | 5.1 |
| West Bengal | 24.7 | 21.4 | 20.7 | 21.2 | 19.9 | 15.1 | 27.2 | 19.4 | 24.5 | 20.8 | 7.3 | 19.1 | 13.9 |
| Other NE States | 4.4 | 11.1 | | 11.1 | 7.8 | 6.5 | 7.9 | – | 7.9 | 7.1 | 5.8 | 8.9 | 7.2 |
| Rest ST and UT | 20.1 | 13.9 | 7.3 | 11.2 | 11.7 | 17.9 | 11.2 | 17.9 | 15.5 | 9.5 | 21.0 | 18.1 | 10.0 |
| All-India | 12.0 | 11.2 | 12.8 | 12.0 | 12.0 | 9.9 | 11.4 | 11.1 | 11.2 | 10.5 | 9.0 | 10.4 | 9.4 |

*Source:* Unit level data of employment and unemployment schedule of 43rd (1987–8), 50th (1993–4), and 55th (1999–2000) Rounds of NSSO.

**Table A3.39**   Unemployment Rates by States, Current Daily Status, by Sex, Metro, and Non-metro

| States | Male | | | | | | | | | Female | | | | | | | | |
|---|---|---|---|---|---|---|---|---|---|---|---|---|---|---|---|---|---|---|
| | 1987–8 | | 1993–4 | | 1999–2000 | | 2004–5 | | | 1987–8 | | 1993–4 | | 1999–2000 | | 2004–5 | | |
| | NM | M | NM | M | NM | M | NM | M | TU | NM | M | NM | M | NM | M | NM | M | TU |
| Andhra Pradesh | 10.4 | 6.8 | 8.0 | 3.6 | 7.2 | 7.2 | 8.5 | 4.6 | 7.8 | 13.8 | 7.5 | 9.7 | 5.7 | 8.6 | 11.0 | 8.6 | 6.9 | 8.3 |
| Assam | 5.8 | – | 6.5 | – | 9.9 | – | 8.1 | – | 8.1 | 22.6 | – | 25.7 | – | 21.9 | – | 14.0 | – | 14.0 |
| Bihar | 8.1 | – | 8.3 | – | 9.0 | 7.2 | 9.5 | 13.7 | 10.0 | 7.0 | – | 12.3 | – | 10.7 | 29.1 | 5.8 | 25.1 | 6.1 |
| Gujarat | 5.7 | 11.3 | 6.0 | 5.1 | 4.5 | 3.1 | 3.7 | 4.8 | 4.2 | 6.3 | 4.0 | 6.8 | 10.2 | 6.7 | 3.0 | 5.1 | 9.8 | 7.2 |
| Haryana | 6.8 | – | 6.5 | – | 4.5 | – | 6.8 | 1.5 | 5.8 | 8.8 | – | 7.3 | – | 4.9 | – | 14.8 | – | 13.1 |
| Jammu and Kashmir | 6.1 | – | 7.1 | – | 6.0 | – | 4.6 | – | 4.6 | 15.1 | – | 14.0 | – | 13.4 | – | 15.2 | – | 15.2 |
| Karnataka | 9.4 | 9.5 | 5.6 | 5.7 | 5.7 | 4.2 | 5.4 | 4.3 | 5.1 | 11.1 | 10.7 | 7.6 | 15.6 | 4.9 | 8.1 | 6.4 | 17.6 | 9.4 |
| Kerala | 22.4 | – | 14.1 | – | 15.5 | – | 17.4 | – | 17.4 | 40.0 | – | 27.8 | – | 28.2 | – | 42.3 | – | 42.3 |
| Madhya Pradesh | 6.1 | – | 7.4 | 4.9 | 7.0 | 8.9 | 6.3 | 8.0 | 6.6 | 7.8 | – | 5.6 | 7.4 | 6.0 | 3.9 | 6.4 | 6.5 | 6.4 |
| Maharashtra | 7.6 | 9.7 | 6.0 | 5.9 | 7.3 | 8.1 | 8.8 | 7.4 | 8.1 | 6.9 | 11.8 | 6.4 | 9.2 | 8.4 | 11.7 | 15.0 | 7.8 | 11.2 |
| Orissa | 8.6 | – | 9.9 | – | 9.8 | – | 11.9 | – | 11.9 | 14.7 | – | 9.3 | – | 8.2 | – | 27.1 | – | 27.1 |
| Punjab | 6.9 | – | 4.5 | 1.1 | 5.8 | 1.1 | 6.5 | 1.8 | 5.4 | 12.5 | – | 6.6 | – | 6.0 | 1.7 | 19.7 | 3.7 | 17.7 |
| Rajasthan | 7.3 | – | 2.9 | 1.1 | 4.9 | 3.5 | 6.2 | 6.9 | 6.3 | 4.1 | – | 1.6 | 0.6 | 3.7 | 1.9 | 6.1 | 2.8 | 5.0 |
| Tamil Nadu | 11.4 | 16.2 | 8.4 | 9.6 | 9.0 | 8.8 | 8.5 | 6.4 | 8.1 | 12.7 | 15.9 | 12.2 | 15.1 | 9.5 | 5.9 | 10.4 | 4.4 | 9.8 |
| Uttar Pradesh | 5.3 | 4.8 | 4.8 | 5.3 | 5.8 | 7.5 | 6.6 | 5.0 | 6.3 | 3.5 | 2.3 | 5.2 | 1.5 | 4.9 | 5.5 | 7.2 | 3.9 | 6.5 |
| West Bengal | 12.2 | 10.5 | 10.8 | 8.4 | 11.0 | 7.6 | 10.6 | 7.7 | 9.9 | 22.2 | 15.7 | 21.7 | 17.0 | 14.9 | 11.5 | 14.1 | 12.5 | 13.7 |
| Other NE States | 4.8 | – | 4.7 | – | 5.8 | – | 8.2 | – | 8.2 | 7.8 | – | 7.1 | – | 7.2 | – | 18.6 | – | 18.6 |
| Rest ST and UT | 11.5 | 4.4 | 8.6 | 1.6 | 9.9 | 3.1 | 7.4 | 5.8 | 6.1 | 14.6 | 10.4 | 16.4 | 6.1 | 18.9 | 3.8 | 17.2 | 9.2 | 11.9 |
| All-India | 8.6 | 9.4 | 7.2 | 5.2 | 7.6 | 6.5 | 8.0 | 6.2 | 7.5 | 12.0 | 12.1 | 10.6 | 10.0 | 9.7 | 8.3 | 12.8 | 8.3 | 11.6 |

*Source:* Unit level data of employment and unemployment schedule of 43rd (1987–8), 50th (1993–4), 55th (1999–2000), and 61st (2004–5) Rounds of NSSO.

**Table A4.2**   Education Levels (Age 7+), Females, 1987–8

(in per cent)

| States | < 50,000 | | | | | 50,000–200,000 | | | | | 200,000–1 million | | | | |
|---|---|---|---|---|---|---|---|---|---|---|---|---|---|---|---|
| | Illiterate | Primary & below | Up to middle | Up to secondary | Graduate & above | Illiterate | Primary & below | Up to middle | Up to secondary | Graduate & above | Illiterate | Primary & below | Up to middle | Up to secondary | Graduate & above |
| Andhra Pradesh | 50.1 | 34.6 | 8.7 | 5.6 | 1.0 | 45.8 | 33.6 | 10.9 | 7.9 | 1.8 | 39.3 | 32.8 | 12.0 | 12.7 | 3.3 |
| Assam | 22.7 | 35.6 | 22.8 | 16.2 | 2.7 | 18.2 | 36.7 | 20.5 | 18.4 | 6.3 | 25.5 | 39.9 | 11.3 | 17.5 | 5.8 |
| Bihar | 57.2 | 29.1 | 8.0 | 4.7 | 1.1 | 49.1 | 29.9 | 11.2 | 8.3 | 1.6 | 44.9 | 27.5 | 12.3 | 9.1 | 6.2 |
| Gujarat | 39.3 | 37.4 | 9.5 | 10.7 | 3.0 | 31.9 | 40.5 | 14.2 | 11.7 | 1.7 | 27.0 | 40.6 | 10.5 | 14.6 | 7.3 |
| Haryana | 33.4 | 34.6 | 10.5 | 17.2 | 4.3 | 30.4 | 29.2 | 12.9 | 18.5 | 9.0 | 51.3 | 24.8 | 5.3 | 16.3 | 2.1 |
| Jammu and Kashmir | 53.4 | 24.2 | 10.2 | 9.7 | 2.6 | | | | | | 46.5 | 21.7 | 10.2 | 13.4 | 8.3 |
| Karnataka | 41.1 | 34.2 | 12.2 | 10.4 | 2.0 | 38.7 | 33.2 | 15.7 | 9.9 | 2.5 | 33.0 | 33.5 | 13.0 | 17.6 | 2.9 |
| Kerala | 13.3 | 42.1 | 25.3 | 15.5 | 3.9 | 12.7 | 37.8 | 21.5 | 23.7 | 4.4 | 11.3 | 33.9 | 25.0 | 20.8 | 9.0 |
| Madhya Pradesh | 47.4 | 32.4 | 8.3 | 8.6 | 3.3 | 38.2 | 36.5 | 8.9 | 10.7 | 5.8 | 29.0 | 35.9 | 12.6 | 14.8 | 7.7 |
| Maharashtra | 41.0 | 34.2 | 12.6 | 10.3 | 2.0 | 34.5 | 36.6 | 11.9 | 13.8 | 3.3 | 29.5 | 39.7 | 12.5 | 14.5 | 3.7 |
| Orissa | 41.8 | 34.4 | 16.3 | 6.1 | 1.5 | 30.4 | 39.3 | 16.7 | 11.2 | 2.4 | 40.1 | 29.9 | 13.5 | 11.3 | 5.3 |
| Punjab | 37.4 | 28.9 | 10.8 | 17.8 | 5.2 | 32.7 | 31.7 | 12.5 | 17.7 | 5.4 | 28.5 | 32.1 | 12.5 | 19.3 | 7.7 |
| Rajasthan | 61.3 | 24.1 | 7.4 | 5.9 | 1.3 | 48.9 | 29.0 | 8.7 | 9.2 | 4.1 | 43.8 | 29.6 | 10.4 | 9.1 | 7.0 |
| Tamil Nadu | 36.1 | 41.8 | 11.3 | 8.6 | 2.1 | 30.4 | 39.5 | 14.5 | 13.4 | 2.2 | 30.8 | 41.0 | 12.1 | 14.5 | 1.6 |
| Uttar Pradesh | 61.3 | 22.2 | 6.1 | 7.4 | 2.9 | 49.2 | 29.3 | 8.1 | 8.9 | 4.5 | 42.4 | 28.3 | 9.0 | 11.8 | 8.5 |
| West Bengal | 37.4 | 39.2 | 12.8 | 7.2 | 3.4 | 33.1 | 36.9 | 15.5 | 8.8 | 5.7 | 23.6 | 44.1 | 12.7 | 11.4 | 8.2 |
| Other NE states | 24.8 | 39.5 | 21.0 | 11.8 | 2.8 | 16.0 | 39.0 | 23.8 | 14.7 | 6.5 | | | | | |
| Rest ST and UT | 29.1 | 41.1 | 13.2 | 13.0 | 3.5 | 24.5 | 39.8 | 16.3 | 14.1 | 5.3 | 17.8 | 38.5 | 12.1 | 18.6 | 13.1 |
| All-India | 44.5 | 33.2 | 10.9 | 9.0 | 2.5 | 37.0 | 35.0 | 12.8 | 11.4 | 3.7 | 34.6 | 33.6 | 11.9 | 13.6 | 6.2 |

(contd.)

**Table A4.2** (contd.)

| States | 50,000–1 million | | | | | Urban Total | | | | |
|---|---|---|---|---|---|---|---|---|---|---|
| | Illiterate | Primary & below | Up to middle | Up to secondary | Graduate & above | Illiterate | Primary & below | Up to middle | Up to secondary | Graduate & above |
| Andhra Pradesh | 42.9 | 33.2 | 11.4 | 10.0 | 2.5 | 44.0 | 34.4 | 10.5 | 9.0 | 2.2 |
| Assam | 21.6 | 38.2 | 16.2 | 18.0 | 6.1 | 22.3 | 36.6 | 20.2 | 16.9 | 4.0 |
| Bihar | 47.0 | 28.7 | 11.7 | 8.7 | 3.9 | 51.2 | 28.8 | 10.2 | 7.0 | 2.8 |
| Gujarat | 29.5 | 40.6 | 12.4 | 13.1 | 4.4 | 32.2 | 41.5 | 9.5 | 12.6 | 4.3 |
| Haryana | 35.1 | 28.2 | 11.2 | 18.0 | 7.4 | 34.5 | 30.4 | 11.0 | 17.7 | 6.4 |
| Jammu and Kashmir | 46.5 | 21.7 | 10.2 | 13.4 | 8.3 | 49.0 | 22.6 | 10.2 | 12.1 | 6.2 |
| Karnataka | 36.2 | 33.3 | 14.6 | 13.2 | 2.7 | 35.9 | 33.9 | 13.8 | 13.8 | 2.6 |
| Kerala | 11.7 | 35.2 | 23.9 | 21.7 | 7.5 | 12.5 | 38.8 | 24.6 | 18.5 | 5.6 |
| Madhya Pradesh | 32.8 | 36.1 | 11.1 | 13.1 | 6.9 | 38.3 | 34.7 | 10.0 | 11.4 | 5.5 |
| Maharashtra | 32.1 | 38.1 | 12.2 | 14.2 | 3.5 | 29.3 | 39.2 | 10.9 | 16.1 | 4.5 |
| Orissa | 34.8 | 35.0 | 15.3 | 11.2 | 3.7 | 38.2 | 34.7 | 15.8 | 8.7 | 2.6 |
| Punjab | 29.9 | 32.0 | 12.5 | 18.8 | 6.9 | 32.6 | 30.9 | 11.9 | 18.4 | 6.3 |
| Rajasthan | 45.5 | 29.4 | 9.9 | 9.1 | 6.1 | 53.0 | 26.9 | 8.7 | 7.6 | 3.8 |
| Tamil Nadu | 30.5 | 40.0 | 13.8 | 13.7 | 2.0 | 31.5 | 40.4 | 13.4 | 12.3 | 2.5 |
| Uttar Pradesh | 45.0 | 28.7 | 8.6 | 10.7 | 7.0 | 49.7 | 27.3 | 8.0 | 9.6 | 5.4 |
| West Bengal | 30.5 | 38.9 | 14.7 | 9.5 | 6.4 | 30.8 | 38.4 | 14.2 | 9.9 | 6.8 |
| Other NE states | 16.0 | 39.0 | 23.8 | 14.7 | 6.5 | 20.8 | 39.3 | 22.3 | 13.2 | 4.5 |
| Rest ST and UT | 22.1 | 39.3 | 14.7 | 15.7 | 8.1 | 24.7 | 33.4 | 11.7 | 18.6 | 11.5 |
| All-India | 35.8 | 34.4 | 12.4 | 12.5 | 4.9 | 36.7 | 34.8 | 11.7 | 12.3 | 4.6 |

*Source:* Unit level data of employment and unemployment schedule of 43rd (1987–8) Round of NSSO.

**Table A4.3**   Education Levels (Age 7+), Metro and Non-metro 1987–8, Male

(in per cent)

| States | Non-metro | | | | | Metro | | | | | Metro literacy/ Non-metro litearcy |
|---|---|---|---|---|---|---|---|---|---|---|---|
| | Illiterate | Primary & below | Up to middle | Up to secondary | Graduate & above | Illiterate | Primary & below | Up to middle | Up to secondary | Graduate & above | |
| Andhra Pradesh | 21.3 | 37.7 | 16.6 | 18.1 | 6.4 | 12.1 | 38.2 | 16.2 | 21.5 | 12.0 | 1.12 |
| Assam | 9.7 | 34.7 | 22.2 | 23.3 | 10.1 | | | | | | |
| Bihar | 24.4 | 33.9 | 16.4 | 17.9 | 7.4 | | | | | | |
| Gujarat | 16.1 | 43.7 | 16.4 | 16.8 | 6.9 | 11.3 | 54.8 | 4.1 | 19.5 | 10.3 | 1.06 |
| Haryana | 15.2 | 41.4 | 14.1 | 21.2 | 8.2 | | | | | | |
| Jammu and Kashmir | 29.5 | 28.3 | 14.9 | 18.3 | 9.0 | | | | | | |
| Karnataka | 19.6 | 38.1 | 17.4 | 19.1 | 5.8 | 14.4 | 33.9 | 18.9 | 25.4 | 7.5 | 1.06 |
| Kerala | 4.4 | 40.2 | 28.6 | 19.0 | 7.8 | | | | | | |
| Madhya Pradesh | 16.1 | 41.0 | 16.4 | 15.6 | 10.8 | | | | | | |
| Maharashtra | 14.8 | 38.3 | 17.0 | 23.1 | 6.8 | 7.8 | 43.1 | 9.8 | 28.4 | 10.9 | 1.08 |
| Orissa | 15.5 | 40.1 | 20.9 | 15.7 | 7.9 | | | | | | |
| Punjab | 17.8 | 35.7 | 15.9 | 23.4 | 7.2 | | | | | | |
| Rajasthan | 20.6 | 39.2 | 13.9 | 17.0 | 9.4 | | | | | | |
| Tamil Nadu | 12.8 | 46.3 | 17.5 | 17.9 | 5.5 | 12.8 | 35.1 | 21.5 | 21.8 | 8.8 | 1.00 |
| Uttar Pradesh | 30.3 | 32.7 | 13.0 | 16.0 | 8.1 | 13.7 | 37.9 | 17.4 | 17.9 | 13.1 | 1.24 |
| West Bengal | 15.6 | 43.4 | 16.1 | 17.1 | 7.9 | 10.9 | 39.4 | 17.9 | 16.9 | 15.0 | 1.06 |
| Other NE states | 8.3 | 38.4 | 23.4 | 20.7 | 9.2 | | | | | | |
| Rest ST and UT | 9.8 | 41.4 | 15.9 | 22.9 | 10.0 | 13.3 | 32.8 | 14.9 | 22.7 | 16.2 | 0.96 |
| All-India | 18.8 | 38.9 | 16.5 | 18.3 | 7.6 | 11.1 | 39.3 | 14.3 | 23.2 | 12.1 | 1.09 |

*Source:* Unit level data of employment and unemployment schedule of 43rd (1987–8) Round of NSSO.

**Table A4.4**  Education Levels (Age 7+), Metro and Non-metro 1987–8, Female

(in per cent)

| States | Non-metro | | | | | Metro | | | | | Metro Literacy/ Non-metro Litearcy |
|---|---|---|---|---|---|---|---|---|---|---|---|
| | Illiterate | Primary & below | Up to middle | Up to secondary | Graduate & above | Illiterate | Primary & below | Up to middle | Up to secondary | Graduate & above | |
| Andhra Pradesh | 45.6 | 33.8 | 10.4 | 8.4 | 1.9 | 31.9 | 38.8 | 11.1 | 13.7 | 4.5 | 1.25 |
| Assam | 22.3 | 36.6 | 20.2 | 16.9 | 4.0 | | | | | | |
| Bihar | 51.2 | 28.8 | 10.2 | 7.0 | 2.8 | | | | | | |
| Gujarat | 33.7 | 39.2 | 11.2 | 12.1 | 3.8 | 27.2 | 48.5 | 4.3 | 14.2 | 5.8 | 1.10 |
| Haryana | 34.8 | 30.4 | 10.8 | 17.7 | 6.2 | | | | | | |
| Jammu and Kashmir | 49.0 | 22.6 | 10.2 | 12.0 | 6.2 | | | | | | |
| Karnataka | 38.8 | 33.8 | 13.3 | 11.8 | 2.3 | 25 | 34 | 15.7 | 21.5 | 3.9 | 1.23 |
| Kerala | 12.6 | 38.8 | 24.6 | 18.5 | 5.6 | | | | | | |
| Madhya Pradesh | 38.5 | 34.7 | 10.0 | 11.3 | 5.5 | | | | | | |
| Maharashtra | 35.4 | 36.6 | 12.3 | 12.7 | 2.9 | 20.9 | 42.8 | 8.9 | 20.8 | 6.6 | 1.22 |
| Orissa | 38.3 | 34.6 | 15.7 | 8.7 | 2.7 | | | | | | |
| Punjab | 32.6 | 30.8 | 11.9 | 18.4 | 6.3 | | | | | | |
| Rajasthan | 53.1 | 26.9 | 8.7 | 7.6 | 3.8 | | | | | | |
| Tamil Nadu | 33.1 | 40.8 | 12.7 | 11.4 | 2.1 | 25.3 | 38.6 | 15.9 | 15.7 | 4.4 | 1.12 |
| Uttar Pradesh | 51.7 | 26.0 | 7.6 | 9.3 | 5.3 | 26.2 | 42.3 | 12.9 | 11.9 | 6.7 | 1.53 |
| West Bengal | 33.0 | 39.1 | 14.0 | 8.7 | 5.3 | 24.9 | 36.9 | 14.7 | 12.9 | 10.6 | 1.12 |
| Other NE states | 20.8 | 39.3 | 22.3 | 13.1 | 4.5 | | | | | | |
| Rest ST and UT | 25.1 | 40.1 | 14.1 | 14.5 | 6.1 | 24.6 | 31.6 | 11 | 19.8 | 13.1 | 1.01 |
| All-India | 39.5 | 33.8 | 11.7 | 11.0 | 3.9 | 24.3 | 38.9 | 11.5 | 17.7 | 7.6 | 1.25 |

*Source:* Unit level data of employment and unemployment schedule of 43rd (1987–8) Round of NSSO.

**Table A4.5**  Education Levels (Age 7+), Males, 1993–4

(in per cent)

| States | < 50,000 | | | | | 50,000–200,000 | | | | | 200,000–1 million | | | | |
|---|---|---|---|---|---|---|---|---|---|---|---|---|---|---|---|
| | Illiterate | Primary & below | Up to middle | Up to secondary | Graduate & above | Illiterate | Primary & below | Up to middle | Up to secondary | Graduate & above | Illiterate | Primary & below | Up to middle | Up to secondary | Graduate & above |
| Andhra Pradesh | 25.0 | 35.2 | 15.9 | 17.8 | 6.2 | 19.3 | 31.4 | 17.2 | 23.6 | 8.6 | 19.5 | 32.9 | 14.3 | 24.6 | 8.8 |
| Assam | 7.6 | 29.6 | 28.6 | 23.6 | 10.6 | 6.4 | 24.1 | 22.6 | 36.1 | 10.8 | 10.8 | 27.8 | 18.5 | 29.0 | 14.0 |
| Bihar | 27.1 | 33.0 | 15.8 | 17.2 | 6.9 | 21.6 | 29.0 | 15.8 | 21.9 | 11.7 | 13.6 | 27.7 | 18.8 | 25.0 | 14.9 |
| Gujarat | 13.7 | 47.1 | 15.5 | 17.9 | 5.8 | 7.4 | 30.4 | 16.7 | 30.0 | 15.5 | 12.0 | 43.6 | 19.3 | 20.0 | 5.1 |
| Haryana | 16.9 | 36.6 | 14.0 | 27.2 | 5.4 | 14.6 | 34.1 | 17.5 | 21.8 | 11.9 | 17.3 | 29.1 | 15.7 | 27.6 | 10.4 |
| Jammu and Kashmir | 10.4 | 33.4 | 18.1 | 29.1 | 9.1 | | | | | | 6.9 | 28.4 | 13.6 | 35.5 | 15.7 |
| Karnataka | 19.9 | 31.0 | 15.3 | 24.5 | 9.3 | 15.3 | 32.7 | 19.3 | 25.8 | 6.9 | 14.4 | 30.5 | 17.1 | 24.9 | 13.1 |
| Kerala | 2.7 | 41.6 | 30.1 | 20.6 | 5.0 | 4.3 | 35.8 | 27.2 | 25.8 | 6.9 | 3.8 | 30.7 | 32.3 | 20.4 | 12.8 |
| Madhya Pradesh | 18.7 | 43.0 | 10.7 | 20.9 | 6.7 | 10.6 | 41.2 | 14.0 | 23.5 | 10.7 | 12.1 | 39.7 | 12.9 | 22.7 | 12.6 |
| Maharashtra | 15.0 | 35.8 | 23.4 | 20.3 | 5.6 | 8.9 | 33.9 | 23.8 | 24.4 | 9.0 | 10.1 | 33.5 | 22.8 | 24.1 | 9.5 |
| Orissa | 18.8 | 30.9 | 19.5 | 20.4 | 10.4 | 15.0 | 31.8 | 21.6 | 20.2 | 11.3 | 11.9 | 29.1 | 20.2 | 25.5 | 13.3 |
| Punjab | 20.4 | 33.2 | 12.6 | 26.5 | 7.3 | 16.1 | 32.4 | 14.6 | 27.3 | 9.7 | 16.1 | 35.8 | 13.3 | 24.8 | 10.0 |
| Rajasthan | 23.9 | 36.2 | 16.5 | 17.0 | 6.3 | 23.7 | 34.6 | 14.7 | 19.5 | 7.5 | 13.0 | 33.6 | 17.4 | 22.2 | 13.8 |
| Tamil Nadu | 12.0 | 44.6 | 17.9 | 20.6 | 5.0 | 12.4 | 43.5 | 18.4 | 19.9 | 5.9 | 11.4 | 43.8 | 16.5 | 21.3 | 7.0 |
| Uttar Pradesh | 28.7 | 34.4 | 13.8 | 15.7 | 7.5 | 20.1 | 37.0 | 14.4 | 19.1 | 9.4 | 20.7 | 31.7 | 13.0 | 19.9 | 14.8 |
| West Bengal | 15.7 | 41.3 | 17.4 | 17.5 | 8.2 | 12.4 | 37.4 | 17.3 | 20.6 | 12.4 | 11.6 | 37.9 | 14.3 | 20.9 | 15.3 |
| Other NE states | 8.8 | 36.9 | 24.4 | 21.8 | 8.1 | 3.0 | 30.8 | 19.8 | 31.1 | 15.2 | | | | | |
| Rest ST and UT | 9.3 | 33.6 | 16.3 | 31.9 | 8.8 | 11.1 | 34.6 | 14.2 | 28.9 | 11.1 | 11.5 | 33.1 | 11.7 | 27.4 | 16.4 |
| All-India | 18.6 | 37.7 | 17.2 | 19.7 | 6.9 | 14.3 | 35.5 | 17.4 | 23.0 | 9.9 | 14.1 | 34.0 | 16.9 | 23.0 | 12.1 |

(contd.)

**Table A4.5** (contd.)

| States | 50,000–1 million | | | | | Urban Total | | | | |
|---|---|---|---|---|---|---|---|---|---|---|
| | Illiterate | Primary & below | Up to middle | Up to secondary | Graduate & above | Illiterate | Primary & below | Up to middle | Up to secondary | Graduate & above |
| Andhra Pradesh | 19.4 | 32.0 | 15.9 | 24.0 | 8.7 | 19.8 | 33.2 | 15.9 | 21.9 | 9.2 |
| Assam | 8.6 | 26.0 | 20.5 | 32.5 | 12.4 | 8.1 | 28.0 | 25.0 | 27.5 | 11.4 |
| Bihar | 16.3 | 28.2 | 17.8 | 24.0 | 13.8 | 19.5 | 29.6 | 17.2 | 22.0 | 11.8 |
| Gujarat | 8.4 | 33.3 | 17.3 | 27.9 | 13.2 | 10.5 | 40.5 | 15.8 | 23.2 | 10.1 |
| Haryana | 15.3 | 32.8 | 17.1 | 23.3 | 11.5 | 15.7 | 33.9 | 16.2 | 24.3 | 9.8 |
| Jammu and Kashmir | 6.9 | 28.4 | 13.6 | 35.5 | 15.7 | 8.5 | 30.7 | 15.7 | 32.5 | 12.6 |
| Karnataka | 14.8 | 31.6 | 18.2 | 25.3 | 10.0 | 15.9 | 30.1 | 17.2 | 26.6 | 10.2 |
| Kerala | 4.0 | 33.1 | 29.9 | 23.0 | 10.1 | 3.3 | 37.8 | 30.0 | 21.7 | 7.3 |
| Madhya Pradesh | 11.2 | 40.6 | 13.5 | 23.2 | 11.5 | 14.3 | 40.7 | 11.9 | 23.3 | 9.8 |
| Maharashtra | 9.7 | 33.7 | 23.2 | 24.2 | 9.3 | 9.7 | 32.2 | 22.0 | 25.6 | 10.6 |
| Orissa | 13.2 | 30.3 | 20.8 | 23.3 | 12.5 | 15.6 | 30.5 | 20.2 | 22.1 | 11.6 |
| Punjab | 16.1 | 34.2 | 13.9 | 26.0 | 9.9 | 16.0 | 33.9 | 14.5 | 26.5 | 9.1 |
| Rajasthan | 18.2 | 34.1 | 16.1 | 20.9 | 10.7 | 19.0 | 34.3 | 16.6 | 19.6 | 10.6 |
| Tamil Nadu | 11.9 | 43.6 | 17.6 | 20.5 | 6.3 | 11.5 | 41.7 | 17.6 | 21.8 | 7.4 |
| Uttar Pradesh | 20.4 | 34.0 | 13.6 | 19.5 | 12.5 | 22.6 | 34.1 | 13.6 | 18.5 | 11.2 |
| West Bengal | 12.1 | 37.6 | 16.1 | 20.7 | 13.6 | 12.2 | 37.7 | 17.3 | 20.3 | 12.6 |
| Other NE states | 3.0 | 30.8 | 19.8 | 31.1 | 15.2 | 6.4 | 34.4 | 22.5 | 25.6 | 11.0 |
| Rest ST and UT | 11.3 | 33.6 | 12.6 | 27.9 | 14.6 | 15.6 | 31.8 | 11.9 | 23.7 | 17.1 |
| All-India | 14.2 | 34.7 | 17.1 | 23.0 | 11.0 | 14.7 | 35.1 | 17.0 | 22.6 | 10.6 |

*Source*: Unit level data of employment and unemployment schedule of 50th (1993–4) Round of NSSO.

**Table A4.6**  Education Levels (Age 7+), Females, 1993–4

(in per cent)

| States | < 50,000 | | | | | 50,000–200,000 | | | | | 200,000–1 million | | | | |
|---|---|---|---|---|---|---|---|---|---|---|---|---|---|---|---|
| | Illiterate | Primary & below | Up to middle | Up to secondary | Graduate & above | Illiterate | Primary & below | Up to middle | Up to secondary | Graduate & above | Illiterate | Primary & below | Up to middle | Up to secondary | Graduate & above |
| Andhra Pradesh | 50.1 | 29.6 | 10.4 | 7.8 | 2.1 | 39.5 | 33.4 | 12.4 | 11.5 | 3.2 | 34.3 | 35.8 | 12.2 | 13.3 | 4.4 |
| Assam | 16.2 | 34.0 | 26.5 | 18.4 | 4.9 | 17.2 | 31.3 | 21.3 | 23.7 | 6.5 | 19.9 | 31.4 | 19.7 | 21.6 | 7.4 |
| Bihar | 53.2 | 26.0 | 9.0 | 9.8 | 2.1 | 44.4 | 25.7 | 13.9 | 11.5 | 4.6 | 35.2 | 28.6 | 12.4 | 17.0 | 6.8 |
| Gujarat | 33.9 | 40.7 | 11.0 | 12.0 | 2.5 | 20.6 | 31.3 | 17.7 | 22.1 | 8.4 | 29.7 | 36.1 | 12.0 | 18.1 | 4.1 |
| Haryana | 38.6 | 30.8 | 8.9 | 18.3 | 3.5 | 30.6 | 32.8 | 8.5 | 20.2 | 7.8 | 27.4 | 40.5 | 10.7 | 13.1 | 8.4 |
| Jammu and Kashmir | 23.0 | 31.6 | 15.5 | 22.3 | 7.7 | | | | | | 20.1 | 25.6 | 15.1 | 28.2 | 11.1 |
| Karnataka | 36.9 | 30.2 | 13.5 | 15.5 | 3.9 | 34.0 | 29.5 | 18.5 | 15.5 | 2.6 | 30.1 | 28.5 | 14.8 | 19.9 | 6.7 |
| Kerala | 10.1 | 38.0 | 28.3 | 19.8 | 3.8 | 9.6 | 35.6 | 26.7 | 20.4 | 7.8 | 9.4 | 32.3 | 27.4 | 24.5 | 6.4 |
| Madhya Pradesh | 44.1 | 35.3 | 7.7 | 10.3 | 2.6 | 30.3 | 37.2 | 10.1 | 15.9 | 6.5 | 31.7 | 34.3 | 11.1 | 13.7 | 9.2 |
| Maharashtra | 36.3 | 32.9 | 16.8 | 11.4 | 2.6 | 29.0 | 33.3 | 19.2 | 14.1 | 4.5 | 28.0 | 31.2 | 20.4 | 15.9 | 4.6 |
| Orissa | 39.3 | 29.8 | 14.3 | 12.2 | 4.5 | 32.2 | 34.2 | 16.5 | 9.5 | 7.6 | 27.7 | 28.3 | 22.0 | 17.6 | 4.5 |
| Punjab | 32.5 | 29.9 | 9.9 | 22.0 | 5.8 | 25.0 | 29.2 | 14.3 | 23.9 | 7.6 | 23.6 | 34.4 | 11.0 | 23.3 | 7.7 |
| Rajasthan | 54.0 | 28.7 | 8.7 | 6.7 | 1.9 | 55.5 | 24.2 | 8.5 | 8.7 | 3.1 | 31.1 | 34.0 | 14.9 | 12.3 | 7.7 |
| Tamil Nadu | 28.7 | 41.0 | 13.3 | 14.6 | 2.5 | 30.4 | 38.2 | 14.8 | 14.7 | 1.9 | 25.7 | 40.7 | 13.5 | 16.3 | 3.8 |
| Uttar Pradesh | 52.2 | 26.1 | 8.2 | 9.7 | 3.8 | 42.2 | 29.6 | 10.4 | 13.2 | 4.6 | 36.0 | 28.6 | 10.6 | 15.7 | 9.1 |
| West Bengal | 33.0 | 39.2 | 13.3 | 10.8 | 3.8 | 24.1 | 36.5 | 16.8 | 14.4 | 8.3 | 23.6 | 35.6 | 15.7 | 16.1 | 9.1 |
| Other NE states | 21.0 | 40.3 | 20.5 | 15.1 | 3.2 | 11.0 | 33.1 | 22.8 | 25.4 | 7.8 | | | | | |
| Rest ST and UT | 21.3 | 34.0 | 15.1 | 23.8 | 5.7 | 32.5 | 27.6 | 10.7 | 21.8 | 7.5 | 20.4 | 35.0 | 13.9 | 20.7 | 10.0 |
| All-India | 38.5 | 33.2 | 12.8 | 12.4 | 3.1 | 32.0 | 32.9 | 14.4 | 15.3 | 5.3 | 29.4 | 32.8 | 14.5 | 16.5 | 6.8 |

(contd.)

**Table A4.6** (contd.)

| States | 50,000–1 million | | | | | Urban Total | | | | |
|---|---|---|---|---|---|---|---|---|---|---|
| | Illiterate | Primary & below | Up to middle | Up to secondary | Graduate & above | Illiterate | Primary & below | Up to middle | Up to secondary | Graduate & above |
| Andhra Pradesh | 37.3 | 34.4 | 12.3 | 12.3 | 3.7 | 40.0 | 32.7 | 11.9 | 11.8 | 3.7 |
| Assam | 18.6 | 31.3 | 20.5 | 22.6 | 7.0 | 17.3 | 32.8 | 23.8 | 20.3 | 5.8 |
| Bihar | 38.4 | 27.6 | 12.9 | 15.1 | 6.0 | 43.0 | 27.1 | 11.7 | 13.4 | 4.8 |
| Gujarat | 22.4 | 32.2 | 16.5 | 21.3 | 7.6 | 26.8 | 37.0 | 12.9 | 17.4 | 5.9 |
| Haryana | 29.9 | 34.7 | 9.0 | 18.5 | 7.9 | 32.1 | 33.7 | 9.0 | 18.5 | 6.8 |
| Jammu and Kashmir | 20.1 | 25.6 | 15.1 | 28.1 | 11.1 | 21.5 | 28.5 | 15.3 | 25.4 | 9.5 |
| Karnataka | 32.1 | 29.1 | 16.7 | 17.6 | 4.5 | 31.2 | 29.2 | 16.4 | 18.4 | 4.9 |
| Kerala | 9.5 | 33.8 | 27.1 | 22.6 | 7.1 | 9.8 | 36.2 | 27.7 | 21.1 | 5.3 |
| Madhya Pradesh | 30.9 | 35.9 | 10.5 | 15.0 | 7.7 | 35.6 | 35.7 | 9.0 | 13.5 | 6.2 |
| Maharashtra | 28.3 | 32.0 | 19.9 | 15.2 | 4.6 | 24.9 | 31.8 | 18.1 | 18.5 | 6.8 |
| Orissa | 29.8 | 31.1 | 19.4 | 13.8 | 6.0 | 34.0 | 30.5 | 17.1 | 13.1 | 5.3 |
| Punjab | 24.3 | 31.8 | 12.7 | 23.6 | 7.7 | 25.6 | 31.3 | 12.2 | 23.0 | 7.9 |
| Rajasthan | 42.8 | 29.3 | 11.8 | 10.6 | 5.5 | 45.4 | 29.2 | 10.4 | 10.2 | 4.7 |
| Tamil Nadu | 28.5 | 39.2 | 14.3 | 15.4 | 2.7 | 27.5 | 38.7 | 14.3 | 15.9 | 3.6 |
| Uttar Pradesh | 38.7 | 29.1 | 10.5 | 14.6 | 7.1 | 42.2 | 28.1 | 9.8 | 13.2 | 6.6 |
| West Bengal | 23.9 | 36.1 | 16.4 | 15.0 | 8.6 | 24.6 | 37.5 | 15.6 | 14.4 | 8.0 |
| Other NE states | 10.9 | 33.1 | 22.8 | 25.4 | 7.8 | 16.8 | 37.3 | 21.4 | 19.4 | 5.1 |
| Rest ST and UT | 24.6 | 32.5 | 12.8 | 21.1 | 9.1 | 26.4 | 25.9 | 10.8 | 21.2 | 15.7 |
| All-India | 30.8 | 32.9 | 14.5 | 15.9 | 6.0 | 31.4 | 32.7 | 13.9 | 15.9 | 6.2 |

*Source:* Unit level data of employment and unemployment schedule of 50th (1993–4) Round of NSSO.

**Table A4.7**  Education Levels (Age 7+), Metro and Non-metro 1993–4, Male

(in per cent)

| States | Non-metro | | | | | Metro | | | | | Metro Literacy/ Non-metro Litearcy |
|---|---|---|---|---|---|---|---|---|---|---|---|
| | Illiterate | Primary & below | Up to middle | Up to secondary | Graduate & above | Illiterate | Primary & below | Up to middle | Up to secondary | Graduate & above | |
| Andhra Pradesh | 21.2 | 33.1 | 15.9 | 21.9 | 7.8 | 7.8 | 34.6 | 15.7 | 21.9 | 20.1 | 1.17 |
| Assam | 8.0 | 28.0 | 25.1 | 27.5 | 11.4 | | | | | | |
| Bihar | 19.6 | 29.6 | 17.2 | 21.9 | 11.7 | | | | | | |
| Gujarat | 10.7 | 39.2 | 16.5 | 23.6 | 10.0 | 10.2 | 43.2 | 14.3 | 22.2 | 10.1 | 1.01 |
| Haryana | 15.7 | 33.9 | 16.2 | 24.4 | 9.8 | | | | | | |
| Jammu and Kashmir | 8.6 | 30.7 | 15.7 | 32.4 | 12.5 | | | | | | |
| Karnataka | 17.2 | 31.3 | 16.9 | 25.0 | 9.7 | 11.0 | 25.3 | 18.5 | 33.1 | 12.2 | 1.07 |
| Kerala | 3.3 | 37.9 | 30.0 | 21.6 | 7.2 | | | | | | |
| Madhya Pradesh | 14.6 | 41.7 | 12.3 | 22.1 | 9.3 | 12.8 | 34.8 | 9.4 | 30.3 | 12.6 | 1.02 |
| Maharashtra | 11.7 | 34.4 | 23.2 | 22.7 | 7.9 | 7.5 | 29.5 | 20.5 | 28.8 | 13.7 | 1.05 |
| Orissa | 15.6 | 30.5 | 20.2 | 22.0 | 11.6 | | | | | | |
| Punjab | 17.3 | 33.9 | 13.6 | 26.1 | 9.2 | 10.1 | 33.7 | 19.0 | 28.4 | 8.9 | 1.09 |
| Rajasthan | 20.6 | 35.0 | 16.2 | 19.3 | 8.9 | 9.8 | 30.3 | 18.5 | 21.3 | 20.1 | 1.14 |
| Tamil Nadu | 12.0 | 44.0 | 17.7 | 20.5 | 5.8 | 9.8 | 33.4 | 17.2 | 26.5 | 13.1 | 1.03 |
| Uttar Pradesh | 23.8 | 34.1 | 13.7 | 18.0 | 10.5 | 14.3 | 34.0 | 12.9 | 22.1 | 16.8 | 1.12 |
| West Bengal | 13.1 | 38.7 | 16.5 | 19.7 | 12.0 | 8.5 | 34.2 | 20.2 | 22.4 | 14.7 | 1.05 |
| Other NE states | 6.5 | 34.5 | 22.6 | 25.6 | 11.0 | | | | | | |
| Rest ST and UT | 10.5 | 33.6 | 14.1 | 29.5 | 12.3 | 16.9 | 31.3 | 11.3 | 22.2 | 18.3 | 0.93 |
| All-India | 15.9 | 35.9 | 17.2 | 21.7 | 9.4 | 10.8 | 32.5 | 16.5 | 25.6 | 14.6 | 1.06 |

*Source:* Unit level data of employment and unemployment schedule of 50th (1993–4) Round of NSSO.

**Table A4.8**  Education Levels (Age 7+), Metro and Non-metro 1993–4, Female

(in per cent)

| States | Non-metro | | | | | Metro | | | | | Metro Literacy/ Non-metro Litearcy |
|---|---|---|---|---|---|---|---|---|---|---|---|
| | Illiterate | Primary & below | Up to middle | Up to secondary | Graduate & above | Illiterate | Primary & below | Up to middle | Up to secondary | Graduate & above | |
| Andhra Pradesh | 41.7 | 32.8 | 11.7 | 10.7 | 3.2 | 25.4 | 31.9 | 13.6 | 20.6 | 8.5 | 1.28 |
| Assam | 17.3 | 32.8 | 23.8 | 20.3 | 5.8 | | | | | | |
| Bihar | 43.1 | 27.1 | 11.7 | 13.4 | 4.8 | | | | | | |
| Gujarat | 27.2 | 35.8 | 14.2 | 17.4 | 5.4 | 26.1 | 40.0 | 9.6 | 17.2 | 7.1 | 1.02 |
| Haryana | 32.1 | 33.7 | 9.0 | 18.4 | 6.8 | | | | | | |
| Jammu and Kashmir | 21.5 | 28.4 | 15.3 | 25.4 | 9.5 | | | | | | |
| Karnataka | 34.3 | 29.6 | 15.2 | 16.6 | 4.3 | 18.7 | 27.4 | 20.9 | 25.5 | 7.5 | 1.24 |
| Kerala | 9.8 | 36.1 | 27.7 | 21.0 | 5.2 | | | | | | |
| Madhya Pradesh | 36.8 | 35.7 | 9.3 | 12.9 | 5.4 | 29.0 | 36.2 | 7.0 | 17.3 | 10.5 | 1.12 |
| Maharashtra | 31.4 | 32.3 | 18.8 | 13.8 | 3.8 | 17.1 | 31.2 | 17.3 | 24.2 | 10.2 | 1.21 |
| Orissa | 34.0 | 30.5 | 17.1 | 13.0 | 5.3 | | | | | | |
| Punjab | 26.5 | 31.3 | 11.9 | 23.2 | 7.1 | 20.5 | 31.7 | 13.7 | 22.2 | 11.9 | 1.08 |
| Rajasthan | 47.7 | 29.0 | 10.5 | 8.9 | 4.0 | 32.5 | 30.4 | 9.5 | 18.4 | 9.2 | 1.29 |
| Tamil Nadu | 28.5 | 40.0 | 13.8 | 15.0 | 2.6 | 22.9 | 33.8 | 16.3 | 19.5 | 7.6 | 1.08 |
| Uttar Pradesh | 44.2 | 27.8 | 9.6 | 12.6 | 5.8 | 27.5 | 29.9 | 11.4 | 17.9 | 13.3 | 1.30 |
| West Bengal | 26.6 | 37.0 | 15.5 | 13.8 | 7.2 | 16.4 | 39.5 | 16.0 | 16.9 | 11.2 | 1.14 |
| Other NE states | 16.9 | 37.3 | 21.4 | 19.3 | 5.1 | | | | | | |
| Rest ST and UT | 23.3 | 33.0 | 13.7 | 22.1 | 7.9 | 27.2 | 23.9 | 9.9 | 21.0 | 18.0 | 0.95 |
| All-India | 33.8 | 33.0 | 13.8 | 14.5 | 4.9 | 22.4 | 31.7 | 14.1 | 21.0 | 11.0 | 1.17 |

*Source:* Unit level data of employment and unemployment schedule of 50th (1993–4) Round of NSSO.

**Table A4.9**  Education Levels (Age 7+), Male, 1999–2000

(in per cent)

| States | < 50,000 | | | | | 50,000–1 million | | | | | Total Urban | | | | |
|---|---|---|---|---|---|---|---|---|---|---|---|---|---|---|---|
| | Illiterate | Primary & below | Up to middle | Up to secondary | Graduate & above | Illiterate | Primary & below | Up to middle | Up to secondary | Graduate & above | Illiterate | Primary & below | Up to middle | Up to secondary | Graduate & above |
| Andhra Pradesh | 21.9 | 33.4 | 10.7 | 26.0 | 8.0 | 16.9 | 32.1 | 15.3 | 22.5 | 13.2 | 17.2 | 31.6 | 14.4 | 24.2 | 12.7 |
| Assam | 8.6 | 34.8 | 22.8 | 23.9 | 10.0 | 6.0 | 24.9 | 18.5 | 31.4 | 19.2 | 7.4 | 30.4 | 20.9 | 27.2 | 14.1 |
| Bihar | 23.8 | 29.5 | 16.7 | 19.9 | 10.2 | 18.4 | 31.1 | 12.5 | 23.0 | 15.1 | 19.7 | 29.0 | 13.8 | 22.5 | 15.0 |
| Gujarat | 11.9 | 34.9 | 20.1 | 23.5 | 9.6 | 10.6 | 35.9 | 18.8 | 24.0 | 10.7 | 9.7 | 32.4 | 21.1 | 25.7 | 11.0 |
| Haryana | 18.9 | 33.7 | 14.3 | 27.2 | 6.0 | 12.9 | 29.0 | 19.1 | 27.6 | 11.4 | 14.6 | 30.3 | 17.7 | 27.5 | 9.9 |
| Jammu and Kashmir | 14.6 | 32.9 | 17.2 | 22.8 | 12.4 | 10.0 | 27.5 | 17.9 | 31.6 | 13.0 | 12.0 | 29.8 | 17.6 | 27.9 | 12.7 |
| Karnataka | 16.6 | 29.2 | 21.5 | 24.2 | 8.5 | 11.6 | 25.2 | 17.5 | 29.7 | 16.0 | 12.3 | 25.2 | 19.4 | 29.4 | 13.7 |
| Kerala | 3.1 | 35.5 | 31.9 | 24.5 | 5.1 | 2.9 | 28.3 | 33.1 | 26.7 | 8.9 | 3.0 | 32.2 | 32.4 | 25.5 | 6.9 |
| Madhya Pradesh | 15.2 | 38.1 | 14.9 | 20.6 | 11.2 | 11.5 | 37.7 | 14.5 | 21.8 | 14.5 | 13.9 | 37.4 | 14.8 | 21.0 | 12.9 |
| Maharashtra | 10.8 | 33.9 | 25.4 | 22.3 | 7.7 | 8.8 | 30.6 | 21.4 | 27.2 | 12.0 | 7.6 | 30.6 | 22.8 | 27.7 | 11.4 |
| Orissa | 16.9 | 33.9 | 18.9 | 20.7 | 9.6 | 12.7 | 30.7 | 22.5 | 22.7 | 11.5 | 14.6 | 32.2 | 20.9 | 21.8 | 10.6 |
| Punjab | 19.0 | 35.7 | 13.6 | 26.0 | 5.8 | 13.7 | 31.4 | 14.7 | 29.4 | 10.8 | 15.4 | 33.3 | 14.6 | 27.5 | 9.2 |
| Rajasthan | 14.2 | 39.5 | 16.1 | 22.3 | 8.0 | 15.8 | 35.5 | 16.8 | 21.1 | 10.8 | 13.9 | 34.7 | 16.3 | 22.4 | 12.8 |
| Tamil Nadu | 11.9 | 36.4 | 18.4 | 26.2 | 7.1 | 8.9 | 34.8 | 18.2 | 26.4 | 11.8 | 9.2 | 34.4 | 19.0 | 27.1 | 10.4 |
| Uttar Pradesh | 29.4 | 34.4 | 14.3 | 15.2 | 6.7 | 19.5 | 31.0 | 15.1 | 21.2 | 13.3 | 22.0 | 32.3 | 15.1 | 19.4 | 11.3 |
| West Bengal | 14.7 | 34.4 | 19.0 | 17.2 | 14.8 | 12.0 | 32.9 | 18.8 | 21.9 | 14.4 | 12.6 | 32.6 | 18.6 | 20.0 | 16.2 |
| Other NE states | 7.5 | 37.8 | 21.6 | 24.4 | 8.7 | 4.1 | 24.7 | 22.1 | 31.1 | 18.0 | 6.1 | 32.2 | 21.8 | 27.3 | 12.7 |
| Rest ST and UT | 8.6 | 29.8 | 15.7 | 35.1 | 10.9 | 14.1 | 28.7 | 15.6 | 29.7 | 11.9 | 9.2 | 26.0 | 16.6 | 27.9 | 20.3 |
| All-India | 16.6 | 34.6 | 18.1 | 22.1 | 8.6 | 13.2 | 31.8 | 17.6 | 24.5 | 12.9 | 13.2 | 31.7 | 18.2 | 24.4 | 12.4 |

*Source:* Unit level data of employment and unemployment schedule of 55th (1999–2000) Round of NSSO.

**Table A4.10**  Education Levels (Age 7+), Female, 1999–2000

(in per cent)

| States | < 50,000 | | | | | 50,000–1 million | | | | | Total Urban | | | | |
|---|---|---|---|---|---|---|---|---|---|---|---|---|---|---|---|
| | Illiterate | Primary & below | Up to middle | Up to secondary | Graduate & above | Illiterate | Primary & below | Up to middle | Up to secondary | Graduate & above | Illiterate | Primary & below | Up to middle | Up to secondary | Graduate & above |
| Andhra Pradesh | 40.7 | 30.4 | 12.2 | 13.1 | 3.7 | 33.7 | 27.2 | 16.3 | 16.1 | 6.8 | 33.8 | 28.1 | 15.3 | 16.2 | 6.6 |
| Assam | 21.8 | 30.9 | 23.2 | 19.6 | 4.6 | 14.1 | 25.2 | 22.6 | 25.9 | 12.3 | 18.2 | 28.1 | 22.9 | 22.6 | 8.3 |
| Bihar | 47.1 | 28.1 | 9.6 | 11.9 | 3.3 | 38.3 | 27.3 | 13.3 | 14.9 | 6.3 | 41.7 | 25.7 | 11.1 | 15.6 | 5.9 |
| Gujarat | 27.5 | 30.2 | 16.5 | 19.0 | 6.9 | 22.8 | 34.0 | 17.4 | 19.5 | 6.2 | 23.0 | 31.8 | 17.6 | 20.1 | 7.6 |
| Haryana | 39.5 | 31.8 | 7.2 | 15.4 | 6.0 | 29.2 | 26.4 | 14.4 | 20.8 | 9.3 | 32.4 | 28.0 | 12.2 | 19.1 | 8.3 |
| Jammu and Kashmir | 38.6 | 24.8 | 13.0 | 19.7 | 4.0 | 28.5 | 23.4 | 12.2 | 27.8 | 8.1 | 32.8 | 24.0 | 12.5 | 24.3 | 6.4 |
| Karnataka | 32.0 | 28.1 | 19.1 | 16.9 | 3.9 | 22.5 | 24.8 | 18.0 | 26.5 | 8.3 | 23.6 | 25.3 | 18.3 | 24.9 | 8.0 |
| Kerala | 9.3 | 32.6 | 31.6 | 21.6 | 5.0 | 7.6 | 29.1 | 28.5 | 28.1 | 6.8 | 8.5 | 31.0 | 30.2 | 24.5 | 5.8 |
| Madhya Pradesh | 35.7 | 34.1 | 11.2 | 14.5 | 4.6 | 29.2 | 34.0 | 12.3 | 15.9 | 8.6 | 32.1 | 33.9 | 11.7 | 15.2 | 7.1 |
| Maharashtra | 27.7 | 32.4 | 21.5 | 14.8 | 3.5 | 22.8 | 30.5 | 20.5 | 19.1 | 7.2 | 20.9 | 32.1 | 19.6 | 19.2 | 8.2 |
| Orissa | 38.0 | 30.8 | 14.4 | 12.3 | 4.5 | 28.5 | 31.1 | 20.3 | 15.1 | 5.0 | 32.8 | 30.9 | 17.6 | 13.8 | 4.8 |
| Punjab | 33.4 | 28.5 | 11.9 | 21.6 | 4.6 | 24.0 | 26.7 | 10.2 | 27.3 | 11.9 | 27.5 | 27.1 | 10.7 | 25.1 | 9.7 |
| Rajasthan | 47.4 | 29.1 | 9.1 | 10.4 | 4.0 | 38.5 | 32.2 | 11.2 | 12.2 | 5.9 | 39.2 | 30.1 | 10.7 | 13.1 | 6.9 |
| Tamil Nadu | 24.8 | 37.2 | 15.7 | 17.1 | 5.3 | 22.6 | 35.5 | 15.4 | 19.0 | 7.5 | 22.3 | 35.8 | 15.9 | 18.9 | 7.1 |
| Uttar Pradesh | 48.3 | 29.8 | 8.3 | 10.1 | 3.4 | 36.4 | 27.3 | 9.3 | 16.1 | 10.9 | 38.1 | 30.1 | 9.7 | 14.3 | 7.8 |
| West Bengal | 28.8 | 34.7 | 14.9 | 15.0 | 6.7 | 23.7 | 34.9 | 17.3 | 16.6 | 7.4 | 24.1 | 33.4 | 16.3 | 17.3 | 8.9 |
| Other NE states | 16.5 | 36.9 | 21.8 | 19.3 | 5.6 | 11.5 | 29.9 | 23.0 | 23.4 | 12.1 | 14.4 | 33.9 | 22.3 | 21.1 | 8.4 |
| Rest ST and UT | 19.2 | 32.5 | 16.1 | 22.6 | 9.5 | 24.8 | 33.5 | 12.8 | 20.9 | 8.0 | 19.9 | 28.5 | 12.5 | 22.3 | 16.8 |
| All-India | 33.6 | 31.7 | 14.9 | 15.2 | 4.6 | 27.8 | 30.1 | 15.7 | 18.6 | 7.9 | 27.8 | 30.7 | 15.3 | 18.2 | 7.9 |

*Source:* Unit level data of employment and unemployment schedule of 55th (1999–2000) Round of NSSO.

**Table A4.11**  Education Levels (Age 7+), Metro and Non-metro 1999–2000, Male

(in per cent)

| States | Non-metro | | | | | Metro | | | | | Metro Literacy/ Non-metro Litearcy |
| --- | --- | --- | --- | --- | --- | --- | --- | --- | --- | --- | --- |
| | Illiterate | Primary & below | Up to middle | Up to secondary | Graduate & above | Illiterate | Primary & below | Up to middle | Up to secondary | Graduate & above | |
| Andhra Pradesh | 18.1 | 32.4 | 14.2 | 23.4 | 11.9 | 12.9 | 28.4 | 15.1 | 28.0 | 15.7 | 1.06 |
| Assam | 7.5 | 30.5 | 20.9 | 27.2 | 14.0 | | | | | | 1.06 |
| Bihar | 20.4 | 30.5 | 14.1 | 21.8 | 13.2 | 15.6 | 19.8 | 12.4 | 26.5 | 25.7 | 1.06 |
| Gujarat | 11.2 | 35.5 | 19.4 | 23.8 | 10.2 | 6.9 | 26.8 | 24.4 | 29.3 | 12.5 | 1.05 |
| Haryana | 14.6 | 30.4 | 17.7 | 27.5 | 9.8 | | | | | | |
| Jammu and Kashmir | 11.9 | 29.8 | 17.6 | 27.9 | 12.8 | | | | | | |
| Karnataka | 13.9 | 27.0 | 19.3 | 27.2 | 12.6 | 7.6 | 19.7 | 19.4 | 36.2 | 17.2 | 1.07 |
| Kerala | 3.0 | 32.2 | 32.4 | 25.5 | 6.8 | | | | | | 0.96 |
| Madhya Pradesh | 13.5 | 37.9 | 14.7 | 21.2 | 12.7 | 17.0 | 33.2 | 15.4 | 20.1 | 14.3 | 1.04 |
| Maharashtra | 9.4 | 31.5 | 22.5 | 25.8 | 10.8 | 5.8 | 29.7 | 22.9 | 29.6 | 11.9 | 1.04 |
| Orissa | 14.6 | 32.2 | 20.8 | 21.8 | 10.6 | | | | | | |
| Punjab | 15.4 | 32.8 | 14.3 | 28.3 | 9.1 | 15.3 | 35.3 | 16.1 | 23.8 | 9.5 | 1.00 |
| Rajasthan | 15.1 | 37.2 | 16.5 | 21.6 | 9.6 | 6.5 | 19.4 | 14.8 | 27.0 | 32.4 | 1.10 |
| Tamil Nadu | 10.2 | 35.5 | 18.3 | 26.3 | 9.7 | 6.4 | 31.4 | 20.8 | 29.2 | 12.2 | 1.04 |
| Uttar Pradesh | 23.8 | 32.5 | 14.7 | 18.6 | 10.4 | 17.7 | 31.9 | 16.0 | 21.1 | 13.3 | 1.08 |
| West Bengal | 12.7 | 33.3 | 18.8 | 20.6 | 14.5 | 12.3 | 30.7 | 17.9 | 18.2 | 20.9 | 1.00 |
| Other NE states | 6.1 | 32.3 | 21.8 | 27.2 | 12.6 | | | | | | |
| Rest ST and UT | 12.3 | 29.0 | 15.6 | 31.4 | 11.6 | 7.5 | 24.4 | 17.2 | 26.0 | 25.0 | 1.05 |
| All-India | 14.5 | 32.9 | 17.8 | 23.6 | 11.2 | 9.7 | 28.5 | 19.3 | 26.8 | 15.8 | 1.06 |

*Source:* Unit level data of employment and unemployment schedule of 55th (1999–2000) Round of NSSO.

**Table A4.12**   Education Levels (Age 7+), Metro and Non-metro 1999–2000, Female

(in per cent)

| States | Non-metro | | | | | Metro | | | | | Metro Literacy/ Non-metro Literarcy |
|---|---|---|---|---|---|---|---|---|---|---|---|
| | Illiterate | Primary & below | Up to middle | Up to secondary | Graduate & above | Illiterate | Primary & below | Up to middle | Up to secondary | Graduate & above | |
| Andhra Pradesh | 35.4 | 28.0 | 15.3 | 15.3 | 6.0 | 26.5 | 28.6 | 15.4 | 20.3 | 9.1 | 1.14 |
| Assam | 18.2 | 28.2 | 22.9 | 22.5 | 8.2 | | | | | | |
| Bihar | 41.6 | 27.6 | 11.9 | 13.7 | 5.1 | 42.1 | 15.1 | 6.8 | 25.9 | 10.1 | 0.99 |
| Gujarat | 24.7 | 32.4 | 17.0 | 19.3 | 6.5 | 19.6 | 30.5 | 18.6 | 21.6 | 9.7 | 1.07 |
| Haryana | 32.2 | 28.0 | 12.3 | 19.2 | 8.3 | | | | | | |
| Jammu and Kashmir | 32.8 | 24.0 | 12.5 | 24.3 | 6.3 | | | | | | |
| Karnataka | 26.9 | 26.3 | 18.5 | 22.0 | 6.3 | 15.2 | 22.7 | 17.5 | 32.0 | 12.6 | 1.16 |
| Kerala | 8.5 | 31.0 | 30.2 | 24.5 | 5.8 | | | | | | |
| Madhya Pradesh | 32.6 | 34.0 | 11.7 | 15.2 | 6.5 | 28.4 | 33.2 | 11.7 | 15.7 | 11.0 | 1.06 |
| Maharashtra | 24.3 | 31.1 | 20.8 | 17.8 | 6.1 | 17.5 | 33.1 | 18.5 | 20.7 | 10.3 | 1.09 |
| Orissa | 32.8 | 31.0 | 17.7 | 13.8 | 4.8 | | | | | | |
| Punjab | 27.0 | 27.3 | 10.7 | 25.4 | 9.5 | 30.3 | 26.4 | 10.1 | 22.7 | 10.5 | 0.95 |
| Rajasthan | 42.3 | 30.9 | 10.3 | 11.4 | 5.1 | 18.2 | 24.9 | 13.3 | 24.8 | 18.8 | 1.42 |
| Tamil Nadu | 23.6 | 36.2 | 15.5 | 18.1 | 6.5 | 18.5 | 34.3 | 17.0 | 21.3 | 8.9 | 1.07 |
| Uttar Pradesh | 41.5 | 28.4 | 8.9 | 13.5 | 7.7 | 29.9 | 34.3 | 11.6 | 16.1 | 8.1 | 1.20 |
| West Bengal | 25.1 | 34.9 | 16.6 | 16.2 | 7.2 | 21.4 | 29.3 | 15.2 | 20.6 | 13.6 | 1.05 |
| Other NE states | 14.4 | 33.9 | 22.3 | 21.0 | 8.4 | | | | | | |
| Rest ST and UT | 23.2 | 33.2 | 13.8 | 21.4 | 8.4 | 17.9 | 25.7 | 11.8 | 22.8 | 21.8 | 1.07 |
| All-India | 30.1 | 30.7 | 15.4 | 17.3 | 6.6 | 21.6 | 30.4 | 15.3 | 21.1 | 11.6 | 1.12 |

*Source:* Unit level data of employment and unemployment schedule of 55th (1999–2000) Round of NSSO.

**Table A4.13**   Education Levels (Age 7+), 2004–5, Metro and Non-metro, Male

(in per cent)

| States | Non-metro | | | | | Metro | | | | | Metro Literacy/ Non-metro Litearcy |
|---|---|---|---|---|---|---|---|---|---|---|---|
| | Illiterate | Primary & below | Up to middle | Up to secondary | Graduate & above | Illiterate | Primary & below | Up to middle | Up to secondary | Graduate & above | |
| Andhra Pradesh | 16.9 | 30.6 | 15.4 | 26.3 | 10.9 | 12.4 | 26.3 | 14.6 | 22.0 | 24.7 | 1.05 |
| Assam | 6.7 | 29.9 | 21.8 | 24.8 | 16.8 | | | | | | |
| Bihar | 13.7 | 28.3 | 17.1 | 25.9 | 15.1 | 3.9 | 26.8 | 15.3 | 32.9 | 21.2 | 1.11 |
| Gujarat | 7.0 | 32.7 | 21.5 | 28.3 | 10.6 | 6.9 | 29.1 | 18.9 | 32.4 | 12.7 | 1.00 |
| Haryana | 12.7 | 32.2 | 11.7 | 31.2 | 12.3 | 7.8 | 32.5 | 18.1 | 32.3 | 9.4 | 1.06 |
| Jammu and Kashmir | 14.5 | 28.4 | 20.5 | 28.1 | 8.4 | | | | | | |
| Karnataka | 9.7 | 30.3 | 17.9 | 29.9 | 12.2 | 8.5 | 21.9 | 22.3 | 32.2 | 15.1 | 1.01 |
| Kerala | 3.4 | 31.4 | 29.3 | 26.5 | 9.4 | | | | | | |
| Madhya Pradesh | 12.2 | 37.1 | 13.4 | 24.0 | 13.4 | 6.5 | 34.8 | 11.9 | 23.0 | 23.8 | 1.06 |
| Maharashtra | 9.0 | 28.5 | 24.7 | 27.3 | 10.5 | 5.6 | 24.5 | 25.6 | 30.5 | 13.8 | 1.04 |
| Orissa | 12.6 | 28.0 | 21.0 | 25.1 | 13.3 | | | | | | |
| Punjab | 12.4 | 29.7 | 12.3 | 34.0 | 11.6 | 14.7 | 37.2 | 17.1 | 21.1 | 9.9 | 0.97 |
| Rajasthan | 18.3 | 33.8 | 16.8 | 19.4 | 11.6 | 14.8 | 33.0 | 18.7 | 21.6 | 11.9 | 1.04 |
| Tamil Nadu | 8.3 | 36.5 | 18.3 | 27.5 | 9.4 | 4.0 | 22.7 | 14.4 | 29.9 | 29.0 | 1.05 |
| Uttar Pradesh | 19.9 | 34.3 | 14.8 | 19.9 | 11.2 | 16.5 | 28.4 | 14.3 | 22.8 | 18.1 | 1.04 |
| West Bengal | 9.2 | 33.5 | 19.0 | 25.2 | 13.1 | 11.2 | 28.3 | 18.8 | 22.5 | 19.2 | 0.98 |
| Other NE states | 4.9 | 31.0 | 22.7 | 28.1 | 13.4 | | | | | | |
| Rest ST and UT | 8.1 | 30.1 | 13.8 | 32.4 | 15.5 | 7.6 | 29.6 | 16.3 | 26.9 | 19.6 | 1.01 |
| All-India | 12.2 | 32.4 | 18.0 | 25.7 | 11.7 | 8.6 | 27.5 | 19.1 | 27.6 | 17.2 | 1.04 |

*Source:* Unit level data of employment and unemployment schedule of 61st (2004–5) Round of NSSO.

**Table A4.14**  Education Levels (Age 7+), 2004–5, Metro and Non-metro, Female

(in per cent)

| States | Non-metro | | | | | Metro | | | | | Metro Literacy/ Non-metro Litearcy |
|---|---|---|---|---|---|---|---|---|---|---|---|
| | Illiterate | Primary & below | Up to middle | Up to secondary | Graduate & above | Illiterate | Primary & below | Up to middle | Up to secondary | Graduate & above | |
| Andhra Pradesh | 34.1 | 31.3 | 14.0 | 14.6 | 6.0 | 26.3 | 21.3 | 11.6 | 28.4 | 12.4 | 1.12 |
| Assam | 14.0 | 30.6 | 23.5 | 23.7 | 8.2 | | | | | | |
| Bihar | 31.1 | 30.4 | 14.7 | 16.9 | 6.8 | 18.1 | 32.6 | 19.7 | 27.7 | 1.8 | 1.19 |
| Gujarat | 18.6 | 32.8 | 22.5 | 19.9 | 6.2 | 19.8 | 23.1 | 20.0 | 24.4 | 12.7 | 0.99 |
| Haryana | 24.4 | 26.0 | 12.5 | 25.6 | 11.4 | 36.7 | 27.9 | 7.1 | 22.6 | 5.7 | 0.84 |
| Jammu and Kashmir | 31.4 | 25.1 | 15.4 | 20.6 | 7.4 | | | | | | |
| Karnataka | 25.5 | 27.1 | 18.4 | 22.2 | 6.8 | 15.7 | 23.2 | 17.7 | 29.3 | 14.1 | 1.13 |
| Kerala | 8.2 | 30.1 | 26.3 | 25.8 | 9.6 | | | | | | |
| Madhya Pradesh | 29.0 | 34.3 | 11.4 | 17.4 | 7.9 | 16.1 | 28.9 | 17.5 | 18.3 | 19.1 | 1.18 |
| Maharashtra | 22.2 | 28.6 | 21.9 | 20.6 | 6.7 | 14.8 | 29.4 | 21.6 | 21.2 | 13.1 | 1.10 |
| Orissa | 26.5 | 29.0 | 18.5 | 17.7 | 8.3 | | | | | | |
| Punjab | 21.1 | 27.1 | 8.5 | 30.4 | 12.9 | 24.5 | 23.5 | 11.0 | 26.8 | 14.3 | 0.96 |
| Rajasthan | 38.3 | 30.3 | 12.3 | 11.5 | 7.5 | 44.1 | 22.5 | 17.2 | 11.6 | 4.5 | 0.91 |
| Tamil Nadu | 20.5 | 35.2 | 16.2 | 21.1 | 7.0 | 13.7 | 28.1 | 19.5 | 24.7 | 14.0 | 1.09 |
| Uttar Pradesh | 35.3 | 31.8 | 11.5 | 14.2 | 7.3 | 23.6 | 28.6 | 12.7 | 19.7 | 15.3 | 1.18 |
| West Bengal | 19.3 | 37.9 | 17.7 | 15.7 | 9.4 | 17.0 | 27.6 | 19.7 | 19.3 | 16.3 | 1.03 |
| Other NE states | 11.6 | 33.2 | 21.9 | 24.0 | 9.2 | | | | | | |
| Rest ST and UT | 17.9 | 27.8 | 13.1 | 27.9 | 13.3 | 19.0 | 29.1 | 12.0 | 24.3 | 15.6 | 0.99 |
| All-India | 25.9 | 31.6 | 16.1 | 18.7 | 7.8 | 19.6 | 27.3 | 17.2 | 22.4 | 13.5 | 1.09 |

*Source:* Unit level data of employment and unemployment schedule of 61st (2004–5) Round of NSSO.

(in per cent)

**Table A4.15**  Education Levels (Age 7+), 2004–5, Total Urban

| States | Male | | | | | Female | | | | |
|---|---|---|---|---|---|---|---|---|---|---|
| | Illiterate | Primary & below | Up to middle | Up to secondary | Graduate & above | Illiterate | Primary & below | Up to middle | Up to secondary | Graduate & above |
| Andhra Pradesh | 16.1 | 29.8 | 15.3 | 25.5 | 13.4 | 32.6 | 29.4 | 13.6 | 17.2 | 7.2 |
| Assam | 6.7 | 29.9 | 21.8 | 24.8 | 16.8 | 14.0 | 30.6 | 23.5 | 23.7 | 8.2 |
| Bihar | 12.3 | 28.1 | 16.8 | 26.8 | 15.9 | 29.6 | 30.6 | 15.3 | 18.2 | 6.2 |
| Gujarat | 6.9 | 31.2 | 20.4 | 30.0 | 11.5 | 19.1 | 28.9 | 21.5 | 21.7 | 8.8 |
| Haryana | 11.7 | 32.2 | 13.0 | 31.4 | 11.7 | 26.6 | 26.4 | 11.6 | 25.1 | 10.4 |
| Jammu and Kashmir | 14.5 | 28.4 | 20.5 | 28.1 | 8.4 | 31.4 | 25.1 | 15.4 | 20.6 | 7.4 |
| Karnataka | 9.4 | 28.1 | 19.0 | 30.5 | 13.0 | 23.1 | 26.1 | 18.2 | 23.9 | 8.6 |
| Kerala | 3.4 | 31.4 | 29.3 | 26.5 | 9.4 | 8.2 | 30.1 | 26.3 | 25.8 | 9.6 |
| Madhya Pradesh | 11.2 | 36.7 | 13.1 | 23.8 | 15.2 | 26.8 | 33.4 | 12.4 | 17.6 | 9.8 |
| Maharashtra | 7.2 | 26.4 | 25.1 | 29.0 | 12.2 | 18.4 | 29.0 | 21.7 | 20.9 | 9.9 |
| Orissa | 12.6 | 28.0 | 21.0 | 25.1 | 13.3 | 26.5 | 29.0 | 18.5 | 17.7 | 8.3 |
| Punjab | 12.8 | 31.3 | 13.3 | 31.2 | 11.3 | 21.7 | 26.5 | 8.9 | 29.7 | 13.2 |
| Rajasthan | 17.5 | 33.6 | 17.3 | 19.9 | 11.7 | 39.8 | 28.3 | 13.6 | 11.5 | 6.8 |
| Tamil Nadu | 7.5 | 33.9 | 17.6 | 28.0 | 13.0 | 19.3 | 33.9 | 16.8 | 21.7 | 8.3 |
| Uttar Pradesh | 19.1 | 33.0 | 14.7 | 20.5 | 12.7 | 32.6 | 31.1 | 11.8 | 15.5 | 9.1 |
| West Bengal | 9.7 | 32.2 | 19.0 | 24.5 | 14.6 | 18.8 | 35.5 | 18.1 | 16.5 | 11.0 |
| Other NE states | 4.9 | 31.0 | 22.7 | 28.1 | 13.4 | 11.6 | 33.2 | 21.9 | 24.0 | 9.2 |
| Rest ST and UT | 7.7 | 29.7 | 15.8 | 27.9 | 18.9 | 18.7 | 28.8 | 12.2 | 25.0 | 15.2 |
| All-India | 11.2 | 31.0 | 18.3 | 26.2 | 13.3 | 24.2 | 30.4 | 16.4 | 19.7 | 9.4 |

*Source:* Unit level data of employment and unemployment schedule of 61st (2004–5) Round of NSSO.

**Table A5.1**   Percentage Households Having Access to Tap Water Supply, 1993, 1998, and 2008–9

| State | 1993 | | | 1998 | | | 2008–9 | | | |
|---|---|---|---|---|---|---|---|---|---|---|
| | < 50,000 | 50,000 to 200,000 | 200,000 to 1 million | < 50,000 | 50,000 to 200,000 | 200,000 to 1 million | < 50,000 | 50,000 to 1 lakh | 1 lakh to 5 lakh | 5 lakh to 1 million |
| Andhra Pradesh | 55.5 | 82.5 | 75.0 | 67.3 | 64.3 | 83.2 | 77.5 | 66.9 | 78.6 | 84.4 |
| Assam | 38.3 | 63.3 | 38.7 | 40.4 | 47.7 | 41.8 | 26.4 | 41.9 | 65.2 | 45.7 |
| Bihar | 17.9 | 51.4 | 66.9 | 23.2 | 37.6 | 51.8 | 31.4 | 20.8 | 31.0 | 63.7 |
| Gujarat | 76.0 | 84.3 | 96.0 | 91.5 | 83.1 | 94.8 | 72.0 | 83.5 | 83.4 | 88.9 |
| Haryana | 59.3 | 88.4 | 89.7 | 74.4 | 79.1 | 96.8 | 84.2 | 74.8 | 84.6 | |
| Jammu and Kashmir | 85.1 | – | 99.6 | 90.0 | – | 98.7 | 88.2 | 90.7 | | 95.2 |
| Karnataka | 53.6 | 84.3 | 90.6 | 65.5 | 79.8 | 88.1 | 92.2 | 77.6 | 91.9 | 95.3 |
| Kerala | 23.2 | 22.1 | 84.8 | 27.3 | 39.5 | 66.9 | 27.8 | 27.1 | 47.5 | 73.9 |
| Madhya Pradesh | 52.8 | 72.5 | 72.9 | 73.0 | 63.7 | 81.0 | 63.8 | 71.0 | 63.1 | 77.9 |
| Maharashtra | 85.8 | 74.1 | 95.3 | 76.7 | 91.2 | 89.3 | 89.6 | 89.5 | 88.3 | 60.6 |
| Orissa | 40.9 | 43.1 | 61.9 | 7.4 | 62.0 | 60.4 | 61.9 | 57.7 | 82.1 | 78.4 |
| Punjab | 54.4 | 72.1 | 60.5 | 70.5 | 68.1 | 67.1 | 82.7 | 87.8 | 79.9 | 79.0 |
| Rajasthan | 78.0 | 84.3 | 84.9 | 91.8 | 88.9 | 81.7 | 85.5 | 83.4 | 95.7 | 94.7 |
| Tamil Nadu | 61.2 | 75.8 | 79.7 | 70.3 | 78.8 | 88.3 | 89.5 | 93.8 | 83.9 | 83.4 |
| Uttar Pradesh | 40.7 | 54.6 | 66.9 | 44.1 | 61.1 | 48.9 | 38.9 | 55.0 | 57.6 | 74.4 |
| West Bengal | 27.0 | 65.8 | 72.4 | 33.6 | 68.2 | 58.2 | 52.7 | 55.3 | 76.6 | |
| Other NE States | 65.3 | 78.1 | – | 52.8 | 51.8 | – | 65.2 | 52.4 | 83.3 | |
| Rest ST and UT | 82.1 | 93.5 | 100.0 | 82.9 | 96.7 | 97.5 | 75.9 | 94.5 | 91.3 | 99.1 |
| All-India | 52.6 | 71.6 | 78.0 | 57.9 | 69.6 | 76.2 | 69.2 | 72.0 | 76.9 | 78.2 |

*Source*: Unit level data of housing condition and migration schedule of 49th Round (1993), common property, sanitation, and hygiene schedule of 54th Round (1998), and housing condition schedule of 65th Round (2008–9).

**Table A5.2**   Percentage Households Having Access to Tap Water Supply, Metro, Non-metro and Total, 1993, 1998, 2002, and 2008–9

| State | 1993 | | | 1998 | | | 2002 | | | 2008–9 | | |
|---|---|---|---|---|---|---|---|---|---|---|---|---|
| | Non-metro | Metro | Total Urban | Non-metro | Metro | Total Urban | Non-metro | Metro | Total Urban | Non-metro | Metro | Total Urban |
| Andhra Pradesh | 71.9 | 95.4 | 74.4 | 69.8 | 95.2 | 75.1 | 75.5 | 96.8 | 78.3 | 76.9 | 93.8 | 79.5 |
| Assam | 43.6 | – | 43.6 | 42.2 | – | 42.2 | 35.5 | 0.0 | 0.0 | 40.3 | | 40.3 |
| Bihar | 44.4 | – | 44.4 | 34.1 | 43.3 | 35.4 | 35.7 | 64.9 | 39.8 | 32.1 | 76.7 | 39.6 |
| Gujarat | 82.4 | 92.7 | 85.5 | 87.8 | 97.0 | 91.1 | 87.9 | 96.9 | 91.7 | 80.9 | 90.4 | 84.9 |
| Haryana | 81.8 | – | 81.8 | 80.5 | – | 80.5 | 76.5 | 83.7 | 77.3 | 83.9 | 68.2 | 80.6 |
| Jammu and Kashmir | 92.6 | – | 92.6 | 94.6 | – | 94.6 | 94.4 | 0.0 | 94.4 | 92.9 | | 92.9 |
| Karnataka | 70.9 | 89.8 | 74.8 | 76.6 | 99.9 | 80.9 | 85.4 | 97.6 | 88.5 | 91.1 | 98.5 | 92.7 |
| Kerala | 40.3 | – | 40.3 | 40.2 | – | 40.2 | 42.6 | 0.0 | 42.6 | 45.7 | | 45.7 |
| Madhya Pradesh | 63.4 | 84.4 | 66.3 | 72.6 | 93.8 | 76.1 | 63.6 | 64.9 | 63.8 | 66.9 | 74.1 | 67.9 |
| Maharashtra | 86.2 | 96.1 | 90.9 | 86.6 | 99.3 | 92.0 | 87.7 | 95.0 | 91.7 | 81.1 | 97.0 | 89.5 |
| Orissa | 48.0 | – | 48.0 | 38.7 | – | 38.7 | 55.4 | 0.0 | 55.4 | 70.2 | | 70.2 |
| Punjab | 62.8 | 84.5 | 67.7 | 68.2 | 55.4 | 64.4 | 74.7 | 93.4 | 78.4 | 81.8 | 91.4 | 84.5 |
| Rajasthan | 81.6 | 96.9 | 83.8 | 87.4 | 77.4 | 85.4 | 78.9 | 88.1 | 80.5 | 90.1 | 82.9 | 88.5 |
| Tamil Nadu | 71.0 | 51.1 | 67.1 | 78.2 | 59.7 | 74.0 | 85.2 | 75.5 | 83.3 | 88.3 | 53.8 | 83.9 |
| Uttar Pradesh | 53.8 | 56.4 | 54.1 | 50.6 | 12.9 | 43.2 | 52.3 | 43.2 | 50.1 | 54.4 | 49.3 | 53.3 |
| West Bengal | 53.8 | 84.7 | 61.0 | 52.7 | 67.0 | 56.0 | 55.0 | 72.7 | 59.5 | 69.7 | 87.8 | 74.6 |
| Other NE States | 70.2 | – | 70.2 | 52.4 | – | 52.4 | 69.0 | 0.0 | 69.0 | 69.9 | | 69.9 |
| Rest ST and UT | 91.8 | 89.2 | 90.0 | 92.2 | 93.6 | 93.2 | 89.0 | 85.9 | 87.0 | 86.8 | 93.7 | 90.7 |
| All-India | 66.1 | 85.1 | 70.5 | 67.2 | 78.9 | 70.1 | 69.7 | 83.8 | 73.6 | 73.8 | 85.8 | 76.9 |

*Source*: Unit level data of housing condition and migration schedule of 49th Round (1993), common property, sanitation, and hygiene schedule of 54th Round (1998), and housing condition schedule of 58th (2002) and 65th Rounds (2008–9).

**Table A5.3**  Percentage Households Having Drinking Water Within Premises, 1993, 1998, and 2008–9

| State | 1993 | | | 1998 | | | 2008–9 | | | |
|---|---|---|---|---|---|---|---|---|---|---|
| | < 50,000 | 50,000 to 200,000 | 200,000 to 1 million | < 50,000 | 50,000 to 200,000 | 200,000 to 1 million | < 50,000 | 50,000 to 1 lakh | 1 lakh to 5 lakh | 5 lakh to 1 million |
| Andhra Pradesh | 42.4 | 37.3 | 52.6 | 21.8 | 33.1 | 54.6 | 61.7 | 69.5 | 60.5 | 73.0 |
| Assam | 79.3 | 78.4 | 84.8 | 75.4 | 90.5 | 72.3 | 87.2 | 95.8 | 98.8 | 93.5 |
| Bihar | 64.4 | 67.0 | 67.6 | 47.4 | 50.4 | 87.7 | 68.7 | 69.9 | 84.8 | 78.1 |
| Gujarat | 68.0 | 72.5 | 82.4 | 78.5 | 72.8 | 86.1 | 82.7 | 91.3 | 86.0 | 90.4 |
| Haryana | 73.8 | 81.2 | 52.2 | 69.8 | 87.2 | 85.8 | 79.7 | 75.0 | 86.1 | |
| Jammu and Kashmir | 82.0 | – | 96.6 | 57.6 | – | 94.8 | 86.0 | 96.7 | | 95.9 |
| Karnataka | 42.1 | 61.0 | 80.2 | 44.7 | 44.2 | 80.2 | 58.3 | 48.3 | 66.3 | 82.6 |
| Kerala | 69.1 | 82.3 | 79.0 | 73.6 | 72.3 | 64.8 | 80.3 | 87.8 | 78.3 | 80.9 |
| Madhya Pradesh | 50.1 | 65.1 | 46.1 | 59.7 | 54.9 | 69.4 | 53.4 | 61.6 | 54.1 | 57.6 |
| Maharashtra | 67.1 | 76.0 | 72.6 | 58.7 | 84.5 | 69.3 | 74.1 | 80.9 | 78.8 | 50.3 |
| Orissa | 33.2 | 47.8 | 67.5 | 32.9 | 40.8 | 69.6 | 50.7 | 37.8 | 62.2 | 70.1 |
| Punjab | 93.3 | 90.8 | 90.5 | 98.0 | 86.9 | 94.9 | 91.9 | 89.8 | 95.8 | 97.3 |
| Rajasthan | 64.0 | 77.3 | 73.4 | 83.5 | 85.1 | 78.9 | 80.6 | 90.2 | 95.3 | 97.6 |
| Tamil Nadu | 41.6 | 47.0 | 61.5 | 35.5 | 52.2 | 43.4 | 51.4 | 73.1 | 67.3 | 74.1 |
| Uttar Pradesh | 76.3 | 83.5 | 81.5 | 77.1 | 87.5 | 86.6 | 79.9 | 87.4 | 85.1 | 92.9 |
| West Bengal | 39.6 | 55.9 | 53.4 | 34.6 | 59.5 | 47.2 | 35.6 | 57.3 | 52.5 | |
| Other NE States | 60.3 | 72.4 | – | 39.2 | 73.5 | – | 59.3 | 73.2 | 88.4 | |
| Rest ST and UT | 75.1 | 83.8 | 95.0 | 84.2 | 83.1 | 67.3 | 87.4 | 94.0 | 82.9 | 92.7 |
| All-India | 57.3 | 64.5 | 69.4 | 55.5 | 63.5 | 69.8 | 66.0 | 75.6 | 71.3 | 77.5 |

*Source*: Unit level data of housing condition and migration schedule of 49th Round (1993), common property, sanitation, and hygiene schedule of 54th Round (1998), and housing condition schedule of 65th Round (2008–9).

**Table A5.4**  Percentage Households Having Water Supply Within Premises, Metro, Non-metro, and Total, 1993, 1998, 2002, and 2008–9

| State | 1993 | | | 1998 | | | 2002 | | | 2008–9 | | |
|---|---|---|---|---|---|---|---|---|---|---|---|---|
| | Non-metro | Metro | Total Urban | Non-metro | Metro | Total Urban | Non-metro | Metro | Total Urban | Non-metro | Metro | Total Urban |
| Andhra Pradesh | 43.8 | 79.9 | 47.7 | 35.3 | 74.2 | 43.5 | 52.4 | 80.6 | 56.2 | 64.6 | 92.3 | 68.9 |
| Assam | 80.3 | – | 80.3 | 77.7 | – | 77.7 | 87.9 | 0.0 | 87.9 | 91.9 | | 91.9 |
| Bihar | 66.2 | – | 66.2 | 55.3 | 76.6 | 58.3 | 67.8 | 91.7 | 71.2 | 74.8 | 91.6 | 77.6 |
| Gujarat | 71.9 | 87.1 | 76.3 | 76.7 | 82.3 | 78.7 | 88.8 | 86.8 | 87.9 | 87.1 | 92.1 | 89.2 |
| Haryana | 70.7 | – | 70.7 | 82.8 | – | 82.8 | 83.3 | 93.1 | 84.4 | 83.6 | 87.9 | 84.5 |
| Jammu and Kashmir | 89.5 | – | 89.5 | 77.4 | – | 77.4 | 90.2 | 0.0 | 90.2 | 93.6 | | 93.3 |
| Karnataka | 56.7 | 73.3 | 60.2 | 55.3 | 82.1 | 60.2 | 62.8 | 72.2 | 65.2 | 64.2 | 92.4 | 70.6 |
| Kerala | 74.5 | – | 74.5 | 71.0 | – | 71.0 | 76.6 | 0.0 | 76.6 | 81.2 | | 81.2 |
| Madhya Pradesh | 54.1 | 63.6 | 55.4 | 60.9 | 49.6 | 59.1 | 61.4 | 40.3 | 58.1 | 55.5 | 69.7 | 57.5 |
| Maharashtra | 71.8 | 75.6 | 73.6 | 70.2 | 89.1 | 78.2 | 68.7 | 84.0 | 77.1 | 70.0 | 84.9 | 77.8 |
| Orissa | 47.3 | – | 47.3 | 45.7 | – | 45.7 | 61.8 | 0.0 | 61.8 | 56.0 | | 56.0 |
| Punjab | 91.4 | 97.8 | 92.8 | 92.1 | 98.5 | 94.0 | 92.3 | 98.3 | 93.5 | 94.0 | 99.8 | 95.6 |
| Rajasthan | 70.1 | 89.2 | 72.8 | 82.3 | 77.5 | 81.4 | 75.4 | 84.7 | 77.0 | 89.9 | 82.6 | 88.3 |
| Tamil Nadu | 48.3 | 54.8 | 49.6 | 43.1 | 68.9 | 48.9 | 52.7 | 66.3 | 55.3 | 61.4 | 70.3 | 62.6 |
| Uttar Pradesh | 80.0 | 75.9 | 79.4 | 83.0 | 52.8 | 77.1 | 84.1 | 71.6 | 81.1 | 85.3 | 76.2 | 83.3 |
| West Bengal | 49.6 | 69.6 | 54.3 | 47.2 | 50.1 | 47.9 | 51.0 | 50.4 | 50.8 | 49.4 | 64.2 | 53.4 |
| Other NE States | 64.9 | – | 64.9 | 53.6 | – | 53.6 | 67.5 | 0.0 | 67.5 | 69.7 | | 69.7 |
| Rest ST and UT | 84.2 | 86.1 | 85.6 | 78.5 | 85.4 | 83.3 | 84.0 | 79.4 | 81.0 | 87.9 | 86.0 | 86.9 |
| All-India | 63.1 | 76.3 | 66.2 | 62.3 | 76.0 | 65.7 | 67.8 | 76.8 | 70.3 | 71.3 | 83.6 | 74.5 |

*Source:* Unit level data of housing condition and migration schedule of 49th Round (1993), common property, sanitation, and hygiene schedule of 54th Round (1998), and housing condition schedule of 58th (2002) and 65th Rounds (2008–9).

**Table A5.5**  Percentage Households Not Sharing Drinking Water Source, 1993, 1998, and 2008–9

| State | 1993 | | | 1998 | | | 2008–9 | | | |
|---|---|---|---|---|---|---|---|---|---|---|
| | < 50,000 | 50,000 to 200,000 | 200,000 to 1 million | < 50,000 | 50,000 to 200,000 | 200,000 to 1 million | < 50,000 | 50,000 to 1 lakh | 1 lakh to 5 lakh | 5 lakh to 1 million |
| Andhra Pradesh | 21.3 | 17.4 | 16.3 | 12.9 | 12.8 | 26.4 | 32.0 | 20.2 | 21.5 | 30.2 |
| Assam | 51.6 | 65.6 | 48.6 | 64.6 | 67.6 | 23.4 | 65.3 | 60.2 | 81.0 | 50.9 |
| Bihar | 47.7 | 30.9 | 46.1 | 33.3 | 31.1 | 54.9 | 31.6 | 45.3 | 53.6 | 48.8 |
| Gujarat | 50.7 | 58.7 | 46.2 | 65.7 | 44.1 | 54.3 | 61.9 | 51.7 | 66.9 | 79.7 |
| Haryana | 52.8 | 59.5 | 32.8 | 40.0 | 51.9 | 78.9 | 54.1 | 61.0 | 61.3 | |
| Jammu and Kashmir | 47.0 | – | 60.0 | 47.6 | – | 84.1 | 57.7 | 84.5 | – | 59.3 |
| Karnataka | 21.9 | 28.5 | 41.9 | 26.3 | 23.8 | 52.6 | 37.1 | 28.4 | 38.4 | 57.8 |
| Kerala | 58.8 | 67.0 | 54.1 | 63.1 | 57.3 | 73.6 | 60.5 | 76.3 | 59.9 | 67.5 |
| Madhya Pradesh | 33.9 | 38.4 | 29.0 | 37.1 | 29.2 | 56.9 | 38.0 | 32.7 | 38.5 | 36.3 |
| Maharashtra | 39.3 | 35.2 | 47.0 | 33.3 | 47.3 | 49.7 | 50.7 | 53.5 | 55.2 | 37.7 |
| Orissa | 23.1 | 27.5 | 50.1 | 12.4 | 31.4 | 40.7 | 38.8 | 31.5 | 36.5 | 34.4 |
| Punjab | 73.4 | 65.5 | 49.2 | 76.7 | 76.2 | 51.9 | 66.5 | 69.8 | 77.6 | 57.1 |
| Rajasthan | 38.6 | 44.9 | 45.0 | 50.4 | 59.0 | 47.1 | 53.2 | 55.4 | 65.2 | 62.2 |
| Tamil Nadu | 15.8 | 21.7 | 17.5 | 18.0 | 29.4 | 17.6 | 25.0 | 42.0 | 32.8 | 25.3 |
| Uttar Pradesh | 52.3 | 62.5 | 48.8 | 53.7 | 51.4 | 54.5 | 55.3 | 65.2 | 57.4 | 64.3 |
| West Bengal | 20.5 | 35.9 | 31.2 | 23.8 | 37.8 | 25.0 | 23.2 | 36.0 | 32.3 | |
| Other NE States | 31.7 | 43.7 | – | 34.7 | 36.9 | – | 38.1 | 41.3 | 47.8 | |
| Rest ST and UT | 45.1 | 55.8 | 75.2 | 59.9 | 64.0 | 50.7 | 55.7 | 72.8 | 59.9 | 68.6 |
| All-India | 36.1 | 39.6 | 39.2 | 37.2 | 38.5 | 45.4 | 42.1 | 45.8 | 44.3 | 48.1 |

*Source*: Unit level data of housing condition and migration schedule of 49th Round (1993), common property, sanitation, and hygiene schedule of 54th Round (1998), and housing condition schedule of 65th Round (2008–9).

**Table A5.6**  Percentage Households Not Sharing Drinking Water Source, Metro, Non-metro, and Total, 1993, 1998, 2002, and 2008–9

| State | 1993 | | | 1998 | | | 2002 | | | 2008–9 | | |
|---|---|---|---|---|---|---|---|---|---|---|---|---|
| | Non-metro | Metro | Total Urban | Non-metro | Metro | Total Urban | Non-metro | Metro | Total Urban | Non-metro | Metro | Total Urban |
| Andhra Pradesh | 18.2 | 27.8 | 19.3 | 16.2 | 32.4 | 19.6 | 17.7 | 40.8 | 20.8 | 24.1 | 24.3 | 24.1 |
| Assam | 53.8 | – | 53.9 | 55.2 | – | 55.2 | 54.6 | – | 54.6 | 64.3 | – | 64.3 |
| Bihar | 42.0 | – | 42.0 | 35.9 | 36.1 | 35.9 | 40.9 | 35.9 | 40.2 | 42.5 | 49.9 | 43.7 |
| Gujarat | 54.0 | 69.0 | 58.4 | 53.9 | 68.6 | 59.2 | 59.5 | 74.0 | 65.6 | 63.8 | 75.8 | 68.8 |
| Haryana | 49.9 | – | 49.9 | 52.8 | – | 52.8 | 50.3 | 56.0 | 50.9 | 59.2 | 45.3 | 56.3 |
| Jammu and Kashmir | 53.7 | – | 53.7 | 67.0 | – | 67.0 | 68.4 | – | 68.4 | 62.3 | – | 62.2 |
| Karnataka | 28.7 | 54.2 | 34.1 | 33.5 | 67.9 | 39.8 | 33.4 | 48.9 | 37.3 | 39.3 | 73.2 | 47.0 |
| Kerala | 59.1 | – | 59.1 | 64.7 | – | 64.7 | 61.5 | – | 61.5 | 65.0 | – | 65.0 |
| Madhya Pradesh | 34.3 | 34.1 | 34.3 | 40.0 | 28.3 | 38.1 | 38.5 | 28.5 | 36.9 | 37.1 | 37.0 | 37.1 |
| Maharashtra | 41.1 | 56.0 | 48.1 | 44.9 | 58.1 | 50.5 | 45.0 | 61.6 | 54.2 | 48.9 | 61.4 | 55.4 |
| Orissa | 32.6 | – | 32.6 | 26.1 | – | 26.1 | 32.7 | – | 32.7 | 36.0 | – | 36.0 |
| Punjab | 61.3 | 64.0 | 61.9 | 66.6 | 33.5 | 56.9 | 62.1 | 55.9 | 60.9 | 66.6 | 39.5 | 59.2 |
| Rajasthan | 42.1 | 68.0 | 45.7 | 51.6 | 44.5 | 50.2 | 44.9 | 45.8 | 45.0 | 59.0 | 57.8 | 58.8 |
| Tamil Nadu | 18.3 | 20.0 | 18.7 | 21.6 | 19.2 | 21.0 | 28.9 | 23.2 | 27.8 | 29.2 | 29.0 | 29.2 |
| Uttar Pradesh | 53.7 | 42.6 | 52.1 | 53.3 | 35.9 | 49.9 | 56.7 | 53.1 | 55.8 | 59.1 | 52.3 | 57.7 |
| West Bengal | 29.5 | 25.4 | 28.5 | 29.5 | 13.6 | 25.8 | 30.3 | 26.2 | 29.2 | 30.7 | 30.1 | 30.6 |
| Other NE States | 36.2 | – | 36.2 | 61.2 | – | 35.6 | 28.0 | – | 28.0 | 41.5 | – | 41.5 |
| Rest ST and UT | 57.8 | 50.4 | 52.5 | 58.4 | 64.0 | 62.2 | 52.3 | 53.9 | 53.3 | 61.6 | 61.4 | 61.5 |
| All-India | 38.1 | 47.1 | 40.2 | 40.0 | 45.1 | 41.3 | 40.8 | 51.5 | 43.8 | 44.5 | 54.3 | 47.0 |

*Source:* Unit level data of housing condition and migration schedule of 49th Round (1993), common property, sanitation, and hygiene schedule of 54th Round (1998), and housing condition schedule of 58th (2002) and 65th Rounds (2008–9).

**Table A5.7**  Percentage Households Stating Adequacy of Drinking Water Availability, 1993, 1998, and 2008–9

| State | 1993 | | | 1998 | | | 2008–9 | | | |
|---|---|---|---|---|---|---|---|---|---|---|
| | < 50,000 | 50,000 to 200,000 | 200,000 to 1 million | < 50,000 | 50,000 to 200,000 | 200,000 to 1 million | < 50,000 | 50,000 to 1 lakh | 1 lakh to 5 lakh | 5 lakh to 1 million |
| Andhra Pradesh | 82.4 | 76.8 | 85.8 | 72.1 | 73.6 | 74.8 | 89.8 | 94.0 | 94.0 | 86.4 |
| Assam | 95.2 | 87.5 | 78.6 | 100.0 | 100.0 | 92.7 | 96.9 | 99.9 | 100.0 | 91.8 |
| Bihar | 88.1 | 84.4 | 86.7 | 82.3 | 70.0 | 94.1 | 90.1 | 89.3 | 99.1 | 97.3 |
| Gujarat | 74.4 | 78.6 | 92.8 | 90.0 | 77.9 | 72.7 | 96.0 | 99.4 | 92.2 | 98.9 |
| Haryana | 96.5 | 79.6 | 85.6 | 88.8 | 79.4 | 43.1 | 96.7 | 82.2 | 92.9 | |
| Jammu and Kashmir | 97.7 | – | 87.6 | 59.8 | – | 92.9 | 76.2 | 93.2 | | 81.7 |
| Karnataka | 64.9 | 74.5 | 83.5 | 80.1 | 82.7 | 75.0 | 76.0 | 85.5 | 90.9 | 89.4 |
| Kerala | 85.6 | 91.0 | 94.3 | 78.7 | 89.9 | 92.5 | 84.0 | 87.8 | 96.1 | 95.8 |
| Madhya Pradesh | 80.9 | 91.6 | 91.0 | 91.6 | 80.0 | 82.1 | 81.8 | 78.7 | 72.6 | 82.5 |
| Maharashtra | 83.6 | 78.4 | 85.3 | 85.0 | 70.0 | 86.9 | 81.2 | 90.3 | 87.5 | 68.0 |
| Orissa | 84.5 | 88.2 | 75.5 | 86.0 | 87.4 | 97.2 | 88.3 | 77.3 | 89.9 | 83.0 |
| Punjab | 97.0 | 86.9 | 97.2 | 95.9 | 99.9 | 91.5 | 88.6 | 93.6 | 95.3 | 93.5 |
| Rajasthan | 89.5 | 77.8 | 94.2 | 75.2 | 80.3 | 94.1 | 80.6 | 87.4 | 76.3 | 93.3 |
| Tamil Nadu | 71.2 | 81.8 | 64.4 | 80.8 | 86.6 | 87.4 | 94.4 | 89.1 | 96.6 | 94.3 |
| Uttar Pradesh | 95.1 | 94.8 | 89.4 | 88.9 | 93.6 | 94.9 | 94.6 | 92.3 | 91.9 | 99.7 |
| West Bengal | 67.0 | 93.0 | 71.7 | 97.5 | 97.9 | 95.8 | 92.5 | 98.8 | 96.0 | |
| Other NE States | 79.1 | 77.3 | – | 86.4 | 73.5 | – | 76.7 | 58.9 | 77.8 | |
| Rest ST and UT | 86.4 | 89.0 | 99.6 | 89.0 | 82.7 | 86.6 | 90.5 | 95.8 | 86.5 | 99.3 |
| All-India | 81.3 | 84.3 | 84.7 | 85.1 | 83.0 | 87.2 | 88.8 | 90.5 | 91.1 | 89.0 |

*Source:* Unit level data of housing condition and migration schedule of 49th Round (1993), common property, sanitation, and hygiene schedule of 54th Round (1998), and housing condition schedule of 65th Round (2008–9).

**Table A5.8**   Percentage Households Stating Adequacy of Drinking Water Availability, Metro, Non-metro, and Total, 1993, 1998, 2002, and 2008–9

| State | 1993 | | | 1998 | | | 2002 | | | 2008–9 | | |
|---|---|---|---|---|---|---|---|---|---|---|---|---|
| | Non-metro | Metro | Total Urban | Non-metro | Metro | Total Urban | Non-metro | Metro | Total Urban | Non-metro | Metro | Total Urban |
| Andhra Pradesh | 81.4 | 71.9 | 80.4 | 73.5 | 56.5 | 69.9 | 88.8 | 94.8 | 89.6 | 92.2 | 99.1 | 93.3 |
| Assam | 89.9 | – | 89.9 | 98.2 | – | 98.2 | 95.4 | | 95.4 | 96.5 | 96.5 | 96.5 |
| Bihar | 86.4 | – | 86.5 | 78.9 | 95.5 | 81.3 | 88.7 | 95.4 | 89.6 | 93.4 | 95.4 | 93.7 |
| Gujarat | 78.6 | 92.0 | 82.6 | 82.1 | 82.7 | 82.3 | 93.0 | 93.1 | 93.0 | 96.2 | 97.3 | 96.7 |
| Haryana | 85.4 | – | 85.4 | 76.6 | – | 76.6 | 90.6 | 74.1 | 88.9 | 93.4 | 90.0 | 92.7 |
| Jammu and Kashmir | 92.5 | – | 92.5 | 77.4 | – | 77.4 | 92.5 | | 92.5 | 81.9 | | 81.7 |
| Karnataka | 72.1 | 89.4 | 75.7 | 79.3 | 96.8 | 82.5 | 90.1 | 79.9 | 87.5 | 86.0 | 98.5 | 88.8 |
| Kerala | 88.6 | – | 89.1 | 84.6 | – | 84.6 | 86.8 | | 86.8 | 90.7 | | 90.7 |
| Madhya Pradesh | 86.5 | 72.0 | 84.5 | 86.3 | 73.9 | 84.2 | 81.7 | 73.6 | 80.4 | 78.8 | 63.2 | 76.7 |
| Maharashtra | 82.8 | 89.8 | 86.1 | 82.3 | 91.6 | 86.3 | 77.3 | 94.3 | 86.6 | 80.9 | 95.2 | 88.4 |
| Orissa | 82.5 | – | 82.5 | 89.6 | – | 89.6 | 92.5 | | 92.5 | 85.8 | | 85.8 |
| Punjab | 93.5 | 96.5 | 94.2 | 95.8 | 90.5 | 94.3 | 95.0 | 100.0 | 96.0 | 92.4 | 96.0 | 93.4 |
| Rajasthan | 87.8 | 75.8 | 86.2 | 83.4 | 87.1 | 84.1 | 86.3 | 92.8 | 87.4 | 82.6 | 93.6 | 85.1 |
| Tamil Nadu | 73.5 | 45.0 | 67.9 | 84.6 | 95.9 | 87.1 | 86.6 | 79.3 | 85.2 | 93.9 | 98.9 | 94.5 |
| Uttar Pradesh | 93.0 | 95.9 | 93.4 | 92.1 | 95.3 | 92.7 | 97.0 | 97.3 | 97.1 | 94.5 | 94.7 | 94.6 |
| West Bengal | 79.0 | 88.5 | 81.3 | 97.3 | 96.6 | 97.1 | 92.9 | 88.9 | 91.9 | 95.5 | 98.2 | 96.2 |
| Other NE States | 78.4 | – | 78.4 | 81.0 | – | 81.0 | 81.4 | | 81.4 | 75.7 | | 75.7 |
| Rest ST and UT | 91.0 | 95.2 | 94.0 | 86.1 | 69.0 | 74.3 | 90.5 | 86.7 | 88.0 | 91.4 | 89.5 | 90.3 |
| All-India | 83.2 | 85.2 | 83.7 | 85.0 | 85.4 | 85.1 | 88.8 | 90.4 | 89.2 | 89.9 | 94.5 | 91.1 |

*Source:* Unit level data of housing condition and migration schedule of 49th Round (1993), common property, sanitation, and hygiene schedule of 54th Round (1998), and housing condition schedule of 58th (2002) and 65th Rounds (2008–9).

**Table A5.9**  Percentage Households Having Access to Bathroom Facility, 1993, 1998, and 2008–9

| State | 1993 | | | 1998 | | | 2008–9 | | | |
|---|---|---|---|---|---|---|---|---|---|---|
| | < 50,000 | 50,000 to 200,000 | 200,000 to 1 million | < 50,000 | 50,000 to 200,000 | 200,000 to 1 million | < 50,000 | 50,000 to 1 lakh | 1 lakh to 5 lakh | 5 lakh to 1 million |
| Andhra Pradesh | 41.1 | 49.8 | 56.1 | 63.0 | 69.8 | 75.2 | 81.4 | 89.2 | 84.3 | 89.7 |
| Assam | 74.9 | 72.2 | 76.2 | 83.9 | 93.5 | 86.9 | 89.8 | 98.5 | 99.6 | 96.1 |
| Bihar | 41.4 | 35.2 | 48.1 | 35.5 | 27.6 | 81.9 | 53.0 | 52.0 | 59.8 | 86.9 |
| Gujarat | 53.0 | 60.5 | 64.9 | 78.0 | 61.9 | 77.8 | 70.2 | 91.7 | 83.1 | 83.9 |
| Haryana | 56.5 | 64.3 | 42.9 | 70.5 | 69.5 | 83.7 | 84.6 | 85.4 | 89.7 | |
| Jammu and Kashmir | 45.7 | – | 72.6 | 86.0 | – | 82.7 | 77.9 | 96.8 | 82.0 | 89.1 |
| Karnataka | 48.8 | 67.3 | 75.3 | 57.5 | 73.2 | 75.7 | 70.4 | 64.3 | 82.0 | 95.0 |
| Kerala | 64.4 | 71.7 | 86.9 | 81.9 | 91.8 | 93.1 | 91.6 | 92.8 | 88.3 | 92.2 |
| Madhya Pradesh | 41.3 | 53.8 | 46.1 | 55.8 | 46.9 | 69.5 | 65.9 | 69.7 | 63.5 | 73.3 |
| Maharashtra | 36.5 | 52.8 | 51.4 | 49.6 | 79.4 | 62.7 | 69.9 | 81.8 | 78.9 | 84.7 |
| Orissa | 26.6 | 30.5 | 54.8 | 31.1 | 53.2 | 59.7 | 59.1 | 35.0 | 66.1 | 74.7 |
| Punjab | 67.5 | 73.9 | 66.6 | 73.3 | 73.8 | 74.9 | 86.3 | 83.8 | 91.9 | 86.1 |
| Rajasthan | 43.1 | 53.6 | 60.8 | 66.1 | 63.5 | 66.6 | 69.5 | 86.0 | 89.1 | 95.5 |
| Tamil Nadu | 49.4 | 56.9 | 65.6 | 62.0 | 63.5 | 74.9 | 73.3 | 86.0 | 84.8 | 88.9 |
| Uttar Pradesh | 31.2 | 42.6 | 46.4 | 38.4 | 62.1 | 66.6 | 59.6 | 75.3 | 72.3 | 89.0 |
| West Bengal | 37.0 | 59.5 | 52.9 | 51.1 | 63.6 | 57.6 | 63.5 | 71.2 | 78.6 | |
| Other NE States | 47.7 | 63.8 | – | 52.4 | 70.4 | – | 63.5 | 97.6 | 77.0 | |
| Rest ST and UT | 61.7 | 76.2 | 84.0 | 66.8 | 75.5 | 69.1 | 87.8 | 87.8 | 91.2 | 90.9 |
| All-India | 44.3 | 55.3 | 57.3 | 56.4 | 64.1 | 70.3 | 70.7 | 80.4 | 79.9 | 87.5 |

*Source:* Unit level data of housing condition and migration schedule of 49th Round (1993), common property, sanitation, and hygiene schedule of 54th Round (1998), and housing condition schedule of 65th Round (2008–9).

**Table A5.10**  Percentage Households Having Access to Bathroom Facility, Metro, Non-metro, and Total, 1993, 1998, 2002, and 2008–9

| State | 1993 | | | 1998 | | | 2002 | | | 2008–9 | | |
|---|---|---|---|---|---|---|---|---|---|---|---|---|
| | Non-metro | Metro | Total Urban | Non-metro | Metro | Total Urban | Non-metro | Metro | Total Urban | Non-metro | Metro | Total Urban |
| Andhra Pradesh | 49.2 | 85.63 | 53.17 | 69.2 | 81.4 | 71.8 | 72.8 | 94.2 | 75.6 | 85.8 | 98.0 | 87.7 |
| Assam | 74.6 | – | 74.61 | 86.6 | – | 86.6 | 88 | | 88 | 94.2 | | 94.2 |
| Bihar | 41.8 | – | 41.72 | 39.7 | 60.3 | 42.6 | 53.1 | 67.6 | 55.2 | 57.9 | 61.2 | 58.4 |
| Gujarat | 58.1 | 62.8 | 59.43 | 70.2 | 71.8 | 70.8 | 86.2 | 85.1 | 85.7 | 81.5 | 82.6 | 82.0 |
| Haryana | 56.0 | – | 56 | 71.8 | – | 71.8 | 76.6 | 88.1 | 77.9 | 88.0 | 92.7 | 89.0 |
| Jammu and Kashmir | 59.5 | – | 59.51 | 84.3 | – | 84.3 | 87.3 | | 87.3 | 87.4 | | 87.2 |
| Karnataka | 60.3 | 77.26 | 63.86 | 67.6 | 96.8 | 73 | 75 | 85.5 | 77.7 | 78.5 | 94.7 | 82.2 |
| Kerala | 72.2 | – | 72.18 | 86.8 | – | 86.8 | 84.8 | | 84.8 | 91.3 | | 91.3 |
| Madhya Pradesh | 46.3 | 63.91 | 48.72 | 57.0 | 77.1 | 60.2 | 62.9 | 64.5 | 63.2 | 66.9 | 93.7 | 70.6 |
| Maharashtra | 46.9 | 47.35 | 47.13 | 63.4 | 56.9 | 60.6 | 56.7 | 51.4 | 53.8 | 78.7 | 60.1 | 68.9 |
| Orissa | 36.3 | – | 36.35 | 45.8 | – | 45.8 | 57.5 | | 57.5 | 60.6 | | 60.6 |
| Punjab | 69.4 | 82.55 | 72.29 | 74.1 | 57.5 | 69.3 | 71.1 | 96.8 | 76.1 | 87.1 | 99.0 | 90.3 |
| Rajasthan | 51.0 | 72.2 | 53.94 | 65.5 | 67.6 | 66 | 65 | 88 | 69 | 83.2 | 92.3 | 85.2 |
| Tamil Nadu | 56.0 | 80.69 | 60.85 | 66.2 | 87.3 | 70.9 | 70.1 | 94.9 | 74.9 | 79.9 | 95.4 | 81.9 |
| Uttar Pradesh | 39.6 | 49.44 | 40.98 | 54.0 | 52.1 | 53.6 | 59.5 | 63.4 | 60.5 | 71.8 | 79.2 | 73.4 |
| West Bengal | 50.2 | 53.38 | 50.91 | 57.5 | 75.4 | 61.6 | 63 | 76.9 | 66.5 | 74.8 | 87.2 | 78.1 |
| Other NE States | 53.7 | – | 53.74 | 59.9 | – | 59.9 | 60.7 | | 60.7 | 70.5 | | 70.5 |
| Rest ST and UT | 73.9 | 57.5 | 62.24 | 70.4 | 76.7 | 74.7 | 78.4 | 74.1 | 75.6 | 89.3 | 82.4 | 85.4 |
| All-India | 51.6 | 59.85 | 53.51 | 63.0 | 69.8 | 64.7 | 67.6 | 70.8 | 68.5 | 78.3 | 79.2 | 78.5 |

*Source:* Unit level data of housing condition and migration schedule of 49th Round (1993), common property, sanitation, and hygiene schedule of 54th Round (1998), and housing condition schedule of 58th (2002) and 65th Rounds (2008–9).

**Table A5.11** Percentage Households Having No Drainage Facility, 1993, 1998, and 2008–9

| State | 1993 | | | 1998 | | | 2008–9 | | | |
|---|---|---|---|---|---|---|---|---|---|---|
| | < 50,000 | 50,000 to 200,000 | 200,000 to 1 million | < 50,000 | 50,000 to 200,000 | 200,000 to 1 million | < 50,000 | 50,000 to 1 lakh | 1 lakh to 5 lakh | 5 lakh to 1 million |
| Andhra Pradesh | 52.0 | 34.1 | 32.7 | 26.6 | 24.5 | 18.7 | 17.2 | 12.2 | 19.9 | 15.5 |
| Assam | 51.7 | 40.3 | 45.8 | 46.1 | 3.7 | 36.0 | 34.4 | 10.6 | 13.3 | 13.1 |
| Bihar | 36.4 | 34.2 | 21.9 | 50.9 | 43.9 | 7.1 | 31.0 | 12.7 | 27.5 | 15.3 |
| Gujarat | 28.3 | 30.3 | 6.1 | 27.5 | 29.8 | 7.3 | 24.3 | 3.3 | 8.6 | 3.8 |
| Haryana | 11.5 | 14.2 | 38.5 | 25.0 | 18.4 | 11.1 | 8.3 | 18.4 | 5.8 | |
| Jammu and Kashmir | 16.3 | – | 14.6 | 4.8 | – | 3.3 | 17.8 | 0.7 | | 5.0 |
| Karnataka | 34.0 | 21.9 | 22.4 | 32.2 | 15.8 | 7.6 | 26.8 | 19.9 | 10.7 | 1.3 |
| Kerala | 92.6 | 84.1 | 57.3 | 66.2 | 45.4 | 11.1 | 47.6 | 62.0 | 63.4 | 50.7 |
| Madhya Pradesh | 35.2 | 29.2 | 37.5 | 24.3 | 26.2 | 24.9 | 19.9 | 14.5 | 20.5 | 11.9 |
| Maharashtra | 44.0 | 42.2 | 16.9 | 23.7 | 8.2 | 12.1 | 18.9 | 14.4 | 7.1 | 39.2 |
| Orissa | 54.8 | 45.6 | 46.9 | 51.5 | 26.4 | 23.1 | 37.5 | 46.9 | 32.3 | 33.4 |
| Punjab | 12.1 | 8.5 | 19.5 | 3.9 | 8.1 | 10.7 | 7.4 | 9.2 | 7.4 | 15.7 |
| Rajasthan | 16.2 | 15.0 | 17.4 | 16.7 | 22.8 | 30.5 | 20.1 | 14.9 | 8.1 | 2.7 |
| Tamil Nadu | 39.3 | 25.7 | 21.5 | 45.1 | 26.4 | 47.2 | 28.0 | 23.8 | 13.6 | 10.0 |
| Uttar Pradesh | 15.1 | 7.1 | 7.7 | 9.7 | 3.3 | 9.5 | 10.8 | 4.2 | 7.8 | 2.4 |
| West Bengal | 77.8 | 43.3 | 32.6 | 42.4 | 26.4 | 18.2 | 50.1 | 27.8 | 21.8 | |
| Other NE States | 50.5 | 31.2 | – | 47.7 | 22.5 | – | 41.3 | 24.1 | 23.8 | |
| Rest ST and UT | 34.4 | 20.4 | 9.6 | 37.9 | 17.9 | 10.3 | 14.9 | 8.7 | 2.1 | 1.0 |
| All-India | 40.6 | 29.6 | 23.5 | 32.2 | 21.6 | 18.3 | 24.5 | 16.9 | 15.7 | 16.9 |

*Source*: Unit level data of housing condition and migration schedule of 49th Round (1993), common property, sanitation, and hygiene schedule of 54th Round (1998), and housing condition schedule of 65th Round (2008–9).

**Table A5.12**  Percentage Households Having No Drainage Facility, Metro, Non-metro, and Total, 1993, 1998, 2002, and 2008–9

| State | 1993 | | | 1998 | | | 2002 | | | 2008–9 | | |
|---|---|---|---|---|---|---|---|---|---|---|---|---|
| | Non-metro | Metro | Total Urban | Non-metro | Metro | Total Urban | Non-metro | Metro | Total Urban | Non-metro | Metro | Total Urban |
| Andhra Pradesh | 39.0 | 3.6 | 35.2 | 23.7 | 5.6 | 19.9 | 22.7 | 2.8 | 20.0 | 17.2 | 0.7 | 14.6 |
| Assam | 47.9 | – | 48.0 | 33.8 | – | 33.8 | 23.6 | – | 23.6 | 22.6 | – | 22.6 |
| Bihar | 30.8 | – | 30.9 | 41.0 | 10.7 | 36.7 | 24.1 | 3.4 | 21.2 | 25.2 | 4.5 | 21.7 |
| Gujarat | 26.6 | 5.8 | 20.5 | 26.1 | 1.9 | 17.4 | 16.4 | 3.8 | 11.1 | 11.2 | 4.2 | 8.3 |
| Haryana | 20.9 | – | 20.9 | 18.9 | – | 18.9 | 17.0 | 6.9 | 15.9 | 7.3 | 2.4 | 6.3 |
| Jammu and Kashmir | 15.4 | – | 15.4 | 4.0 | – | 4.0 | 16.8 | – | 16.8 | 7.6 | – | 7.8 |
| Karnataka | 28.0 | 8.2 | 23.8 | 20.0 | 0.9 | 16.5 | 16.9 | 2.9 | 13.3 | 15.1 | 0.4 | 11.7 |
| Kerala | 80.8 | – | 80.9 | 47.4 | – | 47.4 | 57.4 | – | 57.4 | 54.0 | – | 54.0 |
| Madhya Pradesh | 33.7 | 29.5 | 33.2 | 24.9 | 38.6 | 27.2 | 20.3 | 31.5 | 22.1 | 18.0 | 4.7 | 16.2 |
| Maharashtra | 32.8 | 9.4 | 21.8 | 14.1 | 2.8 | 9.2 | 21.5 | 9.3 | 14.8 | 20.2 | 2.5 | 10.9 |
| Orissa | 50.2 | – | 50.2 | 36.0 | – | 36.0 | 43.4 | – | 43.4 | 36.7 | – | 36.7 |
| Punjab | 13.8 | 2.1 | 11.2 | 8.4 | 2.4 | 6.6 | 16.7 | 0.4 | 13.5 | 10.2 | 0.4 | 7.5 |
| Rajasthan | 16.2 | 8.9 | 15.2 | 23.3 | 37.9 | 26.2 | 20.5 | 5.3 | 17.8 | 12.3 | 1.1 | 9.8 |
| Tamil Nadu | 30.0 | 21.2 | 28.3 | 39.6 | 5.9 | 32.1 | 25.0 | 8.8 | 21.9 | 22.0 | 4.2 | 19.7 |
| Uttar Pradesh | 10.3 | 7.8 | 10.0 | 7.7 | 19.1 | 10.0 | 7.1 | 6.6 | 7.0 | 7.2 | 4.8 | 6.7 |
| West Bengal | 52.8 | 6.3 | 42.0 | 30.6 | 9.9 | 25.8 | 34.9 | 8.3 | 28.1 | 28.2 | 2.9 | 21.4 |
| Other NE States | 43.2 | – | 43.2 | 37.5 | – | 37.5 | 25.6 | – | 25.6 | 34.4 | – | 34.4 |
| Rest ST and UT | 21.6 | 4.5 | 9.4 | 22.4 | 4.3 | 9.9 | 13.3 | 8.7 | 10.3 | 8.1 | 3.7 | 5.6 |
| All-India | 32.0 | 9.2 | 26.8 | 24.6 | 8.5 | 20.6 | 22.4 | 8.1 | 18.5 | 19.0 | 2.9 | 14.8 |

*Source:* Unit level data of housing condition and migration schedule of 49th Round (1993), common property, sanitation, and hygiene schedule of 54th Round (1998), and housing condition schedule of 58th (2002) and 65th Rounds (2008–9).

**Table A5.13**  Percentage Households Having Access to Pucca Covered or Underground Drainage,* 1993, 1998, and 2008–9

| State | 1993 | | | 1998 | | | 2008–9 | | | |
|---|---|---|---|---|---|---|---|---|---|---|
| | < 50,000 | 50,000 to 200,000 | 200,000 to 1 million | < 50,000 | 50,000 to 200,000 | 200,000 to 1 million | < 50,000 | 50,000 to 1 lakh | 1 lakh to 5 lakh | 5 lakh to 1 million |
| Andhra Pradesh | 12.2 | 20.1 | 12.4 | 6.8 | 19.9 | 21.5 | 48.3 | 37.8 | 56.1 | 61.1 |
| Assam | 2.2 | 9.2 | 0.5 | 0.0 | 5.1 | 3.6 | 5.5 | 19.1 | 15.6 | 13.8 |
| Bihar | 8.9 | 13.0 | 32.8 | 4.0 | 8.2 | 16.8 | 25.7 | 16.0 | 43.9 | 34.1 |
| Gujarat | 64.3 | 64.8 | 35.5 | 37.6 | 37.6 | 71.0 | 65.6 | 76.0 | 67.4 | 91.6 |
| Haryana | 18.2 | 35.2 | 7.4 | 16.0 | 34.9 | 71.9 | 21.8 | 66.1 | 61.8 | |
| Jammu and Kashmir | 1.6 | – | 11.2 | 4.2 | – | 65.0 | 6.0 | 14.6 | | 44.7 |
| Karnataka | 15.1 | 31.7 | 67.7 | 13.8 | 5.2 | 59.3 | 46.1 | 61.7 | 75.9 | 86.6 |
| Kerala | 17.0 | 23.7 | 45.9 | 9.7 | 18.4 | 45.9 | 60.0 | 69.6 | 65.0 | 88.8 |
| Madhya Pradesh | 27.4 | 32.3 | 41.6 | 11.8 | 13.8 | 11.4 | 30.7 | 40.3 | 26.7 | 51.7 |
| Maharashtra | 11.2 | 35.0 | 44.6 | 16.1 | 52.5 | 43.5 | 44.5 | 63.9 | 61.9 | 81.3 |
| Orissa | 9.4 | 0.9 | 52.9 | 3.5 | 6.3 | 16.0 | 30.6 | 19.2 | 46.3 | 74.8 |
| Punjab | 22.8 | 26.5 | 46.3 | 9.6 | 16.9 | 46.9 | 52.4 | 68.4 | 81.1 | 80.1 |
| Rajasthan | 23.2 | 12.7 | 29.3 | 24.3 | 16.0 | 29.7 | 35.8 | 40.2 | 46.4 | 88.8 |
| Tamil Nadu | 15.9 | 30.2 | 23.7 | 6.8 | 21.2 | 15.0 | 29.7 | 45.2 | 34.3 | 58.1 |
| Uttar Pradesh | 17.9 | 37.9 | 28.3 | 27.5 | 21.1 | 34.8 | 30.0 | 39.8 | 48.6 | 54.1 |
| West Bengal | 24.0 | 6.2 | 2.6 | 1.7 | 5.8 | 3.5 | 7.7 | 12.0 | 21.0 | |
| Other NE States | 1.2 | 3.4 | – | 3.6 | 7.7 | – | 10.0 | 4.2 | 7.2 | |
| Rest ST and UT | 20.2 | 62.8 | 100.0 | 38.3 | 43.5 | 54.1 | 56.6 | 66.5 | 70.5 | 89.6 |
| All-India | 20.0 | 29.8 | 33.2 | 13.6 | 20.9 | 32.5 | 35.9 | 46.8 | 50.3 | 67.5 |

*Source:* Unit level data of housing condition and migration schedule of 49th Round (1993), common property, sanitation, and hygiene schedule of 54th Round (1998), and housing condition schedule of 65th Round (2008–9).

*Note:* *Of those having access to drainage.

**Table A5.14**  Percentage Households Having Access to Pucca Covered or Underground Drainage,* Metro, Non-metro, and Total, 1993, 1998, 2002, and 2008–9

| State | 1993 | | | 1998 | | | 2002 | | | 2008–9 | | |
|---|---|---|---|---|---|---|---|---|---|---|---|---|
| | Non-metro | Metro | Total Urban | Non-metro | Metro | Total Urban | Non-metro | Metro | Total Urban | Non-metro | Metro | Total Urban |
| Andhra Pradesh | 15.4 | 90.6 | 27.6 | 16.6 | 79.6 | 29.9 | 42.2 | 98.2 | 51.4 | 51.6 | 99.8 | 60.2 |
| Assam | 3.5 | – | 3.5 | 2.1 | – | 2.1 | 10.8 | | 10.8 | 11.6 | | 11.6 |
| Bihar | 19.0 | – | 19.1 | 7.8 | 27.0 | 10.6 | 25.8 | 52.4 | 30.5 | 30.0 | 88.6 | 41.9 |
| Gujarat | 60.0 | 94.7 | 72.1 | 41.7 | 87.3 | 58.1 | 73.5 | 98.7 | 85.0 | 73.6 | 98.2 | 84.5 |
| Haryana | 24.1 | – | 24.1 | 35.7 | – | 35.7 | 58.3 | 79.0 | 60.8 | 50.6 | 46.6 | 49.8 |
| Jammu and Kashmir | 6.6 | – | 6.6 | 36.6 | – | 36.6 | 28.0 | | 28.0 | 31.8 | | 31.8 |
| Karnataka | 34.2 | 71.7 | 43.8 | 25.0 | 97.1 | 38.3 | 41.9 | 84.7 | 54.0 | 68.8 | 97.2 | 76.0 |
| Kerala | 36.0 | – | 36.3 | 21.0 | – | 21.0 | 47.9 | | 47.9 | 71.5 | | 71.5 |
| Madhya Pradesh | 31.9 | 50.4 | 34.6 | 12.2 | 25.7 | 14.5 | 35.7 | 47.8 | 37.4 | 34.6 | 70.9 | 40.4 |
| Maharashtra | 33.1 | 68.1 | 52.2 | 38.8 | 63.5 | 49.3 | 38.2 | 73.9 | 59.2 | 61.8 | 88.3 | 77.0 |
| Orissa | 21.8 | – | 21.8 | 7.9 | – | 7.9 | 42.5 | | 42.5 | 44.0 | | 44.0 |
| Punjab | 32.6 | 61.7 | 39.8 | 27.4 | 51.6 | 34.5 | 53.4 | 55.5 | 53.9 | 69.5 | 78.6 | 72.2 |
| Rajasthan | 22.2 | 29.7 | 23.4 | 23.9 | 32.6 | 25.7 | 36.6 | 40.1 | 37.3 | 50.6 | 72.7 | 56.1 |
| Tamil Nadu | 23.5 | 92.7 | 38.5 | 13.8 | 76.7 | 27.9 | 38.8 | 94.4 | 51.4 | 38.6 | 91.8 | 46.7 |
| Uttar Pradesh | 27.1 | 44.7 | 29.7 | 27.9 | 41.1 | 30.5 | 43.9 | 66.2 | 49.2 | 42.5 | 59.6 | 46.3 |
| West Bengal | 7.9 | 63.4 | 29.0 | 3.7 | 45.3 | 13.4 | 16.6 | 67.3 | 33.1 | 18.3 | 63.6 | 33.3 |
| Other NE States | 2.2 | – | 2.2 | 5.3 | – | 5.3 | 7.7 | | 7.7 | 8.5 | | 8.5 |
| Rest ST and UT | 63.4 | 60.2 | 61.1 | 45.1 | 55.9 | 52.5 | 62.7 | 60.0 | 60.9 | 67.6 | 75.3 | 72.0 |
| All-India | 27.5 | 68.0 | 39.1 | 21.5 | 60.2 | 31.2 | 40.8 | 74.0 | 51.2 | 48.4 | 82.7 | 58.5 |

*Source*: Unit level data of housing condition and migration schedule of 49th Round (1993), common property, sanitation, and hygiene schedule of 54th Round (1998), and housing condition schedule of 58th (2002) and 65th Rounds (2008–9).

*Note*: *Of those having access to drainage.

**Table A5.15** Percentage Households Not Having Access to Toilets, 1993, 1998, and 2008–9

| State | 1993 | | | 1998 | | | 2008–9 | | | |
|---|---|---|---|---|---|---|---|---|---|---|
| | < 50,000 | 50,000 to 200,000 | 200,000 to 1 million | < 50,000 | 50,000 to 200,000 | 200,000 to 1 million | < 50,000 | 50,000 to 1 lakh | 1 lakh to 5 lakh | 5 lakh to 1 million |
| Andhra Pradesh | 52.3 | 40.5 | 28.5 | 49.8 | 38.0 | 21.3 | 19.4 | 10.3 | 13.6 | 10.5 |
| Assam | 7.9 | 2.0 | 9.7 | 1.0 | 1.9 | 4.3 | 1.6 | 0.0 | 0.0 | 0.8 |
| Bihar | 41.7 | 35.4 | 27.9 | 57.0 | 55.3 | 9.6 | 36.0 | 41.8 | 24.2 | 8.3 |
| Gujarat | 27.4 | 33.5 | 14.9 | 19.6 | 33.9 | 16.8 | 14.3 | 6.5 | 9.4 | 10.3 |
| Haryana | 45.4 | 20.5 | 37.5 | 44.8 | 32.0 | 16.6 | 15.8 | 16.9 | 6.2 | |
| Jammu and Kashmir | 49.4 | – | 16.9 | 16.2 | – | 7.7 | 25.5 | 3.6 | | 8.2 |
| Karnataka | 59.5 | 27.5 | 19.7 | – | 25.0 | 30.1 | 29.2 | 21.0 | 8.1 | 1.2 |
| Kerala | 23.8 | 9.3 | 5.6 | 8.5 | 1.4 | 0.9 | 0.7 | 1.6 | 3.6 | 0.7 |
| Madhya Pradesh | 54.1 | 38.0 | 37.4 | 57.6 | 39.3 | 24.9 | 37.8 | 23.8 | 30.2 | 10.5 |
| Maharashtra | 48.2 | 31.5 | 23.8 | 47.2 | 19.4 | 15.5 | 18.0 | 11.1 | 6.8 | 4.9 |
| Orissa | 65.7 | 65.2 | 33.1 | 44.9 | 29.2 | 29.3 | 36.2 | 48.9 | 17.8 | 16.9 |
| Punjab | 32.8 | 21.7 | 25.5 | 25.7 | 18.8 | 13.8 | 12.6 | 5.7 | 4.3 | 3.4 |
| Rajasthan | 49.5 | 38.4 | 32.6 | 29.6 | 16.8 | 25.8 | 29.1 | 13.5 | 5.1 | 4.8 |
| Tamil Nadu | 52.0 | 33.8 | 31.5 | 48.0 | 31.7 | 34.5 | 24.4 | 19.8 | 12.7 | 3.3 |
| Uttar Pradesh | 44.5 | 27.3 | 23.6 | 39.5 | 16.8 | 18.8 | 26.4 | 10.8 | 12.7 | 4.5 |
| West Bengal | 36.4 | 18.8 | 25.4 | 26.1 | 10.8 | 15.9 | 15.7 | 6.9 | 4.9 | |
| Other NE States | 3.0 | 1.2 | – | 3.0 | 1.7 | – | 0.5 | 1.2 | 0.0 | |
| Rest ST and UT | 31.0 | 20.7 | 10.4 | 18.5 | 25.7 | 30.5 | 4.9 | 4.4 | 3.8 | 0.6 |
| All-India | 44.7 | 30.3 | 25.6 | 39.3 | 27.2 | 20.4 | 22.6 | 14.7 | 10.6 | 5.6 |

*Source:* Unit level data of housing condition and migration schedule of 49th Round (1993), common property, sanitation, and hygiene schedule of 54th Round (1998), and housing condition schedule of 65th Round (2008–9).

**Table A5.16**  Percentage Households Not Having Access to Toilets, Metro, Non-metro, and Total, 1993, 1998, 2002, and 2008–9

| State | 1993 | | | 1998 | | | 2002 | | | 2008–9 | | |
|---|---|---|---|---|---|---|---|---|---|---|---|---|
| | Non-metro | Metro | Total Urban | Non-metro | Metro | Total Urban | Non-metro | Metro | Total Urban | Non-metro | Metro | Total Urban |
| Andhra Pradesh | 40.1 | 9.2 | 36.8 | 37.2 | 7.0 | 30.9 | 22.6 | 2.1 | 19.8 | 13.1 | 0.6 | 11.2 |
| Assam | 7.0 | – | 7.0 | 2.0 | – | 2.0 | 1.8 | – | 1.8 | 0.9 | – | 0.9 |
| Bihar | 35.1 | – | 35.2 | 48.5 | 26.6 | 45.4 | 35.7 | 2.7 | 31.0 | 31.0 | 5.7 | 26.7 |
| Gujarat | 28.8 | 23.8 | 27.4 | 26.1 | 12.1 | 21.1 | 9.5 | 3.2 | 6.8 | 10.3 | 3.3 | 7.3 |
| Haryana | 31.6 | – | 31.6 | 32.9 | – | 32.9 | 15.5 | 11.0 | 15.0 | 9.6 | 3.9 | 8.4 |
| Jammu and Kashmir | 32.1 | – | 32.5 | 11.7 | – | 11.7 | 12.6 | | 12.6 | 11.9 | 0.4 | 11.8 |
| Karnataka | 41.2 | 12.7 | 35.2 | 61.3 | 1.1 | 30.0 | 25.9 | 3.2 | 20.1 | 14.5 | 0.4 | 11.3 |
| Kerala | 15.7 | – | 15.7 | 5.1 | – | 5.1 | 3.7 | – | 3.7 | 1.5 | – | 1.5 |
| Madhya Pradesh | 45.3 | 30.5 | 43.3 | 44.8 | 47.1 | 45.2 | 34.1 | 38.2 | 34.8 | 29.3 | 4.4 | 25.9 |
| Maharashtra | 33.8 | 11.1 | 23.2 | 24.5 | 4.0 | 15.8 | 24.2 | 7.9 | 15.2 | 9.9 | 2.2 | 5.9 |
| Orissa | 55.4 | – | 55.4 | 35.8 | – | 35.8 | 32.9 | | 32.9 | 29.1 | | 29.1 |
| Punjab | 26.1 | 3.6 | 21.1 | 18.1 | 7.0 | 14.8 | 14.2 | 0.8 | 11.6 | 6.8 | 0.0 | 5.0 |
| Rajasthan | 41.5 | 11.0 | 37.4 | 24.7 | 28.6 | 25.5 | 34.6 | 11.8 | 30.7 | 14.5 | 6.0 | 12.6 |
| Tamil Nadu | 40.4 | 18.4 | 36.1 | 38.9 | 10.4 | 32.5 | 26.3 | 3.9 | 21.9 | 18.2 | 0.6 | 16.0 |
| Uttar Pradesh | 32.5 | 32.5 | 32.5 | 26.5 | 35.2 | 28.2 | 18.2 | 11.8 | 16.7 | 15.5 | 6.7 | 13.6 |
| West Bengal | 26.4 | 4.4 | 21.2 | 17.8 | 6.6 | 15.2 | 14.3 | 2.0 | 11.2 | 7.3 | 0.8 | 5.6 |
| Other NE States | 2.3 | – | 2.3 | 0.7 | – | 2.4 | 0.4 | | 0.4 | 0.4 | | 0.4 |
| Rest ST and UT | 21.0 | 29.8 | 27.3 | 37.4 | 8.4 | 13.5 | 8.7 | 7.2 | 7.7 | 3.9 | 1.3¹ | 2.5 |
| All-India | 34.5 | 17.5 | 30.6 | 44.8 | 12.7 | 25.5 | 21.8 | 7.5 | 17.9 | 14.4 | 2.5 | 11.3 |

*Source:* Unit level data of housing condition and migration schedule of 49th Round (1993), common property, sanitation, and hygiene schedule of 54th Round (1998), and housing condition schedule of 58th (2002) and 65th Rounds (2008–9).

**Table A5.17** Percentage Households Having Individual Access to Toilets,* 1993, 1998, and 2008–9

| State | 1993 | | | 1998 | | | 2008–9 | | | |
|---|---|---|---|---|---|---|---|---|---|---|
| | < 50,000 | 50,000 to 200,000 | 200,000 to 1 million | < 50,000 | 50,000 to 200,000 | 200,000 to 1 million | < 50,000 | 50,000 to 1 lakh | 1 lakh to 5 lakh | 5 lakh to 1 million |
| Andhra Pradesh | 61.0 | 53.6 | 53.7 | 57.7 | 63.6 | 65.8 | 66.2 | 52.9 | 65.3 | 72.4 |
| Assam | 73.1 | 73.9 | 62.9 | 79.4 | 76.9 | 37.2 | 81.0 | 69.8 | 79.3 | 62.5 |
| Bihar | 72.5 | 51.7 | 66.7 | 75.9 | 59.4 | 78.1 | 53.3 | 74.2 | 70.0 | 69.3 |
| Gujarat | 61.7 | 76.9 | 60.8 | 82.0 | 71.5 | 66.5 | 69.0 | 58.9 | 73.2 | 90.1 |
| Haryana | 75.3 | 53.1 | 69.9 | 63.7 | 75.0 | 98.0 | 72.4 | 69.0 | 75.3 | |
| Jammu and Kashmir | 57.1 | – | 53.9 | 53.7 | – | 87.9 | 77.5 | 95.7 | | 73.3 |
| Karnataka | 51.0 | 54.3 | 57.5 | 65.5 | 64.9 | 55.8 | 70.9 | 73.0 | 67.4 | 70.5 |
| Kerala | 92.8 | 85.6 | 73.3 | 85.9 | 85.9 | 86.5 | 86.6 | 91.5 | 83.8 | 89.6 |
| Madhya Pradesh | 74.4 | 67.0 | 59.2 | 78.2 | 64.2 | 82.2 | 79.1 | 66.5 | 71.1 | 68.3 |
| Maharashtra | 48.5 | 35.2 | 51.7 | 42.5 | 53.0 | 55.2 | 59.6 | 67.5 | 62.3 | 48.2 |
| Orissa | 91.8 | 72.0 | 81.2 | 66.8 | 73.9 | 79.4 | 82.0 | 68.4 | 79.5 | 68.3 |
| Punjab | 82.7 | 75.9 | 54.5 | 85.9 | 87.7 | 56.5 | 75.6 | 82.7 | 81.6 | 57.1 |
| Rajasthan | 62.0 | 58.7 | 64.1 | 67.7 | 69.7 | 67.7 | 76.5 | 67.3 | 72.9 | 66.9 |
| Tamil Nadu | 50.9 | 53.5 | 52.3 | 73.5 | 66.2 | 57.2 | 64.7 | 58.8 | 72.3 | 51.1 |
| Uttar Pradesh | 71.7 | 74.4 | 61.3 | 77.1 | 53.0 | 67.0 | 73.8 | 76.6 | 70.4 | 72.3 |
| West Bengal | 65.3 | 63.2 | 48.3 | 79.0 | 58.1 | 42.1 | 65.5 | 68.9 | 59.4 | |
| Other NE States | 76.0 | 67.9 | – | 70.1 | 51.7 | – | 72.6 | 59.1 | 66.4 | |
| Rest ST and UT | 55.0 | 83.8 | 66.9 | 60.5 | 81.4 | 78.4 | 55.3 | 71.5 | 72.7 | 69.5 |
| All-India | 66.2 | 61.7 | 58.7 | 72.1 | 64.5 | 63.9 | 69.4 | 66.5 | 68.4 | 65.9 |

*Source:* Unit level data of housing condition and migration schedule of 49th Round (1993), common property, sanitation, and hygiene schedule of 54th Round (1998), and housing condition schedule of 65th Round (2008–9).

*Note:* *Of those having toilet facility.

**Table A5.18** Percentage Households Having Individual Access to Toilets,* Metro, Non-metro, and Total, 1993, 1998, 2002, and 2008–9

| State | 1993 | | | 1998 | | | 2002 | | | 2008–9 | | |
|---|---|---|---|---|---|---|---|---|---|---|---|---|
| | Non-metro | Metro | Total Urban | Non-metro | Metro | Total Urban | Non-metro | Metro | Total Urban | Non-metro | Metro | Total Urban |
| Andhra Pradesh | 55.5 | 47.9 | 54.3 | 62.9 | 63.3 | 63.0 | 49.9 | 67.3 | 52.2 | 63.8 | 50.3 | 61.5 |
| Assam | 71.1 | – | 71.1 | 68.9 | – | 68.9 | 80.2 | – | 80.2 | 74.9 | – | 74.9 |
| Bihar | 64.0 | – | 64.0 | 70.4 | 53.7 | 67.3 | 41.0 | 55.4 | 43.1 | 64.1 | 58.9 | 63.0 |
| Gujarat | 68.2 | 74.7 | 70.2 | 75.3 | 71.6 | 73.8 | 67.3 | 80.6 | 72.9 | 71.2 | 74.8 | 72.8 |
| Haryana | 61.9 | – | 61.9 | 76.8 | – | 76.8 | 61.8 | 60.5 | 61.6 | 74.2 | 65.2 | 72.2 |
| Jammu and Kashmir | 55.1 | – | 55.1 | 72.7 | – | 72.7 | 64.5 | – | 64.5 | 77.5 | – | 77.6 |
| Karnataka | 54.3 | 65.0 | 57.3 | 62.0 | 70.1 | 64.1 | 49.5 | 71.9 | 55.2 | 69.1 | 83.8 | 72.9 |
| Kerala | 85.0 | – | 85.0 | 86.1 | – | 86.1 | 84.4 | – | 84.4 | 87.7 | – | 87.7 |
| Madhya Pradesh | 67.9 | 55.1 | 65.8 | 76.6 | 83.3 | 77.8 | 46.6 | 51.8 | 47.4 | 72.7 | 66.6 | 71.6 |
| Maharashtra | 46.1 | 39.2 | 42.3 | 52.4 | 40.6 | 46.7 | 44.6 | 41.8 | 43.1 | 58.4 | 47.2 | 52.3 |
| Orissa | 83.3 | – | 83.3 | 73.2 | – | 73.2 | 40.7 | – | 40.7 | 76.1 | – | 76.1 |
| Punjab | 69.1 | 58.7 | 66.3 | 74.5 | 35.7 | 62.1 | 67.7 | 47.4 | 63.7 | 72.4 | 39.9 | 63.0 |
| Rajasthan | 61.8 | 84.6 | 66.4 | 68.3 | 56.6 | 66.0 | 46.2 | 59.0 | 48.4 | 71.8 | 72.7 | 72.0 |
| Tamil Nadu | 52.4 | 56.1 | 53.3 | 65.9 | 45.8 | 59.9 | 45.9 | 56.8 | 48.0 | 62.3 | 63.7 | 62.5 |
| Uttar Pradesh | 68.2 | 56.8 | 66.6 | 65.7 | 68.7 | 66.2 | 61.2 | 65.6 | 62.2 | 72.7 | 74.1 | 73.0 |
| West Bengal | 60.4 | 24.8 | 50.2 | 61.4 | 34.1 | 54.4 | 49.3 | 45.3 | 48.3 | 61.4 | 47.2 | 57.4 |
| Other NE States | 72.9 | – | 72.9 | 62.2 | – | 62.2 | 67.1 | – | 67.1 | 69.6 | – | 69.6 |
| Rest ST and UT | 71.0 | 51.6 | 57.7 | 72.8 | 57.9 | 61.9 | 54.9 | 52.0 | 53.0 | 65.2 | 62.8 | 63.9 |
| All-India | 62.2 | 48.9 | 58.6 | 66.8 | 52.4 | 62.5 | 53.0 | 54.9 | 53.5 | 67.9 | 59.5 | 65.5 |

*Source:* Unit level data of housing condition and migration schedule of 49th Round (1993), common property, sanitation, and hygiene schedule of 54th Round (1998), and housing condition schedule of 58th (2002) and 65th Rounds (2008–9).

*Note:* *Of those having toilet facility.

**Table A5.19**   Percentage Households Having Toilets Inside Premises,* 1993 and 1998

| State | 1993 | | | | | 1998 | | | | |
|---|---|---|---|---|---|---|---|---|---|---|
| | < 50,000 | 50,000 to 200,000 | 200,000 to 1 million | > 1 million | Total Urban | < 50,000 | 50,000 to 200,000 | 200,000 to 1 million | > 1 million | Total Urban |
| Andhra Pradesh | 85.6 | 75.2 | 77.9 | 97.0 | 81.6 | 100.0 | 95.1 | 90.4 | 92.2 | 94.1 |
| Assam | 95.2 | 82.2 | 97.6 | – | 92.8 | 88.6 | 98.5 | 96.6 | – | 92.5 |
| Bihar | 76.1 | 87.3 | 85.9 | – | 83.1 | 97.7 | 97.1 | 99.3 | 100.0 | 98.3 |
| Gujarat | 71.7 | 89.5 | 75.2 | 88.1 | 82.5 | 92.3 | 92.3 | 99.5 | 84.2 | 89.6 |
| Haryana | 98.6 | 95.2 | 96.7 | – | 96.2 | 94.5 | 100.0 | 99.7 | – | 98.8 |
| Jammu and Kashmir | 94.4 | – | 97.7 | – | 96.5 | 59.8 | – | 99.7 | – | 82.0 |
| Karnataka | 77.8 | 88.5 | 89.2 | 80.9 | 83.9 | 94.1 | 88.5 | 95.9 | 92.7 | 92.7 |
| Kerala | 84.1 | 97.0 | 97.4 | – | 91.1 | 98.1 | 100.0 | 98.3 | – | 98.5 |
| Madhya Pradesh | 88.1 | 92.8 | 80.9 | 88.2 | 88.1 | 97.9 | 91.3 | 94.7 | 99.8 | 95.9 |
| Maharashtra | 72.0 | 59.6 | 62.9 | 63.1 | 63.6 | 81.4 | 92.4 | 73.8 | 71.7 | 75.9 |
| Orissa | 97.4 | 84.1 | 95.3 | – | 94.0 | 99.8 | 97.8 | 61.4 | – | 87.1 |
| Punjab | 98.4 | 92.9 | 95.2 | 98.3 | 96.0 | 96.6 | 99.7 | 96.0 | 99.7 | 98.3 |
| Rajasthan | 90.3 | 97.0 | 92.2 | 97.3 | 93.7 | 98.1 | 91.1 | 97.3 | 100.0 | 96.5 |
| Tamil Nadu | 73.9 | 83.2 | 87.5 | 95.2 | 84.9 | 92.3 | 93.3 | 89.5 | 95.1 | 92.8 |
| Uttar Pradesh | 92.6 | 90.3 | 94.4 | 85.9 | 91.7 | 100.0 | 97.3 | 98.2 | 95.2 | 97.9 |
| West Bengal | 81.8 | 90.3 | 89.1 | 87.8 | 87.6 | 95.7 | 92.0 | 88.3 | 91.3 | 91.9 |
| Other NE States | 87.8 | 90.2 | – | – | 88.7 | 95.1 | 99.2 | – | – | 96.8 |
| Rest ST and UT | 78.9 | 81.9 | 95.4 | 77.2 | 79.7 | 97.1 | 95.8 | 96.0 | 82.1 | 85.9 |
| All-India | 83.1 | 85.5 | 85.6 | 79.6 | 83.4 | 94.8 | 94.6 | 89.7 | 85.9 | 91.0 |

*Source:* Unit level data of housing condition and migration schedule of 49th Round (1993) and common property, sanitation, and hygiene schedule of 54th Round (1998).

*Note:* * Of those having toilet facilities.

**Table A5.20**   Percentage Households Reported Garbage Collection by Local Authority, 1998, 2002, and 2008–9

| State | 1993 | | | | | | 1998 | | |
|---|---|---|---|---|---|---|---|---|---|
| | < 50,000 | 50,000 to 200,000 | 200,000 to 1 million | Non-metro | Metro | Total Urban | Non-metro | Metro | Total Urban |
| Andhra Pradesh | 17.8 | 16.9 | 8.1 | 15.0 | 12.4 | 14.5 | 65.4 | 87.2 | 68.3 |
| Assam | 1.9 | 0.7 | 11.6 | 4.0 | – | 4.0 | 26.8 | | 26.8 |
| Bihar | 0.2 | 5.1 | 0.2 | 2.3 | 0.4 | 2.0 | 30.2 | 68.3 | 35.6 |
| Gujarat | 12.8 | 22.0 | 36.2 | 20.1 | 44.3 | 28.8 | 52.4 | 46.7 | 50.0 |
| Haryana | 20.9 | 0.0 | 24.4 | 8.4 | – | 8.4 | 33.2 | 59.8 | 36.1 |
| Jammu and Kashmir | 0.5 | – | 65.8 | 35.3 | – | 35.3 | 57.7 | | 57.7 |
| Karnataka | 12.2 | 15.6 | 13.2 | 13.5 | 50.7 | 20.4 | 58.0 | 93.6 | 67.0 |
| Kerala | 0.0 | 12.1 | 0.0 | 2.4 | – | 2.4 | 23.1 | | 23.1 |
| Madhya Pradesh | 1.4 | 4.7 | 18.3 | 6.5 | 1.9 | 5.7 | 49.5 | 52.6 | 50.0 |
| Maharashtra | 4.8 | 1.6 | 13.6 | 8.5 | 4.7 | 6.9 | 66.4 | 92.4 | 80.7 |
| Orissa | 0.2 | 0.0 | 10.2 | 3.0 | – | 3.0 | 51.2 | | 51.2 |
| Punjab | 8.5 | 3.6 | 4.5 | 4.8 | 0.1 | 3.4 | 44.8 | 52.8 | 46.4 |
| Rajasthan | 14.5 | 14.5 | 16.2 | 15.1 | 15.0 | 15.1 | 44.3 | 42.5 | 44.0 |
| Tamil Nadu | 10.7 | 26.6 | 17.6 | 17.8 | 18.1 | 17.9 | 74.9 | 84.8 | 76.8 |
| Uttar Pradesh | 19.2 | 25.4 | 6.5 | 17.1 | 3.3 | 14.4 | 57.7 | 46.8 | 55.1 |
| West Bengal | 22.1 | 15.2 | 26.2 | 20.4 | 56.3 | 28.7 | 42.3 | 86.7 | 53.6 |
| Other NE States | 0.7 | 10.8 | – | 5.0 | – | 5.0 | 23.4 | | 23.4 |
| Rest ST and UT | – | 33.2 | 29.7 | 21.6 | 13.1 | 15.7 | 55.2 | 52.6 | 53.5 |
| All-India | 10.3 | 14.4 | 14.3 | 12.8 | 16.2 | 13.7 | 53.9 | 72.3 | 59.0 |

*Source*: Unit level data of common property, sanitation and hygiene schedule of 54th Round (1998) and housing condition schedule of 58th (2002) and 65th Rounds (2008–9).

**Table A5.21** Percentage of Households Reported Garbage Collection by Local Authority, 2008–9

| State | < 50,000 | 50,000 to < 1 lakh | 1 lakh to < 5 lakh | 5 lakh to < 1 million | Non-metro | Metro | Total Urban |
|---|---|---|---|---|---|---|---|
| Andhra Pradesh | 53.0 | 53.5 | 69.5 | 81.6 | 65.7 | 60.8 | 64.9 |
| Assam | 23.0 | 55.8 | 27.4 | 29.5 | 28.8 | | 28.8 |
| Bihar | 14.7 | 32.2 | 30.4 | 37.6 | 24.8 | 61.2 | 30.9 |
| Gujarat | 46.9 | 43.9 | 53.2 | 48.4 | 48.2 | 76.3 | 60.1 |
| Haryana | 22.5 | 42.2 | 29.4 | | 28.2 | 38.0 | 30.2 |
| Jammu and Kashmir | 48.4 | 82.4 | | 74.5 | 69.2 | | 69.3 |
| Karnataka | 57.1 | 65.0 | 63.3 | 79.9 | 63.6 | 96.0 | 70.9 |
| Kerala | 9.2 | 14.1 | 12.4 | 47.9 | 22.4 | | 22.4 |
| Madhya Pradesh | 51.5 | 44.8 | 56.7 | 84.6 | 57.0 | 33.0 | 53.7 |
| Maharashtra | 61.8 | 76.0 | 77.8 | 55.6 | 67.2 | 92.9 | 80.7 |
| Orissa | 31.0 | 34.6 | 66.9 | 61.1 | 47.8 | | 47.8 |
| Punjab | 49.1 | 43.0 | 33.5 | 28.0 | 38.2 | 84.9 | 51.1 |
| Rajasthan | 44.3 | 59.0 | 74.0 | 57.0 | 58.5 | 74.4 | 62.1 |
| Tamil Nadu | 64.3 | 85.9 | 82.7 | 73.0 | 72.4 | 95.3 | 75.3 |
| Uttar Pradesh | 64.0 | 72.7 | 59.0 | 54.6 | 61.5 | 56.4 | 60.4 |
| West Bengal | 12.5 | 44.1 | 68.7 | | 54.8 | 85.9 | 63.1 |
| Other NE States | 11.2 | 37.3 | 48.9 | | 25.3 | | 25.3 |
| Rest ST and UT | 58.3 | 59.2 | 65.5 | 30.3 | 56.7 | 55.4 | 56.0 |
| India | 48.7 | 58.2 | 61.9 | 60.3 | 56.7 | 77.2 | 62.0 |

*Source*: Unit level data of housing condition schedule of 65th Round (2008–9).

**Table A6.1**  Work Participation Rates by Usual (Principal + Subsidiary) Status, Metro and Non-metro, 2009–10

| State | Male | | | Female | | |
|---|---|---|---|---|---|---|
| | Non-metro | Metro | Total Urban | Non-metro | Metro | Total Urban |
| Andhra Pradesh | 55.1 | 49.7 | 54.2 | 18.6 | 12.6 | 17.6 |
| Assam | 52.8 | | 52.8 | 9.3 | | 9.3 |
| Bihar | 46.3 | 39.2 | 45.1 | 6.6 | 3.6 | 6.1 |
| Gujarat | 56.5 | 56.1 | 56.3 | 14.5 | 14.1 | 14.3 |
| Haryana | 55.5 | 56.5 | 55.7 | 14.0 | 7.5 | 13.0 |
| Jammu and Kashmir | 54.2 | | 54.2 | 13.8 | | 13.8 |
| Karnataka | 56.4 | 61.4 | 57.6 | 16.2 | 19.3 | 17.0 |
| Kerala | 54.7 | | 54.7 | 19.4 | | 19.4 |
| Madhya Pradesh | 49.4 | 51.8 | 49.8 | 13.4 | 13.1 | 13.3 |
| Maharashtra | 56.7 | 58.4 | 57.5 | 14.2 | 17.9 | 15.9 |
| Orissa | 56.8 | | 56.8 | 11.9 | | 11.9 |
| Punjab | 55.4 | 65.2 | 56.8 | 13.2 | 7.3 | 12.4 |
| Rajasthan | 50.3 | 54.8 | 51.0 | 12.5 | 9.5 | 12.0 |
| Tamil Nadu | 57.2 | 55.4 | 56.9 | 21.0 | 8.6 | 19.1 |
| Uttar Pradesh | 50.4 | 50.1 | 50.3 | 8.0 | 8.7 | 8.2 |
| West Bengal | 57.9 | 60.5 | 58.4 | 14.3 | 13.3 | 14.1 |
| Other NE States | 49.0 | | 49.0 | 16.9 | | 16.9 |
| Rest ST and UT | 56.3 | 53.5 | 54.0 | 15.2 | 5.8 | 7.9 |
| All-India | 53.9 | 55.3 | 54.3 | 14.2 | 12.4 | 13.8 |

*Source:* Unit level data of employment and unemployment schedule of 66th (2009–10) Round of NSSO.

**Table A6.2**  Nature of Employment, Usual (Principal + Subsidiary) Status, Male, 2009–10

| State | Non-metro | | | Metro | | | Total Urban | | |
|---|---|---|---|---|---|---|---|---|---|
| | SE | RE | CL | SE | RE | CL | SE | RE | CL |
| Andhra Pradesh | 35.6 | 46.6 | 17.7 | 31.0 | 55.9 | 13.1 | 35.0 | 48.0 | 17.0 |
| Assam | 49.0 | 45.0 | 6.0 | | | | 49.0 | 45.0 | 6.0 |
| Bihar | 52.1 | 26.4 | 21.5 | 61.0 | 35.2 | 3.9 | 53.4 | 27.7 | 18.8 |
| Gujarat | 41.7 | 38.7 | 19.6 | 47.5 | 44.8 | 7.6 | 44.5 | 41.7 | 13.8 |
| Haryana | 39.0 | 47.7 | 13.4 | 20.7 | 69.9 | 9.4 | 35.5 | 51.8 | 12.6 |
| Jammu and Kashmir | 46.2 | 42.6 | 11.2 | | | | 46.2 | 42.6 | 11.2 |
| Karnataka | 38.9 | 36.5 | 24.6 | 41.1 | 47.2 | 11.8 | 39.5 | 39.3 | 21.2 |
| Kerala | 34.5 | 28.8 | 36.7 | | | | 34.5 | 28.8 | 36.7 |
| Madhya Pradesh | 46.1 | 32.6 | 21.4 | 33.5 | 53.4 | 13.1 | 44.2 | 35.7 | 20.2 |
| Maharashtra | 35.5 | 46.4 | 18.1 | 30.1 | 64.7 | 5.2 | 32.9 | 55.2 | 11.9 |
| Orissa | 40.5 | 38.9 | 20.6 | | | | 40.5 | 38.9 | 20.6 |
| Punjab | 42.5 | 38.7 | 18.8 | 36.0 | 58.8 | 5.3 | 41.4 | 42.1 | 16.5 |
| Rajasthan | 47.4 | 35.6 | 17.0 | 43.8 | 44.6 | 11.6 | 46.8 | 37.1 | 16.1 |
| Tamil Nadu | 31.9 | 41.0 | 27.1 | 25.7 | 49.5 | 24.7 | 31.0 | 42.3 | 26.7 |
| Uttar Pradesh | 52.5 | 29.9 | 17.6 | 47.6 | 35.1 | 17.3 | 51.4 | 31.1 | 17.5 |
| West Bengal | 49.7 | 36.2 | 14.1 | 39.2 | 40.2 | 20.6 | 47.3 | 37.1 | 15.6 |
| Other NE States | 45.6 | 43.0 | 11.3 | | | | 45.6 | 43.0 | 11.3 |
| Rest ST and UT | 30.5 | 56.8 | 12.7 | 44.9 | 53.0 | 2.2 | 42.2 | 53.7 | 4.1 |
| All-India | 42.0 | 38.1 | 19.9 | 38.7 | 51.8 | 9.5 | 41.1 | 41.9 | 17.0 |

*Source:* Unit level data of employment and unemployment schedule of 66th (2009–10) Round of NSSO.

**Table A6.3**   Nature of Employment, Usual (Principal + Subsidiary) Status, Female, 2009–10

| State | Non-metro | | | Metro | | | Total Urban | | |
|---|---|---|---|---|---|---|---|---|---|
| | SE | RE | CL | SE | RE | CL | SE | RE | CL |
| Andhra Pradesh | 43.8 | 30.8 | 25.4 | 30.2 | 62.6 | 7.2 | 42.2 | 34.5 | 23.3 |
| Assam | 48.7 | 36.7 | 14.6 | | | | 48.7 | 36.7 | 14.6 |
| Bihar | 38.4 | 29.9 | 31.8 | 35.2 | 64.8 | | 38.0 | 33.4 | 28.6 |
| Gujarat | 31.9 | 40.0 | 28.1 | 37.5 | 38.6 | 23.8 | 34.6 | 39.3 | 26.1 |
| Haryana | 41.0 | 46.0 | 13.0 | 25.0 | 72.0 | 3.0 | 39.5 | 48.4 | 12.1 |
| Jammu and Kashmir | 49.4 | 44.7 | 5.9 | | | | 49.4 | 44.7 | 5.9 |
| Karnataka | 33.4 | 35.4 | 31.2 | 36.1 | 52.2 | 11.7 | 34.1 | 39.9 | 26.0 |
| Kerala | 32.9 | 48.2 | 19.0 | | | | 32.9 | 48.2 | 19.0 |
| Madhya Pradesh | 45.5 | 28.5 | 25.9 | 18.7 | 66.3 | 15.0 | 41.2 | 34.6 | 24.2 |
| Maharashtra | 42.2 | 36.2 | 21.6 | 29.7 | 65.6 | 4.7 | 35.7 | 51.4 | 12.8 |
| Orissa | 43.9 | 22.3 | 33.8 | | | | 43.9 | 22.3 | 33.8 |
| Punjab | 43.1 | 46.2 | 10.7 | 52.8 | 47.2 | | 43.9 | 46.3 | 9.8 |
| Rajasthan | 59.2 | 28.1 | 12.7 | 39.7 | 57.7 | 2.6 | 56.7 | 31.8 | 11.5 |
| Tamil Nadu | 38.5 | 30.4 | 31.1 | 18.4 | 63.7 | 17.9 | 37.2 | 32.6 | 30.2 |
| Uttar Pradesh | 58.2 | 27.8 | 14.0 | 65.3 | 27.4 | 7.2 | 59.9 | 27.7 | 12.4 |
| West Bengal | 56.5 | 29.9 | 13.6 | 33.7 | 59.7 | 6.6 | 51.6 | 36.2 | 12.1 |
| Other NE States | 54.2 | 38.5 | 7.3 | | | | 54.2 | 38.5 | 7.3 |
| Rest ST and UT | 22.4 | 64.5 | 13.1 | 21.2 | 78.8 | | 21.7 | 72.7 | 5.6 |
| All-India | 43.3 | 33.9 | 22.8 | 33.5 | 57.2 | 9.3 | 41.1 | 39.3 | 19.6 |

*Source*: Unit level data of employment and unemployment schedule of 66th (2009–10) Round of NSSO.

**Table A6.4**  Distribution of Workers by Industrial Categories, Usual (Principal + Subsidiary) Status, Male, 2009–10

| State | Non-metro | | | Metro | | | Total Urban | | |
|---|---|---|---|---|---|---|---|---|---|
| | P | S | T | P | S | T | P | S | T |
| Andhra Pradesh | 5.5 | 35.4 | 59.1 | | 25.7 | 74.2 | 4.7 | 34.0 | 61.3 |
| Assam | 4.6 | 18.6 | 76.8 | | | | 4.6 | 18.6 | 76.8 |
| Bihar | 13.1 | 27.0 | 59.8 | 5.4 | 26.5 | 68.0 | 12.0 | 26.9 | 61.1 |
| Gujarat | 7.6 | 36.7 | 55.7 | 1.0 | 40.0 | 59.0 | 4.3 | 38.3 | 57.3 |
| Haryana | 4.6 | 43.3 | 52.0 | 1.2 | 56.9 | 41.9 | 4.0 | 45.9 | 50.1 |
| Jammu and Kashmir | 9.0 | 33.3 | 57.7 | | | | 9.0 | 33.3 | 57.7 |
| Karnataka | 11.4 | 34.0 | 54.6 | | 33.1 | 66.9 | 8.4 | 33.8 | 57.8 |
| Kerala | 12.7 | 33.3 | 54.0 | | | | 12.7 | 33.3 | 54.0 |
| Madhya Pradesh | 11.6 | 30.2 | 58.2 | 1.6 | 35.2 | 63.2 | 10.1 | 31.0 | 58.9 |
| Maharashtra | 7.0 | 33.7 | 59.3 | 1.3 | 33.2 | 65.5 | 4.2 | 33.5 | 62.3 |
| Orissa | 9.4 | 31.1 | 59.5 | | | | 9.4 | 31.1 | 59.5 |
| Punjab | 7.2 | 35.4 | 57.4 | | 55.0 | 45.0 | 6.0 | 38.7 | 55.3 |
| Rajasthan | 4.3 | 33.8 | 62.0 | 0.7 | 30.6 | 68.7 | 3.7 | 33.2 | 63.1 |
| Tamil Nadu | 12.2 | 38.3 | 49.5 | 4.1 | 26.6 | 69.3 | 11.0 | 36.6 | 52.4 |
| Uttar Pradesh | 8.9 | 33.6 | 57.6 | 5.9 | 37.3 | 56.9 | 8.2 | 34.4 | 57.4 |
| West Bengal | 5.2 | 33.0 | 61.8 | 0.3 | 32.6 | 67.1 | 4.1 | 32.9 | 63.0 |
| Other NE States | 14.1 | 19.0 | 66.9 | | | | 14.1 | 19.0 | 66.9 |
| Rest ST and UT | 6.2 | 28.8 | 65.0 | 0.2 | 32.6 | 67.1 | 1.3 | 31.9 | 66.8 |
| All-India | 8.7 | 33.8 | 57.5 | 1.6 | 34.4 | 64.0 | 6.7 | 34.0 | 59.3 |

*Source: Unit level data of employment and unemployment schedule of 66th (2009–10) Round of NSSO.*

**Table A6.5**  Distribution of Workers by Industrial Categories, Usual (Principal + Subsidiary) Status, Female, 2009–10

| State | Non-metro | | | Metro | | | Total Urban | | |
|---|---|---|---|---|---|---|---|---|---|
| | P | S | T | P | S | T | P | S | T |
| Andhra Pradesh | 12.2 | 42.9 | 45.0 | | 21.9 | 78.1 | 10.7 | 40.4 | 48.9 |
| Assam | 5.6 | 24.2 | 70.1 | | | | 5.6 | 24.2 | 70.1 |
| Bihar | 27.1 | 15.8 | 57.1 | 1.0 | 34.8 | 64.2 | 24.5 | 17.7 | 57.8 |
| Gujarat | 17.6 | 23.8 | 58.6 | 2.8 | 37.5 | 59.8 | 10.6 | 30.3 | 59.1 |
| Haryana | 12.8 | 30.5 | 56.7 | 2.1 | 41.8 | 56.1 | 11.8 | 31.6 | 56.6 |
| Jammu and Kashmir | 21.5 | 33.3 | 45.1 | | | | 21.5 | 33.3 | 45.1 |
| Karnataka | 21.2 | 30.4 | 48.4 | | 54.8 | 45.2 | 15.6 | 36.9 | 47.6 |
| Kerala | 9.4 | 25.8 | 64.8 | | | | 9.4 | 25.8 | 64.8 |
| Madhya Pradesh | 17.1 | 40.0 | 42.9 | 3.2 | 32.5 | 64.3 | 14.8 | 38.8 | 46.3 |
| Maharashtra | 15.4 | 21.6 | 63.0 | 1.1 | 21.7 | 77.2 | 8.0 | 21.6 | 70.4 |
| Orissa | 24.4 | 44.0 | 31.6 | | | | 24.4 | 44.0 | 31.6 |
| Punjab | 22.9 | 21.5 | 55.6 | | 65.0 | 35.0 | 21.1 | 25.0 | 53.9 |
| Rajasthan | 27.4 | 34.7 | 37.9 | 15.5 | 7.6 | 76.9 | 25.9 | 31.3 | 42.7 |
| Tamil Nadu | 25.9 | 40.5 | 33.5 | | 31.8 | 68.2 | 24.2 | 39.9 | 35.9 |
| Uttar Pradesh | 16.0 | 38.1 | 45.9 | 8.4 | 56.5 | 35.1 | 14.2 | 42.4 | 43.3 |
| West Bengal | 6.2 | 40.0 | 53.8 | | 21.2 | 78.8 | 4.9 | 36.0 | 59.1 |
| Other NE States | 21.7 | 13.6 | 64.7 | | | | 21.7 | 13.6 | 64.7 |
| Rest ST and UT | 6.6 | 19.2 | 74.2 | | 17.1 | 82.9 | 2.8 | 18.0 | 79.2 |
| All-India | 17.8 | 33.6 | 48.6 | 2.0 | 30.8 | 67.1 | 14.2 | 32.9 | 52.9 |

*Source:* Unit level data of employment and unemployment schedule of 66th (2009–10) Round of NSSO.

**Table A6.6**   Distribution of Workers by Occupational Categories, Usual (Principal + Subsidiary) Status, Male, 2009–10

| State | Non-metro | | | Metro | | | Total Urban | | |
|---|---|---|---|---|---|---|---|---|---|
| | A/P | C | ML | A/P | C | ML | A/P | C | ML |
| Andhra Pradesh | 23.5 | 28.4 | 48.1 | 27.9 | 36.0 | 36.1 | 24.2 | 29.5 | 46.3 |
| Assam | 35.3 | 41.5 | 23.3 | | | | 35.3 | 41.5 | 23.3 |
| Bihar | 25.5 | 26.7 | 47.9 | 22.0 | 40.3 | 37.6 | 24.9 | 28.7 | 46.4 |
| Gujarat | 25.1 | 27.2 | 47.6 | 42.2 | 21.3 | 36.6 | 33.4 | 24.3 | 42.2 |
| Haryana | 31.8 | 21.2 | 47.0 | 18.0 | 15.6 | 66.4 | 29.2 | 20.2 | 50.6 |
| Jammu and Kashmir | 19.0 | 36.8 | 44.2 | | | | 19.0 | 36.8 | 44.2 |
| Karnataka | 36.1 | 19.1 | 44.8 | 43.2 | 24.8 | 32.0 | 38.0 | 20.6 | 41.4 |
| Kerala | 22.5 | 23.0 | 54.5 | | | | 22.5 | 23.0 | 54.5 |
| Madhya Pradesh | 23.9 | 30.2 | 46.0 | 38.3 | 22.6 | 39.1 | 26.0 | 29.1 | 44.9 |
| Maharashtra | 27.5 | 28.5 | 44.1 | 36.7 | 30.9 | 32.3 | 31.9 | 29.7 | 38.4 |
| Orissa | 21.8 | 32.6 | 45.6 | | | | 21.8 | 32.6 | 45.6 |
| Punjab | 28.2 | 25.8 | 46.0 | 24.0 | 28.1 | 48.0 | 27.5 | 26.2 | 46.3 |
| Rajasthan | 29.5 | 29.1 | 41.4 | 43.7 | 26.7 | 29.6 | 31.9 | 28.7 | 39.4 |
| Tamil Nadu | 20.1 | 24.1 | 55.8 | 33.7 | 26.9 | 39.4 | 22.1 | 24.5 | 53.4 |
| Uttar Pradesh | 25.2 | 28.6 | 46.2 | 20.9 | 33.2 | 45.9 | 24.3 | 29.6 | 46.1 |
| West Bengal | 19.5 | 36.4 | 44.1 | 22.8 | 40.9 | 36.3 | 20.2 | 37.4 | 42.4 |
| Other NE States | 26.8 | 32.3 | 40.8 | | | | 26.8 | 32.3 | 40.8 |
| Rest ST and UT | 34.1 | 30.4 | 35.5 | 44.4 | 24.0 | 31.7 | 42.5 | 25.2 | 32.4 |
| All-India | 25.5 | 27.8 | 46.7 | 35.6 | 28.3 | 36.1 | 28.3 | 28.0 | 43.8 |

*Source*: Unit level data of employment and unemployment schedule of 66th (2009–10) Round of NSSO.

**Table A6.7** Distribution of Workers by Occupational Categories, Usual (Principal + Subsidiary) Status, Female, 2009–10

| State | Non-metro | | | Metro | | | Total Urban | | |
|---|---|---|---|---|---|---|---|---|---|
| | A/P | C | ML | A/P | C | ML | A/P | C | ML |
| Andhra Pradesh | 18.5 | 27.9 | 53.5 | 31.9 | 42.9 | 25.2 | 20.1 | 29.7 | 50.2 |
| Assam | 41.1 | 30.8 | 28.1 | | | | 41.1 | 30.8 | 28.1 |
| Bihar | 28.7 | 32.3 | 39.0 | 34.6 | 50.6 | 14.8 | 29.3 | 34.2 | 36.5 |
| Gujarat | 21.8 | 38.8 | 39.4 | 41.0 | 32.1 | 26.8 | 30.9 | 35.6 | 33.4 |
| Haryana | 30.9 | 28.1 | 41.0 | 37.6 | 30.8 | 31.6 | 31.5 | 28.4 | 40.1 |
| Jammu and Kashmir | 30.3 | 17.0 | 52.7 | | | | 30.3 | 17.0 | 52.7 |
| Karnataka | 32.9 | 19.9 | 47.2 | 36.2 | 26.8 | 37.0 | 33.8 | 21.7 | 44.5 |
| Kerala | 29.3 | 39.2 | 31.5 | | | | 29.3 | 39.2 | 31.5 |
| Madhya Pradesh | 20.8 | 22.6 | 56.5 | 27.9 | 45.2 | 27.0 | 22.0 | 26.3 | 51.8 |
| Maharashtra | 31.3 | 38.1 | 30.6 | 35.6 | 49.5 | 14.9 | 33.5 | 44.0 | 22.5 |
| Orissa | 15.9 | 19.8 | 64.3 | | | | 15.9 | 19.8 | 64.3 |
| Punjab | 30.6 | 26.3 | 43.1 | 23.0 | 23.1 | 53.9 | 30.0 | 26.0 | 44.0 |
| Rajasthan | 26.9 | 16.9 | 56.2 | 60.0 | 17.7 | 22.3 | 31.0 | 17.0 | 52.0 |
| Tamil Nadu | 21.2 | 17.5 | 61.3 | 34.9 | 40.8 | 24.3 | 22.1 | 19.1 | 58.8 |
| Uttar Pradesh | 30.0 | 22.9 | 47.1 | 17.8 | 23.3 | 58.9 | 27.1 | 23.0 | 49.9 |
| West Bengal | 22.6 | 32.2 | 45.2 | 38.2 | 49.2 | 12.6 | 26.0 | 35.9 | 38.2 |
| Other NE States | 27.7 | 37.5 | 34.8 | | | | 27.7 | 37.5 | 34.8 |
| Rest ST and UT | 36.6 | 42.6 | 20.8 | 42.5 | 45.7 | 11.8 | 40.0 | 44.4 | 15.7 |
| All-India | 25.6 | 26.8 | 47.7 | 35.6 | 40.4 | 24.1 | 27.9 | 29.9 | 42.2 |

*Source*: Unit level data of employment and unemployment schedule of 66th (2009–10) Round of NSSO.

**Table A6.8**  Unemployment Rates by States, Usual (Principal + Subsidiary) Status

| State | Usual Status | | | | | | CDS | | | | | |
|---|---|---|---|---|---|---|---|---|---|---|---|---|
| | Male | | | Female | | | Male | | | Female | | |
| | NM | M | TU | NM | M | TU | NM | M | TU | NM | M | TU |
| Andhra Pradesh | 2.0 | 5.0 | 2.4 | 4.2 | 11.0 | 5.1 | 4.1 | 5.4 | 4.3 | 8.7 | 14.9 | 9.5 |
| Assam | 4.0 | | 4.0 | 12.5 | | 12.5 | 4.6 | – | 4.6 | 10.9 | – | 10.9 |
| Bihar | 4.5 | 13.3 | 6.0 | 12.7 | 24.4 | 14.1 | 6.1 | 14.1 | 7.4 | 20.4 | 36.3 | 22.7 |
| Gujarat | 1.8 | 1.3 | 1.5 | 3.5 | 2.7 | 3.1 | 3.5 | 1.9 | 2.7 | 6.9 | 3.3 | 5.3 |
| Haryana | 2.1 | 3.0 | 2.2 | 2.9 | 11.8 | 3.8 | 4.0 | 4.4 | 4.1 | 4.7 | 12.9 | 5.5 |
| Jammu and Kashmir | 4.7 | | 4.7 | 10.9 | | 10.9 | 5.5 | – | 5.5 | 14.5 | – | 14.5 |
| Karnataka | 2.0 | 3.4 | 2.4 | 4.2 | 3.5 | 4.0 | 4.4 | 4.4 | 4.4 | 6.1 | 5.5 | 6.0 |
| Kerala | 2.9 | | 2.9 | 16.8 | | 16.8 | 12.1 | – | 12.1 | 21.3 | – | 21.3 |
| Madhya Pradesh | 3.1 | 0.5 | 2.8 | 2.7 | 6.0 | 3.3 | 5.9 | 1.4 | 5.3 | 4.7 | 6.8 | 5.0 |
| Maharashtra | 1.9 | 3.7 | 2.8 | 4.9 | 5.1 | 5.0 | 4.7 | 5.2 | 5.0 | 8.7 | 8.0 | 8.3 |
| Orissa | 4.0 | | 4.0 | 5.3 | | 5.3 | 5.7 | – | 5.7 | 9.9 | – | 9.9 |
| Punjab | 4.0 | 6.2 | 4.4 | 5.9 | 13.5 | 6.6 | 6.6 | 7.7 | 6.8 | 8.6 | 14.7 | 9.2 |
| Rajasthan | 1.5 | 2.5 | 1.7 | 4.1 | 6.4 | 4.4 | 3.7 | 3.1 | 3.6 | 5.0 | 7.1 | 5.3 |
| Tamil Nadu | 2.2 | 3.9 | 2.4 | 4.3 | 18.9 | 5.4 | 6.9 | 7.9 | 7.0 | 10.0 | 21.9 | 11.0 |
| Uttar Pradesh | 2.5 | 4.3 | 2.9 | 4.2 | 0.9 | 3.4 | 4.5 | 4.9 | 4.6 | 6.8 | 1.5 | 5.4 |
| West Bengal | 3.7 | 2.9 | 3.5 | 6.2 | 7.4 | 6.5 | 6.1 | 4.5 | 5.7 | 11.4 | 8.6 | 10.8 |
| Other NE States | 5.5 | | 5.5 | 15.1 | | 15.1 | 6.4 | – | 6.4 | 17.1 | – | 17.1 |
| Rest ST and UT | 2.9 | 2.6 | 2.7 | 7.7 | 2.2 | 4.6 | 5.4 | 3.3 | 3.7 | 10.5 | 2.4 | 5.9 |
| All-India | 2.6 | 3.4 | 2.8 | 5.7 | 5.7 | 5.7 | 5.4 | 4.6 | 5.1 | 9.5 | 7.8 | 9.1 |

*Source:* Unit level data of employment and unemployment schedule of 66th (2009–10) Round of NSSO.

**Table A6.9**   Education Levels (Age 7+), 2009-10, Metro and Non-metro, Male

(in per cent)

| State | Non-metro | | | | | Metro | | | | | Total Urban | | | | |
|---|---|---|---|---|---|---|---|---|---|---|---|---|---|---|---|
| | Illiterate | Primary & below | Up to middle | Up to secondary | Graduate & above | Illiterate | Primary & below | Up to middle | Up to secondary | Graduate & above | Illiterate | Primary & below | Up to middle | Up to secondary | Graduate & above |
| Andhra Pradesh | 13.3 | 23.5 | 15.0 | 29.1 | 19.1 | 8.5 | 21.9 | 15.2 | 31.8 | 22.6 | 12.5 | 23.2 | 15.0 | 29.6 | 19.6 |
| Assam | 2.9 | 25.5 | 19.0 | 33.8 | 18.8 | | | | | | 2.9 | 25.5 | 19.0 | 33.8 | 18.8 |
| Bihar | 14.7 | 32.0 | 12.9 | 27.0 | 13.3 | 6.7 | 34.2 | 9.5 | 26.7 | 23.0 | 13.3 | 32.4 | 12.3 | 27.0 | 15.0 |
| Gujarat | 7.9 | 29.1 | 21.0 | 30.9 | 11.1 | 5.2 | 29.2 | 15.6 | 33.1 | 17.0 | 6.5 | 29.2 | 18.4 | 32.0 | 14.0 |
| Haryana | 12.1 | 29.4 | 12.6 | 32.6 | 13.3 | 11.6 | 26.5 | 14.8 | 37.0 | 10.1 | 12.0 | 28.8 | 13.1 | 33.5 | 12.7 |
| Jammu and Kashmir | 13.5 | 22.7 | 17.6 | 33.2 | 13.0 | | | | | | 13.5 | 22.7 | 17.6 | 33.2 | 13.0 |
| Karnataka | 9.6 | 23.4 | 17.3 | 33.8 | 15.8 | 7.1 | 17.1 | 15.0 | 36.6 | 24.1 | 9.0 | 21.8 | 16.7 | 34.5 | 17.9 |
| Kerala | 2.5 | 25.4 | 29.1 | 31.5 | 11.5 | | | | | | 2.5 | 25.4 | 29.1 | 31.5 | 11.5 |
| Madhya Pradesh | 8.2 | 31.0 | 17.3 | 27.2 | 16.4 | 5.0 | 30.0 | 12.7 | 20.9 | 31.4 | 7.7 | 30.8 | 16.6 | 26.3 | 18.6 |
| Maharashtra | 5.8 | 25.1 | 20.6 | 34.8 | 13.7 | 3.3 | 21.1 | 19.2 | 34.8 | 21.7 | 4.6 | 23.2 | 19.9 | 34.8 | 17.5 |
| Orissa | 9.1 | 27.1 | 22.9 | 23.5 | 17.5 | | | | | | 9.1 | 27.1 | 22.9 | 23.5 | 17.5 |
| Punjab | 14.2 | 29.0 | 13.4 | 30.8 | 12.5 | 7.7 | 27.2 | 16.2 | 38.0 | 10.9 | 13.3 | 28.7 | 13.9 | 31.8 | 12.3 |
| Rajasthan | 12.3 | 30.4 | 15.9 | 26.9 | 14.5 | 12.4 | 21.9 | 12.0 | 27.9 | 25.8 | 12.3 | 29.0 | 15.3 | 27.1 | 16.3 |
| Tamil Nadu | 8.4 | 29.2 | 19.5 | 31.5 | 11.5 | 5.4 | 24.1 | 15.3 | 33.4 | 21.8 | 7.9 | 28.4 | 18.8 | 31.8 | 13.1 |
| Uttar Pradesh | 16.9 | 29.6 | 15.7 | 23.4 | 14.4 | 11.5 | 27.0 | 13.2 | 28.3 | 20.0 | 15.7 | 29.0 | 15.1 | 24.5 | 15.7 |
| West Bengal | 8.2 | 36.3 | 15.2 | 23.7 | 16.7 | 7.5 | 30.6 | 14.2 | 23.9 | 23.9 | 8.0 | 35.0 | 14.9 | 23.7 | 18.3 |
| Other NE States | 3.6 | 28.4 | 22.3 | 31.3 | 14.4 | | | | | | 3.6 | 28.4 | 22.3 | 31.3 | 14.4 |
| Rest ST and UT | 5.2 | 24.7 | 15.2 | 32.5 | 22.4 | 6.3 | 24.7 | 14.2 | 35.9 | 18.9 | 6.1 | 24.7 | 14.4 | 35.3 | 19.5 |
| All-India | 10.3 | 28.4 | 17.5 | 29.1 | 14.6 | 6.4 | 24.8 | 15.5 | 32.5 | 20.9 | 9.2 | 27.4 | 17.0 | 30.0 | 16.3 |

*Source:* Unit level data of employment and unemployment schedule of 66th (2009–10) Round of NSSO.

**Table A6.10** Education Levels (Age 7+), 2009–10, Metro and Non-metro, Female

(in per cent)

| State | Non-metro | | | | | Metro | | | | | Total Urban | | | | |
|---|---|---|---|---|---|---|---|---|---|---|---|---|---|---|---|
| | Illiterate | Primary & below | Up to middle | Up to secondary | Graduate & above | Illiterate | Primary & below | Up to middle | Up to secondary | Graduate & above | Illiterate | Primary & below | Up to middle | Up to secondary | Graduate & above |
| Andhra Pradesh | 26.3 | 25.6 | 15.4 | 22.1 | 10.5 | 19.4 | 22.9 | 14.3 | 30.0 | 13.5 | 25.2 | 25.2 | 15.3 | 23.4 | 11.0 |
| Assam | 8.9 | 27.1 | 19.8 | 30.6 | 13.5 | | | | | | 8.9 | 27.1 | 19.8 | 30.6 | 13.5 |
| Bihar | 29.8 | 30.7 | 12.8 | 20.2 | 6.5 | 12.2 | 37.3 | 14.9 | 23.8 | 11.7 | 26.7 | 31.9 | 13.2 | 20.8 | 7.4 |
| Gujarat | 19.8 | 30.0 | 17.8 | 23.5 | 8.8 | 15.9 | 26.2 | 16.7 | 24.3 | 16.9 | 18.0 | 28.2 | 17.2 | 23.9 | 12.7 |
| Haryana | 26.5 | 29.6 | 11.3 | 20.0 | 12.7 | 28.7 | 25.4 | 6.0 | 31.8 | 8.1 | 26.8 | 28.9 | 10.5 | 21.8 | 12.0 |
| Jammu and Kashmir | 28.6 | 18.1 | 15.8 | 26.4 | 11.0 | | | | | | 28.6 | 18.1 | 15.8 | 26.4 | 11.0 |
| Karnataka | 21.6 | 23.0 | 16.4 | 30.3 | 8.7 | 14.8 | 16.4 | 18.6 | 31.3 | 18.9 | 20.0 | 21.4 | 16.9 | 30.5 | 11.1 |
| Kerala | 5.7 | 26.6 | 25.6 | 30.3 | 11.7 | | | | | | 5.7 | 26.6 | 25.6 | 30.3 | 11.7 |
| Madhya Pradesh | 22.2 | 31.4 | 13.3 | 22.8 | 10.3 | 13.9 | 24.5 | 9.2 | 33.1 | 19.4 | 20.8 | 30.2 | 12.6 | 24.5 | 11.9 |
| Maharashtra | 16.8 | 25.8 | 19.8 | 27.8 | 9.8 | 11.1 | 21.7 | 18.1 | 28.3 | 20.8 | 14.2 | 23.9 | 19.0 | 28.0 | 14.9 |
| Orissa | 24.7 | 26.1 | 18.1 | 20.7 | 10.4 | | | | | | 24.7 | 26.1 | 18.1 | 20.7 | 10.4 |
| Punjab | 22.0 | 25.9 | 10.3 | 27.5 | 14.3 | 14.0 | 27.7 | 13.4 | 32.2 | 12.8 | 20.9 | 26.2 | 10.7 | 28.1 | 14.1 |
| Rajasthan | 31.5 | 30.6 | 11.3 | 16.8 | 9.9 | 22.9 | 23.2 | 10.3 | 21.7 | 22.0 | 30.2 | 29.4 | 11.1 | 17.6 | 11.8 |
| Tamil Nadu | 18.8 | 29.7 | 17.0 | 25.7 | 8.8 | 10.0 | 26.3 | 16.9 | 29.2 | 17.7 | 17.5 | 29.2 | 17.0 | 26.2 | 10.1 |
| Uttar Pradesh | 30.9 | 28.2 | 11.4 | 18.1 | 11.3 | 24.7 | 22.4 | 9.8 | 24.8 | 18.3 | 29.5 | 27.0 | 11.1 | 19.6 | 12.9 |
| West Bengal | 18.4 | 34.7 | 14.5 | 21.5 | 10.9 | 12.7 | 28.0 | 15.9 | 26.9 | 16.5 | 17.1 | 33.1 | 14.8 | 22.8 | 12.2 |
| Other NE States | 8.2 | 31.2 | 24.7 | 26.8 | 9.1 | | | | | | 8.2 | 31.2 | 24.7 | 26.8 | 9.1 |
| Rest ST and UT | 13.9 | 25.0 | 13.6 | 30.8 | 16.7 | 14.9 | 25.6 | 11.4 | 29.8 | 18.3 | 14.7 | 25.5 | 11.9 | 30.0 | 18.0 |
| All-India | 22.3 | 28.3 | 15.5 | 23.6 | 10.3 | 15.2 | 24.1 | 14.7 | 27.8 | 18.2 | 20.5 | 27.2 | 15.3 | 24.7 | 12.3 |

*Source:* Unit level data of employment and unemployment schedule of 66th (2009–10) Round of NSSO.

**Table A6.11** Monthly APCE (Current Prices), Metro, Non-metro, and Total Urban, 2009–10

| State | Non-metro | Metro | Total Urban | Metro to Non-metro ratio |
|---|---|---|---|---|
| Andhra Pradesh | 1956.80 | 2111.32 | 1982.23 | 1.08 |
| Assam | 1540.27 | – | 1540.27 | – |
| Bihar | 1159.34 | 1467.22 | 1205.46 | 1.27 |
| Gujarat | 1702.20 | 2036.28 | 1859.01 | 1.20 |
| Haryana | 1955.62 | 1642.97 | 1898.18 | 0.84 |
| Jammu and Kashmir | 1653.90 | – | 1653.90 | – |
| Karnataka | 1488.43 | 2425.13 | 1716.38 | 1.63 |
| Kerala | 2663.45 | – | 2663.45 | – |
| Madhya Pradesh | 1301.01 | 2300.69 | 1445.34 | 1.77 |
| Maharashtra | 1744.67 | 2760.65 | 2231.98 | 1.58 |
| Orissa | 1425.41 | – | 1425.41 | – |
| Punjab | 2034.86 | 1763.04 | 1992.68 | 0.87 |
| Rajasthan | 1398.96 | 3052.87 | 1669.50 | 2.18 |
| Tamil Nadu | 1561.11 | 2344.40 | 1678.69 | 1.50 |
| Uttar Pradesh | 1289.74 | 1720.21 | 1377.81 | 1.33 |
| West Bengal | 1520.82 | 2494.27 | 1735.66 | 1.64 |
| Other NE States | 1482.04 | – | 1482.04 | – |
| Rest ST and UT | 2744.78 | 2181.98 | 2294.99 | 0.79 |
| All-India | 1603.51 | 2301.83 | 1785.81 | 1.44 |
| Coefficient of Variation | 25.59 | 20.99 | 20.67 | |

*Source*: Unit level data of consumption expenditure—Type 1 schedule of 66th (2009–10) Round of NSSO.

# Bibliography

Ahmed, Ahsan and Carmen Pages (2008) 'Some Implications of Regional Differences in Labor-Market Outcomes in India', in D. Mazumdar and S. Sarkar (eds), *Globalization, Labor Markets and Inequality in India*, Routledge, London, pp. 93–120.

Deaton, A. (2003) 'Prices and Poverty, 1987–2000', *Economic and Political Weekly*, 34: 362–68.

Deyin, Y. and S. Zongfen (1982) 'The Strategic Objective of Urban Development in China', in O.P. Mathur (ed.), *Small Cities and National Development*, UN Centre for Regional Development, Nagoya.

Drèze, J. and A. Sen (1995) *India: Economic Development and Social Opportunity*, Oxford University Press, Delhi.

Expert Group on the Commercialisation of Infrastructure (1996) *The India Infrastructure Report: Policy Imperatives for Growth and Welfare*, Ministry of Finance, Government of India, New Delhi.

Government of India [GoI] (1993) *Report of the Expert Group on Estimation of Proportion and Number of Poor*, Planning Commission, Perspective Planning Division, New Delhi.

Hansen, Niles (1982) 'The Role of Small and Intermediate Cities in National Development Process and Strategies', in O.P. Mathur (ed.), *Small Cities and National Development*, UN Centre for Regional Development, Nagoya.

Hardoy, Jorge E. and David Satterthwaite (1986), 'Why Small and Intermediate Urban Centres?' in Jorge E. Hardoy and David Satterthwaite (eds), *Small and Intermediate Urban Centres—Their Role in Regional and National Development in the Third World*, Hodder and Stoughton, London, Sydney, Auckland, Toronto, pp. 1–17.

High Powered Expert Committee (2011), *Report on Indian Urban Infrastructure and Services*, HPEC, available at http://niua.org/projects/hpec/FinalReport-hpec.pdf (accessed on 9 March 2011).

Kundu, A. and S. Bhatia (2001), *Industrial Growth in Small and Medium Towns and their Vertical Integration: The Case of Gobindgarh, Punjab, India*, Management of Social Transformations—MOST Discussion Paper No. 57, UNESCO, available at unesdco.unesco.org/images/0012/001252/125232eo.pdf. (accessed on 9 March 2011).

Kundu, A. and. P.C. Mohanan (2009) 'Employment and Inequality Outcomes in India', Paper presented at the OECD seminar on 'Employment Outcomes and Inequality: New Evidence, Links and Policy Responses in Brazil, China and India', 8 April, Paris.

Kundu, A. and N. Sarangi (2005) 'Issues of Urban Exclusion', *Economic and Political Weekly*, 40 (13): 3642–46.

Kundu, D. and D. Samanta (2011), 'Redefining the Inclusive Urban Agenda in India', *Economic and Political Weekly*, 46 (5): 55–63.

Mahadevia, D. (2001) 'Informalisation of Employment and Poverty in Ahmedabad', in A. Kundu and A.N. Sharma (eds), *Informal Sector in India—Perspectives and Policies*, Institute for Human Development and Institute for Applied Manpower Research, New Delhi, pp. 142–59.

———. (2002) 'Interventions in Development: A Shift towards a Model of Exclusion', in A. Kundu and D. Mahadevia (eds), *Poverty and Vulnerability in a Globalising Metropolis: Ahmedabad*, Manak Publishers, Delhi, pp. 80–132.

———. (2006a) 'NURM and the Poor in Globalising Mega Cities', *Economic and Political Weekly*, 41(31): 3399–403.

———. (2006b) 'Municipal Finances and Development in Small and Medium Towns: Gujarat', in R. Parthasarathy and Sudarshan Iyengar (eds), *New Development Paradigms & Challenges for Western & Central India*, for Gujarat Institute of Development Research, Ahmedabad, Concept, New Delhi, pp. 217–60.

———. (2008) 'Metropolitan Employment in India', in D. Mahadevia (ed.), *Inside the Transforming Urban Asia: Policies, Processes and Public Actions*, Concept, New Delhi, pp. 56–93.

———. (2009) 'Urban Land Market and Access of the Poor', in India, Ministry of Housing and Urban Poverty Alleviation (ed.) *India: Urban Poverty Report 2009*, Oxford University Press, New Delhi, pp. 199–221.

———. (2010a) 'Urban Reforms in Three Cities: Bangalore, Ahmedabad, and Patna', in Vikram Chand (ed.), *Public Service Delivery in India: Understanding the Reform Process*, Oxford University Press, New Delhi, pp. 226–95.

———. (2010b) 'Tenure Security and Urban Social Protection Links: India', *IDS Bulletin*, 41 (4): 52–62.

———. (2011) 'Branded and Renewed? Policies, Politics and Processes of Urban Development in the Reform Era', *Economic and Political Weekly*, 46 (31): 56–64.

Mahadevia, D. and A. Mukherjee (2003) 'Infrastructure Financing through Municipal Bonds: Ahmedabad Experience', *Spatio-economic Development Record*, 9 (6): 19–31.

Mahadevia, D. and P. Shah (2009) 'Tenure Security and Urban Poverty', *Social Protection and Shelter*, Newsletter 4, of Social Protection in Asia, available at http://www.socialprotectionasia. org/newsletter_4/Tenure-Security-and-Urban-Poverty.html. (accessed on 9 March 2011).

Mazumdar, D. and S. Sarkar (2004), *Measurement and Determinants of Poverty in Pre and Post-Reform Period in India: An Analysis for India and Major States*, Institute of Human Development Working Paper No. 22, New Delhi.

———. (2007) 'Growth of Employment and Earnings in Tertiary Sector, 1983–2000', *Economic and Political Weekly*, 42 (11): 973–81.

———. (2008) *Globalisation, Labour Markets and Inequality in India*, Routledge, London.

———. (2009) 'The Employment Problem in India and the Phenomenon of Missing Middle', *Indian Journal of Labour Economics*, January–March 52 (1): 43–55.

McKinsey Global Institute (2010) *India's Urban Awakening: Building Inclusive Cities, Sustaining Economic Growth*, McKinsey & Company, April, available at http://www.mckinsey.com/mgi/ reports/freepass_pdfs/india_urbanization/ MGI_india_urbanization_fullreport.pdf (accessed on 15 February 2011).

Minocha, A.C. and H.S. Yadav (1989) *Small and Medium Towns and Their Role in Regional Development*, Gian Publishing House, New Delhi.

National Sample Survey Office (2010) 'Some Characteristics of Urban Slums, 2008–09', NSS 65th Round (July 2008–June 2009), Report No. 534 (65/0.21/1), National Statistical Organisation, Ministry of Statistics and Programme Implementation, Government of India, May.

National Sample Survey Organisation (2007) *Employment and Unemployment Situation in Cities and Towns in India 2004–2005*, Report No. 520, Ministry of Statistics and Programme Implementation, Government of India, New Delhi, March.

Planning Commission (2009) *Report of The Expert Group to Review the Methodology for Estimation of Poverty*, Government of India, New Delhi, November.

Press Information Bureau (1997) *Estimates of Poverty*, Perspective Planning Division, Planning Commission, Government of India, New Delhi, March.

———. (2007) *Poverty Estimates for 2004–5*, Government of India, New Delhi, March.

Sarkar, S. and B.S. Mehta (2010) 'Income Inequality in India: Pre and Post Reform Period', *Economic and Political Weekly*, 45 (37): 45–55.

Sen, A. and Himanshu (2004) *Poverty and Inequality in India—Getting Closer to the Truth*, (mimeo).

Sundaram, K. and S.D. Tendulkar (2003) 'Poverty has Declined in 1990s: A Resolution of Comparability Problems in NSS Consumption Expenditure Data', *Economic and Political Weekly*, 38 (4): 327–37.

United Nations Population Fund (UNFPA) (2007) *State of World Population, 2007—Unleashing the Potential of Urban Growth*, UNFPA, www.unfpa. org/swp/2007/presskit/pdf/sowp2007_eng. pdf (accessed on 9 March 2011).

# Glossary

**Administrative and Professional services** Consist of employment as legislators, senior officials, administrative officials, managers, professionals, technicians, and associate professionals.

**Casual labour** A person who is casually engaged in others' farm or non-farm enterprises (both household and non-household) and in return receives wages according to the terms of the daily or periodic work contract.

**Clerical services** Consist of clerks, service workers, and sales workers in shops and markets.

**Current daily activity status** The activity pattern of the population, particularly in the informal sector, is such that during a week, and sometimes even during a day, a person can pursue more than one activity. Moreover, many people can even undertake both economic and non-economic activities on the same day of a reference week. The current daily activity status for a person was determined on the basis of his/her activity status on each day of the reference week.

**Current weekly activity status** The current weekly activity status of a person is the activity status obtaining for a person during a reference period of seven days preceding the date of survey.

**Economic activity** Any activity resulting in production of goods and services that add value to the national product was considered an economic activity for the employment and unemployment surveys of the NSS. It includes (i) all the market activities performed for pay or profit which result in production of goods and services for exchange, and (ii) non-market activities relating to the primary sector which result in production (including free collection) of primary goods for own consumption and the activities relating to the own-account production of fixed assets, such as construction of own house, and machinery, tools, for household enterprises and construction of any private or community facilities free of charge.

**Employed** Being engaged in an economic activity.

**High level of education** Graduate and above.

**Household** A group of persons who normally live together and take food from a common kitchen constitute a household.

**Literate** If he/she can both read and write a simple message with understanding in at least one language.

**Low level of education** Up to primary school level.

**Manual labour** Consists of skilled agriculture and fishery workers, craft and related trade workers, plant and machine operators, and elementary occupations in agriculture, mining, manufacturing, construction, transport, and sales and services.

**Metropolis or Metro** An urban centre with population more than 1 million.

**Primary sector** Includes cultivators, agriculture labour, those in fishing, livestock, etc., and mining and quarrying.

**Regular employed** Persons who work on others' farm or in others' non-farm enterprises (both household and non-household) and in return receive salary or wages on a regular basis (that is, not on the basis of the daily or periodic renewal of the work contract).

**Secondary sector** Includes those in manufacturing, household or non-household, electricity, gas and water production, and construction.

**Self-employed** Persons who operate their own farm or non-farm enterprises or are engaged independently in a profession or trade on own-account or with one or a few partners.

**Tertiary sector** Includes those in transport, storage, communication services, and wholesale and retail trade including those vending/hawking on the streets, finance and real estate services,

personnel services, public administration, and social services.

**Unemployed** Not being engaged in any economic activity (work) but either making tangible efforts to seek 'work' or being available for 'work' if the 'work' is available.

**Urban** Settlements declared urban in the Indian census and which have an urban local government.

**Usual principal activity status** The usual activity status relates to the activity status of a person during the reference period of 365 days preceding the date of survey. The activity status on which a person spent relatively longer time (that is, major time criterion) during the 365 days preceding the date of survey is considered as the usual principal activity status of the person.

**Usual subsidiary economic activity status** A person whose usual principal status is determined on the basis of the major time criterion could have pursued some economic activity for a shorter time throughout the reference year of 365 days preceding the date of survey or for a minor period, which is not less than 30 days, during the reference year.

**Worker** One who is engaged in an economic activity or who, despite his/her attachment to economic activity, abstained from work for reason of illness, injury or other physical disability, bad weather, festivals, social or religious functions, or other contingencies necessitating temporary absence from work.

# Index